WALK A MILE

EXPERIENCING AND UNDERSTANDING DIVERSITY IN CANADA

Theresa Anzovino
Niagara College

Deborah Boutilier
Niagara College

1914–2014
Nelson Education celebrates 100 years of Canadian publishing

NELSON
EDUCATION
CELEBRATE LIFELONG LEARNING

NELSON / EDUCATION

Walk a Mile: Experiencing and Understanding Diversity in Canada

by Theresa Anzovino and Deborah Boutilier

Vice President, Editorial Higher Education:
Anne Williams

Executive Editor:
Maya Castle

Marketing Manager:
Terry Fedorkiw

Developmental Editor:
Jessica Freedman

Photo Researcher:
Eva Svec

Permissions Coordinator:
Eva Svec

Content Production Manager:
Christine Gilbert

Production Service:
Cenveo Publisher Services

Copy Editor:
Elspeth McFadden

Proofreader:
Kavitha

Indexer:
Kevin Broccoli
BIM Publishing Services

Design Director:
Ken Phipps

Managing Designer:
Franca Amore

Interior Design:
Dave Murphy

Interior Design Element Credits:
In Their Shoes box: Leonard McLane/Getty Images; Picture This box: Michal Strzelecki/Getty Images

Cover Design:
Jennifer Leung

Cover Image:
Kristina Gruzdeva/Thinkstock; Tusumaru/Shutterstock

Compositor:
Cenveo Publisher Services

Library and Archives Canada Cataloguing in Publication Data

Anzovino, Theresa, author
    Walk a mile : experiencing and understanding diversity in Canada / Theresa Anzovino, Niagara College, Deborah Boutilier, Niagara College.
— First edition.

Includes bibliographical references and index.
ISBN 978-0-17-655711-9 (pbk.)

    1. Multiculturalism—Canada—Textbooks. 2. Ethnic groups—Canada—Textbooks. 3. Canada—Civilization—Textbooks.
I. Boutilier, Deborah, author
II. Title.

HM1271.A59 2014
305.800971   C2013-908615-3

PKG ISBN-13: 978-0-17-655711-9
PKG ISBN-10: 0-17-655711-3

For my son, Daniel, who inspires me with his courage to continue to live the life he imagined as a healer of others.

For my mother, who first taught me to fight for equity, justice, and inclusion—Theresa

For my wild and wonderfully diverse family, with love—Deborah

Foreword by Craig and Marc Kielburger

For us, "walking a mile in someone else's shoes" is only half metaphor.

Our international development work through Free The Children often leads us to remote communities where the only way to travel is by foot. In Ecuador, for example, the road stops halfway up the Andean mountains, and we walk the rest of the way. Beside us are our friends from the mountaintop villages, and the mules carrying cement, lumber, and other school-building materials. We would offer to trade our comfortable hiking shoes for our friends' bare feet, but we know if they accepted we'd never keep up.

An even more challenging walk is with groups of Maasai women and children in Kenya to collect their families' water from the nearest source stream. On the return trip—often two kilometres or more—we balance a 40-litre jerry can of water on our heads like the others, some of whom are as young as six. It's a powerful experience that reaffirms our commitment to clean water projects in communities like theirs, to ensure their walk is much shorter and the children can go to school.

We've learned innumerable lessons by travelling great and difficult distances, literally and figuratively, with our diverse overseas partners. Understanding other ways of living, thinking, and doing has enriched our own life experience and made our work projects more effective and impactful.

It has also inspired us to share these experiences with as many people as possible because we are convinced that a whole generation of diversity-competent global citizens can change the world.

We've now travelled with thousands of young people who want not simply to appreciate diversity, but to *live* it. On our overseas volunteer trips, one-third of participants' time is dedicated to cultural immersion in the communities we visit. We eat traditional local meals, participate in centuries-old celebrations, and most importantly, contribute to daily chores like the water walk.

When they return home, our volunteers pursue a better world with renewed vigour. Some have even organized a fundraising "*Mamas'* Water Walk." This past Mother's Day in Waterloo, Ontario, 15 teams of students from various local schools collected pledges and completed a two-kilometre walk with water jugs on their backs.

Leaving their comfort zones to truly connect with their fellow human beings, our volunteer travellers gain a deeper appreciation of our world's diversity; an understanding of how that diversity plays out in power, privilege, and hardship; and a lifelong sense of empathy, compassion, and dedication to justice and equity.

Now, living diversity doesn't necessarily require international travel. We Canadians have the great fortune of living in one of the world's most diverse nations, brimming with opportunities to meet people with different backgrounds and experiences from our own. It's not far outside our comfort boxes that we can find culturally different foods, music, or community festivals. Even take a look around your own neighbourhood, workplace, or social group, and see people of different gender, age, ability, sexual orientation, income level, and countless other identities than yours. For the truly adventurous, visit a local temple, mosque, or church and get a glimpse into a new way of seeing the world that will expand your mind.

There are also more tangible benefits to becoming diversity competent, in the enhanced prospects for your career and social life. Imagine opening your job search to the world—we regularly encounter fellow Canadians working in banks in China, overseeing construction projects in Africa, or running development programs in South America. If you can learn a second language, Salary.com finds that bilingual employees earn between 5 and 20 percent more than their unilingual co-workers. And a 2008 University of California–Berkeley study even showed that people with culturally diverse social groups have lower levels of the stress hormone cortisol, which lowers their risk of cancer, heart disease, and Type 2 diabetes.

For all these reasons, we are ecstatic to see this book in classrooms across Canada, and we congratulate Professor Boutilier and Professor Anzovino for translating their decades of experiential learning and teaching into a practical guide to diversity competency. The knowledge and active reflection provoked in these pages will help a generation of young Canadians to understand their own identity, the place of identity in our relationships with our fellow global citizens, and our responsibility to take action for a more equitable and just world.

We therefore urge you to see this book as just the beginning. Let it be your guide to a world of opportunity, of understanding, of experiences, of action. You don't have to walk a mile with a jug of water on your head, but don't let the title of this book remain a simple metaphor. Try not to just see the world through someone else's eyes, but to *live* it. Live diversity, and it won't be just your life that is better for it.

Craig and Marc Kielburger

About the Authors

THERESA ANZOVINO

Theresa Anzovino has completed a Masters of Arts degree in Sociology (York University, 1994), Bachelor of Arts Degree in Sociology (University of Waterloo, 1985) and Teaching Adults Certificate (Niagara, 1989). Her academic areas of interest include feminist jurisprudence, migration, diversity, human rights, and universal design for learning. She is a proud mother to son Daniel. Anzovino is a professor in the School of Liberal Arts and Sciences at Niagara College and the 2013 recipient of the Teaching Excellence Award at Niagara College. Prior to this, she worked as a CEO for a large organization within the non-profit sector dedicated to refugee protection and resettlement. This work earned her numerous humanitarian and leadership awards. When she invites you to walk a mile in her shoes, it will be barefoot on a beach connecting with the earth.

DEBORAH BOUTILIER

Deborah Boutilier holds a Doctorate of Education degree in Sociology and Equity Studies (University of Toronto, 2008); Master's degrees in Sociology (State University of New York at Buffalo, 1987) and Education (Brock University, 1998) and a Baking Certificate (Niagara College, 2013). Her academic areas of interest include diversity and social inclusion, social constructions of gender and homicide, and the learning processes of information technology in the practice of cross-cultural computer-mediated exchanges. When she is not teaching in the School of Liberal Arts and Sciences at Niagara College, she loves reading, writing, baking, and walking her dog, Bubba. She invites you to take a walk in her favourite shoes, but warns you that they leak!

Brief Table of Contents

Detailed Table of Contents

A Unique Learning System

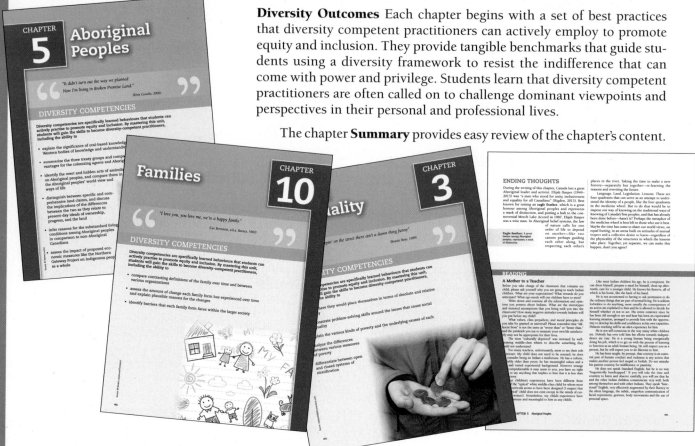

Diversity Outcomes Each chapter begins with a set of best practices that diversity competent practitioners can actively employ to promote equity and inclusion. They provide tangible benchmarks that guide students using a diversity framework to resist the indifference that can come with power and privilege. Students learn that diversity competent practitioners are often called on to challenge dominant viewpoints and perspectives in their personal and professional lives.

The chapter **Summary** provides easy review of the chapter's content.

TWO TYPES OF BOXES

In Their Shoes uses students' stories to give an authentic voice to the lived experience of "real" people that other students can identify with.

Picture This ... uses carefully chosen photographs to speak to the undiscovered themes in each chapter as students consider the historical and future implications of each photograph.

KEY TERMS

Every term is carefully defined and is conveniently located in the text margins beside the section where the term is first introduced. A complete glossary of all key terms is included at the end of the text.

END-OF-CHAPTER SKILL-BUILDING MATERIAL

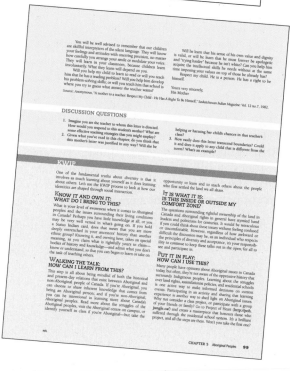

Each chapter ends with a reading, followed by several discussion questions that instructors can use as the basis for a written assignment, an oral discussion, or a class debate. The K.W.I.P. feature closes each chapter by leading students through a process of reflective questioning using the following steps:

    K: Know it and own it—What do I bring to this?

    W: Walk the talk—How can I learn from this?

    I: It is what it is—Is this inside or outside my comfort zone?

    P: Put it in play—How can I use this?

Students can respond to these questions on the accompanying online study platform, CourseMate, and submit their answers to their instructor through the technology.

CourseMate

Nelson Education's *Walk a Mile* CourseMate brings course concepts to life with interactive learning and exam preparation tools that integrate with the printed textbook. Students activate their knowledge through quizzes, games, and flashcards, among many other tools.

CourseMate provides immediate feedback that enables students to connect results to the work they have just produced, increasing their learning efficiency. It encourages contact between students and faculty: you can select to monitor your students' level of engagement with **CourseMate**, correlating their efforts to their outcomes. You can even use **CourseMate**'s quizzes to practise "Just in Time" teaching by tracking results in the Engagement Tracker and customizing your lesson plans to address their learning needs.

Engagement Tracker. How do you assess your students' engagement in your course? How do you know your students have read the material or viewed the resources you've assigned?

Good practice encourages frequent contacts between students and faculty. With **CourseMate**, you can use the included Engagement Tracker to assess student preparation and engagement.

Consult the tracking tools to see progress for the class as a whole or for individual students. Identify students at risk early in the course. Uncover which concepts are most difficult for your class. Monitor time on task. Keep your students engaged.

Interactive Teaching and Learning Tools. **CourseMate** includes interactive teaching and learning tools:

- Flashcards
- *Picture This* with reflection questions
- *The Daily* with critical thinking questions
- The KWIP framework with reflection questions
- …and more!

The variety of tools in **CourseMate** respect diverse ways of learning and give students ample opportunity to actively engage with the course concepts. Students receive prompt feedback, which helps them to focus their learning efforts on the concepts they have yet to master. Time plus energy equals learning, and **CourseMate** offers an engaging way for students to increase their time on task.

Interactive Ebook. In addition to interactive teaching and learning tools, **CourseMate** includes an interactive eBook. Students can take notes, highlight, search, and interact with embedded media specific to their book. Use it as a supplement to the printed text, or as a substitute—the choice is your students' with **CourseMate**.

Preface

INTRODUCTION

With over 50 combined years of working and teaching in the areas of diversity, equity, and justice, we have tested our fair share of teaching strategies. Some have been more successful than others, but we have found that the best ones have always been those that have involved a *balance* of theory *and* content with plenty of experiential (or in-class, and *increasingly* online) sharing and learning. Finding a resource that combines those principles, written at a level that engages students at both college and university, has been problematic, so a few years ago we created a course manual. Thanks to the brilliant vision and bulldog tenacity of Maya Castle, our publisher at Nelson Education, *Walk a Mile: Experiencing and Understanding Diversity in Canada* is the evolution of that initial manual. It has been enriched by the thoughtful, thorough suggestions provided by reviewers from across the country. Their feedback has been instrumental in creating this resource, which aims to balance student engagement activities, theoretical material, and critical thinking and self-reflection exercises, written in an inviting style so that every learner becomes part of the learning experience.

> *Our Reviewers Write …*
>
> *I have been reviewing books for a new … Diversity course and this manual is the first text book that attempts to go "beneath the tip of the iceberg." It is not just a text full of theory and concepts, but attempts to capture the real life application and significance of the people whose lives they are supposed to address.*

GOALS OF THIS BOOK: WHEN STUDENTS WALK A MILE THEY WILL BE ABLE TO …

Our goals as authors of this textbook were to create a text that would help students to:

- Define diversity as a framework that acknowledges difference, power, and privilege using principles of social equity, social justice, and anti-oppression

- Actively engage in examining issues of diversity including social inequality, race, ethnicity, immigration, religion, gender, sexuality, appearance, ability, age, family, and technology in ways that are relevant to the lives of students today
- Extend learning beyond the classroom to the real world and diverse experiences of affected persons and communities
- Enjoy the interactive experience of learning about diversity in a nontraditional manner
- Understand diversity through greater self-awareness, knowledge, and empathy for those who experience prejudice and discrimination, and competent practice
- Reflect critically upon their role as a diversity-competent practitioner in both their personal and professional life
- Model ways of being in the world that value diversity and help to promote awareness, respect, and inclusiveness in building positive relationships with diverse communities
- Critically analyze roots of oppression and inequality for historically disadvantaged and underrepresented communities and make connections with systemic discrimination experienced by these communities in contemporary society
- Devise sustainable and inclusive strategies to eliminate barriers to full participation of diverse communities

WALK A MILE IN THE CLASSROOM

As educators, we make many decisions—including if and how we want to use a textbook. One of the features that we often look at is the textbook's fit with our course plan. *Walk a Mile* was designed to provide you, as an instructor, with a balanced presentation of information in steps that mirror the process of becoming diversity-competent. The intention of its design was to give you ideas to help with the development of course plans including course goals, student learning objectives, assessment plans, units of instruction, and course schedule. For those instructors with an established syllabus, *Walk a Mile* can be customized to include specific chapters to meet your needs and provide you with the content required to cover your course's topics.

Our Reviewers Write …

The materials, concepts and pedagogical techniques in this text are everything I would want to include in a diversity course.

Walk a Mile welcomes your students into an invitational learning environment where content and pedagogy interact in nontraditional ways. More than a compendium of intellectual content, this text will engage your students through an active learning approach that makes diversity relevant to their personal and professional lives. Students "must talk about what they are learning, write about it, relate it to past experiences, and apply it to their daily lives. They must make what they learn part of themselves" (Chickering & Gamson, March 1987). *Walk a Mile* uses pedagogical elements to tap into the voices, experiences, creativity, and passion of post-secondary students, infusing it with content relevant to students' own lives. *Walk a Mile* is shaped by a belief that experiential activities are among some of the most powerful teaching and learning tools available. For example, the pedagogical element entitled *In Their Shoes* shares powerful experience narratives of students as tools for empathy, while the pedagogical element entitled *KWIP* facilitates reflection on experience and action. Together these elements awaken in students an understanding that learning scaffolds on experience and reflection. Most of our reviewers identify *Walk a Mile's* uniqueness and strength as its ability to engage students through its active learning approach.

Our Reviewers Write …

I especially like this text because it takes the hassle out of teaching. These authors have done a lot of the work for faculty: the book is full of good ideas for developing and supporting a syllabus, it has plenty of in-class activity ideas, and opportunities for students to engage with the material outside of the class room and through the Internet.

Walk a Mile's CourseMate website is designed to help instructors facilitate interaction with the textbook's pedagogical elements. As an instructor, the website can help you to create and align assessment whether the course is delivered online, through blended learning or face-to-face in the classroom. Students can interact with the pedagogical elements

of the textbook in an online environment designed to encourage active learning through tools such as discussion boards, journals, blogs, and wikis. This creates online opportunities for students to empathize with other students' stories from *In Their Shoes*, to engage in reflective practices through *KWIP*, to evaluate and problem-solve the hot topics revealed in *Picture This*, to interpret numerical data and analyze findings presented through *The Daily*, and to use their sociological imaginations in creating change for *Diversity Competencies*. Go to **login.cengage.com** to access these resources, and look for this icon ⚡**Course**Mate which denotes a resource available within CourseMate.

PEDAGOGICAL FRAMEWORK

Walk a Mile is a text that supports the implementation of active learning based upon research on best practices in learning environments (Michael, 2006). The hallmarks of active learning include: a holistic approach that involves cognitive and affective domains of learning; embracing diversity and students' unique ways of knowing, learning, and experiencing; making connections between academic knowledge and practice; emphasizing reflective practice; and active engagement in critical thinking processes that involve analysis of concepts, forming opinions, synthesizing ideas, questioning, problem-solving, and evaluating information (McKeachie & Svinicki, 2006).

Our Reviewers Write …

The pedagogy integrating academic and experiential learning tools is inspiring. It has the ability to motivate students and teachers to actively engage (think, reflect, and reflex) with the text and issues of diversity in the real world.

As the title indicates, *Walk a Mile: Experiencing and Understanding Diversity in Canada* requires learning in the cognitive and affective domains. It is not a book that focuses exclusively on the intellectual journey and content because learning about diverse communities also requires empathy and understanding that are culled from experience.

Opening Lyrics. Each chapter begins with a line from a song that relates to the specific theme in each chapter. Why do we use song lyrics and not a quotation from a book or article? Music unites people and builds a commonality at the outset of the chapter. Music also makes us feel—its lyrics help us relate to the experience as we take in the emotional aspects of a song. And feeling, as we know, is an important part of the process of becoming diversity competent.

In Their Shoes. *In Their Shoes* is a pedagogical tool that uses students' stories to give an authentic voice to the lived experience of "real" people that other students can identify with. *In Their Shoes* consists of a piece of original work written by a college or university student on the specific theme of each chapter. The student authors come from a variety of different programs and institutions. With courage and integrity, they shared their personal narratives so that readers might grow in empathy, understanding, and knowledge as they walk a mile "in their shoes". Many of the student authors saw the writing of their stories as an opportunity to engage in the political act of storytelling. Their hope has been that a dialogue might begin about the validity of lived experience as a form of knowledge and about the importance of teaching and learning empathy. Student readers actively engage with these stories because they are relevant to their lives here and now.

Diversity Competencies. Each chapter begins with a set of best practices that diversity-competent practitioners can actively employ to promote equity and inclusion. They provide tangible benchmarks that guide students in using a diversity framework to resist the indifference that can come with power and privilege. Students learn that diversity-competent practitioners are often called on to challenge dominant viewpoints and perspectives in their personal and professional lives. Chapter by chapter, as students learn and practice these diversity competencies, they come to understand that the enterprise of diversity is to construct a society where *all* people can experience the world as just; where *all* people are treated fairly; where *all* people have equivalent access to opportunities; where *all* people, including those historically underserved and underrepresented, feel valued, respected, and able to live lives free of oppression; and where *all* people can fully participate in the social institutions that affect their lives.

'K.W.I.P.' leads students through a process of reflective questioning at the conclusion of each chapter using the following steps:

K: Know it and own it—What do I bring to this? Here students come to terms with who, what, and where they are in their life and accept themselves just the way they are. This feature emphasizes the simple realization that until you get a firm grounding of who you are, you really can't understand and respect anyone else and where they may be coming from.

W: Walk the talk—How can I learn from this? This question establishes the intention to learn about diversity. A huge barrier to understanding and experiencing diversity lies in our fear of the unknown. Learning doesn't necessarily involve reading or listening to a lecture. It can mean learning through experiential affinity (a feeling of fellowship with others who have had similar experiences). Once students set an intention to learn, they can begin to "walk the talk". Mahatma Gandhi, whose leadership in India's struggle for independence from Britain in the early 20th century exemplified the practice of non-violent resistance to oppression, said "You must be the change that you want to see in the world". Walking the talk is all about being that change.

I: It is what it is—Is this inside or outside my comfort zone? Here students are required to honestly confront the fact that we get uncomfortable when we encounter perspectives that are different than our own. Becoming diversity competent requires that we step outside our comfort zone to see things from another point of view. Students discover the wisdom that journalist James Surowiecki, author of *The Wisdom of Crowds*, outlines: The best decisions come from difference and discussion, not from like-minded individuals sharing the same experiences.

P: Put it in play—How can I use this? This last question is a call for students to move from social analysis to social action—by knowing and owning who they are; by establishing the intention to learn about new things; by recognizing the value of diversity; and by choosing to become involved as diversity-competent individuals. Through this process, students are engaged to think beyond the scope of their private selves to consider the implications of public occurrences in the world—in other words, to develop their "sociological imagination".

Picture This... Does a picture say a thousand words? The pictures in *Walk a Mile* have been selected to evoke meaningful critical thought in the minds of students and in their discussions with their peers. *Picture This* uses carefully chosen photographs to speak to the undiscovered themes in each chapter as students consider the historical implications and future implications of each photograph. This feature provides a perfect opportunity for students to use their sociological imaginations.

Readings and Discussion Questions. Our experience has been that readings can form the basis of lively classroom discussions, so every chapter includes a reading carefully chosen to encourage students to make connections between the chapter's themes and its key concepts and ideas. Each reading is followed by several discussion questions that instructors can use as the basis for a written assignment, an oral discussion, or a class debate. We have found that students who work on these active learning exercises are better able to process what they've read and to focus on important information.

CHAPTER HIGHLIGHTS

The key issues and topics, inspired by students, covered in each chapter are outlined below. These highlights begin with action verbs reflective of the active process of learning required in becoming diversity competent.

Chapter 1 Diversity and Identity

- Evaluate the concept of diversity in a Canadian context as a framework for equity and social justice
- Understand the concept and the process of becoming diversity competent beginning with an analysis of identity and increased self-awareness
- Analyze the complex and fluid concepts of personal and social identity in the context of your relational map of the world
- Distinguish between concepts of equality and equity
- Reflect upon how to create socially inclusive and equitable environments

Chapter 2 Forms of Oppression

- Discover the hidden ways oppression manifests itself in everyday life
- Interpret the intersectionality of systems of privilege through the "ism" prism
- Identify mechanisms within society that cause or reinforce different forms of oppression
- Evaluate the consequences of privilege that dominant groups have over the population
- Reflect upon implicit bias as a step towards greater self-awareness

Chapter 3 Social Inequality

- Develop an understanding of what stratification is and how it works
- Demonstrate problem-solving skills around the issues that cause social inequality
- Explain the types and causes of poverty at a national and global level
- Analyze the differences between various measures of poverty
- Reflect upon ways that social stratification and social inequality have impacted your life

Chapter 4 Race as a Social Construct

- Describe racism as a hierarchical system of power and privilege
- Evaluate the effects of racial stereotypes, racial prejudice, and racial discrimination on diverse groups
- Examine the role racialized, ethnic, and multiple cultural identities have on interpersonal encounters and community relationships
- Reflect upon your own privilege and bias and how this can be relevant to anti-racism practices in the workplace

Chapter 5 Aboriginal Peoples

- Explain the significance of oral-based knowledge systems in relation to Western bodies of knowledge and understanding
- Summarize the three treaty groups and compare the advantages and disadvantages for

the colonizing agents and Aboriginal groups involved

- Identify both the overt and hidden acts/Acts of assimilation/oppression forced on Aboriginal peoples and compare them in terms of increasing costs to the Aboriginal peoples' world view and ways of life
- Distinguish between specific and comprehensive land claims and discuss the implications of the differences between the two as they relate to present day ideals of ownership, progress, and the land
- Infer reasons for the substandard living conditions among Aboriginal peoples in comparison to non-Aboriginal Canadians and assess the impact of proposed economic measures like the Northern Gateway Project on Indigenous peoples as a whole

Chapter 6 Religion

- Demonstrate awareness of the changing religious demographics in Canada and the factors contributing to these changes
- Demonstrate knowledge of the history of Canada's religious communities and minorities
- Identify the main components of religious accommodation as dictated by provincial laws
- Identify "fault lines" where religious accommodation laws and personal freedoms collide
- Reflect upon whether or not religion is compatible with the modern world

Chapter 7 Gender and Sexuality

- Distinguish between the biological determination of sex and the social construction of gender as they relate to an individual's expression of their own sexuality
- Describe the culturally appropriate roles that define masculine and feminine and explain the consequences of straying from these defined roles
- Analyze gender inequality on a national and global scale
- Reflect upon how sexualities are represented across culture, time, race, ethnicity, class, gender, age, and ability and why they are labeled as straight, gay, lesbian, bisexual, queer, or transgender

Chapter 8 Mind and Body

- Assess strategies for the civic engagement of all citizens through an understanding that persons with disabilities may experience limited opportunities for social inclusion in the activities of their communities and social institutions
- Reconstruct attitudes and approaches whereby persons with disabilities move from being "objects" of charity, medical treatment, and social protection to instead being "subjects" with rights to make their own decisions and actively contribute to their community
- Appraise universal design practices and principles as an approach to social inclusion and accessibility
- Reflect upon the universalizing implications of the World Health Organization's definition of disability as something every human being can experience at some point in their lifetime

Chapter 9 Generations and Technology

- Summarize the differing characteristics that identify each generation from Traditionalists to Baby Boomers to Generation X, Generation Y, and Generation AO
- Assess the role of technology in each generation
- Determine the barriers and benefits of technology as they relate to each generation
- Reflect upon the role that technology plays in shaping your own lived experiences

Chapter 10 Families

- Compare contrasting definitions of the family and implications of conceptualizing family in different ways
- Analyze trends, characteristics, and diversities of families in Canada within a historical and contemporary context
- Critically analyze challenges facing families in Canada today
- Reflect upon how self-awareness and knowledge of various family traditions and values can expand our world view and influence our relationships with diverse populations

Chapter 11 Immigration

- Examine historic and contemporary patterns of immigration and resettlement in Canada
- Analyze issues associated with Canada's immigration system that impact settlement and integration of ethnic groups
- Assess barriers to acculturation faced by newcomers to Canada
- Differentiate between the experiences of immigrants and refugees and the impact those experiences have on individuals and families
- Reflect upon your own personal migration history and locate it within the context of Canadian immigration history

Chapter 12 Multiculturalism

- Trace the history and various definitions of multiculturalism
- Distinguish between multiculturalism and diversity
- Assess whether or not multiculturalism is working in Canada
- Reflect upon multiculturalism as a unifying and inclusive national identity and as a divisive and marginalizing reality

Chapter 13 Practicing Diversity

- Scaffold increased self-awareness and knowledge to develop diversity-competent practices for the purpose of achieving equity and justice at a personal, professional, and global level
- Analyze tools for social change that challenge injustice and embrace social inclusion and equity in local, national, and global systems
- Construct strategies to combat prejudice and discrimination against diverse populations
- Reflect upon the ways that you can move from social analysis to social action to make a difference in the world you live in

ANCILLARIES

About the Nelson Education Teaching Advantage (NETA)

The Nelson Education Teaching Advantage (NETA) program delivers research-based instructor resources that promote student engagement and higher-order thinking to enable the success of Canadian students and educators.

Instructors today face many challenges. Resources are limited, time is scarce, and a new kind of student has emerged: one who is juggling school with work, has gaps in his or her basic knowledge, and is immersed in technology in a way that has led to a completely new style of learning. In response, Nelson Education has gathered a group of dedicated instructors to advise us on the creation of richer and more flexible ancillaries and online learning platforms that respond to the needs of today's teaching environments. Whether your course is offered in-class, online, or both, Nelson is pleased to provide pedagogically driven, research-based resources to support you.

In consultation with the editorial advisory board, Nelson Education has completely rethought the structure, approaches, and formats of our key textbook ancillaries and online learning platforms. We've also increased our investment in editorial support for our ancillary and digital authors. The result is the Nelson Education Teaching Advantage and its key components: *NETA Engagement, NETA Assessment, NETA Presentation,* and *NETA Digital.* Each component includes one or more ancillaries prepared according to our best practices and may also be accompanied by documentation explaining the theory behind the practices.

NETA Engagement presents materials that help instructors deliver engaging content and activities to their classes. Instead of Instructor's Manuals that regurgitate chapter outlines and key terms from the text, NETA Enriched Instructor's Manuals (EIMs) provide genuine assistance to teachers. The EIMs answer questions like *What should students learn?, Why should students care?,* and *What are some common student misconceptions and stumbling blocks?* EIMs not only identify the topics that cause students the most difficulty, but also describe techniques and resources to help students master these concepts. Dr. Roger Fisher's *Instructor's Guide to Classroom Engagement (IGCE)* accompanies every Enriched Instructor's Manual. (Information about the NETA Enriched Instructor's Manual prepared for *Walk a Mile* is included in the description of the IRCD below.)

NETA Presentation has been developed to help instructors make the best use of PowerPoint® in their classrooms. With a clean and uncluttered design developed by Maureen Stone of StoneSoup Consulting, NETA Presentation features slides with improved readability, more multi-media and graphic materials, activities to use in class, and tips for instructors on the Notes page. A copy of *NETA Guidelines for Classroom Presentations* by Maureen Stone is included with each set of PowerPoint slides. (Information about the NETA PowerPoint® prepared for *Walk a Mile* is included in the description of the IRCD below.)

NETA Digital is a framework based on Arthur Chickering and Zelda Gamson's seminal work "Seven Principles of Good Practice In Undergraduate Education" (AAHE Bulletin, 1987) and the follow-up work by Chickering and Stephen C. Ehrmann, "Implementing the Seven Principles: Technology as Lever" (AAHE Bulletin, 1996). This aspect of the NETA program guides the writing and development of our digital products to ensure that they appropriately reflect the core goals of contact, collaboration, multimodal learning, time on task, prompt feedback, active learning, and high expectations. The resulting focus on pedagogical utility, rather than technological wizardry, ensures that all of our technology supports better outcomes for students.

INSTRUCTOR RESOURCES

Key instructor ancillaries are provided at **www.nelson.com/site/walkamile1e**, giving instructors the ultimate tool for customizing lectures and presentations. The Instructor Resources include:

- **NETA Enriched Instructor's Manual and Test-bank:** The Enriched Instructor's Manual and Testbank was written by Cindy Gervais, Fleming College. It is organized according to the textbook chapters and addresses seven key educational concerns, such as typical stumbling blocks students face and how to address them.

- **NETA Presentation:** Microsoft® PowerPoint® lecture slides for every chapter have been created by Sheila Gordon, St. Clair College. There is an average of 35 slides per chapter, many featuring key figures, tables, and photographs from *Walk a Mile*. NETA principles of clear design and engaging content have been incorporated throughout.

- **Image Library:** This resource consists of digital copies of figures, short tables, and photographs used in the book. Instructors may use these jpegs to create their own PowerPoint presentations.

- **DayOne:** Day One—Prof InClass is a PowerPoint presentation that you can customize to orient your students to the class and their text at the beginning of the course.

ACKNOWLEDGMENTS

Heartfelt thanks to our students who have influenced and contributed to the creation of this textbook. You were the spark that inspired us to create something different. Your feedback, both inside and outside of the classroom, helped us to refine our content in ways relevant to your lives, here and now. With courage and integrity, you shared the stories of your lived experience so that we might grow in empathy, understanding, and knowledge as we walked in your shoes. This book was not only written *for* students, it was written *with* students so that *Walk a Mile* could provide unique insights that would not have been otherwise achievable without you.

We're very lucky to have had our brilliant colleague and friend, Samah Marei, participate as a contributing author to *Walk a Mile*. As a scholar, she graduated from UCLA and spent years travelling, studying, and teaching throughout the Middle East. The richness of her writing is infused by diverse life experiences, for she was born in Egypt, raised in California, employed as a diversity trainer for policing organizations, and is now working both as a professor and the operator of a self-sustaining organic farm. We also thank her beautiful children Dawoud, Munajat, and Selma for their patience and understanding when we needed more of Mommy's time.

We would like to express our gratitude to the following reviewers, who provided constructive and candid feedback that helped to shape the focus, content, and pedagogical elements of *Walk a Mile*:

Michele Lemon, Sheridan College

Patricia Kaye, Fanshawe College

Blake Lambert, Humber College

Stephen Decator, St. Clair College

Sean Ashley, Simon Fraser University

James R. Vanderwoerd, Redeemer University College

Francis Adu-Febiri, Camosun College and University of Victoria

David Aliaga Rossel, Vancouver Island University

Cindy Haig, Fleming College

Tara Gauld, Confederation College

Anastasia Blake, St. Clair College of Applied Arts and Technology

In addition, we acknowledge Niagara College of Applied Arts and Technology.

We would like to acknowledge the extraordinary talent and dedication of everyone we worked with at Nelson Education Ltd. Special thanks go to Executive Editor Maya Castle, who believed in the vision of this book when it was nothing more than a course manual. Developmental Editor Jessica Freedman's work was amazing, brilliant, and extremely generous—especially in the late stages. We are very grateful to both editors and the rest of the team: Christine Gilbert, Content Production Manager, Terry Fedorkiw, Marketing Manager, Eva Svec, Freelance Permissions Researcher, Lynn McLeod, Permissions Manager, Elspeth McFadden, Copy Editor, and Sangeetha, Project Manager.

How inspiring would it be to *walk a mile* in the shoes of the Kielburger brothers, Marc and Craig? They are the embodiment of what it means to be socially conscious global citizens committed to changing the world through social action premised on equity, justice, diversity, and inclusion. As educators, we have had the opportunity to witness the transformative change they inspire in people's lives. We are especially honoured to have Craig and Marc Kielburger author the foreword to *Walk a Mile*.

To our family members, friends, and colleagues who supported us along the way—heartfelt thanks, and yes, we're finally finished!

PREFACE REFERENCES

Chickering, A. W., & Gamson, Z. F. (March 1987). Seven principles for good practice. *AAHE Bulletin* 39 (7), 3–7.

Collins, P. H. (2000). *Black feminist thought: Knowledge, consciousness and the politics of empowerment* (2nd ed.). New York: Routledge.

Keller, H. (1903). *Optimism: An essay*. New York: Crowell and Company.

McKeachie, W., & Svinicki, M. (2006). *Teaching tips: Strategies, research, and theory for college and university teachers*. Belmont, CA: Wadsworth.

Michael, J. (2006). Where's the evidence that active learning works? *Advances in Physiology Education*, 30(4), 159–167.

Diversity and Identity

> *"Sing it loud, so everyone knows who you are."*
>
> *(k.d. lang, 2011)*

DIVERSITY COMPETENCIES

Diversity competencies are specifically learned behaviours that students can actively practise to promote equity and inclusion. By mastering this unit, students will gain the skills to become diversity-competent practitioners, including the ability to

- examine diversity in Canadian society from a variety of perspectives as a basis for equitable relationships

- understand the concept and the process of becoming diversity-competent

- know your own map and how it forms and informs your personal and social identity

- further your understanding of the complexity, multiplicity, intersectionality (interactions), fluidity, and contextuality of personal and social identity

- understand and critique personal identity formation, which includes differentiating between the perceptions of others (ascribed identity) and subjective truth (avowed identity)

- analyze the social construction of "other" in identity formation, and analyze the privileging of some identities over others

- examine beliefs, values, and behaviours that form individual and community identities, and locate personal identity within a national and global context

It is incredible how different we all are as human beings. To prove this, Timothy Allen, a photographer for the BBC series *Human Planet* (2011), captured in stunning imagery the diversity of human experience as he travelled to over 40 countries and some of the world's most extreme environments—from the BaAka villagers in the jungle of Congo Valley in the Central African Republic to the Kazakh hunter with his golden eagle perched in the remote mountains of western Mongolia, and from the Laotian fishers on the raging Mekong River to the Bajan Laut people of Malaysia, who don't set foot on land. Allen's adventure was the dream of most sociocultural anthropologists, and the human element of his extraordinary photos chronicled the great social and cultural diversity of our species.

For many people, the concept of **diversity** exists in a global context. In this text, we define diversity more broadly than a concept of culture based on a person's race, ethnicity, language, or country of birth. Diversity is also more than difference based on salient aspects of our identity. We define diversity as an anti-oppression framework built on principles that value social equity, social justice, social inclusion, and global citizenship. In fact, using a diversity framework is a means of resisting the indifference that can come with power and privilege. It is only then that we can unlock the human potential for every person on this planet to contribute in a positive way to the social world they live in. Imagine a Canada without the contributions of people like Craig and Mark Kielburger, Tommy Douglas, Lincoln Alexander, Margaret Atwood, Michaëlle Jean, Chris Hadfield, Roméo Dallaire, Adrienne Clarkson, Anne Murray, k.d. lang, Rita McNeil, David Suzuki, Alexander Graham Bell, Chief Big Bear, Pierre Trudeau, Jack Layton, Stephen Lewis, Chief Dan George, George Stroumboulopoulos, Jean Vanier, Rick Hanson, Russell Peters, John Diefenbaker, Raymond Moriyama, Terry Fox, and Peter Mansbridge. Suppose their social identities had marginalized and socially excluded them from participating in and contributing to the society they lived in? While acknowledging the legacy of these great Canadians, we recognize that the potential to actively participate and contribute in a significant way to our community, our nation, and our world is within all of us; it is not solely limited to people of power, heads of state, monarchs, or celebrities.

We have also found Canadian heroes in students who had the courage to share their personal stories and who asked you to walk a mile in their shoes. Each chapter in this volume features the narrative of one such student. Engaging in the political act of storytelling, these students shared their narratives in the hopes that a dialogue will begin about the validity of lived experience and the importance of empathy. Their narratives are a poignant reminder that the enterprise of diversity is to construct a society where *all* people can experience the world as just: where *all* people are treated fairly; where *all* people have equivalent access to opportunities; where *all* people, including those historically **underserved** and under-represented, feel valued, respected and able to live lives free of oppression; and where *all* people can be fully participatory in the social institutions that affect their lives.

THE EVOLUTION OF DIVERSITY AS A CONCEPT

Twenty years ago, colleges and universities taught courses on cultural sensitivity that focused on being respectful of different cultures, ethnicities, and races. We rolled out courses in cross-cultural studies that focused on the differences in the **material culture** (the physical aspects of a culture or society) and **non-material culture** (the non-physical aspects of culture or society) of people from other countries. As technology and globalization changed the modern workplace, employees required communication skills and cultural savvy to provide service to consumers in different cultures and to do business in a global context. Courses began focusing on developing skills in verbal and nonverbal communication. Corporate training taught employees the cultural faux pas, with HSBC's series of commercials being the most memorable. The persistence of this approach is owing to the fact that some of the major demographic changes in Canada are due to ethnic and racial diversification resulting from immigration.

Our idea of diversity then evolved into the concept of an **intercultural** perspective that began to look at more than cultural differences; Canada's idea of diversity began to develop concepts of cultural

Diversity: A framework used to acknowledge difference-based guiding principles of social equity, social justice, and anti-oppression.

Underserved: Disadvantaged because of structural barriers and disparities.

Material culture: The physical aspects of a culture or society; for example, food, clothes, buildings, religious objects, homes, places of worship, music, art and so on.

Non-material culture: The non-physical aspects of culture or society, including customs, traditions, symbols, language, values, beliefs, norms, and sanctions.

Intercultural: Relating to different cultural groups.

cooperation, examining the commonalities between cultures for the purpose of bridging cultures. Later, this viewpoint evolved to a **transcultural** perspective, still used widely today, that transcends difference and extends among all cultures. For example, Madeleine Leininger is credited with developing the concept known as transcultural nursing, now a discipline within nursing that uses a comparative study of culture to understand similarities and differences across human groups (Leininger & McFarland, 2002). As a result of Leininger's work, people involved in health care—be they nurses, social workers, human resource managers, business executives, or police officers—are developing **cultural competency**; they are learning to interact in a manner that is respectful of and consistent with a person's culture. In Canada, **multiculturalism**, which is the practice of creating harmonious relations between different cultural groups as an ideology and policy to promote cultural diversity, continues to be an intrinsic component of our national identity. The success of this practice is evidenced in the World Values Survey. Compared with other countries, Canada received an "A" grade for acceptance of diversity (see Figure 1.1).

The term diversity was for a time used interchangeably with *culture*, with the definition of diversity being limited to concepts of race, ethnicity, and culture. Then a fundamental change in an understanding of the term diversity occurred, and the term now includes all aspects of personal and community identity under its banner. Diversity can be defined as a framework used to acknowledge difference-based guiding principles of social equity, social justice, and anti-oppression. Broadening focus beyond different cultures, languages, and countries, diversity as

a concept includes all forms of visible and invisible **difference**, including gender, age, socio-economic status, mental and physical abilities, sexual orientation, religion, spirituality, language, accent, family status, educational background, literacy, appearance, organizational role, group affiliation, ethnicity, race, citizenship, values, belief systems, country of birth, and so on (see Figure 1.2).

There are visible differences, such as physical capability, body size, age, gender, ethnicity, and race, to which we socially attach meaning; and these visible differences can serve as the basis for various forms of prejudice and discrimination in a particular society. These forms of discrimination—abelism, sizeism, ageism, sexism, heterosexism, and racism, for example—are discussed in subsequent chapters. There are also invisible differences, differences which are not immediately apparent, that can also serve as a basis for prejudice and discrimination. If we use the metaphor of an iceberg, there is a part of the iceberg that is visible above the surface of the water (see Figure 1.3). We see it, it is apparent, and we react to it. Below the waterline, there are very large pieces of the iceberg which are not immediately apparent, but which are

Transcultural: Transcending cultural differences.

Cultural competency: The ability of an organization or individual to practise in a manner that is respectful of and consistent with a client's or a patient's culture.

Multiculturalism: The practice of creating harmonious relations between different cultural groups.

Difference: In a social context, it is a term used to refer to difference in social characteristics.

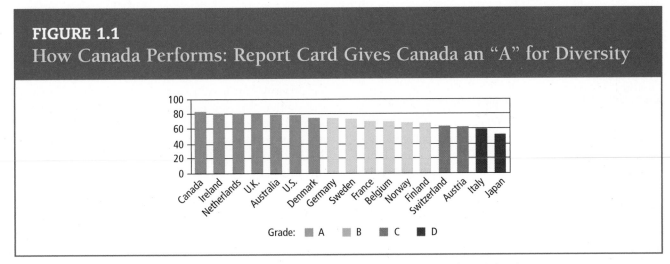

FIGURE 1.1
How Canada Performs: Report Card Gives Canada an "A" for Diversity

Grade: ■ A ■ B ■ C ■ D

Source: How Canada Performs, "Acceptance of Diversity, 2011 or Most Recent Year," The Conference Board of Canada (2013).

FIGURE 1.2
Diversity Defined beyond Culture, Language, and Country

accent
gender
literacy
religion female appearance
language familystatus samesex
cognitiveability young mentalability
physicalabilities rich sexualorientation
older organizationalrole
birthcountry age groupaffiliation
transgender ethnicity spirituality
single poor
race
citizenship
educational
divorced

Diversity as a concept includes all forms of visible and invisible differences.

FIGURE 1.3
The Diversity Iceberg: The Waterline of Visible and Invisible Difference

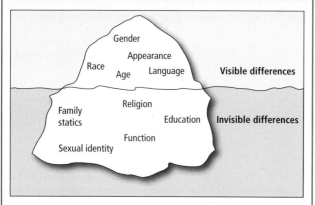

Identity is like an iceberg; part of it is readily visible, but part of it is beneath the surface.

Equality: Fairness and justice achieved through same treatment.

Equity: Principle based on fairness, justice, access, opportunity, and advancement for everyone, while recognizing historically underserved and unrepresented populations, identifying conditions needed to provide effective opportunities for all groups, and eliminating barriers to their full participation.

aspect of a person's identity that can be visible or invisible depending on the circumstances. Physical disabilities can also be visible or invisible. Some parts of non-visible identity, such as sexual orientation, can make you a target for discrimination. Even if someone merely suspects that you are homosexual, bisexual, or transgendered, you may experience discrimination.

Diversity means a great deal more than celebrating difference, just as multiculturalism means a great deal more than saris, samosas, and steel bands. The journey towards diversity competency requires an acknowledgment of the power and privilege that are central in the social construction of our identities. So the concept of diversity—particularly in the public sector—began to evolve as an anti-oppression framework, using concepts like **power**, **privilege**, and **marginalization** to analyze the social construction of "other" as different from the **dominant group**, or the group with social power in a society. Power is the ability to do what you want even in the face of opposition, while marginalization is the process of pushing groups with less social power to the margins of society.

This framework recognized that as certain characteristics became valued and created privilege, other characteristics were devalued and served to marginalize people, thereby creating social structures of domination and oppression expressed in practices of classism, sexism, racism, ageism, ableism, heterosexism, and so on, as illustrated in Table 1.1.

Walk a Mile in My Shoes: One Size Never Fits All

So how do we construct a society where all people can experience the world as just? Where all people are treated fairly? Where all people have equivalent access to opportunities? Where all people, including those historically underserved and under-represented, feel valued, respected, and able to live lives free of oppression? And where all people can fully participate in the social institutions that affect their lives? The conservative approach to anti-oppression is fairness and justice through **equality**, meaning that everyone is treated the same way. The liberal approach to anti-oppression sees diversity as **difference**, meaning that everyone is included despite differences in social characteristics. Neither of these approaches is about **equity** (Sen, 2010).

A diversity banner that uses either the *sameness* or *difference* approach serves to keep the standards of the dominant group intact. If you are discriminated against because you are a woman, is the solution to be treated the *same* as a man? Or is the solution a *difference* approach that means justifying special treatment

of immense importance. The same is true with respect to who we are and how others perceive us.

There are times when certain characteristics may float above the surface of the water to become visible and other times where those same characteristics will be submerged and become invisible. Religion is one

TABLE 1.1
Dominant and Non-Dominant Groups in Canada Based on Aspects of Social Identity

Social Identity	Dominant Group	Non-Dominant Group
Age	Ages 30–60	Youth and seniors
Ability	Able-bodied people	People who are mentally and/or physically disabled
Language of origin	English language	Non-English languages
Faith/Religion	Christianity	Non-Christians
Gender	Male and cisgender*	Female and transgender
Socio-economic status	Middle- and upper-class people	Working class, low-income people, people living in poverty
Race	White people	People of colour and Aboriginal people
Sexual orientation	Heterosexual people	Lesbian, gay, and bisexual people

* The term *cisgender* means having a gender perception that matches one's physical gender.

Source: Ontario Council of Agencies Serving Immigrants (2012). Positive Spaces Initiative's Online Training Course. Retrieved from Ontario Learn: http://learnatwork.ca

for you because you are a woman and explaining the need to deviate from the norm? According to law professor Catherine MacKinnon (1989), neither approach works:

> You can't change the relationship between those who are equal and those who are unequal by giving them the same things ... the relation between the two stays the same, and it is the relation that defines the inequality. The dominant measure is set by advantaged people ... sameness and difference is not the issue of inequality. It never has been. To make this the issue conceals, among other things, the way that the dominant group becomes the measure of everything, including the measure of the disadvantaged group's entitlement to equal treatment. (pp. 5–7)

So can we use the concept of diversity as more than an approach that recognizes differences—instead, as a framework for achieving social equity? To accomplish this requires an understanding of what social equity means and how it is differentiated from the concept of equality. Both equality and equity try to achieve a fair outcome for all people. Equality implies that everyone gets the same thing; but because everyone is different,

treating everyone the same in all situations is not necessarily fair and can lead to unequal results. Social equity is trying to achieve equitable outcomes for all people by ensuring everyone gets what is *right for them*. To provide an applied definition as an example, equity in health can be defined as "the absence of systematic disparities in health (or in the major social determinants of health) between social groups who have different levels of underlying social advantage/disadvantage" (Braveman & Gruskin, 2003). You can see from this definition that equity is a "more flexible measure allowing for equivalency" that accounts for the effects of social disadvantage and does not use the socially advantaged position as the measure of sameness (University of Melbourne, 2013). The process for determining and achieving this **equivalency** requires self-definition and the ability for marginalized communities to share power and leadership in creating change.

A good illustration of the difference between the concepts of equality and equity came from a professor at the University of Waterloo. In class one day, he invited everyone to sit in a circle. He then asked each student to remove his or her right shoe and throw it into a pile in the centre of the circle. The

Equivalency: State of being equal to another.

professor then randomly redistributed the shoes, one shoe to each student, and asked the students to put on their new shoes. Of course, everyone was somewhat perplexed, and very few students were actually happy with the shoe they had been given. A student then asked the professor to explain the point of this exercise.

"I want to treat you all equally and I have, because everyone has one shoe for their right foot and one shoe for their left foot," the professor said. "What's the problem with this? Seems fair."

The student responded, "I think the point you are making is that the solution is never one size fits all. We need the shoes that each fit us best individually."

The inference was not lost on this student, who had summed up the difference between equality and equity. *Equality* means that in order to be fair and just, you give all people the same thing or treat them in the same way, regardless of their individual needs. This approach presumes that everyone is on a level playing field. In the classroom exercise, everyone ended up with the same thing (two shoes), regardless of their individual needs (like shoe size, width, comfort, etc.); so they were treated equally. *Equity* also aims to promote fairness and justice, but it does so by trying to understand and give people what they need individually. In order for the classroom exercise to demonstrate equity, it is no longer about everyone getting "a" shoe; it is about getting the shoe that fits the individual student.

At the end of this classroom experiment, the professor asked the students to return the right shoes into the centre of the circle. "Now I want *you* to choose the shoe that fits you best individually," he said.

Chaos erupted as the students ran to grab their own shoes. In the end, everyone was happy to have chosen his or her own shoe. Then something quite extraordinary happened: Two students with the same size shoes began to barter with one another, and a pair of stilettos was traded for a pair of runners. Seeing that both parties were happy, a few more trades ensued. Everyone left class happy with the shoes they were wearing. Not only were the students' choices in this exercise self-determined, but they also had had the power to collaborate on change if they wished. Ultimately, the second exercise was fair because the students all got the shoes that fit their individual needs and because they were given the power to define what that was. While the process in the second part of the exercise was a more chaotic one, everyone was a lot happier with the result.

Not all diversity initiatives are about equity. Many people believe that the goal of multiculturalism in Canadian society is to use diversity as a unifying banner where all members of diverse communities are invited to sit at the table and participate. While this form of social **inclusion** is certainly a good step, it is not necessarily a full commitment to equity. Why? Consider the example of **tokenism**. As long as organizations with power are reaching out to marginalized communities to get affected members to embrace their agendas, then oppression can continue under a diversity banner. As a leading figure in the racial justice movement, Rinku Sen uses a critique of diversity initiatives that "get white organizations reaching out to racialized communities to get communities of colour to embrace white agenda and leadership" (2010). She notes that the problem is about shared power and equity. What is required is for marginalized communities to share both the power and the leadership to shape the agenda that moves forward a strategy that has results for the affected community (Sen, 2010). Equity can only be achieved when marginalized communities are fully participatory in creating change.

EXAMINING DIVERSITY FROM A VARIETY OF PERSPECTIVES

One of the bases for establishing equitable relationships is the understanding that there is not just one *who* nor just one *how to*. Who you are, how you interpret the world around you, how you live your life, how you know what you know, and how you've come to value and believe in certain things over others are all relative to particular forms of social power and privilege. Reading this textbook, for example, you will find personal stories that come from other Canadian post-secondary students who ask you to walk a mile *in their shoes*. What becomes apparent from the diversity of lived experiences that these students share is that we are all human beings who live in a social world that is shaped by **culture**, with culture referring to everything

Inclusion: Creating an environment that embraces diversity and where everyone is made to feel welcome, invited to participate, and valued and respected for their contributions.

Tokenism: The practice of including one or a small number of members of a minority group to create the appearance of representation, inclusion, and non-discrimination, without ever giving these members access to power.

Culture: The total of everything in our social environment that we learn through socialization, that is passed down from one generation to the next, and that continues to change throughout our lives.

that characterizes our species. The concept of culture is often used interchangeably with the concept of ethnicity, but this is erroneous. Culture is many things: it is learned and transmitted from one generation to the next; it is our way of interpreting the world around us; it is the ideas, beliefs, values, methods, and means by which we live our lives; it is the activity valued by social groups; it is the social institutions that we shape and that shape our lives; and it is always changing.

The concept of **cultural relativism** suggests that cultural context is critical to an understanding of a person's experience, values, beliefs, and actions (Howson, 2009). The concept of cultural relativism denies that any **standpoint** or world view is uniquely privileged over another (Howson, 2009). Imagine what would happen if professionals were to see their own world view as correct and their clients' or patients' views as deviant, problematic, or pathological.

The diversity-competent practitioner examines the role of power and privilege in people's lives. This requires them to shed **false consciousness** about living in a society that is **socially stratified**. The diversity-competent practitioner understands that having power and privilege in a society is not predetermined; power and privilege are socially constructed and create advantages and disadvantages based on race, class, gender, ability, age, sexual orientation, family status, and so on. As the diversity-competent practitioner arrives at a new awareness of how social power works, he or she begins to challenge dominant viewpoints and perspectives that contribute to the oppression and marginalization of others. This might be accomplished through strategies whereby marginalized communities share power and leadership in creating social change for affected communities. This might also be accomplished through the strategies of "becoming an ally," outlined by author Anne Bishop (2002). Whatever the strategy, this new awareness can shake the foundation of what the practitioner had accepted as truth and reality. Take, for example, the person who believes that people are poor because they are lazy. Then something changes the material circumstances of that person's life—maybe the person loses his or her job through downsizing, experiences a change in health status, gets divorced, or has an accident that affects his or her ability. This change in the material circumstances of life may contribute to an understanding of poverty from a different perspective—one rooted in the shortcomings of the economic, social, or political systems within a society.

Consider the movie *The Matrix*, as an allegory of the awakening from false consciousness that can blind us to the systemic oppression of those deemed "less than." For those who haven't seen the movie, Thomas Anderson, a computer hacker who calls himself Neo, meets a leader of a rebellion, named Morpheus, who presents him with a choice. He can take the blue pill and continue to live happily in his fabricated existence inside the Matrix or he can take the red pill, escape the Matrix, and discover the truth of the real world. The truth is that all life on earth is an elaborate computer-generated façade created by machines with artificial intelligence, who dominate the "real" world and use human bodies to create energy, imprisoning their minds within an artificial reality known as the Matrix.

In the movie, Neo takes the red pill and joins the rebellion to overthrow the Matrix. False consciousness keeps the rebels imprisoned inside the Matrix. As they become conscious of their oppression, they can unplug from the Matrix. Change comes about through the resistance of the rebels against the dominance of the machines. In this way, the Matrix is an allegory for diversity-competent practitioners who are called to shed their false consciousness and challenge the systemic marginalization and oppression of those deemed "lesser than" in a socially stratified society. Unlike the Matrix, this does not mean the solution lies in "the One" saviour; but it does mean challenging systems of dominance.

It can be hard to acknowledge that social power and privilege provide advantages (often unearned) to some people and disadvantages to others. How is it fair, just, or equitable that being born in one part of Canada means you don't have access to safe, clean drinking water? How is it fair, just, or equitable that being born in one part of the world might mean you could be forced to work at four years of age? How is it fair, just, or equitable that being born in one family over another makes the difference in being able to afford tuition for your post-secondary education? The social change strategies used to address inequity require a framework that is open to diversity of thought, innovation, and new discoveries; it needs to be

Cultural relativism: The idea that no cultural standpoint is privileged over another.

Standpoint: Using the experiences of social groups as the basis of a theory or explanation.

False consciousness: Friedrich Engels originally coined this term to attach thought to social action, but it becomes problematic when used in the context of victim/saviour. In a modern context, false consciousness refers to a view of social problems as the fault of the individual rather than society.

Socially stratified: Refers to the hierarchical social layers of a society where those at the top have the greatest amount of social power and privilege and those underneath have descending levels of power and privilege.

Social change often requires people to unplug from the "Matrix," examine their social location based on power and privilege, and open themselves to diversity of thought and experience.

rooted in a cultural context that shares power and is grounded in the affected community's understanding and experience. "The fallacy is that we live in one world, with one solution to all available problems" (Ignatieff, 1994, pp. 82–83).

Go Global, Live Local

Diversity-competent practitioners are able to think globally and to consider issues from a variety of perspectives. As agents of social change, they are generally characterized as courageous idealists, meaning individuals with the courage to act on worthy goals. Nelson

Social enterprise: A business organization whose primary mission is social benefit to people or the environment as opposed to making profit.

Mandela was willing to lay down his life for his ideals of liberation and equality, as you can appreciate in his famous "Speech from the Dock" at the Rivonia treason trial on April 20, 1964:

> I have fought against white domination, and I have fought against black domination. I have cherished the ideal of a democratic and free society in which all persons live together in harmony and with equal opportunities. It is an ideal which I hope to live for and to achieve, but if needs be, it is an ideal for which I am prepared to die. (Nelson Mandela Centre of Memory, 2013)

Now, let's look at some other agents of change in our world. Consider the case of Malala Yousafzai, a teenage girl from Pakistan, who had the courage to fight for the educational rights of women, despite an assassination attempt. And think about Iqbal Masih, also from Pakistan. Forced to work at the age of four, Iqbal spent six years of his childhood chained to a carpet-weaving loom. He had the courage to speak out to defend the rights of children against forced labour. He was silenced at the age of 12 when he was murdered. His story was the spark used by Canadian social activists Craig and Marc Kielburger to inspire a new generation of world changers. In founding the international children's charity Free The Children, the Kielburger brothers use a unique approach that challenges the ageism that exists within social development. They recognize the potential of young people to be problem-solvers and agents of change. Rather than working *for*, they work *with*, thereby empowering "youth to remove barriers that prevent them from being active local and global citizens" (Free the Children, 2013). One of the core values of this movement is that youth are shameless idealists who will stop at nothing to change the world (Free the Children, 2013). The Kielburger brothers' **social enterprises** "Me to We" and "We Days" create a new social consciousness of service to others in things that are larger than oneself. According to Craig Kielburger, change can begin through simple acts that all of us can do in our everyday lives (Kielburger, 2012). He describes this as a simple mathematical equation of Issue + Gift = Better World:

> Your issue can be something that sparks your interest, something that you saw as wrong and decided you needed to do something about. The second part of the equation, your gift, is also critical. Everyone has a gift. Whatever your gift, when it is nurtured and applied to an issue, this equates to a better world. (Kielburger, 2012)

Started in 2007, We Day is an annual empowerment event that has brought together from across Canada and the United States hundreds of thousands of youth who commit to volunteering and active citizenship.

There is no one recipe with standard measurements that can serve as a diversity strategy for all organizations or groups. Strategies need to be tailored to the self-determined needs of affected groups, recognizing that there is no "one way" of developing a diversity strategy. But there appear to be some basic ingredients that are important to the process of building a successful and sustainable diversity strategy, and these include commitment, champions, shared power, concrete strategies for implementation, and full participation (Anzovino, Brown, & Rackauskas, 2005). In order to eliminate barriers that exclude all members from fully participating, there is a requirement for a new power arrangement whereby affected communities define their issues, develop their own solutions, and determine their own leadership structures. It is not enough simply to invite representatives of diverse populations to belong. Nor can those in power create a solution *for* diverse populations.

This evolution toward self-determination has characterized international development models. The victim/rescuer **paradigm** was about having development *done to* communities. Well-intentioned individuals and nations would go into communities in need of assistance and "rescue" them by transplanting solutions onto them. Consider the case of a community in Latin America where a water well was built *for* them by an international group, but the community did not have the parts to fix the pump that was needed to draw the water. Without ownership, development projects break down very quickly. If affected communities are not the author of their own solutions, then development initiatives are generally not sustainable.

The empowerment paradigm, on the other hand, appreciates the resourcefulness of local communities.

Development initiatives undertaken using this approach shift the power to local communities to define their own goals, their own solutions, and the resources needed. They own it, build it, and sustain it.

How can this broader perspective enrich our lives? Meeting people in different social locations with different maps of experience and knowledge helps to inform our own "map"—our perspective of how we see the world, our place within it as **global citizens**, and our willingness to learn from the experiences of others around the world. Within this broader perspective is an increased awareness that our sense of identity and our material lives are interconnected with all of humanity. As world citizens, our relationship to others carries with it the responsibility to value diversity, achieve social equity, struggle for social justice, and find ways to coexist in a sustainable way that respects all things living. In doing so, we enrich our framework, our view of the world we live in, and the choices available to us. This broad perspective is a call to action that can make a difference in community at a range of levels from local to global. Sometimes it as simple as connecting the dots between the choices you make in your daily life on a local level with their effect upon the earth's environment and every person's right to live in it.

THE PROCESS OF BECOMING DIVERSITY-COMPETENT

The term *cultural competency* has been used in academia and the workplace to refer to the ability of an organization or an individual to practise in a manner that is respectful of and consistent with a client's or a patient's culture. Culture has generally referred to race, ethnicity, nationality, and language group. The term **diversity competency** takes this approach a step further in considering all forms of diversity, including (but not limited to) those related to age, gender, race, ethnicity, nationality, culture, ability, sexual orientation, class, marital status, family structure, education, and occupation. As a framework for achieving social equity and justice, diversity must be located within the structures of power

Paradigm: A model, typical pattern, or framework.

Global citizenship: Developing the competencies to actively engage with the world, and help to make it a more just, equitable, and sustainable place to live in.

Diversity competency: The ability to work effectively with diverse populations in a manner that protects and preserves their dignity and recognizes, affirms, and values differences, similarities, and worth.

and privilege belonging to individuals and organizations. Diversity competence is a dynamic, lifelong process of "becoming" (see Figure 1.4)—you cannot simply "be" diversity-competent as the result of a training day event, for example.

In the workplace, diversity competence is essential in providing effective and responsive services to diverse populations. The ability to work with diverse members of the community is considered an essential skill by most employers, whether in health care, business, education, law, or the social sector. How important do you think it is for nurses, personal support workers, or dental hygienists to be able to understand the health-care practices and beliefs of their patients? How important do you think diversity competence is for police officers involved in community policing?

Diversity Competence at the Systemic or Organizational Level

At a systemic level, diversity competence refers to the ability of a system or organization to practise in a manner that is equitable, just, respectful, and consistent with the needs of diverse populations, addressing issues of power, leadership, and participation. A diversity-competent organization defines diversity broadly (beyond concepts of culture, ethnicity, race, and language) and recognizes that diversity competency is continuously changing and developing. Diversity-competent organizations might consider the following:

1. The institutionalization of diversity competency values within organizational philosophy and organizational culture, which may translate into formal initiatives at all organizational levels, including codification in mission statements, strategic plans, directional documents, policy reviews, and service delivery models (Alberta Health Services: Healthy Diverse Populations, 2008).
2. Organizational infrastructure for the promotion and practice of diversity competency that might target issues such as workforce diversification, recruitment and retention, human resource policies, leadership, professional development, workplace environment, and financial resources.

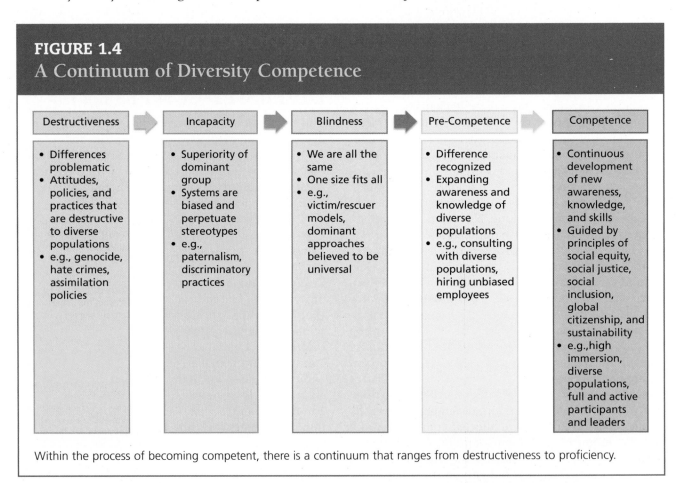

FIGURE 1.4
A Continuum of Diversity Competence

Destructiveness	Incapacity	Blindness	Pre-Competence	Competence
• Differences problematic • Attitudes, policies, and practices that are destructive to diverse populations • e.g., genocide, hate crimes, assimilation policies	• Superiority of dominant group • Systems are biased and perpetuate stereotypes • e.g., paternalism, discriminatory practices	• We are all the same • One size fits all • e.g., victim/rescuer models, dominant approaches believed to be universal	• Difference recognized • Expanding awareness and knowledge of diverse populations • e.g., consulting with diverse populations, hiring unbiased employees	• Continuous development of new awareness, knowledge, and skills • Guided by principles of social equity, social justice, social inclusion, global citizenship, and sustainability • e.g.,high immersion, diverse populations, full and active participants and leaders

Within the process of becoming competent, there is a continuum that ranges from destructiveness to proficiency.

Source: Cross, T. B., *Towards A Culturally Competent System of Care*, Washington, D.C.: Georgetown University Child Development Centre, 1989.

3. Best practice models for service delivery that are evidence-based, provide equitable and accessible programs and services for all individuals, and involve diverse populations in the planning, delivery, and evaluation of services.

Diversity-competent organizations are made up of employees who are diversity-competent and can provide service or care in a manner consistent with diversity competency values, best practices, policies, and standards. Diversity-competent practitioners can also be powerful agents for organizational and social change.

Workplace Diversity

The creation and implementation of workplace diversity initiatives in Canada can provide rich examples of **best practice** for private and public sectors, as well as examples of those strategies to avoid. Some of these diversity initiatives are detailed in Chapter 13, "Practising Diversity." Many organizations have encouraged employees to participate in diversity training programs and, while they may be a good first step in creating awareness, they do not necessarily ensure a commitment to equity. When diversity training in the workplace is mandatory, designed to prevent lawsuits, or prescribed in the settlement of a discriminatory suit, it can often have a negative effect on employees because it is forced upon unwilling participants (Bregman, 2012).

Diversity training using the sameness and difference approach can also be problematic when it serves to keep the standards of a dominant group intact. When a goal of diversity training in the workplace is to help employees learn how to "accept and tolerate difference," it implies that there is a need to learn how to put up with things that are different from the dominant group. Diversity training designed to "celebrate difference" in the workplace falls prey to the same trivialization that "celebrating multiculturalism" in Canada in the 1970s did.

Perhaps the least effective diversity training opportunities were those that used the approach of diversity as difference and required participants to identify with a particular affinity group. One such exercise, called "The Diversity Parade," had participants choose one category of identity to belong to as a means of illustrating the idea of diversity as difference. Participants could choose to sit on imaginary floats identified as the women's float, the LGBT float, the differently-abled float, the African-Canadian float, the First Nations float, and so on, as they "celebrated" their differences.

The exercise simplified the complexity, **intersectionality**, and **fluidity** of our identities as human beings and reinforced stereotypical labels. Some of the training participants felt they needed to be riding multiple floats at the same time, while others felt there was no value in attaching themselves to these labels.

At the end of the training exercise, the facilitator brought out two eggs, one white and one brown, and cracking them open, poured them into a pan. As she walked around the room displaying the contents of the pan, she discussed what is often referred to as the sameness approach: like the eggs, we may differ on the outside, but we are all the same underneath the skin. This sameness approach can serve to keep the standards of a dominant group intact, however, by denying the social construction of difference and the lived experiences of those who are marginalized and excluded in society because of these differences.

Successful diversity management initiatives have generally included principles that

- promote fair treatment as the basis for respectful relationships in the workplace
- create an inclusive working environment where all employees feel valued and can fully contribute their talents
- promote equity in access to opportunities for growth, advancement, and leadership for all employees
- remove institutionalized barriers that prevent full participation of historically under-represented populations in the workplace (Anzovino, Brown, & Rackauskas, 2005)

In the private sector, the goals of diversity initiatives may be to increase a company's competitiveness in the global marketplace, to maximize profits, or to respond to demographic changes in the consumer market. That does not imply that the private sector is not committed to diversity as equity. IBM is an example of a company that was practising diversity long before it was the "thing to do." For IBM, diversity is a corporate value and practice that goes beyond fair human

Best practice: A benchmark, process, strategy, system, approach, policy, procedure, program, or design that has been proven to work well and produce positive outcomes and then is used as a model or optimal standard.

Intersectionality: Refers to the way various aspects of identity interact on multiple and often simultaneous levels; can include how identity interacts with multiple systems of oppression.

Fluidity: Characteristic of identity that describes it as something that can change and be shaped.

2013 Canada's Best Diversity Employers

PRESENTED BY

BMO ◆ Financial Group

Some of the most prominent initiatives are recognized annually by Canada's Best Diversity Employers competition, sponsored annually by the BMO Financial Group and *The Globe and Mail*.

resource policy. The opportunities for IBM employees to be fully participatory have earned them numerous diversity awards. Employees are supported in defining and addressing issues affecting marginalized communities they identify with. Corporate networking groups include IBM Global Asian Diversity Network Group, IBM Global Black Network Group, IBM Native Diversity Network, LGBT at IBM, and Women at IBM. These groups function as more than affinity groups; they provide opportunities for mentorship, leadership, and organizational change. IBM is just one of many corporate examples of diversity initiatives in Canada, each with varying goals and outcomes.

Best Practice in the Provision of Diversity-Competent Service or Care

Part of the ongoing journey towards becoming a diversity-competent practitioner is asking whether you have the awareness, knowledge, attitude, skills, and experience to work equitably and justly with diverse populations. Diversity competency is a lifelong process; it is not a course you take or a training certificate you acquire (see Figure 1.5). It requires knowledge and skills to be able to interact effectively with all people. It requires an awareness and openness to differing perspectives to create a welcoming and inclusive environment to live, work, play, and study in. The competent practitioner must also locate diversity within the structures of power. Once this analysis begins, the practitioner can no longer say, "I'm not really comfortable talking about the role oppression has played in people's lives, so we will just pretend we are all the same." To do so denies the history of disadvantaged populations and the consequences of discrimination in their lives.

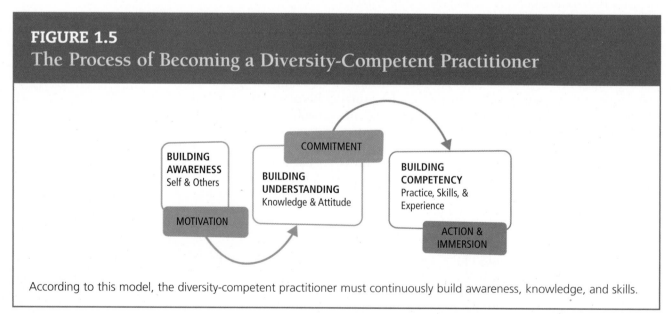

FIGURE 1.5

The Process of Becoming a Diversity-Competent Practitioner

According to this model, the diversity-competent practitioner must continuously build awareness, knowledge, and skills.

Source: Campinha-Bacote, J., *The Process of Cultural Competence in the Delivery of Healthcare Services*, 1991.

To understand diversity in the social world around us, it is important to develop a level of self-awareness that can interpret the social forces that have shaped our personal and social identities. In building self-awareness, diversity-competent practitioners reflect upon their own identity, become conscious of their personal reactions to others whom they perceive as different, and honestly examine their own biases, stereotypes, and prejudices. In building awareness of others, we are able to recognize the validity of other perspectives and world views. Diversity-competent practitioners also make a commitment to building an understanding about diversity and human interaction by expanding their knowledge of diverse populations and by critically analyzing attitudes that marginalize them. Finally, each practitioner looks at how he or she can practise diversity by developing skills needed to be a diversity-competent professional. This is most effective with high-immersion encounters and meaningful interaction with members of diverse populations (Conference Board of Canada, 2006).

KNOWING YOUR OWN STORY

One of the fundamental truths about diversity is that it involves as much learning about oneself as it does learning about others. We each have a map of the world created through knowledge and experience—a map that shows our social location relative to the world we live in. For most of us, there are huge gaps in our map—sometimes gaps we are not even conscious of. The world itself is infinitely complex, so we do have to make choices about what we are going to look at and what we are not going to look at. Part of the process of becoming diversity-competent is a discovery of your own evolving story and where it fits in your map of the world (Ward, 2013; see Figure 1.6). As we reflect on the multiple identities that form who we are as individuals, that define us as members of families and communities, and that locate our place in the world, a relationship map emerges.

What you value makes a great deal of difference in terms of how you perceive your location and purpose in this world. Boundaries of your personal map change, and pathways through it are as unique as the individual. The self is not always at the centre location. The target or focus of our personal map is dynamic. At times, the centre target of your map can be family.

FIGURE 1.6
Our Relationship Map

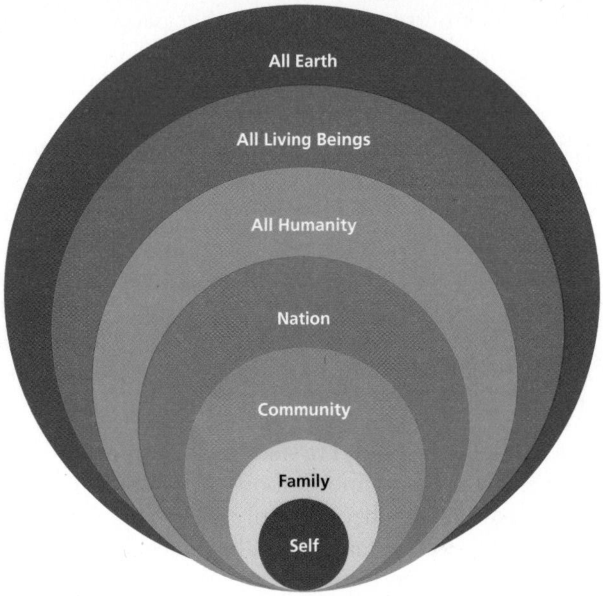

All Earth
All Living Beings
All Humanity
Nation
Community
Family
Self

We each have a map of the world created through knowledge and experience.

Source: Adapted from Tim Ward, "Finding Your Map," (Welland, Ontario, Canada: Presentation made at Niagara College, September 2013).

In the story that follows it is the value of shared power that places community at the centre of the relationship map that guides these children:

An anthropologist had been studying the habits and customs of this tribe … so he proposed a game for the children to play. He'd bought lots of candy and sweets in the city, so he put everything in a basket with a beautiful ribbon attached. He placed it under a solitary tree, and then he called the kids together. He drew a line on the ground and explained that they should wait behind the line for his signal. And that when he said "Go!" they should rush over to the basket and the first to arrive there would win all the candies. When he said "Go!" they all unexpectedly held each other's hands and ran off towards the tree as a group. Once there, they simply shared the candy with each other and happily ate it. The anthropologist was very surprised. He asked them why they had all gone together, especially if the first one to arrive at the tree could have won everything in the basket—all the sweets. A young girl simply replied: "How can one of us be happy if all the others are sad?" (Tutu, 2011)

This story demonstrates the meaning of *Ubuntu*—a word that comes from a Zulu proverb. *Ubuntu* means a person is a person because of other people and that we seek to work for the common good because the best expression of our humanity is our relationship with our community (Tutu, 2011). It is a philosophy succinctly described in the expression "I am because we are," and Archbishop Desmond Tutu believes that it is part of the gift that Africa will give to the world (Tutu, 2011).

For some people, at certain times in life, nation may be at the centre of their personal map. Take, for example, the acceptance speech made by k.d. lang at the 2013 Canadian Juno Awards as she was inducted into the Canadian Music Hall of Fame:

> I think the fact that I'm standing here receiving this award says more about Canada than it does about me, because only in Canada could there be such a freak as k.d. lang receiving this award. Only in Canada could there be people like Stompin' Tom Connors and Rita MacNeil. So I am here to tell you, my friends and my countrymen, that it is OK to be you. It is OK to let your freak flags fly. Embrace the quirkmeister that is inside all of us. And I'm not even just talking artists; every single person in this nation has the right to be themselves, live life. Go team go. (K.D. Lang, Juno acceptance speech. Copyright © K.D. Lang, 2013)

Recognizing that people experience the world differently based on their own map helps us to improve understanding and competence.

Who Am I?

We often use the word **identity** in everyday conversation, but as a concept, identity is a bit of an enigma. We know that it links social identifiers in complex ways to help us develop a sense of ourselves and our relationships with others (Fearon, 1999). We also know that due to a range of influences—from

the writings of Michel Foucault to the debate on multiculturalism—the historical and cultural construction of identity is at the centre of many lively interdisciplinary discussions (Fearon, 1999). So, when you begin the intellectual journey of analyzing issues in diversity, a good place to start is by examining your own identity. This includes knowing your own story and where it fits in your personal map of the world. The term **personal identity** (or individual identity) is used to refer to a person's self-concept based on personal attributes (Hogg & Tindale, 2005). For example, if a person says, "I am well-educated," he or she is referring to personal identity. The term **social identity** (sometimes referred to as group identity or community identity) is a person's self-concept based on the attributes of a group he or she aligns with (Hogg & Tindale, 2005). Saying "we are a happy family" refers to social identity. Social identity can change depending on the social context you are in and whom you are with. As we move to different groups, our identity usually changes. For example, as an employee a woman will act differently than she would as a mother. Intercultural studies in communication also use the terms of avowed and ascribed identity.

Proud to be Canadian and flanked by Mounties, k.d. lang is inducted into the Canadian Music Hall of Fame at the 2013 Canadian Juno Awards.

Source: THE CANADIAN PRESS/Liam Richards

Identity: Social construction of a person's sense of self that is based upon social categories that influence self-perception and the perception of others.

Personal identity: The part of person's identity determined by his or her individual attributes and characteristics.

Social identity: The part of a person's identity that is determined by attributes and characteristics of groups the person aligns him- or herself with.

Avowed identity is self-selected and refers to the image we have of ourselves. Tiger Woods has an avowed identity that he has termed "Cablinasian"—it is a way of defining who he is based on his Caucasian, black, Indian, and Asian ancestry. **Ascribed identity** refers to an identity that is assigned to us by others. It is based on how other people see us. Ascribed identity is often influenced by physical appearance and stereotypes and can become a barrier in dialogue with diverse populations.

What is common to all forms of identity is that they are socially constructed. Society constructs the social meaning that is given to the characteristics and attributes that are used to define us. Even aspects of our identity that we believe we are born with, like race, are in fact social constructs. We now have scientific proof that the concept of race is a biological myth. But we also know that the concept of race is real in terms of its social consequences. Certain aspects of our identity may afford us the privilege of belonging to the dominant group within a society. Other aspects of our identities may have the effect of "othering us." The social construction of difference as "other" has the effect of marginalizing

Source: Stonewall: The Lesbian, Gay and Bisexual Charity.

Yes, that is Gandalf. Actor Sir Ian McKellen is a vocal LGBT rights activist.

individuals and groups of people within a society. In the reading found later in this chapter, David Suzuki talks about travelling to Japan and belonging because of his appearance, but being "othered" as a "gaijin" because he could not speak Japanese. The premise is that if aspects of identity can be socially constructed in a way that marginalizes, they then can also be reconstructed in a way that creates belonging and inclusion.

Stereotypes are distorted generalizations, made about an individual or group, that assume all members of a particular group share the same characteristics (Diller, 2007). Stereotypes are often used in ascribing identity to someone. The problem with stereotypes is that they are often used in ways that reinforce prejudice and justify discriminatory behaviour. If you think you know what a person is going to do or say because you've met "their type" before or because all of "those people" are the same, then you are engaging in stereotyping (National Vet E-Learning, 2013). Let's use an example to further illustrate this concept. Once a term, students enrolled in a course on diversity at our college are asked to participate in a classroom exercise to look at the concept of stereotyping. This exercise is, of course, staged with the cooperation of former students. Let's look at a recent example.

While standing at the front of a large lecture hall, a young man saunters in and sits down in the middle of the room. His skin is tanned and he is wearing a t-shirt, swim shorts, and flip-flops that smack against the concrete floors as he walks—for effect. No one misses his entrance. He sits down and flips back his sun-bleached dreadlocks. Other students can now see that he has earphones on that appear to be connected to an iPod. A disapproving glare is sent his way to signal that the reaction to his appearance is a negative one. As the lecture turns to the topic of stereotyping, the young man is invited to come to the front of the room and face the class. Students are asked what identity they would ascribe to him. After a few moments of silence, one student yells out, "Surfer dude." This breaks the floodgates for a number of negative labels from "lazy bum" to "loser." Students are then asked if they were a teacher, what would be their expectations of him as a learner? Again, students yell out a number of negative comments like "not much" and "would never come to class if the sun was shining." Finally, the students are asked what behaviour they are anticipating based on his appearance. The students respond with "drunk all the time" and "partier." One student resists and

---

Avowed identity:
Identity based on traits and characteristics that individuals use to define themselves.

Ascribed identity:
Identity based on traits and characteristics that others use to define an individual.

says, "That's mean!" Our "guest" is then invited to speak to the class for a few minutes on any subject of interest to him. He begins by saying, "At the moment, I am involved in cancer research. I am reading research on the effect of manganese superoxide dismutase overexpression from the mitochondria, possibly playing a role in protecting against radiation-induced cell death. Mitochondrial manganese superoxide dismutase overexpression was shown to reduce damage caused by reactive oxygen species, which may play a role in prevention of cell death caused by radiation" (Motoori, 2001).

In the debriefing of this exercise, students talk about the power of labelling and stereotyping in everyday life. They are able to see the pathway leading from negative stereotypes to prejudice and discrimination. Students are able to see how stereotypes negate the complexity, multiplicity, intersectionality, fluidity, and contextuality of a person's identity. It is this same concern that has a student organization at Ohio University called STARS (Students Teaching About Racism in Society) challenging the stereotypical costumes people wear on Halloween. The poster series

PICTURE THIS...

Source: Ohio University STARS, "We're a Culture Not a Costume" campaign (2013).

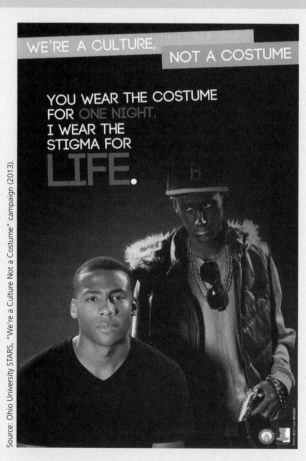 

Some students claim this poster campaign by students at Ohio University reveals political correctness gone too far. Other students, in rebuttal, have stated that if you are not a member of that group, then you should not be able to dictate how painful that stereotype might be to its members. Other students suggest that since stereotypes are not a person's entire identity, it is not funny or clever to suggest they are. **What do you think?**

PICTURE THIS highlights the way that stereotypes can reduce an entire ethnicity to a caricature.

Examining Dimensions of Identity Using the Diversity Wheel

If we use the **Diversity Wheel** (see Figure 1.7) as an analytical tool, we can examine the dimensions of diversity that shape our lives in very powerful ways at home, work, school, and within the larger society (Loden, 1995). While the Diversity Wheel cannot describe our inner feelings and thoughts, it can help describe the complexity of our personal identity and social identity. If we view it as a dynamic tool, we can see the multiple ways that dimensions of our identity intersect with one another and change. Together, all of these aspects contribute to a concept of self as an integrated whole.

Diversity Wheel: A tool developed by Marilyn Loden to analyze different social aspects and dimensions of a person's identity.

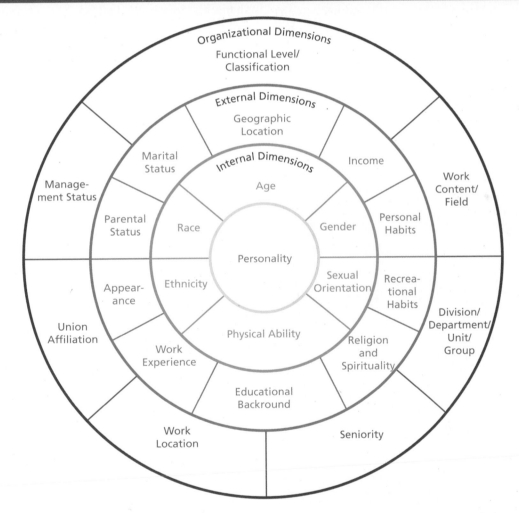

FIGURE 1.7
The Dimensions of Diversity

The Diversity Wheel is a model that helps us to examine the primary (internal) and secondary (external) dimensions of diversity that add layers of complexity to individual identity.

Source: U.S. Department of Health and Human Services: Health Resources and Services Administration.

Intersecting and Dynamic Dimensions of Identity

Personal and social identities are complex. There is no one single social category that can define us. The lived experience of the poverty-stricken, pagan, lesbian living in rural Manitoba will undoubtedly be different from a middle-class, Christian, heterosexual woman living in Newfoundland. Identity is not a static concept; it is not fixed. Identity is fluid, and as such, it is important to recognize that all social forces and social positions are relational, cross-cutting one another (Collins, 2000). This concept is referred to as *intersectionality* (Collins, 2000). Our identities are multifaceted and multidimensional, arising out of our lived experience in different social contexts, which are defined by different forms of power. Therefore, there is no homogeneous identity that can define a collective standpoint (Collins, 2000). Someone can't say that because she is a woman, she speaks on behalf of all women everywhere. The concept of a universal sisterhood that constructs gender oppression as sole determinant is deficient. Our social identities are too complex for this kind of analysis.

It is one dimensional to suggest some groups are more oppressed than others. We have seen this argument emerge in the arena of competing human rights. The Supreme Court of Canada has been clear that there is no hierarchy of Charter rights, stating that no right is inherently superior to another right (Dagenais v. Canadian Broadcasting Corp., 1994). It is similarly one dimensional to suggest that a white woman living in poverty is a privileged person. Since each person is not just one thing, our identities interact and impact each other. Some aspects of our identity can also be invisible, so we may enjoy social power provided we do not disclose these parts of our identity in social contexts that might discriminate if they were visible. In using the Diversity Wheel model, it is important to remember that these social dimensions of identity are not static. Each time our social context changes, the negotiation of new identities begins again. This change also occurs over time, creating moments when certain aspects of one's personal or social identity may be more salient than others.

As you walk a mile in the shoes of the student who shares his story in the In Their Shoes feature, consider just how fluid our identities can be and how quickly they can change. While he faces his own mortality, he remains driven by a call to something larger than himself, to realize a dream of being a healer for others. His struggle to survive is interwoven with a struggle to live life defined by more than a master status ascribed to him by his brain tumour. He wants to be recognized as more than "you know, the guy with the tumour." Not only does he face changes in his social context, but he also faces the possibility of personality changes from treatment, all of which leaves him wondering who he will be when it is all over. Whoever that is, he will fight to have others recognize that we are always more than our physical and cognitive abilities.

ENDING THOUGHTS

To live and work in a way that honours a framework for diversity requires an awareness of who we see ourselves to be, an understanding of how we live our lives, and a competency in terms of how we treat others. Diversity is an anti-oppression framework built on a commitment to social equity, social justice, social inclusion, and global citizenship that looks to create a society and social institutions that respect the dignity of every human being. In utilizing diversity as an anti-oppression framework, we must assume the responsibility of actively challenging privilege and oppression in its many forms. According to sociologist Allan G. Johnson,

> To perpetuate privilege and oppression, we don't have to do anything consciously to support it. Just our silence is crucial for ensuring its future, for the simple fact is that no system of privilege can continue to exist without

Source: © Samuel Killermann

Speech bubble: Sorry, Teacher, but where do the kids whose most salient identity isn't gender and instead self-identify as "awesome" line up?

What are some of the ways we are asked in daily life to define the most salient aspects of our identity? What would social life be like if we stopped identifying people by gender, race, ethnicity, age, ability, and so on?

IN THEIR SHOES

If a picture can say a thousand words, imagine the stories your shoes could tell! Try this student story on for size – have you walked in this student's shoes?

I invite you to walk a mile in my shoes, or in my head, as my story shows how your personal and social identity can change within a day. On February 17, 2013, I am a twenty-one-year-old post-secondary student studying kinesiology and dreaming of practising rehabilitative medicine one day. My friends and family nicknamed me "Mr. Healthy" because of my lifestyle. Some people call me "driven," but I live my life according to the perform-ance goals I have set for myself. A year and a half ago, I began experiencing headaches and was referred to a neurologist who misdiagnosed me with migraines. On February 17, 2013, I experience what I think is a migraine and then I lose all feeling on my left side of my body. Suspecting something neurological, the doctor at Urgent Care orders a CT scan for the morning—in retrospect, this is part of what saved my life. I spend Family Day with my Mom sitting in the emergency room of my local hos-pital waiting for the CT scan. Once it is finished, I wait for the doctor who comes in and tells me very directly that I have a mass. I say, "I have what?" He repeats that I have a "mass." Translation: I have a brain tumour. He tells me it is being analyzed by a neurosurgeon as we speak and that I will have to go to Hamilton General Hospital tomorrow for a consultation with a neurosurgeon. In two minutes my life changed. Was this real or a dream?

I meet with a great neurosurgeon the next day at Hamilton General. His words are "We don't have a choice. We have to remove this tumour. If left to con-tinue … bottom line is you won't survive." Everything else seemed irrelevant but the words "you have a tumour and you won't survive this *unless*." You face your own mortality like never before and everything changes. My family and friends are very emotional—not so much for me—I think I was pretty clear on what had to be done and there was no choice but to face it head on. It sounds cliché, but it is all the support from my wonderful family and great friends that sees me through.

The following day is game time. As I am rolled into the OR, my MRI results are up on the screen and the tumour is massive. The neurosurgeon is explaining to his team the strategy—people are moving quickly. I do remember the OR prep, but after that there is nothing. No transition to sleep or death. That portion of memory does not exist. Wake up in recovery and everything is a haze. Wave at my Mom and my uncle. Wake up again later in the step down unit. Surgeon says he is happy with the outcome and I feel more at ease.

Death is not something I was afraid of. I knew it was a possibility but it wasn't something I could control. If I survive, great. If I die, so be it. Things will play out as they will. You just find peace. It makes you strong because the anxiety of life and death does not wear on you. People associate death with this negative aura and it does not feel like that to me. The recovery from neurosurgery is pretty intense. My concentration was limited; my short-term memory had declined. In order to reduce brain edema, I have to take a corticosteroid and I get almost every side effect possible from this drug. Most discour-aging is the muscle atrophy—years spent in the gym feel like they are gone in a matter of weeks. I was known in the gym as the power and strength guy—my max bench press was 385 lbs, leg press 1300 lbs, deadlift 500 lbs, squat 500. Now I can only dream of getting under a load like that. I was also a fairly gifted sprinter. Running is joy for me and I conditioned for 200 and 400 sprints. Now I am winded just walking up the stairs.

People look at me differently and they are often uncomfortable around me. I feel like this tumour is starting to define me. It's almost dehumanizing in a sense. People don't look at me like me anymore—I'm the tumour boy. Yes, I know my disability is very visible at the moment, with this incision on the side of my head. I've literally watched people walk into doors as they stare at me.

I feel like this journey has dramatically changed who I am and the context by which others now define me. But I am still me—just because I have this tumour doesn't mean I am any different than who I was. As soon as you tell someone though, or they see your scar, it's like you are no longer normal. On a physiolo-gical level this is partly true, but I am still me. It's like accidental discrimination.

I've come to learn that brain tumours don't discriminate—they can affect anyone, at any age. It has become hard to plan for a future that you may not have. What I do know is that I have more neurosurgery in a few weeks, followed by six weeks of radiation therapy. I will lose my short-term memory. There is a good chance my personality will change. Brain seizures mean I can't drive right now, so I have lost some independence. But I am alive and determined. I am inspired by my neurosur-geon Dr. T. Gunnarsson, and know that one day I will find a way to use my knowledge and skills to help heal others. I know it is what I was destined to do in life. I have learned that "who we are" can change in a matter of seconds. The "ability" to learn at whatever college or university you are studying at is truly a privilege. I dream of the day when I can join you there again.

most people choosing to remain silent about it. … As such, we can only choose how to be involved—whether to be part of the problem or also to be part of the solution. That's where our power lies, and also our responsibility. (Johnson, 2005)

Transformation change is possible when we begin to reflect critically upon how inclusive our thoughts and actions really are. When we encounter inequity and injustice, are we silent or do we know that we are socially responsible for being part of a solution that envisions a just and equitable world for all people?

READING

ANCESTORS: THE GENETIC SOURCE

By David Suzuki

My genes can be traced in a direct line to Japan. I am a pure-blooded member of the Japanese race. And whenever I go there, I am always astonished to see the power of that biological connection. In subways in Tokyo, I catch familiar glimpses of the eyes, hairline smile of my Japanese relatives. Yet when those same people open their mouths to communicate, the vast cultural gulf that separates them from me becomes obvious: English is my language, Shakespeare is my literature, British is what I learned and Beethoven is my music.

For those who believe that in people, just as in animals, genes are the primary determinant of behaviour, a look at second- and third-generation immigrants to Canada gives powerful evidence to the contrary. The overriding influence is environmental. We make a great mistake by associating the inheritance of physical characteristics with far more complex traits of human personality and behaviour.

Each time I visit Japan, I am reminded of how Canadian I am and how little the racial connection matters. I first visited Japan in 1968 to attend the International Congress of Genetics in Tokyo. For the first time in my life, I was surrounded by people who all looked like me. While sitting in a train and looking at the reflections in the window, I found that it was hard to pick out my own image in the crowd. I had grown up in a Caucasian society in which I was a minority member. My whole sense of self had developed with that perspective of looking different. All my life I had wanted large eyes and brown hair so I could be like everyone else. Yet on that train, where I did fit in, I didn't like it.

On this first visit to Japan I had asked my grandparents to contact relatives and let them know I was coming. I was the first in the Suzuki clan in Canada to visit them. The closest relative on my father's side was my grandmother's younger brother, and we arranged to meet in a seaside resort near his home. He came to my hotel room with two of his daughters. None of them spoke any English, while my Japanese was so primitive as to be useless. In typical Japanese fashion, they showered me with gifts, the most important being a package of what looked like wood carved in the shape of bananas! I had no idea what it was. (Later I learned the package contained dried tuna fish from which slivers are shaved off to flavour soup. This is considered a highly prized gift.) We sat in stiff silence and embarrassment, each of us struggling to dredge up a common word or two to break the quiet. It was excruciating! My great uncle later wrote my grandmother to tell her how painful it had been to sit with her grandson and yet be unable to communicate a word.

To people in Japan, all non-Japanese people—black, white or yellow—are *gaijin* or foreigners. While *gaijin* is not derogatory, I find that its use is harsh because I sense doors clanging shut on me when I'm called one. The Japanese do have a hell of a time with me because I look like them and can say in perfect Japanese, "I'm a foreigner and I can't speak Japanese." Their reactions are usually complete incomprehension followed by sputtering, "What do you mean? You're speaking Japanese." And finally a pejorative, "Oh, a *gaijin*!"

Once when my wife, Tara, who is English, and I went to Japan we asked a man at the travel bureau at the airport to book a *ryokan*—a traditional Japanese inn—for us in Tokyo. He found one and booked it for "Suzuki-san" and off we went. When we arrived at the inn and I entered the foyer, the owner was confused by my terrible Japanese. When Tara entered, the shock was obvious in his face. Because of my name, they had expected a "real" Japanese. Instead, I was a *gaijin* and the owner told us he wouldn't take us. I was furious and we stomped off to a phone booth where I called the agent at the airport. He was astonished and came all the way into town to plead our case with the innkeeper. But the innkeeper stood firm and denied us a room. Apparently, he had accepted *gaijin* in the past with terrible consequences.

As an example of the problem, Japanese always take their shoes off when entering a *ryokan* because the straw mats (*tatami*) are quickly frayed. To a Japanese, clomping into a room with shoes on would be comparable to someone entering our homes and spitting on the floor. Similarly, the *ofuro*, or traditional tub, has hot clean water that all bathers use. So one must first enter the bathroom, wash carefully and rinse off before entering the tub. Time in the *ofuro* is for relaxing and soaking. Again, Westerners who lather up in the tub are committing a terrible indiscretion.

To many Canadians today, the word "Jap" seems like a natural abbreviation for Japanese. Certainly for newspaper headlines it would seem to make sense. So people are often shocked to see me bristle when they have used the word Jap innocently. To Japanese Canadians, Jap or Nip (from "Nippon") were epithets used generously during the pre-war and war years. They conjure up all of the hatred and bigotry of those times. While a person using the term today may be unaware of its past use, every Japanese-Canadian remembers.

The thin thread of Japanese culture that does link me to Japan was spun out of the poverty and desperation of my ancestors. My grandparents came to a Canadian province openly hostile to their strange appearance and different ways. There were severe restrictions on how much and where they could buy property. Their children, who were born and raised in Canada, couldn't vote until 1948 and encountered many barriers to professional training and property ownership. Asians, regardless of birthplace, were third-class citizens. That is the reality of the Japanese-Canadian experience and the historical-cultural legacy that came down to the third and fourth generations—to me and my children.

The first Japanese immigrants came to Canada to make their fortunes so they could return to Japan as people of wealth. The vast majority were uneducated and impoverished. But in the century spanning my grandparents' births and the present, Japan has leapt from an agrarian society to a technological and economic giant.

Now, the Japanese I meet in Japan or as recent immigrants to Canada come with far different cultural roots. Present-day Japanese are highly educated, upper-middle class and proud of their heritage. In Canada they encounter respect, envy and curiosity in sharp contrast to the hostility and bigotry met by my grandparents. Japanese immigrants to North America have names that signify the number of generations in the new land (or just as significantly, that count the generational distance away from Japan). My grandparents are *Issei*, meaning the first generation in Canada. Most *Issei* never learned more than a rudimentary knowledge of English. *Nisei*, like my parents, are the second generation here and the first native-born group. While growing up they first spoke Japanese in the home and then learned English from playmates and teachers. Before the Second World War, many *Issei* sent their children to be educated in Japan. When they returned to Canada, they were called *Kikanisei* (or *Kibei* in the United States). Most have remained bilingual, but many of the younger *Nisei* now speak Japanese with difficulty because English is their native tongue. My sisters and I are *Sansei* (third generation); our children are *Yonsei*. These generations, and especially *Yonsei*, are growing up in homes where English is the only spoken language, so they are far more likely to speak school-taught French as their second-language than Japanese.

Most *Sansei*, like me, do not speak Japanese. To us, the *Issei* are mysteries. They came from a cultural tradition that is a hundred years old. Unlike people in present-day Japan, the *Issei* clung tightly to the culture they remembered and froze that culture into a static museum piece like a relic of the past. Not being able to cut off from each other. My parents dutifully visited my grandparents and we children would be trotted out to be lectured at or displayed. These visits were excruciating, because we children didn't understand the old culture, and didn't have the slightest interest—we were Canadians.

My father's mother died in 1978 at the age of ninety-one. She was the last of the *Issei* in our family. The final months of her life, after a left-hemisphere stroke, were spent in that terrible twilight—crippled, still aware, but unable to communicate. She lived the terminal months of her life, comprehending but mute, in a ward with Caucasian strangers. For over thirty years I had listened to her psychologically blackmailing my father by warning him of her imminent death. Yet, in the end, she hung on long after there was reason to. When she died, I was astonished at my own reaction, a great sense of sadness and regret at the cleavage of my last link with the source of my genes. I had never been able to ask what made her and others of her generation come to Canada, what they felt when they arrived, what their hopes and dreams had been, and whether it was worth it. And I wanted to thank her, to show her that I was grateful that, through them, I was born a Canadian.

Source: David Suzuki, *Metamorphosis: Stages in a Life.* © David Suzuki, 1987.

DISCUSSION QUESTIONS

1. Suzuki raises the age-old debate surrounding nature vs. nurture and argues that it is environmental factors that play a larger role in shaping an individual's fate. Do you agree with him?
2. Is it becoming more difficult for third- and fourth-generation immigrants to keep the culture of their ancestors alive? Why? Are you in a position to carry on family traditions? How will you do this?
3. Although Suzuki resembles his relatives physically, he cannot communicate with them verbally. How does this language barrier exclude him from the rest of Japanese society? How do you imagine that he feels?

KWIP

KNOW IT AND OWN IT: WHAT DO I BRING TO THIS?

The fact is that we live in a social world where human diversity shapes our social structures and our daily lived experiences. This lived experience helps us to shape our own personal map, which helps us to navigate our way in the world. Meeting people in different social locations with different maps of experience and knowledge helps to inform our own maps—how we see ourselves and how we view the world we live in. So when you begin the intellectual journey of analyzing issues in social diversity, a good place to start is by examining your identity. Who are you? How did you become who you are? When and how did you first become aware of different aspects of your identity? How is your identity shaped by your everyday experiences? How much of your identity is defined by you and how much is defined by others with whom you interact? For example, do interactions with friends shape who you are? How does being labelled a "student" influence how other people treat you? Are there significant life events that have defined who you are and how others react to you? As you begin to examine your responses to these questions, you will bring to the dialogue greater self-awareness with respect to your own identity and a consciousness of your personal reactions to people who are "different." You will be able to reflect upon who you are, and you will be able to examine honestly your own biases, stereotypes, and prejudices.

WALKING THE TALK: HOW CAN I LEARN FROM THIS?

We all have personal and community identities that are complex, fluid, and shaped by social context. While certain aspects of our identity may be more salient than others, there is never one single identifier that can define who we are. We also have multiple social identities that change over time and at different stages of our life. How does your own identity shape your interactions with others who may be oppressed because of age, race, ethnicity, gender, abilities, sexual orientation, education, work, income, marital status, parental status, religious beliefs, geographical location, or language? Are there certain aspects of who you are that give you an advantage in society? Are there certain aspects of who you are that mean people are less likely to include you socially and more likely to discriminate against you?

IT IS WHAT IT IS: IS THIS INSIDE OR OUTSIDE YOUR COMFORT ZONE?

How comfortable are you with your sense of self? At the 2103 Canadian Music Awards, k.d. lang said to the audience that "it is OK to let your freak flags fly. Embrace the quirkmeister that is inside all of us." Where are you now? Can you let your own freak flag fly? What challenges or difficulties still remain with respect to your comfort with who you are? What kind of power do you have? In what ways does your identity position you as both "oppressor" and "oppressed"? What experiences have you had of being "othered" or of "othering" others? Have you been bullied because of this, or have you bullied others because of the social power you possess?

PUT IT IN PLAY: HOW CAN I USE THIS?

As diversity-competent practitioners, we know that an important part of the journey is developing greater self-awareness. Our sense of self is developed in relation to our sense of family, our connection to our community, our national identity as Canadians, and how we define ourselves as global citizens. How does having a global perspective enrich your life? What personal choices are available when you have a broader perspective? Can you envision a society where difference no longer "others" people as "freaks" or "quirkmeisters"? If you are interested in reflecting upon the issues of social identity and how to create socially inclusive and equitable environments, try the free online certificate course on the OCASI Learn at Work website called *Positive Spaces*.

Located at www.nelson.com/site/walkamile1e

- Consolidate your knowledge with the **Flashcards**.
- Gauge your understanding with **Picture This** and accompanying questions for reflection.
- Develop your critical thinking skills by working through **The Daily**.
- Apply your understanding with **KWIP** interactive!
- Develop your critical reading skills through compelling **Readings** and accompanying short answer questions.

REFERENCES

Alberta Health Services: Healthy Diverse Populations. (2008). *Best practices in diversity competency.* Alberta, Canada. Retrieved from http://www.calgaryhealthregion.ca/programs/diversity/diversity_resources/research_publications/diversity_comp_rprt_2009.pdf

Allen, T. Audio Slideshow: Human Planet. *BBC Human Planet.* Retrieved from BBC News World.

Anzovino, T., Brown, M., & Rackauskas, L. (Directors). (2005). *It's snowing in small town Ontario* [Motion Picture].

Bishop, A. (2002). *Becoming an ally: Breaking the cycle of oppression in people.* Halifax: Fernwood Publishing.

Braveman, P., & Gruskin, S. (2003). Defining equity in health. *J Epidemiol Community Health*, 57, 254–258.

Bregman, P. (2012). Diversity training doesn't work. *Harvard Business Review*. Retrieved from http://blogs.hbr.org/bregman/2012/03/diversity-training-doesnt-work.html

Campinha-Bacote, J. (1991). The process of cultural competence in the delivery of healthcare services. Retrieved from *Transcultural C.A.R.E.*: http://www.transculturalcare.net/Cultural_Competence_Model.htm

Collins, P. H. (2000). *Black feminist thought: Knowledge, consciousness and the politics of empowerment* (2nd ed.). New York: Routledge.

Conference Board of Canada. (2006, December). Report on diversity: Priorities, practices and performance in Canadian organizations. Retrieved from http://www.conferenceboard.ca/e-library/abstract.aspx?did=1828

Cross T., Bazron, B., Dennis, K., & Isaacs, M. (1989). *Towards a culturally competent system of care.* Volume I. Washington, D.C.: Georgetown University Child Development Center, CASSP Technical Assistance Center.

Dagenais v. Canadian Broadcasting Corp. [1994]. 3 S.C.R. 835.

Diller, J. V. (2007). *Cultural diversity: A primer for human services* (3rd ed.). Belmont: Thomson Brooks/Cole.

Fearon, J. D. (1999). *What is identity (as we now use the word)?* Stanford: Stanford University.

Free The Children. (2013). Our mission, our model: Why we are different. Retrieved from *Free The Children*: http://www.freethechildren.com/about-us/our-model/why-were-different/

Hogg, M., & Tindale, R. (2005). Social identity, influence and communication in small groups. In J. Hartwood & H. Giles, *Intergroup communication: Multiple perspectives* (pp. 141–164). New York: Peter Lang.

Howson, A. (2009). Cultural relativism. EBSCO Research Starters, pp. 1–5.

Huffington Post. (2013, April 22). k.d. Lang Junos speech: Singer enters Canadian Music Hall of Fame. Retrieved from *Huffpost Music*: http://www.huffingtonpost.ca/2013/04/21/kd-lang-juno-speech-2013_n_3129280.html#slide=2362688

Ignatieff, M. (1994). *Blood and belonging.* London: Vintage.

Johnson, A.G. (2005, February). Who me? Retrieved from http://www.agjohnson.us/essays/whome/

Kielburger, C. (2012, February 4). Interview with Free The Children and Me to We co-founder Craig Kielburger. (A. McLean, Interviewer).

Leininger, M., & McFarland, M. R. (2002). *Transcultural nursing: Concepts, theories, research and practice.* USA: McGraw-Hill Companies.

Loden, M. (1995). *Implementing diversity: Best practices for making diversity work in your organization.* McGraw-Hill Education.

MacKinnon, C. (1989). Equality rights: An overview of equality theories. Ottawa: National Meeting of Equality Seeking Groups.

Motoori, S. E. (2001). Overexpression of mitochondrial manganese superoxide dismutase protects against radiation-induced cell death in the human hepatocellular carcinoma cell line HLE. *Cancer research*, 61:5382–5388.

National Vet E-Learning. (2013, May 22). Barriers to effective communication: Stereotypes. Retrieved from *Flexible Learning Toolboxes*: http://toolboxes.flexiblelearning.net.au/demosites/series9/903/content/resources/03_effective_communication/08_barriers/page_002.htm

Nelson Mandela Centre of Memory. (2013). Life and times of Nelson Mandela. Retrieved from http://www.nelsonmandela.org/content/page/biography

Ontario Council of Agencies Serving Immigrants. (2012). Positive Spaces Initiative's online training course. Retrieved from http://learnatwork.ca

Sen, R. (2010). Popularizing racial justice: Building clarity, unity and strategy to move us forward [Facing Race 2010's Closing Plenary]. Chicago.

Statistics Canada (2005). Study: Canada's visible minority population in 2017. Retrieved from http://www.statcan.gc.ca/daily-quotidien/050322/dq050322b-eng.htm

Suzuki, David. Ancestors—the genetic source. In *Metamorphosis: Stages in a life.* Toronto: Stoddart. 1987. 13–17.

Tutu, A. D. (2011). The age of Ubuntu. Retrieved from *University of Diversity*: http://www.harisingh.com/UbuntuAge.htm

University of Melbourne. (2013, April 19). What is social equity? (B. McSherry, Editor) Retrieved from Melbourne Social Equity Institute: http://www.socialequity.unimelb.edu.au/what-is-social-equity/

Ward, T. (2013, September). Finding your map [Presentation made at Niagara College]. Welland, Ontario.

> *"Let's make one thing crystal clear: we don't want no ism here"*
>
> *(Dog Eat Dog, 1996)*

DIVERSITY COMPETENCIES

Diversity competencies are specifically learned behaviours that students can actively practise to promote equity and inclusion. By mastering this unit, students will gain the skills to become diversity-competent practitioners, including the ability to

- critically evaluate themselves and the world around them to uncover the hidden ways oppression manifests itself in everyday life

- analyze the ways in which oppression is linked to issues of identity and diversity

- identify the formal and informal mechanisms within society (both past and present) that cause or reinforce different forms of oppression

- identify and respond to the consequences of privilege that dominant groups have over the rest of the population (for example, male privilege, class privilege, etc.)

- understand and identify the intersectionality (interactions) of systems of privilege through the "ism" prism, and consider the implications for social change

- understand the social, psychological, and political effects of stereotypes, prejudice, discrimination, and oppression on diverse groups

Source: Paul Campbell/Shutterstock.com

In 1955, Rosa Parks was tired—tired of giving in to an unjust system that discriminated against black people in Montgomery, Alabama. So when the bus driver told her to give up her seat to a white passenger, she refused—and set in motion a series of events that would forever change the world, simultaneously jumpstarting the career of one of the greatest humanitarians of all time (Shipp, 2005). When she was arrested for her act of defiance, Parks called the preacher of the local Baptist Church to assist her. Martin Luther King, Jr. was only too glad to help.

Dr. King had spent his life fighting prejudice and discrimination. In response to Parks's arrest, he organized a boycott of the bus company, and these actions eventually lead to a United States Supreme Court decision declaring the state's bus segregation laws unconstitutional. In 1963, eight years after Parks's act of defiance, King made his famous "I have a dream" speech, in which he told hundreds of thousands of listeners about his hope that "my four little children will one day live in a nation where they will not be judged by the colour of their skin, but by the content of their character." As a civil rights activist, King spoke to all oppressed minorities, sending a message that promoted understanding, intergroup dialogue, and non-violent resistance to injustice. He won world recognition in 1964 when he was awarded the Nobel Peace Prize. But in 1968, at the age of 39, Martin Luther King, Jr. was assassinated in Memphis, Tennessee, where he was planning to lead a protest march to assist striking garbage workers (Nobelprize.org, 2012). Did his dream die with him?

Flash forward to June 1991. Stopped by police for driving erratically through a suburban neighbourhood in Los Angeles, Rodney King (no relation to Martin Luther King, Jr.), intoxicated and on probation, resisted arrest and was brutally beaten by four officers. The whole scene was caught on videotape. A year later, when a mostly white jury acquitted three of the officers on trial for assaulting King, the response in Los Angeles was a race riot that left 55 people dead and cost the city an estimated one billion dollars in damages. In the midst of the riots, Rodney King was filmed by television crews, pleading, "Can we all get along?" Twenty troubled years passed for King until June 17, 2012, when his fiancée found him dead in his swimming pool. Police ruled out foul play (CBC News, 2012). King was dead before he was 50. Is King's iconic question just as relevant today?

Two men named King died in the midst of racial tension—men with the mightiest of names rendered powerless because of discrimination and oppression. Before her death at the age of 92, Rosa Parks was recognized as the "first lady of civil rights" (Pub.L. 106–26). Each of these three people experienced racial discrimination and saw it brought to the forefront as the key social issue that it was. Is racial discrimination still a problem?

We all have prejudices, stereotypes, and biases about members of groups that are unlike us. However, we must recognize that we are not acting fairly if we treat people differently because of these judgments. Imagine, if you will, holding a glass prism up to the light and watching the light refract into many different colours. Using this metaphor, imagine how stereotypes refract through a prism of oppression to become racism, ageism, sexism, classism, ableism, heterosexism, and many other "isms."

We know how important it is to stand up against injustice and fight the discrimination that has served as the precursor to persecution, violence, and genocide. We know that each one of us deserves to be considered a unique human being—and not just because it's the law. Think of these things as you read this chapter and see the effects that stereotyping, prejudice, discrimination, and oppression have on all of us. In doing so, ask yourself these questions: What is to be done about it? Can we all get along?

THE SOCIAL CONSTRUCTION OF REALITY

The culture that was resisted by Dr. Martin Luther King, Jr. and by the civil rights movement is one of the most prominent examples of oppression in history, but it is only one of countless instances. Stereotypes, prejudice, and discrimination grow from the unequal distribution of power, creating dominant and subordinate groups in society and allowing the subjugation of one in favour of the other. The relationships that exist between groups may be real in and of themselves, but all of the players within the groups create or "socially construct" their own realities of those relationships. The **social construction of reality** refers to the sociological theory that proposes that the way we present ourselves in any given situation is shaped by the interactions of our all our past relations and the social interactions that we have with others. How we see a situation depends entirely on the interactions that we have with the individuals involved and how those interactions

> **Social construction of reality:** The sociological theory that proposes that how we present ourselves in any given situation is shaped by the interactions of our all our past relations and the social interactions that we have with others.

relate with our own beliefs, values, and experiences. We define everyday situations continually and differently, consciously and unconsciously, throughout our waking lives. Each individual's definition varies from the definition of others according to his or her own interactions and history (Berger & Luckmann, 1966). So, for example, if two people were to witness an accident in the street, though their accounts of the accident may be similar, there's very little chance that the two individuals would give identical versions of the same scene. Their stories will be shaped by their own histories, the interactions they may have had prior to seeing the accident, and a host of other values, beliefs, and experiences.

When you see someone panhandling for change on the street, for example, why is it that some passersby will donate and others will not? The answer depends on how the passersby have socially constructed the situation. Some might be sympathetic, some might be disgusted, and some might ignore the situation all together. These reactions stem from the fact that they have stereotyped street people as "homeless" or "lazy" and treat them accordingly. Almost exclusively, people with power impose stereotypes on those who are powerless. American sociologist W. I. Thomas suggests, "It is not important whether or not the interpretation is correct—if men define situations as real they are real in their consequences" (Thomas, 1927). So, if the privileged avoid street people or tell them to "get a job," street people are reminded that they are not welcomed by the larger part of society. Street people then begin to define their situations based on the interactions they have with passersby, and they may eventually come to believe that they are indeed unwanted.

The consequences of power are manifest in every interaction in society, at all levels. Regardless of whether power is expressed between individuals (a bully abusing a weaker individual), or by a dominant group imposing its beliefs and values on a minority group (society celebrating Christian holidays to the exclusion of other religions), the end result is the same: unfair and in many cases illegal and often inhumane treatment. Power refers to the ability to get your own way, even in the face of adversity. Those who hold power in society are able to label, stereotype, and discriminate against weaker individuals or groups, whether that weakness is real or perceived.

Stereotype: A stereotype is a label that may have some basis in fact, but that has been grossly overgeneralized and applied to a particular segment of the population, or situation.

Stereotypes

We routinely use labels to categorize people, places, and things. However, stereotypes generalize about the behaviours and characteristics associated with members of those categories. We often use stereotypes because doing so is easy: we do not have to think as hard when we use them. For example, if you were asked for words to describe rock concerts, senior citizens, tattoos, and school, you would likely use stereotypes ("rowdy," "frail," "edgy," "cliquey") as part of your descriptions.

So what's wrong with using stereotypes? Well, **stereotypes** have been described as "'mental cookie cutters'—they force simple patterns on a complex mass and assign a limited number of characteristics to all members of a group" (Nachbar & Lause, 1992). While stereotypes may have some basis in fact, they have been grossly overgeneralized and applied to an entire segment of the population or an entire situation. When we stereotype, we ignore all individual characteristics about the individuals in that group or about the specific situation. For example, if we say that women are bad drivers or sociology lectures are boring, we fail to take into account the number of women who are excellent drivers, and the sociology lectures that are fun and exciting.

The media play a role in creating stereotypes as well. People learn about the world through varying forms of the media, such as television, magazines, movies, and the Internet. The collective media shape young minds today through overgeneralized, value-laden images that perpetuate stereotypical myths about different cultural groups (Chung, 2007). For example, did you grow up watching Disney movies? They have been a part of our lives for what seems like forever. How old were you when you began to realize that the characters in those movies had certain predictable qualities? One group of researchers analyzed 26 popular Disney movies and found consistent use of stereotypes in the presentation of male and female characters. Disney's males express their emotions through physical actions; they cannot restrain of their sexual responses; they are strong and heroic by nature; they do not perform domestic work; and if overweight they are slow and unintelligent. In contrast, Disney's females are valued more for their beauty than their intellect; they are helpless and need male protection; their work focuses on household chores and their goals focus on marriage; and if overweight they are mean, ugly, and unattached (Towbin, Haddock, Zimmerman, Lund, & Tanner, 2003). Though stereotypes seem harmless, when children grow up watching these images repeatedly, they can begin to believe that every woman should be like Cinderella, Belle, or Snow White, and every man should act like Aladdin or John Smith, because these images help to establish what pass for norms in our society. The mass media, in all their various forms, teach society what the acceptable and normal roles are for both men and women (Hammer, 2009).

Similarly, advertising plays a big part in shaping how we perceive groups and individuals in society today. A research study at Keele University in the U.K. investigated the extent to which advertising affects our subconscious. The study showed by the time they are 12, children consciously understand how commercials use celebrities to promote their brands. Subconsciously, though, the children in the study were still susceptible to the emotional lures of advertisements (Keele University, 2012). Other research has been done by Jean Kilbourne, who for decades has studied advertising and the impact that it has on social values, relationships, and commitment to civic life (Kilbourne, 1999). Results from her work have consistently shown that "the self-esteem of girls plummets as they reach adolescence partly because they cannot possibly escape the message that their bodies are objects, and imperfect objects, at that" (Kilbourne, 1999, p. 27). Boys, in contrast, "learn that masculinity requires a kind of ruthlessness, even brutality" (Kilbourne, 1999, p. 27).

Comedy shows are another platform for perpetuating stereotypes. Several minority groups at Michigan University think that stereotype-based comedy routines, like those made famous by comedian Dave Chappelle, perpetuate negative images of the group being depicted. Sha Duncan, Coordinator of the Office of Multi-Ethnic Student Affairs, believes that "the stereotyping jokes on different ethnicities are often brought to life when groups outside of the black community embrace what they see and think is black culture." She states, "They think they are being friends when they say, 'Wut up dawg!' But people don't do that. I speak proper English" (Kan, 2004). In contrast, Azhar Usman thinks differently about stereotypes. A Chicago-based attorney, lecturer, and community activist turned comedian, Usman uses his stand-up routines to fight negative stereotyping of Muslims and Arabs in America. In 2004, Usman and two friends launched their "Allah Made Me Funny" tour to describe what it is like to be Muslim in a predominantly non-Muslim society (Elshinnawi, 2009). Canadian comedian Russell Peters is another example of an entertainer who uses stereotypes to deflate them, often drawing on his own Indian background.

Is it possible to have comedy shows without stereotyping? How do you handle ethnic-based humour? Do you see the use of stereotypes in comedy as derogatory or as educational tools? For experts as different as psychology professor Lawrence Hirschfeld and

How would the stereotypes surrounding body modifications affect your interactions with this businessman?

Tony Fox, vice president of Comedy Central, the jury is still out. Both note that there is no scientific evidence to suggest that viewers take stereotypes as truth (Kan, 2004).

Prejudice

In his seminal book *The Nature of Prejudice*, American psychologist Gordon Allport defines prejudice as "an antipathy [negative feeling] based on faulty and inflexible generalization. It may be felt or expressed. It may be directed toward a group or an individual of that group" (Allport, 1954, p. 9). **Prejudice** is very similar to stereotyping but it involves a prejudging component, and prejudice is often a precursor to discriminatory behaviour. When individuals are prejudiced, they have preconceived notions—usually negative—about a group of people, based on their physical, cultural, or social characteristics. So, if you have a problem with your roommate

Prejudice: A negative attitude based on learned notions about members of selected groups, based on their physical, social, or cultural characteristics.

because he or she is messy ("Chris is a slob"), you are likely not guilty of prejudice. However, if you stereotype your roommate because of his or her religion, gender, or ethnicity, that is a form of prejudice.

Sociological and psychological works from 1890–1925 examined individual differences between whites and blacks, and between men and women, but many of the studies were conducted to support the stereotypes that men were superior to women and whites were superior to blacks. However, during this period some sociologists and psychologists—men like G. T. W. Patrick, W. I. Thomas, and Josiah Morse—adopted a more theoretical approach to prejudice. When their works were analysed by contemporary sociologists Russell J. Webster, Donald A. Saucier, and Richard J. Harris, the modern researchers found four main characterizations of prejudice:

1. It can be defined as "an undue judgment, favourable or unfavourable, toward an object, person, or thing."
2. No one is free, either consciously or unconsciously, from prejudice.
3. Prejudice is a "normal" human attribute arising from cognitive processes that occur naturally—processes that can assist a person who holds a prejudice by conserving mental energy but that can also have damaging results.
4. Because of its complexity, prejudice is difficult to control or eliminate (Webster, Saucier, & Harris, 2010).

What do you make of these findings today? Do you believe that everyone holds prejudicial attitudes? Are they a normal part of our cognitive thought processes? Can we avoid making prejudgments about anything or anyone?

Today, studies in prejudicial attitudes investigate in-group and out-group behaviours, using Allport's foundational work in categorization. Allport (1954) argued that prejudice stems partially from the conscious and unconscious mental processes that automatically categorize information as we take it in. He asserted that "the human mind must think with the aid of categories.... Once formed, categories are the basis for normal prejudgment. We cannot possibly avoid this process. Orderly living depends upon it" (Allport, 1954, p. 20).

Ethnocentrism: Refers to a tendency to regard one's own culture and group as the standard, and thus superior, whereas all other groups are seen as inferior.

The categorizing of information seems useful and natural for us. As we go about our days, we consciously and unconsciously file and sort information into "folders" in our brains so we can process it. However, it can become a problem when some of the information is blurred and hard to categorize—for example, when we encounter biracial or intersex individuals. Our brain might not easily know how to classify a man with breasts who is undergoing gender reassignment surgery because that individual does not neatly fit into one of our mental folders. By automatically sorting information, we unconsciously develop sets of in-groups (things that are like us) and out-groups (things that aren't like us). This sorting isn't limited to things that look like us. Our brain processes everything, so everything—sound, sight, smell, or taste—gets placed into in-group and out-group folders.

In one example of this sorting process at work, 78 German students volunteered to participate in a project that was described to them as being about the development of a social robot prototype. Researchers split the students into two groups. They told the first group that the machine had a typical German name (Armin) and was German-designed. They told the second group that the robot's name was Arman (a typical Turkish name, from the largest minority group in Germany) and that it was developed in Turkey. Both groups were shown identical pictures of the robot. The students from the first group felt more attachment to Armin than students from the second group felt for Arman. The first group's members were more likely to describe Armin as warm, intelligent, and well designed than were the students evaluating the "Turkish-built" Arman. But the students' evaluations showed more than a basic preferential bias for the German robot: they also saw Armin as more human, stating said they felt psychologically close to Armin and expressing more of a willingness to live with it than did students from the second group who evaluated Arman. For these students, Armin belonged to the in-group folder, and Arman to the out-group. If individuals can form such attitudes about an inanimate object, we can see how easily perceptions about out-group members of society, such as the homeless, might develop (Eyssel & Kuchenbrandt, 2012).

Sometimes prejudice can result from ethnocentric attitudes, or **ethnocentrism**. This refers to the practice of assuming that the standards of your own culture are universally normal and superior to other cultures. Do you know Dr. Seuss's story of the Sneetches? The Sneetches were yellow bird-like creatures who lived on the beach. Some of them had green stars on their bellies and others were plain-bellied. The star-bellied Sneetches thought they were much better than the plain-bellied Sneetches and treated them rather

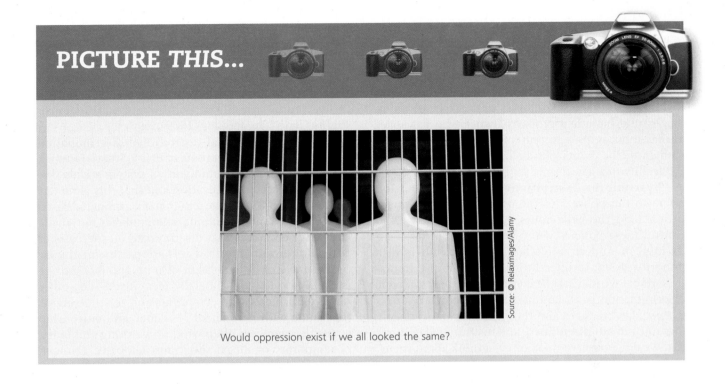

Would oppression exist if we all looked the same?

Source: © Relaximages/Alamy

unfairly. They called them names and forbade them from attending their marshmallow roasts. One day Mr. McBean came to the beach with a machine that could put stars on the plain-bellied Sneetches—for a fee, of course. The original star-bellied Sneetches then decided it was much better to be plain-bellied, and Mr. McBean obliged in removing their stars—for a larger fee, of course. The foolishness of adding and removing stars went on until the Sneetches had no money left at all. At the end of the story, all of the Sneetches realized the folly of their poor treatment of their fellow Sneetches and agreed it was much better to accept each other as they were, regardless of the number or placement of their stars (Seuss, 1961). In writing *The Sneetches,* Theodore Geisel (Dr. Seuss) created a children's book that became a timeless classic. More importantly, he told a story of prejudice and discrimination that reflected the experience of Jews in Nazi Germany and German-occupied nations through the 1930s and the Second World War: they were forced to wear yellow stars to differentiate them from their neighbours.

Having an ethnocentric attitude separates you from others. However, research has found that increasing an in-group member's amount of contact with out-group members can reduce prejudices of all types, including those based on sexual orientation, mental illness, race, age, and physical disability (Pettigrew & Tropp, 2006).

Discrimination

Prejudice is an attitude that often leads to **discrimination**—the unequal treatment of individuals or groups based on their characteristics or behaviours. In most cases, the treatment is negative, though some theorists (those who do not espouse a critical social justice perspective) believe that discrimination in favour of a positive outcome can also occur. The Canadian Charter of Rights and Freedoms (1982) promises equality under the law and ensures that "[e]very individual ... has the right to the equal protection and equal benefit of the law without discrimination and, in particular, without discrimination based on race, national or ethnic origin, colour, religion, sex, age, or mental or physical disability" (Department of Justice, 2012). Writing about the Canadian Charter and various provincial charters, sociologist Denise Helly explains that "[t]he right to equality protected by these documents is fourfold: equality before the law, equality in the application of the law, equality of protection afforded by the law, and equal benefit of the law" (Helly, 2004).

Discrimination can exist on many different

> **Discrimination:** The unequal treatment of individuals or groups based on their characteristics or behaviours. It involves actions or practices of dominant group members that have a harmful impact on members of a subordinate group.

levels. **Individual or direct discrimination** is an individual's deliberate exclusion of other individuals or groups based on race, ethnicity, and so on (Helly, 2004, p. 25). It also refers to the denial of a right or freedom by an individual against another individual, institution, or group. Examples of this type of prejudice would include a property owner who has space available but refuses to rent an apartment to a single woman or the owner of a hall who refuses to rent to the facility to a gay couple for their wedding.

Systemic or institutionalized discrimination refers to the policies of the dominant group's institutions and the behaviours of the individuals who control these policies with the tendency of having a harmful or undesirable effect on the members of a minority group. It differs from individual discrimination in that we may not be conscious of it, for systemic discrimination is an "unintentional secondary effect of everyday practices and thinking that are so deeply ingrained in our disciplinary and institutional cultures that we don't observe them or even think about them" (Neuman, 2003). One example is the former height requirement of many police forces, which indirectly discriminated against individuals of Asian descent who are on average shorter than people of European origin.

Institutional discrimination can often be observed in exclusionary hiring practices. Philip Oreopoulos of the University of British Columbia was interested in finding out why immigrants who were allowed into Canada based on their skills still struggled in the labour market. He sent out six thousand fake resumés in response to online job postings across Toronto for a variety of occupations. Oreopoulos found that applicants with English-sounding names received almost 40 percent more callbacks from employers than those with Chinese-, Indian-, or Pakistani-sounding names. Further, English-named applicants with Canadian education and experience were over three times more likely to receive interview requests than applicants whose resumés gave Chinese, Indian, or Pakistani names and foreign education and experience. Oreopoulos notes that these practices and others in his findings are illegal under the Ontario Human Rights Code (Oreopoulos, 2009).

Another example of institutional discrimination can be found in immigration policies. Stuart Tannock believes that Canada's immigration system openly discriminates based on education and that this is no different from policies of the past that discriminated based on race. For Tannock, immigration policies in Canada and other countries that discriminate on the basis of education eventually lead to national inequality by promoting a two-tier system of immigrants. One tier is highly skilled and officially recognized. The other tier is denied access to civil rights and the protections that come with permanent residency and citizenship status; its members often wind up working and living in temporary or illegal situations. Globally, Tannock claims, education-based immigration policies in wealthier countries contribute to inequality by "brain-draining" highly skilled and educated people from poorer nations (Tannock, 2011).

Structural discrimination differs from both systemic and individual discrimination. Institutional policies of the dominant groups and the behaviour of the individuals who control the policies are neutral in intent but end up having a differential or harmful effect on minority groups. Structural discrimination, on the other hand, is difficult to identify and clouded, especially by the concept of "intent." Take, for example, companies whose lay-off policies are based on seniority or length of employment. The policy doesn't seem to be deliberately discriminatory, except when you reflect that minority workers are more likely to be recent immigrants with low seniority than members of the dominant group (Pincus, 1996).

OPPRESSION

Stemming from the most blatant abuse of power and prejudice, **oppression** describes policies, practices, norms, and traditions that systemically exploit one group at the expense of another (Pharr, 1997). Unlike discrimination, which can take place at the individual level, oppression occurs when institutional and social powers support prejudice (Sensoy & Diangelo, 2009).

The women's suffrage movement, for example, arose as a response to oppression. Even though women nearly equalled men in numbers, they did not have the right to vote in Canada until

Individual or direct discrimination: The denial of a right or freedom, by an individual, against another individual, institution, or group.

Systemic or institutionalized discrimination: The policies of the dominant group's institutions and the behaviours of the individuals who control these policies, which tend to have a harmful or undesirable effect on the members of a minority group.

Structural discrimination: The policies in the institutions of the dominant groups and the behaviour of the individuals who control the policies are neutral in intent, but end up having a differential or harmful effect on the minority groups.

Oppression: Describes policies, practices, norms, and traditions that systemically exploit one group at the expense of another.

1918. Even then, there were questions as to how far women's rights extended: under Canadian law, were they "persons" entitled to sit in the Senate? In 1927, the "Famous Five"—Nellie McClung, Emily Murphy, Irene Parlby, Louise McKinney, and Henrietta Muir Edwards—asked the Supreme Court of Canada to answer the question, "Does the word 'person' in Section 24 of the B.N.A. [British North America] Act include female persons?" (Status of Women Canada, 2009). After weeks of debate, the Supreme Court of Canada decided that for the purpose of eligibility to be appointed to the Senate, the word "person" did *not* include women. Though shocked by the decision of the court, the Famous Five didn't give up their battle. Instead, they took their case to the Privy Council in Britain, at that time the highest court of appeal for Canadians. The Privy Council overturned the Supreme Court decision on October 18, 1929. It is worth noting that regardless of how hard they fought for equal rights, women could not grant themselves equality; only men held the institutional power to do so. Even though both men and women could be prejudiced against each other, only men's prejudice against women carried with it the history of patriarchy, the laws of the country, and the norms of society, giving men the power to oppress women (Sensoy & Diangelo, 2009). As this example shows, for a situation to be oppressive there must be an abuse of power, coupled with prejudice.

It its most extreme form, oppression results in acts of physical and psychological brutality—sometimes even genocide—against subordinate groups. Contemporary examples of oppression include Nazi Germany's treatment of European Jews during the 1930s and 1940s, culminating in the Holocaust; South Africa's policy of Apartheid or racial separation between 1948 and 1990; and slavery in the American South, from early colonial history to its abolition in 1865, with damaging consequences up to the present day (Axner, 2012).

Young (2004) suggests that oppression has five faces, all involving the abuse of power:

1. **Exploitation**, which involves the unfair use of people's time or labour and failure to compensate them fairly (for example, workers in sweatshops).
2. **Marginalization**, which refers to an act of exclusion that forces minority groups to the fringes of society and is most commonly based on race (for example, Aboriginal peoples).
3. **Powerlessness**, which occurs when the dominant group leaves the subordinate group with virtually no access to the rights and privileges enjoyed by the powerful (for example, immigrants). When the subordinate group comes to believe that they deserve this unfair treatment, its members are described as living in a "culture of silence."
4. **Cultural imperialism**, which describes the condition when the dominant group has made their beliefs and values the norms of a society (for example, heterosexuality or Christianity).
5. **Violence**, which is the most insidious form of oppression, instilling fear in some groups (for example, gays, blacks). (Young, 2004)

The weight of oppression sits heavily on the minds of all those in society who oppose subjugation and inequality. Though we often think of oppression as an abuse of power against groups in society, anyone who has felt the shame of being bullied, abused, or discriminated against knows on a personal level what oppression feels like. Do you remember the street people at the start of the chapter? Based on their interactions with passersby, they can eventually come to believe that they are worthless individuals who don't deserve anything from society. When this phenomenon occurs—either with individuals or on a larger scale with a minority group of

Exploitation: The unfair use of people's time or labour without compensating them fairly.

Marginalization: An act of exclusion that forces minority groups to the fringes of society, most commonly based on race.

Powerlessness: Occurs when the dominant group has left the subordinate group with virtually no access to the rights and privileges that the dominant group enjoys.

Cultural imperialism: A form of oppression where the dominant group has made their beliefs and values the norms of a society (for example, heterosexuality or Christianity).

Source: Barry Winiker/Getty

These bronze shoes are the very symbol of oppression. They line the Danube River in Budapest as a memorial to Jews in the Second World War who were rounded up by fascist soldiers, taken to the riverside and ordered to take off their shoes, then shot, their bodies disappearing into the river.

people—those who experience oppression come to internalize it. **Internalized oppression** occurs when targeted people or groups begin to believe the negative stereotypes and misinformation that the larger society communicates to them.

"Ism" Prism

The injustices done by the powerful to the powerless can be seen as rays of light through the lens of a prism: we see them refract into a set of "isms" that are synonymous with discrimination and oppression (see Figure 2.1). For example, age, when refracted through the prism, becomes ageism. It transforms from a concept to an "ism," altered by the influences and biases of social interactions, self-perceptions, power relations, and a host of other effects that determine how people relate to each other based on age. Characteristics such as class, race, ability, gender, and size go through the same process, passing through the prism to become "isms" in their own way, determined perhaps by family relations, ethnicity, religion, and (always) power. The "isms" that exist in society multiply in number as dominant groups increasingly marginalize groups that are different from the norm, groups that lack the power and resources to resist the stereotyping and prejudice that lead to discrimination. The examples listed below are merely a few of the common "isms" that exist today.

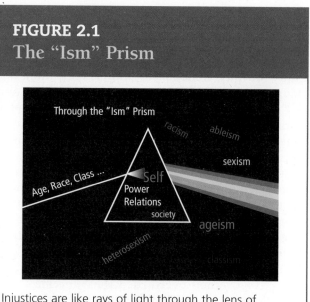

FIGURE 2.1
The "Ism" Prism

Injustices are like rays of light through the lens of a prism; they refract in a set of "isms" that are synonymous with discrimination and oppression.

ABLEISM

Ableism refers to the set of attitudes and behaviours that allocate inferior status and value to individuals who have developmental, emotional, physical, or psychiatric disabilities. The authors of one study looked at over 300 000 records of employment and found that it is not just the disability itself that causes discrimination, but also the stigma that surrounds it. These authors found that it did not matter whether the disability was apparent or existed in a record of employment: it still had an effect on workplace discrimination. Workers with current or previous disabilities, including mental illness, epilepsy, diabetes, and PTSD, experienced discrimination that affected hiring, promotion, reinstatement, and reasonable accommodation (Draper, Hawley, McMahon, & Reid, 2012).

AGEISM

The term **ageism** refers to the stereotyping of and prejudice and discrimination against individuals or groups because of their age. Examples include the tendency to view seniors as unable to work, confused, and fragile, and young people as undisciplined and erratic. Discriminating against people based on their age is illegal, whether it involves a landlord who refuses to rent an apartment to a young couple or a business that refuses to hire a qualified older person for a job. Age is protected by the Canadian Charter of Rights and Freedoms.

Age discrimination is difficult to prove in a court of law, but that doesn't stop those being treated unfairly from trying. In London, Ontario, seven women aged 60 or more are taking an age-discrimination suit against their former employer, InStore Focus, to the Ontario Human Rights Tribunal. Employed as "brand ambassadors" who offered product samples to customers, the women had between 3 and 15 years of service with the company. However, they were let go after being told that they didn't fit the image the store wanted. According to one woman, "My manager called me and said, 'I have

Internalized oppression: Occurs when targeted people internalize (or begin to believe) the negative stereotypes and misinformation that the larger society communicates to them, either as individuals or part of a larger group.

Ableism: The set of attitudes and behaviours that allocate inferior status and or value to individuals who have developmental, emotional, physical, or psychiatric disabilities.

Ageism: Stereotyping, prejudice, and discrimination against individuals or groups because of their age; it also refers to the tendency to view seniors as unable to work, confused, and fragile.

some bad news, (the store) is profiling and they no longer want to use you. They want soccer moms, they feel soccer moms shop for children'" (Hensen, 2012). The women lost needed income, suffered serious blows to their self-esteem, and now face the daunting task of finding new employment.

Seeking a new job is becoming increasingly difficult for older workers because of a new strategy some companies (most notably in the United States) are using to recruit employees. In red print at the bottom of many ads for employment positions is the statement, "Client will not consider/review anyone NOT currently employed regardless of the reason." This strategy especially discriminates against job-seekers—often older workers—who are unemployed because of the recession. Employers argue that they are looking for employees who are "happy where they are" rather than anxious because of prolonged unemployment; and with approximately 5.5 people available for every U.S. job, employers can afford to be choosy. The disclaimer saves them from wading through the resumés of people that they deem unsuitable (that is, "old"). Currently the practice is not illegal, though some U.S. states have passed bills trying to make it so (Bassett, 2010).

However, age discrimination is not limited to older adults. The President and CEO of Volunteer Canada reports that young volunteers today feel the sting of discrimination "while seeking, and receiving volunteer responsibilities. They feel discounted by other volunteers and say they are given the simpler types of tasks that nobody else would want to do" (Volunteer Canada, 2012).

Classism

Classism refers to the systematic oppression of subordinate classes by dominant class groups in order to gain advantage and strengthen their own positions. Examples of classist attitudes include the belief that one occupation is better than another, that poor people are impoverished because they don't budget their money properly, and that working class people are less intelligent than upper class people (OPIRG, 2012). Over thirty years ago, economist Bradley R. Schiller found empirical evidence of classism when he measured the relative socio-economic achievements of black and white adolescents. Schiller's research showed that class discrimination was potentially as evident and harmful as racial discrimination to black youths who came from impoverished backgrounds (Schiller, 1971).

Classist attitudes are the basis for class discrimination, and they affect everyone. For example, have you ever had to complete a peer evaluation at work or school? In one study, almost 250 students answered a range of questions aimed at measuring their class biases, including the statement "During an in-class presentation, I would rate a poor person's performance lower than a wealthier person's performance." Analysis of the results of the study found that some students demonstrated negative biases toward classmates they perceived to be poor. In addition, students evaluating their peers allocated lower grades to students who were financially poor but higher-performing—grades that differed greatly than assigned by the teachers, while female students were more likely to grade harshly than males (Sadler & Good, 2006; Moorman & Wicks-Smith, 2012).

Heterosexism

Heterosexism refers to the belief in the natural superiority of heterosexuality as a way of life and its logical right to social dominance. Comprised of a system of ideas and institutionalized beliefs, it leads to the oppression of any non-heterosexual form of behaviour, identity, relationship, or community.

One well-known example of heterosexism concerns the experience of Canadian teenager Marc Hall, who took the Durham (Ontario) Catholic District School Board to court in 2002 after his principal refused to allow Hall to bring his boyfriend to prom. On the day of the prom, Justice Robert McKinnon issued an injunction that ordered the school to allow Hall to go the prom with the date of his choice. Eventually, though, Hall dropped the case against the school board in 2005 when he learned it would likely take years to resolve the case (Kennedy, 2012). His story was portrayed in the television movie *Prom Queen* in 2004. But while Hall's initiative had a positive outcome, the suicide of Ottawa teenager Jamie Hubley, who took his life in 2011 after enduring years of anti-gay bullying in school, demonstrates the devastating consequences heterosexism can have (CBC News, 2011).

Racism

Racism is a set of ideas that asserts the supremacy of one group over others

---

Classism: The systematic oppression of dominant class groups on subordinate classes in order to gain advantage and strengthen their own positions.

Heterosexism: The belief in the natural superiority of heterosexuality as a way of life and therefore its logical right to dominance. Comprised of a system of ideas and institutionalized beliefs, it leads to the oppression of any non-heterosexual form of behaviour, identity, relationship, or community.

Racism: A set of ideas that entails the supremacy of one social group over another based on biological or cultural characteristics, combined with the power to put these beliefs into practice to the exclusion of minority men and women.

based on biological or cultural characteristics, accompanied by the power to put these beliefs into practice to the exclusion of minority men and women. While scientists argue that race has no genetic basis, the concept of "race" is real enough in its consequences. Basically, it comes down to how race is socially constructed as a label attached to a system of power that has the ability to oppress or privilege, depending on the meanings and values assigned to it and on who is doing the assigning.

Fashion magazines provide excellent examples of race as a social construct. In countless instances, dark-skinned and Hispanic models and celebrities, such as Queen Latifah, Beyoncé, Tyra Banks, Rihanna, Halle Berry, and Jennifer Lopez, are "whitewashed" through digital enhancement and given lighter skin to appeal to the dominant demographic of the fashion market (Kite, 2011). And it's not just in advertising—where there's profit to be had—that those in power manipulate individual and collective perceptions of race. In 2012, Mark Carney, then governor of the Bank of Canada, issued a formal apology for mishandling the design of the new polymer $100 bill (Isfeld, 2012). The original design showed an Asian-looking woman peering into a microscope. However, before the design was released, focus groups indicated that some people thought portraying a scientist as Asian reflected an ethnic stereotype as well as being unfair in representing only one ethnic group on a denomination of money. In response, the bank ordered the bill to be redrawn with the image of a woman of "neutral ethnicity"—who in fact appeared to be Caucasian (The Canadian Press, 2012). It was a public relations fiasco.

How would you define "neutral ethnicity"? Do you see the Bank of Canada's re-imaging as anything different from the "whitewashing" that's done in the advertising industry? Do you think that, in a society espousing multiculturalism and ethnic diversity, the Bank of Canada's action was narrow-minded? Does it constitute racism?

Sexism: The attitudes or behaviours based on the belief that one sex is superior to the other, often resulting in the discrimination or devaluation of that sex and the roles related to it.

Sizeism: Discrimination against individuals based on their body size, including height and weight

SEXISM

Sexism refers to attitudes and behaviours based on the belief that one gender is superior to the other. Sexism often results in discrimination against or the devaluation of that gender and the roles related to it.

How prevalent is sexism? Results from a recent study reveal startling information about gender bias in the sciences. Researchers sent out 127 fake resumés to male and female science professors throughout the United States. The resumés contained application materials from a fictional undergraduate student applying for the position of lab manager. On 63 applications, the student's name was John; on 64 applications, the student's name was Jennifer. Every other piece of the application was identical—the resumé, GPA, references, and portfolio. The researchers also made sure to match the groups of professors receiving the resumés in terms of age distribution, scientific fields, proportion of males and females, and tenure status. Both male and female professors consistently regarded the female student applicant as less competent and less hireable than the identical male student. On a scale of 1 to 5, the average competency rating for the male applicant was 4.05, compared to 3.33 for the female applicant. The average salary offered to the male was $30 238.10, while the female was offered $26 507.94 (Moss-Racussin, Dovidio, Brescoll, Graham, & Handelsman, 2012). Could these discrepancies offer a reasonable explanation for differences between the numbers of men and women who practise in the physical sciences such as biology, chemistry, physics, and astronomy?

When we think of sexism, we have a tendency to think of men discriminating against women, but that's not always the case. American Derek Hunter is in the process of suing his local firing range. The last time he practised he paid his usual $15 fee, but he noticed a sign that announced it was Ladies Day when women could practise for free. Hunter accused the firing range of reverse sexism and filed a $200 000 lawsuit. According to Hunter's attorney, "The special court of appeals outlawed gender discrimination and ladies' night activities in 1986. … You can't offer one benefit to one group and not to the other group based on sex" (Ellin, 2012).

SIZEISM

Sizeism refers to discrimination against individuals based on their body size, including height and weight; it is generally seen as prejudice against those who are overweight. Social consequences experienced by persons with obesity include inequities in employment, barriers in education, compromised health care, and negative portrayals in the media, to the extent that the Canadian Obesity Network reports weight bias and discrimination are more prevalent than discrimination based on race, gender, or sexual orientation (Canadian

IN THEIR SHOES

If a picture can say a thousand words, imagine the stories your shoes could tell! Try this student story on for size – have you walked in this student's shoes?

My name is Cameron. I am told by my grandmother that I was a very happy child until about the age of 5 or so. Then I became very depressed and very withdrawn. This was because of a major depressive episode that ended up lasting 11 years. This was brought on by two mentally and physically abusive family members and severe bullying at school. I would get kicked down two flights of concrete stairs by other students several times a day. I would be physically assaulted sometimes in the middle of class and often I would be chased home with knives and baseball bats, and no one ever tried to stop it—not teachers, not parents, not even the principal.

At age 10 a neighbour began to abuse me physically, mentally, and sexually—this went on most days for 4 years. I never said anything because he and his friends said they would frame me for the same thing if I ever spoke about it. In grade 8 I went to a private school to get away from my public school problems. The principal hated little boys and decided to take this out on me every morning all school year long. She would haul me into her office and scream at me because she hated me for about an hour. After which point I would be locked in a windowless broom closet for the rest of the day without bathroom breaks until one of the secretaries would unlock the door and say "I've distracted her, run boy the last bus for home is leaving."

I always had a rough home life. My mom would make it her mission to get us all to fight every day and then patch things up by the end of the evening only to get into an unwarranted screaming match the next day. She would often call up my father at work and tell him I had done something bad which I had not. He would come racing home from work and scream at me and sometimes threaten to beat me up. My brother who is much older was just as manipulative as my mom. He moved out young and I would visit him most weekends. He spent the entire time I was with him telling me how he was planning on taking as much cash as he could from my parents and then just disappearing into the night and he expected me to do the same eventually. He left 4 years ago. I speak to him maybe 4 times a year for a few minutes each time.

I had a series of abusive relationships with other men. All but one was abusive in many different ways. One had attempted to rape me and get me to contract AIDS. I would have been 14 at the time. Fortunately I was able to escape him. When I was 16, I developed wildly fluctuating bipolar disorder. Also that year I had what is known medically as a first episode psychosis or as it's more commonly known a complete mental breakdown. I spent 6 weeks in the psychiatric ward of my local hospital where I attempted suicide several times. I had my second overdose at this point (my first was at age 10). I began self mutilating in addition to the anorexia I had had since grade 6. This gave me a way to punish myself. I felt if this many people had tried to hurt me, I must have done something to deserve it. I was diagnosed with bipolar type 2 with psychotic features, a rather severe case of post traumatic stress disorder, generalized anxiety disorder. It took 6 months for everything to stabilize, and then an additional 3.5 years spent in a "walking coma" before I was fully healed.

This is extremely hard to write all of this. It is hard to remember everyone I've told my life story to—absolutely hundreds of mental health professionals, teachers, professors, and everyday people and it never gets any easier. I am shaking from head to toe and I feel sick, but this has to be mentioned. I refuse to live in silence. It is unfortunate how we live in a society where when someone gets a physical illness that almost ends their lives people automatically rush in with love and support, but if I was to tell people something small like that I suffer from bipolar disorder or I take psychiatric medications they will always look at me with fear and hate, like I am a beast who must live his days in exile. All this over what other people willingly and consciously chose to do to me starting at a very young age. Society had me marked for death.

So please, I ask just one thing of you: I sincerely hope and pray that after reading this you will be kind when someone seems a little strange, or if they mention they suffer from mental illness, be a kind ear and a warm heart, then maybe my words, and my life will not have been in vain.

Obesity Network, 2011). But our willingness to act against sizeism is a recent development: it was only in 2011 that doctors, public health policymakers, government representatives, educators, and activists gathered for Canada's first-ever conference on weight discrimination.

Jennifer Portnick knows all about sizeism. Seeking both a fitness instruction job and the purchase of a franchise with Jazzercise, a Carlsbad, California based-based company that markets what it calls "the world's leading dance-fitness program," she was denied both applications. In rejecting Portnick, Jazzercise officials cited the company's policy that instructors possess a "fit appearance" (Ackman, 2002). "Jazzercise sells fitness," the company's director of franchise programs wrote to Portnick. "Consequently, a Jazzercise applicant must have a high muscle-to-fat ratio and look leaner than the public" (Brown, 2002). Portnick, a 109-kg, 172-cm (240-pound, 5-foot-8) aerobics teacher, had been taking aerobics classes for 15 years without having her skills questioned. She brought her case before the San Francisco Human Rights Commission, which enforces that city's ordinance barring discrimination based on height or weight, and won. On May 6, 2002, Jazzercise announced that it would stop requiring applicants to be fit in appearance.

In Canada, there is currently no legal recourse for acts of discrimination based on size. The Canadian Human Rights Act does not include protection against sizeism or discrimination based on weight, nor has anyone fought an employment discrimination case based solely on the issue of weight (Immen, 2012). Similarly, in the United States, no federal legislation exists to protect individuals with obesity from discrimination based on weight. Michigan and a few localities, including San Francisco, prohibit weight-based discrimination. Some people with obesity have tried to seek legal recourse under the Americans with Disabilities Act, but few of these cases have been successful (Puhl, Heuer, & Sarda, 2011).

ENDING THOUGHTS

Power is at the root of every stereotype, prejudicial thought, or act of discrimination. But power is also a relative concept, for no one has absolute power. Individuals can choose to exercise what little or great amounts of power they possess, including the power to change themselves or the world.

Sometimes we have a notion that to be powerful, you must also be rich or occupy a high position. Do you think these notions are based on stereotypes? Rosa Parks's refusal to give up her bus seat lead to monumental change in American society, but she lost her job as a seamstress because of her action. On the day he made his famous "I have a dream" speech, Martin Luther King, Jr. had hundreds of thousands of people listening to his every word, yet a few years later it took only one man with a gun to silence him. When Rodney King was captured on film appealing to Los Angeles rioters to stop the destruction, his words reached millions. None of them was highly positioned or rich, but each used what power he or she had to resist discrimination and oppression.

Research suggests that individuals are capable of "self-regulating" their responses to stereotypes in an attempt to hide prejudicial attitudes, especially in inter-group settings (Plant & Devine, 2009). We can only hope that the ability to "hide" prejudicial attitudes carries over into real-life settings as well. Gaining a greater understanding of the power that you have to create or crush stereotyping, prejudice, and discrimination is the first step in the journey to fight oppression—a journey that might one day culminate in the realization of the dream of Martin Luther King, Jr.

READING

JAIL GUARD COMPENSATED FOR RACIAL TAUNTS 23 YEARS LATER

By Ashante Infantry

After 23 years, jail guard Mike McKinnon's human rights complaint against the Ministry of Community Safety and Correctional Services has finally been resolved, but he's not crowing about the "substantial" out-of-court settlement.

"I feel betrayed by the government for allowing this to happen all these years," said McKinnon, 55. "I'm still fielding calls from people that are in the system saying, 'Mike, you are so lucky that you're not here, it's just as bad or worse, in some situations.'"

Shortly after joining Toronto East Detention Centre in 1977, the Scarborough native of Cree descent found himself the subject of racial taunts.

"I was called 'chief,' conversations were referred to as 'powwows'; my wife, who was then my girlfriend was referred to as a 'squaw,'" recalled McKinnon who never hid his native ancestry, as some of his colleagues did.

"I self-identified. People asked me my background; I told them what it was. I'm proud of my ancestry, but I wasn't prepared for what was going to happen."

And he was further disappointed by his superiors' response.

"They seemed shocked that somebody would actually identify it and bring it forward," said McKinnon. "You could see in their reaction, 'Do you really want to come forward? You're going to cause problems for yourself. Try and fit in. Be part of the team.'

"I indicated I didn't want to be part of that team and I wanted to be treated with respect and for whatever reason management dug in their heels."

He witnessed or heard of similar experiences from black, gay and female staffers throughout the system.

"It is a cesspool of inequity," said McKinnon. "People are reluctant to come forward. When I first put my complaint in, there was no mechanism in my collective agreement to deal with it. I had to go to the human rights commission which is going outside.

"At hearings, I was finding out more stuff from people giving evidence. I was being referred to as "The FBI"—The f---ing big Indian. One manager indicated that he understood the native culture because when he was a little boy he used to watch cowboys and Indians on TV."

A decade later, in 1998, the human rights board of inquiry ruled in McKinnon's favour, finding that the centre was "poisoned by racial harassment and discrimination."

Since then, McKinnon has been fighting for proper implementation of the tribunal's orders, such as a human rights training program.

The intricacies of the case contributed to its length, said Ontario Human Rights Commission spokesperson Rosemary Bennett.

"We're not thrilled with the time it took, but given the number of cases and counter cases we're not surprised," she

said. "This was not a garden variety race case. It was a systemic case, which are always more complex, involving such a large institution and [it] involved a whole lot of little cases."

In February, the tribunal ruled that the ministry "deliberately withheld information and documents that were vital to the case" and for the first time in its history, requested that the Divisional Court consider whether a deputy minister, Jay Hope, was in contempt of its orders.

Not long after, McKinnon's lawyer, Kate Hughes, was approached for mediation which resulted in last week's settlement, ending all legal proceedings. There is a gag order on the details, but it must be sizable to compensate McKinnon and his wife, Vicki Shaw-McKinnon, who are raising two children and will not return to the Corrections jobs they have been on paid leave from since 2002.

"It was too dangerous to go back in," said McKinnon. "In that type of environment you have to be able to depend on your colleagues to react immediately and effectively; and if somebody were to turn a blind eye for a few seconds, I might be stabbed, strangled, whatever. You're dealing with maximum security inmates. We feared for our safety in that setting."

McKinnon would like to see a royal commission forged to address the racism he says is rampant throughout Corrections.

Greg Flood, a spokesman for the Ministry of Community Safety and Correctional Services, said the ministry recognizes that "this has been a very difficult and trying matter for Mr. McKinnon and his spouse.

"We hope that this settlement brings them not only the closure they deserve, but also presents an opportunity to enhance professionalism within the ranks of Correctional Services in Ontario," he said.

Flood said the ministry has agreed to "undertake and continue a number of actions focused on enhancing accountability, recruitment and training with respect to Aboriginal employees. The ministry will be working closely with the Ontario Human Rights Commission to ensure that our objectives are met and Deputy Minister Hope will continue to play an integral role in that regard." (http://www.thestar.com/news/article/1042778)

Source: Reprinted with permission—Torstar Syndication Services.

DISCUSSION QUESTIONS

1. Do you think that this case would have taken so long to reach resolution if the charges had been levied against a private firm, rather than the government?
2. Try your best to add up (excluding the settlement) how much money this has cost taxpayers over the last 23 years. What are the ramifications of these costs and wait times?

3. Does the type of discrimination that Mr. McKinnon experienced in 1977 still exist in workplaces today? If so, why hasn't anything been done to prevent it? If not, what measures have been put in place to curtail it?

KNOW IT AND OWN IT: WHAT DO I BRING TO THIS?

What do you do when someone tells a joke that's based on a stereotype? Do you laugh, or keep silent? Do you speak out and tell the person that his or her words are not appreciated—that the attempt at humour is at the cost of someone else's feelings? Your answers to these questions will help you understand how likely you are to engage in stereotyping. Reflect on your thoughts and consider your beliefs, words, and deeds as they relate to how you treat people who belong to different groups than you.

WALKING THE TALK: HOW CAN I LEARN FROM THIS?

Identifying the differences between stereotyping, prejudice, and discrimination is the first step in overcoming the thoughts and feelings that lead to the practice of each. By catching yourself and others when this behaviour is evident and bringing it out in the open, you will create greater awareness of prejudiced behaviour and contribute to its eventual decline.

IT IS WHAT IT IS: IS THIS INSIDE OR OUTSIDE MY COMFORT ZONE?

Standing up for what's right is always a bit uncomfortable, but putting an end to oppression can be as easy as spending time with people you don't usually spend time with. Breaking down borders and getting to know people from different cultures is the first step in eliminating stereotypes and prejudice.

PUT IT IN PLAY: HOW CAN I USE THIS?

Do you think that you are free from bias and judgment? You might be surprised at the thoughts that run through your mind—thoughts of which you're not really consciously aware. Check out the research going on at Project Implicit (**https://implicit.harvard.edu/implicit/**), where millions of people have taken tests to determine their implicit biases about race, gender, weight, mental health, and other characteristics.

CourseMate Study Tools

Located at www.nelson.com/site/walkamile1e

- Consolidate your knowledge with the **Flashcards**.
- Gauge your understanding with **Picture This** and accompanying questions for reflection.
- Develop your critical thinking skills by working through **The Daily**.
- Apply your understanding with **KWIP** interactive!
- Develop your critical reading skills through compelling **Readings** and accompanying short answer questions.

REFERENCES

Ackman, D. (2002, May 9). The case of the fat aerobics instructor. Retrieved from *Forbes*: http://www.forbes.com/2002/05/09/0509portnick.html

Allport, G. (1954). *The nature of prejudice*. Reading, Massachusetts: Addison-Wesley.

Axner, M. (2012). Healing from the effects of internalized oppression. Retrieved from *The Community Tool Box*: http://ctb.ku.edu/en/tablecontents/sub_section_main_1172.aspx

Bassett, L. (2010, June 4). Disturbing job ads: 'The unemployed will not be considered.' Retrieved from *Huffington Post*: http://www.huffingtonpost.com/2010/06/04/disturbing-job-ads-the-un_n_600665.html

Berger, P., & Luckmann, T. (1966). *The social construction of reality: A treatise in the sociology of knowledge*. Garden City, New York: Double Day.

Brown, P. L. (2002, May 8). 240 pounds, persistent and Jazzercise's equal. Retrieved from *New York Times*: http://www.nytimes.com/2002/05/08/us/240-pounds-persistent-and-jazzercise-s-equal.html

Canadian Obesity Network. (2011, January 17). Canadian Summit on Weight Bias and Discrimination summit report. Retrieved from *Canadian Obesity Network*: http://www.obesitynetwork.ca/files/Weight_Bias_Summit_Report.pdf

Canadian Press. (2012, August 17). Asian-looking woman scientist image rejected for $100 bills. Retrieved from *CBC*

News: http://www.cbc.ca/news/politics/story/2012/08/17/pol-cp-100-dollar-bills-asian-scientist-image.html

CBC News. (2011, June 18). Gay Ottawa teen who killed himself was bulled. Retrieved from *CBC News*: http://www.cbc.ca/news/canada/ottawa/story/2011/10/18/ottawa-teen-suicide-father.html

CBC News. (2012, June 17). Rodney King, symbol of 1992 L.A. riots, dies. Retrieved from *CBC News*: http://www.cbc.ca/news/world/story/2012/06/17/rodney-king-obit.html

Chung, S. (2007). Deconstructing lesbian and gay stereotypes in the media. *Journal of Art and Design Education*, 98–107.

Department of Justice. (2012, August 14). *Canadian Charter of Rights and Freedoms*. Retrieved from *Department of Justice*: http://laws-lois.justice.gc.ca/eng/Const/page-15.html#h-39

Dog Eat Dog. (1996). Isms.

Draper, W., Hawley, C., McMahon, B., & Reid, C. (2012). Workplace discrimination and the record of employment. *Journal of Vocational Rehabilitation*, 199–206.

Ellin, A. (2012, August 24). Maryland man sues firing range for 'reverse sexism'. Retrieved from *ABC News*: http://abcnews.go.com/Business/maryland-man-sues-firing-range-reverse-sexism-women/story?id=17067299#.UDe67qPCRe4

Elshinnawi, M. (2009, January 8). American Muslim comic fights stereotypes with humor. Retrieved from *The Muslim Observer*: http://muslimmedianetwork.com/mmn/?p=3456

Eyssel, F., & Kuchenbrandt, D. (2012, March 5). Robot prejudice. Retrieved from *British Psychological Society–Research Digest*: http://bps-research-digest.blogspot.ca/2012/03/robot-prejudice.html

Hammer, T. (2009). Controlling images, media, and women's development: A review of the literature. *Journal of Creativity in Mental Health*, 202–216.

Helly, D. (2004). Are Muslims discriminated against in Canada since September 2001? *Canadian Ethnic Studies*, 24–48.

Hensen, M. (2012, August 20). Fired 'soccer mom' seniors launch human rights battle. Retrieved from *The Daily Observer*: http://www.thedailyobserver.ca/2012/08/20/fired-soccer-mom-seniors-launch-human-rights-battle

Immen, W. (2012, August 23). The skinny on weight discrimination. Retrieved from *The Globe and Mail*: http://www.theglobeandmail.com/report-on-business/careers/career-advice/the-skinny-on-weight-discrimination/article4311089/

Infantry, A. (2011, August 22). 23 years later, jail guard compensated for racial taunts. Retrieved from *Toronto Star*: http://www.thestar.com/news/gta/2011/08/22/23_years_later_jail_guard_compensated_for_racial_taunts.html

Isfeld, G. (2012, August 20). Bank of Canada's Mark Carney apologizes for way removal of Asian woman on $100 bill was handled. Retrieved from *National Post*: http://business.financialpost.com/2012/08/20/bank-of-canadas-mark-carney-apologizes-for-way-removal-of-asian-woman-on-100-bill-was-handled/

Kan, M. (2004, April 12). Stereotypes in comedy: Harm or humor? Retrieved from *The Michigan Daily*: http://www.michigandaily.com/content/stereotypes-comedy-harm-or-humor

Keele University. (2012, May 1). Can children resist the subconscious advertising allure of Cheryl Cole? Retrieved from *Keele University*: http://www.keele.ac.uk/pressreleases/canchildrenresistthesubconsciousadvertisingallureofcherylcole.php

Kennedy, J. R. (2012, September 25). 10 years later, Marc Hall is much more than 'the prom guy.' Retrieved from *Global Toronto*: http://www.globaltoronto.com/10+years+later+marc+hall+is+much+more+than+the+prom+guy/6442721676/story.html

Kilbourne, J. (1999). *Can't buy my love: How advertising changes the way we think and feel*. New York: Simon & Schuster.

Kite, L. (2011, February 28). Beauty whitewashed: How white ideals exclude women of color. Retrieved from *Beauty Redefined*: http://www.beautyredefined.net/beauty-whitewashed-how-white-ideals-exclude-women-of-color/

Moorman, D., & Wicks-Smith, D. (2012). Poverty discrimination revealed through student evaluations. *College Student Journal*, 141–150.

Moss-Racussin, C., Dovidio, J., Brescoll, V., Graham, M., & Handelsman, J. (2012, September 17). Science faculty's subtle gender biases favor male students. Retrieved from *Proceedings of the National Academy of Sciences*: http://www.pnas.org/content/early/2012/09/14/1211286109

Nachbar, J., & Lause, K. (1992). Breaking the mold: The meaning and significance of stereotypes in popular culture. In J. Nachbar & K. Lause, *Popular culture: An introductory text* (pp. 236-256). Bowling Green, Ohio: Bowling Green State Popular Press.

Neuman, S. (2003). Systemic discrimination and the Canada Research Chairs: Diagnosis and treatment. *Clinical & Investigative Medicine*, 35–37.

Nobelprize.org. (2012). Biography of Martin Luther King, Jr. Retrieved from *The Official Website of the Nobel Prize*: http://www.nobelprize.org/nobel_prizes/peace/laureates/1964/king.html

Ontario Public Interest Research Group (OPIRG). (2012). Anti-oppression. Retrieved from *OPIRG*: http://opirg.ca/ao/Op_Classism.html

Oreopoulos, P. (2009). Why do skilled immigrants struggle in the labor market? A field experiment with six thousand resumés. Retrieved from *Ideas*: http://www.nber.org/papers/w15036.pdf

Pettigrew, T., & Tropp, L. (2006). A meta-analytic test of intergroup contact theory. *Journal of Personality and Social Psychology*, 751–783.

Pharr, S. (1997). *Homophobia: A weapon of sexism*. Inverness, California: Chardin Press.

Pincus, F. (1996). Discrimination comes in many forms. *American Behavioral Scientist,* 186–195.

Pub.L. 106-26. 106th Congress Public Law 26. May 4, 1999. http://www.gpo.gov/fdsys/pkg/PLAW-106publ26/html/PLAW-106publ26.htm

Sadler, P., & Good, E. (2006). The impact of self and peer grading on student learning. *Educational Assessment,* 1–31.

Schiller, B. (1971). Class discrimination vs. racial discrimination. *The Review of Economics and Statistics,* 263–269.

Sensoy, O., & Diangelo, R. (2009). Developing social justice literacy. *Phi Delta Kappan,* 345–352.

Seuss, D. (1961). *The Sneetches and other stories.* New York: Random House.

Shipp, E. R. (2005, October 25). Rosa Parks, 92, founding symbol of civil rights movement, dies. Retrieved from *The New York Times*: http://www.nytimes.com/2005/10/25/us/25parks.html?_r=1

Status of Women Canada. (2009, October 9). Governor General's awards in commemoration of the persons case. Retrieved from *Status of Women Canada*: http://www.swc-cfc.gc.ca/dates/gg/case-affaire-eng.html

Tannock, S. (2011). Points of prejudice: Education-based discrimination in Canada's immigration system. *Antipode,* 1330–1356.

Thomas, W. (1927). Situational analysis: The behaviour pattern and the situation. *Publications of the American Sociological Society,* 1–13.

Towbin, M., Haddock, S., Zimmerman, T., Lund, L., & Tanner, L. (2003). Images of gender, race, age, and sexual orientation in Disney feature-length animated films. *Journal of Feminist Family Therapy,* 19–44.

Volunteer Canada. (2012, February 29). Canadian youth perceive age discrimination while volunteering . Retrieved from *Volunteer Canada*: http://volunteer.ca/media-centre/news-releases/canadian-youth-perceive-age-discrimination-while-volunteering

Webster, R., Saucier, D., & Harris, R. (2010). Before the measurement of prejudice: Early psychological and sociological papers on prejudice. *Journal of the History of the Behavioral Sciences,* 300–313.

Young, I. (2004). Five faces of oppression. In L. Heldke, & P. O'Connor, *Oppression, privilege, and resistance* (pp. 39-65). Boston: McGraw-Hill.

Social Inequality

> *"Sleepin' on the street there ain't a damn thing funny"*
>
> (Beastie Boys, 1989)

DIVERSITY COMPETENCIES

Diversity competencies are specifically learned behaviours that students can actively practise to promote equity and inclusion. By mastering this unit, students will gain the skills to become diversity-competent practitioners, including the ability to

- rank where they would place themselves in terms of absolute and relative poverty

- demonstrate problem-solving skills around the issues that cause social inequality

- explain the various kinds of poverty and the underlying causes of each

- analyze the differences between various measures of poverty

- differentiate between open and closed systems of stratification

Have you ever been hungry and wondered where your next meal was coming from? In 2010, 925 million people worldwide were hungry every day (World Hunger, 2012). Have you ever experienced sleepless nights worrying about paying your rent? The Canada Mortgage and Housing Corporation reports that a studio apartment in Vancouver rents for $855 a month, and a one-bedroom apartment goes for $965 (BCLA, 2012). Why are so many post-secondary students, billed as the future of Canada, living below the poverty line? Perhaps it's because undergraduate students paid an average of $5366 in tuition fees in 2011–2012 (Statistics Canada, 2011). Have you or has someone in your immediate family ever used a food bank? In 2011, food banks were used by 851 014 individuals in Canada (Hunger Count, 2011).

Social inequality:
The unequal distribution of tangible or intangible goods or services to individuals or groups in society.

If you've ever grappled with these issues, you're not alone. **Social inequality** exists in the unequal distribution of tangible or intangible goods or services to individuals or groups in society. About a tenth of Canadians—more than three million people—are living in poverty (Shapcott, 2010), and that situation is having a devastating impact on their physical and mental health. Single individuals living on social assistance in Canada receive roughly $600 a month to cover all of their expenses—rent, food, utilities, and entertainment. Students receiving funding through the Ontario Student Assistance Program (OSAP) are allocated roughly $7.50 a day for food. Could you stay within these financial guidelines and still follow the nutritional requirements of Canada's Food Guide? Not only is it a matter of eating healthy foods, but think about what those monetary restrictions would do to your social life—we often take the social processes that surround mealtime for granted. Without money to eat out or entertain at home, mealtime can be an isolating process.

In 2010, six prominent Canadians took up a one-week challenge through the "Do the Math Campaign" to live on food that came only from the local food bank (Bielski, 2010). The purpose of the challenge was to show what it's like to eat at the end of the month when all of your monthly social assistance cheque has gone for rent, transportation, and clothing. Michael MacMillan, a former CEO, ran out of his food rations after four days, so his meals for the rest of the week consisted of hotdog/wiener rice pilaf and SpaghettiOs—meals that were not what he what used to. This campaign is just one of many (Ontario Coalition Against Poverty; MakePovertyHistory.ca; Campaign Against Child Poverty) that exist to heighten the understanding of poverty in Canada and to bring increased awareness to the government and policymakers that we are a nation in need of change.

When comparing overall child poverty rates, a 2010 UNICEF report (UNICEF Canada, 2010) ranked Canada 18th out of 35 industrialized countries—indicating that 17 countries fare better when it comes to providing for the well-being of their children and, essentially, the future of their nations. While the gap between the rich and poor in Canada continues to grow, the disparity between nations also increases. Of the total world income, the richest 10% of the population receive 42% of the resources, while the poorest 10% receive just 1% (Conference Board of Canada, 2012).

The Long Walk to Justice, better known as Live 8 (2005), was a monumental social movement that sought to bring global awareness to poverty issues, with the sole purpose of ending world hunger. Over 3 billion people watched a series of simultaneous

Student poverty issues are bigger than tuition. How does your living space affect your grades?

Source: © Jaimie Duplass/Thinkstock

concerts in ten countries, highlighted by the reunion of Pink Floyd in London's Hyde Park. Had a group of brilliant musicians started a movement that would see more done to alleviate world poverty than what governments all over the world had only promised to do?

In this chapter, you'll learn about social inequality—in all its various forms—as you discover the differences between absolute and relative poverty and the impacts they have on those who experience poverty. Once you investigate the relationships between the rich and poor, mental illness and homelessness, and inequality among nations, your thoughts on inequality may or may not change; but anything that sparks a discussion surrounding the inequalities that exist in our society is a very good thing. It's a starting point for social action that begins in the mind of one person—a person just like you—and that's all it takes to create change.

SOCIAL STRATIFICATION

The reality is that even though we live in one of the wealthiest countries in the world, where we might think that we can achieve anything, the inequalities that exist are such that the odds are stacked against certain individuals. This doesn't mean those individuals can never realize their dreams; it just means that they might have to work a little harder to see them come true. Social inequality occurs when individuals or groups have unequal access to varying resources. It is present between individuals, like when your friend has more than you do; it is evident nationally in Canada, when we see homeless people living on the streets; and it is real on a global scale, as evidenced by the famine that exists in underfunded nations.

In the mid-1800s, Horatio Alger wrote "rags to riches" stories about young men who rose to the top through hard work and determination, and today, the term "rags to riches" is still commonly used. Consider, for example, Guy Laliberté—he's the founder of Cirque de Soleil, a serious poker player, a humanitarian, and a space traveller. Though he was born to middle-class parents, he began his career by busking on the streets. Even though he barely finished high school, he travelled throughout Europe and ended up studying with street artists there and in Quebec. In 1984, with the help of a Canadian government contract, he staged a grand provincial tour to celebrate the 450th anniversary of the discovery of Canada. In 1987, he took a big risk and hauled his entire troupe to a Los Angeles Arts Festival—he had his hopes, dreams, and all his money invested in this event. In fact, if it failed, he would have no money to bring everyone with the show back home. Cirque de Soleil was a great success, and the rest is history (Wong, 2009). How often do you think of "rags to riches" stories? Do you think if you work hard enough, you'll be able to claim the same kinds of victories that Guy Laliberté has? Can everyone realize their dreams? Is our society structured so that individuals have the same opportunities that will lead them down the road to success, or do some people have certain advantages over others? That Guy Laliberté was able to move from his humble beginnings as a street performer to become a wealthy entrepreneur reflects the level of openness we experience in Canada—he was able to move from one social class to a much higher one.

The existence of classes in Canada means that we live in a socially stratified society. **Social stratification** is a common feature in systems of shared social inequality; it is common when its members are divided into categories or strata that are rewarded unequally in terms of power, property, and prestige (Berreman, 1972). The ability to move between or within strata is usually determined by an individual's status. An **ascribed status** is given at birth—for example, gender, age, or race. An **achieved status** is a non-birth status—for example, occupation, education, or marital status. In an **open system society**, where status is based largely on achievement, individuals have the ability to move between and within different strata; but in a **closed system society**, where status is based largely on ascription, individuals are restricted in their movements between and within strata.

The **caste system** in India is an example of a closed stratified system premised on ascription or birth. The caste system itself is actually thousands of caste systems that vary village by village across the subcontinent, but all these local caste systems represent closed,

Social stratification: Division of people into categories or strata that are rewarded unequally in terms of power, property, and prestige.

Ascribed status: Status given at birth, such as gender, age, or race.

Achieved status: A status that is not given at birth; for example, occupation, education, or marital status.

Open system society: Society where status is based largely on achievement and individuals have the ability to move between and within different strata.

Closed system society: Society where status is based largely on ascription and individuals are restricted in their movements between and within strata.

Caste system: A closed stratified system in India that is premised on ascription or birth.

hierarchical stratification designs (Syed, 2002). **Castes** are fixed groups and individuals are born into a particular caste based on their societal roles, which become an unalterable social status, passed on through heredity. Hindus believe in reincarnation, so the inability to move between castes during your physical life on earth doesn't mean that your soul can't transcend to a different caste once you've transitioned to the spirit world. The caste system is comprised of four ranked castes called *varnas*. They are the Brahim, made up largely of priests, teachers, and scholars; the Kshatriya, comprised of warriors, rulers, and property owners; the Vaisya, consisting of farmers, traders, and artisans; and the Sudra, who are tenant farmers and servants. Below the Sudras is a fifth category, ati-Sudras—today known as Untouchables, Harijans, or Dalits. Dalits are not actually one caste; rather, Dalits make up a category that includes many hierarchically arranged castes, all of which are considered by upper castes to be ritually polluted, or untouchable (Syed, 2002). Untouchables can only work in jobs involving animal carcasses, leather, and scavenging. In many cases, they have to make sure that they never come into physical contact with higher-caste people and may even have to ensure that they don't touch anything that will be touched by higher-caste people, so they can't go near eating places or water sources. Some have to sweep the ground where they've walked to remove the pollution of their footsteps. Estimates put the number of Dalits in India at between 180 million and 220 million, or 16–20 percent of the total population. Of these, it is further estimated that some 40 million are bonded workers, which means that they are working as slaves to pay off debts incurred by their ancestors, often many generations ago (Ninian, 2008). It is believed that if individuals perform well and live according to the rules during their physical lives, they may enter a higher caste when they are reborn. Although the formal caste system was abolished after India's independence (which granted equal status and fundamental rights to all people), the system still exists in traditional villages (V, 2012). The only way to move from caste to caste is through reincarnation. Each individual is born into a certain caste—an excellent example of a closed system of stratification based on ascription.

A different form of stratification—a system based on ethnicity—existed in South Africa from 1948 to 1994. Prior to 1948, an informal segregation based on race existed in South Africa, but in that year, apartheid became an official government policy. **Apartheid** refers to any system or policy that divides people based on their race. Though the supremacy of whites was traditionally accepted, the mandate of apartheid included the further and formal segregation of the races—not just between whites and non-whites, but also of non-whites from each other (Columbia Electronic Encyclopedia, 2011). Access to housing, education, and health care was limited for non-whites, while whites enjoyed the privileges of all those services and more. Interracial marriages were illegal, and non-whites were not allowed to vote. On an international level, such blatant racial discrimination was deemed unacceptable. Countries began boycotting goods and services from South Africa because of its racial policies, and, eventually, South Africa yielded to global pressure. In 1994, the world celebrated as Nelson Mandela became the first democratically elected president of South Africa, eliminating the last trace of white minority rule (Klotz, 1995). Apartheid is another example of a closed stratification system based on ascription or birth, but one that's dependent on ethnicity where the colour of your skin could severely limit your chances of achieving any success in your life.

In Canada, we have an open stratified system, divided into social classes. A **social class** is any group of people who share the same situations in a common social structure. We usually measure social class in economic terms—according to individuals' annual income, occupation, or combined resources. The social class rankings themselves can become quite complex and might also include an individual's level of educational attainment. Sociologist Daniel Rossides (1997) uses a five-levelled model to distinguish the classes that exist in a capitalist society. They include the upper class, the upper middle class, the lower middle class, the working class, and the lower class (Rossides, 1997). The distinctions between the classes are not as clear-cut as those between castes, but there are marked differences between the divisions. Membership to the upper class in Canada is limited to the extremely wealthy. These individuals belong to exclusive clubs and social circles and generally associate with people of the same social standing. Conversely, members of the lower class find it difficult to find regular work, or must make do with low-paying employment. The difference between the classes is stark when you compare them in quantitative terms. The average after-tax income of the top 10% of income earners

Castes: Fixed groups that individuals are born into based on their societal roles; a caste is an unalterable social status, passed on through heredity.

Apartheid: Any system or policy that divides people based on their race.

Social class: Any group of people who share the same situations in a common social structure.

in Canada in 2007 was $165 322, while the average after-tax income of the lowest 10% of income earners that same year was $9790 (Fraser, 2012). When we look at an even smaller piece of the upper echelon, the magnitude of the difference is overwhelming. Canadians in the richest 1% of income tax filers made a minimum of $169 300 in 2007; however, the average income of this class was $404 500. The richest 0.1% of tax filers included 24 600 Canadians who had a minimum income of $621 300 and an average income of $1.49 million. The richest 0.01% of Canadians made a minimum of $1.845 million. The average income of the 2500 people in this rarefied group was $3.833 million (Yalnizyan, 2010). By 2009, the top 20% of the population accounted for more than half of Canada's income, and the bottom 20% accounted for only 1% (Fraser, 2012); and research indicates that the gap that exists between these two classes is only growing larger.

According to Rossides (1997), the upper middle class consists mainly of professionals such as doctors and lawyers, while those with less affluent occupations, such as nurses and teachers, reside in the lower middle class. Though not everyone in the lower middle class may hold a university degree, they share the common goal of sending their children to university. The working class are individuals who earn their living in blue-collar jobs, generally involving manual labour. The lower class is comprised mainly of individuals who are precariously employed (in part-time or contract labour), and who are continually looking for permanent full-time work that pays a decent salary. When you identify yourself in terms of class standing, in which of these classes would you place yourself now? Do you see your position changing 20 years from now? To what extent does your class standing affect your future life chances? Studies indicate that a higher social standing might mean a lower body weight (McLaren, 2007), a lower likelihood of smoking (Ward, Tarasuk, & Mendelson, 2007), and diminished physical activity (Kuhle & Veugelers, 2008). Do you think that your class standing has helped or hindered your current social position in any way? Do you think you might be a "rags to riches" story?

Social Mobility

Social mobility refers the degree of opportunity that individuals have to move from one position in a stratified system to another. Those moves can be vertical (upward or downward mobility), or horizontal—movement within a class. When sociologists measure social mobility, they do so in terms of **intergenerational mobility** (mobility between an individual's family of origin and an individual's own class) and **intra-generational mobility** (the mobility measured over an individual's career, such as someone's first job compared to his or her last job). So, one way to measure social mobility is by looking at rich parents and determining if their children are also rich, or conversely, looking at poor parents and determining if their children are also poor. In some cases, the incomes of the two may be completely unrelated (Wilkinson & Pickett, 2009). If we go back to Guy Laliberté, we can see that he has experienced both intergenerational and intra-generational mobility. Laliberté's father was a public relations executive at Alcan Aluminum and his mother was a nurse. Since he has surpassed his parents' occupational status and class standing, he has experienced intergenerational mobility. Though he was briefly employed at a hydro-electric dam, he spent much of his youth busking and is now CEO of Cirque du Soleil, so he has experienced intra-generational mobility as well (Wong, 2009). In an open society, where social mobility is possible, social status will strongly affect an individual's life chances. We live in an open, class-based society, and we have the ability to move from one class to another through achievement. But just how hard is it to transcend classes?

MEASURING INEQUALITY

By 12:00 noon on January 3, 2012, the first official working day of the year, Canada's Elite 100 CEOs had already pocketed $44 366—what it takes the average person an entire year, working full-time, to earn (based on 2010 figures) (Hennessy, 2012). Can you imagine having earned that much money by lunchtime? How many days or weeks would you work before you'd made enough money to survive on for the year? Your answer will likely depend on what you've been used to spending and what kind of lifestyle you hope to have in the future. The bridge that spans upper and lower classes is one that you can travel in any class-based society; but in Canada, crossing that bridge is becoming a more difficult journey each year.

Social mobility: The degree of opportunity that individuals have to move from one position in a stratified system to another; these moves can be vertical (upward or downward mobility) or horizontal (movement within a class).

Intergenerational mobility: Mobility between an individual's family of origin and an individual's own class.

Intra-generational mobility: Mobility measured over an individual's career, such as someone's first job compared to his or her last job.

Canada doesn't have an official definition for *poverty*, so when we measure inequality in Canada, we use three different measures. The **low income cut-off** (LICO) is established by Statistics Canada annually and refers generally to what people call a poverty line. It represents the income level at which a family may face hardship because it has to spend a greater proportion of its after-tax income on food, shelter, and clothing than the average family of similar size. There are separate cut-offs for seven sizes of family (from unattached individuals to families of seven or more persons) and for five community sizes (from rural areas to urban areas with a population of more than 500 000). For example, single individuals in Toronto would be considered to have a low income if their 2009 after-tax income was below $18 421 (Employment and Social Development, 2013).

Created for making international comparisons, the **low-income measure** (LIM) is another commonly used measure. The LIM compares a household's income against the median of an equivalent family. Any family whose income is less than half that median is defined as poor. The LIM adjustment for family sizes reflects the fact that a family's needs increase as the number of members increases. Most would agree that a family of five has greater needs than a family of two. Similarly, the LIM allows for the fact that it costs more to feed a family of five adults than a family of two adults and three children (Employment and Social Development, 2013).

Created in 2001, the **Market Basket Measure** (MBM) is a measure of low income based on the cost of a specified basket of goods and services representing a modest, basic standard of living in comparison to the standards of its community. It includes the costs of food, clothing, footwear, transportation, shelter, and other expenses for a reference family of two adults aged 25 to 49 and two children (aged 9 and 13) (Employment and Social Development, 2013). It was designed to complement the LICO and LIM measures and allows for different costs for rural areas in the different provinces. The LICO and LIM are relative measures, while the MBM is an absolute measure of poverty. It is important, however, to understand that there is no perfect measure. The three measures produce different results. In 2009, according to each measure, the following numbers of Canadians were living in low income:

- LICO—3.2 million (9.6 percent of the population)
- MBM—3.5 million (10.6 percent)
- LIM—4.4 million (13.3 percent) (Conference Board of Canada, 2011)

Measuring poverty becomes increasingly important when we consider that there are varying kinds of poverty. Usually we think of poverty in terms of rich and poor and only in terms of the individuals who affect us in our cities or towns. Society as a whole encounters poverty on different levels and in different ways that further serve to divide it. When we talk about poverty, we generally refer to a lack of resources. Economic poverty is the most obvious kind of poverty, but people can also experience spiritual, mental, and cultural poverty. For example, people who live in cultural poverty feel marginal, helpless, or dependent, and experience a sense of not belonging. They are like aliens living in their own country, who are convinced that societal institutions do little to help them. They feel powerless, and it might not have anything to do with economics (Lewis, 1998).

When studying poverty, we generally classify it into two major types—absolute and relative poverty. **Absolute poverty** refers to a situation where an individual lacks even the basic resources necessary for survival. People who live in absolute poverty live without food, clothing, or a roof over their heads. This is most common in developing countries, where finding necessities such as clean water for drinking and food to stave off hunger are daily struggles. **Relative poverty** refers to an individual's or group's lack of basic resources for survival when compared with other people in society as a whole. In other words, it refers to an individual's standard of living relative to someone else's. We see this in many forms in the cities that we live in. The disparities that exist highlight the difference between those families who can afford to eat three nutritious meals a day and dress their children in the latest fashions, and those families who struggle to eat one meal a day and hope that their children have winter coats.

Low-income cut-off (LICO): Measure established by Statistics Canada annually that refers generally to what people call a poverty line; it represents the income level at which a family may face hardship because it has to spend a greater proportion of its after-tax income on food, shelter, and clothing than the average family of similar size.

Low-income measure (LIM): A measure of poverty that is commonly used for making international comparisons.

Market basket measure (MBM): A measure of low income based on the cost of a specified basket of goods and services representing a modest, basic standard of living in comparison to the standards of its community.

Absolute poverty: Situation where an individual lacks even the basic resources that are necessary for survival; people who live in absolute poverty live without food, clothing, or a roof over their heads.

Relative poverty: Situation where an individual or group lacks basic resources for survival when compared with other people in the society as a whole; relative standard of living when measured to others.

POVERTY

Child Poverty

To understand poverty wholly in absolute and relative terms requires us to go beyond the sterile definitions and apply them to an everyday situation. Consider the responses in the following example, where a teacher asked a class of Grade 4 and 5 students in North Bay, Ontario, what poverty meant to them (Interfaith Social Assistance Reform Coalition, 1999):

Source: Interfaith Social Assistance Reform Coalition, *Our Neighbours' Voices: Who Will Listen?* (Toronto: Lorimer, 1998).

Poverty Is...

Not being able to go to McDonald's

Getting a basket from the Santa Fund

Feeling ashamed when my dad can't get a job

Not buying books at the book fair

Not getting to go to birthday parties

Hearing my mom and dad fight over money

Not ever getting a pet because it costs too much

Wishing you had a nice house

Not being able to go camping

Not getting a hot dog on hot dog day

Not getting pizza on pizza day

Not being able to have your friends sleep over

Pretending that you forgot your lunch

Being afraid to tell your mom that you need gym shoes

Not having breakfast sometimes

Not being able to play hockey

Sometime crying really hard because my mom gets scared and she cries

Not being able to go to Cubs or play soccer

Not being able to take swimming lessons

Not being able to afford a holiday

Not having pretty barrettes for your hair

Not having your own private backyard

Being teased for the way you are dressed

Not getting to go on school trips

Can you tell which experiences on the list are examples of absolute poverty and which are indicative of relative poverty? The words of these children tell stories of absolute poverty (e.g., pretending that you forgot your lunch) and relative poverty and exclusion (e.g., not being able to play hockey) (deGroot-Magetti, 2002). What does it tell us about the world when we have to use children to explain what poverty is? Could you identify with any of the experiences on that list?

The number of children who continue to live in impoverished conditions continues to be a growing concern both nationally and internationally. How can we expect children to grow and become successful, productive adults, when they begin their lives in poverty? In 2009, about 1 in 10 or 639 000 Canadian children were living in poverty (Family Service Toronto, 2011). Growing up without basic necessities affects all areas of life, but it is especially linked to mental and physical health. Poverty is a key determinant of good or poor health because we know that children growing up in poverty

- are more likely to have low birth weights, asthma, and type 2 diabetes, and suffer from malnutrition;
- are unlikely to have family benefit plans for prescription drugs or vision or dental care;
- are more likely to have learning disabilities, emotional disabilities, and behavioural problems; and
- are 2.5 times more likely to have a disability than children from wealthier families (Family Service Toronto, 2010).

New research links childhood poverty to poor performance in school and later on in life. Evans and Schamberg (2009) found strong connections between childhood poverty, physiological stress, and adult memory. The findings of their research can explain, in part, why impoverished children consistently perform worse than their middle-class peers in school, and eventually in adult life (Evans & Schamberg, 2009). Impaired health, poorer health, and school achievement are just some of the consequences children living in poverty experience.

A 2010 UNICEF report compared the state of child poverty in various countries and showed that some of the world's wealthiest countries were more successful in raising children out of poverty, despite having similar economic performances, even in challenging times. Although one would think that all wealthy countries would be successful in diminishing child poverty, UNICEF's analysis shows that the risk of poor child development is affected by government policy and spending priorities. Scandinavian countries and the Netherlands have the lowest rates of child poverty, while Japan and the United States have among the highest. The child poverty rate ranges from 5% in Iceland to 25% in Romania. Canada ranks in the middle with 14%. To improve its standing, Canada must make two important changes. First, it must make children a priority in budget spending and allocations (UNICEF Canada, 2010). Government-regulated child care in Canada is only available for 17.2% of children aged 0–12 years (Raphael, 2010). Additionally, Canada invests $40.4 billion in elderly benefits, almost three times the amount it invests in children. The second necessary change is that Canada needs an official definition of poverty, as well as a national strategy to eliminate poverty, with a focus specifically on children (UNICEF Canada, 2010).

World Hunger and Poverty

Perhaps on July 2, 2005, you were witness to the Live 8 Concerts, dubbed the Long Walk to Justice The purpose of the Live 8 initiative was to pressure G8 leaders to increase aid and cancel the foreign debts of some of the world's poorest nations. According to Bono, lead singer of U2, "It is this movement of church people and trade unionists, soccer moms and student activists, that will carry the spirit of Live 8 on … it is this movement, not rock stars that will make it untenable in the future to break promises to the most vulnerable people on this planet" (Vox, 2005). Has the challenge of solving world hunger and poverty fallen into the hands of those who may be at risk of falling into the poverty trap themselves?

The most commonly used measure of income inequality is the **Gini index** (also known as the Gini coefficient or ratio), which is measured on a scale of 0 to 1. A Gini index of 0 represents exact equality (that is, every person in a certain society or nation has the same amount of income), while a Gini index of 1 represents total inequality (that is, one person has all the income and the rest of the society has none; Conference Board of Canada, 2011). In the 1980s, Canada reduced its degree of inequality, reaching a low Gini index of 0.281 in 1989. Income inequality rose in the 1990s and has remained around 0.32 into the 2000s (Conference Board of Canada, 2011). You might think that sounds good; but when you consider that number in relation to the Gini index numbers of other countries, it gives you a better picture of the level of inequality in Canada. Out of 17 peer countries, Canada ranks 12th in terms of inequality, which means income inequality is higher in Canada than in 11 other countries. The countries with the lowest Gini index scores are Denmark (0.232) and Sweden (0.234). Canada's score (0.317) is not as high as that of the United States (0.381), but it's not nearly as low as the scores for France (2.70), Norway (2.76), or Finland (2.69) (Conference Board of Canada, 2011).

Gini index: A commonly used measure of income inequality, which measures inequality on a scale of 0 to 1; a Gini index of 0 represents exact equality (i.e., every person in a certain society or nation has the same amount of income), while a Gini index of 1 represents total inequality (i.e., one person has all the income and the rest of the society has none).

PICTURE THIS...

Source: © Kevin Carter/Sygma/Corbis

What will it take to end world hunger?

In 2000, at United Nations Headquarters in New York, world leaders from 189 countries created a new global partnership committed to reducing extreme poverty. They adopted a series of eight goals, to be achieved by 2015. The purposes of the **Millennium Development Goals** (MDG), as they were labelled, are as follows:

- eradicate extreme poverty and hunger
- achieve universal primary education
- promote gender equality and empower women
- reduce child mortality
- improve maternal health
- combat HIV/AIDS, malaria, and other diseases
- ensure environmental sustainability
- develop a global partnership for development (United Nations Development Program, 2012)

The 2012 Millennium Report indicates that with just three years to the deadline, broad progress has been made (United Nations, 2012). Here are some of the advancements:

- The number of people living on less than $1.25 a day fell from 47% in 1990 to 24% in 2008—a reduction from over 2 billion to less than 1.4 billion (United Nations, 2012).
- The number of people using an improved water source rose from 76% in 1990 to 89% in 2010—in those 20 years, more than 2 billion people saw an improvement in their drinking water and/or their access to it (United Nations, 2012).
- Enrolment rates of children of primary school age increased in sub-Saharan Africa, from 58% to 76% between 1999 and 2010 (United Nations, 2012).
- Tuberculosis rates have fallen since 2002, and current projections suggest that the 1990 death rate from the disease will be halved by 2015 (United Nations, 2012).

Since 2000, the Canadian International Development Agency (CIDA) has contributed to the MDG project in a number of different ways. With its additional $1.1 billion commitment to maternal, newborn, and child health through the Muskoka G8 Initiative, Canada's total commitment to reducing child mortality and improving maternal health will be $2.85 billion from 2010 to 2015 (Foreign Affairs, 2012). And Canada's contribution does not stand alone. Many organizations work endlessly to stop world hunger (e.g., From Hunger to Hope, Stop Hunger Now, and UNICEF). Remember our story of Guy Laliberté? The non-profit organization he established in 2007, ONE DROP, has so far changed the lives of 300 000 people by ensuring accessibility to water. Many organizations exist in the hopes of eliminating world poverty, but we are far from creating nations that are more equitable. Can you think of any goals to add to the Millennium Development Goals?

Women and Poverty

In 2010, 9.3% of females in Canada—over 1.5 million in total—were living on a low income (Statistics Canada, 2012). Women experience poverty in greater numbers than men for many reasons, but two of the main reasons are related to work—both paid and unpaid.

First, women spend more time doing unpaid work such as child care and domestic labour, which leaves them less

> **Millennium Development Goals (MDG):** A set of eight goals established by a global partnership committed to reduce extreme poverty by 2015; the goals are to eradicate extreme poverty and hunger, to achieve universal primary education, to promote gender equality and empower women, to reduce child mortality, to improve maternal health, to combat HIV/AIDS, malaria, and other diseases, to ensure environmental sustainability, and to develop a global partnership for development.

Something as simple as clean water can mean the difference between life and death for millions of people.

Source: © ChandrashekarReddy/ Thinkstock

time to engage in the paid work force. Women are still expected to perform the majority of household chores and child care. Results of the General Social Survey of 2010 indicate the stark difference between the time that men and women spend on these responsibilities (see Table 3.1). When respondents were asked to report the number of hours spent on unpaid child care in the household, women generally reported a higher number of hours per week than men: men reported spending, on average, 8.3 hours on unpaid domestic work, while women spent more than one and a half times this amount—13.8 hours (see Table 3.2; Milan, Keown, & Covadonga, 2012).

Women also face a wage gap. In 2011, women's average earnings ($32 100) were only 66.7% of their male counterparts' earnings ($48 100) (Statistics Canada, 2013). Since they don't earn as much as men,

women are at risk of falling into poverty, especially if they have children and then find themselves single through separation, divorce, or widowhood. Then, they're less likely—and less able—to save for retirement and end up poverty-stricken in their senior years. To avoid this fate, many women will stay in abusive relationships, despite the dangers. Women are also often involved in part-time or precarious employment. They account for 70% of part-time employees and two-thirds of the Canadians who work for minimum wage. Even though there are more working mothers now than at any other time in history, 36% of mother-led families still live below the poverty line and 43% of children who live in a low-income family live with a single mother (YWCA, 2009). In the "In Their Shoes" feature, a single mother discusses her experience with poverty.

TABLE 3.1
Time Spent on Household Domestic Work, by Working Arrangement, Canada, 2010

Working Arrangement	Women	Men
	Average number of hours per week	
All women and men	13.8	8.3*
Working arrangement		
Respondent was working		
Dual earner couples; respondent working full-time	13.9	8.6*
Dual earner couples; respondent working part-time	21.0	11.8*
Single earner couples; respondent working	15.2	8.8*
Singles; respondent working	7.7	6.1*
Respondent was not working		
Single earner couples; respondent not working	23.4	14.6*
Couples; neither partner working	17.3	10.6*
Singles; respondent not working	10.0	6.3*

* statistically significant difference between women and men at p < 0.05

Source: Statistics Canada, Time spent on household domestic work, by working arrangement, Canada, 2010. Reproduced and distributed on an "as is" basis with the permission of Statistics Canada.

TABLE 3.2

Time Spent on Unpaid Care of a Child in the Household, by Working Arrangement and Age of Youngest Child, Canada, 2010

Working Arrangement and Age of Youngest Child	Women	Men
	Average number of hours per week	
All women and men	50.1	24.4*
Working arrangement		
Respondent was working		
Dual earner couples; respondent working full-time	49.8	27.2*
Dual earner couples; respondent working part-time	59.4	40.5*
Single earner couples; respondent working	50.8	25.5*
Lone parents; respondent working	26.9	12.0*
Respondent was not working		
Single earner couples; respondent not working	81.3	36.9*
Couples; neither partner working	59.5	36.3E*
Lone parents; respondent not working	30.0	8.1E*
Age of youngest child in the household		
0 to 4	67.5	30.2*
5 to 14	37.7	19.7*

* statistically significant difference between women and men at $p < 0.05$

Source: Statistics Canada, Time spent on unpaid care of a child in the household, by working arrangement and age of youngest child, Canada, 2010. Reproduced and distributed on an "as is" basis with the permission of Statistics Canada.

HOMELESSNESS

Before the 1980s, the word *homelessness* didn't exist—really (Hulchanski, 2009). Before then, we referred to individuals who didn't have homes as "the homeless"; but the term homelessness as an abstract concept is now used to refer not to a subset of individuals in society but rather to the multiple blights on the social, economic, and political systems in society. The cutbacks in social housing and related housing programs and policies began in 1984. In the 1990s, the government ended federal and provincial housing programs, decreased social assistance rates, and reduced social spending. Forced onto the streets and into makeshift shelters, at-risk individuals, had few, if any, social services or supports available to them. Diseases like tuberculosis returned, and the number of homeless deaths began to increase (Crowe, 2012). With a failure to provide adequate housing, income, and support services came a need to shift the focus on "the homeless" to the concept of homelessness (Hulchanski, 2009). Now, in a very broad sense, **homelessness** refers to a social category that includes anyone who cannot obtain and sustain long-term, adequate, and risk-free shelter—for any reason.

How would you define homelessness? When you think of a homeless person, who automatically comes to mind? Is it as simple as someone who doesn't have

Homelessness: Social category that includes anyone who cannot obtain and sustain long-term, adequate, and risk-free shelter, for any reason.

IN THEIR SHOES

If a picture can say a thousand words, imagine the stories your shoes could tell! Try this student story on for size – have you walked in this student's shoes?

DEAR PUBLIC AUTHORITY:

Recently, we had a public meeting where you wanted to hear from different sectors of the community about poverty, the obstacles faced, and how we could deal with them. There were many people from different social agencies speaking on behalf of others, but you also wanted to hear from a single parent. I was chosen as that single parent. I apologize for having to bring my son with me, but this was firsthand experience for you on how difficult it is to find child care, especially on the spur of the moment (as was my case). I explained that as a single mom on Ontario Works, it wasn't often that I could do things on my own. Child care is expensive and a luxury I could not afford.

I believe that when I started to speak, you were shocked because you had already judged me as being lazy and looking for a handout. I also believe that you were shocked because my son sat quietly in the corner for over an hour. I would like to explain to you that not all mothers on social assistance are drug addicts or addicts of any sort and that even though I don't work, I love my son very much and I have raised him well. I would also like you to know that I am highly intelligent, have passed on that intelligence to my son, and that I have decided to further my education in the social services field.

I want you to know that when I am actively employed in the field, I will take the lesson you taught me to every job. That lesson is that you don't prejudge someone just by the label that is placed on them. I may be a single mom, but I am every bit as ambitious and capable as you. I hope that with our meeting, you too learned a valuable lesson. Most people in my position are only asking for a hand up, not a handout.

I wish you luck as you move through the different ministries and I hope that together we can make a difference.

Yours truly,
A Single Mom

Source: Patti Pringle.

Absolute homelessness: Situation of individuals who live either in emergency shelters or on the street.

Hidden or concealed homelessness: State of those without a place of their own who live in a car, with family or friends, or in a long-term institution such as a prison.

Relative homelessness: State of those who have housing, but who live in substandard or undesirable shelter and/or who may be at risk of losing their homes.

a place to stay, or is it far more complicated than that? Is it the stereotypical panhandler, asking passersby for change? Is it a squeegee kid washing windshields? Or is it the person in the seat next to you, who sleeps in his car and showers at the gym? Just as in Canada there is no formal definition for poverty, neither is there one way of categorizing those who live in less-than-desirable housing conditions. No single definition of homelessness is official in Canada. Most officials take into account the specific housing situation and the duration and/or frequency of homeless episodes (Echenberg & Jensen, 2012). If we look at homelessness on a continuum based specifically on types of shelter, at one end, there's **absolute homelessness**, which refers to the situation of individuals who live either in emergency shelters or on the street. These individuals are typically the people that you see on the streets, often panhandling for change. **Hidden or concealed homelessness** refers to those people without a place of their own, who live in a car, with family or friends, or in a long-term institution such as a prison. Increasingly, these are new immigrants to Canada, who stay with family until they can afford a place of their own. These individuals fall in the middle of the continuum. At the other end of the continuum is **relative homelessness**, which refers to those individuals who have housing, but who live in substandard or undesirable shelter and/or who may be at risk of losing their homes (Girard, 2006). This might include a woman who lives with an abusive husband but stays because she and maybe her children have nowhere else to go. We can think of this continuum as a pyramid (see Figure 3.1).

FIGURE 3.1
Homelessness Pyramid

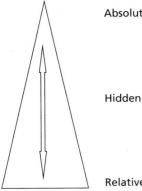

Absolute homelessness

Hidden homelessness

Relative homelessness

The homelessness pyramid reminds us of an iceberg: although there's a proportion of the homeless we can see, the real numbers of homeless are hidden or difficult to detect.

Source: Parliament of Canada Information Services, Defining and Enumerating Homelessness in Canada (17 May 2012).

The individuals who live on the streets have typically become the face of the homeless, but some suggest that for every one individual living in absolute homelessness, there are between 4 and 23 individuals whose homelessness is hidden (Condon & Newton, 2007; Hwang, 2010). Counting the homeless is a difficult process because of methodological issues such as defining the population and sample size; even conservative estimates suggest that between 200 000 and 300 000 Canadians spend their nights in shelters, on the streets, or couch surfing (Bramham, 2008). Risk factors that contribute to homelessness for the mainstream population include the lack of affordable housing, poverty and low income, mental illness, domestic violence, and drug abuse/addiction. Not all of these factors affect each individual, and some factors affect some individuals more than others. Homeless people and the issue of homelessness itself are very complex issues. Studying them as multi-layered identities and events is critical to their understanding and ultimately solution.

Immigrants

Recent immigrants are increasingly expanding the number of individuals who belong to the ranks of the hidden homeless. The increasing cost of rent, discrimination in the workplace, and language barriers all contribute to the fact that many newcomers who enter Canada live in shared, overcrowded housing, often for extended periods. In Toronto, where the average income is $69 000 and the monthly rent on a bachelor apartment is close to $800, the income of most newcomers is under $20 000. Most newcomers spend more than 50 percent of their income on housing, with 15 percent spending 75 percent or more (Preston et al., 2011).

Race

The Aboriginal population is overrepresented among the homeless in Canada. They make up less than 4% of Canada's total population but represent 10% of the homeless (Sider, 2005). In urban centres, the numbers vary significantly. The city of Winnipeg has the largest self-identified Aboriginal population, with 8.4% (55 755). In 2001, an estimated 60–70% of the homeless population in Winnipeg was Aboriginal. Aboriginal people living in Vancouver represent about 2% of the city's people, but 30% of the homeless people. The numbers for other major cities are similar (Native Women's Association, 2007). A history of disenfranchisement, oppression, and colonization has led to disparities in health care, income, and education among the Aboriginal population in Canada. This has no doubt contributed to the increased numbers in homelessness (United Native Nations Society, 2001). Though Aboriginal people experience the same risk factors for homelessness as the mainstream population, the fallout from the years spent in residential schools continues to haunt many Aboriginal people and their children.

Mental Illness

The deinstitutionalization movement started in the 1960s. With the discovery of new medications coupled with the use of psychotherapy to help treat mental disorders, the general belief was that people with mental illnesses would fare better in the community, or back with their families, than in government-funded institutions. Consequently, the government decided to start removing psychiatric beds from mental health institutions and hospitals. Between 1960 and 1976, 27 630 beds were eliminated, reducing the number of available beds by 57% (Casavant, 1999). Unfortunately, in many cases, families were not prepared to care for their loved ones, social services were inadequate, and the community supports just fell through, leaving an extremely vulnerable population to fend for themselves. Left with no long-term mental health treatment programs and little family or community support, many people with mental illnesses were unable to control their symptoms and ended up homeless. Recent statistics show that an estimated 25–50% of the homeless population have a mental illness and that up to 70% of those with a severe mental illness have substance abuse issues (CMHA, 2009).

Youth

Public Health Canada (Government of Canada, 2012) conducted a major longitudinal study (1993–2003) on homeless youth in Canada that likely provides the most comprehensive picture of that portion of the Canadian homeless population. Highlights from this study of some 5000 homeless youths in seven urban centres found the following information:

- Most homeless youth had histories of family poverty and unstable housing.
- Fifteen percent came from families that had been homeless at some point.
- Close to half had been in foster care (45 percent), and almost 50 percent had lived in a group home at some point.
- Many had experienced violence at home (Eva's Initiatives, 2012).

Additionally, results indicated that in terms of ethnic background, the majority of street youth were Caucasian (60%); Aboriginal youth made up the second largest group (30%); and African, Middle Eastern, and Asian or other ethnicities comprised the rest.

Recent work shows that street youth are exposed to a number of factors that may detrimentally affect their health, including unsafe sexual practices, drug use, poor diet, inadequate shelter, exposure to violence, low levels of social support, and limited access to medical care (Boivin, Roy, Haley, & du Fort, 2005). Almost a third of Canada's homeless are youths aged 16–24 (CMHA, 2009).

Women and Young Girls

Homelessness affects thousands of women and young girls, and this subset of the population presents itself with a very specific set of characteristics, since in many cases, unplanned pregnancy is an issue, which brings about an increased need for health care (Reid, Berman, & Forchuk, 2005). Additionally, violence often touches the lives of homeless females through their family histories or current situations. In Toronto,

physical and sexual violence is a leading cause of homelessness, especially for women and youth—in 2007, 35% of homeless people reported being assaulted in the past year, and two-thirds of those admitted to being beaten more than once (Wellesley Institute, 2007). A U.S. study reveals that the most significant risk factor for violent victimization as an adult is a pattern of physical, emotional, and sexual abuse as a child. Many of the young homeless girls and young women studied were permanently scarred by their childhood victimization and had an extremely warped sense of what constitutes "normal" when it comes to relationships with men. Additionally, results showed that American homeless women are far more likely to experience violence of all kinds than other American women are (Jasinski, Wesely, Mustaine, & Wright, 2005). Some young women and girls will trade sex for money, shelter, and other necessities just to survive. Survival sex is literally just that—a young woman or girl's only way of surviving on the streets; and though it may bring in enough money to live on, the risk of pregnancy, sexually transmitted diseases, or assault expose young women to great dangers (Montgomery, 1994).

ENDING THOUGHTS

While you may not become the next Guy Laliberté, do you think you'll be able to climb from the class in which you were born, or do you think that climbing to the top will prove to be a bigger challenge than you ever imagined? For some, the climb may not be so far, while others have a long journey ahead of them. Do you think we live in an open society, where individuals can achieve whatever they set their mind to? And to what extent does your ascribed status advantage or disadvantage you?

When you think about social inequality, it is important to remember the distinction between absolute and relative poverty and the perceptions that surround both. The stereotypes that surround those who live in poverty lead us to believe that poverty and homelessness are choices. We are led to believe that there are shelter beds to sleep in that alleviate the need to sleep on the street, that there are food banks to eat from and there is no need to starve, that people go hungry because they can't budget their money properly—but that is not the reality. A study conducted in 2002 defined panhandlers as people who were soliciting donations of money for personal use from passersby without providing any goods or services in return, and the authors found that 70% of the panhandlers in Toronto would prefer a minimum-wage job in order to have a steady income or to get off the street (Bose & Hwang, 2002). The average monthly income that a panhandler received from passersby was $300; the average total monthly income was just over $600—including loans from friends and family.

The reality is that no one (or very few people) chooses a life of poverty—no one chooses mental illness, domestic violence, or addiction. Would you choose to live on the streets or to live on social assistance and bear the social stigma that is attached to it? The next time that you see a street person asking for a donation, think about the others you can't see. And, then think about the millions who exist beyond the streets you live in. Remember the differences between absolute and relative poverty. Are you better or worse off than this person?

THE SINGER SOLUTION TO WORLD POVERTY

By Peter Singer

In the Brazilian film "Central Station," Dora is a retired schoolteacher who makes ends meet by sitting at the station writing letters for illiterate people. Suddenly she has an opportunity to pocket $1,000. All she has to do is persuade a homeless 9-year-old boy to follow her to an address she has been given. (She is told he will be adopted by wealthy foreigners.) She delivers the boy, gets the money, spends some of it on a television set and settles down to enjoy her new acquisition. Her neighbor spoils the fun, however, by telling her that the boy was too old to be adopted—he will be killed and his organs sold for transplantation. Perhaps Dora knew this all along, but after her neighbor's plain speaking, she spends a troubled night. In the morning Dora resolves to take the boy back.

Suppose Dora had told her neighbor that it is a tough world, other people have nice new TV's too, and if selling the kid is the only way she can get one, well, he was only a street kid. She would then have become, in the eyes of the audience, a monster. She redeems herself only by being prepared to bear considerable risks to save the boy.

At the end of the movie, in cinemas in the affluent nations of the world, people who would have been quick to condemn Dora if she had not rescued the boy go home to places far more comfortable than her apartment. In fact, the average family in the United States spends almost one-third of its income on things that are no more necessary to them than Dora's new TV was to her. Going out to nice restaurants, buying new clothes because the old ones are no longer stylish, vacationing at beach resorts—so much of our income is spent on things not essential to the preservation of our lives and health. Donated to one of a number of charitable agencies, that money could mean the difference between life and death for children in need.

All of which raises a question: In the end, what is the ethical distinction between a Brazilian who sells a homeless child to organ peddlers and an American who already has a TV and upgrades to a better one—knowing that the money could be donated to an organization that would use it to save the lives of kids in need?

Of course, there are several differences between the two situations that could support different moral judgments about them. For one thing, to be able to consign a child to death when he is standing right in front of you takes a chilling kind of heartlessness; it is much easier to ignore an appeal for money to help children you will never meet. Yet for a utilitarian philosopher like myself—that is, one who judges whether acts are right or wrong by their consequences—if the upshot of the American's failure to donate the money is that one more kid dies on the streets of a Brazilian city, then it is, in some sense, just as bad as selling the kid to the organ peddlers. But one doesn't need to embrace my utilitarian ethic to see that, at the very least, there is a troubling incongruity in being so quick to condemn Dora for taking the child to the organ peddlers while, at the same time, not regarding the American consumer's behavior as raising a serious moral issue.

In his 1996 book, *Living High and Letting Die*, the New York University philosopher Peter Unger presented an ingenious series of imaginary examples designed to probe our intuitions about whether it is wrong to live well without giving substantial amounts of money to help people who are hungry, malnourished or dying from easily treatable illnesses like diarrhea. Here's my paraphrase of one of these examples:

Bob is close to retirement. He has invested most of his savings in a very rare and valuable old car, a Bugatti, which he has not been able to insure. The Bugatti is his pride and joy. In addition to the pleasure he gets from driving and caring for his car, Bob knows that its rising market value means that he will always be able to sell it and live comfortably after retirement. One day when Bob is out for a drive, he parks the Bugatti near the end of a railway siding and goes for a walk up the track. As he does so, he sees that a runaway train, with no one aboard, is running down the railway track. Looking farther down the track, he sees the small figure of a child very likely to be killed by the runaway train. He can't stop the train and the child is too far away to warn of the danger, but he can throw a switch that will divert the train down the siding where his Bugatti is parked. Then nobody will be killed—but the train will destroy his Bugatti. Thinking of his joy in owning the car and the financial security it represents, Bob decides not to throw the switch. The child is killed. For many years to come, Bob enjoys owning his Bugatti and the financial security it represents.

Bob's conduct, most of us will immediately respond, was gravely wrong. Unger agrees. But then he reminds us that we, too, have opportunities to save the lives of children. We can give to organizations like UNICEF or Oxfam America. How much would we have to give one of these organizations to have a high probability of saving the life of a child threatened by easily preventable diseases? (I do not believe that children are more worth saving than adults, but since no one can argue that children have brought their poverty on themselves, focusing on them simplifies the issues.) Unger called up some experts and used the information they provided to offer some plausible estimates that include the cost of raising money, administrative expenses and the cost of delivering aid where it is most needed. By his calculation, $200 in donations would help a sickly 2-year-old transform into a healthy 6-year-old— offering safe passage through childhood's most dangerous years. To show how practical philosophical argument can be, Unger even tells his readers that they can easily donate funds by using their credit card and calling one of these toll-free numbers: (800) 367-5437 for UNICEF; (800) 693-2687 for Oxfam America. [http://supportUNICEF.org/forms/whichcountry2.html for UNICEF and http://www.oxfam.org/eng/donate.htm for Oxfam —PS]

Now you, too, have the information you need to save a child's life. How should you judge yourself if you don't do it? Think again about Bob and his Bugatti. Unlike Dora, Bob did not have to look into the eyes of the child he was sacrificing for his own material comfort. The child was a complete stranger to him and too far away to relate to in an intimate, personal way. Unlike Dora, too, he did not mislead the child or initiate the chain of events imperiling him. In all these respects, Bob's situation resembles that of people able but unwilling to donate to overseas aid and differs from Dora's situation.

If you still think that it was very wrong of Bob not to throw the switch that would have diverted the train and saved the child's life, then it is hard to see how you could deny that it is also very wrong not to send money to one of the organizations listed above. Unless, that is, there is some morally important difference between the two situations that I have overlooked.

Is it the practical uncertainties about whether aid will really reach the people who need it? Nobody who knows the world of overseas aid can doubt that such uncertainties exist. But Unger's figure of $200 to save a child's life was reached after he had made conservative assumptions about the proportion of the money donated that will actually reach its target.

One genuine difference between Bob and those who can afford to donate to overseas aid organizations but don't is that only Bob can save the child on the tracks, whereas there are hundreds of millions of people who can give $200 to overseas aid organizations. The problem is that most of them aren't doing it. Does this mean that it is all right for you not to do it?

Suppose that there were more owners of priceless vintage cars—Carol, Dave, Emma, Fred and so on, down to Ziggy—all in exactly the same situation as Bob, with their own siding and their own switch, all sacrificing the child in order to preserve their own cherished car. Would that make it all right for Bob to do the same? To answer this question affirmatively is to endorse follow-the-crowd ethics—the kind of ethics that led many Germans to look away when the Nazi atrocities were being committed. We do not excuse them because others were behaving no better.

We seem to lack a sound basis for drawing a clear moral line between Bob's situation and that of any reader of this article with $200 to spare who does not donate it to an overseas aid agency. These readers seem to be acting at least as badly as Bob was acting when he chose to let the runaway train hurtle toward the unsuspecting child. In the light of this conclusion, I trust that many readers will reach for the phone and donate that $200. Perhaps you should do it before reading further.

Now that you have distinguished yourself morally from people who put their vintage cars ahead of a child's life, how about treating yourself and your partner to dinner at your favorite restaurant? But wait. The money you will spend at the restaurant could also help save the lives of children overseas! True, you weren't planning to blow $200 tonight, but if you were to give up dining out just for one month, you would easily save that amount. And what is one month's dining out, compared to a child's life? There's the rub. Since there are a lot of desperately needy children in the world, there will always be another child whose life you could save for another $200. Are you therefore obliged to keep giving until you have nothing left? At what point can you stop?

Hypothetical examples can easily become farcical. Consider Bob. How far past losing the Bugatti should he go? Imagine that Bob had got his foot stuck in the track of the siding, and if he diverted the train, then before it rammed the car it would also amputate his big toe. Should he still throw the switch? What if it would amputate his foot? His entire leg?

As absurd as the Bugatti scenario gets when pushed to extremes, the point it raises is a serious one: only when the sacrifices become very significant indeed would most people be prepared to say that Bob does nothing wrong when he decides not to throw the switch. Of course, most people could be wrong; we can't decide moral issues by taking opinion polls. But consider for yourself the level of sacrifice that you would demand of Bob, and then think about how much money you would have to give away in order to make a sacrifice that is roughly equal to that. It's almost certainly much, much more than $200. For most middle-class Americans, it could easily be more like $200 000.

Isn't it counterproductive to ask people to do so much? Don't we run the risk that many will shrug their shoulders and say that morality, so conceived, is fine for saints but not for them? I accept that we are unlikely to see, in the near or even medium-term future, a world in which it is normal for wealthy Americans to give the bulk of their wealth to strangers. When it comes to praising or blaming people for what they do, we tend to use a standard that is relative to some conception of normal behavior. Comfortably off Americans who give, say, 10 percent of their income to overseas aid organizations are so far ahead of most of their equally comfortable fellow citizens that I wouldn't go out of my way to chastise them for not doing more. Nevertheless, they should be doing much more, and they are in no position to criticize Bob for failing to make the much greater sacrifice of his Bugatti.

At this point various objections may crop up. Someone may say: "If every citizen living in the affluent nations contributed his or her share I wouldn't have to make such a drastic sacrifice, because long before such levels were reached, the resources would have been there to save the lives of all those children dying from lack of food or medical care. So why should I give more than my fair share?" Another, related, objection is that the Government ought to increase its overseas aid allocations, since that would spread the burden more equitably across all taxpayers.

Yet the question of how much we ought to give is a matter to be decided in the real world —and that, sadly, is a world in which we know that most people do not, and in the immediate future will not, give substantial amounts to overseas aid agencies. We know, too, that at least in the next year, the United States Government is not going to meet even the very modest United Nations-recommended target of 0.7 percent of gross national product; at the moment it lags far below that, at 0.09 percent, not even half of Japan's 0.22 percent or a tenth of Denmark's 0.97 percent. Thus, we know that the money we can give beyond that theoretical "fair share" is still going to save lives that would otherwise be lost. While the idea that no one need do more than his or her fair share is a powerful one, should it prevail if we know that others are not doing their fair share and that children will die preventable deaths unless we do more than our fair share? That would be taking fairness too far.

Thus, this ground for limiting how much we ought to give also fails. In the world as it is now, I can see no escape from the conclusion that each one of us with wealth surplus to his or her essential needs should be giving most of it to help people suffering from poverty so dire as to be life-threatening. That's right: I'm saying that you shouldn't buy that new car, take that cruise, redecorate the house or get that pricey new suit. After all, a $1,000 suit could save five children's lives.

So how does my philosophy break down in dollars and cents? An American household with an income of $50 000 spends around $30 000 annually on necessities, according to the Conference Board, a non-profit economic research organization. Therefore, for a household bringing in $50 000 a year, donations to help the world's poor should be as close as possible to $20 000. The $30 000 required for necessities holds for higher incomes as well. So a household making $100 000 could cut a yearly check for $70 000. Again, the formula is simple: whatever money you're spending on luxuries, not necessities, should be given away.

Now, evolutionary psychologists tell us that human nature just isn't sufficiently altruistic to make it plausible that many people will sacrifice so much for strangers. On the facts of human nature, they might be right, but they would be wrong to draw a moral conclusion from those facts. If it is the case that we ought to do things that, predictably, most of us won't do, then let's face that fact head-on. Then, if we value the life of a child more than going to fancy restaurants, the next time we dine out we will know that we could have done something better with our money. If that makes living a morally decent life extremely arduous, well, then that is the way things are. If we don't do it, then we should at least know that we are failing to live a morally decent life—not because it is good to wallow in guilt but because knowing where we should be going is the first step toward heading in that direction.

When Bob first grasped the dilemma that faced him as he stood by that railway switch, he must have thought how extraordinarily unlucky he was to be placed in a situation in which he must choose between the life of an innocent child and the sacrifice of most of his savings. But he was not unlucky at all. We are all in that situation.

Source: Peter Singer, "The Singer Solution to World Poverty," (5 September 1999).

DISCUSSION QUESTIONS

1. What would happen if everyone took Singer's advice and donated all of their "extra" money to charitable organizations? Would this indeed create more equality among nations? What would happen to the industries that produced the luxury items that Singer suggests that individuals abandon?

2. Like many of the advertisements that we see on television, Singer suggests that individuals have a moral obligation to assist others who are less fortunate. When you compare this strategy of fundraising to different approaches that feature philanthropic efforts like large donations made by Bill Gates and Warren Buffet or the high-profile activities of celebrities like Angelina Jolie and Brad Pitt, which initiative is more effective for you? What are the pros and cons of each approach and which strategy is likely to raise more money? Why?

3. Imagine that you had to debate the merit of Singer's ideas. How would you convince the opposing team that his solution to world poverty was sound?

KNOW IT AND OWN IT: WHAT DO I BRING TO THIS?

Do you have a firm understanding of the differences between absolute and relative poverty, as they relate to your own life? Have you ever gone hungry or wondered how you would pay for your rent or tuition? How often do you donate your time or money to charitable organizations or street people? Knowing your own situation as it relates to issues of social inequality will bring a greater understanding as you consider the concepts introduced in this chapter.

WALKING THE TALK HOW CAN I LEARN FROM THIS?

Once you have a good understanding of where you stand in terms of your own personal wealth, put it in absolute and relative terms as you apply it to those close to you and those who live very far from you. Try to determine the reasons that both of those populations experience poverty and in what ways. The next time that you see homeless people or a food bank, remind yourself of what you've learned and maybe you'll be moved to help!

IT IS WHAT IT IS: IS THIS INSIDE OR OUTSIDE MY COMFORT ZONE?

Social inequality is never fair, and the consequences of it wreak havoc on those who are on the receiving end of unjust treatment. Perhaps you are hungry, but you have never had the nerve to ask for help because you are too afraid or embarrassed.

If you're not in a situation where poverty is a concern, then you might be that person who gets to hold out a hand and offer a kind word, some information, or a non-judgmental greeting—a smile. Levelling the playing field is often the first step in achieving equality, regardless of the real or perceived barriers that exist in any relationship.

PUT IT IN PLAY: HOW CAN I USE THIS?

If you've never had to live on a strict budget, try surviving by playing on Playspent.org, or go to dothemath.thestop.org and see how your income compares to someone who lives on social assistance. See how long you can survive on the Spent site, and then turn it into a contest among your friends.

Located at www.nelson.com/site/walkamile1e

- Consolidate your knowledge with the **Flashcards**.
- Gauge your understanding with **Picture This** and accompanying questions for reflection.
- Develop your critical thinking skills by working through **The Daily**.
- Apply your understanding with **KWIP** interactive!
- Develop your critical reading skills through compelling **Readings** and accompanying short answer questions.

REFERENCES

BCLA. (2012, June 28). CMHC rental housing report: Affordability is still a big issue in Vancouver. B.C. Landlords Association. Retrieved from http://bclandlords .ca/2012/06/29/cmhc-rental-housing-report-affordability -is-still-a-big-issue-in-vancouver/

Berreman, G. (1972). Race, caste, and other invidious distinctions in social stratification. *Race and Class*, 385–414.

Bielski, Z. (2010, April 13). Living on a welfare diet. Retrieved from *The Globe and Mail*: http://www .theglobeandmail.com/life/living-on-a-welfare-diet/ article4314633/

Boivin, J., Roy, E., Haley, N., & du Fort, G. G. (2005). The health of street youth: A Canadian perspective. *Canadian Journal of Public Health*, 432–437.

Bose, R., & Hwang, S. (2002). Income and spending patterns among panhandlers. *Canadian Medical Association Journal*, 477–479.

Bramham, D. (2008, April 19). Homeless crisis grows while Canada prospers; the economy is strong, provinces run budget surpluses, yet we turn our backs on the destitute. *The Vancouver Sun*, p. A4.

Casavant, L. (1999, January 1). Composition of the homeless population. Retrieved from *Parliamentary Research*

Branch: http://publications.gc.ca/Collection-R/LoPBdP/modules/prb99-1-homelessness/composition-e.htm

CMHA. (2009, January 1). Out of the shadows forever: Annual Report 2008-2009. Retrieved from *Canadian Mental Health Association*: http://www.cmha.ca/public_policy/out-of-the-shadows-forever-annual-report-2008-2009/#.T-smZMUfh40

Columbia Electronic Encyclopedia. (2011). Apartheid. In *Columbia Electronic Encyclopedia* (pp. 1–2). New York: Columbia University Press.

Condon, M., & Newton, R. (2007). In the proper hands: SPARC BC research on homelessness and affordable housing. Vancouver: Social Planning and Research Council of British Columbia.

Conference Board of Canada. (2011, July 1). Canadian income inequality. Retrieved from *Conference Board of Canada*: http://www.conferenceboard.ca/hcp/hot-topics/canInequality.aspx

Conference Board of Canada. (2012, January 1). World income inequality. Retrieved from *Conference Board of Canada*: http://www.conferenceboard.ca/hcp/hot-topics/worldinequality.aspx

Crowe, C. (2012, June 8). Toronto Disaster Relief Committee: 14 years of advocacy, activism and action. Retrieved from *Toronto Disaster Relief Committee*: http://tdrc.net/uploads/tdrc14years.pdf

deGroot-Magetti. (2002, March 1). A measure of poverty in Canada. Retrieved from *Citizens for Public Justice*: http://action.web.ca/home/cpj/attach/A_measure_of_poverty.pdf

Echenberg, H., & Jensen, H. (2012, May 7). Defining and enumerating homelessness in Canada. Retrieved from *Library of Parliament Research Publications*: http://www.parl.gc.ca/Content/LOP/ResearchPublications/prb0830-e.htm

Employment and Social Development Canada. (2013, August 9). Poverty profile. Retrieved from *Employment and Social Development Canada*: http://www.hrsdc.gc.ca/eng/communities/reports/poverty_profile/2007.shtml

Evans, G., & Schamberg, M. (2009). Childhood poverty, chronic stress, and adult working memory. Proceedings of the National Academy of Sciences, Vol. 106, 13.

Eva's Initiatives. (2012, January 1). National profile–Homeless youth: Who are they and why are they on the street? Retrieved from *Eva's Phoenix Toolkit*: http://phoenixtoolkit.evasinitiatives.com/homeless-youth-background/national-profile/

Family Service Toronto. (2010, January 1). 2010 report card on child and family poverty in Canada. Retrieved from *Campaign 2000*: http://www.campaign2000.ca/reportCards/provincial/Ontario/2010OntarioReportCardEnglish.pdf

Family Service Toronto. (2011, January 1). 2011 report card on child and family poverty in Canada. Retrieved from *Campaign 2000*: http://www.campaign2000.ca/reportCards/national/2011EnglishRreportCard.pdf

Foreign Affairs, Trade and Development Canada. (2012, May 10). Millennium development goals. Retrieved from *Foreign Affairs, Trade and Development Canada*: http://www.acdi-cida.gc.ca/acdi-cida/acdi-cida.nsf/eng/JUD-13173118-GPM

Fraser, J. (2012, May 27). Mind the gap; Canada income inequality: An infographic. Retrieved from *Huffington Post*: http://www.huffingtonpost.ca/2012/05/27/income-inequality-infographic_n_1548973.html

Girard, M.-C. (2006). Determining the extent of the problem: The value and challenges of enumeration. *Canadian Review of Social Policy*, 104.

Government of Canada. (2012, February 2). Street youth in Canada. Retrieved from *Government of Canada Publications*: http://publications.gc.ca/collections/Collection/HP5-15-2006E.pdf

Hennessy, T. (2012, January 1). The clash for the cash: CEO vs. average Joe. Retrieved from *Canadian Centre for Policy Alternatives*: http://www.policyalternatives.ca/ceo

Hulchanski, D. J. (2009, February 18). Homelessness in Canada: Past, present, future. Retrieved from *Growing Home: Housing and Homelessness in Canada*: http://www.cprn.org/documents/51110_EN.pdf

Hunger Count. (2011, January 1). Food banks Canada. Retrieved from *Hunger Count 2011*: http://www.foodbankscanada.ca/getmedia/dc2aa860-4c33-4929-ac36-fb5d40f0b7e7/HungerCount-2011.pdf.aspx

Hwang, S. (2010, November 1). Housing vulnerability and health: Canada's hidden emergency. Retrieved from *St. Michael's*: http://www.stmichaelshospital.com/crich/housing-vulnerability-and-health.php

Interfaith Social Assistance Reform Coalition. (1998). *Our neighbours' voices: Will we listen?* Toronto: James Lorimer and Company.

Jasinski, J., Wesely, J., Mustaine, E., & Wright, J. (2005, November 1). The experience of violence in the lives of homeless women: A research report. Retrieved from *National Criminal Justice Reference Service*: https://www.ncjrs.gov/pdffiles1/nij/grants/211976.pdf

Klotz, A. (1995). *Norms in international relations: The struggle against apartheid*. Ithaca, New York: Cornell University Press.

Kuhle, S., & Veugelers, P. (2008). Why does the social gradient in health not apply to overweight? Health Reports, *Statistics Canada*, 7–15.

Lewis, O. (1998). The culture of poverty. *Society*, 7–9.

McLaren, L. (2007). Socioeconomic status and obesity. *Epidemiologic Reviews*, 29–48.

Milan, A., Keown, L., & Covadonga, R. U. (2012, February 4). Families, living arrangements and unpaid work. Retrieved from *Statistics Canada*: http://www.statcan.gc.ca/pub/89-503-x/2010001/article/11546-eng.htm#a12

Montgomery, C. (1994). Swimming upstream: The strengths of women who survive homelessness. *Advances in Nursing*, 34–45.

Native Women's Association (2007, June 22). Aboriginal women and homelessness. Retrieved from *Newfoundland*

Labrador: Labrador Affairs Office: http://www.laa.gov
.nl.ca/laa/naws/pdf/nwac-homelessness.pdf

Ninian, A. (2008). India's untouchables: The Dalits.
Contemporary Review, 186–192.

Preston, V., Murdie, R., D'Addario, S., Sibbanda, P.,
Murnaghan, A., Logan, J., et al. (2011, December 1).
Precarious housing and hidden homelessness among
refugees, asylum seekers, and immigrants in the Toronto
Metropolitan Area. Retrieved from *CERIS—The Ontario
Metropolis Centre*: http://www.ceris.metropolis.net/
wp-content/uploads/pdf/research_publication/working
_papers/wp87.pdf

Raphael, D. (2010). Health equity in Canada. *Social
Alternatives*, 41–49.

Reid, S., Berman, H., & Forchuk, C. (2005). Living on the
streets in Canada: A feminist narrative study of girls and
young women. *Issues in Comprehensive Pediatric Nursing*,
237–256.

Rossides, D. (1997). *Social stratification: The interplay of
class, race, and gender*. Upper Saddle River, New Jersey:
Prentice Hall.

Shapcott, M. (2010, November 24). More than three million
Canadians forced to live in poverty: 2010 child and
family poverty report card. Retrieved from *Wellesley
Institute*: http://www.wellesleyinstitute.com/news/more
-than-three-million-canadians-forced-to-live-in-poverty
-2010-child-and-family-poverty-report-card/

Sider, D. (2005, May 1). A sociological analysis of root causes
of homelessness in Sioux Lookout. Retrieved from
Canadian Race Relations Foundation: http://www.crr.ca/
divers-files/en/pub/rep/ePubRepSioLoo.pdf

Singer, P. (1999, September 5). The Singer solution to world
poverty. *The New York Times Magazine*, 60–63.

Statistics Canada. (2009, June 3). Low income cut-offs for
2008 and low income measures for 2007. Retrieved from
Income Research Paper Series: http://www.statcan.gc.ca/
pub/75f0002m/75f0002m2009002-eng.htm

Statistics Canada. (2011, September 16). University tuition
fees. Retrieved from *The Daily*: http://www.statcan.gc.ca/
daily-quotidien/110916/dq110916b-eng.htm

Statistics Canada. (2012, June 15). Persons in low income
families. Retrieved from Table 202-0802, *Statistics
Canada*: http://www5.statcan.gc.ca/cansim/a21

Statistics Canada. (2013, June 27). Average female and
male earnings, and female-to-male earnings ratio, by
work activity, 2010 constant dollars. Retrieved from
Statistics Canada: http://www5.statcan.gc.ca/cansim/
a05?lang=eng&id=2020102

Syed, A. (2002). Collective and elective ethnicity: Caste
among urban Muslims in India. *Sociological Forum*,
593–620.

UNICEF Canada. (2010, January 1). Poverty ... the
one line we want our kids to cross. Retrieved
from *UNICEF Report Card 10: Measuring Child
Poverty*: http://www.UNICEF.ca/sites/default/files/

imce_uploads/DISCOVER/OUR%20WORK/ADVOCACY/
DOMESTIC/RESEARCH%20AND%20POLICY/DOCS/
canadian_companion_fa.pdf

United Nations Development Program. (2012, July 2).
The Millennium Development Goals Report 2012.
Retrieved from *UNDP*: http://www.undp.org/
content/undp/en/home/librarypage/mdg/
the-millennium-development-goals-report-2012/

United Nations. (2012, July 2). We can end poverty 2015.
Retrieved from *Millennium Development Goals Report
2012*: http://www.un.org/millenniumgoals/pdf/MDG%20
Report%202012.pdf

United Native Nations Society. (2001, June 1). Aboriginal
homelessness in British Columbia. Retrieved
from *Homeless Hub*: http://www.homelesshub.ca/
%28S%280oinij454xdtat555ztjoheb%29%29/Resource/
Frame.aspx?url=http%3a%2f%2fwww.urbancenter
.utoronto.ca%2fpdfs%2felibrary%2fUNNS_Aboriginal
_Homelessn.pdf&id=36039&title=Aboriginal+Home
lessness+in+British+Columbia&owner=121

V, J. (2012, May 26). The Hindu caste system. Retrieved from
Hindu Website: http://www.hinduwebsite.com/hinduism/
h_caste.asp

Vox, B. (2005, December 1). Live 8. Retrieved from *Live 8*:
http://www.live8live.com/

Ward, H., Tarasuk, V., & Mendelson, R. (2007).
Socioeconomic patterns of obesity in Canada: Modeling
the role of health behaviour. *Applied Physiology, Nutrition
and Metabolism*, 206–216.

Wellesley Institute. (2007, August 24). Physical and sexual
violence rates for homeless many times higher than for
housed. Retrieved from *Wellesley Institute*: http://www
.wellesleyinstitute.com/publication/physical_and_sexual
_violence_rates_for_homeless_many_times_higher_than
_housed/

Wilkinson, R., & Pickett, K. (2009). *The spirit level: Why equality
is better for everyone*. London, England: Penguin Books.

Wong, J. (2009, October 1). Guy Laliberté; Cirque du
Soleil founder: From busker to spaceman. Retrieved
from *CBC News*: http://www.cbc.ca/news/arts/theatre/
story/2009/10/01/f-guy-laliberte-backgrounder.html

World Hunger. (2012, January 1). 2012 world hunger
and poverty facts and statistics. Retrieved from *World
Hunger Education Service*: http://www.worldhunger
.org/articles/Learn/world%20hunger%20facts%202002
.htm#Number_of_hungry_people_in_the_world

Yalnizyan, A. (2010, January 1). The rise of Canada's
richest 1%. Retrieved from *Canadian Centre for Policy
Alternatives*: http://ywcacanada.ca/data/research
_docs/00000192.pdf

YWCA. (2009, January 20). Broad investments: Counting
women into the federal budget. Retrieved from *YWCA
Canada*: http://ywcacanada.ca/data/publications/
00000006.pdf

Race as a Social Construct

> "Until the colour of a man's skin Is of no more significance than the colour of his eyes—Me say war."
>
> *(Bob Marley, 1976)*

DIVERSITY COMPETENCIES

Diversity competencies are specifically learned behaviours that students can actively practise to promote equity and inclusion. By mastering this unit, students will gain the skills to become diversity-competent practitioners, including the ability to

- describe racism as a hierarchical system of power and privilege

- evaluate the effects of racial stereotypes, racial prejudice, and racial discrimination on diverse groups

- examine the role racialized, ethnic, and multiple cultural identities have on interpersonal encounters and community relationships

- reflect upon your own privilege and bias and how this can be relevant to anti-racism practices in the workplace

Source: David McGlynn/Getty

Consider the case of a student named Samuel, who found that as a black student studying in Canada, he was reminded every day that he was black. In fact, he described every day of his life in Canada as a personal experience in understanding **racism**. When asked what that meant, Samuel described daily experiences where people reminded him they didn't see the colour of his skin yet they stared at him, touched his hair, held their purses a little tighter, asked him where he came from, called upon him to speak for all black people, told him he was a role model for other students like him, and declared they were **anti-racist** because they had friends who were black. Samuel also described a heated discussion on racism in a class where he was one of two black students, during which time most students stared at him for his reaction. During the discussion, he listened while a white student used the **reverse discrimination** and so-called **race-card** arguments, and he thought to himself ... try walking a day in my shoes. This is, in part, the inspiration for the title of this book.

More than fifty years ago, John Howard Griffin did just that. Wanting to understand the experience of **Jim Crow racism** in the southern United States, this white novelist darkened his skin with sun lamps and medication and travelled from New Orleans to Alabama as a black man. The book he wrote in 1961 is based on a journal of his experiences and is titled *Black Like Me*. The book sold ten million copies and became a modern classic. In the book, Griffin confronted his own racism and challenged white readers to face their own denial. Upon its release, effigies of Griffin were hung and burned—even in his hometown.

Gerald Early, a professor of English and of African and Afro-American Studies at Washington University, writes (as cited in Watson, 2011), "*Black Like Me* disabused the idea that minorities were acting out of paranoia. There was this idea that black people said certain things about racism, and one rather expected them to say these things. Griffin revealed that what they were saying was true. It took someone from outside coming in to do that." It is interesting to note that it was a white man, making himself appear black for a short period of time, who gave legitimacy (in the eyes of the dominant white culture) to the voice and experience of black oppression at that time.

Fifty years later, is the book still relevant? Some have argued that *Black Like Me* has only ever been relevant to those who are white. From a historical perspective, some have asked, "does the book mean the same in the age of Obama as it did in the age of Jim Crow?" (Watson, 2011) Some would argue its continued relevancy in a country that remains racially stratified with whites at the top of its hierarchy.

The documentary *Race 2012* looks at the issues around **race** and politics in the United States in 2012, and as Rich Benjamin, author of *Searching for Whitopia*, states, "[We] thought that with the election of Barack Obama we would have a post-racial society. Obviously we don't have that." Building racial equality in the United States will take more than the election of its first black president, when we know that racism is complex, systemic, institutionalized, and socially constructed. In the same way, we know that building gender equality in a country takes more than the election of a female political leader, when patriarchy is complex, systemic, institutionalized, and socially constructed. But the question that remains unanswered is: How do we build a post-racial society? Is the answer as complex as the construction of oppression itself? Or is the answer as simple as the one that actor Morgan Freeman proposed in a famous *60 Minutes* interview with Mike Wallace? He said the answer was that we just stop talking about it (Freeman, 2005). Until we do find answers, one thing is clear—the war that Bob Marley sang about will continue.

ACKNOWLEDGING THE EXISTENCE OF RACISM IN CANADA TODAY

In the United States, discussions of racism are often characterized as a black-and-white binary issue, with legitimate historical roots in slavery. In Canada today, discussions of racism are often truncated by the denial of its existence, or by assertions of its unintentional nature, limited by perception of racism as something

Racism: Negative attitudes of a person or group of people using a socially constructed concept of race; racism can manifest itself as feelings or behaviours that can give advantages, privilege, and power to certain groups of people, and conversely, can disadvantage or limit the opportunities of racialized individuals or racialized groups.

Anti-racist: Against or opposed to racism.

Reverse discrimination: Discrimination against whites, usually in the form of affirmative action, employment equity, and diversity policies; the concept of reverse discrimination, specifically reverse racism, is considered by many to be impossible because of existing power structures in society.

Race card: Term that refers to the use of race to gain an advantage.

Jim Crow racism: Anti-black racism that existed in the United States during the period of 1877–1960s; Jim Crow laws enforced racial segregation and a racialized social order that resulted in the subjugation, oppression, and death (through lynching and other violence) of African Americans.

that happened in the past, something that happens in other parts of the world, or as isolated incidents against **people of colour** (often termed by Statistics Canada as "**visible minorities**"). Jennifer Roy writes for the Canadian Race Relations Foundation:

> there appears to be a refusal to recognize that racism is an issue in Canada, both presently and historically … [W]hen we think of the main examples of racism historically, the images that often spring to mind are of slavery in the United States, apartheid in South Africa or the Holocaust. … Inherent in this limited understanding is a tendency to assume both that these problems are in the past and that they do not occur in Canada. (Roy, 2012)

We would like to think of ourselves as a nation differentiated from the United States, hinged to the myth that slavery did not exist in Canada. As historian Afua Cooper (2006) states, slavery is "Canada's best kept secret, locked within the National closet." At times, we like to believe that racism is now neatly tucked away as a part of history we won't repeat. Government officials have apologized for historical racism:

- The mayor of Halifax apologized for the evictions and razing of the African-Canadian community of Africville.
- Prime Minister Stephen Harper apologized to the Indo-Canadian community for the 1914 *Komagata Maru* incident, in which immigrants were denied entry based on racist legislation. Ship passengers remained on board for months, and were denied food and water.
- The Canadian government apologized to Aboriginal peoples for Canada's role in the Indian Residential School System, where children were separated from their parents and subjected to abuse.
- The Canadian government apologized to Japanese Canadians for their internment and seizure of their property during World War II.
- The Canadian government apologized to Inuit families for their relocation from Inukjuak, Quebec, to the high Arctic.
- The Canadian government apologized to Chinese Canadians for the head tax they were forced to pay and that prevented family reunification.

So we have acknowledged and apologized to racialized groups affected by some of the racism that is a part of Canada's past. But we know the past informs both the present and the future, so how have we changed?

As Canadians we have also acknowledged that overcoming racism is of international importance. In this context, we vocalize our objections and sometimes act on them. There are many examples that attest to this practice. Many Canadians, horrified by the Holocaust, sacrificed their lives in the fight against Nazi Germany. Canada is a signatory to the United Nations International Convention on the Elimination of All Forms of Racial Discrimination, which requires us as a nation to commit to the elimination of racial discrimination, promote interracial understanding, legislate against hate speech, and criminalize membership in racist organizations (United Nations, 2011). In 2010, Canada also signed the United Nations Declaration on the Rights of Indigenous Peoples.

At the 2012 Olympic Games, Canadians generally supported the expulsion of Greek triple jumper Paraskevi Papachristou for her Twitter post making reference to immigrants in Athens that stated "with so many of Africans in Greece, the West Nile virus mosquitoes will at least be eating some homemade food" (Toronto Star, 2012). One of the International Olympic Committee's fundamental principles of Olympism is that "any form of discrimination with regard to a country or a person on grounds of race, religion, politics, gender or otherwise is incompatible with belonging to the Olympic Movement" (International Olympic Committee, 2011). Canadians were similarly outraged and supported the expulsion of Swiss soccer player Michel Morganella from the 2012 Olympic Games for an offensive Twitter post about the people of South Korea (Dunbar, 2012).

On the International Day for the Elimination of Racial Discrimination, held each year on March 21 to commemorate the anniversary of the 1960 Sharpeville, South Africa, massacre, Canadians renew their commitment to fight for racial equality. In 2012, that day's theme was proclaimed by the United Nations as "Racism and Conflict" to highlight ways in which **racial prejudice**, **racial discrimination**, and **xenophobia** are often at the root of conflict,

People of colour: Term intended to be more positive and inclusive of people than the terms "non-white" or "visible minorities"; refers to people who may share common experiences of racism.

Visible minorities: Term used primarily in Canada by Statistics Canada to refer to a category of persons who are non-Caucasian in race or non-white in colour and who do not report being Aboriginal.

Racial prejudice: Prejudgment or negative attitude based on a set of characteristics associated with the colour of a person's skin.

Racial discrimination: Behaviour that has a discriminatory effect based on race; there does not have to be an intention to discriminate.

Xenophobia: Hostility to anything considered foreign.

Source: Paul McKinnon/Shutterstock.com

Demonstrators walk to Parliament Hill as part of Idle No More movement.

genocide, **ethnic cleansing**, and **war crimes** (United Nations, 2012). As Canadians, we have been awarded the Nansen Peace Medal for our efforts in helping refugees fleeing from this form of conflict. But what about right now? At home in our own country? Can we acknowledge racism in the here and now?

As Canadians, we are also known to challenge individual acts we perceive as racist. Consider, for example, the former Toronto police officer and his friend who attended a Halloween party at Campbellford's Royal Canadian Legion and walked away with first prize for their two-man costume. One man dressed in a Ku Klux Klan robe with a white hood, Confederate flag cape, and a rope attached to the neck of his friend, whose face has been covered in black make-up (what is known as "blackface" and is symbolic of the Jim Crow era). Royal Canadian Legion officials closed the branch for a short period of time (Globe and Mail, 2010). In September 2011, students at a business school in Montreal were caught on film wearing blackface and chanting with Jamaican accents about smoking marijuana. Students alleged they were doing a skit to honour Jamaican sprinter Usain Bolt. A spokesperson claimed that these French-speaking Canadians were unaware of the history and significance of blackface (Wade, 2012). In November 2012, a bathroom stall at the University of Ottawa's Law School was defaced with racist graffiti (CBC News, 2012).

It is difficult to acknowledge that racism is not simply isolated incidents perpetrated by unknowing individuals. Racism is also embedded in the everyday life of our social systems and structures. Students like Samuel can narrate the experience of everyday racism in Canada, while at the same time, many who belong to the dominant culture question whether racism still exists in Canada today. Most of us who have ever engaged in a dialogue about racism have heard the arguments of reverse discrimination, especially in relationship to employment. These differing perceptions make the work of anti-racist educators and activists challenging.

The first step in understanding racism in Canada is to acknowledge that it is real, that it is a serious issue at both the individual and systemic levels, and that it is pervasive.

The Concept of Race as a Biological Myth

So what is **race**? Some have used the concept of race to mean a biological division of humans based on physical attributes such as skin colour and other physical traits. And for hundreds of years, we have used these differences to draw a colour line that has categorized people into four or five groups we call races. Academics have erroneously equated biology with destiny for many years, usually with the effect of reinforcing white superiority.

During the 1820s and 1830s, American physician and scientist Samuel Morton conducted a systematic analysis of hundreds of human skulls from all over the world to confirm his hypothesis that there were differences among races not only in terms of their origin, but also in terms of their brain size. Morton created a hierarchy among different racial groups of their brain capacity based on skull measurements. Morton assigned the largest brain capacity to English Europeans and the smallest brain capacity to Africans and Australian Aborigines (American Anthropological Association, 2011). Neuroscience research today refutes the validity of Morton's findings, and we know that what Morton did was attempt to use science to legitimate a socially constructed inequality.

Genocide: The intentional extermination or killing of an identifiable group.

Ethnic cleansing: The process or policy of eliminating unwanted ethnic, racial, or religious groups by deportation, forcible displacement, mass murder, or threats of such acts, with the intention of creating a homogenous population.

War crimes: Serious violations of international law applicable during armed conflict, such as ill treatment of prisoners of war, killing of prisoners of war, and so on; as of 2002, those arrested for war crimes have been tried in the International Criminal Court.

Race: Concept no longer recognized as valid except in terms of its social consequences; for many years, the concept of race referred to biological divisions between human beings based primarily on their skin colour.

After Morton, the work of early "race scientists" such as Josiah Nott, George Gliddon, and Louis Agassiz continued to attempt to prove that blacks and whites did not originate from the same species (American Anthropological Association, 2011).

In 1927, University of Toronto professor Peter Sandiford attempted to prove that racial and ethnic differences in IQ scores should be used by Canada as a selection criteria for new immigrants, encouraging the recruitment of the British, German, and Dutch, who scored well on IQ tests, and discouraging the recruitment of Poles, Italians, Greeks, and Asians who did not score as well on IQ tests (Walker, 2008). According to Sandiford (cited in Walker, 2008:197), Canada needed to protect itself from becoming a "dumping ground for misfits and defectives."

In the late 1980s, Philippe Rushton, a Canadian psychologist and professor at the University of Western Ontario, continued in the vein of earlier race scientists with theories about race and intelligence, suggesting that he had scientific evidence to prove whites are more intelligent than blacks and that Asians are the smartest of all. In a televised debate on the University of Western Ontario's campus in 1989, geneticist David Suzuki said Rushton's ideas were "monstrous": "I did not want to be here. I do not believe that we should dignify this man and his ideas in public debate ... his claims must be denounced, his methodology discredited, his grant revoked and his position terminated at this university, this is not science" (CBC Digital Archives, 1989).

We find the theme of race as a biological myth illuminated in popular culture as well. In American

IN THEIR SHOES

If a picture can say a thousand words, imagine the stories your shoes could tell! Try this student story on for size – have you walked in this student's shoes?

WHAT ARE YOU?

I've been asked that question countless times. Whenever I meet someone new, they are immediately itching to find out my background. You'd think it would get annoying after a while, but in all honesty, I'd rather people ask than make assumptions.

I'm of mixed race. My father is African and my mother is European. People always comment on how unique that sounds and I always tell them it's not unique at all. The world's mixed-race population is growing faster than ever in the 21st century. But despite all the strides it has made, things are still far from perfect.

Most people of mixed race have been fortunate enough not to have crises of identity. I, on the other hand, wasn't that lucky. All my life I have been pushed and pulled in different directions to identify myself as either white or black. The problem with this is I'm both and neither.

Many other mixed-race individuals have fought this battle, and I will say this: it's hard to find your own identity when everyone else is trying to create one for you.

I have never wanted to be associated with any particular race. I am proud to be what I am and I don't need to feel part of a "whole." I have never wanted to be labelled just black or just white or anything else that I am not, and I fail to understand why people can't acknowledge that fact.

I found it slightly shocking that the One Drop Rule is still referenced and relevant today. For those who may not know, the One Drop Rule stated that a person with as little as one drop of black blood in their heritage was to be considered black—a slightly racist idea, don't you think?

And so we have the rule, an echo of the United States' racist past used today, albeit unmentioned, to classify a person of mixed race as black.

People have the right to determine their racial, sexual, and national identities. No one, not even society, should have the right to tell anyone who or what they are. It is up to us to determine that for ourselves.

There are people of mixed race who feel more comfortable associating themselves with one side of their heritage, and there is really nothing wrong with that. But when all of us are expected to pick and choose, or just fall in line with illusionary expectations, then it becomes a violation of our freedom.

comedian Dave Chappelle's parody titled "Racial Draft," Chappelle mocks the absurdity of racial classification as the Black delegation drafts Tiger Woods, the Jewish delegation drafts Lenny Kravitz, the Latino delegation drafts Elian Gonzalez, the White delegation drafts Colin Powell, and the Chinese delegation drafts the Wu Tang Clan. The writer of the "In Their Shoes" feature describes why the concept of race is not real in his life other than in terms of its social consequences: "All my life I have been pushed and pulled in different directions to identify myself as either white or black. The problem with this is I'm both and neither."

Every day, as you walk the halls of your academic institution, you can see with your own eyes that human beings look different from one another. The shape of the face, the colour of the hair, the shape of the body, or the colour of the skin—all point to human physical variation. But this does not mean that we can neatly tuck everyone into a handful of groups based on these physical characteristics and then correlate these groups with attributes such as brain size, intelligence, or athletic ability. Nor does racism refer to the visceral reaction you may have to someone who has a different physical appearance. We have come to understand that the concept of race is not real—that there is no biological basis to the social categorizations we have constructed and used for the past several hundred years. Racism is really about how people assign meaning to that appearance. This is learned behaviour; and if we can learn it, we can unlearn it. If we want to create the world that Bob Marley sings about, where the colour of people's skin is of no more significance than the colour of their eyes, we must deconstruct the social hierarchy of privilege based on skin colour.

The concept of race is focused on the social construction of difference between groups, with the effect of marginalizing and oppressing some of these groups within a

Racial stereotyping: Using the concept of race or ethnicity to attach a generalized concept that all members of a group have a particular characteristic or ability.

Hate crimes: Crimes that are committed against people or property that are motivated by hate or prejudice against a victim's racial, ethnic, religious, or sexual identity; they can involve intimidation, harassment, destruction of property, vandalism, physical force or threat of physical force, or inciting hatred in other people.

Individual racism: Individual discriminatory attitudes or behaviour motivated by negative evaluation a person or group of people using a socially constructed concept of race.

Systemic racism: Behaviour, policies, or practices that disadvantage racialized persons; can be intentional or unintentional.

society. According to biological anthropologist Alan Goodman,

> To understand why the idea of race is a biological myth requires a major paradigm shift, an absolute paradigm shift, a shift in perspective. And for me, it's like seeing, you know, what it must have been like to understand that the world isn't flat … in fact, that race is not based on biology but race is rather an idea that we ascribe to biology. (Adelman, 2003)

Race was really about the creation of a dominant group within society. According to historian Robin D.G. Kelley (PBS, 2005), "[R]ace was never just a matter of categories. It was a matter of creating hierarchies. … or the creation of racism, was really about the invention of a dominant group." This dominant group develops the social, cultural, economic, and political power to define its own particular history and culture as representative of all. We see an example of a response to this kind of dominance in the creation of the Africentric Alternative School in Toronto. It was believed that the high dropout rate affecting students of African descent was related in part to the relevancy of school curriculum and its failure to represent anything other than the history and culture of the English and French.

If we now understand that there is no scientific basis to the concept of race, then we know racism is not about the category you belong to; rather, it is about the power of particular groups of people to construct and assign negative meaning to that category. That meaning can lead to a range of social responses— from **racial stereotyping** to **hate crimes** and violence.

The hope for anti-racist educators and activists is rooted in this idea: if racism is socially constructed, then we might have the ability to deconstruct it as well as the desire to do so, when it is one of the root causes of human inequality (Roy, 2012).

By looking at the different forms in which racism is manifest, we can begin to understand some of the problems in uncovering racism in Canada. **Individual racism** is often the easiest to identify and is found in the prejudicial attitudes and discriminatory behaviours of individuals (Roy, 2012). Examples of individual racism can include a wide range of behaviours and attitudes from hate crimes and violence to insults, name-calling, offensive jokes, or shunning of racialized people. **Systemic racism** operates at a structural level in the "policies and practices of organizations, which directly or indirectly operate to sustain the advantages of peoples of certain social races" (Roy, 2012). Systemic racism is often more difficult to identify and address than individual racism, as it is often hidden with the implicit policies of social institutions. Examples of systemic racism may include the following: racial profiling by law enforcement officers, lack of representation of racialized people within an organization and at all levels of that organization, curriculum in an educational institution that is not inclusive of all racialized persons, and the assumption that racialized people have been hired within an organization because of employment equity or diversity policies. **Cultural racism** is the basis for both individual and systemic racism, as "it is the value system which is embedded in society which supports and allows discriminatory actions based on perceptions of racial difference, cultural superiority and inferiority" (Roy, 2012).

There are often references made to forms of racism based on intention—a categorization of racism as implicit versus explicit or conscious versus unconscious. But this kind of characterization presumes that dominant white culture in North America has not yet experienced any awareness of their privilege. Students often ask, "Isn't racism just ignorance, people simply not knowing any better?" A favourite quotation used to respond to this question comes from an interview with Robin D.G. Kelley, an American professor, who states:

> When I teach about racism the first thing I say to my students is that racism is not ignorance. Racism is knowledge. Racism in some ways is a very complicated system of knowledge, where science, religion, philosophy, is used to justify inequality and hierarchy. That is foundational. ... And that is why you can't think of racism as simply "not knowing." That is not the case at all—on the contrary. (PBS, 2005)

It is important to understand that racism is knowledge, attitude, and behaviour that serve to marginalize and oppress some people at an individual level but also marginalize and oppress people at a systemic level, most notably in systems of criminal justice, policing, education, health, media, immigration, and employment (Roy, 2012). Racism can be simply defined as an equation: "racism = prejudice + discrimination + power" (Fleras and Elliott, 1999, p. 440).

White Privilege and Forms of Its Denial

The picture featured at the beginning of this chapter is a political response to the peach-coloured crayon in the Crayola crayon box that, up until 1962, was called "flesh." Some suggest this naming is symbolic of the invisible system of privilege that has conferred dominance on those perceived as white (McIntosh, 1989).

Anti-racism educator Tim Wise (2011), reflecting upon his own privilege as a white man, writes, "[T]o be white is to be born into an environment where one's legitimacy is far less likely to be questioned than would the legitimacy of a person of color, be it in terms of where one lives, where one works, or where one goes to school."

Not surprising is the fact that any challenge to white privilege and its concomitant power is not popular among white people. One of the ways in which we reinforce white privilege in multicultural Canada is the creation of a society where white people can still assume that their social institutions, their political structures, their economy, and their neighbourhoods will still work for them as long as they play by the rules (Wise, 2010a). There still exists a pathology of isolation that creates and maintains racially and ethnically segregated neighbourhoods across Canada. The *Toronto Star* recently published an article on the city of Brampton that some suggest is experiencing a phenomenon referred to as "white flight"—where former white mainstream communities are not comfortable becoming the minority population:

> While the visible-minority segment has exploded to represent two-thirds of Brampton's population, white residents are dwindling. Their numbers went from 192 400 in 2001 to 169 230 in 2011. That's a loss of more than 23 000 people, or 12 per cent, in a decade when the city's population rose by 60 per cent. That's hardly a picture of the multicultural ideal so celebrated in this country. (Grewal, 2013)

Duke University Professor Eduardo Bonilla-Silva (2012) asserts that white isolation produces racialized perceptions and behaviour that limit the skills to interact with people of colour and that normalize racial inequality. Tim Wise (2010b) concurs, noting that the effects of raising children in environments where no one discusses racism can result in those children growing up to believe that racial inequalities are natural and that marginalization is not a systemic issue but one based on individual deficiencies. More generally across society, whiteness is reinforced by a kind of code that attacks equity in matters like tax exemption for First Nations people, immigration policies, **employment equity**, and

Cultural racism:
Includes both individual and systemic forms of racism.

Employment equity:
Requirement under the Employment Equity Act of Canada that employers use proactive employment practices to increase representation of four designated groups: women, people with disabilities, Aboriginal peoples, and racialized communities in the workplace. Employment equity mandates the accommodation of difference with special measures when needed.

inclusive language, and a kind of code that does not respond appropriately to racial discrimination, **racial profiling**, **racial harassment**, and **language-related discrimination**. Professor Bonilla-Silva suggests that the defence of white privilege sounds something like this: "I am all for equal opportunity; I want people to be judged by the content of their character and not by the colour of their skin; therefore, I am against affirmative action because it is discrimination in reverse" (Bonilla-Silva, 2012). He goes on to suggest that systemic white privilege is maintained by the language of liberalism: "they don't even process that because they think that they are beyond race. So they are the normative people. They are the universal people. They are the raceless people" (Bonilla-Silva, 2012).

White students often respond to Samuel's story with disbelief, blame, and certainly advice about his alleged attempts to use the so-called "race card"—as if that is something that confers real privilege. For example, a student named Ashley responded to Samuel's story by asking why he feels the need to walk around all the time thinking about race: "I don't go around thinking about my race all the time. We all belong to one race—the human race. Colour shouldn't matter." Some students in the class applauded after Ashley's statement. One African-Canadian student was suspect of the validity of Samuel's experience and questioned his racial authenticity, commenting on Samuel's "shade of blackness." The translation: Samuel is not black enough to have experienced the kind of daily racism he describes. This brings us to the concept of shadeism.

SHADEISM

In 2010, five students from Ryerson University created a short documentary film that looked at the privileging of lighter skin tones among persons of colour and titled it *Shadeism*. In an interview with the *Toronto Star*, Nayani Thiyagarajah, the director of this documentary, noted that "in a lot of communities this issue of shadeism isn't given a name, but it is something that has become normalized" (Hinkson, 2013, p. GT4). She found that women in the film with lighter skin acknowledged this skin tone as a privilege that cut across all ethnic and racial boundaries (Hinkson, 2013). **Shadeism**, sometimes referred to as colourism, is a form of intra-racial discrimination that is privileging people with lighter skin tones. Ryerson University Professor Camille Hernandez-Ramdwar notes that this has not always been true: "as the black power movement gained momentum in the 1960s and 1970s, it brought with it the 'black is beautiful' mentality, favouring dark skin, naturally curly hair and other 'black' features. But the pendulum has swung back to the 'white is light is right' message" (Hinkson, 2013, p. GT4).

Pigmentocracy—a social hierarchy based on skin pigmentation that places light skin on the top—has long been considered the motivator for the alleged use of skin-lightening products by celebrities like Michael Jackson and Beyoncé Knowles. But the concept of pigmentocracy extends beyond the social construction of ideal beauty types. A group of high school students in Oshawa, Ontario, are trying to raise awareness about this form of discrimination as something that they deal with on a daily basis. In an interview with the

Inclusive language: A policy or practice that uses language that includes and reflects the diversity of communities in an accurate and respectful way.

Racial profiling: Any action undertaken for reasons of safety, security, or public protection that relies on stereotypes to treat a person differently; while it is most often relevant in policing practices, it is not limited to the context of criminal justice.

Racial harassment: Pattern of behavioural conduct that isolates, humiliates, or intimidates racialized individuals; can include name calling, slurs based on racial or ethnic stereotypes, racial or ethnic jokes, cartoons, drawings or graffiti based on demeaning stereotypes, unwanted letters or phone calls of a racist nature, vandalism or damage to your property, spreading rumours, or staring at someone in an intimidating manner because of their race or colour.

Language-related discrimination: Discrimination that is based on a person's accent or some manner of speech (such as a person's fluency).

Shadeism: Intra-racial discrimination based on skin tone that currently privileges lighter skin tones.

Pigmentocracy: A social hierarchy based on skin pigmentation that places light skin on the top.

Source: © Breonca Trofort/www.btrofortphotography.com

Shadeism is fuelling a particular beauty myth and an accompanying international market of skin lightening products, worth billions of dollars.

Toronto Star, they describe pigmentocracy's many forms, such as the following examples:

- The hashtags #TeamDarkSkin or #TeamLightSkin are employed by Twitter users.
- Others try to get their attention by referring to them as "darkie" or "light skin" instead of by their first names.
- On Instagram, girls sometimes use filters to lighten photos of themselves before sharing them (Hinkson, 2013, p. GT1).

COLOURBLINDNESS

Racial discourse will often use words like "colourblind" to describe the phenomenon that a person is oblivious to race and therefore not racist. Racialized persons commonly hear statements that sound something like this: "I don't care if you are black, brown, white, green, or blue." Or "When I see you, I don't see you as black (or insert any other racial category here)." Julian Bond, a civil rights legend and the former chairman of the NAACP (the National Association for the Advancement of Colored People), said it best when he stated colorblindness really means being blind to the consequences of colour. Colourblind policies can actually worsen the problem of racial injustice (Wise, 2010b).

So why do people say "when I see you, I don't see colour." It is a question posed by Jane Elliott, an anti-racist activist and educator, in a workshop with college student participants that was captured in a documentary film (Elliott & Elliott Eye, 2001) titled *Angry Eye*. Elliott is the teacher who created the famous "blue-eyed/brown-eyed exercise" with her grade-school children following the assassination of Martin Luther King, Jr. In this exercise, Elliott divided the children based on their eye colour and then set out a system of discrimination based on eye colour. The purpose of Elliot's exercise was to expose the children to the experience of prejudice and discrimination based on a socially constructed hierarchy. Years later, having divided a college classroom in a blue-eyed and brown-eyed exercise, Elliott taught participants that colourblindness is a form of racism. "When you say to a person of colour, 'when I see you I don't see you black, I just see everybody the same' ... you don't have the right to say to a person, 'I don't see you as you are, I want to see you as I would be more comfortable seeing you' ... you are denying their reality" (Elliott & Elliott Eye, 2001).

Some suggest that the insistence on colourblindness is rooted in a fear of being labelled as a racist. But the point that Elliott makes is that noticing a person's race doesn't make you racist. What does make you racist is adopting attitudes and behaviours that make you believe and act upon the belief that certain characteristics are related to the race you think that person is. It is hard to overcome this behaviour when we are bombarded with racist messages through agents of socialization in our society, including families, the media, and so on.

So how can we say that race does not matter? It might not be a biological reality, but it is very real in terms of social consequences and impact on people's lived experience. As long as racism exists within a society, race will still matter. Pretending otherwise negates the experience of Samuel and other people of colour in Canada.

RACISM AND THE LAW

White Supremacy and Racially Motivated Hate Crimes

Hate crimes are a focus of concern around the world. Canada works with other countries to monitor and combat hate crime (Allen & Boyce, 2013). A hate crime is a criminal act motivated by hate. The Criminal Code of Canada, under sections 318 and 319, defines four specific offences as hate crimes: advocating genocide, public incitement of hatred, willful promotion of hatred, and mischief in relation to religious property. The Criminal Code of Canada, section 718.2(a)(i), also allows for increased penalties in sentencing when there is evidence that the crime was motivated by prejudice or hatred toward a particular group. Hate crimes can affect not only individual victims of the crime, but also the groups targeted (Allen & Boyce, 2013). Hate crimes can be either violent in nature, such as assault, or they can be non-violent in nature, such as mischief (Allen & Boyce, 2013).

Some of the most notable Canadian hate crime cases include verdicts against Don Andrews, James Keegstra, and Ernst Zundel. In cases such as these relating to hate, Section 2 of the Canadian Charter of Rights and Freedoms is often cited as justification for hate speech. Section 2 of the Charter guarantees the fundamental freedom of thought, belief, opinion, and expression, including freedom of the press and other media of communication. In the case of hate crimes, courts have ruled that although section 319(2) of the Canadian Criminal Code *does* limit free speech by preventing people from expressing their opinions, Section 1 of the Charter of Rights and Freedoms can restrict those freedoms granted in the Charter by making them subject "only to such reasonable limits prescribed by law as can be demonstrably justified in a free and democratic society." Canadian courts have ruled that in a democratic society like Canada, it is reasonable that we limit speech that may incite hatred against others. An example is the recent unanimous decision of the Supreme Court of Canada in the case of William Whatcott of Saskatchewan, which reaffirms the Canadian approach to freedom of speech: "that it can be limited by law to address the problem of hate speech, unlike the American approach, in which speech cannot be limited except in the most extreme circumstances" (Brean, 2013).

While the number of hate crime incidents in Canada varies from year to year, what is consistent is the fact that race or ethnicity remains the most common motivation for hate crime (Allen & Boyce, 2013). In fact, hate crimes motivated by race or ethnicity represented half (52%) of all police-reported hate crime incidents in 2011 (Allen & Boyce, 2013). Black populations are the most frequent targets of racially-motivated hate crimes, representing 21% of *all* hate crimes in Canada (Allen & Boyce, 2013). A recent example of a racially-motivated hate crime is the conviction under Canada's hate crime laws of Justin and Nathan Rehberg for burning a cross on the lawn of an interracial couple in Windsor, Nova Scotia (CBC News, 2011).

White supremacy is an ideology that supports the superiority of whites over all others and is embraced by members of white supremacist organizations. The beliefs of the white supremacist movement are examples of **overt racism**, and they cultivate hate (Canadian Race Relations Foundation, 2012). The ideology is premised on the myth that whites are racially superior to people of colour, Jews, and other minority populations (Canadian Race Relations Foundation, 2012). While hate-motivated acts based on race, ethnicity, religion, and sexual orientation are often associated with organized white supremacist groups, some racially-motivated hate crimes are also carried out by individuals who are not associated with such groups (Canadian Race Relations Foundation, 2012).

The laws and institutions of Canadian society designed to protect the rights of all citizens are contradictory to the declared goals of the white supremacist movement (Canadian Race Relations Foundation, 2012). Perhaps this is why **white nationalism** has recently emerged as a more sophisticated political ideology incorporating a collective racialized identity for white people, premised on separatism. Examples of this are evidenced in the challenges to immigration policies, human rights, and racial integration by white nationalist organizations such as the Aryan Guard, the Canadian Heritage Alliance, and the National Socialist Party of Canada. **Neo-Nazism** is an ideology that promotes white racial superiority as well as anti-Semitism specifically. Examples of groups that operate under anti-Semitic ideologies in Canada include the Northern Alliance Canada, Blood and Honour, Canadian Heritage Alliance, Northern Hammerskins, the Final Solution Skins, and the Aryan Resistance Movement.

Law enforcement personnel use tattoos as one means of identifying membership in some white supremacist organizations. Tattoos will often include swastikas as representative of neo-Nazi ideology. Tattoos also use numbers to code specific references. For example, the number 8 signifies the eighth letter of the alphabet (H), so 88 becomes HH or "Heil Hitler." Another example is 311: the letter K is the 11th number of the alphabet, and using it three times would translate to "KKK." The number "100%" can signify racial purity. Tattoos with the number 4/20 are sometimes used to commemorate Hitler's birthday (however, in some cases, 4/20 can also be a reference to marijuana). Colour of the shoelaces can also indicate membership in a racially motivated group: shoelace colour can indicate whether a member has been involved in acts of racial violence (e.g., red shoe laces can indicate spilled blood).

Race and Law Enforcement

There is perhaps no issue more controversial in racial discourse in Canada today than that of racial profiling within the Canadian criminal justice system, and specifically by the police. Law professor David Tanovich (2006), in the opening line of his book *The Colour of Justice: Policing Race in Canada,* states, "The colour of justice in Canada is White." Reference to this phenomenon is engrained in popular culture, rooted in historical events in North America, and revealed in academic research.

White supremacy: An ideology that supports the superiority of whites over all others and is embraced by members of white supremacist organizations.

Overt racism: Racism that is direct, open, and often public; examples include hate crimes, the ideology of white superiority as voiced in white power music, and blatantly racist statements.

White nationalism: A political ideology that advocates for a racialized identity for "white people."

Neo-Nazism: A post–World War II movement related to the white nationalist and white power skinhead movements, which seeks to revive elements of Nazi ideology such as racism, xenophobia, homophobia, holocaust denial, and anti-Semitism.

Racial profiling in the United States has been widespread. The brutal beating of Rodney King by four white officers was caught on video and the initial acquittal of the these officers sparked the 1992 Los Angeles race riots, which left 53 people dead, 2000 people injured, and over a billion dollars in property damage. King's public plea in the question of "Can't we all get along?" is often still quoted in racial discourse today. Filmmaker Michael Moore released *The Awful Truth—The African American Wallet Exchange* as a satire of the New York Police Department's racial profiling of the black community. More recently, the son of a NYPD police officer posted on YouTube an audio recording of a verbal exchange between himself and NYPD officers as alleged evidence of racial profiling under the title "The Hunted and the Hated: An Inside Look at the NYPD's Stop-and-Frisk Policy." In 2012, unarmed black teenager Trayvon Martin was shot by neighbourhood watch volunteer George Zimmerman, and Zimmerman's subsequent acquittal in 2013 has become a lightning rod for issues of alleged racism in the American criminal justice system. Black comedians like Dave Chappelle and Chris Rock use the concept of racial profiling and white privilege in the criminal justice system as fodder for much of their comedic material. But it is an all-too-serious issue.

In Canada, in 1995, during a peaceful protest by First Nations representatives at Ipperwash Provincial Park, Dudley George, an unarmed protestor, was shot dead by a member of the Ontario Provincial Police. The Ontario government called for an inquiry into the death of Dudley George, to make recommendations to avoid violence in similar circumstances in the future. Inquiry Commissioner Sidney B. Linden made the following statement:

> To many Aboriginal People, the shooting of Dudley George, the first Aboriginal person to be killed in a land-rights dispute in Canada since the 19th century, was the inevitable result of centuries of discrimination and dispossession. Many Aboriginal people also believed that the explanation for killing an unarmed Aboriginal occupier was rooted in racism. From this perspective, Ipperwash revealed a deep schism in Canada's relationship with its Aboriginal People and was symbolic of a sad history of government policies that harmed their long-term interests. (Linden, 2007)

Commissioner Linden's findings include the assertion that Ontario Premier Mike Harris made the racist comment: "I want the f---ing Indians out of the park," and found that racism among some members of the Ontario Provincial Police contributed to the lack of a timely, peaceful resolution to the Ipperwash dispute (Linden, 2007). The incident at Ipperwash is layered upon years of **historical disadvantage** represented in treaty violations, colonialism, residential schools, and apprehension and adoption of Aboriginal children into non-Aboriginal families.

It is important to note that Aboriginal communities identify the concepts of racial profiling and racism rooted in a different dynamic from that of racialized communities, as they have a unique and historical reality that is different from ethnic minorities in Canada (Ontario Human Rights Commission, 2003).

Racial profiling in Canada is highlighted in these specific incidents and in research:

- Musician K'Naan, in an interview with Craig Keilburger, discussed his youth in Toronto and the use of the Trespass to Property Act in a manner that was discriminatory to black Somali youth (K'Naan, 2010), a practice confirmed in a report by the Toronto Community Housing Corporation (Ontario Human Rights Commission, 2003).
- On October 14, 2007, Polish immigrant Robert Dziekanski died in the Vancouver International Airport after being repeatedly tasered by four RCMP officers. A video of the event revealed persons in the airport waiting area advising the RCMP officers that the agitated Dziekanski spoke no English. Without ever having had the benefit of assistance from someone who spoke his language, Dziekanski was repeatedly tasered by the RCMP. An inquiry into Dziekanski's death found that the RCMP were not justified in using a taser against him, that the RCMP officers misrepresented their actions to investigators, and that the Canadian Border Security Agency needed to make changes in arrival procedures for sponsored immigrants (Braidwood Commission, 2010).
- The freezing deaths of three Aboriginal men, Neil Stonechild, Rodney Naistus, and Lawrence Wegner, and the experience of Darrel Night in Saskatoon has created a great deal of controversy around the alleged police practice known as **starlight tours**, in which police pick up Aboriginal people and take them to some location far way, leaving them there to get home on their own (Comack, 2012).

Historical disadvantage: Disadvantage related to past historical discriminatory actions combined with current disadvantage to contribute to systemic discrimination.

Starlight tours: Alleged police practice of picking up Aboriginal people and taking them to some location far way and leaving them there to get home on their own.

- A report on the victims of serial killer Robert Pickton identified unintentional systemic bias as partly to blame, as "The women were poor, they were addicted, vulnerable, aboriginal. They did not receive equal treatment by police" (Oppal, 2012).
- Racialized communities have long alleged profiling by police through use of stop-and-search procedures, a phenomenon often referred to in popular culture as "driving while black (DWB)." Rawle Maynard was awarded $40 000 by the Human Rights Tribunal of Ontario after it was found he was racially profiled by a Toronto Police Service officer. Stop-and-search practices of Kingston, Ontario, police officers reveal racial profiling by officers, confirmed in a study conducted by Scot Wortley, a criminology professor at the University of Toronto. The study found that black people were four times more likely to be pulled over than whites, that Aboriginal people were 1.4 times more likely to be pulled over by police than whites, and that 40 percent of black males between the ages of 15 and 24 were stopped by police during the study year, compared to 11 percent of their white counterparts (Wortley & Marshall, 2005).

So what does racial profiling really mean? While the definition of racial profiling is usually given in a law enforcement context, it is important to note that this is not the only context in which the concept can be applied. The Ontario Human Rights Commission, as one example, defines racial profiling as "any action undertaken for reasons of safety, security or public protection that relies on stereotypes about race, colour, **ethnicity**, ancestry, religion, or place of origin rather than on reasonable suspicion, to single out an individual for greater scrutiny or different treatment" (Ontario Human Rights Commission, 2012). Profiling can occur in many contexts involving safety, security, and public protection issues. Consider these examples heard at the Inquiry into Racial Profiling in Ontario:

- A law enforcement official assumes someone is more likely to have committed a crime because he is black.
- A bar refuses to serve Aboriginal patrons because of an assumption that they will get drunk and rowdy.
- A criminal justice system official refuses bail to a Latin American person because of a belief that people from that part of the world are violent.

Ethnicity: A person's or his or her ancestors' country of origin; includes material and non-material aspects associated with a culture and social identity.

- During the SARS (severe acute respiratory syndrome) crisis of 2003, a landlord asks a Chinese student to move out because she believes that the tenant will expose her to SARS, even though the tenant has not been to any hospitals, facilities, or countries associated with a high risk of SARS. (Ontario Human Rights Commission, 2003)

Source: © Queen's Printer for Toronto, 2003. Reproduced with permission.

In a law enforcement context, racial profiling is often defined more specifically as something that occurs when an officer consciously or unconsciously uses race or racial stereotypes associated with criminality in suspect selection for investigation, police stop-and-search practices, Canadian Border Security Agency searches at ports of entry, police patrols of racialized communities, gathering criminal intelligence that link racialized groups with particular forms of criminality, suspect treatment upon arrest and detention, and so on (CBC News, 2005).

Does racial profiling by the police in Canada exist? Some scholars (Tanovich, 2006; Tator & Henry, 2006) suggest that the evidence is so overwhelming that we need to move on from the discussion about whether or not it exists. In 1988, the Ontario Race Relations and Policing Task Force concluded that visible minorities believed they were policed differently. One of the findings of Stephen Lewis's 1992 Report to the Premier on Racism in Ontario was that visible minorities, particularly black Canadians, experienced discrimination in policing and the criminal justice system (Ontario Human Rights Commission, 2012). Following this finding, the Ontario government established the Commission on Systemic Racism in the Ontario Criminal Justice System to study all aspects of the Ontario criminal justice system.

The Ontario Human Rights Commission recently released its report from the Racial Profiling Inquiry, which documents the existence of racial profiling in the public sectors, including police services across the province (including the OPP and the RCMP), all levels of the criminal justice system (e.g., crown counsels, justices of the peace, judges, prison guards and officials, and those involved in parole and probation), all levels of the education system (e.g., school board officials, school administrators, principals, teachers, guidance counsellors, and Ministry of Education officials), and the Canada Revenue Agency, as well as within the private sector (Ontario Human Rights Commission, 2012).

The landscape is evolving. It has taken leadership from Aboriginal communities, racialized communities, and policing agencies to make this evolution possible. It has taken government support like that in the form of the 2003 National Forum on

Policing in a Multicultural Society sponsored by the Multiculturalism Directorate of the Department of Canadian Heritage. Today, there are countless examples of police agencies across Canada that have adopted formal policies, frameworks, and best practices for hiring from and interfacing with Aboriginal and racialized communities. One such example is the Ontario Provincial Police's Framework for Police Preparedness for Aboriginal Critical Incidents. Through this framework, the OPP explicitly acknowledges its intention to work with Aboriginal relations teams and liaison officers. A great start that will require ongoing dialogue and participation with Aboriginal and racialized communities, public transparency, and vigilance in practice (Commission on Systemic Racism in the Ontario Criminal Justice System, 1995).

THE COLOUR OF POVERTY

One of the greatest illuminators of colourblindness as blindness to the consequence of colour is Canadian statistics on poverty. If race doesn't matter, then why do Aboriginal and **racialized persons** have a higher risk of living in poverty compared to non-racialized persons in Canada? According to Statistics Canada, 3 million Canadians, or 9.0% of the population, lived in low income in 2010 (Statistics Canada, 2012). One of the most vulnerable groups in Canada is Aboriginal children, with one in every four living in poverty (National Council of Welfare, 2012). Food security issues in communities like Iqaluit and Arctic Bay, Nunavut, exist due to the price of food and the cost of living in general (Food Banks Canada, 2012). It's hard for most people to imagine paying $12 for milk or $29 for cheese spread, but these costs are common in northern communities (Food Banks Canada, 2012).

Racialized communities also experience ongoing, disproportionate levels of poverty (22%) and are more likely to fall below the poverty line and experience problems like poor health, lower education, and fewer job opportunities than those from European backgrounds (National Council of Welfare, 2012). In two of Canada's largest cities, more than half of those living in poverty are from racialized groups: 58 percent of people living in poverty in Vancouver are from racialized groups, and 62 percent of people living in poverty in Toronto are from racialized groups (National Council of Welfare, 2012). The problem is most severe among new immigrants, the vast majority of whom belong to racialized groups (National Council of Welfare, 2012). The rates of poverty for Aboriginal children, new immigrant children, and children from racialized communities are cause for concern among Canadians. Figure 4.1 outlines the rates of child poverty for various groups.

The colour of poverty creates a relationship between income and reduced opportunities as a result of individual and systemic racism in Canada. Discrimination means that Aboriginal and racialized communities are less likely to get jobs when equally qualified, less likely to receive equal pay for equal work, less likely to have good working conditions, and less likely to have access to health care (Block & Galabuzi, 2011).

A POST-RACIAL SOCIETY

So how then, do we eliminate racism? How do we create the world that Bob Marley sings about—a world where the colour of someone's skin has no greater importance that the colour of his or her eyes? Morgan Freeman in his *60 Minutes* interview with Mike Wallace proposed a solution to the problem of racism: stop talking about it:

Wallace: Black History Month you find …
Freeman: Ridiculous.
Wallace: Why?
Freeman: You're going to relegate my history to a month.
Wallace: Come on …
Freeman: What do you do with yours? Which month is White History Month?
Wallace: (stutters) … I'm Jewish.
Freeman: Ok. Which month is Jewish History month?
Wallace: There isn't one.
Freeman: Oh. Why not? Do you want one?
Wallace: No. No. No.
Freeman: I don't either. I don't want a Black History Month. Black history is American history.
Wallace: How are we going to get rid of racism?
Freeman: Stop talking about it. I'm going to stop calling you a white man and I'm going to ask you to stop calling me a black man. I know you as Mike Wallace; you know me as Morgan Freeman. (Freeman, 2005).

Freeman raises a valid criticism of the need to relegate the history of one race to a designated month known as **Black History Month**.

> **Racialized persons or communities:** Persons or communities of persons, other than Aboriginal peoples, who are non-Caucasian in race or non-white in colour.
>
> **Black History Month:** Observed during the month of February in Canada, the United States, and the United Kingdom to commemorate the important people and events and history of the African diaspora.

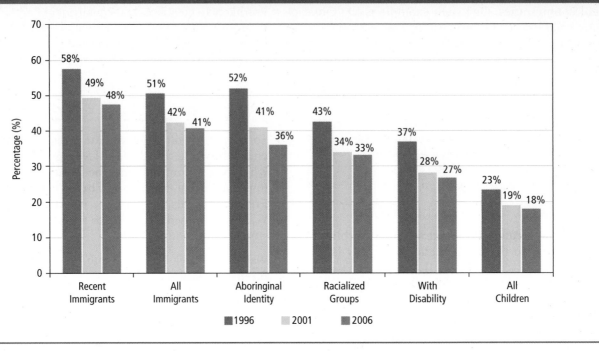

FIGURE 4.1

Child Poverty Rates for Selected Social Groups in Canada: Children 0–14 Years, 1996–2006

Percentage (%)

Recent Immigrants: 58% (1996), 49% (2001), 48% (2006)
All Immigrants: 51% (1996), 42% (2001), 41% (2006)
Aboriginal Identity: 52% (1996), 41% (2001), 36% (2006)
Racialized Groups: 43% (1996), 34% (2001), 33% (2006)
With Disability: 37% (1996), 28% (2001), 27% (2006)
All Children: 23% (1996), 19% (2001), 18% (2006)

■ 1996   ■ 2001   ■ 2006

Source: Campaign 2000, "2010 Report Card on Child and Family Poverty in Canada."

Asian Heritage Month: Observed annually in Canada (and the United States where it is called Asian-Pacific American Heritage Month) in May. The purpose of the month is to learn about and acknowledge the historical and contemporary contributions made by Canadians of Asian heritage.

National Aboriginal History Month: Observed annually in Canada during the month of June to recognize the past and present contributions of First Nations, Inuit, and Métis peoples to the birth and development of Canada.

Tokenism: The practice of including one or a small number of members of a minority group to create the appearance of representation, inclusion, and non-discrimination, without ever giving these members access to power.

As teachers rush to "celebrate" black history during the month of February, the abbreviated curriculum tells an incomplete story, focusing solely on slave narratives, civil rights, and the historical figures of Martin Luther King Jr., Rosa Parks, George Washington Carver, Frederick Douglass, Harriet Tubman, Eli Whitney, Malcolm X, and Nelson Mandela. Can we make the same argument in Canada as Freeman makes in the United States? Is black history Canadian history? The government of Canada acknowledges that our history books do not reflect the history of African Canadians:

> Despite a presence in Canada that dates back farther than Samuel de Champlain's first voyage down the St. Lawrence River, people of African descent are often absent from Canadian history books. There is little mention of the fact that slavery once existed in the territory that is now Canada, or that many of the Loyalists who came here after the American Revolution and settled in the Maritimes were Blacks. (Citizenship and Immigration Canada, 2009)

Is the solution the creation of a designated month? It can acknowledge the absence of the history of designated groups of people, but what happens when the month is over? Should teachers say to their students in March, "Well, it's back to white history again." Should they say the same to students when **Asian Heritage Month** concludes in May or when **National Aboriginal History Month** concludes in June? Some suggest that these observances are merely a kind of **tokenism** used to mask real issues of power, equity, inclusion, and justice. Perhaps the most important question is how do we instead ensure that the history we share and the narratives we tell every day include the experiences, events, and voices of all people as subjects—and not just the objects—of our interest? This is much harder to achieve, as it requires the dominant group in a society to move beyond token change to break the cycle of oppression and to eliminate **institutionalized racism**. So, ultimately, it is an issue of power. Making only token changes risks trivializing, racially stereotyping, or demeaning the histories of **racialized groups** as "other" and "less than."

ENDING THOUGHTS

Most anti-oppression and anti-racism frameworks include elements of structural analysis, institutional change, self-awareness, and constant vigilance. Is the strategy for creating a post-racial society as simple as Morgan Freeman suggests—a kind of racial transcendence that comes when we stop talking about race, and when we stop assigning meaning to the colour of skin? Perhaps someday.

How, then, do we address the structural inequity that creates social injustice and oppression? The vision of a society free of oppression is perhaps most articulately described in Dr. Martin Luther King Jr.'s "I Have a Dream" speech, given in 1963 at the Lincoln Memorial, as he inspired the crowd: "I have a dream that my four little children will one day live in a nation where they will not be judged by the color of their skin, but by the content of their character." As a civil rights activist, Dr. King spent his life fighting prejudice and discrimination. Rodney King's question—"Can't we all get along?"—highlights the dream of Dr. King and others that we can one day live in a society where equality and justice make getting along possible. Ironically, this goal becomes harder in a country like Canada that has been generally respected for its human rights record and has begun to acknowledge and redress some parts of its racist history. How do we as a nation begin to understand that this racist history is still echoed in modern policy and practice (Roy, 2012)? The conservative approach to racism has been colourblindness and the liberal approach has been a framework of diversity that invites racialized communities to participate and be included under the same banner of existing power structures. Neither approach is about equity.

When we no longer socially construct power differences among racialized groups, then Samuel will be free to live in a post-racial society and he will be judged by the content of his character and not the colour of his skin—where racism will no longer be a part of his everyday life.

> **Institutionalized racism:** Direct and intentional system of inequality based on race, which is built into societal institutions.
>
> **Racialization:** The way in which society makes the concept of race seem real; used to differentiate groups of people as unequal.

DON'T CALL ME THAT WORD

By Lawrence Hill

Growing up in the 1960s in the affluent, almost all-white Don Mills, Ont., I was told by my black father that education and professional achievement were the only viable options for black people in North America. He laid down three rules as if they had been received from the mouth of God: (1) I was to study like the dickens; (2) anything less than complete success in school or at work was to be regarded as failure; (3) if anybody called me "nigger," I was to beat the hell out of him.

This is the legacy of being black in Canada. You overcompensate for the fluke of your ancestry, and stand on guard against those who would knock you down. Over 400 years of black history here, we have had to overcome numerous challenges: the chains of slave vessels, the wrath of slave owners, the rules of segregation, the killing ways of police bullets, our own murderous infighting, and all the modern vicissitudes of polite Canadian oppression.

Blacks in Canada, like our metaphorical brothers and sisters all over the world, have a vivid collective memory. We know what our ancestors have been through, and we know what our children still face. Most of us cringe when we hear the word "nigger." No other word in the English language distills hatred so effectively, and evokes such a long and bloody history. These days, more people than ever are talking about the word "nigger," as a result of the publication this year of the book *Nigger: The Strange Career of a Troublesome Word*, by Randall Kennedy, a black American law professor at Harvard University. It's a fascinating read, but it raises a troublesome argument that I ultimately reject; Kennedy praises "African American innovators" (by which he means comedians and hip hop stylists) for "taming, civilizing, and transmuting 'the filthiest, dirtiest, nastiest word in the English language.'" Some misguided white people have bought into this same way of thinking. We have hit the pinnacle of absurdity when white teenagers sling their arms around black friends and ask, "Whassup my nigger?" And some white people seem to want a piece of that word, and feel the need to apply it to their own difficult experiences. The Irish have been referred to as "the niggers of Europe." In the 1970s, Québécois writer Pierre Vallieres titled one of his books *White Niggers of America*. And just the other night, when I visited a drop-in centre catering mostly to black junior high and high school students in Toronto's Kensington Market area, a white teenager decked out in baggy pants and parroting what he imagined to be blackspeak complained that some kids accused him of being a "wigger"—an insulting term for whites who are trying to act black. Whatever that means. As Randall Kennedy rightly asserts, the word abounds in contemporary black urban culture. True, when it crops up in hip-hop lyrics, it's not intended to carry the hate of the racist. It signals an in-group, brotherly, friendly trash talk. This is well known in American culture but it has penetrated black Canadian culture, too.

Choclair, a leading black Canadian hip hop artist, uses the word "nigga"—a derivation of "nigger"—frequently in his lyrics. Some people might say that the N-word is making a comeback. That the old-style, racist use of the word has faded into history and that it's now kosher to use the word in ordinary conversation. This argument fails on two counts. First, racists and racism haven't disappeared from the Canadian landscape. The comeback argument also fails because it suggests that reappropriating the word reflects a new linguistic trend. This is naive. As a way of playing with the English language's most hateful word, black people—mostly young black males—have called themselves "nigger" for generations. The difference now is that these same young blacks have broadcast the word, via music and TV, to the whole world. In the middle-class black cultures I've encountered in Canada and the United States, such a young man usually gets slapped or tongue-lashed by his mother, at just about that point, and he learns that the only time it's safe to use that word is when he's chilling on the street with his buddies. Black people use the word "nigger" precisely because it hurts so much that we need to dance with our own pain, in the same way that blues music dives straight into bad luck and heartbreak. This is very much part of the black North American experience: we don't run from our pain, we roll it into our art.

But does that take the sting out of the word? No. And what's the proof of that? We don't use the word around our mothers, our teachers, the people we fall in love with, or our children. "Nigger" is a word that young black men use on each other. But the word still pains most black Canadians. Let me share an image of just how much the word hurts. A friend of mine—a black woman, community activist and graduate student—was dying to read Kennedy's book. She bought it last week, but couldn't bring herself to start devouring it on the subway to work until she had ripped off the cover: she wouldn't allow herself to be seen on the subway with the word "nigger" splashed on the cover of a book, so close to her face.

Source: Adapted from *Black Berry, Sweet Juice: On Being Black and White in Canada* © 2001 by Lawrence Hill. Published by HarperCollins Publishers Ltd. All Rights Reserved.

DISCUSSION QUESTIONS

1. We have seen recent attempts by black comedians like Dave Chappelle and Chris Rock and hip hop artists like rapper Nas try to reclaim the "n-word" and strip it of its power as hate speech. Do you agree with Lawrence's Hill perspective in this article that the "n-word" should never be used by anyone, ever?

2. We have seen many changes in racial terminology from the use of the word "Negro" in the 1970s to newer terms in popular language culture, like "African Canadian" and "black." The author of this article has also written a famous book in Canada titled *The Book of Negroes*. The Book of Negroes is a historical document, a book containing a list of slaves who moved from New York to Nova Scotia in 1783. The cover of this book was recently burned by a Dutch anti-slavery group who objected to the use of the term "Negro" in the title (they did not burn the content). The same book had to be published under a different title in the United States, where it is called *Somebody Knows My Name*. Do you think racial terms should be used if they are historically accurate or direct quotations? Why or why not?

3. It is sometimes argued that members of an identified group have the right to use language that non-members do not have. For example, members of Queer Nation and other LGBT communities have reclaimed the word "queer" and turned it from a term used to oppress, to a term used to empower. It is argued that black urban youth culture has done the same with the "n-word." Is the political correctness of identity terms based on membership in that group?

Let's use the KWIP process to develop our awareness about the way in which our racialized identities are part of a hierarchical system of power and privilege based on our "blackness" or "whiteness" or "brownness" and consider how we might work toward a post-racial society.

KNOW IT AND OWN IT:
WHAT DO I BRING TO THIS?

As Tim Wise (2006) suggests, the beginning of honest dialogue is the acknowledgement of the way things actually are, rather than the way we would like them to be. So where does your race land you in the hierarchy of power and privilege in our society? Does the social construction of race mean you are marginalized and discriminated against? Or does your race afford you certain privileges and power that you may not even be fully conscious of?

WALKING THE TALK:
HOW CAN I LEARN FROM THIS?

An honest dialogue begins with the acknowledgement that racism exists in Canada. Historical events prove that racism is not something new. The Indian Act and residential schools, Africville, the internment of Japanese Canadians, and the Chinese head tax provide evidence of systemic racism in Canada. So how do we know that racism still exists today? It requires an openness to the lived experiences of people of colour in Canada today as a complex and dynamic narrative. It requires a reliance on scholarly research evidence. It requires a critical analysis of current events. When we stop the denial of racism as a hierarchical system of power and privilege present in individual, organizational, and systemic contexts, then we can begin a meaningful dialogue. In order to walk the talk, ask yourself, "How willing am I to listen and to learn from the experiences of others"? Can you imagine a post-racial society where the colour of a person's skin is no longer correlated with yearly earnings, employment status, social class, incarceration rates, graduation from high school, and matriculation in post-secondary education?

IT IS WHAT IT IS:
IS THIS INSIDE OR OUTSIDE YOUR COMFORT ZONE?

If your race positions you in the upper echelons of a society's hierarchy of power and privilege, you may land outside your comfort zone in this chapter. How open are you to hearing about claims of racism and listening to both narratives and scholarly evidence of racial inequality and injustices?

PUT IT IN PLAY:
HOW CAN I USE THIS?

So how do we one day construct the type of post-racial society that Bob Marley described where "the colour of a man's skin is of no more significance that the colour of his eyes"? We know the diversity-competent person begins by developing greater self-awareness. Take the Project Implicit test designed to examine unconscious attitudes and biases that can influence your perception and action at **https://implicit.harvard.edu/implicit/demo/takeatest.htm**.

CourseMate Study Tools

Located at www.nelson.com/site/walkamile1e

- Consolidate your knowledge with the **Flashcards**.
- Gauge your understanding with **Picture This** and accompanying questions for reflection.
- Develop your critical thinking skills by working through **The Daily**.
- Apply your understanding with **KWIP** interactive!
- Develop your critical reading skills through compelling **Readings** and accompanying short answer questions.

REFERENCES

Adelman, L. (Director). (2003). *Race: The power of an illusion* [Motion Picture]. United States: California Newsreel.

Allen, M., & Boyce, J. (2013, July 11). *Police-reported hate crime in Canada, 2011*. Retrieved from *Statistics Canada*: http://www.statcan.gc.ca/pub/85-002-x/2013001/article/11822-eng.pdf

American Anthropological Association. (2011). One race or several species. Retrieved from *Race: Are We So Different?*: http://www.understandingrace.org/history/science/one_race.html

Benjamin, R. (2009). *Searching for Whitopia: An improbable journey to the heart of white America*. Hyperion Books.

Block, S., & Galabuzi, G. (2011). Canada's colour coded labour market: The gap for racialized workers. Ottawa: Canadian Centre for Policy Alternatives.

Bonilla-Silva, E. (2012). *Race 2012*. PBS. Retrieved from http://video.pbs.org/video/2289501021/

Braidwood Commission on the Death of Robert Dziekanski. (2010, May). WHY? The Robert Dziekanski tragedy. British Columbia: Provincial Government of British Columbia.

Brean, J. (2013, February 27). Supreme Court upholds Canada's hate speech laws in case involving anti-gay crusader. Retrieved from *National Post*: http://news.nationalpost.com/2013/02/27/supreme-court-upholds-canadas-hate-speech-laws-in-case-involving-anti-gay-crusader/

Canadian Charter of Rights and Freedoms. (1982). Part I of the Constitution Act, 1982, RSC 1985, app. II, no. 44.

Canadian Race Relations Foundation. (2012, July 30). *CRRF facts about ... Facing hate in Canada*. Retrieved from http://www.crr.ca/divers-files/en/pub/faSh/ePubFaShFacHateCan.pdf

CBC Digital Archives. (1989). The Rushton–Suzuki debate. London, Ontario. Retrieved from http://www.cbc.ca/archives/categories/arts-entertainment/media/david-suzuki-scientist-activist-broadcaster-1/the-rushton-suzuki-debate.html

CBC News. (2005, May 26). In depth: Racial profiling. Retrieved from http://www.cbc.ca/news/background/racial_profiling/

CBC News. (2011, Jan 11). *Cross-burning brother gets 2 months in jail*. Retrieved from *CBC Canada*: http://www.cbc.ca/news/canada/nova-scotia/story/2011/01/11/ns-justin-rehberg-sentencing.html

CBC News. (2012, November 9). Racist bathroom graffiti angers students. Ottawa, Ontario. Retrieved from http://www.cbc.ca/news/canada/ottawa/story/2012/11/08/ottawa-racist-bathroom-graffiti-shock-university-ottawa-students.html

Citizenship and Immigration Canada. (2009, August 31). About black history. Retrieved from *Government of Canada*: http://www.cic.gc.ca/english/multiculturalism/black/background.asp

Comack, E. (2012). *Racialized policing: Aboriginal people's encounters with the police*. Winnipeg: Fernwood Publishing.

Commission on Systemic Racism in the Ontario Criminal Justice System. (1995). *Report of the Commission on Systemic Racism in the Ontario Criminal Justice System*. Toronto: Queen's Printer for Ontario.

Cooper, A. (2006). *The untold story of Canadian slavery and the burning of old Montreal*. Toronto, Ontario, Canada: Harper Perennial.

Criminal Code, R.S.C. 1985, c. C-46, s. 318, s. 319. S. 718.2. Retrieved from *Department of Justice Canada*: http://laws.justice.gc.ca

Dunbar, G. (2012, July 30). London 2012: Swiss expel soccer player, Michel Morganella posted offensive tweet after losing to South Korea. Retrieved from *Thestar.com*.

Elliot & Elliott Eye (producer), & Golenbock, S. A. (Director). (2001). *The Angry Eye* [Motion Picture].

Fleras, A., & Elliott, J. L. (1996). *Unequal relations: An introduction to race, ethnic and Aboriginal dynamics in Canada*. Scarborough: Prentice Hall Canada.

Food Banks Canada. (2012). Hungercount 2012: A comprehensive report on hunger and food bank use in Canada and recommendations for change. Toronto: Food Banks Canada.

Freeman, M. (2005, December 15). *60 Minutes*. (M. Wallace, Interviewer).

Globe and Mail. (2010, November 04). Not a racist, KKK costume a mistake, says former cop who wore blackface. Campbellford, Ontario. Retrieved from http://www.theglobeandmail.com/news/national/not-a-racist-kkk-costume-a-mistake-says-former-cop-who-wore-blackface/article1241264/

Grewal, S. (2013, May 30). Brampton suffers identity crisis as newcomers swell city's population. Retrieved from *The Star*: http://www.thestar.com/news/gta/2013/05/24/brampton_suffers_identity_crisis_as_newcomers_swell_citys_population.html

Griffin, J. H. (1961). *Black like me*. Houghton Mifflin.

Hill, L. (2001). *Black berry, sweet juice: On being black and white in Canada*. Toronto: Harper Flamingo Canada.

Hinkson, K. (2013, May 20). High school students put spotlight on shadeism. *Toronto Star*, p. GT1 & 4.

International Olympic Committee. (2011). Olympic charter. Switzerland: International Olympic Committee.

K'Naan. (2010, October 11). Shameless idealists. (C. Keilburger, Interviewer).

Linden, S. B. (May 31, 2007). Commissioner's statement. Forest: Ontario Ministry of the Attorney General Ipperwash Inquiry. Retrieved from http://www.attorneygeneral.jus.gov.on.ca/inquiries/ipperwash/index.html

McIntosh, P. (1989, July/August). White privilege: Unpacking the invisible knapsack. *Peace and Freedom*, pp. 9–10.

The Nation. (2012, October 12). *The hunted and the hated: An inside look at the NYPD's stop-and-frisk policy.* Retrieved October 20, 2013 from http://www.youtube.com/watch?v=7rWtDMPaRD8

National Council of Welfare. (2012). Poverty profile: A snapshot of racialized poverty in Canada. Ottawa: Government of Canada.

Ontario Human Rights Commission. (2003). Inquiry report: Paying the price: The human cost of racial profiling. Toronto: Ontario Human Rights Commission.

Ontario Human Rights Commission. (2012). What is racial profiling? Retrieved from *Ontario Human Rights Commission*: http://www.ohrc.on.ca/en/paying-price-human-cost-racial-profiling/what-racial-profiling

Oppal, T. H. (2012, November 19). Forsaken: Missing Women Commission of Inquiry. British Columbia: The Missing Women Commission of Inquiry.

PBS. (2005, February). Race: The Power of Illusion: Interview with Robin D.G. Kelley. Retrieved from http://www.pbs.org/race/000_About/002_04-background-02-05.htm

R. v. Andrews, [1990] 3 S.C.R. 870

R. v. Keegstra, [1996] 1 S.C.R. 458

R. v. Zundel, [1992] 2 S.C.R. 731

Roy, J. (2012). Acknowledging racism. Retrieved from *Canadian Race Relations Foundation*: http://www.crr.ca

Statistics Canada. (2012, June 18). The Daily. Income of Canadians 2010. Retrieved from http://www.statcan.gc.ca/daily-quotidien/120618/dq120618b-eng.htm

Tanovich, D. M. (2006). *The colour of justice: Policing race in Canada*. Toronto: Irwin Law.

Tator, C., & Henry, F. (2006). *Racial profiling in Canada: Challenging the myth of a few bad apples*. Toronto: University of Toronto Press.

Toronto Star. (2012, July 25). Greece expels Olympic athlete over racist tweets about immigrants. Toronto, Ontario: *Thestar.com*

United Nations. (2011, January 12). International Convention on the Elimination of All Forms of Racial Discrimination. Retrieved from *Canadian Heritage*: http://www.pch.gc.ca/pgm/pdp-hrp/docs/cerd/rpprts_17_18/index-eng.cfm

United Nations. (2012, March 21). International Day for the Elimination of Racial Discrimination March 21. Retrieved from *United Nations*: http://www.un.org/en/events/racialdiscriminationday/

Wade, L. (2012, October 12). Race themed events at colleges. Retrieved from *Sociological Images: Inspiring Sociological Imaginations Everywhere*: http://thesocietypages.org/socimages/2012/10/20/individual-racism-alive-and-well/

Walker, B. (2008). *The history of immigration and racism in Canada*. Toronto: Canadian Scholars' Press.

Watson, B. (2011, October). Black like me: Fifty years later. *Smithsonian Magazine, Arts and Culture*. Retrieved from http://www.smithsonianmag.com/arts-culture/Black-Like-Me-50-Years-Later.html

Wise, T. (2006). *Beyond diversity: The hidden curriculum of privilege*. Retrieved from *YouTube*: http://www.youtube.com/watch?v=D30GOWsnVuA&list=PL64A999D2C184E259

Wise, T. (2010a). *Colorblind: The rise of post-racial politics and the retreat from racial equity*. San Francisco: City Lights Open Media.

Wise, T. (2010b, June 18). Colourblind ambition. Retrieved from *Tim Wise*: http://www.timwise.org/2010/06/colorblind-ambition-the-rise-of-post-racial-politics-and-the-retreat-from-racial-equity/

Wise, T. (2011). *White like me: Reflections on race from a privileged son*. Berkeley: Soft Skull Press.

Wortley, S., & Marshall. L. (2005). Race and police stops in Kingston, Ontario: Results of a pilot project. Kingston: Kingston Police Services Board.

CHAPTER 5

Aboriginal Peoples

> *"It didn't turn out the way we planned
> Now I'm living in Broken Promise Land."*
>
> *(Elvis Costello, 2006)*

DIVERSITY COMPETENCIES

Diversity competencies are specifically learned behaviours that students can actively practise to promote equity and inclusion. By mastering this unit, students will gain the skills to become diversity-competent practitioners, including the ability to

- explain the significance of oral-based knowledge systems in relation to Western bodies of knowledge and understanding

- summarize the three treaty groups and compare the advantages and disadvantages for the colonizing agents and Aboriginal groups involved

- identify the overt and hidden acts of assimilation and oppression forced on Aboriginal peoples, and compare them in terms of increasing costs to the Aboriginal peoples' world view and ways of life

- distinguish between specific and comprehensive land claims, and discuss the implications of the differences between the two as they relate to present-day ideals of ownership, progress, and the land

- infer reasons for the substandard living conditions among Aboriginal peoples in comparison to non-Aboriginal Canadians

- assess the impact of proposed economic measures like the Northern Gateway Project on Indigenous people as a whole

Will you be celebrating June 21? Not only is it the summer solstice (the day with the most daylight), it's also National Aboriginal Day. Certain employees in the Northwest Territories will enjoy a paid holiday. Some Canadians will eat fry bread and moose stew while delighting in the summer solstice festivals and attending traditional drumming and dancing ceremonies. Most, however, will let the day pass unnoticed, unaware of its existence. How much do you know about Canada's first peoples? Scientists now have evidence that First Nations people lived in what is now Canada over 12 000 years ago and this knowledge is also reflected in many of their creation myths (Canada's First Peoples, 2007).

Without doubt, Canada is one of the most beautiful countries in the world, and we have our Aboriginal peoples to thank for initially respecting and nourishing this land. Though other interpretations exist, some believe that Canada is a word taken from the Cree language (Cardinal, 1977). Stemming from the Cree word *Ka-Kanata*, it translates literally to mean "that which is clean." The full Cree term to describe the country is *Ka-Kanata-Aski*—"the land that is clean" (Cardinal, 1977). The connection of the Aboriginal peoples to the land, often told through the tradition of oral storytelling, has kept the history of Canadian life very much alive within Aboriginal and non-Aboriginal populations. Over time, however, connections to the land have been crossed, lost, and misunderstood.

The history that accompanies the rustic imagery of the heritage of these initial settlers, however, is anything but peaceful. Rife with continual negotiations, misunderstandings, and confrontations, Aboriginal peoples (First Nations, Inuit, and Métis) in Canada have struggled to maintain any semblance of peace between their own communities and the larger Canadian society (AANDC, 2012c). This was evidenced long ago by the **Indian Act** (1876), not so long ago by the Royal Commission on Aboriginal Peoples (1996), and recently by the Idle No More Campaign (2012). Through these examples, this chapter will investigate the past, present, and future relationships between Aboriginal and non-Aboriginal people in Canada.

THE LANGUAGE

Using the Right Words

There are many terms that are related to **Indigenous** people, and the terminology associated with **Aboriginal peoples—First Nations**, **Inuit**, and **Métis**—can be fraught with confusion, anxiety, and misinformation. Using the right word in the right context is important in any conversation, but it becomes especially so when the chosen words belie a history where the terminology may not have been chosen by the very groups involved. Consider, for example, "status" and "non-status Indians," which are the legally defined terms under the Indian Act (First Nations Study Program, 2009). It is important to be mindful of correct terminology and to be respectful of appropriate representation; but what becomes of paramount importance is that we continue to have many conversations, in every conceivable form, and carry on discussing the relations that exist between and among Aboriginal peoples, the rest of society, and our collective Canada.

The Role of Storytelling in Aboriginal Communities

The importance of language cannot be understated for Aboriginal peoples. There are over 60 different Aboriginal languages, grouped into 12 distinct language families, currently spoken in Canada. According to the 2011 census, nearly 231 400 people reported speaking an Aboriginal language most often, or regularly at home (Statistics Canada, 2012). Language is a way for Aboriginal groups to talk among themselves, but it is also a way to communicate with the earth and share their history, through oral storytelling.

What stories did your parents read to you? What lessons did they teach you? For the children of First Nations, Métis, or Inuit descent, storytelling was likely a different experience altogether.

Indian Act: Assimilatory Canadian federal legislation, first passed in 1876, and subsequently amended, which details certain federal government obligations and regulates the management of reserve lands, money, and other resources previously negotiated with Canada's first peoples.

Indigenous: Term used to describe a variety of Aboriginal groups and, in very broad terms, refers to any group of people who are known to have initially settled in an area.

Aboriginal peoples: The original peoples of North America and their descendants, consisting of three groups of people—First Nations, Inuit, and Métis.

First Nations: A term used to refer to those Aboriginal people who are of neither Inuit or Métis descent; First Nations refers to the ethnicity, while a band may be a grouping of individuals within that ethnicity (e.g., Seneca or Oneida).

Inuit: The Aboriginal peoples who live in the far north or Arctic regions of Canada.

Métis: People with mixed Aboriginal and European ancestry.

Oral-based knowledge systems are prevalent among First Nations (Hanson, 2009a), and exist among all Aboriginal peoples. First Nations people focus on creation stories, which give them their identity, and which focus on their philosophy of life and the importance of values and traditional beliefs (Sinquin, 2009). These stories are often told as evening family entertainment, to pass along local or family knowledge. They might include titles such as *Raven Steals the Light* (Reid & Bringhurst, 1988) and *Path with No Moccasins* (Cheechoo, 1991).

The sacred stories of the Métis tell of their own customs and traditions, relating to the creation stories using mythical figures, flowers, trees, plants, and animals as characters. Increasingly, stories recounting details from the life and leadership of Louis Riel have become a part of the understanding of how the Métis define and record the events of their history (Lombard, 2009). Métis children might hear stories like *The Flower Beadwork People* (Racette, 1991) or *I Knew Two Métis Women* (Scofield, 1999).

From birth, Inuit children have listened to their parents tell stories and sing songs in the Inuktitut language, and then have gone on to share those same songs and lessons with their own children (Silou, 2009). Inuit stories teach children about their ancestors and how they lived, and often address larger themes, such as death and respect. Stories from the Inuit culture include *Qasiagssaq, The Great Liar* (Norman, 1990) and *The Sea Goddess Sedna* (Kennedy & Moss, 1997).

Though each group of Aboriginal people has their own set of cultural values and traditions, they share common beliefs that are passed on through oral traditions. Many of the creation and recreation stories that are told reflect the interdependent relationship between humans and all of nature—not just the land. Though their stories are filled with spirits, animals, and sea creatures (all or none of which may come of life), they are deeply based in spirituality.

Common in many Aboriginal cultures is the belief that the Great Spirit created the Earth and its inhabitants. Others, however, think that humans came from the sky (or Sky-Woman), and that all living things have spirits that must be respected and cherished (Directorate of Human Rights and Diversity, 2008).

This holistic view of human and natural life, where everything and everyone is interconnected, is exemplified by the "circle of life," as depicted by a **shaman**'s medicine wheel. The **medicine wheel** demonstrates how all life travels on a circular journey. The small, inner-circle part of the wheel represents Mother Earth and the Creator, and the wheel is divided into four sections. Four quadrants of the medicine wheel represent the four cardinal directions (north, south, east, and west); the four colours of humans (red, yellow, black, and white); the four faces of man (physical, mental, emotional, and spiritual); the four seasons (fall, winter, summer, and spring); the four sacred medicines (sweet grass, tobacco, sage, and cedar); and the four stages of life (child, teen, adult, elder). There are many variations of the medicine wheel, and evidence in Alberta of a large structure for the medicine wheel, built and arranged on the land, dates back 4500 years. The large medicine wheels that were built on the land were thought to be structures to commemorate the death place of, or the last tipi occupied by, a famous warrior (Royal Alberta Museum, 2005). Other uses are thought to have included astronomical rituals, healing, and teaching.

Similarly, **totem poles** are often used to document certain stories and histories that are familiar

Oral-based knowledge systems: Ways of knowing that provide an account of a group's origins, history, and spirituality, passed on through the tradition of oral storytelling.

Shaman: Aboriginal healer or spiritual counsellor.

Medicine wheel: Ceremonial tool of the Indigenous people of North America; symbolizes the interconnected, circular journey of all living things.

Totem pole: A pole or post usually carved from red cedar and painted with symbolic figures, erected by Indigenous people of the northwest coast of North America.

Among other things, the medicine wheel teaches the importance of balance in our lives—mentally, emotionally, spiritually, and physically. Would you visit practitioners who use the medicine wheel as part of their diagnosis, treatment, or learning plans? Why or why not?

to community members or particular family or clan members. Usually carved from red cedar and painted with symbolic figures, they were erected by Indigenous people of the northwest coast of North America (Applied History Research Group, 2001). For example, some Kwakwaka'wakw families of northern Vancouver Island belonging to the Thunderbird clan will feature a Thunderbird crest and familial legends on their poles. Other common crests among coastal First Nations include the wolf, eagle, grizzly bear, killer whale, frog, raven, and salmon (Malin, 1986). You can find them in various shapes and sizes at trading posts, on reserves, and in small tourist towns all over North America (Ramsey, 2011).

To the unaware, the designs on a totem pole may appear to be confusing; but on closer examination, you will see that they are very intricate and complex. Each object on the pole represents an animal, a human, or a mythological creature; the skill lies in identifying them. Every item on the pole also has meaning—the choice of colour, animal, and crest all mean something special to the family or community that is represented on the pole. Generally, totem poles serve one of four purposes:

1. Crest poles give the ancestry of particular family.
2. History poles record the history of a clan.
3. Legend poles illustrate folklore or real-life experiences.
4. Memorial poles commemorate a particular individual. (National Park Service, 2013)

Totem poles are courageous statements that speak of the identities and histories of the people who carved them. The "raising" of a totem pole is surrounded with much ceremony and gaiety. Author Hilary Stewart describes a Haida pole-raising ceremony on the coast of British Columbia:

> Different groups had (and still practice) varying traditions for the pole-raising ceremonies: a popular Haida one is for the carver to dance with his tools tied around his person. Among all groups, the owner of the pole (or a speaker representing him) explains in detail the stories and meaning behind all the carved figures, and those assembled to witness the event are expected to remember what they see and hear. A particularly fine pole calls for praise, criticism and comparison, enhancing the status of the owner and the reputation of the carver. Feasting and potlatching follow in celebration, as one more carved monument stands tall and splendid against the sky. (Stewart, 1993, p. 28)

Source: © Tammy Lucniow

Totems are a distinct and important piece of Aboriginal heritage. Can you identify any figures in this Haida totem? What markers or crests signify your family's lineage?

Tools like the medicine wheel and the totem pole, combined with ceremonies and rituals, contribute to a rich oral history that is part of the Aboriginal peoples' shared philosophy and way of understanding how life exists. It's critical to recognize that their system of knowing differs from other systems of knowledge within a Western framework, but it is no less valid or reliable.

This knowledge system is being recognized more frequently: it was legitimated by the Supreme Court of Canada, illustrated in the landmark case of *Delgamuukw v. British Columbia*. In this case, the Gitksan and Wet'suwet'en peoples argued that they had Aboriginal title to the lands in British Columbia that make up their traditional territories. To show that they had title to this land, they had to provide evidence that they had been living there for thousands of years, but they had no written documentation of this. To prove their title, Gitksan and Wet'suwet'en hereditary chiefs presented their oral histories—by telling stories, performing dances, giving speeches, and singing songs in court (Hanson, 2009a). Though the Gitskan and Wet'suwet'en nations had to appeal the first decision, eventually they won a precedent-setting victory for oral history to be given weight as legal evidence. Since then, a number of cases (*Squamish Indian Band v. Canada*; *R. v. Ironeagle*; FJA, 2013) have won the same right—for oral histories to be heard as legal evidence in a court of law—but there are often stipulations, and each case is heard individually.

The legal right to use oral tradition in a court of law today is but one battle won in a struggle that began long ago. Fighting to keep their land, traditions, and culture alive has been a decades-long battle for those who have overcome assimilationist policies and practices for generations in Canada and for those who continue to work to get back their rights and titles. As early as the 1700s, Canada's Aboriginal peoples have had to wrestle with increasingly oppressive agencies, who have tried very hard to change them. Though gradual at first, the quest to integrate Aboriginal communities into "civilized" society became an open political agenda when in 1887 Prime Minister John A. Macdonald declared, "The great aim of our legislation has been to do away with the tribal system and assimilate the Indian people in all respects with the other inhabitants of the Dominion as speedily as they are fit to change" (Montgomery, 1965, p. 25).

The challenge for the prime minister then was the same as it is for the prime minister now: Aboriginal peoples have every right to maintain their own identity, an identity forged with the lands of our nation. Will Canada remain a land that is, ironically, unsettled by those who initially settled it? For all of our multiculturalism, industry, and pride, our Canada is not at peace. Some say we are a peaceful nation, but we are not—not when it comes to Aboriginal rights. How in our separate but collective worlds did this happen?

TREATIES

When the Europeans came to the Americas, Aboriginal peoples had already inhabited the land and permitted the Europeans full access to it, in accordance with their own **world view**. The Aboriginal peoples' first contacts with Europeans were mainly through the participation and partnerships they had in the fisheries and in the fur trade (Henry & Tater, 2006); however, they believed that "The Creator placed Aboriginal people upon this land first for a reason, and that, as the first ones on the land, they were placed in a special relationship to it"

World view: The ways in which a group of people perceive and understand their place in the universe, often in relation to their interconnectedness with others.

Treaty: A formal agreement between two parties that has been negotiated, concluded, and ratified.

(Government of Manitoba, 2013). In keeping with this world view, they saw their relationship to the land in broad conceptual terms, in that they marked time by seasons rather than by the clock, for example. Consequently, this approach supported their world view that they were inherently and innately bound to the earth. The land and their identity—as a people—were intricately woven as one, and since they had inhabited this land before anyone else, they felt (and still do) as though they had certain rights and access to it (Government of Manitoba, 2013).

In line with the Aboriginal peoples' world view, they saw the Europeans as visitors and expected them to respect the obligations of that status. During the initial encounters between the Aboriginal peoples and the Europeans, however, cultural barriers led to many misunderstandings (Applied History Research Group, 2001). These misinterpretations often centred on land issues, since Europeans had a very traditional understanding of private ownership of land, based on capitalism, while Aboriginal peoples (mainly First Nations at this time) felt that no one could own the land. Confusion also existed because of language barriers. Although there were interpreters, it's important to remember that the Aboriginal peoples had (and continue to have) a different world view and their understanding of the protocols of trading was not in sync with the Europeans. They didn't think that they were selling the land; to them, the land didn't belong to anyone, so it could not be sold. The land was a gift from their Creator, and they were its Guardians, not its owners (Roberts, 2006). Although **treaties** existed among First Nations in oral form, long before the arrival of the Europeans, historians generally classify the First Nations treaties into three major groups: pre-Confederation treaties, the Numbered Treaties, and land claims.

The Royal Proclamation of 1763 and the Pre-Confederation Treaties

The Peace and Friendship Treaties occurred between 1725 and 1779 when the British and French were vying for control over land in North America. Each respective power formed allegiances with various First Nation bands to help them advance their own interests (AANDC, 2010d). One of the very first Peace and Friendship Treaties was reached in present-day Nova Scotia between the British and the Mi'kmaq First Nation band. In return for the Mi'kmaq's neutrality in any conflicts with the French, the British agreed to help with the advancement of trade in the area, and promised to prevent any European interference with traditional Mi'kmaq hunting, trapping, or fishing practices (Roberts, 2006).

After the Seven Years War in 1763, Britain's King George III enacted the **Royal Proclamation of 1763**, a powerful piece of legislation that remains in effect and is legally binding to this day. Often referred to as the "Magna Carta of Indian Rights," one of the main purposes of the Royal Proclamation was to pave the way for the treaty process that would enable only the Crown to purchase Aboriginal land—and then, if settlers and newcomers wanted, they could buy it from the Crown. Key here is that the Crown names Aboriginal peoples as original holders of the land and deeds title to them. The Royal Proclamation explicitly states that Aboriginal title to the land has existed and continues to exist, and that all land would be considered Aboriginal land until **ceded** (surrendered or forfeited; Applied History Research Group, 2001). Essentially, a **monopoly** (exclusive control) was granted over land sales in Canada to the Crown, since it could be the only legal purchaser of Aboriginal land.

The treaty process at this time, though legalized by the Royal Proclamation, was largely ceremonial for the First Nations; and though the treaty process may have differed from band to band, the negotiations followed the same basic pattern. It always consisted of three parties—the Crown (or its representative), the First Nation party, and the Creator as witness. Introductions would be followed by gift giving and time spent getting to know one another. As a signal of agreement and to formalize the meeting, a pipe would be smoked. Many First Nations' cultures considered this process as a way of building relationships with the European traders, settlers, and treaty commissioners; indeed, it was used to establish protocols between First Nation and non-First Nation parties (Treaty Relations Commission of Manitoba, 2013).

Other treaties negotiated during this time included the Upper Canada Treaties (1764–1862) and the Vancouver Island Treaties (1850–1854). Under these treaties, in exchange for benefits that might have included land reserves, annual payments or other types of payment, and certain hunting and fishing rights, First Nations peoples exchanged their interests in present-day Ontario and British Columbia (AANDC, 2010d). The British became enormously wealthy from this venture—in some of the earlier treaties in Ontario, for example, the Crown would purchase land for three pence (six cents) an acre from a First Nations band, and sell it for as much as 15 pence to a private investor (Roberts, Boyington, & Kazarian, 2008). Figure 5.1 presents a map representing some of the early treaties.

The Numbered Treaties

Since they were actually numbered 1 to 11, the treaties made between 1871 and 1921 are referred to as the Numbered Treaties. Covering Northern Ontario, Manitoba, Saskatchewan, Alberta, and parts of the Yukon, Northwest Territories, and British Columbia, these treaties were signed between the government of Canada and the First Nations peoples (AANDC, 2010d).

Although there has been much written about the good or bad intentions of the government and the early victimization of the First Nations, the reality is that both parties had their own reasons for entering the treaties and saw them as necessary elements in achieving their very different goals (Applied History Research Group, 2001). The government was looking to obtain land and resources so that it could build a railroad and create arable areas for settlers. The extension and expansion of Canada from shore to shore was another goal in the government's search for and use of the land's natural resources. For members of the First Nations, and later, the Métis, treaties promised reserve lands, hunting and fishing rights, money, annual payments, and help with medical care and education. As hunting and food supplies became scarce, more and more First Nations peoples became dependent on food rations from the government, trading with immigrants, and agriculture, rather than the traditional methods they were used to. Some treaties promised specific rights or privileges (Government of Manitoba, 2008). For example, among the exchange of land in the present-day prairies for cash, farm animals, and tools, Treaty 6 also guaranteed that a medicine chest would be kept in the home of the "Indian agent" (government official) for the use of the First Nation peoples (Roberts, 2006). This remains to be contentious, as it stands as the basis for free health care for all Aboriginal peoples, and serves to remind us that not all promises have been respected.

Since one of the main reasons for the treaty agreements was the building of the railroad, between 1881 and 1885, many Aboriginal people were uprooted from their traditional migratory lifestyle and moved onto settlements or reserves in exchange for land, farming supplies, and an annuity. Along with the building of the railroad came immigrants,

Royal Proclamation of 1763: One of the most important documents pertaining to Aboriginal land claims.

Cede: Surrender or forfeit possession of something, usually by treaty.

Monopoly: Situation where someone has exclusive control over goods or services, allowing them to set any price.

FIGURE 5.1
Map of Canada during Confederation

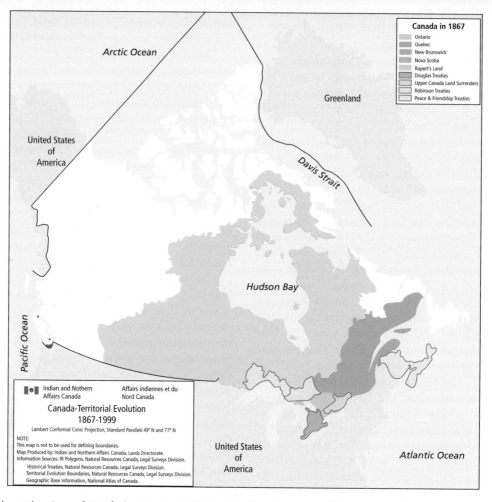

This is Canada at the time of Confederation in 1867. By the time Nova Scotia, New Brunswick, Ontario, and Quebec form the Dominion of Canada, the Robinson Treaties, the Upper Canada Land Surrenders, and the Peace and Friendship Treaties are already in place.

Source: Map of Canada during Confederation 1867, Aboriginal Affairs and Northern Development Canada, 2010. Reproduced with the permission of the Minister of Public Works and Government Services Canada, 2013.

including additional Europeans, and also a host of diseases that spread throughout the First Nations populations. Resigned to living in sheltered areas and often on infertile lands, many of the First Nations people found it difficult to survive in regions that were losing their natural wildlife to the "industrialization" of the incoming railway. In many cases, First Nations bands felt as though they had no choice but to agree to a treaty agreement—in order to survive (Government of Manitoba, 2008).

The whole treaty process was problematic for a number of reasons. Of particular note was the difference in communication and translation. It was not just a matter of mistranslations—the bargaining factions were not even on the same levels in terms of world view. There was also the questionable interpretation of the oral versus the written terms of the treaty. New research shows that recorded promises existed and were never written into treaty documents—documents that were signed by individuals who couldn't read. A final problem was in gathering the required signatures themselves. Many Aboriginal nations were left out of the treaty process simply because the government did not know that they were there (Roberts, Boyington, & Kazarian, 2008). Figure 5.2 illustrates how the map of Canada changes following the numbered treaties.

FIGURE 5.2
Map of Canada during Treaty 11

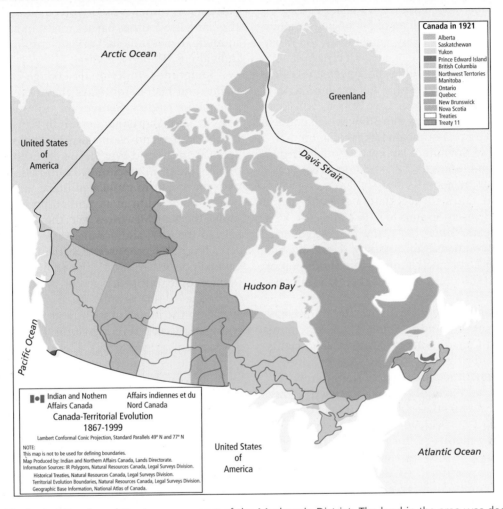

Treaty No. 11, the last Numbered Treaty, covers most of the Mackenzie District. The land in the area was deemed unsuitable for agriculture, so the federal government was reluctant to conclude treaties. Immediately following the discovery of oil at Fort Norman in 1920, however, the government moved to begin treaty negotiations.

Source: Map of Canada in 1921, Aboriginal Affairs and Northern Development Canada, 2010. Reproduced with the permission of the Minister of Public Works and Government Services Canada, 2013.

Even more difficult to comprehend was the idea that the treaties were going to be about something much bigger than the land. The question remains: When the Aboriginal peoples bargained in what they thought was good faith, did they realize that they bargained away the rights to their own identities, along with the land?

LAND CLAIMS

The issues surrounding Aboriginal title, treaty rights, and land claims remain debatable today, and many claims are still being resolved. Generally, there are two kinds of Aboriginal claims in Canada, commonly called land claims. **Comprehensive claims** are the modern day treaty-making process where Aboriginal land rights have not been dealt with by past treaties or through other legal means. They always involve matters related to the land, whereas **specific claims**

Comprehensive claims:
A modern-day "treaty-making process," where Aboriginal land rights have not been dealt with by past treaties or through other legal means.

Specific claim:
Process to deal with past grievances, mainly of First Nations; related to unfairly distributed treaty lands or mismanagement of First Nations funds by the Crown.

are not necessarily land-related (AANDC, 2010c). Specific land claims are usually negotiated through the provincial court system and deal with matters that are not tied directly to the land. For example, a specific claim might address the failure to provide the right amount of land that was promised in a historic treaty or it might address the mishandling of First Nation money by the Crown. Whereas treaty agreements (or other formal agreements) cannot be opened for renegotiation, fulfilling the terms surrounding the agreements often makes specific land claims possible. For example, a 2010 settlement involved the Bigstone Cree Nation. This First Nation band adhered to Treaty 8 in 1899, which entitled it to an area of land proportional to its population; however, the promised amount of land was not delivered at the time. The band received $259.4 million in both cash and land as a settlement.

The time it takes to negotiate a specific claim varies, but new legislation aims to have claims resolved within three years. Since 1974, the federal government has paid compensation totalling over $2.6 billion to settle 343 specific claims, while hundreds of other claims are still outstanding (Gobeil & Monpetit, 2011; AANDC, 2011).

Comprehensive claims deal with the unfinished business of treaty-making in Canada. These claims arise in areas of Canada where Aboriginal land rights have not been addressed by past treaties or through other legal means; they are used to define how traditional lands and resources can be used today. Unlike specific claims, these claims can take decades to negotiate, and on average, are settled within 15 years. Often they involve treaties from the 1800s and address hunting and fishing rights, resources, and Aboriginal self-government (AANDC, 2010c). In an October 2012 comprehensive claim that addressed self-government, John Duncan, the Minister of Aboriginal Affairs and Northern Development, signed an agreement with the Sioux Valley Dakota Nation, allowing them to have greater control over elections, membership, financial management, education, health, social development, child and family matters, culture, economic matters, lands, environment protection, transportation, and enforcement on Sioux Valley Dakota Nation lands. Since 1973, 24 comprehensive land claims and 2 stand-alone self-government agreements have been concluded and are being implemented. Of the 24 concluded claims, 18 included provisions related to self-government (AANDC, 2012b). Though the claims are lengthy in process, most are resolved without incident.

One of the problems arising when resolving land claims pertains to the number and kind of parties involved in the process. Often both federal and provincial governments are involved, and, depending on the claim itself, other parties might include regional or municipal governments, private corporations, or even individuals (Roberts, 2006).

Sometimes, individuals change the course of a claim (and history) in ways they never thought possible. Take Dudley George, for example. In 1995, he was the first Aboriginal person in Canada to be killed by police in a land-claims dispute that started decades ago. During World War II, the government attempted to buy land from the Stoney Point First Nation people, with the intent to build a military camp. The land in question was a burial ground and not up for sale; but under the **War Measures Act**, the government expropriated the land and compensated the people $15 an acre. They also promised that the land (referred to as Camp Ipperwash) would be returned to the Stoney Point people, but it never was. At the end of the war, the Stoney Point people asked to enter into negotiations for the return of their land, but the military was still using it as a training camp. In 1986, the federal government agreed to pay $2.4 million to the Stoney Point band as compensation for the use of the land over the years and agreed to return it, after an environmental assessment. Cleaning the land after decades of military use proved to be a costly venture for the Department of National Defence, so once again, the Stoney Point people were denied their land. It would continue as a training camp under tri-annual review and only when deemed unnecessary, returned to the First Nation band. In 1992, the Standing Committee on Aboriginal People recommended to the federal government that the land be returned. Again, the recommendation failed. On September 4, 1995, unarmed Stoney Point protestors moved onto the property known as Camp Ipperwash. About 30 people planned a peaceful demonstration to occupy the land, but Ontario Premier Mike Harris did not want them there, and he insisted that they be removed from the park. Two days later, under the cover of darkness, the Ontario Provincial Police (OPP) attempted to forcefully remove the protestors by way of a night-time raid. A single, unarmed, Ojibwa protestor was shot (and later died) by acting Sergeant Kenneth Deane. The protestor's name was Dudley George (Salomons, 2009; Roberts, Boyington, & Kazarian, 2008).

A formal inquiry into the Ipperwash crisis didn't start until 2003, eight years after the event, and it finished up in 2006. Key findings and evidence from

War Measures Act: 1914 statute that gives emergency powers to the federal government, which allows it to govern by orders when there's a real or perceived threat of war or invasion.

the inquiry included surveillance tapes and audio evidence, painting certain members of the OPP and Ontario government as racist. Former Attorney General Charles Harnick testified before the inquiry that Mike Harris had stated, "I want the f---ing Indians out of the park" only hours before Dudley George was shot, although Harris denies making that statement. The Inquiry concluded that the OPP and the provincial and federal governments all bore some responsibility in what transpired (Salomons, 2009). In June 2007, an Ontario Ministry of Aboriginal Affairs was established. In 2010, the Ontario government took the final legislative step in relinquishing control of Ipperwash Provincial Park and putting it back in Aboriginal hands. The actual transfer of the park is still years away, but provincial officials say that once the land becomes part of the reserve, the First Nation will have complete control over its use (Ogilvie, 2010).

The Ipperwash crisis was not the first time that the claims for land became violent. The Oka crisis took place in 1990. This confrontation resulted in an armed stand-off between the Mohawk community of Kanasetake, the Quebec police, and the Canadian army, in the village of Oka, Quebec. Plans to extend an existing privately owned golf course in Oka infringed on lands that the First Nations band had used as a burial ground. The Mohawks had previously filed both comprehensive and specific land claims stating that the extension of the golf course would include the ancestral burial ground and sacred grove, but both claims had been turned down (in 1975 and 1986) due to lack of evidence for specific legal requirements. Essentially, a plan to extend a nine-hole golf course to eighteen holes by acquiring and incorporating a municipally owned tract of land—which the Mohawks claimed they owned—became the catalyst for the heated battle. Mohawks erected barricades around the contested area and ignored two court injunctions to remove them.

On July 11, 1990, Mayor Ouellette requested that the Quebec Provincial Police tear down the barricades—which they did, using tear gas and flash bang grenades. Soon enough, an exchange of gunfire erupted and Corporal Marcel Lemay was shot and later died from his injuries. More fighting and bigger weaponry ensued. Finally, the confrontation ended without further bloodshed. Military troops tried to water-hose the Mohawks, but found they didn't have enough pressure. Then they threw water balloons at them, but the result was much the same. Ultimately, the Mohawk warriors dismantled their weapons and burned them in a ceremonial fire. For 78 days, Canada watched this national stand-off in disbelief, wondering how it could have happened.

Since the Oka crisis, there have been negotiations to address the historical grievances of the Mohawks

PICTURE THIS...

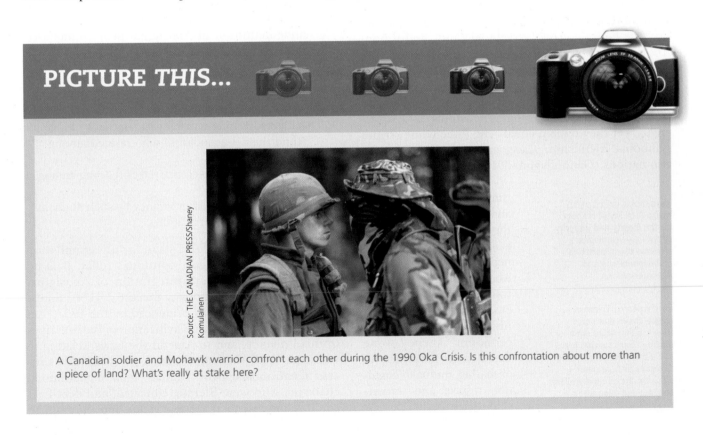

Source: THE CANADIAN PRESS/Shaney Komulainen

A Canadian soldier and Mohawk warrior confront each other during the 1990 Oka Crisis. Is this confrontation about more than a piece of land? What's really at stake here?

of Kanesatake and bring greater certainty in the Kanesatake/Oka area and the surrounding municipalities. These negotiations have led to fruition in many cases—for example, the construction of a Mohawk youth centre, elder home, and police station. On April 14, 2008, Canada accepted the claim of the Mohawk Council of Kanesatake under the Specific Claims Policy and formally offered to negotiate the claim, restating its willingness to move forward on resolving this historical grievance through negotiations (AANDC, 2010b; Miller, 1991; Canada History, 2012).

LEGISLATION

The Two-Row Wampum Belt

Aboriginal leaders craft the **two-row wampum belt** to mark an important agreement. The two-row wampum belt is a treaty of respect for the dignity and integrity of both parties involved, and it stresses the importance of independence and non-interference. The belt itself consists of two rows of purple **wampum** beads set on a background of white wampum beads. Wampum beads are white or purple shells that come from whelk (white ones) or quahog clams (purple ones). The beads have a multitude of meanings and uses in Aboriginal cultures, which include healing, jewellery, and decoration. In the case of negotiations with the Europeans, two stripes of purple beads signify the course of two vessels—a canoe and a non-Aboriginal ship travelling down the river of life together, side by side but never touching. This arrangement suggests that neither side will try to steer the other's vessel. Each boat is filled with people who follow their own laws, religion, customs, and sovereignty, yet they remain equal. The three white stripes symbolize friendship, peace, and respect between the two nations (Ganondagon, 2012).

Two-row wampum belt: A treaty of respect for the dignity and integrity of both parties involved; stresses the importance of independence and non-interference.

Wampum: White or purple shells that come from whelk (white ones) or quahog clams (purple ones); has a multitude of meanings and uses in Aboriginal cultures, including jewellery, healing, and decoration.

As negotiations continue between Aboriginal and non-Aboriginal parties, the two-row wampum belt is a symbol to express the needs and wants of the Aboriginal groups, who want a relationship that emphasizes their own Aboriginal sovereignty and economic agency—one that includes the principles of sharing, mutual recognition, respect, and partnership (Borrows, 2002).

Aboriginal Identity

With all of the treaty signing and legislation that has occurred, however, that is not exactly what happened. Somehow, the waters got muddied and in the obscurity, the issues of land and identity got caught up in the fray. Up until about 1850, virtually all of the dealings between Aboriginal and non-Aboriginal factions related specifically and overtly to land issues, though assimilation had always been a covert and ever-present objective. The question of identity as it related to the land became problematic as land poachers or "squatters" began settling in areas that were specifically designated for those Aboriginal groups who had rightfully gone through the treaty process. In an attempt to protect the rights of the legally assigned reserve land, colonial officials had to know who was fully entitled to it, and who was not. To this end, in 1850, two important acts were put in place that would attempt to determine who was of Aboriginal descent. Both of these acts—"An Act for the Better Protection of the Lands and Property of the Indians in Lower Canada" and "An Act for the Protection of the Indians in Upper Canada from Imposition and the Property Occupied or Enjoyed by Them from Trespass or Injury"—virtually gave all responsibility for leasing Aboriginal land and collecting rents to the Commission of Indian Land. They also represented the first attempts at defining who was "Indian" and which rights and responsibilities went with that status (Belanger, 2010). The first legislative definition of Aboriginal peoples included the following stipulations:

- all persons of "Indian" blood who were known to belong to a specific band, living on specific land, with their descendants
- all persons intermarried with any such "Indians" (and their descendants) who resided among them
- all children of mixed marriages residing among such "Indians"
- all persons adopted in infancy by such "Indians" (Frideres & Gadacz, 2008).

These stipulations set the stage for an assimilation process that, many argue, continues today. It is no myth that the complete integration of Aboriginal people into "civilized" society was the goal of colonial operators of the time, as evidenced by the 1857 "Act to Encourage the Gradual Civilization of Indian Tribes in this Province, and to Amend the Laws Relating to Indians." With this act, through the voluntary process of **enfranchisement**, "Indian" men of good moral character, who were literate, educated, and debt-free, could relinquish their reserve rights and the right to live with their families in exchange for the right to vote and all other rights afforded other British subjects.

Only one man applied for enfranchisement, however; and in 1869, the Enfranchisement Act was altered and named "An Act for the Gradual Enfranchisement of Indians, the Better Management of Indian Affairs, and To Extend the Provisions of the Act 31st Victoria." This new act developed the first system of Aboriginal self-government in the form of elective band councils, which remains in effect today. It also granted the Superintendent General of Indian Affairs virtually total control over the status of "Indians." For example, it forbade the sale of alcohol to Aboriginal people (for their own good) and stripped Aboriginal women (and subsequent children) of their cultural identity and legal status if they married non-Aboriginal men—a blatantly discriminatory process, based on gender (Makarenko, 2008). These two acts formed the foundation for the Indian Act of 1876.

The Indian Act

In the Constitution Act of 1867 (originally named the British North America Act), which created Confederation, the federal government was given responsibility for Aboriginal peoples and, as seen in the Enfranchisement Acts, lobbied heavily for the integration of all Aboriginal people into mainstream society (Roberts, 2006). In 1876, with the aim of merging all previous acts into one piece of legislation, the Government of Canada (now an independent nation) created the Indian Act (Makarenko, 2008). Essentially clumping all Aboriginal peoples into one group, not only did this act serve to disregard any distinct cultural differences between bands of Aboriginal people, it also made them wards of the government—effectively forming a **fiduciary** (or parent-like) relationship between them and the government. The problems with the Indian Act (besides the obvious moral and ethical ones) were logistical. As early as 1850, the colonial government began to keep records that identified individual Aboriginal people and the bands to which they belonged. They kept these records in the **Indian Register**, which helped agents of the Crown keep track of who was eligible for treaty and interest benefits and the treaties they were involved in. Working from these records and definitions set out in the previous acts, the Indian Act further defined First Nations people according to an assigned status:

- Status Indians: Those individuals who are registered under the Indian Act on the Indian Register. They are entitled to certain rights and benefits under the law.

- Non-Status Indians: Those individuals who consider themselves to be Aboriginal or First Nation, but are not recognized by Government of Canada as "Indians" under the Indian Act—either because they can't prove their status or because they've lost it. Non-Status Indians don't share the same rights and privileges as Status Indians.
- Treaty Indian: A Status Indian who belongs to a First Nation that signed a treaty with the Crown (AANDC, 2012a).

Assigning First Nations people into categories was discriminatory and exclusionary. In fact, the Indian Act did not recognize Aboriginal peoples as individuals at all: until 1951, the term "person," as defined by the Indian Act, meant "an individual other than an Indian, unless the context clearly requires another construction" (AANDC, 2010d). And, since the Indian Act only applied to Status Indians, it didn't recognize Inuit or Métis groups, resulting in the further marginalization of these cultures. The act itself and several amendments over the years only served to further oppress and discriminate against all Aboriginal peoples. Some of the discriminatory inclusions/amendments are as follows:

- Until 1960, Status Indians were not allowed to vote in Canadian elections, unless they gave up their status and the rights and privileges that went with it.
- In 1884, First Nations people were prohibited from buying arms and alcohol.
- In 1884, First Nations religious ceremonies were made illegal. The banning of **potlatches** and the sun dances clearly interfered with Aboriginal traditions.
- From 1914–1951, Aboriginal people were required to get official permission before appearing in public in traditional clothing.
- In 1920, attendance at Residential Schools for First Nations children was made mandatory.

Enfranchisement: The process whereby an individual gets the right to vote or become a citizen.

Fiduciary: A person who holds power or property in trust for another person—usually for the benefit of the other person.

Indian Register: Document that kept track of all of the existing records of people recognized by the federal government as members of an "Indian" band; started in the 1850s.

Potlatch: Organized meeting for special ceremonies, such as name-giving, birth, rites of passage, treaties, and weddings; practised mainly by First Nations of the west coast.

- In 1927, lawyers were forbidden from pursuing land claim violations on behalf of First Nations peoples without first seeking special permission from the Canadian government, effectively making legal changes to treaty violations impossible.
- In 1930, First Nations people were banned from pool halls.
- From 1951–1985, Indian status was removed from status women who married non-status men (Kunin, 2011).

Although many of the practices originally written into the Indian Act have been repealed or amended, one cannot go back and rewrite the effect that this legislation has had on the peoples' lives. Overtly racist and unapologetic, the Indian Act stands as proof of the government's aim to strip all Aboriginal people of what was rightfully theirs—the land, their identity, and any desire to maintain a formal but independent relationship with government agents.

Residential Schools

In its ongoing quest to assimilate Aboriginal peoples into mainstream society, the federal government decided that the best way to "civilize" Aboriginal peoples was to get them while they were untrained—that is, while they were children—and remove them from their family and communities. Youngsters were malleable, unlike adults, and they were more susceptible to learning the values, language, and identity of a new culture.

To this end, the government institutionalized an education system that tore young Aboriginal children away from their families and traditional cultures to attend newly created residential schools that were located far from their homes. Beginning in 1883–1884, in conjunction with the Anglican, Presbyterian, United, and Roman Catholic churches, schools were built in every province except New Brunswick, Prince Edward Island, and Newfoundland (Belanger, 2010). As wards of the state, the children and their parents were virtually powerless to stop the process of building a "civilized nation." Under the Indian Act, in 1920, it became mandatory for Aboriginal children to attend a residential school and illegal for them to attend any other educational institution. They had to attend until they were 18, but they could not obtain an education further than Grade 8, which was quite

Self-fulfilling prophecy: Situation where a belief in something that's false actually sparks a behaviour that makes the original false assumption come true.

manageable, since they barely received any academic instruction at all. Religious studies took most of the morning, and chores took much of the afternoon. The goal was to assimilate them into mainstream society, and to ensure that they didn't necessarily succeed. The few children who did show academic promise would never have survived in "civilized society," and so they were kept in residential schools to learn the skills that were "appropriate" for them. There was no sense in challenging the status quo of the time. Consequently, the boys were taught farm work, shoemaking, or other manual-skilled trades, and girls were taught sewing, bread-baking, and household tasks (Long & Dickason, 2000).

Financed by the government, but managed by the various churches, all the schools adhered to similar common guidelines:

- Children were forbidden to speak in their native language and were punished if caught doing so.
- All references to and aspects of their customary ways of life were eliminated from school curricula.
- Boys and girls were segregated—brothers and sisters especially so, in an effort to weaken family ties.
- Children were required to cut their hair, eat European food, and wear school uniforms.
- Christian holidays were celebrated and children learned European sports, like soccer and cricket.
- School days were divided between religious classes and training for manual labour. The children were taught practical skills rather than academic skills like reading or writing. (Roberts, 2006; Hanson, 2009b)

The devastating consequences from the residential schools are immeasurable, including the loss of language and the erosion of family values, traditions, and parenting skills. The most negative effects, however, resulted from the various abuses suffered by the children (Long & Dickason, 2000). The physical and sexual abuse—the beatings and whippings—meted out for punishment or pleasure, contributed to the real or perceived "dysfunction" of Aboriginal families and their communities today. By disintegrating any semblance of a family structure, the children grew up without proper socialization or parenting skills, without hopes and dreams to make something of their lives, and without the belief that they were people of worth or substance. The **self-fulfilling prophecy** that was pervasive throughout the residential school system bore fruit as children grew to become men and women destined for the lower rungs of Canadian society, as evidenced here by the voice of a former student: "[T]he residential school system (not just the one that I went to—they were the common form of Indian education all across Canada) was the perfect system for instilling a strong sense of inferiority" (Manuel & Posluns, 1974, p. 67).

The 60s Scoop

The last residential school closed in 1996, but the government started phasing them out in the late 1950s and early 1960s, and continued this process into the 1980s. The government belief at the time was that the children would be better off in the Child Welfare System and integrated into the public school system where they'd receive a better education (First Nations Study Program, 2009). To this end, in what has become known as the "60s Scoop," thousands of children were literally scooped from their homes, often without the knowledge or consent of their families and bands, and put up for adoption. Statistics from the then-named Department of Indian Affairs reveal a total of 11 132 Status Indian children adopted between the years of 1960 and 1990, but it's believed that the actual number is much higher. Seventy percent of these children went to non-Aboriginal homes, and today many of those children are looking for their birth parents (Sinclair, 2011).

In 2008, Prime Minister Stephen Harper issued a formal apology to the former students of residential schools, admitting that the assimilation policy at the time was a "sad chapter" in Canadian history: "The government now recognizes that the consequences of the Indian Residential Schools policy were profoundly negative and that this policy has had a lasting and damaging impact on Aboriginal culture, heritage and language" (AANDC, 2008). Denouncing the residential schools program as racist, in an emotional speech that day, NDP Leader Jack Layton said, "It is the moment where we as a Parliament and as a country assume the responsibility for one of the most shameful eras of our history ... it is the moment to finally say we are sorry and it is the moment where we start to begin a shared future on equal footing through mutual respect and truth" (Canadian Press, 2008). Did two of Canada's most powerful leaders say the same thing that day? Did their words matter? Does an apology for the residential schools exonerate all that has been done to the Aboriginal peoples as a whole?

Aboriginal comedian Ryan MacMahon remembers the time he spent with his grandmother, when she told him of the abuses she suffered in the residential school system. She told him, too, that there were good things—like learning to bead, and three square meals a day. She died before she heard Stephen Harper's apology, and five years later, MacMahon thinks Harper's apology has done little to change the reality facing Indigenous peoples in Canada. Reconciliation is not a reality. And he wonders why all the talk about Aboriginal matters centres around the notion of "moving forward": "As a father ... it is my job to break that cycle and free [my children] of the burden of the past and to teach them," he said. "On Remembrance Day [November 11] ... we say, 'lest we forget.' But in Canada [when discussing residential schools], we are always saying, can't we just all move on? Can't we just forget it already, can't you let it go? But, if we are never supposed to forget those other traumas, why should we forget these ones. ... It is our responsibility to remind people that it is an ugly past and we have to be willing to put it on the line because of that past" (Barrera, 2013).

In an effort to ensure that the travesty of the residential schools is not forgotten, so that all Canadians can learn from the injustices done, the Canadian government formed the Truth and Reconciliation Commission (TRC) in 2008. This was part of the court-approved Residential Schools Settlement Agreement that was negotiated between legal counsel for former students, legal counsel for the churches, the government of Canada, the Assembly of First Nations, and other Aboriginal organizations (CBC News, 2010). With a suggested timeline of five years, and a budget of $60 million, the TRC will document the truth of survivors, families, communities, and anyone who has been personally affected by the residential school experience. It is an action-oriented response to the horrors of the residential schools. Will it make the whole issue disappear? No. It will, however, give Aboriginal peoples their own stake in providing their own solutions in the healing processes—the opportunity to ensure that these times are not forgotten and swept under the rug, but rather used as learning tools for the future, and healing times for those in need.

The White Paper

In 1969, Prime Minster Pierre Trudeau and then Minister of Indian Affairs Jean Chrétien set about to right the wrongs of the Indian Act, by way of dismantling it and doing away with the notion of status as it pertained to Aboriginal peoples. Essentially, their aim was equality for all Canadians, believing that it was the legal status of Aboriginal people that kept them from fully participating in Canadian society. With this new proposal, Aboriginal peoples would no longer have special status as defined by the Indian Act, treaties

IN THEIR SHOES

If a picture can say a thousand words, imagine the stories your shoes could tell! Try this student story on for size – have you walked in this student's shoes?

DEAR GENERAL PUBLIC:

I don't always go to Bingo, drink a lot of beer or come from some sort of violent family. I am sick and tired of the assumptions that people come up with as soon as I say that I'm a Native. You know, I can take a joke very well until people assume that I have a bad family who are all on Ontario Works because they're lazy. Ya, some people in my culture don't make the right decisions but that doesn't mean that everyone is like that. There are lots of white homeless people, so are all white people beggars?

My family is strong, supportive and educated. Just because I am Native doesn't mean that I huff gas or hunt for my dinner. And, just because I am Native doesn't mean that I agree with how they are in Caledonia. I love hearing everyone's opinions but everyone is so scared that I am going to be pro-Native, despite how stupid they are truly being. Also, stop looking so surprised when you find out that I'm in college right after you find out that I'm Native. Anyone can go to college!!! And, stop asking if I'm only into Native men. I don't have control over who I fall in love with. People!!! And, last, but not least: Don't say all these things to me and then use the same mouth and say Natives have it easy and complain too much. How do we have it easy when we get called "wagon burners" or "gas huffers"?

---

would be taken at face value, and the federal responsibility for Aboriginal peoples would be transferred to the provinces (Belanger, 2010).

Many Aboriginal people were incensed by the idea of scrapping much of what had been accomplished to date, but still making them assimilate into the status quo. Others agreed, but also saw it as passing the responsibilities of the federal government on to the provinces. Nullifying the Indian Act would, in essence, dissolve their Aboriginal or "Indian" identities as a whole. Aboriginal peoples wanted to be recognized as First Peoples—not as equal to every other Canadian. Though Trudeau believed the proposed changes would culminate in a more just society, the prevailing belief at the time was exactly the opposite. Harold Cardinal's biting satirical response to something that he equated to **cultural genocide** was to state boldly what he believed was the belief of Deputy Minister John A. MacDonald and Minister Jean Chrétien at the time: "The only good Indian is a non-Indian" (Cardinal, 1969, p. 1). The White Paper provoked wide and organized public outcry from various Aboriginal groups and was withdrawn in 1971.

Cultural genocide:
The deliberate destruction of the cultural heritage and traditions of a group of people or a nation.

Bill C-31

Also known as "A Bill to Amend the Indian Act," Bill C-31 was passed into law in 1985 largely in order to address the gender discrimination included in the Indian Act and to align the Indian Act with the Canadian Charter of Rights and Freedoms. The complex issues of identity that surround all Aboriginal peoples and the land were magnified in the case of Aboriginal women, whose identities are tied to the land and to their culture but who lost those connections along with their Indian status if they married outside their band. Bill C-31 ended this discrimination against Aboriginal women by allowing them to retain their status no matter whom they married. Bill C-31 also proposed other changes to the Indian Act that included the restoration of Indian status to those who had been forcibly deprived of their rights because of previous provisions—for example, if Aboriginal people earned university degrees, or became doctors or lawyers, other provisions meant that they had automatically lost their status. In addition, as a move toward self-government, Bill C-31 made changes in order to allow bands to control their own band membership (First Nations Study Program, 2009).

The Royal Commission on Aboriginal Peoples (RCAP)

The issue of self-government has always been controversial, but for many Aboriginal people, the right to govern themselves equals the right to self-determination (Roberts, 2006). With the ability to manage their own affairs, Aboriginal people would have greater autonomy and decrease their dependence on various government supports, with the goals of self-sufficiency and improved living conditions. To this end, in 1991, the government created the Royal Commission on Aboriginal Peoples to examine the relationships between Aboriginal peoples, the government, and the larger society as a whole. In 1996, the five-volume, 4000-page report was published, with some 440 recommendations, which included the following:

- restructuring the Indian Act
- self-determination through self-government
- the creation of an Aboriginal parliament
- dual citizenship as Aboriginal nationals and Canadians
- Aboriginal economic initiatives through the provision of more land
- the establishment of an Aboriginal national bank (Roberts, 2006)

Although negotiations on many of the recommendations are ongoing, over ten years after the report, how much progress has been made? According to Métis writer Chelsea Vowel, "In the 16 years since the RCAP was released, almost nothing has been accomplished" (Vowel, 2012). The Assembly of First Nations released a Report Card 10 years after the RCAP, pointing out the lack of progress in these areas:

- The Department of Indian Affairs (now AANDC) had yet to be abolished.
- There has been no commitment to train 10 000 Aboriginal professionals in health and social services over 10 years.
- There is no First Nations jurisdiction over housing, no independent administrative tribunal for lands and treaties, and no sustained investment in meeting basic needs in First Nation communities. (Auditor General of Canada, 2006; Vowel, 2012)

LESSONS

How do Aboriginal communities fare in Canada today? In an effort to debunk the myths surrounding Aboriginal peoples, a 2011 study from TD Economics reported that the personal income of Aboriginal people has grown 7.5% a year for the preceding decade, and has increased from $6.9 billion in 2001 to $14.2 billion in 2011 (TD Economics, 2011). Using labour market data from Statistics Canada, the report's authors suggest that there has been a shift toward occupations based in the natural resource sector (oil and gas mining) along with construction and development that accounts for the higher wages, often found in these areas. By 2016, they predict that the combined total income of Aboriginal households, business, and government sectors could reach $32 billion. Though the shift toward gas and oil mining foretells income increases, at what cost will this economic uplift come?

The costs to the land will be detrimental and irreversible, according to the manifesto of the grassroots movement Idle No More: "The taking of resources has left many lands and waters poisoned—the animals and plants are dying in many areas in Canada" (Idle No More, 2012). Started in December 2012 in response to Prime Minister Harper's proposal for a number of **omnibus bills**, the Idle No More movement focuses specifically on Bill-C45, which, in part, proposes changes to the Indian Act, the Navigation Protection Act (the former Navigable Waters Protection Act), and the Environmental Assessment Act.

A major target for the peaceful protestors is the proposed Enbridge Northern Gateway Pipeline project. Enbridge hopes to build twin underground pipelines that will carry tar sands oil from Bruderheim, Alberta, across the Rockies to the northern B.C. port of Kitimat. Giant tankers would transport crude oil to the Asian coast roughly every second day (Nature Canada, 2013). According to Enbridge, the pipelines' construction would only stand to improve Aboriginal peoples' living and community conditions. Promises include a construction workforce comprised of 15% regional Aboriginal people, a 10% share in a $5.5 billion project, a community trust established for Aboriginal and non-Aboriginal communities, and certain communities receiving access to existing Enbridge stewardship and habitat protection initiatives (i.e., the Neutral Footprint Program; Enbridge, 2013).

Many, though not all, Aboriginal communities—through whose land parts of the proposed pipeline will travel—don't buy into Enbridge's deal. They see the pipeline as a risky venture economically, socially, environmentally, and culturally, and perhaps for good reason. In June 2013, as public talks on the proposal came to a close, with the pipeline's future still uncertain, word spread that Enbridge was forced to temporarily shut down two pipelines because of

> **Omnibus bills:** Proposed laws or legislature that can cover a number of different subjects, but are packaged together in one bill.

Source: © Tammy Luciow

Developing gas and oil resources on Aboriginal lands can lead to environmental damage, poverty, and the loss of traditional lifestyles. However, what are the potential benefits (both Aboriginal and non-Aboriginal) from development?

a 750-barrel oil spill into a wetland area and small lake. At a site about 70 kilometres southeast of Fort McMurray, the spill occurred in a major part of the network that serves Alberta's oil sands (Rowland, 2013). Do the Idle No More protestors make sound arguments, or can you see the feasibility of the project from the side of the developers?

If the Idle No More campaign and other such protests brought media attention to the potential harms the Northern Gateway Pipeline project would cause, this media attention was insignificant in comparison to that of Chief Theresa Spence, whose hunger strike brought national attention to Canada's Aboriginal peoples—whether they wanted it or not. The Idle No More campaign and Chief Spence's intent to begin a hunger strike (with the mission to meet with Prime Minister Harper in order to discuss the dismal living conditions of Canada's Aboriginal people) both occurred on the **National Day of Action**. The two events were not part of a coordinated plan, but Spence's 43-day hunger strike raised media attention for both the substandard living conditions in the Attawapiskat First Nation community and for the Idle No More campaign, for which she became an icon (CBC News, 2013). Although Chief Spence's actions brought media attention once again to the crisis in Attawapiskat (it had been declared in a state of emergency in 2011), they brought forward as well the state of Aboriginal affairs in general.

According to a new study from the Canadian Centre for Policy Alternatives, Canada's Indigenous children fall behind other Canadian children in virtually every measure of well-being: family income, educational attainment, water quality, infant mortality, health, suicide, crowding, and homelessness. Arguing that children in poverty fall into three tiers, the authors of this study found that children who experience the lowest rate of 12% are *not* Indigenous, **racialized**, or immigrant. The second tier includes racialized children, with a poverty rate of 22%; first-generation immigrant children, whose poverty rate is 33%; and Métis, Inuit, and non-Status First Nations children, who suffer with a poverty rate of 27%. Most disturbing is the third tier, where fully half—50%—of Canada's Status First Nations children live below the poverty line—a number that grows to 62% in Manitoba and 64% in Saskatchewan (see Figure 5.3; Macdonald & Wilson, 2013).

Adult Aboriginal people—regardless of their band membership—don't fare much better than the children. Consider the following:

- With a First Nation suicide rate twice that of other Canadians (6–11times higher for Inuit), over a third of Aboriginal deaths are self-induced (CMHA, 2013).
- According to the 2006 census, which provides the latest Canadian statistics on the topic, the projected life expectancy for most Canadians in 2017 is 79 years for men and 83 years for women. The numbers are dramatically different for Aboriginal peoples in 2017—at 73–74 for men and 78–80 years for First Nation and Métis women. It is higher than the projected ages of 64 for Inuit men and 73 years for Inuit women.
- In 2006, the employment rate for Aboriginal people of core working age (25 to 54) was 65.8%; it was 81.6% for non-Aboriginal people.

National Day of Action: Day devoted to raising the awareness of serious issues facing Aboriginal people in Canada; first organized on June 29, 2007.

Racialized: Referring to people, other than Aboriginal peoples, who are non-Caucasian in race or non-white in colour, as defined by the Employment Equity Act.

FIGURE 5.3
From Bad to Worse—Child Poverty Rates in Canada

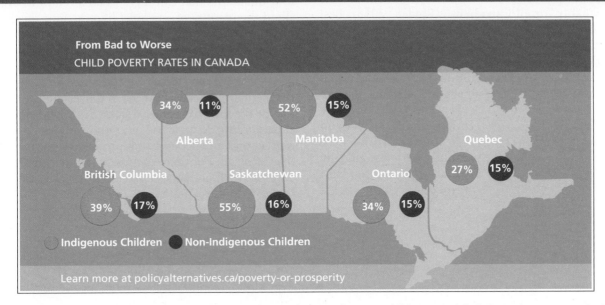

From Bad to Worse
CHILD POVERTY RATES IN CANADA

- 34% 11% Alberta
- 52% 15% Manitoba
- 27% 15% Quebec
- British Columbia
- 39% 17%
- 55% 16% Saskatchewan
- 34% 15% Ontario

◯ Indigenous Children ● Non-Indigenous Children

Learn more at policyalternatives.ca/poverty-or-prosperity

In some cases, child poverty rates between Indigenous and non-Indigenous children are tripled. Sometimes, money isn't the answer. Besides financial assistance, what would you do to address the poverty that Indigenous children suffer?

Source: © Canadian Centre for Policy Alternatives, report by David MacDonald & Daniel Wilson, 2013. Data from 2006 Census, StatsCan. This work is protected by copyright and the making of this copy was with the permission of Access Copyright. Any alteration of its content or further copying in any form whatsoever is strictly prohibited unless otherwise permitted by law.

- In 2006, fully 25% of non-Aboriginal adults had a university degree, compared to 9% of Métis, 7% of First Nations people, and 4% of Inuit.
- Aboriginal people represented 3.1% of all adults 18 years of age and older; however, in 2007/2008, Aboriginal adults accounted for 20% of adults admitted to remand (detention while awaiting trial or sentencing), 25% admitted to provincial/territorial sentenced custody, and 18% of all adults admitted to federal custody.
- The median total income of the Aboriginal population aged 25 to 54 in 2005 was just over $22 000, compared to over $33 000 for the non-Aboriginal population in the same age group.
- Nearly half (45%) of First Nations people living on a reserve in 2006 lived in homes that they identified as needing major repairs; 17% of First Nations people living off reserves indicated that their homes were in need of major repairs (Statistics Canada, 2010).

The substandard living conditions of Aboriginal peoples have existed and continue to exist in Canada, across all measurable indicators, indicative of the systemic discrimination that has kept them from achieving equality with the larger Canadian society.

Earlier queries in this chapter have asked you how this could have happened. Now, we ask you—when and how will this change?

In 1969, Harold Cardinal, a Cree leader, lawyer, and political activist, wrote:

> Canadians worry about their identity. Are they too English? Are they too American? Are they French Canadians or some other kind of hybrid? Indians worry about their identity too. For the most part they like to think of themselves as Canadians. But there are towns and cities in Canada, in every province of Canada, where an Indian dares not forget his identity as an Indian. There are towns and cities in Canada where a Canadian Indian simply does not go ... where simply being an Indian means getting a beating. (Cardinal, 1969, p. 18)

Can Harold Cardinal's words be, in part, an explanation for rifts that exist between Aboriginal and non-Aboriginal Canadians today? To what extent do you think Cardinal's words are still relevant? Is the link between the land and identity the weakest or the strongest link in the chain of forgiveness and acceptance? Only time will tell.

ENDING THOUGHTS

During the writing of this chapter, Canada lost a great Aboriginal leader and activist. Elijah Harper (1949–2013) was "a man who stood for unity, inclusiveness and equality for all Canadians" (Rigden, 2013). Best known for raising an **eagle feather**, which is a great honour among Aboriginal peoples and represents a mark of distinction, and putting a halt to the controversial Meech Lake Accord in 1987, Elijah Harper was a wise man. In Aboriginal belief systems, the law of nature calls for one order of life to depend on another—like two canoes perhaps guiding each other along, but respecting each other's places in the river. Taking the time to make a new history—separately but together—re-learning the reasons and rewriting the future.

Eagle feather: A great honour among Aboriginal peoples; represents a mark of distinction.

Language. Land. Legislation. Lessons. These are four quadrants that can serve as an attempt to understand the identity of a people, like the four quadrants in the medicine wheel. But to do that would be to impose our way of knowing on the traditional ways of knowing of Canada's first peoples, and that has already been done before—hasn't it? Perhaps the metaphor of the medicine wheel is best left to those who use it best. Maybe the time has come to share our world views, on equal footing, in an arena built on attitudes of mutual respect and a collective desire to learn—regardless of the physicality of the structures in which the lessons take place. Together, yet separate, we can make this happen, don't you agree?

READING

A Mother to a Teacher

Before you take charge of the classroom that contains my child, please ask yourself why you are going to teach Indian children. What are your expectations? What rewards do you anticipate? What ego-needs will our children have to meet?

Write down and examine all the information and opinions you possess about Indians. What are the stereotypes and untested assumptions that you bring with you into the classroom? How many negative attitudes towards Indians will you put before my child?

What values, class prejudices, and moral principles do you take for granted as universal? Please remember that "different from" is not the same as "worse than" or "better than," and the yardstick you use to measure your own life satisfactorily may not be appropriate for their lives.

The term "culturally deprived" was invented by well-meaning middle-class whites to describe something they could not understand.

Too many teachers, unfortunately, seem to see their role as rescuer. My child does not need to be rescued; he does not consider being an Indian a misfortune. He has a culture, probably older than yours; he has meaningful values and a rich and varied experiential background. However strange or incomprehensible it may seem to you, you have no right to do or say anything that implies to him that it is less than satisfactory.

Our children's experiences have been different from those of the "typical" white middle-class child for whom most school curricula seems to have been designed (I suspect that this "typical" child does not exist except in the minds of curriculum writers). Nonetheless, my child's experiences have been as intense and meaningful to him as any child's.

Like most Indian children his age, he is competent. He can dress himself, prepare a meal for himself, clean up afterwards, care for a younger child. He knows his Reserve, all of which is his home, like the back of his hand.

He is not accustomed to having to ask permission to do the ordinary things that are part of normal living. He is seldom forbidden to do anything; more usually the consequences of an action are explained to him and he is allowed to decide for himself whether or not to act. His entire existence since he has been old enough to see and hear has been an experiential learning situation, arranged to provide him with the opportunity to develop his skills and confidence in his own capacities. Didactic teaching will be an alien experience for him.

He is not self-conscious in the way many white children are. Nobody has ever told him his efforts towards independence are cute. He is a young human being energetically doing his job, which is to get on with the process of learning to function as an adult human being. He will respect you as a person, but he will expect you to do likewise to him.

He has been taught, by precept, that courtesy is an essential part of human conduct and rudeness is any action that makes another person feel stupid or foolish. Do not mistake his patient courtesy for indifference or passivity.

He does not speak Standard English, but he is no way "linguistically handicapped." If you will take the time and courtesy to listen and observe carefully, you will see that he and the other Indian children communicate very well, both among themselves and with other Indians. They speak "functional" English, very effectively augmented by their fluency in the silent language, the subtle, unspoken communication of facial expressions, gestures, body movements, and the use of personal space.

You will be well advised to remember that our children are skillful interpreters of the silent language. They will know your feelings and attitudes with unerring precision, no matter how carefully you arrange your smile or modulate your voice. They will learn in your classroom, because children learn involuntarily. What they learn will depend on you.

Will you help my child to learn to read or will you teach him that he has a reading problem? Will you help him develop his problem-solving skills; or will you teach him that school is where you try to guess what answer the teacher wants?

Will he learn that his sense of his own value and dignity is valid, or will he learn that he must forever be apologetic and "trying harder" because he isn't white? Can you help him acquire the intellectual skills he needs without at the same time imposing your values on top of those he already has?

Respect my child. He is a person. He has a right to be himself.

Yours very sincerely,
His Mother

Source: Anonymous, "A mother to a teacher: Respect My Child—He Has A Right To Be Himself," *Saskatchewan Indian Magazine*: Vol. 12 no.7, 1982.

DISCUSSION QUESTIONS

1. Imagine you are the teacher to whom this letter is directed. How would you respond to this student's mother? What are some effective teaching strategies that you might employ?
2. Given what you've read in this chapter, do you think that this mother's letter was justified in any way? Will she be helping or harming her child's chances in that teacher's class?
3. How easily does this letter transcend boundaries? Could it and does it apply to any child that is different from the norm? What's an example?

KWIP

One of the fundamental truths about diversity is that it involves as much learning about yourself as it does learning about others. Let's use the KWIP process to look at how our identities are shaped through social interaction.

KNOW IT AND OWN IT: WHAT DO I BRING TO THIS?

What is your level of awareness when it comes to Aboriginal peoples and the issues surrounding their living conditions in Canada? Perhaps you have little knowledge at all, or you may be very well versed in what's going on. If you hold a Status Indian card, does that mean that you are more deeply entrenched in your ancestors' history than another ethnic group? Knowing it, and owning here, takes on special meaning, as you claim what is rightfully yours to claim—bodies of history and knowledge—and admit what you don't know or understand, so that you can begin to learn or take on the task of teaching others.

WALKING THE TALK: HOW CAN I LEARN FROM THIS?

This step is all about being mindful of both the historical and present-day relations that exist between Aboriginal and non-Aboriginal people of Canada. If you're Aboriginal, you can choose to share inherent knowledge that comes from being an Aboriginal person; and if you're non-Aboriginal, you can be intentional in learning more about Canada's Aboriginal peoples. Read more about the struggles of the Aboriginal peoples, visit the Aboriginal centre on campus, or identify yourself in class if you're Aboriginal—but take the opportunity to learn and to teach others about the people who first settled the land we all share.

IT IS WHAT IT IS: IS THIS INSIDE OR OUTSIDE MY COMFORT ZONE?

The questions surrounding rightful ownership of the land in Canada and Aboriginal rights in general have stymied band leaders and politicians for centuries. It would be miraculous if you could think about these issues without feeling confused or uncomfortable. However, regardless of how awkward or difficult the discussion may be, as an individual who respects the principles of diversity and acceptance, it's your responsibility to continue to keep these talks out in the open, for all to see and participate in.

PUT IT IN PLAY: HOW CAN I USE THIS?

Many people have opinions about Aboriginal issues in Canada today, but often, they're not aware of the oppressive history that surrounds Indigenous peoples. Learning about the struggles over land rights, assimilationist policies, and residential schools is one active way to make informed decisions on current events. Participating in an activity and sharing that learning experience is another way to shed light on Aboriginal issues. Why not consider a class project, or participate with a group of your friends or family? Go to Project of Heart (**http://poh.jungle.ca/**) and create a masterpiece that honours those who suffered through the residential school system. It's a brilliant project, and all the steps are there. Won't you take the first one?

CourseMate
Study Tools

Located at www.nelson.com/site/walkamile1e

- Consolidate your knowledge with the **Flashcards**.
- Gauge your understanding with **Picture This** and accompanying questions for reflection.
- Develop your critical thinking skills by working through **The Daily.**
- Apply your understanding with **KWIP** interactive!
- Develop your critical reading skills through compelling **Readings** and accompanying short answer questions.

REFERENCES

AANDC. (2008). Statement of apology. Retrieved from *Aboriginal Affairs and Northern Development Canada*: http://www.aadnc-aandc.gc.ca/eng/1100100015644/1100100015649

AANDC. (2010a, September 15). Chapter 18—An act to amend and consolidate the laws respecting Indians. Retrieved from *Aboriginal Affairs and Northern Development Canada*: http://www.aadnc-aandc.gc.ca/eng/1100100010252/1100100010254

AANDC. (2010b, September 15). Fact sheet—Progress report—Kanesatake. Retrieved from *Aboriginal Affairs and Northern Development Canada*: http://www.aadnc-aandc.gc.ca/eng/1100100016305/1100100016306

AANDC. (2010c, September 15). Land claims. Retrieved from *Aboriginal Affairs and Northern Development Canada*: http://www.aadnc-aandc.gc.ca/eng/1100100030285/1100100030289

AANDC. (2010d, September 15). Treaties with Aboriginal people in Canada. Retrieved from *Aboriginal Affairs and Northern Development Canada*: http://www.aadnc-aandc.gc.ca/eng/1100100032291/1100100032292

AANDC. (2011, September 14). Fact sheet—Settlement agreement with Bigstone Cree Nation. Retrieved from *Aboriginal Affairs and Northern Development Canada*: http://www.aadnc-aandc.gc.ca/eng/1316020893971/1316021019328

AANDC. (2012a, October 1). Words first: An evolving terminology relating to Aboriginal peoples in Canada. Retrieved from *Aboriginal Affairs and Northern Development Canada*: http://www.aadnc-aandc.gc.ca/eng/1100100014642/1100100014643

AANDC. (2012b, October 5). Minister John Duncan congratulates Sioux Valley Dakota Nation on successful self-government agreements community vote. Retrieved from *Aboriginal Affairs and Northern Development*: http://www.aadnc-aandc.gc.ca/eng/1349475217859/1349475288013

AANDC. (2012c, December 5). Aboriginal peoples and communities. Retrieved from *Aboriginal Affairs and Northern Development Canada*: http://www.aadnc-aandc.gc.ca/eng/1100100013785/1304467449155

Anonymous. (1982). A mother to a teacher: Respect my child—he has a right to be himself. *Saskatchewan Indian*, Vol. 12, no. 7, 45–47.

Applied History Research Group. (2001). Canada's first nations. Retrieved from *University of Calgary*: http://www.ucalgary.ca/applied_history/tutor/firstnations/

Assembly of First Nations (2006, November 26). Aboriginal peoples, 10 years after the royal commission. Retrieved June 27, 2013, from *CBC News*: http://www.cbc.ca/news/background/aboriginals/pdf/afn_rcap.pdf

Auditor General of Canada. (2006, May). Management of programs for First Nations. Retrieved from *CBC News*: http://www.cbc.ca/news2/background/auditorgeneral/ag_report200605/20060505ce.pdf

Barrera, J. (2013, June 11). A grandson reflects on Harper's Indian residential school apology and the day his grandmother revealed her story. Retrieved from *APTN*: http://aptn.ca/pages/news/2013/06/11/24358/

Belanger, Y. (2010). *Ways of knowing*. Toronto: Nelson.

Borrows, J. (2002). *Recovering Canada: The resurgence of indigenous law*. Toronto: University of Toronto Press.

Canada History. (2012, January 1). Oka. Retrieved from *Canada History*: http://www.canadahistory.com/old/sections/Eras/pcsinpower/oka.htm

Canada's First Peoples (2007). The first peoples of Canada. Retrieved from *Canada's First Peoples*: http://firstpeoplesofcanada.com/fp_groups/fp_groups_origins.html

Canadian Press. (2008, June 11). PM cites 'sad chapter' in apology for residential schools. Retrieved from *CBC News*: http://www.cbc.ca/news/canada/story/2008/06/11/aboriginal-apology.html

Cardinal, H. (1969). *The unjust society: The tragedy of Canada's Indians*. Edmonton: M.G. Hurtig Publishers.

Cardinal, H. (1977). *The rebirth of Canada's Indians*. Edmonton: Hurtig Publishers.

CBC News. (2010, June 14). Federal commission FAQs: Truth and reconciliation commission. Retrieved from *CBC News*: http://www.cbc.ca/news/canada/story/2008/05/16/f-faqs-truth-reconciliation.html

CBC News. (2013, January 5). 9 questions about Idle No More. Retrieved from *CBC News*: http://www.cbc.ca/news/canada/story/2013/01/04/f-idlenomore-faq.html

Cheechoo, S. (1991). *Path with no moccasins*. West Bay.

CMHA. (2013). Suicide among Aboriginal people in Canada. Retrieved from *CMHA*: http://london.cmha.ca/mental_health/suicide-among-aboriginal-people-in-canada/#.UczgjJz3Nug

Costello, E. (2006). Broken promise land. *The river in reverse*.

Directorate of Human Rights and Diversity. (2008). Religions in Canada. Retrieved from *Government of Canada Publications*: http://publications.gc.ca/collections/collection_2011/dn-nd/D2-147-2008-eng.pdf

Enbridge. (2013). Benefits for Aboriginals. Retrieved from *Enbridge Northern Gateway Pipeline*: http://www.northerngateway.ca/aboriginal-engagement/benefits-for-aboriginals/

First Nations Study Program. (2009, January 1). Bill C-31. Retrieved from *University of British Columbia*: http://indigenousfoundations.arts.ubc.ca/home/government-policy/the-indian-act/bill-c-31.html

Federal Judicial Affairs. (2013, May 17). *Squamish Indian Band v. Canada*, [1996] 3 F.C. 0 Retrieved May 24, 2013, from *Office of the Commissioner for Federal Judicial Affairs Canada*: www.fja-cmf.gc.ca

Frideres, J., & Gadacz, R. (2008). *Aboriginal peoples in Canada*. Toronto: Pearson.

Ganondagon. (2012). The two row wampum. Retrieved from *Ganondagon: Preserving a past; providing a future*: http://www.ganondagan.org/wampum.html

Gobeil, M., & Monpetit, I. (2011, May 11). When the government fails to honour its commitments. Retrieved from *CBC News*: http://www.cbc.ca/news/canada/story/2011/05/30/f-mapping-future-specific-claims.html

Government of Manitoba. (2008, November 24). Numbered treaties. Retrieved from *Education and Literacy*: www.edu.gov.mb.ca/k12/cur/socstud/foundation_gr6/blms/6-1-4f.pdf

Government of Manitoba. (2013). The justice system and Aboriginal people. Retrieved from The *Aboriginal Justice Implementation Commission*: http://www.ajic.mb.ca/volumel/chapter5.html

Hanson, E. (2009a). Oral traditions. Retrieved from *University of British Columbia*: http://indigenousfoundations.arts.ubc.ca/home/culture/oral-traditions.html

Hanson, E. (2009b, January 1). The residential school. Retrieved from *University of British Columbia*: http://indigenousfoundations.arts.ubc.ca/home/government-policy/the-residential-school-system.html

Henry, F., & Tater, C. (2006). *The colour of democracy: Racism in Canadian society*. Toronto: Thomson Nelson.

Idle No More. (2012, January 24). Manifesto. Retrieved from *Idle No More*: http://idlenomore.ca/manifesto

Kennedy, M., & Moss, J. (1997). *Echoing silence: Essays on Arctic narrative*. Ottawa: University of Ottawa Press.

Kunin, J. (2011, May 24). Highlights of the Indian Act. Retrieved from *Educators for Peace and Justice*: http://epjweb.org/resources/lessons/social-sciences/some-highlights-of-the-indian-act/

Lombard, A. (2009, June 18). Our voices, our stories: First Nations, Métis and Inuit stories–Voices of Métis. Retrieved from *Library and Archives Canada*: http://www.collectionscanada.gc.ca/stories/020020-2000-e.html

Long, D., & Dickason, O. (2000). *Visions of the heart*. Toronto: Harcourt.

Macdonald, D., & Wilson, D. (2013, June 22). Poverty or prosperity: Indigenous children in Canada. Retrieved from *Canadian Centre for Policy Alternatives*: http://www.policyalternatives.ca/sites/default/files/uploads/publications/National%20Office/2013/06/Poverty_or_Prosperity_Indigenous_Children.pdf

Makarenko, J. (2008, June 2). The Indian Act: Historical overview. Retrieved from *Maple Leaf Web*: http://www.mapleleafweb.com/features/the-indian-act-historical-overview

Malin, E. (1986). *Totem poles of the Pacific north coast*. Portland: Timber Press.

Manuel, G., & Posluns, M. (1974). *The fourth world: An Indian reality*. Toronto: Collier Macmillan.

Miller, J. R. (1991). Great White Father knows best: Oka and the land claims process. *Native Studies*, 23–52.

Montgomery, M. (1965). The Six Nations and the MacDonald Franchise. *Ontario History*, 25.

National Park Service. (2013, May 15). Sitka National Historical Park. Retrieved from *National Park Service*: http://www.nps.gov/sitk/historyculture/totem-poles.htm

Nature Canada. (2013). Enbridge Northern Gateway Project. Retrieved from *Nature Canada*: http://naturecanada.ca/enbridge_northern_gateway.asp

Norman, H. (1990). *Northern tales: Traditional stories of Eskimo and Indian peoples*. New York: Pantheon.

Ogilvie, G. (2010, March 1). First Nations to reclaim Ipperwash. Retrieved from *The Toronto Star*: http://www.thestar.com/news/ontario/2010/03/01/first_nations_to_reclaim_ipperwash.html

Racette, S. (1991). *The flower beadwork people*. Regina: Gabriel Dumont Institute.

Ramsey, H. (2011, March 31). Totem poles: Myth and fact. Retrieved from *The Tyee*: http://thetyee.ca/Books/2011/03/31/TotemPoles/

Reid, B., & Bringhurst, R. (1988). *Raven steals the light*. Vancouver: Douglas and MacIntyre.

Rigden, M. (2013, May 21). The humble and powerful Elijah Harper will be missed. Retrieved from *APTN*: http://aptn.ca/pages/news/2013/05/21/the-humble-and-powerful-elijah-harper-will-be-missed/

Roberts, J. (2006). *First Nations, Inuit, and Métis peoples*. Toronto: Emond Montgomery Publications.

Roberts, J., Boyington, D., & Kazarian, S. (2008). *Diversity and First Nations in Canada*. Toronto: Emond Montgomery.

Rowland, R. (2013, June 24). First Nations don't have right to direct tankers, Northern Gateway lawyer says. Retrieved from *The Vancouver Sun*: http://www.vancouversun.com/news/metro/First+Nations+have+right+direct+tankers+Northern+Gateway/8571353/story.html

Royal Alberta Museum. (2005). What is a medicine wheel? Retrieved from *Royal Alberta Museum*: http://www.royalalbertamuseum.ca/human/archaeo/faq/medwhls.htm

Scofield, G. (1999). *I knew two Métis women*. Victoria, BC: Polestar Book Publishers.

Silou, S. (2009, June 18). Our voices, our stories: First Nations, Métis and Inuit stories–Inuit oral traditions: The social conscience of Inuit culture. Retrieved from *Library and Archives Canada*: http://www.collectionscanada.gc.ca/stories/020020-3000-e.html

Sinclair, R. (2011). The 60's scoop. Retrieved from *Origins Canada*: http://www.originscanada.org/the-stolen-generation/

Sinquin, A. (2009, June 18). Our voices, our stories: First Nations, Métis and Inuit stories–Voices of First Nations. Retrieved from *Library and Archives Canada*: http://www.collectionscanada.gc.ca/stories/020020-1000-e.html

Salomons, T. (2009, January 1). Ipperwash crisis. Retrieved from *University of British Columbia*: http://indigenousfoundations.arts.ubc.ca/home/community-politics/ipperwash-crisis.html

Statistics Canada. (2010, June 21). Aboriginal statistics at a glance. Retrieved from *Statistics Canada*: http://www.statcan.gc.ca/pub/89-645-x/89-645-x2010001-eng.htm

Statistics Canada. (2012). Census in brief: Aboriginal languages in Canada. Retrieved from *Statistics Canada*: http://www12.statcan.gc.ca/census-recensement/2011/as-sa/98-314-x/98-314-x2011003_3-eng.pdf

Stewart, H. (1993). *Looking at totem poles*. Vancouver: Douglas & McIntyre.

TD Economics. (2011, June 17). Estimating the size of the Aboriginal market. Retrieved from *Canadian Council for Aboriginal Business*: http://www.ccab.com/uploads/File/TD-Economics---Estimating-the-Size-of-the-Aboriginal-Market.pdf

Treaty Relations Commission of Manitoba. (2013). Treaties in Canada. Retrieved from *Treaty Relations Commission of Manitoba*: http://www.trcm.ca/about_treaties.php

Vowel, C. (2012, December 31). Chelsea Vowel: Assimilation is not the answer to the Aboriginal 'problem'. Retrieved from *The National Post*: http://fullcomment.nationalpost.com/2012/12/31/chelsea-vowel-assimilation-is-not-the-answer-to-the-aboriginal-problem/

Religion

> "You strut your rasta wear
> And your suicide poem
> And a cross from a faith that died
> Before Jesus came."
>
> *(Sarah McLachlan, 1997)*

DIVERSITY COMPETENCIES

Diversity competencies are specifically learned behaviours that students can actively practise to promote equity and inclusion. By mastering this unit, students will gain the skills to become diversity-competent practitioners, including the ability to

- demonstrate awareness of the changing religious demographics in Canada and the factors contributing to these changes

- demonstrate knowledge of the history of Canada's religious communities and minorities

- identify the main components of religious accommodation as dictated by provincial laws

- identify "fault lines" where religious accommodation laws and personal freedoms collide

Source: Dimitri Otis/Getty

At a very basic level, religion divides the world into believers and non-believers, the enlightened and the unenlightened, or—at the very least—those who "know" and those who don't. At the same time, it has historically been one of the strongest sources of social cohesion because of that very fact. Communities were united as much in their beliefs and traditions as they were by their exclusion of the "other." And unlike race and gender, religion is—at least to a degree—a matter of choice.

Many Canadians who are open to multiculturalism in theory, draw the line at what they feel is a bending of Canada's laws to accommodate religious minorities. Throw in international and domestic news of religiously fuelled terror plots and child abuse scandals and it is no wonder that religion in the public sphere has become a perennial lightning rod issue. Many Canadians wonder if a united Canada is possible with different groups clinging to their different religious beliefs, values, and practices. This is not a matter like ethnic food or dress—these are fundamental beliefs that periodically come into conflict with "fundamental Canadian values," whatever those are. In fact, when opponents of multiculturalism speak about its failures, the examples they cite tend to revolve around religious disputes—either in the workplace, in domestic situations, or on the legal stage.

Most Canadians have a vague notion that religious freedom is protected by our Constitution, but the details are sketchy. You will often hear people cite the concept of separation of church and state—assuming that Canada's stance is the same as that of the United States. But the history of religious freedom in Canada is different from that in the United States, and the ways in which we have sought to protect it, as well as our successes and failures, are also very different.

EMPTY CHURCHES AND OVERFLOWING TEMPLES

Before delving into issues of **religious accommodation**, or the reasonable duty that employers have to meet the needs of their employees' work and faith requirements, it is important to get an idea of where Canadians stand religiously speaking, according to the latest research. Although the numbers are changing on an almost daily basis because of an aging population and immigration, and although we will see shortly that Canada is entering what some scholars call a "post-Christian" era, where pluralism is more valued than religious **dogma** or fervent belief, the numbers tell an interesting story of our society. As of the 2006 census, the question on religious affiliation was not specifically addressed, so any numbers beyond the 2001 census are scientific and statistical projections. The latest actual data we have are from the 2001 Census.

The Roman Catholic church maintains primacy as the oldest and most adhered-to church in Canada, claiming 43% of the population. But this was not always the case. For more than 100 years, the Protestant churches of Canada far outnumbered the Catholic churches. Studies of immigration patterns made the reasons obvious; until the early 1960s, immigration pools came primarily from Protestant-majority countries.

Protestants remain the second-largest religious group in Canada. Together, Roman Catholics and Protestants represent roughly 70% of Canadians. This percentage may seem high; but it should be noted that in 1851, these two churches claimed 98% of the population. Even in 1951, this number was still 96% (Statistics Canada, 2001).

However, there is a group whose numbers fall below those self-identifying as Catholic but above those claiming Protestantism. One of the fastest-growing groups in Canada is made up of those marking "no religion" on census forms. While lapsed Christians account for much of this number, immigration also plays a role. Of the almost 2 million immigrants to arrive in Canada between 1991 and 2001, fully one-fifth claimed no religious affiliation. This was particularly true of immigrants arriving from China, Hong Kong, and Taiwan. Of those reporting no religious affiliation, younger Canadians are far more represented than older Canadians. For Canadians over the age of 65, 94% reported some degree of religious affiliation in 1991 versus 86% of those between the ages of 15 and 44. Further, those over 65 were more likely to be affiliated with Catholicism, Protestantism, or Judaism. Those between 15 and 44 were more likely to be affiliated with Eastern religions, such as Islam, Hinduism, Buddhism, and Sikhism (Statistics Canada, 2001).

The fastest-growing religious groups in Canada represent the latest immigration demographics.

Between 1991 and 2001, the population of Muslims in Canada doubled from approximately 250 000 to over 500 000. Muslims went from 1% to 2% of the Canadian population in only 10 years (Statistics Canada, 2003). According to Pew Research, the estimated number of Muslims in 2010 was close to 1 million, and projections for 2030 put that number at well over 2 million (Pew Research Center, 2011). Hindu, Sikh, and Buddhist populations also showed significant increases, due mostly to immigration patterns. Each of these groups rose by over 80% between 1991 and 2001, and each represents about 1% of the population. Future projections by Statistics Canada predict that in the near future, one of every six residents in the greater Toronto area will either be Muslim or Hindu, and that together these two groups in Toronto will make up 1 million people (Jedwap, 2005). While these numbers correspond to the increase of immigration from predominantly Muslim and Hindu countries (as well as Sikh and Buddhist countries to a slightly lesser degree), they also represent the age of the immigrants as well as birth rates among them. While the Anglican population is a predominantly aging one, for example, the median age of Muslims, Sikhs, and Hindus in 2001 was 28, 30, and 32 respectively (Statistics Canada, 2003).

Rounding out the major religious denominations in Canada are those who report adherence to one of the Orthodox Christian denominations. Greek, Ukrainian, Serbian, and Russian Orthodox Church members numbered about half a million in 2001, with the latter two denominations more than doubling between 1991 and 2001. Though historically the largest Orthodox groups, both Greek and Ukrainian churches reported a steady decline (Statistics Canada, 2003).

Finally, the number of adherents of the Jewish faith also increased slightly and now accounts for over 1.1% of the Canadian population. Half of these adherents live in Ontario.

Is Canada Post-Christian?

Churches have long been tied to Canadian heritage, and the loss of the central place of their structures has many people worried about the loss of Canadian heritage as a whole. The panic over the disappearance of a Christian Canada may be legitimate. But religious accommodation is not the culprit.

Over the last few decades, mainstream church attendance has declined so steadily that "For Sale" signs on church lawns have become a common sight. A report prepared for the Anglican diocese of British Columbia reiterated the dire findings of a previous study claiming that with current rates of decline, there would only be one Anglican left in Canada by 2061. While the study does not go into specifics of

PICTURE THIS...

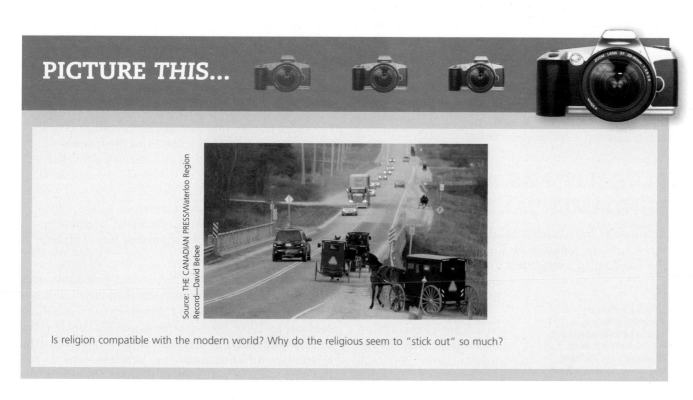

Source: THE CANADIAN PRESS/Waterloo Region Record—David Bebee

Is religion compatible with the modern world? Why do the religious seem to "stick out" so much?

replacement numbers either by birth or immigration, the results—even if taken with a large grain of salt—show that the once socially, morally, and even politically powerful Anglican church has suffered a substantial blow (Valpy, 2012).

In Montreal, the Très-Saint-Nom-de-Jésus Church—once bursting at the seams with over 1000 parishioners—is now barricaded with signs warning of safety hazards as the building's century-old structure crumbles. Its $2.5 million organ is having a hard time finding a new home, despite the church's willingness to give it away for free.

By 1985, the percentage of Canadians between ages 45 and 63 who attended church on a weekly basis had already dropped to 39%. By 2005, this number had plummeted further to only 22% of the population (Lindsay, 2008). The largest Protestant denomination in Canada—the United Church—averages one church closing per week (Peritz, 2010).

These realities and projections have led many observers to call Canada a "**post-Christian**" **society**, a Canada which sees traditional Christianity declining, where Canadians are more likely to call themselves "Christian" rather than ascribe themselves to specific denominations (Grossman, 2010). They are, further, more likely than ever to check the box marked "no religion" on census forms.

Compare these numbers to those of recent immigrants, and a different trend emerges. Canadians who have immigrated in the last 20 years tend to be at least as regular in religious attendance as they were in 1985. It is no wonder that the narrative spun is often one of encroaching foreign traditions taking over Canadian ones. The irony here is that religious accommodation and pluralism are actually a hallmark of that most-Canadian value of all—multiculturalism. And when immigrants come to Canada, they come with this much vaunted value in their minds.

PLURALISM AS A FUNDAMENTAL PRINCIPLE

Among the four fundamental rights guaranteed by the Canadian Charter of Rights and Freedoms is the freedom of conscience and religion. Article 27 states: "This Charter shall be interpreted in a manner consistent with the preservation and enhancement of the multicultural heritage of Canadians." Ideally, this means that everyone

"Post-Christian" society: A society in which the traditional values, beliefs, and symbols of Christianity are declining in meaning, leading toward secularization.

living in Canada is free to believe (or not believe) whatever he or she chooses. It also means that the government is responsible for eliminating barriers for those wishing to practise their religion—even if governmental inconvenience or cost is the result. From a diversity perspective, the problems surface when the borders of one Canadian's rights infringe on the borders of another's. The Supreme Court reviews case after case where individuals or groups deem their rights of religion or conscience to have been violated. We will review some of these cases shortly.

Whether claimed by the French or the British, early Canadians were not seeking religious autonomy from their mother countries. For the most part, French colonists carried on the Roman Catholic traditions of France while their English counterparts held fast to the Church of England. As England gained the political upper hand, Anglicanism also became part of the Canadian identity. In fact, part of the process of "Anglicization" of Aboriginal children included indoctrination of religious beliefs and removal of any beliefs or practices not sanctioned by the Church. Though the Church has since apologized and attempted reparations against the abuses of the residential schools, the message seems to have remained in the cultural ether: to be Canadian meant to belong the Church.

In his book *Foreigners or Canadians*, C. J. Cameron, the 1913 assistant superintendent of the Baptist Home Mission, draws this point out very clearly:

> We must endeavor to assimilate the foreigner. If the mixing process fails, we must strictly prohibit from entering our country all elements that are non-assimilable. It is contrary to the Creator's law for white, black or yellow races to mix together. If the Canadian civilization fails to assimilate the great mass of foreigners admitted to our country, the result will be destruction to the ideals of a free and nominally Christian nation which will be supplanted by a lower order of habits, customs and institutions … we shall Canadianize the foreigner by Christianizing him. (Slater, 1977, p. 29)

With the Charter of Rights and Freedoms, this message was unambiguously knocked down, but not everyone in Canada would disagree with Cameron's notions. In 1985, the Supreme Court of Canada ruled in *R. v. Big M Drug Mart Ltd.* that a law requiring businesses to shut down on Sundays—the Lord's Day Act—was a violation of Charter Rights. While you can still find businesses that choose to close on

Sundays, the court ruled that requiring a business to close on the traditional Christian day of rest was illegal and unconstitutional. Since that case, many of the inherent assumptions about Canada being a "Christian nation" have been challenged. As the faces of immigrants become more and more prominent on the streets of Canada, as city halls across the country add Diwali, Hanukah, and Eid decorations to the traditional nativity scenes, the media reports widespread panic about the loss of a "Canadian identity." Are fundamental Canadian values being threatened by the demise of Christian Canada? Is our social cohesion and democratic way of life being sacrificed to pander to religious diversity? What about issues of gender equality, where foreign values clash with Canadian ones? Religious issues are as important as gender considerations.

LEGISLATING ACCOMMODATION

While the Supreme Court judges large landmark cases that determine the constitutionality of lesser court decisions, the provincial **human rights commissions**, organizations set out to investigate, protect, and advocate for the rights of individuals, do the everyday work of determining the limits and requirements of religious accommodation. These commissions have jurisdiction over issues that arise in the workplace, and in the marketplace, and in accommodations. According to provincial Human Rights Codes (HRCs), discrimination based on creed (religion) is against the law. For example, according to the Ontario Human Rights Commission, it is the responsibility of the employer to accommodate someone's religious requirements, as long as the accommodation does not cause undue hardship, cost, or safety issues (OHRC, 2012). That's the easy part. But everything in between—from defining what constitutes a **creed** to what constitutes hardship and cost—can get murky and inflame tempers like almost no other issue can.

According to the Policy on Creed and Accommodation of Religious Observances, **creed**:

> … is interpreted to mean "religious creed" or "religion." It is defined as a professed system and confession of faith, including both beliefs and observances or worship. A belief in a God or gods, or a single supreme being or deity is not a requisite.
>
> Religion is broadly accepted by the OHRC to include, for example, non-deistic bodies of

faith, such as the spiritual faiths/practices of aboriginal cultures, as well as *bona fide* newer religions (assessed on a case by case basis). (OHRC, 1996, p. 4)

The definition of creed itself is a subjective one. Making matters even more complicated is that the practices people sincerely believe to be necessary to their creedal beliefs are protected—whether that system of beliefs is officially considered a religion or not. For example, Falun Gong—defined and outlawed in its native China as a cult—is given creedal status and its members are protected against discrimination. As a result, in May 2011, Ottawa resident Daiming Huang was awarded $15 000 in damages when the Ontario Human Rights Commission ruled that she had been discriminated against by her local senior centre for practising Falun Gong (CBC News, 2011). At the heart of the law is the prohibition against religious discrimination based on the two parties not sharing the same religion. This applies regardless of whether either or both parties are minority groups or whether one or the other party has no religious beliefs. In other words, religious accommodation laws protect atheists from discrimination too.

The duty to accommodate is most often seen in the workplace in issues of dress, holidays, and break times. We will review specific cases of accommodation; but in general, employers are duty-bound to accommodate unless there are reasonable occupational reasons for them not to do so. As for what constitutes "hardship," this too is considered on a case-by-case basis. There are no universal monetary standards above which an employer is not obligated to expend. Also, what is possible in accommodating one employee with religious requirements may not be possible in future cases with multiple employees. Safety may constitute another form of hardship. If a particular uniform must be worn as part of a job necessity and cannot be modified in such a way as to accommodate religious requirements (e.g., a head covering), then employers may cite this matter as a legitimate lifting of their duty to accommodate.

The duty to accommodate is based in a good faith understanding that the employee's request is a legitimate religious one. The employee is not required to give evidence of the validity or obligatory nature of the accommodation,

Human rights commission: A national or international organized body that investigates, protects, and advocates for the rights of human beings.

Creed: A doctrine or system of beliefs—very much like dogma.

IN THEIR SHOES

If a picture can say a thousand words, imagine the stories your shoes could tell! Try this student story on for size – have you walked in this student's shoes?

Although I am not a religious person, my experience was definitely inspiring. I had a bout with depression and decided to move back in with my mother for a short time to recover. Finding it difficult to find work in my hometown, I was offered a job through my sister-in-law at Digital Attractions at the Falls. It was here that I met two very influential people who would change my life forever. Their names were Siddiq and Ahmed. They were from Pakistan and they were Muslim. Now, my first thoughts on them were stereotypical and disrespectful. Only a few years had passed since 9/11, and it was clear that I had a biased opinion that was more media driven than factual.

After several weeks of working side by side with them, I realized that I had a lot in common with them. We shared common interests like music, sports, news, TV shows, and we all became very close friends.

I was asked to come to an all-you-can-eat Chinese buffet one Saturday night with Siddiq, Ahmed, and another friend from Turkey named Tai. I loaded up my plate, unaware that Muslims do not eat pork. I offered some sweet and sour pork to Tai and he refused, saying that he could not eat it. This is where I began to ask many questions about their faith. I have always been the type of person to seek out knowledge of things I do not fully understand, and Ahmed took a more personal interest. He invited me to come with his wife Sarai and their son Hamad to the Islamic Society of Niagara on the following Friday, to learn about their religion. Naturally, I did not want to feel out of place, so I decided to meet with them at their house for dinner on the Thursday to ensure my understanding of their customs.

It was like stepping into a different world being there. Sarai took me under her wing and taught me an English version of prayer and showed me how to perform *wudu*. Wudu is a cleansing ritual that all Muslims perform before they enter into prayer. She also taught me how to wear a *hijab*, which, I admit, I found constricting and degrading. I was told prior to my visit that I would not be required to wear it, as it is not mandated by the *Qur'an*. It was adopted from the teachings of Muhammad and it is more so a personal choice for modest female dress. Given my want for a full cultural experience, I donned the garb and met with them Friday morning at the mosque.

Now, I felt uncomfortable because I was one of two white women in the building, and I had to pray in a room separate from Ahmed with Sarai. There were speakers in the room so we could hear the Imam and a window that showed the prayer floor. I had originally thought that woman in all Islamic societies were not allowed to pray with the men. On closer inspection, I realized that the reason I was in the room was because Sarai had her young son with her and I was actually in a room for "little ones" who are learning with their mothers. The prayer floor was a myriad of the sexes, although the women were closer to the back, and there wasn't actually any separation or discrimination. I felt ashamed of my preconception and was quite relieved that I was in the room to practise without making a fool of myself for doing any actions wrong.

After the service, it was time to meet in the cafeteria. I had assumed that I would be stared at because of my obvious minority, and the fact that I was having difficulty with my hijab as it kept sliding down the back of my head. I was surprised as I was welcomed by their congregation and the attention was more than surprising. I was lavished with attention and praise, and although I made it clear that I was there for educational understanding, the people were happy that I was taking the time to understand their culture and religion.

Islam is not just a religion to Muslims. It is a way of life and a peaceful understanding of their community. It was not what I thought it was going to be at all. I felt spiritual gratification, which I will admit aided in my depression recovery. I did not need Islam for this spiritual gratification; however, it needed me. I say this because most of the people I talked to after that were disgusted that I was practising Islam, including family members. The words *Al-Qaeda*, *Osama Bin Laden*, *terrorist*, and *anti-Christian* were thrown around regularly. I realized my part in this experience was to educate the Islamophobics on what I had learned. I do not make a habit of preaching religion. I consider myself an atheist; however, this experience helped me understand Islam and help others understand that it's not what the media and word-of-mouth makes it out to be.

My experience has aided in my understanding and appreciation for Islam and I wouldn't have changed it for the world.

Source: Shannon Engemann.

whether in dress code or time off. It is enough that the employee holds a sincere religious belief and holds it consistently in other areas of his or her life. An obvious violation of this trust would be someone asking for religious time off and using that time off to engage in other employment.

What Is Not Covered by the Law

No matter how strongly someone believes in certain political views, these are not protected by religious accommodation laws. An employee cannot demand time off to attend a political rally in which he or she fervently believes. Also not applicable are practices that incite violence against others or in any way violate international human rights standards or national criminal codes. A religious tradition that involves virginal sacrifices on a yearly basis would, by this principle, be as illegal as any other homicide in Canada.

Finally, religious accommodation is not intended to elevate one set of religious practices over another. It is intended to level the playing field so that all Canadians have equal access to the Charter of Rights and Freedoms, regardless of their religious views.

You Be the Judge

Many discussions of Canada's religious accommodation standards fail to recognize how nuanced and well researched the judicial decisions are. Religious accommodation does not mean that anytime anyone—particularly a minority—cries "Religion," the employer involved must immediately cede his or her rights. Looking at some landmark cases gives a fuller picture of Canada's means of accommodating its increasing religious diversity. The success of the Canadian multicultural dynamic has encouraged many European countries to re-evaluate their own policies regarding diversity in recent years.

CASE I: CHAMBLY V. BERGEVIN

In Chambly, Quebec, in1994, three Jewish teachers working for the Catholic school board were given an unpaid day off to celebrate Yom Kippur. The teachers' union raised a grievance, claiming that the loss of pay was discriminatory. The courts agreed. Their finding was that although Good Friday and Christmas had essentially become statutory (non-religious) holidays, they are historically and remain Christian-based holidays, and those who did observe them were not penalized for not working on those days. The Jewish teachers, however, were in essence being monetarily penalized for seeking the same accommodation as their Christian co-workers. Supreme Court Judge Justice Peter Cory explained:

> If a condition of work existed which denied all Asian teachers one day's pay, it would amount to direct discrimination. … The loss of one day's pay resulting from direct discrimination would not be tolerated … and would fly in the face of human rights legislation. Similarly adverse effect discrimination resulting in the same loss cannot be tolerated unless the employer takes reasonable steps to accommodate the affected employees. (OHRC, 1996, p. 13)

The general principle that emerged from this case has and continues to have far-reaching effects. Employers are required to honour employees' requests for religious days off as long as the request does not cause undue hardship. To demonstrate equal treatment requires that at least two (in some cases three) paid days off be available to those requesting religious leave.

CASE II: SAADI V. AUDMAX INC.

In 2009, Seema Saadi brought a religious discrimination suit against Audmax Inc., a corporation that places Canadian newcomers in the workplace. Ms. Saadi's placement with Audmax was terminated because the company deemed that she was not a "good fit." Part of the misfit was caused by Ms. Saadi's wearing of a Muslim hijab or headscarf, which Audmax referred to as a "cap" and inappropriate business attire. Ms. Saadi took her case to the Ontario Human Rights Tribunal, which found that Audmax was guilty of discrimination (CanLII, 2009).

CASE III: JEHOVAH'S WITNESS V. HOSPITAL

In Manitoba, a young Jehovah's Witness claimed that her rights had been violated when she was hospitalized and given a blood transfusion without her consent. Because she was a minor at the time of her hospitalization, her refusal of a transfusion was overruled because the transfusion was deemed a medical necessity. The doctors contacted Manitoba Children's Services, who intervened and got the courts to order the transfusion. In 2009, as an adult, she took matters to the Supreme Court. Although they upheld the original court's decision and the hospital's actions, the judges concluded that future cases would have to take into account a minor's maturity level in cases of enforced treatment and religious refusal (CBC News, 2009).

CASE IV: HUTTERIAN BRETHREN OF WILSON COUNTY V. PROVINCE OF ALBERTA

In 2003, Alberta modified a driver's licence policy that had previously allowed religious groups opposed to having their photograph taken to obtain a photo-less licence—a special condition "G" licence. The new regulations required that a photo be provided and stored in the province's facial recognition data bank. These new regulations were designed to combat the growing problem of driver's licences used in identity theft.

Members of the Hutterian Brethren of Wilson County objected to the photographs on the grounds of religious principle. In their understanding of the Bible, the second commandment prohibits the taking of images. While the Supreme Court did concede that their beliefs were sincerely held and that the taking of the photographs would violate their religious rights, the court ruled in favour of the universal photo requirement anyway. Their decision stated that the province's necessity of a universal photo bank to combat fraud outweighed the religious rights of the Hutterian Brethren. Chief Justice Beverley McLachlin wrote:

> The law does not compel the taking of a photo. It merely provides that a person who wishes to obtain a driver's license must permit a photo to be taken for the photo identification data bank. Driving automobiles on highways is not a right, but a privilege. While most adult citizens hold driver's licenses, many do not, for a variety of reasons. (Ceballos, 2009)

CASE V: FRIESEN V. FISHER BAY SEAFOOD LTD.

The courts have also ruled that someone's sincerely held beliefs requiring them to preach in the workplace are not covered by the Charter of Rights and Freedoms. In Sidney, Vancouver Island, in 2008, Seann Friesen's employment with Fisher Bay Seafood was terminated because he refused to stop preaching to fellow employees. A number of employees complained and even threatened to walk off the job if Mr. Friesen was not stopped. By definition, Friesen's

Arbitration: Occurs when two disputing parties call in a third, neutral party to help them settle their dispute.

termination was religious discrimination because his religious beliefs and practices—not his competence as an employee—ended his employment. However, upon reviewing the case, the British Columbia Human Rights Tribunal found that Fisher Bay Seafood had tried to accommodate Friesen in a reasonable manner: the company allowed him to preach during non-work hours to those employees willing to listen, for example (CanLII, 2009).

Religious Tribunals

In May, 2004, *The Globe and Mail* ran an editorial in which columnist Heather Mallick argued that allowing Islamic law as the basis for family mediation among Muslims was "about the best idea since female foot-binding" (Mallick, 2004).

In 2003, a retired Muslim lawyer, Syed Mumtaz Ali, announced the formation of the Islamic Institute of Civil Justice (IICJ), whose aim was to conduct family arbitration for Muslim families under the guidelines of the Arbitration Act. Ali made subsequent comments to the media, comments which were taken to mean that the IICJ would be the only choice for Muslims who wanted to practise their religion. In correspondence with reporters from *The Toronto Star*, he said that "the Muslim tribunal would use and apply only those provisions of the sharia, which do not clash or conflict with any Canadian law, particularly the Canadian Charter of Rights and Freedoms. The use of the word 'sharia' is a misnomer. ... This is very basic, fundamental and crucial to Muslims because in a faith-oriented, Islamic way of life, as distinct from a secular way of life, to obey the religious laws in this way is crucial. ... One cannot call oneself a real Muslim if one does not obey the Islamic law in such a comprehensive manner (Kamlani & Keung, 2004)." Ontario's court would then be required to enforce the results of the private arbitration.

A predictably volatile public debate ensued, including Mallick's comments. Headlines became dominated with fears of Canadian law becoming overtaken by foreign Islamic law. But what was lost in the verbal firestorm was that the setup of the IICJ was not a new deal brokered between its founders and a governmental group. This group was simply availing itself of a policy that had been used by a number of faith-based groups in Canada (including Catholics and Jews) for many years.

The resulting controversy led Quebec to drop faith-based family **arbitration**, or neutral, third-party intervention, altogether. Ontario established a commission under the leadership of former Attorney

General Marion Boyd to review the Arbitration Act in light of the public's perceived reaction. Although Boyd's recommendation was that the safeguards within the Arbitration Act were sufficient to uphold personal freedom within the context of religious accommodation, the province ended up dropping faith-based arbitration in circumstances where the arbitration was not based on Canadian law (Boyd, 2004). According to the 2006 Family Statute Law Amendment Act, in order for any family arbitration to be enforceable, it must be based on provincial and federal law (Gregory, Predko, & Nicolet, 2005). In November 2005, Premier Dalton McGuinty announced, "There will be no religious arbitration in Ontario. There will be one law for all Ontarians" (Simmons, 2010). Ironically, many women's groups now report that religious arbitration still occurs, but that it is done without the governmental oversight that it received during the years of its inclusion in the Arbitration Act.

Where did faith-based arbitration come from? Does it stipulate different laws for different people? Though we have lived to see the legal ending of faith-based arbitration, in reality, it has existed as long as there have been religions upon which to base it. Following the adoption of International Commercial Arbitration Laws in the 1980s, the Ontario government introduced legislation regulating the use of already-practised domestic arbitration in 1991, with the Arbitration Act. In seven other provinces, arbitration is essentially an alternative to traditional litigation. With arbitration, the litigants are permitted to choose the "judge" based on whatever criteria they deemed suitable, as the Arbitration Act did not originally stipulate a criteria for the choice of arbitrator—only that he or she be a neutral party. With faith-based family arbitration, both parties had to enter willingly and could resolve such issues as divorce, child custody, and family inheritance. Once the arbitrator has ruled—called an arbitral reward—both parties are bound by this ruling. If one party reneges, the other party may take the matter to court and have the ruling enforced.

A few elements of the original Arbitration Act that got lost in the debate would be helpful to highlight in the context of Canada's concessions to religious minorities:

1. Faith-based arbitration is only one category of the Arbitration Act. The two parties can choose virtually any basis for their contract. This could be in the context of a workplace agreement or an ad-hoc agreement between friends. Once this contract is written and agreed upon, it becomes binding on both parties.

2. Anything that would render the contract illegal in the public courts (e.g., one or both of the disputants being under age, intoxicated, or coerced) would also render the private agreement void. Recent additions to family law arbitration stipulate that both parties must be screened independently for signs of domestic abuse of power imbalance (Attorney General, 2010).

3. The arbitrator has no inherent power over the disputants. He or she is only given the authority to judge on disputes brought forth.

4. The arbitrator cannot rule in a way that contravenes Canadian law or the Charter of Rights and Freedoms. For example, polygamy is an offence under the Criminal Code of Canada; as such, no arbitrator can rule in such a way that the ruling permits or assists in perpetuation of polygamy.

5. Finally, some matters may not be open for arbitration. Criminal offences must be taken to the courts, as well as matters that can only be awarded by a civil court. While a religious divorce can be determined through arbitration, a civil divorce (which would have numerous financial implications) would not.

"CAN'T WE ALL GET ALONG?"

Canadians are notorious for their politeness. So it may be surprising to learn that **hate crimes**, targeted against victims belonging to specific social groups, have shown a steadily increasing trend over the last few decades, with a slight decline between 2009 and 2010. Although race and ethnicity continue to be the highest motivators for police-reported hate crimes, religion is a close second. Religion accounts for approximately 29% of all hate crimes, and this percentage did not decrease with the overall decrease in hate crimes between 2009 and 2010. The Jewish community continues to have the highest number of crimes directed towards them, but the percentage of Jewish-targeted crimes has declined, while the number of hate crimes directed towards Muslims (or those "suspected" of being Muslim) has increased significantly over the last few years. Attacks against Muslims and Catholics

Hate crimes: Occur when victims who belong (or are seen to belong) to certain social groups are targeted based solely on their membership to that group. Groups that are most vulnerable include those based on race, ethnicity, religion, sexual orientation, and gender identity.

each represent 17% of religiously motivated hate crimes (Dowden & Brennan, 2013).

In Canada, the number of **interreligious, or interfaith, marriages** continues to climb, with nearly one in five Canadians married to someone from outside their faith tradition. Before we read too much into these numbers, it is important to note that half of these marriages are between Protestants and Catholics. However, even as recently as the middle of the last century, these unions would have been unacceptable to most Canadians. Also increasing in interreligious unions are marriages where one partner—usually the man—is Jewish, while the other partner is not. Sikhs, Hindus, Muslims, and evangelical Protestants were the least likely to be engaged in interreligious marriages, with the latter two groups representing 11% of the total numbers of interreligious marriages. One study notes that when a person's parents are in an interfaith relationship, there is a higher likelihood of that person engaging in an interfaith marriage (Clark, 2006). And as with all types of mixed marriages, the broadening effects of the relationship go far beyond the couple themselves and extend to immediate and distant family members.

The Elephant in the Mosque

It would be disingenuous to pretend that all religions are looked at with equal levels of antipathy and suspicion. The concern with religious identities obstructing national social cohesion and threatening democratic values and principles centres on the fear of an Islamic takeover of the Western world.

Though Muslims have been in Canada since shortly after Confederation, the last few decades have seen a growing unease about their ability to live peaceably and integrate seamlessly in Canada. According to a recent survey (Csillag, 2012), 52% of Canadians distrust their Muslim compatriots. The vast majority blamed Muslims themselves for this distrust; despite the fact that when prodded, "nearly half of those surveyed, 49 percent, listed the Internet as the number one source of racism and prejudice" (Csillag, 2012).

With the Canadian Muslim population expected to triple by 2031 (Pew Research Center, 2011), distrust of nearly 3 million Canadians will only be exacerbated as communities become more isolated, and as rhetoric—especially on anonymous Internet pages—becomes more radical. The facts are a great deal more reassuring: Canadian Muslims, more than their counterparts in Europe and even the United States, report great satisfaction with their lives in Canada. Fully 80% of Canadian Muslims, polled by the CBC and Environics, reported that they were satisfied. This number is higher than the general Canadian satisfaction level, with only 61% of the population reporting satisfaction with their lives. As for how Muslims think they are perceived by their fellow Canadians, only a small minority (17%) felt they were perceived with hostility (CBC, 2007). The picture that emerges from the survey is one of a community that experiences Canada and Canadian values positively and has no intention of isolating itself.

When ghettoization does occur, it is usually for the same reasons we find in other communities—language, culture, and (most importantly) economics. Though not all Canadian Muslims are immigrants, many are, and a sizable number have immigrated under duress, leaving behind war-torn homelands or social conditions in which they were or their families are in danger. Canada witnessed large numbers of Lebanese refugees in the 1980s, and many Somali and Bosnian refugees came to Canada in the 1990s. The circumstances of immigration and landing play a huge role in how long it takes immigrants to establish themselves in their new country. For those who came as refugees, that process naturally takes longer, as basic survival and living needs take precedence over anything else. And though recent studies have shown that there is little evidence of true "ghettoization" in Canada, gateway cities like Toronto, Vancouver, and Montreal do have neighbourhoods that are heavily populated by distinct ethnic communities. For many immigrant Muslims, these neighbourhoods are natural stepping-stones where they find others with whom they can speak their language, eat similar foods, and share similar values, until they are settled enough to branch out away from these neighbourhoods.

Muslim immigrants in Canada face the same economic struggles we see with other immigrants, if not more of them. The result of a major study conducted by University of Toronto professor Jeffrey Reitz found that "skin colour—not religion, not income—was the biggest barrier to immigrants feeling they belonged here. And the darker the skin, the greater the alienation" (Taylor, 2009). As many Muslim immigrants have darker skin, they have to contend with anti-Muslim sentiment as well as general issues of discrimination faced by darker-skinned non-Muslims.

Finally, one of the most commonly cited concerns with regards to the Muslim community in Canada is the accusation that Muslim immigrants will bring with them the stereotypical misogynistic tendencies

Interreligious (interfaith) marriages: Occur when two individuals who believe in different faiths marry.

Where churches once provided not only spiritual answers but social unity, they are now closing down in city after city. Can Canada still call itself a "Christian nation"? What does that mean today?

with which their community has been associated. Will Canada's liberal attitude towards religious minorities lead to gender discrimination, forced veiling and forced marriages, honour killings, and the like? The well-publicized case of Aqsa Parvez, a 16-year-old girl of Pakistani descent who was murdered by her father in a so-called honour killing, certainly shone a spotlight on these fears. Dr. Amin Muhammad, a psychiatrist at Memorial University in St. John's, Newfoundland, suggests that while honour killings have no place in Islamic law, defence teams may be attempting to use the term and its cultural connotations to present a case for more lenient sentences (Cohen, 2010).

For opponents of multiculturalism and diversity, these events—however rare—serve as "proof" of the failure of Muslims to integrate and the dangers of allowing immigration from Muslim countries to continue. It is important to consider that whether or not certain cases of honour killings lead to guilty verdicts, the courts' message must be clear—that there will be no leniency toward misplaced cultural sensitivity when it comes to violating the laws of the land.

ENDING THOUGHTS

What is the future of religion in Canada? Monica Toft, associate professor at Harvard's Kennedy School of Public Policy, argues that religions have outlived any number of social and political ideologies of the past few centuries. The inconvenience and violence caused by religious adherents is less a sign that religion is on its way out than an indication that religion will continue to make itself seen and heard in a modern, **secular** world. As so-called "**theo-cons**" claim Canada's prime minister as one of their own, religion is clearly a major player in the architecture of Canada's public (and foreign) policy—from defining the Canadian family to the limits of religious accommodation of non-Christian immigrants. Those waiting for religion to go away and take with it all the problems that religious differences cause will have to wait a long time. Those who worry that Canada's religious reality will be unrecognizable compared to the demographic realities at the time of Confederation have reason to worry, however; as Canada marches towards **secularism**, its immigrants come with their religious traditions intact, creating more possible fault lines in the multicultural divide, but also creating the growth that diversity can bring (Friesen & Valpy, 2010).

Secular: not related to anything religious or spiritual

Theo-cons: Conservative thinkers who believe that religion (specifically Christianity) should inform public policy.

Secularism: the belief that religion should play no role in public life

READING

WHAT CANADIANS THINK OF SIKHS, JEWS, CHRISTIANS, MUSLIMS …

By John Geddes, *Maclean's* (April 2009)

Canadians like to think of their country as a model for the world of how all sorts of people can get along together. But when it comes to the major faiths other than Christianity, a new poll conducted for *Maclean's* finds that many Canadians harbour deeply troubling biases. Multiculturalism? Although by now it might seem an ingrained national creed, fewer than one in three Canadians can find it in their hearts to view Islam or Sikhism in a favourable light. Diversity? Canadians may embrace it in theory, but only a minority say they would find it acceptable if one of their kids came home engaged to a Muslim, Hindu, or Sikh. Understanding? There's not enough to prevent media images of war and terrorism from convincing almost half of Canadians that mainstream Islam encourages violence.

The poll, by Angus Reid Strategies, surveyed 1,002 randomly selected Canadians on religion at a moment when issues of identity are a hot topic in Ottawa. Immigration Minister Jason Kenney has led a push by the Conservative government to revamp citizenship law, emphasizing the need for real bonds to Canada, and Kenney is looking for ways to encourage immigrants to integrate faster and more fully into Canadian society. But as federal policy strives to encourage newcomers to put down roots and fit in, the poll highlights an equal need for the Canadian majority to take a hard look at its distorted preconceptions about religious minorities. "It astonishes and saddens me as a Canadian," said Angus Reid chief research officer Andrew Grenville, who has been probing Canadians' views on religion for 16 years. "I don't think the findings reflect well on Canada at all."

Those findings leave little doubt that Canadians with a Christian background travel through life benefiting from a broad tendency of their fellow citizens to view their religion more favourably than any other. Across Canada, 72 per cent said they have a "generally favourable opinion" of Christianity. At the other end of the spectrum, Islam scored the lowest favourability rating, just 28 per cent. Sikhism didn't fare much better at 30 per cent, and Hinduism was rated favourably by 41 per cent. Both Buddhism, at 57 per cent, and Judaism, 53 per cent, were rated favourably by more than half the population—but even Jews and Buddhists might reasonably ask if that's a glass-half-full or glass-half-empty result.

Bernie Farber, chief executive officer of the Canadian Jewish Congress, said he was shocked that so many Canadians responding to a poll were willing to be so open about their negative feelings toward minority religions. "It tells me," Farber said, "that our journey from intolerance to tolerance, to where we can actually celebrate each other's cultures, is elusive."

From the perspective of Sikhs and, especially, Muslims, that's putting it mildly. When asked if they thought "the mainstream beliefs" of the major religions "encourage violence or are mostly peaceful," only 10 per cent said they thought Christianity teaches violence. But fully 45 per cent said they believe Islam does, and a sizable 26 per cent saw Sikhism as encouraging violence. By comparison, just 13 per cent perceived violence in Hindu teachings and 14 per cent in Jewish religion. A tiny four per cent said they think of Buddhism as encouraging violence.

Ihsaan Gardee, executive director of the Council on Islamic-American Relations Canada, said "reductive reasoning" in media coverage of armed conflict in largely Islamic countries is a big part of the problem. Violence in countries with Muslim populations is portrayed as rooted in their religions in what Gardee calls a "clash of civilizations" world view. "They're not looking at the social and economic context in which these things are happening," Gardee said. "It can't be reduced to Islam, per se."

Clearly, Islam and Sikhism face the highest hurdles when it comes to persuading many Canadians they are not inherently violent faiths. The problem varies across regions. By far the highest percentage who viewed Islam as encouraging violence was found in Quebec, 57 per cent. Sikh doctrine is mostly likely to be viewed as violent in the province where about half of Canadian Sikhs live: 30 per cent of British Columbians said they think Sikhism encourages violence.

Palbinder Shergill, a Vancouver lawyer who has long represented the World Sikh Organization of Canada on legal matters, said she might have expected such negative opinions about Sikhism in the 1990s. Back then, the 1985 Air India bombing, the work of Sikh separatist terrorists, was still a fresh memory. "Air India has had a very lasting negative legacy for the Sikh community," Shergill said. "The majority of imagery of Sikhs in the media typically associates the community with that sort of violence."

Patient work trying to overcome the widespread view of Sikhs as dangerous seemed to be paying off, she said—until recently. Shergill said Sikhs have lately faced a "huge resurgence" of the sorts of challenges to their distinctive practices that they thought were put to rest 15 years or so ago. In Ontario, a Sikh man is fighting in court for the right to wear a turban, but not a helmet, when he rides his motorcycle. In Montreal last week, Judge Gilles Ouellet found a Sikh boy guilty of having threatened two other boys with a hair pin, used to keep his hair neat under his turban.

But Ouellet said the boy didn't use his kirpan, the small symbolic dagger many Sikh men carry. The judge gave him an unconditional discharge, leaving him with a clean record, and said the case would never have reached his bench if the incident hadn't had a religious dimension. "Too much importance has been given this case," he said. "This matter should end here."

Shergill suspects that many more Canadians read about the initial charge being laid than the remarks of the obviously frustrated judge. And the fact that this episode unfolded in Quebec is not incidental. The province appears to be an incubator of deep suspicions concerning minority faiths.

A mere 17 per cent of Quebecers said they have a favourable opinion of Islam, and just 15 per cent view Sikhism favourably. Only 36 per cent of Quebecers said they hold a favourable opinion of Judaism, far below the national average, and in sharp contrast to neighbouring Ontario, where 59 per cent expressed a favourable view of the Jewish religion. "It's sadly not a shock," Farber said.

Farber said his group, a 90-year-old advocacy organization for Canadian Jews, recently rebranded its Quebec wing as the Quebec Jewish Congress, a bid to highlight its roots in the province and reach out to francophone Quebecers. He said Quebec's perennial anxieties about the survival of the French language play into attitudes toward minorities. "There are built-in fears there that have to be overcome," he said. In fact, all religions were regarded less positively in Quebec than in Canada as a whole, including Christianity, which 67 per cent of Quebecers view favourably, five points below the Canadian average.

A heated debate over how far to go in "reasonable accommodation" of minorities gripped Quebec in 2007 and 2008.

A commission headed by sociologist Gérard Bouchard and philosopher Charles Taylor toured the province holding often controversial hearings on the subject, ultimately concluding in a final report that Quebec needed to adapt, but that its cultural foundations were not at risk.

Angus Reid took that debate national, asking how far governments should go to accommodate minorities. A strong majority of 62 per cent agree with the statement, "Laws and norms should not be modified to accommodate minorities." A minority, 29 per cent, agreed with the alternative statement, "On some occasions, it makes sense to modify specific laws and norms to accommodate minorities." Another nine per cent weren't sure. In Quebec, 74 per cent were against changing laws or norms, the highest negative response rate on the accommodation question in the country.

Recent campaign trail experience in Canada has taught politicians to be cautious about anything that smacks of a concession to religious minorities. John Tory, the former leader of Ontario's Conservatives, was largely expected to win the province's 2007 election, until he pledged to extend public funding to all religious schools. That promise proved deeply unpopular, even with his party's base. The Angus Reid poll suggests that lesson can be broadly applied. It found 51 per cent oppose funding of Christian schools, and the level of opposition soars from 68 per cent to 75 per cent for all other religions. On even hotter-button religious issues, opposition is overwhelming. Only 23 per cent would allow veiled voting, and just three per cent Islamic sharia law—an even lower level of support than the eight per cent who would allow polygamy. There's substantial sympathy for recognizing religious holidays, 45 per cent, but a solid majority still opposes the idea.

Leaders of religious groups contacted by *Maclean's* commonly said their impression is that urban attitudes are more open, especially in Toronto and Vancouver—huge magnets for immigrants. Yet familiarity does not appear to be a reliable predictor of tolerance or acceptance. The Sikh community is prominent on the West Coast, but only 28 per cent of British Columbians surveyed reported a favourable impression of Sikhism. That was well below the figures in provinces where Sikhs are far less numerous, like neighbouring Alberta, where 47 per cent reported a favourable opinion of Sikhism, or Ontario, where Sikhism was rated favourably by 35 per cent.

Still, many advocates for Islamic and Sikh groups optimistically tout fostering personal contact—the sort of bonds that grow into friendships—as the key to creating acceptance of that religion. "The more that people have interactions with Muslims," said Gardee from the Council on American-Islamic Relations Canada, "the more favourable an opinion they have of Muslims."

To try to assess the extent and impact of friendships between Canadians of different faiths, Angus Reid asked, "Do you personally have any friends who are followers of any of these religions or not?" Not surprisingly, given that seven out of 10 Canadians identify themselves as Catholic or Protestant, the vast majority, 89 per cent, said they have Christian friends. Less predictably, given that only two per cent of the population follows Islam, fully 32 per cent of respondents claimed they have a Muslim friend. Only 16 per cent nationally reported having Sikh friends, but 36 per cent of British Columbians do. Across Canada, 45 per cent reported having Jewish friends, from a high of 61 per cent in Ontario to a low of 20 per cent in Quebec.

Digging into that data, Angus Reid checked to see if those who claimed to have friends of a particular religion tended to view that faith more positively. There is a correlation. Among those who said they don't have any Muslim friends, a mere 18 per cent reported that their opinion of Islam is generally favourable. But among those who said they do have Muslim friends, 44 per cent had a favourable opinion of Islam.

For all other religions, well over half of the pool of people who have friends of a certain faith view that faith favourably: for example, 63 per cent of those with Sikh friends view Sikhism favourably, compared with just 23 per cent of those without Sikh friends. And 76 per cent of Canadians with Jewish friends are favourably disposed toward Judaism, while only 34 per cent of people with no Jewish friends have a favourable opinion of Judaism.

Beyond personal contact with adherents of different religions, there's the question of whether Canadians really know much about what the various faiths profess. Asked about their level of knowledge, 86 per cent said they have a "good basic understanding" of Christianity, compared to just 32 per cent who make the same claim regarding Islam, 18 per cent for Hinduism, 12 per cent for Sikhism, 32 per cent for Buddhism and 40 per cent for Judaism. In fact, it's a stretch to imagine that a third of Canadians really have a solid grounding in Islam. Or, to express that skepticism another way, is it likely that Canadians are much more likely to have a grasp of the basic tenets of Islam and Buddhism than of Sikhism and Hinduism?

More likely, the higher reported levels of "good basic understanding" actually represents superficial impressions gleaned from news reports, combined with images—both negative and positive—picked up from popular entertainment. Grenville pointed out that with common Old Testament roots, Christians, Muslims and Jews have a natural starting point for mutual understanding. As for Buddhism, he suggested the sixties cultural touchstones established good press. "Meditation, the Beatles, all these things that feel Buddhist, even if they're not really Buddhist, feel friendly," he said. "There haven't been a lot of Buddhist wars."

Muslims and Sikhs might well envy that vibe. But Buddhism is more than an odd case—it shows that even a fast-growing religion can avoid rubbing Canadians the wrong way. The Buddhist population increased 84 per cent between 1991 and the 2001 national census. Still, that left the total Buddhist population at only about 300 000, or around one per cent of the population—far too small for most Canadians to have anything beyond fleeting direct contact with the religion. Even so, Buddhism's favourability rating of 57 per cent is four points higher than Judaism, a religion with much deeper roots in Canada. Buddhism was the only religion, including Christianity, for which more than half of people who said they don't have a friend of that faith held a favourable opinion of it anyway.

Even among those who profess a broad acceptance of other religions, the prospect of one of your children marrying someone from an unfamiliar background can be a test of tolerance. On this delicate question, though, the poll suggests a paradox. Although only 28 per cent said they have a generally favourable opinion of Islam, fully 39 per cent declared that they would find it acceptable for one of their children to marry a Muslim. The pattern follows for the other minority faiths: Canadians surveyed were more likely to say they would approve of one of their kids marrying a follower of a given religion than tended to view that religion favourably. So while only 30 per cent view Sikhs favourably, 39 per cent wouldn't object to a child marrying one. Similarly, 41 per cent have a favourable opinion of Hinduism, but 46 per cent would find their child's marriage to a Hindu acceptable.

That pattern might signal an intriguing instinct to respect personal choice in marriage over misguided generalizations about religions. Still, the numbers hardly suggest open-armed tolerance: with respect to all three of Islam, Hinduism and Sikhism, less than half of those surveyed said they would find it acceptable for one of their children to marry a follower of those religions. For the marriage question, the results again suggest the usual stratification: Christianity is by far most widely accepted, followed by Judaism and Buddhism, with Islam, Hinduism and Sikhism facing the most negative feelings. A resounding 83 per cent would accept a child marrying a Christian, 53 per cent a Buddhist, and 56 per cent a Jew.

Overall, the findings suggest minority religions aren't getting a fair shake from the majority. But there remain legitimate questions, even misgivings, about the relationship between mainstream believers and fringe extremists. Outsiders, including journalists, sometimes have trouble gauging how many Sikhs support groups that have sometimes resorted to terrorism in their quest to carve a separate state out of India. Earlier this month, for instance, portraits of the assassins of former Indian prime minister Indira Gandhi were reportedly on display in Surrey, B.C., at celebrations of Vaisakhi, the birth of Sikhism, and the images even appeared on T-shirts. Palbinder Shergill responds to questions about this sort of issue by making the simple, but fundamental, point that not everything a particular Sikh espouses should reflect on Sikhism as a whole.

Muslim groups also face a minefield of image challenges, which often flow from international affairs rather than domestic life. Gardee admits, for example, his organization's campaign urging the federal government to bring home Omar Khadr might convey the wrong impressions to some Canadians. After all, Khadr, the Canadian being held by the U.S. at the Guantánamo Bay detention facility, is the son of Ahmed Said Khadr, who was an al-Qaeda financier before he was killed in a gun battle in Pakistan in 2003. Other members of the Khadr family have made outrageous public

comments. "Yes, some of the things his family have said have been troubling and outright disturbing," Gardee said. "But as a Canadian citizen he still has rights. He's a Canadian citizen and he's a Muslim. That puts him squarely within our mandate to deal with."

The problem of how to project a moderate face of Islam to a wider Canadian public is a pressing challenge. Within disparate Muslim communities—and the religion is anything but monolithic—the nature of mosque leadership is a subject of sometimes fierce debate. In fact, that argument is currently raging at Ottawa's largest mosque, just a few minutes drive west of Parliament Hill. An imam recruited last year from Egypt to preach at the mosque is regarded by some who pray there as not fluent enough in English and too out of touch with modern Canadian society for the job. Others say he needs more time to find his place.

Karim Karim, a communications professor at Carleton University in Ottawa, recently released a report based on extensive surveys and focus group sessions in Canada, the U.S. and Britain that found Muslims in all three countries yearn for imams who better understand the West. "There was a lot of admiration for leaders who were engaging in issues of youth, poverty, employment, women's issues," Karim told *Maclean's*, "rather than just knowing the theology and being able to recite the Quran."

Perhaps a new generation of Muslim leaders more attuned to Canadian sensibilities can help bridge the obvious gaps in understanding. Karim points to negative connotations that have built up around a handful of loaded terms. According to him, sharia is a "very malleable, very diverse" set of ethics and values about leading a Muslim life—not a rigid legal code. He describes a fatwa as an "informed opinion by a learned scholar"—not a death edict. And Karim says most Muslims think of jihad as "a daily struggle to be a good Muslim." But he adds, "It would be disingenuous on my part to say that, no, the other side does not exist. It does exist—the taking up of arms for a cause of justice."

His willingness to try to explain details, convey nuances, even underline contradictions—it all suggests that Karim craves dialogue on a level the Angus Reid poll suggests too few Canadians are ready for. Even Grenville, who has long experience tracking all sorts of opinions, finds the landscape of attitude toward unfamiliar faiths bleak. "This runs counter to all we espouse," he said. "We need to face up to the reality of it." No doubt leaders of the fast-growing, little-understood religious minorities need to consider the image they project. But the rest of Canadians might try a little soul-searching, too. For a country that often boasts of modern identity based on acceptance of diversity, this poll suggests that's still a goal to strive toward rather than an achieved reality.

Source: John Geddes, "What Canadians Think of Sikhs, Jews, Christians, Muslims ..." *Maclean's* (April 28, 2009).

DISCUSSION QUESTIONS

1. What are the implications of this study? How do people's feelings towards members of a minority religion effect the real world treatment of minorities? Would you be comfortable living next to (or with) someone whose religion you believed taught violence? How would you handle a situation like this?

2. Do these findings reflect your own social experience? Do you recognize changes in attitudes—for better or worse—towards different religious groups during your lifetime?
3. Who bears the most responsibility for the shifting perceptions (and misperceptions) of minority religions?

Why do you think Christianity is perceived most favourably? Do you think these opinions are based on knowing the theology of the particular religions? If not, what are the perceptions based on?

KWIP

KNOW IT AND OWN IT: WHAT DO I BRING TO THIS?

Religion is one of the most personal choices a person can make. Or is it? Think about your own religious views. Where and when were they formed? How much choice did you have in the matter? Reflect upon how much of your day and life is determined by your religious background or your rejection of that background. Are your views on the various issues brought up in this course determined by religion in any way? Are you open to others having views that are determined by religious views at odds with yours? If you immigrated to Canada from a country with a different degree of public religiosity, do you feel more or less comfortable with Canada's (theoretical) "live and let live" policy?

WALKING THE TALK: HOW CAN I LEARN FROM THIS?

After reading the chapter and the *Maclean's* article, superimpose your own views on religious minorities. Even if you are a member of a religious minority yourself, reflect on how media sources have shaped your views of other communities. Try to speak to others from different religious backgrounds and learn how and whether they have felt accommodated within Canada's laws. Speak to older members of your family and ask them to reflect on how the face of religion in Canada has changed.

IT IS WHAT IT IS: IS THIS INSIDE OR OUTSIDE MY COMFORT ZONE?

Religion tends to make everyone in the room uncomfortable. It is as much a heated debate starter as it is a conversation stopper. Why is this? Are you comfortable talking about your religious views? Are you comfortable with others sharing theirs?

PUT IT IN PLAY: HOW CAN I USE THIS?

Our country's history of and laws regarding religious accommodations are a big part of what defines it. Whether as a student, an employee, an employer, a resident, or in any other role in your adult life, the laws that dictate what and how much religious freedom you have in any public space are, on the one hand, well-defined, and, on the other, subject to modification, as our demographic realities shift and new needs are addressed. Chances are that you will one day be in a situation where your religious needs may be challenged, or where you are challenged to meet someone's religious needs. Know your role and your country's role in both cases.

CourseMate Study Tools

Located at www.nelson.com/site/walkamile1e

- Consolidate your knowledge with the **Flashcards**.
- Gauge your understanding with **Picture This** and accompanying questions for reflection.
- Develop your critical thinking skills by working through **The Daily**.
- Apply your understanding with **KWIP** interactive!
- Develop your critical reading skills through compelling **Readings** and accompanying short answer questions.

REFERENCES

Attorney General. (2010, December 9). Screening for domestic violence and power imbalances. Retrieved from *Ministry of the Attorney General of Ontario*: http://www.attorneygeneral.jus.gov.on.ca/english/family/arbitration/screening.asp

Boyd, M. (2004, December 1). Dispute resolution in family law: Protecting choice, promoting inclusion. Retrieved from *Ministry of the Attorney General*: http://www.attorneygeneral.jus.gov.on.ca/english/about/pubs/boyd/section1.pdf

CanLII. (2009, January 6). *Friesen v. Fisher Bay Seafood and others*, 2009 BCHRT 1. Retrieved from *Canadian Legal Information Institute*: http://www.canlii.org/en/bc/bchrt/doc/2009/2009bchrt1/2009bchrt1.html

CanLII. (2009, October 7). *Saadi v. Audmax*, 2009 HRTO 1627. Retrieved from *Canadian Legal Information Institute*: http://canlii.ca/t/262jc

CBC News. (2007, February 13). Glad to be Canadian, Muslims say. Retrieved from *CBC News*: http://www.cbc.ca/news/canada/story/2007/02/12/muslim-poll.html

CBC News. (2009, June 29). Girl's forced blood transfusion didn't violate rights: Top court. Retrieved from *CBC News*: http://www.cbc.ca/news/canada/story/2009/06/26/supreme-blood026.html

CBC News. (2011, May 5). Falun Gong senior booted from club gets $15K. Retrieved from *CBC News*: http://www.cbc.ca/news/canada/ottawa/story/2011/05/05/ottawa-falun-gong-seniors-347.html

Ceballos, A. (2009, August 7). Province's goals trump religious rights: SCC. *The Lawyer's Weekly*.

Clark, W. (2006, October 1). Interreligious unions in Canada. Retrieved from *Statistics Canada*: http://www.statcan.gc.ca/pub/11-008-x/2006003/9478-eng.htm

Cohen, T. (2010, June 10). "Honour killings" on the rise in Canada: Expert. Retrieved from *The Vancouver Sun*: http://www.vancouversun.com/life/Honour+killings+rise+Canada+Expert/3165638/story.html

Csillag, R. (2012, March 26). 52% of Canadians distrust Muslims, according to latest poll. Retrieved from *Huffington Post*: http://www.huffingtonpost.com/2012/03/26/canadians-distrust-muslims_n_1381239.html

Dowden, C., & Brennan, S. (2013, June 5). Police-reported hate crime in Canada, 2010. Retrieved from *Statistics Canada*: http://www.statcan.gc.ca/pub/85-002-x/2012001/article/11635-eng.htm

Friesen, J., & Valpy, M. (2010, December 10). Canada marching from religion to secularization. Retrieved from *The Globe and Mail*: http://www.theglobeandmail.com/news/national/canada-marching-from-religion-to-secularization/article1833451/

Geddes, J. (2009, April 28). What Canadians think of Sikhs, Jews, Christians, Muslims ... *Maclean's*.

Grossman, C. (2010, February 11). Christian churches in Canada fading out: USA next? Retrieved from *Faith and Reason*: http://content.usatoday.com/communities/Religion/post/2010/02/christian-churches-in-canada-fading-out-usa-next/1#.UbeyAZz3Nug

Jedwap, J. (2005, March 30). Canada's demo-religious revolution: 2017 will bring considerable change to the profile of the Mosaic. Retrieved from *Association for Canadian Studies*: http://www.acs-aec.ca/pdf/polls/30-03-2005.pdf

Kamlani, T. & Keung, N. (2004, August 28). Muslim group opposes sharia law. Retrieved from *Muslim Canadian Congress*: http://muslimcanadiancongress.info/wp-content/uploads/2013/08/Muslim-group-opposes-sharia-law-August-28-2004.pdf

Lindsay, C. (2008, November 21). Canadians attend weekly religious services less than 20 years ago. Retrieved from *Statistics Canada*: http://www.statcan.gc.ca/pub/89-630-x/2008001/article/10650-eng.htm

Mallick, H. (2004, 05 15). Boutique law: It's the latest thing. Retrieved from *The Globe and Mail*: http://www.theglobeandmail.com/incoming/boutique-law-its-the-latest-thing/article743677/

OHRC. (1996, October 26). Policy on creed and the accommodation of religious observances. Retrieved from *Ontario Human Rights Commission*: http://www.ohrc.on.ca/sites/default/files/attachments/Policy_on_creed_and_the_accommodation_of_religious_observances.pdf

OHRC. (2012, May 01). Creed case law review. Retrieved from *Ontario Human Rights Commission*: http://www.ohrc.on.ca/en/creed-case-law-review

Peritz, I. (2010, December 13). As churches crumble, communities fear loss of heritage. Retrieved from *The Globe and Mail*: http://www.theglobeandmail.com/news/national/as-churches-crumble-communities-fear-loss-of-heritage/article1320111/

Pew Research Center. (2011, January 27). The future of the global Muslim population. Retrieved from *Pew Research Religion & Public Life Project*: http://www.pewforum.org/The-Future-of-the-Global-Muslim-Population.aspx

Gregory, J., Predko, A., & Nicolet, J. (2005). Faith-based family arbitration. Retrieved from *Uniform Law Conference of Canada*: http://www.ulcc.ca/en/2005-st-johns-nf/254-civil-section-documents/750-faith-based-family-arbitration

Simmons, H. (2010, September 14). One law for all Ontarians. [Editorial opinion]. Retrieved from *Toronto Star*: http://www.thestar.com/opinion/editorialopinion/2010/09/14/one_law_for_all_ontarians.html

Slater, P. (1977). *Religion and culture in Canada*. Waterloo, Ontario: Waterloo University Press.

Statistics Canada. (2001, June). Religious groups in Canada. Retrieved from *Statistics Canada*: http://www.statcan.gc.ca/pub/85f0033m/85f0033m2001007-eng.pdf

Statistics Canada. (2003, May 13). Religions in Canada. Retrieved from *Census 2001*: http://www12.statcan.gc.ca/english/census01/products/analytic/companion/rel/contents.cfm

Taylor, L. (2009, May 10). Darker the skin, less you fit. Retrieved from *The Star*: http://www.thestar.com/news/gta/2009/05/14/darker_the_skin_less_you_fit.html

Tyshynski, M. (2009, January 6). *Friesen v. Fisher Bay Seafood*. Retrieved from *BC Human Rights Tribunal*: http://www.bchrt.gov.bc.ca/decisions/2009/pdf/jan/1_Friesen_v_Fisher_Bay_Seafood_and_others_2009_BCHRT_1.pdf

Valpy, M. (2012, 02 09). Anglican Church facing the threat of extinction. Retrieved from *The Globe and Mail*: http://www.theglobeandmail.com/news/british-columbia/anglican-church-facing-the-threat-of-extinction/article4352186/

Gender and Sexuality

> *"Well, I'm not dumb but I can't understand why she walked like a woman but talked like a man"*
>
> *(The Kinks, 1970)*

DIVERSITY COMPETENCIES

Diversity competencies are specifically learned behaviours that students can actively practise to promote equity and inclusion. By mastering this unit, students will gain the skills to become diversity-competent practitioners, including the ability to

- distinguish between the biological determination of sex and the social construction of gender as they relate to individuals' expression of their own sexuality

- identify the culturally appropriate roles that define what is masculine and feminine, and explain the consequences of straying from the defined roles, especially as they relate to gender identity

- analyze gender inequality on a national and global scale

Not so long ago, we never thought of gender and sexuality as two separate concepts. In fact, we hardly ever had to think about gender at all. Sexuality—that was relatively easy—we simply referred to it as "sex," and you were either male or female. There was no in-between (biologically, psychologically, or sociologically), and the roles that women and men fulfilled in society were very clear-cut and regimented. Women performed traditionally female tasks, and men did all the things that women wouldn't (or supposedly couldn't) do. In some ways, we've come a long way since then (e.g., some men stay at home and mind their children); but in other ways, we still have a very long way to go (women still don't earn as much as men, for example) before gender and sexuality, these two very separate but highly related issues, are truly understood and accepted in our society.

Historically, as a society, we've always had straight and rigid categories to define what it means to be a man or a woman—segmented, binary groupings into which males and females were supposed to fit. People who strayed from those categories were labelled as deviants and treated as such. Predominantly, we accept heterosexuality as the norm in mainstream society.

Other cultures, however, have different categories. For example, many Native North American subcultures (e.g., the Sioux, Lakota, and Cheyenne) live with two-spirited people as a third gender (Perkins, 2011). And while the men of the Sambia tribe of Papua New Guinea engage in what Western society would call homosexuality, their practices are all part of a rite of passage into becoming a warrior (McKay & McKay, 2010). The rites of the Sambia are "normal" to them—they know nothing about homosexuality, or heterosexuality for that matter—even though the males experience both.

The labels that Western society places on individual practices and preferences come with all sorts of implications, innuendos, and often inhumane treatment to those who find themselves living as part of a category that falls outside of the norm. We see a similar process when we think about the prescribed roles that men and women are supposed to play in their lives. How much pressure do you think society puts on individuals to stay within the socially constructed gender roles that we know as male and female? If you are male, consider this question: If you were in a heterosexual marriage and your wife earned enough for you and your family to live comfortably, would you choose to stay home and take care of your children and the household (in other words, work as a house-husband), while your wife supported your family financially? Over the past 25 years, the overwhelming majority of male students (90%) in one

professor's classes have reported that they would not. Why? Most of them say that it's just not right: men are supposed to be the breadwinners in society; women are supposed to stay home, watch the children, and do the housework.

Gender stereotypes still exist in our society and they affect us in ways that we often don't realize. Men, women, **gay**, **lesbian**, homosexual, transsexual, omni-gendered, questioning—what's in a name? Plenty. These social and biological constructions that have become our identifiers have serious consequences in some cases. Do you know and/or love someone who is gay? **Transgendered**? **Questioning**? Is this person you? Does your sex match your gender identity? Have you found the place in society where you fit in? In this chapter, you'll read about individuals who have chosen to live both within and beyond the borders of convention, as you learn to differentiate between sex, gender, and sexuality.

DO YOU LIVE IN A BINARY WORLD?

Thomas Beatie was hailed as the "world's first pregnant man" by countless newspapers and magazines when he gave birth to baby Susan in 2008. Even though the headlines were no doubt a bit sensational-istic, his story was nonetheless shocking to the world when revealed for the first time on *Oprah* (Oprah Show Info, 2012). How is it possible that a man could have a baby? Thomas was born a biolog-ical female, but he had his breasts removed and kept his reproductive organs. As a female-to-male (FTM) **transsexual,** or a **transman**, he's currently

Gender stereotypes: Exaggerated, one-sided images by which the media repeatedly portray men and women in the same typical roles.

Gay: Someone who is emotionally and physically attracted to a member of the same sex.

Lesbian: A woman who is sexually attracted to women.

Transgender: Category that includes cross-dressing males, cross-dressing females, and inter- or bi-gendered individuals, as well as trans-sexed individuals.

Questioning: Refers to individuals who are uncertain about their gender, sexual identity, or sexual orientation; individuals who may be unsure of their sexuality or are still exploring their feelings.

Transsexual: Person who permanently identifies with the role of the opposite gender or someone who has had sex reassignment surgery to alter his or her external sex organs to those of the opposite sex.

Transman: A transgendered man or a transsexual man; an individual born biologically female who has transitioned into a man.

IN THEIR SHOES

If a picture can say a thousand words, imagine the stories your shoes could tell! Try this student story on for size – have you walked in this student's shoes?

Do you ever wonder whether people are born straight or if they are born gay? I don't really. In the end, it doesn't matter to me if I was born this way or not. It doesn't change who I am and it doesn't make it any more or any less acceptable. All I know is that I am a woman who is in a relationship with a woman. Because of that, I have a different story than most. Growing up, I was one of the lucky ones. I was popular, outgoing, and athletic and while definitely a tomboy, didn't endure any taunting, teasing or even questioning about my sexuality. I dated men and didn't struggle with that. In fact, I never really felt that I had "different" feelings and didn't really feel that I was in any closet. I don't think I was fodder for rumours or speculation and, overall, had a pretty regular life.

In university, one of my friends told me that she was attracted to me. We started a relationship and decided to keep it a secret. We realized that once we were out, it would be tough to shed ourselves of that label if that was what we wanted. Neither of us knew what path we would take in life and neither of us wanted to have to decide immediately. After that relationship ended, I dated men again. I had some wonderful boyfriends and cared very deeply for them. The relationships were genuine and, once again, I didn't feel that I was shut in any closet or bound by any social norms.

I met a woman when I was 24 and knew that it was different. It was also the first time in my life that I started to struggle with the notion of "coming out." When, how, and what was going to happen? I was going through one of the most exciting times and was scared to death to tell people about it.

I was fortunate that my partner had been out for some time, so a lot of our common friends figured it out quickly. The next step was coming out to my family. I was having a tough time—I felt that I was being dishonest—excited, happy and in love, but not sharing it. I started by coming out first to my brother, one of the most important people in my life. Easy—he was supportive and terrific. Next were my mom and my stepdad. It was tough and I was scared because I really didn't know what to expect. My mom's initial reaction was very supportive. She told my stepfather and, to my surprise, he accepted the news happily. As time went on, I saw that he was truly accepting my life and my choices. My mom, on the other hand, was not coping as well. She had a big birthday coming up and I mentioned that "we" would be happy to fly home for the celebration. She told me that I was welcome but that my partner was

not. I was crushed. I was ready and excited to take the step to introduce my partner to my family and I was told that "we" were not welcome. I didn't go to the party. And, for two years, my mother and I rarely spoke.

During this time and after the experience with my mother, I was terrified to tell my father that I was gay. He grew up in a proper, affluent family, and I was worried that my lifestyle would be considered a mark on the family name. When I told him, he said he was thankful that I told him. Three days after, my dad called me to tell me that he "told the family my news." He had called everyone—aunts, uncles, grandmother—and told them that I was a lesbian. My initial reaction was shock but, ultimately, he was doing what he could to make things easier for me. I was proud of him and knew he was of me—it took a lot of pressure off of my shoulders and gave me a sense of peace knowing I wasn't hiding anymore. He flew to Ontario shortly after to meet my partner and was excited to know more about my life. When that relationship ended, my dad was very supportive and did all he could to help me get re-settled.

Since that time, I have grown significantly in terms of my own level of comfort with myself, my choices, and being secure with those decisions. I am in a relationship with a wonderful woman and have been for five years. She has two children and I am proud to be a stepparent to two wonderful boys. I own my own business and have terrific friends. My relationship with my mother has improved drastically and she is now pleased to be a "step-grandparent" and mother-in-law. We are all welcomed into the family like everyone else. My partner's family has also been very supportive and have welcomed me into their family without reservation.

It all sounds rather plain and normal? It is. We work, we go out with friends, we coach soccer, and we watch school plays. We have regular jobs, own a home, and have a dog and a cat. Overall, we really aren't that much different than any other family.

I realize how fortunate I am. I also believe that my family, friends, and others who have been there for me made a tough process a lot easier. What took me some time to realize was that I can't live my life afraid of what others may think—all I can do is live my life the way I choose. Daily, I give thanks for those who make coming out easier and safer for those around them. I truly hope that as our society becomes more understanding and accepting of diversity, others can have similar experiences, free from judgment and full of acceptance!

battling in the courts with his request for a divorce from Nancy, his wife of nine years. They now have three children. Recently, however, a judge ruled that he couldn't get divorced, because there wasn't proof that he was a man when they got married. Though he was born female, when they married, he had undergone a double mastectomy and testosterone hormone therapy. The court argued, however, that the "Beaties never provided records to fully explain what Mr. Beatie actually had done and not done to become a man." Unhappy with the decision and determined to continue his fight, Thomas Beatie argues that this is "the state of Arizona versus transgender people, human reproductive rights, and fairness under law" (Associated Press, 2013).

Canadian male-to-female (MTF) **transwoman** and Grand Prix motorcycle racer Michelle Duff was born Michael Duff, a biological male, in 1939, and successfully competed in a male-dominated sport until he underwent **sex reassignment surgery** in 1984. Today Michelle spends her time writing and dabbling in photography (Duff, 2012).

In the cases of both Thomas Beatie and Michelle Duff, our traditional ideas of what it means to be a male and a female have been tested, as was evidenced by the media that surrounded (and still surrounds) Beatie and the difficulties that Duff faced after her transition. Do your own ideas of what it means to be a man or a woman resemble what we traditionally know to be male and female? Does being a man require the presence of a penis? And, must a woman be born with a vagina to be considered female? In the case of Thomas Beatie, how should the courts decide whether or not he is a man? And how is this affecting his identity, and the lives of his children?

Although these examples may just seem like media hype, the consequences of living outside the traditionally prescribed roles of masculine and feminine are very real indeed. Take for example, the 2012 case of Canadian Miss Universe contestant Jenna Talackova (Raptis, 2012). Although born with a penis, Jenna knew from a very young age that she was a female. She began hormone therapy at 14 years of age and had sex reassignment surgery (SRS) when she was 19 years old. Jenna had already made it to the finals in the Miss Vancouver pageant when officials told her she could no longer continue because "the rules state that each contestant must be a 'naturally born female'" (Pullman, 2012). Jenna knew when she was four years old that she was a girl, even though her anatomical parts didn't match the feelings she was experiencing. She felt she was a "naturally born female," but because her physical self didn't quite fit her gendered self, she was ousted from the competition. It was only after a huge public outcry that the Miss Universe pageant changed its rules to allow transgender women to take part in all of its competitions (Reuters, 2012).

As a society, how do we recognize and reconcile the spaces that exist between male and female, and those that divide masculine and feminine?

Using the Right Language

In recognizing the differences between male and female, let's look at how we define what it means to be a man or a woman in society today. What's the difference between sex and gender? Where does sexuality fit in? Many people confuse the definitions of these terms, and use them interchangeably; however, they have very different meanings. **Sex** refers to the biological components that make up who we are—in short, it refers to mechanical parts. Usually, men are born with a penis and women are born with a vagina. **Gender**, however, is a social construct. It refers to a set of social roles, attitudes, and behaviours that describe people of one sex or the other. Stereotypically, we often attribute or identify a certain set of roles and traits to males; for example, males are expected to demonstrate strength and toughness, and to act as protectors. Attributes like empathetic and caring, and roles like nurturer are typically associated with females. Your own **gender identity** refers to your own perception or conception of yourself, in terms of masculinity or femininity. **Gender roles** are stereotypical images (often perpetuated by the media) that place men and women in positions that they have historically held—for example, the images of mothers who stay at home to care for the children, while men leave the home to earn the family wage. Generally, we think that our sex exists between our legs, but our gender exists

Transwoman: A transgendered woman or a transsexual woman; an individual who is born biologically male who has transitioned into a woman.

Sex reassignment surgery: The surgical procedure where a person's physical appearance and functioning of their sex organs are modified to resemble that of the other sex.

Sex: The biological components that make up who we are.

Gender: The social and/or cultural aspect of masculinity and femininity.

Gender identity: A person's perception or conception of him- or herself, in terms of masculine or feminine.

Gender roles: Preconceived sets of behaviours, norms, and values that are associated with males and females in any given culture.

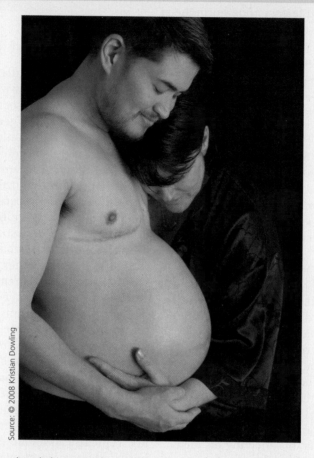

Source: © 2008 Kristian Dowling

Imagine that you're explaining where babies come from to your child. How will you explain the couple in this picture?

Sexuality: All the ways in which individuals experience and express themselves in relation to sex and gender.

Heterosexuality: The state of being sexually attracted to members of the opposite sex.

Sexual orientation: Orientation based on whom a person is attracted to affectionately and sexually.

Bisexual: Sexual orientation in which one is sexually attracted to members of both sexes.

between our ears—it's the mental part of how we feel about ourselves in relation to our masculinity or femininity.

Sexuality is, in some ways, a combination of sex and gender, and refers to all the ways in which individuals experience and express themselves in relation to both. Historically, we used to think of sexuality very differently. **Heterosexuality**

was the norm, and everything else was considered taboo or deviant.

When we refer to someone's sexuality, it can refer to that person's **sexual orientation**. For example, people who are emotionally and physically attracted to people of the same sex are gay. Lesbians are females who are attracted specifically to females, and **bisexual** individuals are attracted to both males and females.

The Kinsey Report and Other Research

In Western society, heterosexuality is the norm, and everything else was considered deviant for a long time.

That changed when Alfred Kinsey, who began his studies as a zoologist, started studying human sexuality in the 1940s and 1950s. Kinsey and his research team interviewed thousands of men and women about their most intimate sexual experiences, and they were among the first to publish the idea that sexuality could be measured on a continuum, suggesting that people weren't necessarily exclusively heterosexual or exclusively homosexual (Kinsey, Pomeroy, & Martin, 1948). Kinsey and his colleagues went on to inform the world that there were many individual lifestyles that fell between the confines of strictly heterosexual and strictly homosexual. Moreover, he suggested that **homosexuality** was neither deviant, damaging, nor something that needed "curing"—a view that was controversial at a time when same-sex relations were considered perversions and sins.

One of Kinsey's major contributions was the creation of a rudimentary scale—the Heterosexual–Homosexual Scale, which allowed individuals to self-identify and categorize their sexual orientation. Kinsey's work was groundbreaking at the time, but his scale had many limitations. It measured only behaviours and took into account behaviours at only one point in a person's life. In 1985, Fritz Klein developed the Klein Sexual Orientation Grid (Klein, 1993), which considers a person's sexuality in the past, present, and an idealized future. Klein's grid contains seven variables that include not only sexual behaviour, but fantasies, emotions, and social behaviour. Many consider this grid to be a far more comprehensive indicator of an individual's sexual orientation.

Gender Ambiguity

Sexual orientation is only one component of what contributes to the concept of sexuality, however. **Transgender** is broad term used to refer to those who struggle with the inner and behavioural differences that exist between their anatomical sex and their gender. Remember that gender is a mindful or ideological concept and sex is a biological thing. Different people make different choices in dealing with the difference between the two. **Transsexuals** are those who permanently identify with the role of the opposite gender. Some transsexuals engage in—or wish to engage in—other-gender activities and behaviours because they feel that they really are the other gender, that they were born with the wrong genitals. They may choose to cope with their "incorrect" biological sex by living as the other gender, and they may choose sex reassignment surgery to align their biological sex with their true gender identity (Ellis & Erickson, 2002). Some may adopt the dress and mannerisms of the other sex, while others may take hormones to adopt the appearance of the sex they desire to become. **Transvestites** are people who express their sexuality by wearing the clothes of the opposite sex (American Psychological Association, 2000). They don't believe that they are the other gender, nor do they want to be. Their behaviours often have nothing to do with their sexual orientation, but rather with sexual excitement and gratification. Individuals who are **androgynous**

Gender roles can often be conflicting, and how we express them is all part of our sexuality. Is this individual male, female, or androgynous? Why does it matter?

Source: © Timothy Large/Thinkstock

Homosexuality: The state of being sexually attracted to members of the same sex.

Transvestites: Men and women who express their sexuality by wearing the clothes of the opposite sex; often, the behaviour has nothing to do with whom they are attracted to physically.

Androgynous: Having the appearance of not being clearly masculine or feminine; applies to someone who could be either or both.

simultaneously portray the physical characteristics of both men and women, so it's often difficult to determine their sex or their gender.

In a neat and tidy world, everyone would fit into specific categories; but the world is not that simple, and we live in a gloriously diverse world. For many individuals, their sex and gender align with the traditional conventions of masculine and feminine, but many individuals are **gender variant**.

Usually, when we're born, our sex matches our gender, but that's not the case with everyone. Occasionally children are born with **ambiguous genitalia**. This condition can be obvious at birth, or it may not appear as an irregularity until much later in adolescence; so estimating exact numbers of affected individuals is difficult. The incidence of children with ambiguous or **intersex** genitalia, is reported to be 2%, but it could be as high as 4% (Preves, 2003). Intersex individuals are those who are born with indeterminate biological sex. They may have a genetic sex that does not match their outward appearance, or they may have genitalia that are ambiguous (Ellis & Erickson, 2002). Years ago, the term for this condition was "hermaphrodite," but that term is no longer used.

In many instances, it's the parents who find themselves in a difficult situation when faced with a child who has ambiguous genitalia. In some cases, it might be a boy born with an abnormally small penis or a girl with an extended clitoris. For these children, their sex may not match their gender and they find themselves "locked inside the wrong body." A boy's gender may be found inside a girl's body or the opposite. Sometimes these children will develop **gender dysphoria**, a condition where someone feels as though his or her physical self contradicts his or her sense of gender identity. This condition is also known as gender identity disorder (GID) or transgenderism. Though GID is currently classified as a psychiatric disorder, the exact cause of it is unknown. Ettner (1999) argues that "that the prevalence of persons with gender dysphoria varies from a range of 3% to 5% to a range of 8% to 10% of the general population" (Ettner, 1999, p. 28). It is diagnosed five times more often in males than in females. In the United Kingdom, roughly one in 4000 males are affected (Blunden & Dale, 2009), and Dr. Kelley Winters estimates that more than one in every 2500 males in the United States has undergone sexual reassignment surgery (SRS) (Winters, 2010).

Sexuality in Different Cultures

Not all people with gender dysphoria have ambiguous genitalia, however. People whose expressions of gender don't conform to the traditional norms of masculine and feminine can also be considered gender variant (Public Health Agency of Canada, 2008). Sixteen-year-old Fred Martinez from Cortez, Colorado, was blessed as a *nadleehi* in his native Navajo culture. In our Western language, we would call Fred transgender, but to his own people, he was a **two-spirited person**. He was a girl in a boy's body, and he grew up believing, as many Aboriginal cultures do, that there are mixed identities. Men and women exist, but so do mixed genders, and Fred grew up with the special gift of "one who constantly transforms"—the translation of the word *nadleehi* (Nibley, 2010).

By all accounts, Fred and those who loved him were comfortable with his sexuality, but unfortunately, not everyone found it easy to accept his refusal to conform to one particular gender role. On June 21, 2001, five days after Fred's mother had reported him missing, two young boys found Fred's bludgeoned body. Shaun Murphy, an 18-year-old who openly bragged to friends that "he beat up a fag" (Associated Press, 2001), pled guilty to second-degree murder (a charge that was upgraded to first-degree murder and classified as a hate crime) and is currently serving a 40-year prison term.

It's not just the North American Aboriginal cultures that have a different understanding from ours of what it is to be male and female. The *waria* in Indonesia are individuals who identify as male but assume certain characteristics of femininity. They wear women's clothing, jewellery, and make-up. Many *waria* are Muslim, but there aren't many mosques or prayer schools where they feel comfortable praying as women, so they attend a Koran school specially set up for *waria*. The word *waria* comes from the Indonesian words "*wanita*" (meaning woman) and "*pria*" (meaning man; BBC News, 2012).

Gender variants: Individuals whose expressions of gender don't conform to the traditional norms of masculine and feminine.

Ambiguous genitalia: A birth defect where the outer genitalia don't have the appearance of either a male or a female.

Intersex: Having the sexual characteristics of both a male and a female.

Gender dysphoria: A condition where a person feels as though their physical self contradicts their sense of gender identity.

Two-spirited: Having a male and female spirit living in the same body; recently, the term was adopted by contemporary gay, lesbian, bisexual, and transgender Native Americans and Canadian First Nations people to describe themselves and the traditional roles they are reclaiming.

The *wakawahine* of the Maori in New Zealand are males who have been "sufficiently compelled by their gender issues to take hormones and/or undergo surgery in order to appear and live as women. These are transsexuals under Western cultural concepts because many of them take hormones to alter their bodies. *Wakawahine* also include feminine boys who are "born like that" and who live as females but don't undergo body changes (Lomax, 2007). For the *Wakawahine*, the identification of the self requires an identity that blends ethnic, gender, and sexual identities. It requires an acceptance of the self as lesbian, gay, transgender, and Maori (Sears, 2005).

Although homosexuality is banned in Iran (and it is still punishable by death), sex reassignment surgery is allowed—and even promoted—as an answer to the gender issue. In fact, it has been legal since 1979. Iran carries out the second highest rate of sex change operations in the world, with only Thailand ranking higher. Filmmaker Tanaz Eshaghian says that in Iran, "if you are a male with female tendencies, they don't see that as something natural or genetic. They see it as someone who is consciously acting dirty." Being diagnosed as a transsexual makes it a medical condition, not a moral one, so it's considered something that can be treated and fixed (Barford, 2008).

Many cultures worldwide recognize a third gender. Table 7.1 outlines some examples of what can be viewed as a third gender in different cultures around the world.

TABLE 7.1
Examples of Alternative Genders

Location	Cultural Group	Alternative Gender(s)
Arctic areas of northern Europe	Saami	The Saami acknowledge the existence of double-sexed wights (or spirits, witches) called *gadniha*.
Benin	Beninese (African)	The *mino* of Benin was a female military troop, with masculine traits, also known as the Dahomey Amazons.
Canada	North Peigan Blackfoot Nation (Native American: most from northern Montana; some from southern Alberta)	These people acknowledge the *ninauposkitzipxpe* or manly-hearted woman as a third gender.
Congo	Bangala (African)	The *shaman* (medicine man/priest) in this culture wore women's trappings as he attempted to solve local crimes.
Dominican Republic	Dominican Republicans	Due to a genetic trait, young girls began developing male traits around the age of 12, leading to a class of *guevedoche*—now identified as a third gender.
Ethiopia	Ethiopian (African)	Among the Maale people, biological women were forbidden to enter the homes of the powerful, so they relied on the *ashtime*—eunuchs (or any male who didn't maintain typical gender roles) to perform traditionally female duties. *Ashtime* still exist today but the terms refers more widely to any type of sexual non-conformity.
Hawaii	Kanaka Maoli people (Pacific Islander)	These people acknowledge the *aikane*—traditionally, homosexual men of lower class who partnered with Hawaiian nobility. In contemporary society, *aikane* refer to a close friend of any sex or gender.

Continued

TABLE 7.1
Continued

Location	Cultural Group	Alternative Gender(s)
India, Pakistan, Bangladesh	South Asian	In India, some 200 000 *hira* or male-to-female transgendered individuals exist, who consider themselves a distinctly third gender; and in Pakistan, the *khusra* refer to the ambiguously gendered—transsexuals, transvestites, eunuchs—also identified as a third gender.
Indonesia	Bugis Tribe	The Bugis society divides their people many ways—they identify three sexes (male, female, and intersex) and four genders (women, men, *calabai*, and *calalai*), plus a fifth mixed-gender group, the *bissu*, who can be all genders or none at all.
Indonesia Southeast Asian	Indonesia	The *waria* are biologically male but take on many feminine mannerisms, and often choose to dress like women.
Iran	Iranian	Since homosexuality is punishable by death in Iran, transgender men are allowed to undergo sex reassignment surgery, acquire new documents, and live their lives as women. Many of these "altered" individuals do so at a huge cost, as they are banished by their families for bringing shame upon them.
Kenya/Tanzania	Kenyan/Tanzanian (African)	*Mashoga* is a term loosely applied to gay men in general, but it also refers to biological males who adopt female gender roles at very young ages. Some of them alternate between male and female clothing and styles, but wear these styles in a distinctly "*mashogan*" fashion.
Kiribati/Micronesia	Butaritari people (Pacific Islander)	Referred to as transgenderism or "gender liminality," the Butaritari people identify the *binabinaaine* (female-gendered men who adopt the guise of women) and the *binabinamane* (male-gendered women, who adopt the guise of men) as alternative genders.
Mexico	Zapotec Nation (Native American)	Identify the *muxes* as a third gender—biological young boys or men who choose to live and identify as women, or who cannot concretely identify with either gender. Many carry out the traditional duties of women.
Myanmar	Burmese (Southeast Asia)	The *acault* are identified as a third gender of men (some are gay) who adopt female gender roles. Other men can engage in sexual relations with an *acault* without breaking the cultural ban on homosexuality (because their genders are different).
Nepal	Nepalese	The *meti* are transgendered people. Many don't view themselves as gay, but rather assume a feminine identity through dress and gender roles.
New Zealand	Maori (Pacific Islander)	The *wakawahine* are biological males who live as females, and the *wakatane* are biological females who live as males in Maori cultures.

Continued

TABLE 7.1
Continued

Location	Cultural Group	Alternative Gender(s)
Philippines	Filipinos	*Baklas* make up a variety of sexual and gender identities, but consist mainly of biological males who present as women—those who are very flamboyant or those who are trying to "pass" as legitimate women.
Oman	Oman (Middle Eastern)	The *xanith* are identified as a third gender here. Born biologically male, the *xanith* do not cross-dress for fear of dishonouring women; rather, they wear pastel colours, part their hair on the side, and wear cosmetics.
Peru	Inca civilization (Native American)	The Incas worshipped a dual-gendered God and shamans called *quariwarmi* acted as liaisons between dichotomous worlds, i.e., past/present.
Polynesia	Tongan and Tahitian (Pacific Islander)	Though they don't consider themselves transgender or gay, the Tongan *fakaleiti* are biological males who adopt female dress, characteristics, and social roles. In Tahiti, they are identified as *mah'u*.
Samoa	Samoan (Pacific Islander)	The *fa'afafine* are identified as a third gender in Samoan culture, though they're not considered "gay," since they have relations with men, women, or other *fa'afafine*. These individuals are biological males who have a strong female orientation, often recognized by their parents early in childhood.
Siberia	The Chukchi, Koryak, and Kamchadal peoples	These cultures identified three genders—men, women, and *shamans*—who, because of their spirit power, were able to marry men as well as women.
Thailand	Thai (Southeast Asia)	The *kathoeys* are seen as belonging to a third gender, if not female. Even though they are born biologically male, they appear outwardly almost exclusively as females.
United States	Lakota, Ktunaxa, and Sioux Nations (Native Americans)	These clans all identify *two-spirited gender* as a biological male who lives as a woman. Lakota identify them as *winkte*.
United States	Mohave Nation (Native American)	Referring to the creation myth that tells of a time when humans were not sorted by sex, they identify four genders—men, women, *hwame* (male-identified females), and *alyha* (female-identified males).
United States	Navajo Nation (Native American)	This cultural group identifies the *nadleehi*—a third gender, where a biologically male person carries both the masculine and feminine spirit. The *dilbaa* refers to a biological female with a more masculine spirit.
United States	Zuni Nation (Native American)	Identifies the *lhamana*, where a person lives as both genders at the same time. Typically, they are biological males who live as females, adopting their dress and performing traditionally female duties.

Source: Adapted from: World Gender Customs (2011). Retrieved 09 02 2013 from https://maps.google.com/maps/ms?ie=UTF8&oe=UTF8&msa=0&msid=210679661112179870040.0004a2e0a49561ae0ff35

Third Gender Table (2011). Retrieved 09 02 2013 from: http://thirdgendertable.blogspot.ca/

GENDER INEQUALITY

Living in a world divided into distinct categories of male and female has very real consequences. When speaking of women's rights, Rama Yade, France's Minister of State for Foreign Affairs and Human Rights, indicated that the international community is "still far from having achieved a victory over inequality regardless of which continent we look at" (UNHR, 2009). Historically and at present, most societies are **patriarchal**. This domination has led to tangible inequities that are now systemically embedded within some of the most important social institutions in society. By looking at major sectors of society and the allocation of power, prestige, or income within them, we can see the gender inequalities that exist.

Global Inequality

Can you imagine how you would feel if your fate depended on the way in which a chicken died? In northern Ghana, more than 1000 women live in Gambaga—a camp for witches that is run by a male chief. They pay him rent and work in his fields in return for his protection. Some of the women have been there for as long as 20 years. The inhabitants of their villages forced them out their homes after accusing them of being witches. With nowhere to go, they journey to Gambaga. When the chief decides that the demon is no longer with them, he cuts a chicken's throat and then releases it into the air. If the dead chicken falls with the wings facing the sky, the demon has left the woman and she can return to her home village. If, however, the wings face the ground, she must stay in Gambaga (Badoe, 2010).

Patriarchy: Historically, any social system that was based on the authority of the heads of the household, which were traditionally male; recently, the term has come to mean male domination in general.

Though we may have thought that the idea of witchcraft was long gone, it is very much a present-day concern. With witchcraft comes all of the ancient stereotypes that surround the dichotomies between good and evil, men and women, powerful and powerless.

For Irina Bokova, Director General of UNESCO, empowering women could be as easy as teaching them to read, if access to education weren't so problematic: "Two in every three of the world's 759 million illiterate adults are women," she says; and there is no justification for it (UNESCO, 2010).

Unequal access to education is only one of the problems that face women and girls all over the world today. Keeping them safe is another. Consider the following:

- Violence against women is a universal phenomenon.
- Women are subjected to different forms of violence—physical, sexual, psychological, and economic—both within and outside their homes.
- Rates of women experiencing physical violence at least once in their lifetime vary depending on where they live.
- In many regions of the world, longstanding customs put considerable pressure on women to accept abuse (UN Women, 2011).
- The International Labour Organization estimates that 98 percent of the people trafficked for sexual exploitation are women and girls (International Labour Organization, 2009).

This kind of abuse is found in Canada as well. On January 29, 2012, Mohammad Shafia, 58, his second wife, Tooba Mohammad Yahya, 41, and their son Hamed Mohammad Shafia, 20, were found guilty of four counts of first-degree murder in the deaths of sisters, Zainab, 19, Sahar, 17, and Geeti Shafia, 13, and Shafia's first wife, Rona Amir Mohammad, 50 (Global News, 2012). It was a case that captured headlines and fascinated Canadians for weeks on end, largely because parents rarely murder their children, but also because, although Shafia denied it, many people believed this to be an "honour killing." Though the great majority of honour killings that take place do not make it into the headlines, the Shafia case made national news because it happened in Canada, and because the perpetrators were convicted of first-degree murder.

According to the United Nations:

Globally, around five thousand women and girls are murdered and abused every year by male relatives as punishment for a range of behaviours judged to have damaged the family

Source: © Yaba Badoe

Ma Hawa is the spokeswoman for the witches of Gambaga. How is it that the practices that define Gambaga can still exist today?

reputation. The so called "honour killings" by relatives are often in response to perceived breaches of traditions governing sexual behaviour; the woman may have been raped; she may have expressed a desire to choose her own husband; said she wanted a divorce; or tried to claim an inheritance. (UNHR, 2010)

Officially, about 5000 women and girls worldwide experience violence each year for bringing shame to their families. Five thousand is both a large number and a small number. When we think about how much violence is acceptable against women, 5000 women seems like a huge number, because, in reality, the only acceptable amount of violence against women is no violence. However, when we look at different kinds of violence against women—like female genital mutilation (FGM)—5000 is a very small number. FGM encompasses all of the procedures comprising partial or total removal of the external female genitalia, plus any other injury to the female genital organs for non-medical reasons (World Health Organization, 2012). Usually, traditional circumcisers or those involved in childbirth carry out the ritual. According to World Vision, "Between 100 and 140 million girls and women worldwide have undergone female genital mutilation (FGM) or cutting, and over 3 million girls under the age of 18 across the African continent are at risk of being cut" (World Vision International, 2011). Though prevalent in Africa, FGM is a worldwide phenomenon, and is a violation against women's human rights.

It is clear that women's oppression is a global concern, and we are still a long way from lessening the inequalities that exist between genders.

Inequality in Canada

Although we like to think, because we live in such a liberal country, that levels of gender inequality are relatively low in Canada. In reality, however, Canada is not immune from gender inequality. In Canada, women have had to struggle for the right to vote, the right for equal pay, and the right to enter male-dominated occupations.

One of this textbook's authors, Deborah Boutilier, took part in one of those struggles, becoming one of the first female machinists in Ontario in the late 1970s and joining a movement that resulted in a large steel mill, Stelco, finally rehiring women in non-traditional jobs (Luxton & Corman, 1991). This struggle wasn't just about hiring the women; it was also about recognizing their skills and presence in the factory: washrooms and change rooms had to be built, equal pay issues had to be addressed, and appropriate behaviour on the shop floor was a situation that had to be constantly monitored. Though Boutilier did not work at Stelco, she did work as a machinist in male-dominated industrial shops. Having her work boots spray-painted pink, the lenses of her safety glasses painted black, and her lathe sabotaged more than once was enough to tell her that women weren't always welcomed in the shop. And apart from Boutilier's personal experiences, national statistics show that although women hold higher levels of education than men, they make less money and are more likely to live in poverty (Statistics Canada, 2010).

Years ago, women did not have the same access to education as men, so men had higher levels of completed education. Many women thought that education was unattainable because from the time they were children, they were "taught to play a serving role, to be docile and submissive, to get what they want by being coy, instead of aggressive. They [were] socialized to expect their lives [would] be spent as housewives ..." (Goldberg, 1970, p. 35). However, that trend has reversed itself, and today the situation is completely different (Turcotte, 2012). Table 7.2 indicates that by 2009, more women than men attained both post-secondary certificates or diplomas and university degrees, indicating their increasing participation in higher education.

Generally, girls fare better in elementary school than boys, by obtaining better marks; but that hasn't always lead to greater advantages in terms of post-secondary education. Even though women are more likely than men to go to college or university, they don't necessarily end up making more money than men when they enter the job market. In general, a higher educational level means a higher income; but when men and women have the same education levels, there is a disparity in their income levels. When women and men working full-time are compared, women's earnings remain at about 71% of men's, a ratio that has fluctuated between 70% and 72% since 1999 (Williams, 2012). The story is much the same if we compare hourly wages between men and women, as opposed to full-time earnings (which can be problematic because of the differing definitions of "full-time work"). In general, women continue to have average hourly wages that are lower than men's, but the gap between the wages of women and men has declined (Williams, 2012). What are the consequences of this disparity? How would you feel knowing that employees working next to you do the same job as you but earn more or less money based solely on whether they are male or female?

Studying the differences in stress levels (work-to-home conflict) between men and women in higher-status jobs, researchers found that "women are

TABLE 7.2
Distribution of Women and Men, by Age Group and Highest Level of Educational Attainment, Canada, 1990 and 2009

Highest Level of Educational Attainment	25 to 34				25 to 54			
	1990		2009		1990		2009	
	Women	Men	Women	Men	Women	Men	Women	Men
	Percentage							
0 to 8 years	3.9	4.6	1.4	1.5	8.6	9.0	2.2	2.7
Some high school	15.5	17.9	5.2	8.0	17.5	18.0	6.6	9.2
High school diploma	27.3	23.0	15.0	19.3	25.4	20.0	19.4	19.7
Some postsecondary	9.9	9.7	7.4	8.2	8.2	8.1	6.3	6.5
Postsecondary certificate/diploma	28.3	29.3	36.7	37.0	26.6	27.8	37.2	36.8
University degree	15.0	15.6	34.3	26.0	13.7	17.1	28.1	25.1
Total population (thousands)	**2466**	**2469**	**2265**	**2280**	**6016**	**6014**	**7262**	**7256**

Source: Statistics Canada, Distribution of women and men, by age group and highest level of educational attainment, Canada, 1990 and 2009. Reproduced and distributed on an "as is" basis with the permission of Statistics Canada.

less likely than men to have executive, skilled, and unskilled occupations and more likely than men to have midlevel professional or sales jobs" (Schieman, Kurashina, & VanGundy, 2006, p. 248). This is partially because women are still graduating from programs that lead to "traditionally female" occupations. According to Statistics Canada, "in 2008, women accounted for over three out of four graduates in education and in health sciences programs. In humanities, in visual and performing arts and communications technologies, as well as in social and behavioural sciences and law, roughly two out of three graduates were women" (Turcotte, 2012, p. 20).

Why do you think this is the case? Are there still strong negative stereotypes that exist around male nurses or female engineers? Is this a matter of socialization—that young girls grow up thinking that their place is in the home? Have you ever noticed the wording in job advertisements? Researchers have found that gender stereotypical wording actually helps to reinforce **gender inequality**. Job advertisements in male-dominated fields use more masculine wording (i.e., words associated with male stereotypes, such as *leader, competitive, dominant*) than advertisements within female-dominated areas. And, more importantly, women found these jobs less appealing (Gaucher, Friesen, & Aaron, 2011). Additional research shows that another explanation might be applicable here. When filling positions for a newly restructured bank, bank management in another study used signs, photographs, and videos that showed men as prestigious personal bankers and women as customer relations managers, positions with lower pay and no supervisory power. In other words, they used gender stereotypical images to determine which person should get which job (Skuratowicz & Hunter, 2004).

Whereas it may have been a matter of socialization years ago, recent research would suggest that there are other conscious or subconscious reasons for the gender segregation that keeps women in traditional occupations. While some women do manage to rise to the top, the numbers in comparison to men are still disproportionately small. Only 17 percent of corporate officers and 13 percent of directors at Canada's top 500 private and public sector companies are

Gender inequality: The disparities (either obvious or hidden) that people experience based on their gender, as opposed to their biological sex.

female, representing a mere gain of 2.8 percent since 2002 (McNish & McFarland, 2010). A recent study shows that in any given year from 1997 to 2009, men were two to three times more likely than women to hold senior positions above the level of director, even though women make up half the Canadian workforce. Men have consistently been 1.5 times more likely than women to hold positions at the middle management level—the most common stepping-stone to executive positions (Wright, 2011). But then women seem to run into the **glass ceiling**.

While there aren't very many women heading up some of Canada's largest corporations, there are even fewer helping to govern our country. Though women represent half the population of Canada, they only fill roughly one-fifth of the seats in federal parliament (Galloway, 2010). How will young girls learn to aspire to be politicians, and how will young boys learn that women can be strong, effective leaders, if women are not actively participating in positions of power and legitimate authority?

Very frequently, women end up working in "**precarious employment**" situations. In 2008, for example, almost 40% of employed women, compared with 30% of employed men, were in non-standard work arrangements, such as part-time, casual, or temporary jobs, as well as self-employment and multiple jobs (Townson, 2009). Although some women voluntarily choose part-time work because they're going to school or caring for others, a substantial number of women work part-time because they cannot find full-time employment. According to Statistics Canada, in 2009, 25.9% of female part-time employees reported wanting full-time employment, but only finding part-time work (Ferrao, 2012).

ENDING THOUGHTS

Sex and gender are complicated subjects, even more complicated when we investigate all the individuals who inhabit the places between the traditional roles of male and female. Do you think life would be any easier if the construct of gender didn't exist at all? What if you could grow up in a world where there was no pressure to conform to either role? That's exactly what is happening to a child named Storm in Toronto. Kathy Witterick gave birth to a baby named Storm in May 2011 and, along with her partner David Stocker, decided to keep the baby's sex a secret. There are only seven people who know if Storm is a boy or a girl, including the baby's two older brothers. After Storm's birth, the parents sent an email to friends and family, telling them they wouldn't be announcing Storm's sex just yet: "A tribute to freedom and choice in place of limitation, a stand up to what the world could become in Storm's lifetime (a more progressive place? …)" (Poisson, 2011). When do you think Storm will decide on who he or she is? Will the parents succeed in raising a child without the societal pressures of gender roles and stereotyping?

Glass ceiling: An invisible barrier that prevents women and minorities from advancement in organizations.

Precarious employment: Employment that differs from the traditional ideal of a stable, full-time job.

READING

FIGURE SKATING IS THE MOST MASCULINE SPORT IN THE HISTORY OF FOREVER

By Julie Mannell

In Judith Butler's novel *Gender Trouble*, she claims that masculine/feminine divisions were built upon homophobic cultural taboos that inform strict societal regulations of individual sexuality. These hetero normative acts serve the purpose of ratifying day-to-day expressions of our individuality as natural identifiers of our gender, and furthermore to marginalize and subjugate desires and expressions that fall outside of these artificial boundaries.

When I was 12 years old I knew nothing of Judith Butler. That was, however, the first year I learned about sexual desire. It began innocently enough. I dreamed of being the first figure skater at the Pelham (Ontario) arena to make it to the Olympics. Fulfilling such a lofty ambition entailed hours on ice, practicing before and after school, special off-ice rehearsals where we jumped in shoes, and learning how to dance with a partner. For a while my partner was an older coach from the former Soviet Union who would say "last chance" every time I went through my waltz routine. One day I thought I'd call him out on giving more chances after saying each was the last, to which he responded, "In Russia when they say last chance, they mean last chance … and then they shoot you." He scared the shit out of me that day and I was excited when I was paired off with a younger boy instead.

His name was Isaac Molowenski, and he was the first boy to put his hand on my hip, rest his chest on mine, and evoke all the passion that could possibly transpire when you're in the sixth grade at a civic center with both of your mothers watching from the wooden bleachers. Even with his shimmering suspenders and elastic waisted technical knit pants, I knew he was the sexiest thing. I felt it might be love.

On the ice he was some sort of free dancing God. He'd just landed his double axel and rumour had it he was starting work on his triple-toe-loop, an elemental feat comparable to driving a Ferrari. Yet, off the ice, the hockey players in neighboring change rooms would mutter "faggot" as they strapped cups on their crotches to protect their balls from one another. The other mothers would whisper over hot chocolate in the lobby, "How could anyone do that to their son?" And at school he was just another kid with an elaborate collection of Pokemon cards. I'd felt I'd discovered a hidden gem in my practices. I may not have been the queen in classroom politics but on the ice I could do a mean flying camel that would even have enticed Rudy Galindo during his sparkly-onesie "Send in the Clowns" phase.

I'd made a plan to coax Isaac's attention by coyly performing backwards spread eagles as he tried to work on his gold skills number. This merely annoyed him. Then I decided to tell my crush to Dolly Laverty who then told her Mom who told Isaac's Mom who giggled about it with my Mom. The plan worked and I'd earned an invitation to his thirteenth birthday party—a hot tub party! I remember braiding my hair in pigtails like Britney Spears in the "Hit Me Baby One More Time" video and purchasing a brand new bikini at the local Giant Tiger. These things meant I was taking the party very seriously. I had sat up late at night dreaming about how the party would go and for some reason I'd made an unfair assumption. With all of the flak poor Isaac had received for somehow breaking with conventional notions of male-normative behaviour, I had assumed that I was the only girl who knew the truth—that he was the sexiest 12 year-old in the history of forever (or at least in Pelham in the spring of 2000). The strength of this assumption had planted a very solid image in my mind of us alone in his jacuzzi, sipping ginger ale, professing our undying passions to each other. Who else knew and could aptly appreciate the decadence of his Russian split or the suave curves to his twizzles?

I arrived ten minutes late and his mother offered me a bowl of chips. "Hurry on outside," she said, and hurry I did—through the living room, the newly refinished kitchen, the set of sliding doors, up the patio steps, and there he was, at the center of the hot tub in all of his white chested titillation. Surrounded by the entire synchro team.

That day Isaac broke my heart. The other girls' chests had filled out more and they too wanted a chance with the boy who could throw them, lift them, and death spiral them into a national championship. I would find a way to get over him, but the feeling would never leave: figure skating is the most masculine sport there is. Figure skating is the sexiest thing a man could do.

I believe the first time I wanked off it had something to do with a fantasy of Elvis Stojko and I behind a Zamboni on our wedding night, but I digress. I do feel inclined to mention that figure skating has a bad rep. Surely there is a place for our Rudys and our Johnny Weirs and, of course, they are masculine as well. This has nothing to do with a specific aim of attraction, it's more in the essence of sexuality as a whole, as an energy you put out into the world that then draws people in. When you are skating you are not an opinion, you are not a conversation, you are a body spinning, a body antagonizing gravity, a body alone against the elements. There are no team members, there are no supports. To watch male singles is to watch a solitary man with the force of the world on his back, a man tied to razor-thin blades, a man at war with nothing and everything, a man and physics, a man and cold air, a man as only a man—fighting himself, fighting the universe.

After Isaac, I moved on to the gutter punks at the local skate park. What amazed me was how, except for the clear disparity in musical accompaniment, what skate boys did after school was very similar to what we did after school. Their jumps had different names, their movements had a different aesthetic, and their tools were boards with wheels—but in essence they were still men jumping and twirling. The evidence is even in the lexicon: "figure skate" abbreviated to "skate," as if they wanted to exclude the bodily element, the figure, and hide what they were doing so that it would somehow be less sentimental, less attached to anything human or feeling. These boys were the cool boys and their coolness came with their blatant disregard for chivalrous conventions—spitting on curbs, showing off scars, and smashing bones against concrete. How were their anti-establishment personae any less anti-establishment than a man putting on a sequined unitard and shamelessly shimmying to "The Samba?" I admire both for their individuality; however, I must confess that I've always been partial to any man who can wear lycra with confidence. For myself, the difference was in the fact that the skater boys were members of a collective with a similar semblance. The figure skaters, like Isaac, often stood alone—talking during ice time was frowned upon, and there was usually only one male anyhow—there wasn't necessarily a community, there wasn't any one ice-skating outfit that they all wore and fit them all. They were artists who used their body like a brush, artists who fashioned their routines and their outfits according to the colors of their movements. There is a sort of bravery in the solitude of men's singles.

In 2010 Skate Canada, basically figure skating's equivalent to the federal government, announced that they were planning to make men's singles more masculine. Essentially their aim was to "degay" the sport in order to attract hockey fans. There are several reasons such a statement is ludicrous. The first that comes to mind is the thought of my homeboys in Pelham—slightly balding, beer-bellied potato people in hockey jerseys, munching nachos on a Saturday sitting on some couch and loudly applauding the footwork of Alexei Yagudin. While the thought brings a smile to my face, it isn't realistically going to happen. These are men who grew up on hockey, men for whom it is entirely an issue of regional pride, familial alliance, and communal tradition, and not about gender performance. To assume these men would switch sports, renegotiate their fandom, simply to inhabit some ideal of their sex is a slap in the face to hockey fans, figure skating enthusiasts, and Canadian sports followers everywhere. I wouldn't want it anyhow.

Instead this assertion reveals our own assumptions of gender. That for one reason or another we've ascribed certain cultural practices to men and women as implicit aspects of who they are as people—then gone so far as to project these assumptions onto sports. The proclamation that figure skating needs a "masculine makeover" in order to draw audiences then illustrates a society where love of sports is less of an individual autonomous act, and more of an effort to exert one's self as a certain kind of person to others. This seems absurd, and when contextualized within the framework of changing certain sports' traditions to better accommodate societal insecurities about sexuality, ultimately the message Skate Canada broadcasts to sports followers everywhere is that masculinity always wins and femininity loses. That the sports we love reveal the people we desire. As if a hockey jersey or a costume can dictate where we put our penis, non-penis, half penis, penis ambition, and so forth.

Both figure skating and hockey have an important place in our collective Canadian nostalgia—a time before we spent nights in Budget Inns, drinking cheap wine and proving some sort of point about who we are as men and women. They conjure memories of a world with twenty-five-cent hot chocolates, pay phones, wooden bleachers, smelly change-room showers and being people with people, doing what they loved because it made them feel good, because it made them a part of something, and for the pure reason that the arena was the center of most communities, a place for mothers to gossip, fathers to drink, and kids to be kids

without the pressure of enacting prescribed gender codes. This is in an ideal world.

I won't ever marry Isaac Molowenski, not because he's gay (he's not), and not because I find him emasculated or defeated (he isn't). I won't ever marry Isaac Molowenski because he's now a successful computer programmer who makes good money, and I'm a lowly writer, with little to give but my words and little to gain but the (maybe) occasional twenty-five dollar cheque from some "up-and-coming" publication. He still skates, he gets many women, and I am happy for him, and would have been happy for him otherwise as well.

Sometimes I still think of Isaac as he was then, and the fact that, however light what I've written might be, I remember the real and excruciating pain he went through at a young age, simply because he preferred toe-loops to slap shots. I also remember how sexy he was to me and to other girls who hung around that rink, how my attraction revealed sexuality's multidimensional character, that it takes on many different forms and how masculinity and femininity are never fully one or the other, and most certainly not static binaries.

Maybe you have a son who favors blades with picks. Maybe you have a daughter who'd rather hang around boys who can dance than boys who can spit, or do kick-flips in Volcom caps. Maybe, if you're lucky, they're really good at what they do and actually make it out of your small Ontario town and into the cast of Stars on Ice. Maybe. Just know that whatever any of it means, none of it is certain, and there is more to all of us than a sequined bow-tie or a goalie mask.

Source: "Figure Skating is the Most Masculine Sport in the History of Forever," Julie Mannell, previously published on The Barnstormer. (www.thebarnstormer.com)

DISCUSSION QUESTIONS

1. Male figure skaters, hockey players, and skate boarders are all extraordinary athletes, yet the labels that differentiate the groups differ significantly. Compile a list of stereotypes that identify each of the groups, and explain the formal and informal consequences they impose.

2. CBC television's *Battle of the Blades* (in its 4th season as this book is being written) pairs female figure skaters and male hockey players and pits the teams against each other in a figure skating competition. As suggested by the article's author, do you think this might have been an attempt to "degay" figure skating for males? Determine the success of this program as a strategy to masculinize the sport of male figure skating.

3. Brendan Burke, the son of Toronto Maple Leafs General Manager Brian Burke, was an advocate for gays in professional sports. Openly gay himself, he tragically died in a 2010 car accident, just as his career as an aspiring social activist started. Sexual orientation seems to be such an issue when it comes to male figure skating, yet in virtually every other sport, heterosexuality is the assumed norm. In 2009, 2% of the Canadian population self-reported to be either gay or bisexual (Statistics Canada, 2011). It's conceivable that some of those individuals are playing in the National Hockey League—or any other professional sports league. Analyze the reasons why we rarely read about homosexuality in professional sports, but often read about drug abuse, gambling, and womanizing.

KWIP

KNOW IT AND OWN IT: WHAT DO I BRING TO THIS?

Are you a person who is comfortable with the skin that you're in, or are you someone who has felt the sting of a

bully's taunts? When you read this chapter, feel grounded in knowing that whatever you feel, or don't feel, about your sexuality, you're likely not alone. Sometimes it takes years to discover who you really are—but you'll get there one day!

WALKING THE TALK: HOW CAN I LEARN FROM THIS?

Are you comfortable living in the "binary" world—when it comes to gender and sexuality—that most of Western society seems to live in? Are you aware of the spaces that exist between the traditional concepts of male and female? When learning about sex and gender, try to imagine the individuals who inhabit this space. You may already know some students who are gay, transgender, or questioning. Talk to these students and see how if they think they live in a "binary" world, and if so, what it's like for them.

IT IS WHAT IT IS: IS THIS INSIDE OR OUTSIDE MY COMFORT ZONE?

Learning about anything new is always a bit uncomfortable, and discussing our sexuality can be intimidating at the best of times. In this chapter, open-mindedness is your best friend as you discover the complexities that are involved with people of all cultures who experience and express their sexuality differently. Traditional Western interpretations of sex, gender, and sexuality may be the norm for you, but that doesn't mean that they are the norm for everyone. Being open to how others choose (or don't choose) to define masculine and feminine is the key in this step. Try living a day without the categories of male and female and just see what happens. How powerful are the labels that we put on people?

PUT IT IN PLAY: HOW CAN I USE THIS?

Go to the *Two Spirits* documentary page on the PBS *Independent Lens* website (**http://www.pbs.org/independentlens/two-spirits/map.html** to launch an interactive map). Explore this website while you visit 25 countries inhabited (or once inhabited) by individuals who live in between masculine and feminine or as a combination of both. Test your comfort levels here and imagine your reaction to the people that you see on this site. How would you feel if you got the chance to meet people from any of these cultures? Would you shy away, willingly learn more, or avoid them altogether.

Located at www.nelson.com/site/walkamile1e

- Consolidate your knowledge with the **Flashcards**.
- Gauge your understanding with **Picture This** and accompanying questions for reflection.
- Develop your critical thinking skills by working through **The Daily.**
- Apply your understanding with **KWIP** interactive!
- Develop your critical reading skills through compelling **Readings** and accompanying short answer questions.

REFERENCES

American Psychiatric Association. (2000). *Diagnostic and statistical manual of mental disorders*, 4th edition. Washington, DC: American Psychiatric Association.

Associated Press. (2001, July 12). Navajo teen death may be hate crime: Retrieved from *Associated Press News Archive*: http://www.apnewsarchive.com/2001/Navajo-Teen-Death-May-Be-Hate-Crime/id-cc5a9389be3e8e4cc808db96be3a6be5

Associated Press. (2013, April 14). 'Pregnant man' vows to continue fighting for divorce with new girlfriend by his side so he can prove to his three children that his transgender marriage was legitimate. Retrieved from *Daily Mail Online*: http://www.dailymail.co.uk/news/article-2303138/Thomas-Beatie-Pregnant-man-vows-fight-divorce-prove-transgender-marriage-legitimate.html

Badoe, Y. (Director). (2010). *The witches of Gambaga* [Motion Picture].

Barford, V. (2008, February 25). Iran's 'diagnosed transsexuals.' Retrieved from *BBC News*: http://news.bbc.co.uk/2/hi/7259057.stm

BBC News. (2012, January 1). In pictures: Indonesia's waria. Retrieved from *BBC News*: http://news.bbc.co.uk/2/shared/spl/hi/picture_gallery/08/asia_pac_indonesia0s_waria/html/2.stm

Blunden, P., & Dale, J. (2009). Gender dysphoria: Time for positive thinking. *Mental Health Practice*, 16–20.

Nibley, L. (Director). (2010, November 3). *Cinema Q, women + film: Two spirits* [documentary film]. Retrieved from *Denver Film Festival*: http://www.denverfilm.org/festival/film/detail.aspx?id=22745&FID=49

Duff, M. (n.d.). Michelle Duff: Racing successes. Retrieved from *Michelle Duff, Writer, Photographer, Publisher, Grand Prix Champion*: http://www.michelle-duff.ca/webpages/sportscareer.html

Ellis, K., & Erickson, K. (2002). Transsexual and transgenderist experiences and treatment options. *The Family Journal*, 289–299.

Ettner, R. (1999). *Gender loving care: A guide to counseling gender-variant clients*. New York: Norton.

Ferrao, V. (2012, February 24). Paid work. Retrieved from *Statistics Canada*: http://www.statcan.gc.ca/pub/89-503-x/2010001/article/11387-eng.htm

Galloway, G. (2010, October 12). Women: Half the population, a fifth the seats in Parliament. Retrieved from *The Globe and Mail*: http://www.theglobeandmail.com/news/national/time-to-lead/women-in-power/part-5-women-half-the-population-a-fifth-the-seats-in-parliament/article1754326/

Gaucher, D., Friesen, K., & Aaron, C. (2011). Evidence that gendered wording in job advertisements exists and sustains gender inequality. *Journal of Personality and Social Psychology*, 109–128.

Global News. (2012, February 8). The Shafia murder timeline. Retrieved from *Global News*: http://www.globalnews.ca/news/170784/timeline-shafia-family-murder-trial

Goldberg, M. P. (1970). The economic exploitation of women. *Review of Radical Political Economics*, 35–47.

International Labour Organization. (2009). *Give girls a chance: Tackling child labour, a key to the future*.

Kinks, The (1970). Lola. *Lola versus powerman and the moneygoround, part 1*.

Kinsey, A., Pomeroy, W., & Martin, C. (1948). *Sexual behaviour in the human male*. Philadelphia: W.B. Saunders.

Klein, F. (1993). *The bisexual option* (2nd ed.). Binghamton, NY: The Haworth Press.

Lomax, T. (2007). Wakawahine—A given or a becoming? In J. Hutchings & C. Aspin, *Sexuality and the stories of Indigenous people*. Wellington Aoteroa: Huia Publishers.

Luxton, M., & Corman, J. (1991). Getting to work: The challenges of getting women back into Stelco. *Labour/Le Travail*, 149–185.

Mannell, J. (2012, July 20). Figure Skating is the most masculine sport in the history of forever. Retrieved from *The Barnstormer*: http://thebarnstormer.com/figure-skating-is-the-most-masculine-sport-in-the-history-of-forever-2/

McKay, B., & McKay, K. (2010, February 21). 8 interesting (and insane) male rites of passage from around the world. Retrieved from *The Art of Manliness*: http://artofmanliness.com/2010/02/21/male-rites-of-passage-from-around-the-world/

McNish, J., & McFarland, J. (2010, October 8). Why the executive suite is the final frontier for women. Retrieved from *The Globe and Mail*: http://www.theglobeandmail.com/news/national/time-to-lead/women-in-power/part-1-why-the-executive-suite-is-the-final-frontier-for-women/article1749955/

Public Health Agency of Canada. (2008, January 1). Questions and answers: Gender identity in schools Retrieved 2012-13-05 from *Public Health Agency of Canada*: http://www.phac-aspc.gc.ca/publicat/qagis-qrise/pdf/qagis-qrise-eng.pdf

Oprah Show Info. (2012). First TV interview: The pregnant man [TV episode]. Retrieved from *Oprah*: http://www.oprah.com/showinfo/First-TV-Interview-The-Pregnant-Man_1

Perkins, R. (1993, December). American Indian gender crossers. *Polare*. Retrieved from *gendercentre*: http://www.gendercentre.org.au/2article5.htm

Poisson, J. (2011, December 26). The 'genderless baby' who caused a Storm of controversy in 2011. Retrieved from *Toronto Star*: http://www.thestar.com/news/article/1105515--the-genderless-baby-who-caused-a-storm-of-controversy-in-2011

Preves, S. E. (2003). *Intersex and identity: The contested self*. New Brunswick, New Jersey: Rutgers University Press.

Pullman, L. (2012, March 24). Booted out for being born a boy: Transgender beauty queen kicked out of Miss Universe. Retrieved from *Mail Online*: http://www.dailymail.co.uk/news/article-2119786/Jenna-Talackova-Transgender-beauty-queen-kicked-Miss-Universe-Canada-pageant.html

Raptis, M. (2012, March 26). Miss Universe Canada disqualifies transsexual beauty queen Jenna Talackova. Retrieved from *National Post*: http://news.nationalpost.com/2012/03/26/jenna-talackova-miss-universe-canada-disqualified/

Reuters. (2012, April 10). Jenna Talackova forces Miss Universe transgender rule change. Retrieved from *National Post*: http://news.nationalpost.com/2012/04/10/jenna-talackova-forces-miss-universe-transgender-rule-change/

Schieman, S., Kurashina, Y., & VanGundy, K. (2006). The nature of work and the stress of higher status. *The Journal of Health and Social Behaviour*, 242-257.

Sears, J. (2005). *Youth, education, and sexualities: An international encyclopedia*, Volume 2. Westport Connecticut: Greenwood.

Skuratowicz, E., & Hunter, L. (2004). Where do women's jobs come from? Job resegregation in an American Bank. *Work and Occupation*, 73–110.

Statistics Canada. (2010, December 16). Women in Canada: Economic well-being. Retrieved July 8, 2012, from *The Daily*: http://www.statcan.gc.ca/daily-quotidien/101216/dq101216c-eng.htm

Statistics Canada. (2011, October 7). Gay pride ... by the numbers. Retrieved July 24, 2012, from *Statistics Canada*: http://www42.statcan.ca/smr08/2011/smr08_158_2011-eng.htm

Statistics Canada. (2012, February 24). Distribution of women and men, by age group and highest level of educational attainment, Canada, 1990 and 2009. Retrieved from *Statistics Canada*: http://www.statcan.gc.ca/pub/89-503-x/2010001/article/11542/tbl/tbl001-eng.htm

Townson, M. (2009, September). Poverty rates still shocking among Canadian women. In Women's poverty and the recession. Retrieved from *Canadian Centre for Policy Alternatives*: http://www.policyalternatives.ca/sites/default/files/uploads/publications/National_Office_Pubs/2009/Womens_Poverty_in_the_Recession.pdf

Turcotte, M. (2012, February 24). Women and education. Retrieved May 13, 2012 from *Statistics Canada*: http://www.statcan.gc.ca/pub/89-503-x/2010001/article/11542-eng.htm

UNESCO. (2010, November). Winners of the UNESCO literary prizes: Power of women's literacy 2010. Retrieved from *UNESCO*: http://unesdoc.unesco.org/images/0018/001891/189122e.pdf

UNHR. (2009, June 8). Inequality before the law. Retrieved from *United Nations Human Rights*: http://www.ohchr.org/EN/NewsEvents/Pages/InequalityBeforeLaw.aspx

UNHR. (2010, May 7). UNHRC. Murder in the name of family honour. Retrieved from *United Nations Human Rights*: http://www.ohchr.org/EN/NewsEvents/Pages/MurderInTheNameOfFamilyHonour.aspx

UN Women. (2011, January). Words to action: Newsletter on violence against women. Retrieved from *United Nations*: http://www.un.org/womenwatch/daw/vaw/Words-to-Action-Issue-No-10-January-2011.pdf

Williams, C. (2012, February 24). Economic well being. Retrieved May 16, 2012, from *Statistics Canada*: http://www.statcan.gc.ca/pub/89-503-x/2010001/article/11388-eng.htm

Winters, K. (2010). GID Reform advocates: Because our identities are not disordered. Retrieved from *GIDReform.org*: http://www.gidreform.org/gid30285.html#numbers

World Health Organization. (2012, February). Female genital mutilation. Retrieved from *World Health Organization*: http://www.who.int/mediacentre/factsheets/fs241/en/

World Vision International. (2011, August). Protecting the girl child from female genital mutilation. Retrieved from *United Nations Human Rights*: http://www2.ohchr.org/english/bodies/cedaw/docs/cedaw_crc_contributions/WorldVisionInternational.pdf

Wright, R. (2011, November 10). Women in senior management: Progress is glacial. Retrieved from *Conference Board of Canada*: http://www.conferenceboard.ca/insideedge/2011/nov2011/nov10-womenseniormgmnt.aspx

Mind and Body

> *"Forgiveness for the ones who cut us deeply and wish that we could love us all the same"*
>
> *Justin Hines, 2011*

DIVERSITY COMPETENCIES

Diversity competencies are specifically learned behaviours that students can actively practise to promote equity and inclusion. By mastering this unit, students will gain the skills to become diversity-competent practitioners, including the ability to

- reflect upon the universalizing implications of the World Health Organization's definition of disability as something every human being can at some point in their lifetime experience

- reconstruct attitudes and approaches whereby people with disabilities move from being "objects" of charity, medical treatment, and social protection to instead being "subjects" with rights to make their own decisions and actively contribute to their community

- assess strategies for the civic engagement of all citizens through an understanding that peoples with disabilities may experience limited opportunities for social inclusion

- appraise universal design practices and principles as an approach to social inclusion and accessibility

- "unlock the possible" by seeing ability, not disability

Consider the following:

- Albert Einstein, a physicist and one of the greatest minds of the 20th century, had a learning disability and didn't speak until age three.
- Ludwig van Beethoven, one of the greatest musical composers in history, was deaf.
- Helen Keller was deaf and blind.
- Vincent Van Gogh, one of the world's most famous painters, lived with depression.
- Christy Brown was an Irish painter and poet who had cerebral palsy. His autobiography, *My Left Foot*, became an Academy Award–winning film.
- John Forbes Nash, the Noble laureate American mathematician and the inspiration for the movie *A Beautiful Mind*, has schizophrenia.
- Brilliant physicist Stephen Hawking has a motor neuron disease.

The simple truth that binds the greatness of these figures is this: disability is not inability. The concept of **disability** is one that is now commonly referred to in discussions about diversity, oppression, and social justice. Disability is an issue of discrimination that relates to the physical, developmental, learning, and mental health aspects of people that results in inequity at a social and individual level (Shier, Sinclair, & Gault, 2011). Disabilities emerged as a government policy issue in Canada during World War I, when many Canadian soldiers returned home injured, and rapid industrialization produced many work-related injuries (Office for Disability Issues HRDC, 2003). Disability issues are present today among all populations in every part of the world, and so everyone should expect to encounter disability issues—both visible and invisible—at work, at school, at home, and in the community (Shier, Sinclair, & Gault, 2011).

In order to work towards a goal of social inclusion for people with disabilities, the diversity-competent practitioner must embrace interventions that break down environmental and social barriers and facilitate equitable opportunities for everyone. As Wu Hongbo, United Nations Under-Secretary-General for Economic and Social Affairs, stated, "It is our responsibility as members of the international community and citizens of our own countries to bring about changes to more than one billion people

Disability: A universal human experience that anyone can experience at any time; disabilities can limit a person's ability to engage in daily activities; disabilities can be visible or invisible, temporary or permanent.

World Health Organization (WHO): United Nations authority on health issues.

Source: Canadian Down Syndrome Society

World Down Syndrome Day uses a poster campaign slogan "See the ability" in addressing attitudinal barriers to social inclusion.

with disabilities worldwide. There is no development when so many people are without equal opportunities and excluded from society" (United Nations, 2012). The goal of the diversity-competent practitioner is to be an agent for social change that "unlocks the possible" through social inclusion. It requires an attitude that we "see the ability," which is now a poster campaign slogan for World Down Syndrome Day.

DEFINING DISABILITY

The International Classification of Functioning, Disability and Health of the **World Health Organization** (WHO) describes disability as a universal human experience, noting that all human beings can at some point in their lifetime experience a problem with mental or physical health and, therefore, some degree of disability (World Health Organization, 2013). This is the broadest description of disability. It removes the dichotomy of ability versus non-ability that reinforces an *us*-versus-*them* approach to disabilities. According to the WHO description, a person might expect his or her abilities to change over the course of a lifetime.

All people live on a continuum that ranges from low to high ability, where some people have greater ability in some aspects of their lives than others (Social Planning Council of Kitchener Waterloo, 2001, p. 8). One's ability at any particular time is dependent on his or her stage of life span development, individual experiences, ecological issues, and even the time of day (Hoyle, 2004).

The Canadian government and its agencies use many different definitions of disability and consequently many different criteria for assessing eligibility for programs and services. Disability programs offered by provinces, territories, and municipalities increase the complexity of defining disability across these different jurisdictions (Office for Disability Issues HRDC, 2003). During public hearings of the House of Common's Subcommittee on the Status of Persons with Disabilities, concerns regarding the definition of disability and eligibility criteria were voiced by professional associations, academics, disability organizations, and people with disabilities (Office for Disability Issues HRDC, 2003). Dr. Dana Hanson, speaking on behalf of the Canadian Medical Association in 2003, said:

> Increasingly, physicians are spending more and more of their time filling out forms … To figure out all the various forms and determine eligibility you almost need to be a physician, a lawyer and tax expert … [T]here is virtually a different definition and a different assessment process for each and every program. A common frustration for physicians is that while a patient qualifies as disabled under one disability program, that same patient does not under another. … There needs to be some consistency and definitions across the various government programs. Let me state very clearly though that this does not mean that eligibility criteria must be identical. However, there must be a way for a more standardized approach. (Office for Disability Issues HRDC, 2003, pp. 53–54)

Disability Perspectives

The lack of consistency among definitions of disability in Canada can be attributed in part to the different perspectives used in understanding this complex and multidimensional concept. When interpreted using a biomedical perspective, the definition of disability is approached as illness or impairment in function that is located within the individual (Office for Disability Issues HRDC, 2003). Using this perspective, disability is viewed as something objective that is fixed in an individual's body or mind and that can be measured in terms of ability to perform specific tasks (Office for Disability Issues HRDC, 2003). When defining disability using a social perspective, the concept can be interpreted as a socially constructed disadvantage that results in a person's social exclusion and possible violation of their legal rights. There is clear evidence at an international level that there is a movement towards including a social perspective within a definition of disability. The **United Nations Convention of the Rights of Persons with Disabilities** includes a social perspective when it defines persons with disabilities as "those who have long-term physical, mental, intellectual or sensory impairments which in interaction with various barriers may hinder their full and effective participation in society on an equal basis" (United Nations, 2006).

How we define disability has evolved over the years through different perspectives that will be referred to as the biomedical perspective, functional limitations perspective, socio-constructionist perspective, socio-economic perspective, legal rights perspective, and the social inclusion perspective (see Table 8.1). These perspectives have influenced the approaches used to accommodate disability within society, including the development of programs and services and their eligibility criteria.

BIOMEDICAL PERSPECTIVE

The biomedical perspective considers disability as an **impairment** to an individual's body or mind that is a result of a health problem, illness, disease, or abnormality (Nixon, 1984). According to this perspective, people with disabilities are sick and therefore require help in the form of medical treatment and specialized care (Bickenbach, 1993). The approach used to accommodate those with disabilities is to fix the individual's impairment through medical interventions focused on the illness or abnormality. An example of this approach is reflected in the branch of psychology referred

United Nations Convention on the Rights of Persons with Disabilities: A human rights instrument adopted by the United Nations in 2006 for the purpose of protecting the human rights and dignity of persons with disabilities; signatories are required to ensure that people with disabilities are equal under the law.

Impairment: According to the biomedical perspective, a medical condition that leads to disability; according to functional perspective, it is any loss or abnormality of physiological, psychological, or anatomical structure or function, whether permanent or temporary.

TABLE 8.1
Disability Perspectives

Perspective	Approach to disability	Critique of perspective
Biomedical	Considers disability as an *impairment* to an individual's body or mind that is a result of a health problem, illness, disease, or abnormality.	Ignores social and environmental factors that affect people with disabilities.
Functional limitations	Quantifies the type and degree of disability a person might have to measure his or her functional limitations and ability to perform certain tasks.	Focuses on individual inability; creates inconsistency in the determination of eligibility for federal programs; approaches disability as pathology (abnormalcy).
Socio-constructionist	Disability is a concept we socially construct as different from the norm; locates disablement issues within society.	Its exclusive focus on the social neglects issues of the physical body and mind.
Socio-economic	Focus on inclusion of people with disabilities within the economic framework of a society; goal of programs is to make people with disabilities more employable.	Does not address impairment nor process of stigmatization experienced by people with disabilities.
Legal rights	Focus is on rights to full participation and non-discrimination for people with disabilities using a human rights and social justice paradigm; perspective used by disability social movement.	Is sometime critiqued for its neglect of individualized experiences of body and mind (medical model) and functional limitation.
Social inclusion	Focus is on contributions all people can make to community as a whole as valued and respected members; challenges the notion of disabled and non-disabled that reinforce an *us*-and-*them* mentality.	Sometimes fails to acknowledge differences arising from intersectionality of identities (e.g., women with disabilities, Aboriginal people with disabilities, people with disabilities from visible minority communities).

to as *abnormal psychology*—a term that pathologizes mental health issues as medically or psychologically abnormal. Criticism of this perspective is that it "locates the defect in a person's body or mind, and that person may be defined as defective, abnormal and by extension biologically or mentally inferior" (Office for Disability Issues HRDC, 2003). In viewing disabilities solely as a medical issue, this perspective ignores social and environmental factors that affect people with disabilities. This can result in the social marginalization and isolation of people with disabilities because this model believes in a service-based approach that focuses on caring for deficiencies using specially trained health professionals (Kretzmann & McKnight, 1993).

FUNCTIONAL LIMITATIONS PERSPECTIVE

The functional limitations perspective, like the biomedical perspective, uses objective standards and is rooted in the concept that impairment of the mind or body is the direct cause of disability (Office for Disability Issues HRDC, 2003). This perspective is used to quantify the degree of disability a person might have and to measure his or her functional limitations (Office for Disability Issues HRDC, 2003). What distinguishes this perspective from the biomedical one is that it utilizes social and environmental criteria in the evaluation of the individual's functional limitations: "Disability is seen as influenced not only by the characteristics of impairments, such as type and severity, but also by how the individual defines a given situation and reacts to it, and how others define that situation through their reactions and expectations" (Office for Disability Issues HRDC, 2003, p. 6). An example of a program that utilizes the functional limitations perspective is the Ontario Disability Support Program. If a person with a disability living in Ontario is applying for financial support through this program, the doctor would be required to complete a medical assessment that includes a Health Status Report and Activities of Daily Living Index. But in addition to the medical assessment, the applicant completes a Self-Report Form that allows him or her to define and describe the situation and detail how the disability affects personal care, participation in the community, and ability to work.

Critiques of the functional limitation perspective have suggested that the attempts to quantify the type and severity of disabilities have contributed to the inconsistency in eligibility criteria for government programs for people with disabilities. Dr. Blake Woodside of the Canadian Psychiatric Association notes that the current system discriminates against those with mental illness because "the use of primitive efforts, phrases such as 'almost all of the time,' 'greater than 90 percent' or 'prolonged,' simply does not address the complex issue of characterizing psychiatric disability" (Office for Disability Issues HRDC, 2003, p. 52). The functional limitations perspective fails to account for recurrent, cyclic, or episodic disabilities, or for the variation in lived experiences of people with disabilities. The other criticism of this perspective is its focus on inability and not ability. Using a standard of "normalcy" for functional assessment, disability is considered pathology, and those people who live outside of these standards become disadvantaged (Oliver, 1990).

SOCIO-CONSTRUCTIONIST PERSPECTIVE

According to this perspective, disability is something that is socially constructed by the ability-orientated and ability-dominant society we live in (Office for Disability Issues HRDC, 2003). The **pathologization** of disability is something that we create socially and it is reinforced through **ableism** it often results in social isolation and marginalization (Bickenbach, 1993). Stereotypes of people with disabilities focus on what we perceive to be different from the "norm"—with the result that similar needs for dignity, friendship, hope for the future, and valuation in the community can then be overlooked (Kretzmann & McKnight, 1993). Our belief about what is normal becomes embedded in our thoughts and is used to legitimize social policies (Oliver, 1990). Ron Mace, founder of the Centre for Universal Design, discusses how socially constructed concepts of normalcy can disadvantage those who fail to measure up:

> We discount people who are less than what we popularly consider to be "normal." To be "normal" is to be perfect, capable, competent and independent. Unfortunately, designers in our society also mistakenly assume that everyone fits this definition of "normal." This just is not the case. (Social Planning Council of Kitchener Waterloo, 2001, p. 1)

According to the social-constructionist perspective, if society constructs disability as inability, then we limit human potential.

Robert Christy writes about his life with cerebral palsy, a life that unlocks the possible and defies the negative labels that others attempt to attach:

> My name is Bob and I have lived and am living a very full, wonderful life as a son, brother, husband, father, father-in-law, and grandfather. I have studied at three post-secondary institutions, received bachelor and master degrees from Canada's two top universities, had a 30-year career with the federal government … yet a close relative thought that I should have been "destroyed at birth," because I have cerebral palsy. I'm a raging extrovert, energized by people and my humorous nature when I am with them. Yet those who paid my salary put me into introvert-natured jobs of research and policy writing, refusing me the opportunity to do the things I knew that I could do best. When I didn't "shine" or meet the potential that those who knew me in my youth thought that I should achieve, people could justifiably say, "What do you expect? He has cerebral palsy" … [N]o matter how clever, diligent or successful I am or may yet become, I will always be judged and known, in a negative non-flattering

Ableism: Discrimination based on ability; occurs when a society has a set of ideas about the "normal" abilities of people.

Pathologization: Characterization as medically or psychologically abnormal.

way as "Bob, the man with cerebral palsy" (Christy, 2001).

One of the contributions of the socio-constructionist perspective is that it locates disablement issues within society and there is the opportunity, therefore, to socially construct meaning and value around abilities (rather than disabilities) that are manifest in ways different from what is socially defined as "normal." A critique of the socio-constructionist perspective of disability is that its exclusive focus on the social neglects issues of the physical body and mind (Hoyle, 2004).

Socio-Economic Perspective

The socio-economic perspective focuses on the inclusion of people with disabilities in the economic framework of society through policies and programs (Hoyle, 2004). Poverty is a significant issue for people with disabilities. In 2006, 48.7 percent of working-age adults with disabilities were unemployed in Canada (Council of Canadians with Disabilities, 2007). Those people with disabilities who must rely on disability support programs often find themselves stigmatized and faced with financial limitations. A forum called "Unlocking the Possible" examined the issue of civic participation for people with disabilities and participants discussed poverty as a barrier:

> Disability dollars don't go far. … For people receiving disability assistance from the government, their disability assistance didn't go far.

The rent that some people paid was more than what was allotted by disability assistance. This meant there was little or no money left for other activities so people stayed home. (Hoyle, 2004)

There is also a relationship between the type of disability a person has and the likelihood of that person living in poverty (see Figure 8.1).

The goal of the socio-economic perspective is to ensure economic well-being, and one of the strategies used by governments to do this is to make people with disabilities more employable (Bickenbach, 1993). In addition to being more likely to live in poverty, people with disabilities have a long history of high unemployment and underemployment in Canada and throughout the world (Council of Canadians with Disabilities, 2007). The International Labour Organization estimates that the exclusion of people with disabilities from the labour market carries with it a price tag of between US$1.37–$1.94 trillion in *annual* loss of global gross domestic product (Council of Canadians with Disabilities, 2007). There are a number of government programs at various jurisdictional levels that are designed to assist with this problem. The Opportunities Fund is a federal government program that uses a socio-economic perspective in helping people with disabilities find employment or self-employment (Office for Disability Issues HRDC, 2003). Another government program, which uses this perspective at the provincial level, is the Disability Related Employment Supports program, which is

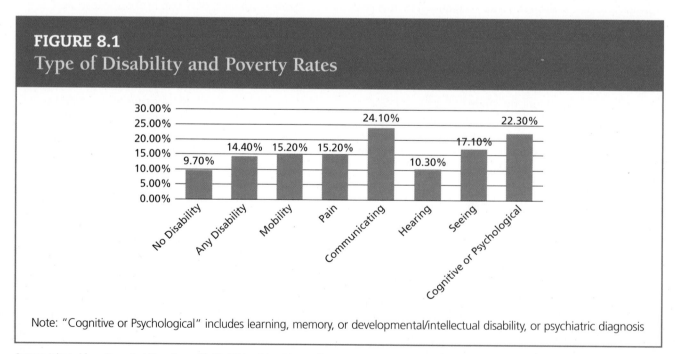

FIGURE 8.1
Type of Disability and Poverty Rates

Note: "Cognitive or Psychological" includes learning, memory, or developmental/intellectual disability, or psychiatric diagnosis

Source: Adapted from Council of Canadians with Disabilities, "As a Matter of Fact: Poverty and Disability in Canada."

administered by Alberta government. This program focuses on job search, educational training, and assistive technology (Government of Alberta, 2010).

One criticism of the socio-economic perspective is that it is rooted in supporting individuals who experience activity limitations and participation restrictions in specific environments such as work, but it does not acknowledge how the socio-economic environment can *create* disability (Hoyle, 2004). While this perspective can change the experience of disability in an employment context, it "does not change the impairment or the process of stigmatization experienced by people with limited functional abilities" (Hoyle, 2004, p. 8).

LEGAL RIGHTS PERSPECTIVE

The legal rights perspective approaches disability as a human rights and social justice issue. The primary concerns of this perspective are the rights to full participation, equity, and non-discrimination for people with disabilities. There are times in Canada's history where discrimination against people with disabilities was entrenched in law. From the time of Confederation until the proclamation of the Immigration and Refugee Protection Act in 2001, potential immigrants with disabilities were defined as an "undesirable class" and deemed inadmissible to Canada. Ena Chadha (2008) in her research on mental disability in Canadian Immigration Law, states:

> By the time of Canada's 50th birthday, a litany of labels, descriptors and conditions, such as idiocy, insanity, imbecility, feeblemindedness, epilepsy, loathsome or dangerous diseases, constitutional psychopathic inferiority, chronic alcoholism, mental defects and illiteracy, were being employed in immigration legislation to justify the discriminatory ban of persons with mental disabilities.

Another example of discrimination against people with disabilities that was rooted in law was the **compulsory sterilization** in Canada of people deemed "unfit" or "mentally defective" (Office for Disability Issues HRDC, 2003). This included people who were institutionalized and deemed "capable of propagating undesirable social characteristics" (Grekul, Krahn, & Odynak, 2004). Two Canadian provinces, Alberta and British Columbia, have a documented history of using compulsory sterilization. The Sexual Sterilization Act of Alberta was in effect in that province from 1929 until 1972 (Grekul, Krahn, & Odynak, 2004); the Sexual Sterilization Act of British Columbia was in effect from 1933 until 1973 (Grekul, Krahn, & Odynak, 2004).

The disability social movement arose in the 1970s as a human rights–based response to the discrimination that people with disabilities face, and was premised on the inherent right for all persons to be treated with human dignity. One organization that has sought to address these issues is the Council of Canadians with Disabilities, which is a coalition that defines itself as "a national human rights organization of people with disabilities working for an accessible and inclusive Canada" (Council of Canadians with Disabilities, 2007).

Canada has adopted a number of laws to ensure that people with disabilities are able to fully participate in society and are protected against discrimination. Canada recently signed the United Nations Convention on the Rights of Persons with Disabilities, which represents a new opportunity for all levels of government to be proactive in eliminating disadvantage and achieving full inclusion for persons with disabilities (Brodsky, Day, & Peters, 2012). The **Canadian Human Rights Act** has guaranteed protection from discrimination based on disability since 1977. The **Canadian Charter of Rights and Freedoms** (1982) guarantees a constitutional right under Section 15 to equal treatment and equal protection against discrimination:

> (1) Every individual is equal before and under the law and has the right to the equal protection and equal benefit of the law without discrimination and, in particular, without discrimination based on race, national or ethnic origin, colour, religion, sex, age, or mental or physical disability.
>
> (2) Subsection (1) does not preclude any law, program or activity that has as its object the amelioration of conditions of disadvantaged individuals or groups including those that are disadvantaged because of race, national or ethnic origin, colour, religion, sex, age or mental or physical disability.

In addition to the guarantees of equal treatment and protection from discrimination, the Charter explicitly recognizes mental disabilities. Until 1982,

Canadian Human Rights Act: Statute passed in 1977 to ensure equal opportunity; protects Canada's citizens against discrimination based on race, national or ethnic origin, colour, religion, age, sex, sexual orientation, marital status, family status, disability, and conviction for a pardoned offence.

Canadian Charter of Rights and Freedoms: Referred to as the Charter, it is a bill of rights and the first part of the 1982 Constitution Act; it is considered the highest law of Canada and, as such, supersedes any other federal or provincial law that conflicts with it.

Canadians with mental disabilities had limited protection (Office for Disability Issues HRDC, 2003). Also important is the fact that "equality" is not defined legally as treating all people the same way; the law recognizes that special measures or special programs are sometimes necessary to correct disadvantage.

One of the critiques of the legal rights perspective is that laws and human rights machinery cannot alone eliminate barriers and reduce discrimination for people with disabilities (Brodsky, Day, & Peters, 2012). In a famous Supreme Court decision (*Eldridge v. British Columbia [Attorney General]*, 1997), the court ruled that failure by the province to pay for and provide sign language interpretation during pregnancy and childbirth to the three appellants who were deaf was discriminatory, as the government had an obligation to address their needs as a disadvantaged group and by failing to do so, denied them equal access to public medical services (Office for Disability Issues HRDC, 2003). In 1999, the Supreme Court of Canada, in two rulings referred to as the *Meiorin* and *Grismer* decisions, reinforced the **duty to accommodate** individuals who cannot meet an employment or serviced delivery standard for any reason related to a ground protected by the Canadian Human Rights Act, such as disability.

Despite all the conventions, laws, and legal decisions made by tribunals and courts, the question remains as to why the largest part of the case load of many human rights commissions continues to be complaints dealing with disability (Brodsky, Day, & Peters, 2012). The complaints to the Canadian Human Rights Commission consistently identify disability as the predominant reason for which a person was discriminated against (see Table 8.2; Canadian Human Right Commission, 2012).

Clearly, discrimination faced by people with disabilities is an enduring facet of their lived experience in Canada. While the legal rights perspective on disability is important in terms of protection of individual legal rights, it has also been important at a broader societal level as it has served as the impetus for disability rights groups. The major criticism of this model is that its focus on the common experience of discrimination fails to consider the individual experiences of one's body as unique and diverse (Wendell, 1989). In its exclusive focus on legal and social aspects of disability, this perspective neglects aspects of the medical model of disability that need to be considered, as well as the lived realities of the physical and mental experiences of disability, such as living with pain and limitations (Hoyle, 1999; Hoyle, 2004).

SOCIAL INCLUSION PERSPECTIVE

Many Canadians with disabilities experience barriers to their full and equal participation in Canadian society (Council of Canadians with Disabilities, 2007). All of the other perspectives differentiate people with disabilities from people without disabilities. Social **accommodation** then focuses on these differences (Hoyle, 2004). The *us-versus-them* dichotomy can lead to ableism, which excludes and discriminates against those who don't measure up to societal norms of ability:

> PWD's [Persons with disabilities] must be seen for who we are: Regular people, neither pathetic poster children nor superheroes "overcoming" the unimaginable. And regular people need regular things: transportation, be it bus or wheelchair; help around the house, be it from their kids or personal assistant; information, be it gleaned from print or sign language or Braille; relief from pain, be it an aspirin or a prescription for morphine; and a decent standard of living, be it from a job or a government check. When all people are provided with such necessities, they will be assured the opportunity for a good quality of life. This is what PWDs deserve and require— tangible assistance that provides freedom, independence, and control over our lives as disabled people, not adulation, pity, or encouragement to focus on a cure that will make us nondisabled. (Wachsler, 2007, p. 14)

In inclusive settings, people with disabilities "have the opportunity to discredit the negative stereotypes and challenge the notions of disabled and non-disabled that reinforce the boundaries between sameness and difference" (Hoyle, 2004). Models for social inclusion recognize that a difference approach separates and disengages persons with disabilities from active participation in their communities. Social inclusion is premised on the belief that all members of a community have a valuable contribution to make (Laidlaw Foundation, 2002–2003): "A true community is only able to grow and strengthen itself by including all of its members and finding room for them to develop their capacities within its own pattern of growth" (Kretzmann & McKnight, 1993).

Duty to accommodate:
A legal principle that requires employers to identify and change any rules, practices, expectations, or procedures that have or may have a discriminatory impact based on the Canadian Human Rights Act's prohibited grounds—namely, race, national or ethnic origin, colour, religion, age, sex (including pregnancy), sexual orientation, marital status, family status, and disability.

Accommodation:
The specialized design of products, environments, and individualized strategies that are uniquely adapted to an identified limitation for the purpose of ensuring access.

TABLE 8.2

Complaints Received by Canadian Human Rights Commission by Grounds of Discrimination Cited,* 2010–2012

	2010		2011		2012	
	#	%	#	%	#	%
Disability	719	38	891	33	746	36
Age	220	12	259	10	146	7
National or ethnic origin	184	10	307	12	217	10
Race	183	10	247	9	182	9
Sex	196	10	408	15	343	17
Family status	121	6	217	8	165	8
Colour	92	5	143	5	92	4
Religion	76	4	76	3	86	4
Marital status	47	2	78	3	43	2
Sexual orientation	42	2	38	1	40	2
A conviction for which a pardon has been granted or a record suspended	3	—	3	—	8	—
Total	**1883**	**100**	**2667**	**100**	**2068**	**100**

* Total number of grounds cited exceeds the total number of received complaints because some complaints dealt with more than one ground.

Source: *Canadian Human Rights Commission 2012 Annual Report*, Canadian Human Rights Commission, 2012. Reproduced with the permission of the Minister of Public Works and Government Services Canada, 2013.

The social inclusion perspective is sometimes criticized for failing to account for the complexity and intersectionality of aspects of identity, such as women with disabilities, Aboriginal people with disabilities, and people with disabilities from visible minority communities. A good example of the social inclusion perspective is the vision statement and action plan for an inclusive and accessible Canada that was developed by the Council of Canadians with Disabilities (see Figure 8.2).

PROFILE OF PEOPLE WITH DISABILITIES IN CANADA

In Canada, we use a number of sources to gather statistical information on disabilities, the two major ones being the Canadian Census and the **Participation and Activity Limitation Survey**. According to the 2006 Canadian Census, which provides the most recent available information, there are almost 4.4 million Canadians, or about one in seven, who reported having a disability (Statistics Canada, 2007). Disability rates vary across provinces and territories, with the province of Nova Scotia having the highest regional percentage (20%) of people with disabilities, and Nunavut having the lowest at 6.7 percent (Statistics Canada, 2007).

Participation and Activity Limitation Survey: A national survey the purpose of which is to gather information on all people whose daily activities are limited by a physical, mental, or other health-related condition or problem.

FIGURE 8.2
A Shared Vision and Action Plan for an Inclusive and Accessible Canada

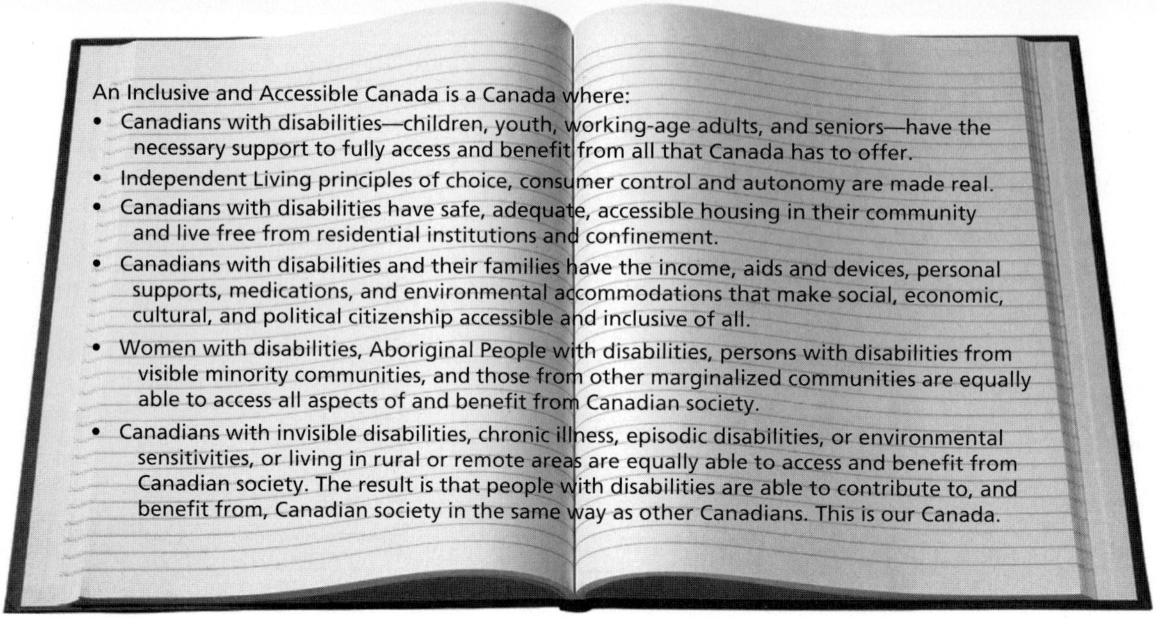

An Inclusive and Accessible Canada is a Canada where:

- Canadians with disabilities—children, youth, working-age adults, and seniors—have the necessary support to fully access and benefit from all that Canada has to offer.
- Independent Living principles of choice, consumer control and autonomy are made real.
- Canadians with disabilities have safe, adequate, accessible housing in their community and live free from residential institutions and confinement.
- Canadians with disabilities and their families have the income, aids and devices, personal supports, medications, and environmental accommodations that make social, economic, cultural, and political citizenship accessible and inclusive of all.
- Women with disabilities, Aboriginal People with disabilities, persons with disabilities from visible minority communities, and those from other marginalized communities are equally able to access all aspects of and benefit from Canadian society.
- Canadians with invisible disabilities, chronic illness, episodic disabilities, or environmental sensitivities, or living in rural or remote areas are equally able to access and benefit from Canadian society. The result is that people with disabilities are able to contribute to, and benefit from, Canadian society in the same way as other Canadians. This is our Canada.

Source: Council of Canadians with Disabilities, 2007.

Disabilities and Age

Disability rates increase steadily with age. In 2006, there were 202 350 children living in Canada with disabilities. Over half of Canadians aged 75 and over reported having a disability (Statistics Canada, 2007). Figure 8.3 outlines the disability rates by age.

Types of Disabilities among Adults in Canada

The most prevalent type of disability reported by Canadian adults is limitation resulting from pain, followed by lack of mobility and reduced agility (see Figure 8.4). The number of adult Canadians reporting disabilities because of limitations related to hearing, seeing, learning, memory, speech, and psychological and developmental issues was relatively smaller by comparison (Statistics Canada, 2007). It is important to note that these rates vary by age group. For example, hearing and memory disabilities were higher among those who were 65 years of age and older (Human Resources and Skills Development Canada, 2011).

Types of Disabilities among School-Aged Children in Canada

Among school-aged children (5–14 years of age), more boys than girls were reported as having disabilities. Learning disabilities were the most common disabilities for boys, while chronic health conditions were the most common disabilities for girls (see Figure 8.5).

IMPACT OF DISABILITIES ON FAMILIES

Caring for children, parents, and other family members with disabilities can result in a great deal of pressure for caregivers and often impacts their employment status. Family members are still the most common source of help for seniors with disabilities, with 66% of seniors still being cared for by family (Statistics Canada, 2007). Ninety-two percent of families of children with disabilities reported that they needed help with things like housework and other family responsibilities, but for a variety of reasons (mostly related to cost), they were not able to get the help they needed

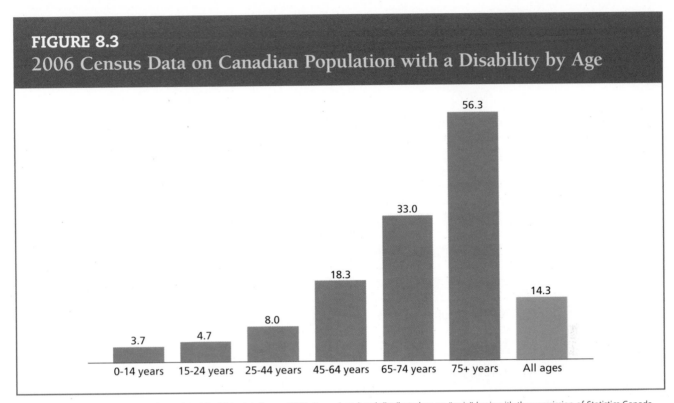

FIGURE 8.3

2006 Census Data on Canadian Population with a Disability by Age

Source: Statistics Canada, Participation and Activity Limitation Survey 2006. Reproduced and distributed on an "as is" basis with the permission of Statistics Canada.

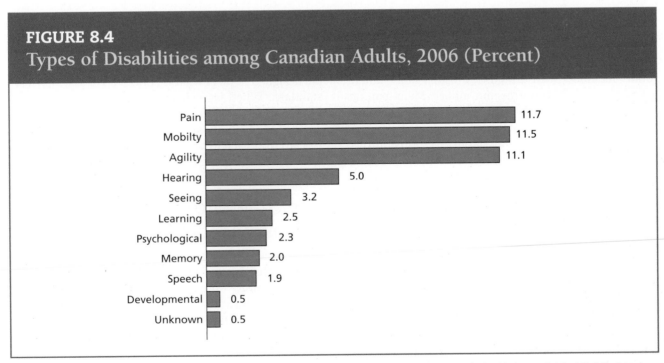

FIGURE 8.4

Types of Disabilities among Canadian Adults, 2006 (Percent)

Source: Statistics Canada, Participation and Activity Limitation Survey 2006. Reproduced and distributed on an "as is" basis with the permission of Statistics Canada.

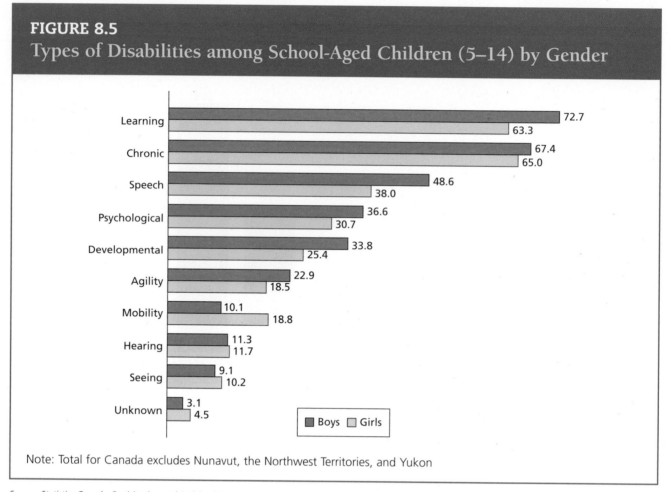

FIGURE 8.5

Types of Disabilities among School-Aged Children (5–14) by Gender

Type	Boys	Girls
Learning	72.7	63.3
Chronic	67.4	65.0
Speech	48.6	38.0
Psychological	36.6	30.7
Developmental	33.8	25.4
Agility	22.9	18.5
Mobility	10.1	18.8
Hearing	11.3	11.7
Seeing	9.1	10.2
Unknown	3.1	4.5

Note: Total for Canada excludes Nunavut, the Northwest Territories, and Yukon

Source: Statistics Canada, Participation and Activity Limitation Survey 2006. Reproduced and distributed on an "as is" basis with the permission of Statistics Canada.

(Statistics Canada, 2007). The pressure of caring for family members with disabilities results in a challenging balance between time and money. Many parents of children with disabilities had to alter their employment arrangements in some way (see Table 8.3).

In addition to juggling family responsibilities, employment, child care, household chores, medical appointments, and caregiving, families with disabled children often struggle with increased financial pressures because of additional medical costs and lost wages.

THE CONTEXT OF DISABILITY WITHIN OUR SOCIAL ENVIRONMENT

When we conceptualize disability as something different from what is "normal," then the approach we use in dealing with disability issues is one that employs

individual accommodations. These accommodations are designed to meet what is conceived of as a "normal" standard. When we conceptualize disability as a universal experience, then the approach we use employs the goals of accessibility and social inclusion for everyone. For any approach to be effective, it is important to begin with the lived experiences of people with disabilities.

The Difference Approach and Accommodation

When disability is constructed as "difference from the norm"—that is, different from the "normal" body or "normal" mind—then the approach used is one that focuses on how to accommodate difference. This approach maintains an *us*-versus-*them* mentality and differentiates people with disabilities from people without disabilities. An accommodation approach often requires people with disabilities to be their own

TABLE 8.3
Employment Modifications for Parents of Children with Disabilities, 2006

Employment impact	Severity		
	Total	Mild to moderate	Severe to very severe
	Percentage		
Not taken a job	26.4	16.4	39.8
Quit working	21.6	13.2	32.9
Changed work hours	36.5	26.9	49.4
Turned down promotion	19.7	10.5	31.9
Worked fewer hours	38.4	29.1	50.8
Worked more hours	9.7	6.4	14.2

Source: Statistics Canada, Participation and Activity Limitation Survey 2006. Reproduced and distributed on an "as is" basis with the permission of Statistics Canada.

advocates in initiating adaptations for their unique needs; it often results in reactive and retro-fit solutions.

Using the familiar context of the post-secondary classroom, what does equal access to learning through individualized accommodations mean for the college or university student with disabilities? Using the approach of recognizing disability as difference from the norm, individualized accommodations rely on the student to initiate the process of having their unique needs met (Dosis, Coffey, Gravel, Ali, & Condra, 2012). Students have to identify themselves as having a disability and provide documentation to their professors and instructors as well as to the institutional service supporting students with disabilities. One of the **barriers** that can be created for students through individualized accommodations is that this approach can leave them feeling as though they are asking for a special favour (Dosis, Coffey, Gravel, Ali, & Condra, 2012). Students may be reluctant to request accommodations as they can feel labelled in a negative way by this process. As one college student states:

I was bullied in high school because of my learning disability. People called me names like "tard and "slow" and I was pushed and punched by a group of girls on a regular basis. They even bullied other people who tried to be friends with me, so I basically spent four years in high school alone. I went away to college so

I could have a fresh start. I just want to fit in, so there is no way I am going to label myself as a student with a disability. I would rather fail than go through that again. (Anzovino, 2012)

Bullying behaviour is rooted in power and aggression and is often based on perceived differences in appearance, sexual orientation, ethnicity, or ability. If disabilities are perceived as different from the norm of ability, then they can reinforce an *us*-versus-*them* mentality that can create a fertile environment for bullying behaviour. Violence in Canadian schools against children with disabilities is a prevalent reality. In *Abilities Magazine*, Melissa Martz details her childhood experiences with bullying:

Bullies can find any reason to target someone—maybe because he or she wears glasses, is overweight or wears hand-me-downs. Children with disabilities are frequently singled out for being different. They may speak differently, walk differently, use assistive devices or have difficulty with social interaction—all of which bullies can turn into jokes. ... It happened to me. While growing up in Kitchener, Ont., I was tormented because I stuttered (something that I still struggle with) and required special education for math and language arts. (Martz, 2008–2009)

The case of Mitchell Wilson has garnered media attention around the issue of bullying children with disabilities. Mitchell Wilson was an 11-year-old boy from Pickering, Ontario, who had muscular dystrophy. Children at his school bullied him socially and physically. Prior to testifying in court, Mitchell committed suicide (Kennedy, 2011). This tragedy has highlighted the issue of bullying of children with disabilities. Approximately 30 percent of parents with school-aged children with disabilities report that their children have been physically assaulted by other children at school, and this number increases to 38 percent for children with severe or very severe disabilities (Statistics Canada, 2007).

In the context of the post-secondary classroom, individualized accommodations in this academic setting can result in retrofit solutions after the program, curriculum, course, and instruction have been designed (Dosis, Coffey, Gravel, Ali, & Condra, 2012). Accommodations such as providing a student with more time to write a test or arranging for a note-taker can become a "one-size fits all" adaptive measure that can ensure equality but not equitable access to education.

When access in society is based on norms of ability, the danger is "it can lead to ableism in policy and practice as it negates the commonalities of our shared lived experiences" (Hoyle, 2004). What if, instead of measuring people against norms of ability, a society reframed itself on a universal acknowledgement that all members can, over the course of their lifetime, expect to experience disability? What if based on this viewpoint, we decided to create a society where everyone would feel included, would be able to develop their own capabilities, and would be valued and contributing members of society based on who they really are and not on some normative ideal physicality?

Nowhere is the social construction of ideal physicality more prominent than in the fashion and beauty industry. It was interesting, then, when a well-known fashion photographer, Rick Guidotti, began to redefine the concept of beauty through his not-for-profit organization called Positive Exposure, using photography to change public perception of people living with genetic, physical, and behavioural differences (Positive Exposure, 2012).

In creating inclusive environments, people can challenge negative stereotypes and the assumption that people with disabilities are a separate social group because of differences in ability (Hoyle, 2004). Social inclusion challenges the "the notions of disabled and non-disabled that reinforce the boundaries between sameness and difference" (Hoyle, 2004). Social inclusion as a perspective helps us to move from accommodation as special treatment for people with disabilities to accessibility as equitable treatment for all.

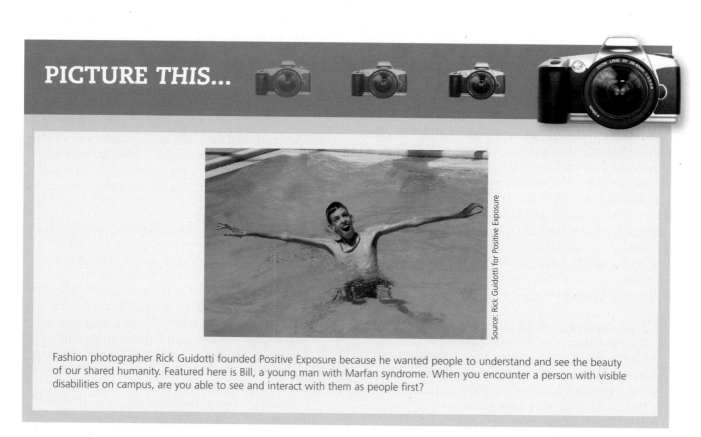

PICTURE THIS...

Source: Rick Guidotti for Positive Exposure

Fashion photographer Rick Guidotti founded Positive Exposure because he wanted people to understand and see the beauty of our shared humanity. Featured here is Bill, a young man with Marfan syndrome. When you encounter a person with visible disabilities on campus, are you able to see and interact with them as people first?

Moving from Accommodations to Accessibility

When developing inclusive policy and practice, it is important that policy and practice be premised on the understanding that **accessibility** is multifaceted. Accessibility can mean different things to different people based on their experiences of the body, their stage of life, their physical environment, and so on. Creating a society where all members can participate fully in their community is one of the goals of accessibility.

A study entitled "Unlocking the Possible" (Hoyle, 2004) is an interesting model of how a municipality might work at becoming more accessible and inclusive to people with disabilities. At a citizen's forum, **barriers** to social inclusion and full participation in civic life were identified:

- *Experiences of the body*, including fear of ridicule over unpredictable body movements and behaviours, variation in physical strength and energy, and personal care needs.
- *Access to physical space*, including both the accessibility of the space itself and how people move within that space in terms of the amount of space, placement of items, transportation, and types of devices available for mobility.
- *Access to time* needed for daily routine, equipment use, and full participation when physical or cognitive issues require this.
- *Access to information*, such as the technological adaptations people needed to listen and communicate.
- *Access to services*, including equitable access to employment, recreation, and health care services.
- *Access to social networking opportunities*, which include being able to make social connections, having a sense of belonging to the community, feeling valued for one's contributions, feeling a sense of interdependence and reciprocity with other citizens, and experiencing a people-first approach (Hoyle, 2004).

This study highlights that accessibility is a multifaceted concept whose practice would eliminate those barriers and would hold the promise of community where all members can fully participate in civic life. Accessibility is a model for practising diversity as a framework for equity and social inclusion at a municipal level.

Accessibility and inclusion can begin with **universal design**, using design principles which can help to eliminate the need for adaptation or specialized accommodation. You may have heard these ideas referred to as barrier-free design, accessible design, adaptable design, trans-generational design, and inclusive design. Universal design considers all members of the community and plans for the full participation of all members. Universal design has been utilized in architecture, urban planning, and education in many ways. There are seven basic principles of universal design:

1. *Equitable use*. The design is useful and marketable to any group of users.
2. *Flexibility in use*. The design accommodates a wide range of individual preferences and abilities.
3. *Simple and intuitive use*. Use of the design is easy to understand, regardless of the user's experience, knowledge, language skill, or current concentration levels.
4. *Perceptible information*. The design communicates necessary information effectively to the user regardless of ambient conditions or the user's sensory abilities.
5. *Tolerance of error*. The design minimizes hazards and adverse consequences of accidental or unintended actions.
6. *Low physical effort*. The design can be used effectively and comfortably and with a minimum of fatigue.
7. *Size and space for approach and use*. Appropriate size and space is provided for approach, reach, manipulation, and use, regardless of user's body size, posture, or mobility (Connell et al., 1997).

In the familiar context of the post-secondary classroom, a universal design for accessibility is a proactive way to remove barriers to learning at the outset, as opposed to a retrofit solution after the fact, thereby reducing the need for individual accommodations (Dosis, Coffey, Gravel, Ali, & Condra, 2012). This proactive approach designs curriculum and instruction to meet the diverse learning styles and needs of students and develops assessment that recognizes that students can express understanding in multiple ways (Dosis, Coffey, Gravel, Ali, & Condra, 2012). The focus of accessible education is to create sustainable access based on the following principles:

Accessibility: The degree to which a product, device, service, or environment is available to as many people as possible.

Barriers: Policies or practices that prevent full and equal participation in society; barriers can be physical, social, attitudinal, organizational, technological, or informational.

Universal design: "The design of products, environments, programs and services to be usable by all people, to the greatest extent possible, without the need for adaptation or specialized design (but does not exclude assistive devices for particular groups of persons with disabilities where this is needed)" (United Nations, 2006).

TABLE 8.4

Accessible Education Approaches to Reducing Barriers for Students with Disabilities

	Barrier	Accessible education approach
Attitudinal	Treating accommodation as a special favour.	Offering multiple ways for students to demonstrate comprehension.
Organizational	Holding office hours in person in a set location.	Providing students with multiple ways to contact the instructor.
Architectural / physical	Creating a classroom layout that is difficult for a student in a wheelchair to navigate.	Taking the needs of students in wheelchairs into account when designing the classroom layout.
Information and communications	Organizing lectures poorly.	Providing clear, well-organized lectures using advanced organizers and summaries.
Technology	Using handouts in formats that do not facilitate the use of assistive technology.	Providing all students with accessible, properly formatted handouts.

Source: Dosis, O., Coffey, K., Gravel, D., Ali, I., & Condra, E. (2012). Accessibility awareness training for educators: Fulfilling our commitment to accessible education. Funded by Colleges Ontario.

- dignity for students, by maintaining privacy and not singling them out;
- equitable opportunities and advantages for all students for learning, not just for information;
- independence for students, so they can complete learning tasks without specialized help; and
- integration, so that each student is able to benefit from the same learning experiences (Dosis, Coffey, Gravel, Ali, & Condra, 2012).

Table 8.4 provides an outline of accessible education approaches that can help reduce barriers for students with disabilities.

Using a universal design for learning is an example of an effective framework for accessible education: it emphasizes flexibility in curriculum design; it uses multiple modes of engaging students, presenting content, and assessing comprehension; and it utilizes technology to maximize equitable learning opportunities for all students (Dosis, Coffey, Gravel, Ali, & Condra, 2012). Ed Roberts Campus in Berkeley, California, is an icon for the disability community worldwide. Using principles of universal design, the campus is an excellent example of how architecture can marry aesthetics, creativity, and universal design to ensure full inclusion for all people. Designed to be functional for as many people as possible, the Ed Roberts Campus includes

Source: Will Nold, courtesy of the Ed Roberts Campus

The Ed Roberts Campus in Berkeley, California, uses the principles of universal design to ensure full inclusion for all people.

universal design features such as wide corridors for people who use wheelchairs to pass one another, a massive circular ramp to the second floor that is the centrepiece of the building's interior, hands-free building systems controls, restrooms that meet a range of abilities, an easy-to-navigate plan for getting around in the building aided by acoustical landmarks, coloured and textured flooring, and more (Arch Daily, 2011).

TABLE 8.5
Examples of Universal Design in Learning

Principles	Examples
Be accessible and fair.	Provide accessibility-checked course website; supply lecture outlines; use variety of media to provide information.
Provide flexibility in use, participation, and presentation.	Use verbal, text, images, audio; use discussion or problem-solving exercises; post exercises and quizzes online.
Be straightforward and consistent.	Use headings consistently; develop concept maps for complex topics; use plain language.
Ensure that course content is explicitly presented and readily perceived.	Ensure PowerPoint materials are easy to read; provide outlines and summaries; consider room conditions.
Provide a supportive learning environment.	Expect students to have varying levels of skills; offer collaborative learning opportunities; review drafts of assignments.
Minimize unnecessary physical efforts or requirements.	Minimize clicking, scrolling, etc., on websites; consider lighting, physical space; have students work in pairs; provide remote access to reading material.
Ensure learning spaces fit students' needs and instructional materials.	Match exercises to course technology; provide videotapes for review; ensure space accommodates mobility and communication needs.

Source: Dosis, O., Coffey, K., Gravel, D., Ali, I., & Condra, E. (2012). Accessibility awareness training for educators: Fulfilling our commitment to accessible education. Funded by Colleges Ontario.

Table 8.5 outlines some examples of universal design in educational settings.

Lived Experience and Experiential Affinity

One of the ways of understanding the context of disability within our social environment is through the lived experiences of people with disabilities. This is the foundation upon which *Walk a Mile* was first conceived. Any strategies used to promote social inclusion of people with disabilities means respecting their lived experiences. Diversity-competent practitioners must honour the voices and lived experiences of people with disabilities, in order to preserve the dignity of all people in a way that does not promote pity (Shier, Sinclair, & Gault, 2011).

Developing **experiential affinity**—that is, an appreciation of someone else's experiential challenges—is another way in which diversity practitioners can better understand the social context of disability (Shier, Sinclair, & Gault, 2011). As diversity practitioners share the experience of simulated disability, they come to a fuller understanding of the experiences of the body, the social construction of norms of ability, and accessibility barriers faced by people with disabilities. Experiential affinity is the premise of the "Dine in the Dark" experience at O.Noir, a restaurant experience in Toronto and Montreal. After an hour or two in complete darkness

Source: O.Noir Restaurant

Moe Alameddine founded O.Noir, Canada's only "Dine in the Dark" restaurant.

Experiential affinity:
A feeling of closeness and understanding that someone has for someone else because of their similar experience.

IN THEIR SHOES

If a picture can say a thousand words, imagine the stories your shoes could tell! Try this student story on for size – have you walked in this student's shoes?

Ever wondered what it would be like living with a disability? Let me tell you that for the most part it is very challenging; I have a physical disability, which can be challenging to say the least. I have had people assume a lot about me before they even get to know me and sometimes it bothers me. For example, I was a spokesperson for an organization that supports disabled children and I went to this one place and it was not accessible to me because of the stairs. I was carried in and out but that is not the point. I guess what I am saying is that not everyone thinks about how to accommodate disabled people in wheelchairs—it is not their fault. Try and think if you were in a wheelchair—what problems would arise? But, more important, how would you solve the problems?

When you interact with a disabled person, there are some little things that you can do to make the situation more enjoyable. First, if the person is in a wheelchair, try to be at the same level, because most people in wheelchairs have to look up to see your eyes, but if you bend down so that your eyes are at the same level, it shows that you do not see yourself above them. Another thing is that most people in wheelchairs have some way of communicating, so if they are with a friend, please don't ask the friend what the person in the wheelchair is thinking. There have been many times where I have been out with friends and a person will come up and ask my friends, "Can he talk?" Or they will ask my friends what I think. Bottom line: you should try to treat someone in a wheelchair the same as anyone else. You may put your foot in your mouth sometimes, and that's OK— everyone does, even me. The biggest tip that I would give anyone is if you are unsure of anything, just ask! You learn more from questions than assuming the answer.

Being in a wheelchair has challenges, but it has some rewards too. You are in the front of lines, most people will help you if you need assistance, and you never need to worry about a seat. For me, the best is when I set a goal that people think I can't reach. When I reach that goal it is the best feeling I have ever felt. When you are in a wheelchair, you have to work harder than most people, and it makes the victory that much sweeter. Remember—the only person that has to believe in you, is you.

Source: Michael Caughell.

(including no flashlights, matches, cellphones, cigarette lighters, or luminous watches), customers gain a better understanding of what it's like to be blind.

ENDING THOUGHTS

When we define *diversity* in a way that privileges the concepts of culture, ethnicity, and race, we further eclipse the lived experiences of people with disabilities in a manner that reinforces their social exclusion as members of our communities. When the concept of *ability* is included in the framework for achieving social equity and justice, we move closer to the goal of social inclusion. As part of this discussion, it becomes important to acknowledge the fact that "all people live on a continuum of ability and disability with our position on this continuum dependent on time of life, the time of day, the situation and the environment … ability is not an either/or situation where one is either able or not able" (Hoyle, 2004). When we consider these universalizing lived experiences, we can begin to look at our shared humanity with a people-first approach that sees ability in everyone.

HUMBLE ABODE: RECOVERY STARTS AT HOME … IF YOU HAVE ONE

By Michelle Mora

When *Los Angeles Times* columnist Steve Lopez asked a homeless street musician if he would consider sleeping indoors, the man said, "Oh, no. I wouldn't want to do that."

This puzzling response is the premise of *The Soloist*, a movie based on Lopez' newspaper and book accounts of that homeless man, Nathaniel Ayers. Ayers (played by Jamie Foxx) was a gifted cellist studying at Julliard when symptoms of schizophrenia forced him to halt his studies. Years later he met Lopez (played by Robert Downey Jr.), a journalist who was stuck for a good story and wanted to know how a man like Ayers ends up living on the street.

Ayers lived on the streets of Los Angeles, and he was loved. His sister, while out of touch, missed him terribly and was heartbroken at the thought of him not having a safe place to live.

Dale L. Johnson, PhD, of Houston knows what it's like. His son, Jay, had schizophrenia and frequently ended up lost or homeless. Sometimes, Johnson and his wife received calls from a police officer who had jailed him to keep him warm for the night. Jay, who had dropped out of Harvard when his illness progressed, escaped from state hospitals. He hitchhiked, slept on the streets, and was often beaten and robbed. This would force him to panhandle for more funds, and the cycle would repeat itself.

Finally, the Johnsons learned of a low-income housing and support facility run by Volunteers of America, which had a vacancy. Once Jay had a home of his own, things started to fall into place. Doctors found him a drug that worked without harsh side effects. He had a roommate he liked. Rather than scrambling for the next meal or hiding place, life became a more stable routine of visiting the library, going to the gym, having coffee at Starbucks, and taking the trolley to the ocean.

Things don't fall into place for people who are homeless, regardless of their mental state. The prognosis is bad. Death rates are high, rape and violence higher.

Sadly, the Johnsons' son died four years ago of natural causes unrelated to his mental illness. But the home he enjoyed in his final years was a blessing to him and to his parents, who visited him in the San Diego area many times. Not all accommodations are so pleasant. People with schizophrenia commonly endure living conditions in community-assisted housing of varying degrees of sanitation, comfort, and safety. The prospect of spending one's adult life in such a place, with little to no personal privacy, can be especially uninviting. But while many leave those homes in hopes of a better life on the street, Johnson believes that is the wrong choice.

"Any group home is better than homelessness," he says. "Any. And some are just dreadful."

Still, carving out one's own existence in some quiet tunnel or under a tree might seem more appealing than relying on the system. Someone like Ayers who is mistrustful of strangers will, understandably, want to be alone. But how long can a person with schizophrenia sustain a life on the street, without access to treatment, privacy and safety? And if a shelter were of questionable help in a person's recovery from mental health, would the prognosis be better in a permanent residence?

Gimme shelter

For a gentle soul like Nathaniel Ayers, the street is not always the worst demon. There's a disturbing scene in *The Soloist* where Ayers, in a flashback to his Julliard days, is beaming with pride in his beautiful new apartment. But he is soon distracted by a voice, then two or three voices, then a barrage of voices, shouting confusing messages all at once in his head. A happy moment turns to anguish as he is reduced to sobbing on his kitchen floor.

We all have voices in our heads: contemplations, reflections, ideas—although not the audible voices many with schizophrenia hear. When we see a homeless person, our voices might say, "Why doesn't he just get a job?" or "Don't my taxes pay for assisted living?" or "If she chooses to sleep there of all places, that's her problem, not mine."

The Soloist explores a complex question: Why would Ayers, or anyone who is afraid, paranoid, and vulnerable, not gravitate to the nearest shelter or try harder to find a permanent home? To the frustration of the well-meaning Lopez, initial attempts to house Ayers fail.

In fairness to Ayers, the local shelter with its long lines of crack addicts, pushers, and other jittery, restless and violent characters, certainly does not seem like a step up from the quiet nook where he sleeps on a tarp next to his shopping cart. But when Lopez finds him a room of his own, to use both as a music studio and as a permanent home, Ayers rejects it, responding with aggression: "I don't want to live here … I don't want to die in here … I want to be in the tunnel and hear the city sounds … I don't belong here. I'm never coming here again."

At Lopez' suggestion that Ayers "should" live there, Ayers becomes extremely agitated, triggered by the "s" word that threatens his independence.

Independence may be the key to "housing first," a type of intervention that is gaining momentum in recent years. In 1992, Sam Tsemberis, PhD, founded Pathways to Housing, Inc. in New York City as he found the previous system sorely lacking. He had been director of a program called the Homeless Emergency Liaison Project (HELP), launched in the 1980s, where his job was to identify the mentally ill homeless people whose health and safety were in jeopardy, and take them to the psychiatric center at Bellevue Hospital—whether or not they wanted to go.

"It was not about consumer choice," he recalls. "It was very intense, clinically driven, and very traumatic for all of us. There was disagreement among the teams about whether we were really helping anybody."

After such an intense process, he says, only one or two of the 30 hungry, exhausted people he saw each day were admitted to hospital. And even those who made it to Bellevue for medical care and a few good meals were back on the street 30 days later, with no follow-up.

Tsemberis felt there was something broken in that system. "We always saw the same people on the streets," he says, "and they made a compelling case that they needed housing above all."

In some cases, people find themselves stepping up through the system's shelters, group homes, boarding homes, and other accommodations before being given the option of a permanent dwelling. Once that opportunity arises, the person must meet certain conditions, such as agreeing to attend weekly group therapy sessions, quit drinking, or take medication.

For those suffering from severe mental illness, that "treatment first" system presents a host of barriers. Housing becomes about what form to fill out, what doctor to see, what diagnosis the person has, what medications were prescribed. Many homeless people are too preoccupied with staying safe or getting their next meal to abide by rigid schedules or show up to meetings on time. Many still do make their way through this system with varying degrees of success. Others wait years for an opportunity to apply for a permanent home; many fall through the cracks.

After many failed attempts at housing those in need, Tsemberis started paying attention to what homeless individuals really wanted. Many said they didn't want facilities with tiny rooms and groups of social workers in the basements. They wanted the freedom to have guests, or pets, and choose what meals to cook, what TV channels to watch. "They had a life before, and they wanted some restoration of that life."

"Housing first" is based on the premise that housing is a basic human right, not a reward for clinical or programmatic success. When staff find someone living under a bridge or on the sidewalk, they ask, "How can we help you find housing?" If the person is ready to talk, staff get to know the person's situation and identify what type of funding he or she is eligible for under disability or social assistance benefits. Then, together, they find a dwelling.

Once housed, the person receives regular visits from a mental health professional who helps set personal goals—such as seeking treatment, or opening a bank account—but imposes no requirements. People respond well to this approach, and being actively involved might be a key factor. They have a say in where they live. They also choose their own furniture and décor from a furniture bank and get to decide where everything goes.

Toronto City Council founded a similar project in 2005. "Streets to Homes" was Canada's first housing model of its kind and several other municipalities have adopted similar programs. New York City has seen a consistent rate of 80 percent of people staying housed through Pathways to Housing. In Toronto, nearly 92 percent stay housed, and 83 percent are still in the original dwelling they chose.

One unique aspect of the housing first model is that if things go wrong, people can try again. That's a welcome change from the alternative system, where a breach of the rules could land them back to the streets indefinitely.

"Some may not make great choices the first go around," says Iain De Jong, Manager of Streets to Homes. "We need to look at homelessness from a recovery lens and acknowledge that relapse is part of recovery. Some relapse into homelessness."

Tsemberis agrees with giving people another chance until they get it right. To anyone who might find this too lenient an approach, he says, "It's just like when rich people go to the Betty Ford clinic. They don't lose their house just because they've relapsed."

Depending on the severity of their illness, some might choose a living arrangement with 24-hour access to care, but many live very well independently. Either way, Tsemberis believes there is little chance for a positive outcome without a home. "People recover more quickly from mental illness than they do from poverty," he says.

Be it ever so humble …

There's no place like home. But here come those voices again: "What if someone with schizophrenia was alone at home and forgot to turn off the stove?" "Would that be fair to other building occupants?" "Is a person utensils?" "Will he not harm himself or others if left to his own devices?"

Tsemberis once had those same apprehensions. Today, he believes that his entire profession has been wrong about what people diagnosed with schizophrenia are able to do.

"We have focused so much on their disabilities, their symptoms, and on classifying them," he says, "we have missed the fact that many are so capable, they can be homeless and on the street and manage to survive."

He no longer wonders if people with mental illness can manage apartments on their own. He has seen their skills in action. "They know when soup lines are serving food, where to sleep, who they can trust, where to go to the bathroom, how not to get arrested. Just by virtue of their survival on the street, there's so much they can figure out for themselves. Then, to take someone with all this capability into an apartment? To them, it's a piece of cake."

It takes a certain degree of trust to grant someone independence. Remarkably, though, that independence can bring great results for the mentally ill. Johnson calls independence "one of the essentials of recovery." It certainly worked for his son, and he has seen countless examples of how well people can live with mental illness when given the dignity of choice and freedom.

He cites as an example Magnificat House, Inc., a supported apartment program where he has worked as a volunteer consultant for 40 years. Founded in 1968 in Houston, it runs nine residential houses and provides immediate and direct aid to anyone who needs a place to live, with few questions asked. About one-third of residents have a serious mental illness.

"It's in the middle of Houston and no one knows it's there," says Johnson. "The residents do all the work. If a toilet is stopped up or the roof leaks, they fix it. They mow the lawns, trim the hedges; have a big garden that produces enough vegetables to feed all the residents and have some left over for the Farmer's Market."

Johnson says it's a place where people want to live, for many years—and many of them do.

What about people like Nathaniel Ayers, who at some point make a conscious decision to live on the street? His decision, like the decisions of many, was likely the result of an untreated brain disease. He may have needed coaxing but once he got used to his permanent home, he stayed.

"His mental health is as precarious as before," says Lopez at the end of the film. Only now he has a bed. A safe place to keep his cello. Dignity. And a friend in Steve Lopez.

Ayers still lives in Los Angeles, where he plays several musical instruments.

Source: Bill Macphee.

"Housing is a powerful motivator," says Tsemberis. "For some people, this is the first time they've had an apartment of their own. They have lived with family, in foster care, in jail or in shelters … but a home of their own gives them a sense of dignity and pride. People care about it and want to get their act together. It's really quite beautiful to observe all of that transformation."

DISCUSSION QUESTIONS

1. According to the Canadian Mental Health Association, people with serious mental illness are disproportionately affected by homelessness (Canadian Mental Health Association, 2013). Research has documented that 30–35 percent of the homeless in general and up to 75 percent of homeless women specifically have a mental illness (Canadian Mental Health Association, 2013). Research also documents that 20–25 percent of homeless people suffer from concurrent disorders (severe mental illness and addictions). People with mental illness remain homeless for longer, have less contact with family and friends, encounter more barriers to employment, and tend to be in poorer health than other homeless people (Canadian Mental Health Association, 2013). Given this evidence, what strategies would you develop to reduce homelessness in this population?

2. Some argue that when we link mental illness as an individual factor to homelessness, we are pathologizing the issue. They argue that we focus on individual factors that are most often personal failures at the expense of looking at homelessness as a social problem. If a well-off individual runs into a personal psychiatric crisis, that person doesn't lose his or her housing. If a poor person runs into a crisis, though, that person does lose his or her housing. It is not the crisis that causes the homelessness; it is the lack of affordable housing. People argue that homelessness has nothing to do with alleged mental illness, but has everything to do with the lack of housing and lack of political will on all levels of government to address poverty issues. Do you agree or disagree?

3. Do you think we should change the term schizophrenia? Bill McPhee, publisher of *SZ* magazine, believes it should be. Why? The term schizophrenia has many negative labels attached to it. People who are diagnosed with schizophrenia are often stigmatized because of it. The word *schizophrenia*, roughly translated, means "splitting of the mind," which is not an accurate description and can explain why people mistake schizophrenia for multiple personality disorder. If you could rename schizophrenia, what would you call it?

KWIP

KNOW IT AND OWN IT: WHAT DO I BRING TO THIS?

One of the fundamental truths about diversity is that it involves as much learning about oneself as it does learning about others. Through reflective practice, begin the process of honestly examining your own biases, stereotypes, and prejudices. Have you had personal experience with disability, either yourself or through someone you know? What effect has this had on your understanding of what the daily lived experiences are for people with disabilities? Have you met students with disabilities at your own college or university? What is done there to ensure students with disabilities have access to education? As you look around your classrooms, do you think students with disabilities are socially included in the learning environment? Do you feel there is an *us*-versus-*them* mentality between students with disabilities and students without disabilities? What have you done personally to facilitate the social inclusion of students with disabilities in your school environment?

WALKING THE TALK: HOW CAN I LEARN FROM THIS?

What can you learn from reflective practice to help you better understand the context of disability within your social environment? In some universities and colleges that use an accommodation model, you can see students with disabilities having to self-identify with teachers to request accommodations that focus on their differences. Common examples of accommodation include extending time allotted for a test or arranging for a note-taker during classes. We also know that while some disabilities are visible and permanent, other disabilities are invisible and temporary. Students with disabilities can be reluctant to self-identify, especially when disabilities are invisible or temporary, because of the stigmatization and disadvantages that result from being labelled as different.

Choose your favourite class and imagine you are now the teacher in this classroom. What will you do to ensure that *all* students in your classroom are included? What will you do to account for differences in learning styles and learning needs?

How will you provide accessible education to your students by removing barriers and reducing the need for individual accommodations? How will you evaluate students' understanding in ways that allow all students to demonstrate what they know?

Or try this exercise. Walk around your campus and do an assessment of its physical structure. See if you can find examples of building design that (a) use universal design, (b) use an accommodated design, and (c) are not accessible. Imagine how you might feel encountering each of the physical aspects of your campus if you were a student with visible disabilities, invisible disabilities, temporary disabilities, and permanent disabilities.

IT IS WHAT IT IS: IS THIS INSIDE OR OUTSIDE YOUR COMFORT ZONE?

How comfortable are you at school, work, or play with people with disabilities? When you define disability as an issue that everyone may potentially experience at some point in their life, then it removes the dichotomy of ability versus non-ability that reinforces an *us*-versus-*them* approach to disabilities. At some point in your life, you are likely to experience a disability, based on age, accident, or circumstance. It can be visible or invisible, temporary or permanent. You will hope you will be able to get to where you need to go. You will not want to be praised for your courage nor will you want to be pitied. You will hope that your friends and loved ones won't treat you differently and begin to withdraw. You will hope that other people you meet won't define you by your disability, but will rather see you as a whole person. As a diversity-competent practitioner, anti-oppression practice moves people with disabilities from being "objects" of charity, medical treatment, and social protection to instead being "subjects" with rights to make their own decisions and actively contribute to their community (Shapiro, 1993).

PUT IT IN PLAY: HOW CAN I USE THIS?

Disablism: A term that is used to refer to discrimination based on disability; while Canadians are more apt to use the term *ableism*, the term *disablism* is used more frequently internationally.

Human rights commissions and tribunals in Canada have reported discrimination based on disability as the predominant type of discrimination for many years now (Canadian Human Rights Commission, 2012). To change this fact, it is

necessary to demonstrate to society the many ways that disability touches people's lives and to promote improved reflective practices within all professions around issues related to ableism and **disablism** (Shier, Sinclair, & Gault, 2011).

Actively listening to the voices of lived experiences of people with disabilities is one means of developing the self-awareness, knowledge, and skills needed as a diversity-competent practitioner. Another is based on the concept of experiential affinity and is premised on the belief that if you walk a mile in the experience of disability, then as a practitioner, you will be more mindful of and committed to addressing issues of ableism (Shier, Sinclair, & Gault, 2011).

So, let's put these ideas into play by trying an exercise in experiential affinity that was developed by Professor Jennifer Hoyle (2004). Working in pairs, Person A will be the person with a simulated disability. Person A will be asked by Person B to do a maze activity. Person B is the person without disability. Person B will put a maze, face up, in front of Person A. Then Person B will place a mirror beside the paper with the maze, so that Person A can see the maze in the mirror. Person B then asks Person A to put a pencil on the start point of the maze and look at this point in the mirror. Person B then asks Person A to follow the maze by looking at it through the mirror. Person B tells Person A that he or she cannot look at the maze itself, but only at its reflection as he or she is given one minute to complete it.

Now debrief. Person A might want to reflect upon what he or she was experiencing, physically, emotionally, and socially while doing this exercise. Person B might consider whether he or she wanted to jump in and help or make suggestions. What would have made the interaction easier for the person with the disability? Both partners may wish to reflect on the ways this experiential learning activity will make them more mindful of and committed to addressing issues of ableism.

As self-reflective practice helps us to examine our biases, stereotypes, and prejudices, we often realize that many of our feelings about disability may be unconscious and unintentional. Harvard University's Project Implicit has developed an online test that takes less than ten minutes to complete (go to **https://implicit.harvard.edu/implicit/user/pimh/index.jsp**). Taking this test will help you examine your attitudes towards people with mental health issues. This activity may be helpful in breaking down assumptions and thoughts about disability and the implications these attitudes have on people with disabilities. As we discover our similarities, recognize what we have in common, and see ability instead of disability, then we begin to unlock the possible.

CourseMate Study Tools

Located at www.nelson.com/site/walkamile1e

- Consolidate your knowledge with the **Flashcards**.
- Gauge your understanding with **Picture This** and accompanying questions for reflection.
- Develop your critical thinking skills by working through **The Daily**.
- Apply your understanding with **KWIP** interactive!
- Develop your critical reading skills through compelling **Readings** and accompanying short answer questions.

REFERENCES

Arch Daily. (2011, March 28). Ed Roberts Campus/Leddy Maytum Stacy Architects. Retrieved from *Arch Daily*: http://www.archdaily.com/122507/

Anzovino, T. (2012). Universal design in the post-secondary learning environment. Unpublished raw data.

Bickenbach, J. E. (1993). *Physical disability and social policy*. Toronto: University of Toronto Press.

Brodsky, G., Day, S., & Peters, Y. (2012, March). Accommodation in the 21st century. Retrieved from *Canadian Human Rights Commission*: http://www.chrc-ccdp .gc.ca/sites/default/files/accommodation_eng.pdf

Canadian Charter of Rights and Freedoms. (1982). Part I of the Constitution Act, 1982, RSC 1985, app. II, no. 44.

Canadian Human Rights Commission. (2012). *Annual report*. Ottawa: Minister of Public Works and Government Services 2013.

Canadian Mental Health Association. (2013). Homelessness. Retrieved from *CMHA*: http://www.cmha.ca/ public-policy/subject/homelessness/

Chadha, E. (2008, winter). "Mentally defectives" not welcome: Mental disability in Canadian immigration law, 1859–1927. *Disability Studies Quarterly, 28* (1).

Christy, R. (2001, February 5). Life with cerebral palsy. *Maclean's*.

Connell, B., Jones, M., Mace, R., Mueller, J., Mullick, A., Ostroff, E., ... Vanderheiden, G. (1997, April 1). The principles of universal design. Retrieved from *The Centre for Universal Design*: http://www.ncsu.edu/ncsu/design/ cud/about_ud/udprinciplestext.htm

Council of Canadians with Disabilities. (2007). From vision to action: Building an inclusive and accessible Canada: A national action plan. Retrieved from *Council of Canadians with Disabilities*: http://www.ccdonline.ca/en/socialpolicy/ actionplan/inclusive-accessible-canada

Dosis, O., Coffey, K., Gravel, D., Ali, I., & Condra, E. (2012). Accessibility awareness training for educators. Fulfilling our commitment to accessible education. Colleges Ontario.

Eldridge v. British Columbia (Attorney General), S.C.R. 624; [1997] S.C.J. No. 86 (Supreme Court of Canada 1997).

Government of Alberta (2010). Training for work: Disability related employment supports. Retrieved from *Government of Alberta: Human Services*: http://www.humanservices. alberta.ca/working-in-alberta/3159.html

Grekul, J., Krahn, A, & Odynak, D. (2004, December). Sterilizing the "feeble-minded": Eugenics in Alberta, Canada, 1929–1972. *The Journal of Historical Sociology, 17* (4), 358–384.

Hoyle, J. (2004). Unlocking the possible: A case for inclusion. Fort Erie: Town of Fort Erie.

Hoyle, J. (1999). Physical activities in the lives of women with disabilities. *Sport and Gender in Canada*, 254–268.

Human Resources and Skills Development Canada. (2011). Disability in Canada: A 2006 profile. Gatineau: Human Resources and Skill Development Canada. Retrieved from http://publications.gc.ca/collections/collection_2011/ rhdcc-hrsdc/HS64-11-2010-eng.pdf

Kennedy, B. (2011, September 26). Disabled Pickering boy took his own life after he was mugged and bullied. Retrieved from *Toronto Star*: http://www.thestar.com/ news/gta/2011/09/26/disabled_pickering_boy_took_his _own_life_after_he_was_mugged_and_bullied.html

Kretzmann, J. P., & McKnight, J. (1993). *Releasing individual capacities. Building communities from the inside out*. ACTA Publications: Chicago.

Laidlaw Foundation. (2002–2003). *Perspective on social inclusion: The working paper series*. Toronto: Laidlaw Foundation.

Martz, M. (2008-2009, Winter). Standing up to bullying. Retrieved from *Abilities Magazine*: http://www.abilities.ca/ learning/2009/02/11/issue77_article_bullying/

Mora, M. (2008). Humble abode: Recovery starts at home ... If you have one. *SZ Magazine*. Retrieved from *Mental Wellness Today*: http://www.mentalwellnesstoday.com/ mental-illnesses/about-schizophrenia/schizophrenia -articles/14-schizophrenia-recovery/23-humble-abode -recovery-starts-at-home-if-you-have-one

Nixon, H. L. (1984). Handicapism and sport: New directions for sport sociology research. *Sport and the sociological imagination*, Nancy Theberge and Peter Donnelly (Eds.), pp. 162–176.

Office for Disability Issues HRDC. (2003). *Defining disability: A complex issue*. Gatineau: Human Resources Development Canada.

Oliver, M. (1990). *The politics of disablement*. London: The MacMillan Press Ltd.

Positive Exposure. (2012). About the program: Our story. Retrieved from *Positive Exposure*: http://positiveexposure. org/about-the-program-2/

Rosenhan, D. (1973). On being sane in insane places. *Science*, 179, 250–258.

Shapiro, J. (1993). *No pity: People with disabilities forging a civil rights movement*. New York: Three Rivers.

Shier, M. L., Sinclair, C., & Gault, L. (2011). Challenging "ableism" and teaching about disability in a social work classroom: A training module for generalist social workers working with people disabled by the social environment. *Critical Social Work* 12(1), 47–64.

Social Planning Council of Kitchener Waterloo. (2001, April). Disabilities: Universal design: Waterloo Region trends research project. Retrieved from *Waterloo Region*: http:// temp.waterlooregion.org/spc/trends/disabilities/design.html

Statistics Canada. (2007). Participation and activity limitation survey 2006: Tables. Ottawa: Statistics Canada.

United Nations. (2006). *United Nations convention on the rights of persons with disabilities*. Geneva: United Nations.

United Nations. (2012, September 12). Seeking to advance rights of people with disabilities, UN treaty review starts in New York. Retrieved from *UN News Centre*: http://www.un.org/apps/news/story.asp?NewsID =42860

Wachsler, S. (2007). The real quality of life issue for people with disabilities. *Journal of Progressive Human Services, 18*(2), 7–14.

Wendell, S. (1989). Towards a feminist theory of disability. *Hypatia*, Vol. 4, No. 2, 104–124.

World Health Organization. (2013). Health topics: Disabilities. Retrieved from *World Health Organization*: http://www.who.int/topics/disabilities/en/

Generations and Technology

> *"For as rich as you are, it's much better by far to be young at heart"*
>
> *(Frank Sinatra, 1954)*

DIVERSITY COMPETENCIES

Diversity competencies are specifically learned behaviours that students can actively practise to promote equity and inclusion. By mastering this unit, students will gain the skills to become diversity-competent practitioners, including the ability to

- summarize the differing characteristics that identify each generation

- assess the role of technology in each generation

- determine the barriers and/or benefits of technology, as they relate to each generation

You probably don't think of age in spans of generations, but when you walk down the busy streets of Toronto or Vancouver, or down the main street of the town where you live, you'll likely pass people from all generations. If you think about them as individuals, they're just a bunch of strangers; but when you think of them as belonging to a certain cohort, you realize that even though they may be strangers, they share common bonds and experiences that link them to each other—even though, in all likelihood, they will never meet.

A **generation** is a cohort or group of people who share similar chronological ages (usually in 15-year time spans) and were shaped by the events, trends, and developments of a particular span of time (McCrindle & Wolfinger, 2010). The world events, inventions, and media that helped shape the individuals in a generation create the bonds that unite those individuals, while simultaneously, they build the barriers that can separate each generation from another. It is important to understand that it is the lived experiences that people have in common—more so than their age—that make them part of a generation. For that reason, you might see different time frames associated with the same cohort. For example, Statistics Canada refers to the **cohort** of individuals born between 1966 and 1971 as "Baby Busters" (Statistics Canada, 2012), but different names and cohort dates are used in the literature (Beach, 2008; Buahene & Kovary, 2007; Zickuhr, 2011; McCrindle & Wolfinger, 2010). The point here is to understand that the concept of generation is open to a number of definitions and interpretations, though most follow the same general themes.

Many things could define a generation. Natural disasters. Heroes. Inventions. Music, for sure. Technology is an excellent example of an artefact that can define a generation. We can see the changes in technology over time and relate them to a certain cohort of people who used a certain technology during any given time period. For example, your grandparents might remember when television became popular, and your parents might remember the advent of the "walkman." Using technology can bring the global world together via the Internet, but only if people have acquired the technological skills to access computers—and if they can afford them.

A viable hypothesis is that younger people are more technologically adept than older people are at using **information communication technology (ICT)**, but does this hypothesis have support in the literature? Would you "friend" your grandmother on Facebook? Do you think your grandfather could beat you in a game like *Call of Duty*? In this sense, we can see how ICT relates to age, but does the interplay between ICT and age become a relationship that promotes inclusivity or exclusivity? Does ICT bring people closer together (which is what communication is really all about) or does it create a divide between the generations, because we think that older people don't know how to use ICT?

In this chapter, you'll learn about the generations of life and some of the challenges that each cohort has faced and has yet to face. Technology becomes an important piece, as we see that present generations and those to come increasingly and unavoidably intertwine with the machinery of the future.

THE GENERATIONS

Traditionalists (Born 1925–1945)

Born from around 1925 to 1945, **traditionalists** are the parents of the Baby Boomers (defined later). Those born specifically between 1939 and 1945 are also known as the World War II generation, and they're the fastest growing cohort in Canada today. This oldest generation makes up 13.8% of Canada's population (Statistics Canada, 2012). Within Canada's senior population, 73% are between the ages of 65 and 79 years and more than one-quarter (27%) are 80 years and older. Immigrants account for approximately 28% of the senior Canadian population, while Aboriginal peoples account for 1% (Butler-Jones, 2010). By 2036, according to a 2010 Statistics Canada projection, between 9.9 million and 10.9 million, roughly 23% of the estimated 40 million Canadians, will be seniors (Statistics Canada, 2010).

In many cases, these are your grandparents, or even your great-grandparents. Individuals growing up during these times experienced such events as the Great Depression, World War II, Pearl Harbor, the Korean War, and the rise of labour unions (Buahene & Kovary, 2007). Many of the men fought in wars, and

Generation: A cohort or group of people who share similar chronological ages (usually in 15-year time spans) and who were shaped by the events, trends, and developments of a particular span of time.

Cohort: Any group of people who share a time-specific period, such as graduating in the same year.

Information communications technology (ICT): The various uses of digital technology in assisting individuals to access, store, transmit, and manipulate information.

Traditionalists: Refers to those born specifically between the years 1925 to 1945.

Does technology divide or unite the generations?

nearly all of them learned to live through desperate times of poverty. Men, women, and children had to learn to survive without food, clothing, or, in some cases, a roof over their heads until they found work. Families stuck together, which resulted in a fierce sense of loyalty, pride, and dedication to each other. If you wanted to get ahead in life, you worked hard and saved your money. School and the church taught the difference between right and wrong, and you obeyed your elders. If you were fortunate and found a good job, then you stayed loyal to the company; you believed that the company would provide for you, so that you could provide for your family (Buahene & Kovary, 2007).

In terms of technology, this was the golden age of radio. Children's stories, comedy skits, and the names of loved ones lost were broadcast through the airwaves (Canadian Communications Foundation, 2001; BBC, 2012). Women's programming and weather reports, along with regular updates about the war, kept families huddled around the "wireless" (radio) to hear the latest news. In Hollywood, movies began to emerge on the silver screen. Silent movies became popular in the 1910s and when members of this generation were in their teens, movies like *The Wizard of Oz, Gone with the Wind*, and *King Kong* would go on to become box office hits (IMDb, 2012). Though telephones were available, not every home had one; and many people read the daily newspaper. The hard times that the Traditionalists lived through defined the individuals that they are today. These are dedicated, frugal, and loyal individuals, who may be set in their ways and averse to change or risk-taking. Ever mindful and respectful of authority, Traditionalists take pride in what they accomplish and are sure to provide for those they love.

TRADITIONALISTS TODAY

Senior Canadians are living longer today and with fewer disabilities than the generations before them, but the majority of them suffer from at least one **chronic disease** or condition (Barratt et al., 2006). Chronic diseases last a long time, and usually they progress very slowly, unlike acute illnesses, which

Chronic disease: A disease that lasts a long time and progresses slowly; examples are arthritis and heart disease.

end quickly. Arthritis or rheumatism is the most frequently reported chronic condition among seniors. Affecting women more than men, in 2003, 44% of 65- to 74-year-olds and 51% of those 75 and over reported having arthritis or rheumatism (Turcotte & Schellenberg, 2007). Though they may present with fewer disabilities and chronic conditions, the reality is that this generation (representing just 14% of the population), uses roughly 40% of hospital services, accounting for about 45% of all provincial and territorial government health spending. In general, the aging population will present more challenges to the health care system in Canada in future years. As indicated, seniors will require both an increase in the services used and the types of services required. Health care planners and providers are considering various ways to meet the needs of the senior population, including an increased focus on prevention and more efficient adoption and use of new technologies (CIHI, 2012).

Social isolation can be problematic for the vast majority (93% in 2001) of Canadian seniors who live at home (CIHI, 2012). Existing social supports outside the home, with friends or family, closely relate to the general overall well-being of seniors. While some seniors have a large network of friends and family, others live in relatively isolated conditions. In 2003, 32% of seniors aged 65 or older reported having no friends that they felt close to, compared to 5% of individuals aged 25 to 54 (Turcotte & Schellenberg, 2007).

Though there is a digital divide between the generations in terms of technological use and literacy, the use of the Internet among seniors continues to grow, thus expanding the social worlds of seniors and increasing their independence. According to Statistics Canada, 89.9% of Canadians aged 65 and over had sent an email in the past twelve months and 19.9% had used a social networking site (Statistics Canada, 2011). Between 1990 and 2003, the number of senior-led households with home Internet access increased from 3.4% to 22.7% (Turcotte & Schellenberg, 2007). As computer clubs for seniors spring up around the country, many seniors are taking advantage of this learning opportunity. Older women (aged 65–74) in one study reported that using the computer decreased their social isolation and increased their awareness about health issues (Malcolm, Mann, Tomita, Fraas, Stanton, & Gitlin, 2001).

Technological advances in the health field can allow seniors to stay in their own homes longer, too. For example, for seniors receiving home care services, a medication-monitoring system equipped with a sensor-trigger system allows family members to monitor which medications are taken when from anywhere in the world (CIHI, 2012).

Of particular concern to the aging population is elder abuse, especially since it is difficult to detect and monitor in cases where the victim is suffering from a **cognitive disorder** (such as Alzheimer's disease or a related dementia) that impairs their perception, memory, or ability to communicate. The Toronto Declaration on the Global Prevention of Elder Abuse defines **elder abuse** as "a single or repeated act, or lack of appropriate action, occurring within any relationship where there is an expectation of trust which causes harm or distress to an older person" (World Health Organization, 2002, p. 2). The abuse can occur in various forms, including physical, psychological/emotional, sexual, or financial. Elder abuse may also manifest itself in the shape of intentional or unintentional neglect. Issues such as under-reporting, confusion surrounding definitions of abuse, limitations in victimization/police data, and a general lack of awareness surrounding the problem make it difficult to determine exactly who is affected by elder abuse. Based on available Canadian data, however, it's estimated that between 4% and 10% of older adults experience some form of elder abuse in their life (National Seniors Council, 2007). Legal in some U.S. states, **"granny cams"** are security cameras that individuals are installing in their senior loved one's living space (residential care unit, apartment, or their own home) to ensure that they can monitor for elder abuse by a caregiver (Meyer, 2011). Does this sound a little like "Big Brother" to you, or is it an acceptable way to decrease abuse? What are the legal and ethical implications here?

Baby Boomers (Born 1946–1964)

Beginning in 1946, the Baby Boom lasted almost 20 years in Canada and saw women giving birth, on average, to 3.7 children, compared to 1.7 in more recent years (Statistics Canada, 2012). The children born at the beginning of this generation have reached the age of 65; and one study projects that by 2031, the proportion of seniors in Canada could reach 23% of the population, compared to 15% in 2011 (Statistics Canada, 2012). Figure 9.1 illustrates the Baby Boom phenomenon.

Cognitive disorders: Category of mental disorders that affect memory, perception, learning, and problem-solving; examples include dementia and Alzheimer's disease.

Elder abuse: A single or repeated act against an older person in which harm or distress is caused.

Granny cams: Security cameras intended to monitor for elder abuse by caregivers.

FIGURE 9.1
Portrait of Generations, Using the Age Pyramid, Canada 2011

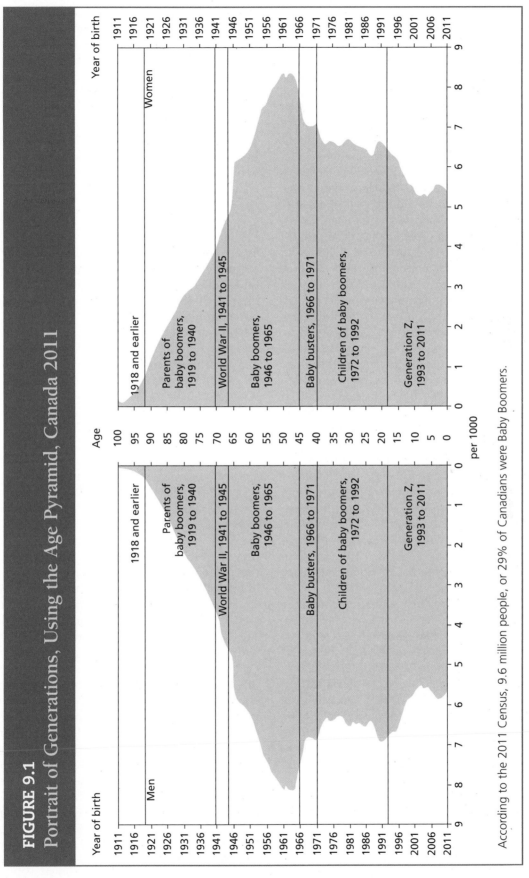

According to the 2011 Census, Portrait of generations, 9.6 million people, or 29% of Canadians were Baby Boomers.

Source: Statistics Canada, Portrait of generations, using the age pyramid, Canada, 2011. Reproduced and distributed on an "as is" basis with the permission of Statistics Canada.

Born between 1946 and 1964 and raised by Traditionalists, **Baby Boomer** children had a very child-focused upbringing (Buahene & Kovary, 2007). Unlike their parents, who lived through the Great Depression, Baby Boomers grew up in an economy that was booming after World War II. They lived in optimistic, idealized times and quickly realized that, just by their sheer numbers alone, they could push for social change—and they did. As these individuals grew into adulthood, they began to challenge the norms of society and question the political institutions in power. Some events that helped to define the lives of these individuals included the civil rights and women's liberation movements, the Quebec Crisis and Bill 101, the Vietnam War, Trudeau's multiculturalism, Woodstock, and Neil Armstrong landing on the moon. The size of this cohort also affected this generation in terms of the workplace. With limited jobs available, competition became fierce and forced many Baby Boomers to question their commitment to social change, rather than conformity, for as much as many of them wanted to picket for peace or around separation issues in Quebec, it didn't pay the bills. Raised with a good work ethic, Baby Boomers soon poured their waning social commitment into their careers. This is the generation that coined the phrase "Thank God it's Monday" (Buahene & Kovary, 2007), and their careers became the symbols of their value and self-worth—until the massive downsizing of the 1980s. A huge wake-up call for many of the Baby Boomers, massive layoffs gave them cause to rethink their lives and redefine who they were. Baby Boomers are optimistic and career-oriented individuals, whose competitive edge drives them to succeed in all their endeavours. They work hard and play hard, enjoying the benefits of their labour by indulging in consumer goods and vacations (Sheppard, 2006).

In terms of technology, this generation saw television ushered in as the newest form of social media (BBC, 2012; Giedd, 2012). Black-and-white television came into its own in the late 1940s and Baby Boomers grew up with shows like *Milton Berle*, *Leave It to Beaver*, *All in the Family*, and *Hockey Night in Canada* (NBC, 2012; CCF, 2001; BBC, 2012). Movies like *To Kill a Mockingbird*, *A Clockwork Orange*, and *Apocalypse Now* were entertaining audiences everywhere (IMDb, 2012). Baby Boomers were in their early teens when the first IBM PCs and Apple computers became popular (Rogers, 2009). It was a bit of a paradox because although Baby Boomers seemed very "high-tech," they still had to rent their phones, and send letters through the post to keep in touch. If they woke up in the middle of the night, they'd see a test pattern on the television; and if their friends moved away, they'd likely lose touch. This generation had mastery over the technology—they used it for data analysis, and word processing, and to make their lives easier, but it didn't define who they were (Rogers, 2009). They were like the pioneers or settlers of technology—setting down the foundation for what was to come—by building the networks and software programs that would fuel the technological revolution that would change the world—and come to define their children.

BABY BOOMERS TODAY

Known to be a bit rebellious in nature, Baby Boomers are just heading into their retirement years and will find it challenging to live comfortably, even if they're financially secure. Though a certain segment of this population will likely continue working well into their 70s, others will end their lives in poverty. But money is just a part of it. As this population ages, the increased use of technology will be a great communication tool.

Author Michael Adams (2010) divides the Baby Boomers into four distinct categories—the Disengaged Darwinists, Connected Enthusiasts, Autonomous Rebels, and Anxious Communitarians. Almost half of the cohort belongs to the first group. They long for the traditional times of old—before the women's liberation movement and multiculturalism "softened us up," and cost us our common sense. Their goals in life are to be financially independent, stable, and secure. They've lost their edge for social change, and they now live with the constant hope that things could be "as they used to be." Conversely, the 21% that comprise the Connected Enthusiasts thrive on the diversity, immigration, and equal opportunity that have come to define Canada. These people love their families and love experiencing new and exciting adventures. The technology that they use allows them to keep up with friends and family, as well as stay on top of world events and satiate their interests in cultures around the world. While it's a bit about immediate gratification and hedonism for the Connected Enthusiasts, it's also about the notion of community. The Anxious Communitarians are the fretful bunch of this generation. They quietly spend their time looking after their families and stay within their own communities. They uphold the traditional values and institutions of this generation and are fearful of change. Vested in maintaining their social status, these Baby Boomers still have a strong need for respect. Finally, the Autonomous Rebels are those who stand for what was supposed to have defined the Baby Boomer generation. Interested

Baby Boomers: Those individuals born between 1946 and 1964 and raised by Traditionalists.

in self-fulfillment and personal autonomy, they also have a strong belief in human rights. Entrepreneurial in spirit, skeptical of authority, and willing to use technology to make their lives more efficient, this group of Baby Boomers lives by its own rules and still hope to create social change—well into their retirement years (Adams, 2010).

Regardless of how they're divided, Baby Boomers have played a large part in changes to the Canadian labour market over the last 30 years. An important trend in recent years for both men and women has been the growth in the employment rate of people 55 and over. For men, the growth represents the reversal of a previous trend, since their employment rate was falling between 1976 and 1997. For women, the growth is the continuation of a trend. From 1997 to 2010, the employment rate of men 55 and over grew from 30.5% to 39.4%, and that of women grew from 15.8% to 28.6% (Carrière & Galarneau, 2011).

Baby Boomers will fundamentally reinvent retirement by living longer and remaining engaged and employed beyond age 65 (O'Keefe, 2010). A new study finds that this cohort is giving up the life of leisure and retirement and choosing to spend more time on the job (Carrière & Galarneau, 2011). One Statistics Canada study finds that a 50-year-old individual employed in 2008 can expect to stay in the labour force another 16 years, 3.5 years longer than would have been the case in the mid-1990s, if the previous year's retirement rates remain stable (LaRose, 2011). Many Baby Boomers have no choice but to work longer than planned because they lost some of their savings in the recession; others will work so that they continue to live the life they're accustomed to, in retirement. Results from one recent study revealed that almost half of today's 50- to 59-year-olds surveyed have less than $100 000 saved for retirement, and many of them plan to use employment income in retirement to make up for lack of savings (CARP, 2012). Another recent poll suggests that 57% of Canadians aged 50–59 say they would prefer to work longer into their retirement years in order to uphold their current lifestyles (Canadian Press, 2012).

Newer trends show that Baby Boomers are also more entrepreneurial. The deputy chief economist at the Canadian Imperial Bank of Commerce says that technology definitely plays a role in the creation of the 150 000 new businesses that he predicts will crop up within the next ten years. Baby Boomers make up the fastest-growing segment of new business owners—nearly 30% of the start-up businesses are started by those aged 50 and older and though 70% of new businesses are started by men, women's businesses are generally more successful. More than one-third of all the self-employed entrepreneurs, regardless of age, have a university degree (Tal, 2012).

Baby Boomers continue to interact with technology. Clearly, 90.3% of those aged 46–64 had sent an email in the past 12 months, 36.7% had used a social networking site, and 62% use online banking services (Statistics Canada, 2012). However, it seems as though the use of social networking sites can be problematic for some Baby Boomers. Many of this generation prefer to make friends in traditional ways and gravely mistrust the sharing of personal information in a public forum like the Internet (Lehtinen, Nasanen, & Sarvas, 2009). Baby Boomers are used to the old ways of interacting socially—without intensive digital interface—and are mistrustful of the instant connections that the younger generations make today. The many Baby Boomers that experience technological shyness will not have a chance to alleviate it as advances in the industry move forward, often without regard for the consumer. Prior to the release of Windows 8 and its bold new interface, "Metro," James Alexander, a senior vice-president of the consulting firm Info-Tech Research Group remarked, "Who cares whether the boomers can make the leap. They're less than 25% of the workforce now. Gen Y, Millennials or whatever you want to call them are going to comprise 50% of the North American workforce by the end of this decade" (Sorenson, 2012). New survey results indicate differently, however. According to the recruiting firm Adecco, "hiring managers are three times more likely to hire a worker that is 50 years old or older, than hire a millennial," stating concern with the younger generations' long-term commitment, professionalism, and reliability as reasons. The firm also offered the top five interview mistakes that Millennials make, which include wearing inappropriate attire, having posted questionable social media content, not researching the firm enough or asking questions during the interview, and appearing overconfident (Goudreau, 2012).

If more aging workers are staying in the workforce, then employers may be willing to accommodate their needs. Since work has become less physically demanding, employers could include offices that are more ergonomic, computer screens that are easier to read, easier-to-use software, and more technological training (Beach, 2008). What's clear is that Baby Boomers don't seem to be the "dinosaurs" with technology that they've often been painted as in the media. Where they may not be up on the latest, greatest, or fastest technology, they'll be a driving force behind the use of information technology in the next decade, especially in the health care industry, one of the largest in our society (Williams, 2011).

IN THEIR SHOES

If a picture can say a thousand words, imagine the stories your shoes could tell! Try this student story on for size – have you walked in this student's shoes?

I was content with my life. The kids had grown and moved out of the house, the grandchildren were a joy to baby sit and we were looking forward to my husband's retirement in two short years. My life was turned upside down when he collapsed at work and died of heart failure on the way to the hospital. The months after his funeral were a blur—flowers, casseroles and sympathy cards in the mail. It wasn't long before I started to notice the bills arriving in the mail as well. My husband had always handled our finances so it was inevitable that I would start falling behind in our payments.

Alone now, I realized that I needed to support myself financially. I realized that I needed to get a job. Prior to having my children I had worked in an office and had excellent keyboarding skills but I was using a typewriter! I couldn't imagine using a computer and doubted that I would even know how to turn one on. So back to school I went.

The fear of being alone was nothing compared to my fear of failing. Coupled with my age and computer illiteracy, I was a basket case. When the teacher started talking, my eyes glazed over. The technical terms and jargon did nothing but confuse me and as I looked around the classroom watching all those kids on their cell phones and laptops, I was ready to give up, but I knew that wasn't an option—I needed to learn this new skill.

I didn't buy a computer right away, because they had them at school and at the local employment office. I focused on using Microsoft Office and spent hours creating a recipe index, address book, cover letter and resumé. I even used Excel to create my monthly budget. Eventually I bought my own computer and began to send emails. I set up a Facebook account. I renewed old friendships and even learned to Skype with my grandkids.

My computer changed my world. I no longer felt isolated and alone. Eventually, I got Linked In and heard of a part-time receptionist position at a local not-for-profit agency. I applied online and was called for an interview. The interviewer was impressed with my computer skills. We laughed about teaching an old dog new tricks. This "old dog" got the job and is now financially secure. I'm so glad that I overcame my insecurities and went back to school.

My future is definitely brighter than it was three years ago and I'm ready for my next challenge—who knows, I might try online dating next!

Generation X (Born 1965–1980)

Many authors—including the authors of this book—consider people born between 1965 and 1980 as **Generation X**, but Statistics Canada has designated it only as 1966–1971: roughly 2.8 million (8% of the total population in 2011) were born between 1966 and 1971 in Canada (Statistics Canada, 2012). These individuals were born at time when the fertility rates were rapidly declining, resulting in a smaller cohort of people. Growing up in the shadow of the Baby Boomers, Generation X wasn't afforded the same attention as its predecessor. Media, marketers, and government were not as concerned with this group of individuals and, consequently, some have labelled Generation X as the "lost" generation. (Buahene & Kovary, 2007).

Generation X: Those individuals born between 1965 and 1980.

MTV/Much Music and personal computers, the Canadian Charter of Rights and Freedoms, the Los Angeles Riots, the Quebec Separation Referendum, the fall of the Berlin Wall, and AIDS—all influenced the Generation X cohort. Since their Baby Boomer parents were often dual-income earners, divorced, or single, this generation became the first "latch-key kids," forcing them to become independent at a very young age. This independence would become a prominent feature of Generation X and form the foundation for other characteristics, including self-reliance, skepticism, and pragmatism (Buahene & Kovary, 2007).

Rather than forming tight-knit family ties, members of this generation developed close friendship networks and non-traditional families by bonding with peers. In the workforce, many Generation X individuals found themselves competing for entry-level positions with downsized Baby Boomers. Realizing that competition for employment was fierce, they focused their energies on job employability rather than on job security and didn't develop the allegiance to companies that the previous generations had. Often, they chose contract work or started their own businesses; they preferred rewards for their efforts, rather than their years of service. If they found that the rewards didn't equal their efforts, this generation had no problem leaving a job to find another. Unlike their parents, the motto of Generation X is "work to live, rather than live to work" (Buahene & Kovary, 2007).

Generation X is, essentially, the first "techno" generation. Moving from a manufacturing-based economy to a service- and knowledge-based economy required the use of forms of technology that were more sophisticated, and this generation embraced virtually every form of gadgetry available. PDAs, cellphones, video games, email, Blackberrys, and laptops intertwined their lives at work and at home (Kane, 2012). *Super Mario*, *Pong*, and the dawn of the computer age are some of the events that helped to shape their lives. Major social issues like the Los Angeles riots took on new meaning, as the availability of information about these events was far more extensive than ever before. Images and news stories broadcast 24 hours a day, available on bulletin boards, via the Internet, in the daily news, and spread through social networks inundated individuals like never before. Undoubtedly, the electronic media was a huge influence on those born in this cohort. Generation X experienced the electronic media just as it was emerging as a social institution; print, radio, film, and television each played equally pivotal roles in modelling the lives of these individuals.

As children, they watched *Sesame Street*, *The Electric Company*, *ABC Afterschool Specials*, and *Schoolhouse Rock* (Garrard, 2008), and at the movies, teens watched films like *Star Wars* and *Pulp Fiction* (IMDb, 2012). Computer-literate, with the ability to multi-task and adapt to new environments, Generation X individuals are extremely results-driven and creative people who focus on creating harmony between their work and home lives.

GENERATION X TODAY

A 1990 *Time* magazine cover story painted a dismal picture of Generation X:

> They have trouble making decisions. They would rather hike in the Himalayas than climb a corporate ladder. They hate yuppies, hippies and druggies. They postpone marriage because they dread divorce. They possess only a hazy sense of their own identity but a monumental preoccupation with all the problems the preceding generation will leave for them to fix. (Gross & Scott, 1990, p. 56)

They were viewed as lost, lazy whiners—like the character George Costanza from the sitcom *Seinfeld*. Psychologically damaged from their parents' divorce and devastated by the suicide of Nirvana lead singer Kurt Cobain, Generation X had the reputation of being a cohort of mostly white slackers, who would buy anything (Mitchell, McLean, & Turner, 2005). Years later, *Time* magazine would revisit that story with an update: "Slackers? Hardly. The so-called Generation X turns out to be full of Go-Getters who are just doing it—but their way" (Hornblower, 1997). Around the turn of the century, the myths that surrounded this generation were debunked as reality checked in, and society took a better look at this educated group of individuals. Generation X entered the labour market in the early 1980s, when jobs were scarce. Since then, this generation has struggled to gain employment due to a weak economy (both in Canada and the United States) and the lack of jobs, which were occupied by the Baby Boomers (Statistics Canada, 2001).

Claiming independence and flexibility as two of their greatest strengths, members of Generation X now find themselves squeezed between the Baby Boomers and the up-and-coming Generation Ys, leading to yet another assumption—that they're suffering from "middle child syndrome." Having to fight for attention and screaming to be heard, any middle child can identify with the pains that this cohort deals with. Too young to mingle with the seasoned professionals and too old to hang with the younger stars on the horizon, this generation may have found work, but they are having trouble making their mark (Ungar, 2012). One interviewee makes an insightful analogy: "We're like the layer in between the cookies. Unless we actually step up to the plate and take management and leadership roles, we will be the forgotten generation" (Lawrence & Zimmett, 2011).

It is hard to be a forgotten generation when you produce people whose members include Google founders Larry Page and Sergey Brin and Facebook Inc., and Facebook's chief operating officer Sheryl Sandberg—all members of Generation X. In terms of technology, Generation X set the stage for introducing innovation and questioning the past. Baby Boomers and many Generation X workers learned what they know about computers while on the job. Smartphones were a sci-fi pipe dream when these individuals entered the workforce (Reisinger, 2010). Generation X Internet users still lead the pack in online shopping. Fully 80% of this cohort's Internet users buy products online, compared with 71% of younger Internet users;

and the same claim can be made for online banking. Generation X individuals are significantly more likely (67%) than any other generation to do their banking online (Jones & Fox, 2009). Findings from one study show, in fact, that the older member of Generation X goes online to accomplish a task and then walks away from the computer (Behrstock-Sherratee & Coggshall, 2010). Essentially, members of Generation X, though computer-savvy, use the technology in ways that support their lifestyles—to make their lives easier. They've got hectic lives, and if shopping and banking can be done online to allow them more time to work and spend time with family, then they use the technology.

Generation Y (Born 1981–2006)

Reared nothing like the Generation X children, the **Generation Y** children (sometimes referred to as Nexters, Millennials, or the Net Generation) were very different from the "latch-key kids." Protective and caring parents, who involved them in virtually all family decisions and got them involved in as many activities as possible, raised these individuals. Born between 1981 and 2006 and growing up in a time when violence in society was rising, parents protected and supervised their Generation Y children, and they treated them like peers, as opposed to offspring (Buahene & Kovary, 2007). Many Generation Y children treat the "lateral" relationship with their parents much the same as they would a relationship with a friend their own age—even referring to their parents by their given names, instead of "Mom" and "Dad."

Life-defining events during this time included the death of Princess Diana, the Oklahoma bombing, the digital age, increased school violence, Y2K, 9/11, and the U.S. War on Terror. Generation Ys were raised in a highly nurturing atmosphere that inspired confidence and hopefulness. Their parents taught them that life was going to be challenging and negotiable, but also collaborative, and they entered the workforce with a positive attitude and high expectations. Unfortunately, their enthusiasm wasn't always reciprocated once employed, and at times, was met with hostility by the older, more experienced workers (Pooley, 2006).

In terms of technology, teenagers and twentysomethings today are growing up in an unparalleled era of interconnectivity. According to recent data collected by the Pew Internet Project, 95% of young people 12 to 17 are online, 76% use social networking sites, and 77% have cellphones

Generation Y: Those individuals born between 1981 and 2006; also known as Millennials.

(Netburn, 2012). Author Donald Tapscott describes Generation Y as the Net Generation "because they were the first to grow up surrounded by digital technology" (Tapscott, 2009, p. 9). They are the first generation in human history to see behaviours such as tweeting and texting, and websites like Facebook, YouTube, Google, and Wikipedia as everyday facets of their lives that play important roles in their search for meaning and understanding in the world. They are racially diverse (and accepting), confident, and less religious than any of the preceding generations (Keeter & Taylor, 2009). Though they're likely to be the most educated of all the generations, they're also the most likely to spend their money on luxury goods. At a time when youth unemployment has been consistently high in Canada, from 2009 to 2011, Generation Y spenders have been the driving force behind national spending on luxury goods, with increased spending on luxury fashion by 33%, travel by 74%, and fine dining by 102%. Does it surprise you that 60% of those shoppers were men (Infantry, 2012)?

GENERATION Y TODAY

Many view teenagers and twentysomethings as a little wild and crazy, but are they given a bad rap in the brains department for making poor choices and bad decisions? Certain traits and annoying behaviours have come to define adolescence, only because they get on our nerves, or put our children in harm's way. Historically, teenagers have had their parents and grandparents shaking their heads, wondering about how much times have changed, and thinking of ways to bridge the ever-widening generation gap. But, what if there were scientific evidence that claimed the decisions that teens make are simply a consequence of the differing ways in which their brains are developing during this period in their lives? Compared to adults, teens do think in different ways when it comes to risk-taking behaviours. Both teens and adults understand that risky behaviours like smoking and unprotected sex carry consequences. However, research has shown that teens give more weight to the rewards than to the costs, and consequently engage in the behaviour anyway. It's not that they don't think things through, or that they don't understand the consequences; rather, they value the reward more heavily than adults do. Often, the stakes of the reward are heightened by social interaction with one's peers. Imagine, for example, the difference between playing a video game by yourself and playing it against a friend with a bunch of your friends watching. The reward in the latter situation is increased because of the perceived peer pressure applied on the teen to win

(Dobbs, 2011). Neuroscientists have discovered that teenagers behave the way they do because their brains are still developing and changing in ways that were never fully investigated before. Dr. Jay Giedd explains that "it's sort of unfair to expect teens to have adult levels of organizational skills or decision-making before their brains are finished being built" (Giedd, 2012).

Perhaps this finding is best exemplified by the myth of multi-tasking that is associated with this younger generation. With ready access to both the skills and machinery of modern technology, Generation Y is both perceived by others and self-perceived as multi-taskers, while they read, tweet, text, talk, eat, and study at the same time. Although there's no doubt that this generation, and much of Generation X, can certainly handle the actions of multi-tasking, there is some doubt as to whether or not they can multi-task effectively.

Several studies have indicated that perhaps the self-perception that Generation Y are multi-tasking marvels is accurate; however, this cohort seems to be in denial about the results of their multi-tasking. The purpose of one such study was to determine the extent to which multi-tasking affected the academic performance of business students. Half of an accounting class was allowed to text messages during a lecture, while the other half had their phones turned off. After the lecture, both groups took the same quiz. The results showed that students who texted during the lecture scored significantly lower on the quiz, compared to those who had their phones turned off (Ellis, Daniels, & Jauregui, 2010).

In another study, psychology students were asked to read a story on a computer. One group used instant messaging before they started reading, another group used it while they were reading, and a third group read the story without using it at all. The group that used instant messaging while reading took between 22% and 59% longer to read the story than the students in the other two groups—and that was after the time spent messaging was subtracted from their reading times (Bowman, Levine, Waite, & Dendron, 2010).

Another team of researchers used spyware to track the number of windows and page names for each of the programs that students had open during a class lecture. Even though students were encouraged to access course-related information, they also had access to "distractive" material, such as games, pictures, email, and instant messaging. Results showed that students had the distractive windows open for as much as 42% of the class time, and these students had significantly lower scores on homework, projects, quizzes, and final course averages. The students who looked at mostly productive windows (i.e., with course-related information) scored better on all markers than the distracted group (Kraushaar & Novak, 2010).

A study for the Kaiser Foundation found a correlation between multi-tasking and risky behaviours. The results of this in-depth study on multi-tasking revealed that sensation seekers (those shown to be more likely to engage in risky behaviours) are more likely to engage in media multi-tasking (Foehr, 2006). In a similar study where researchers examined screen time (computers, televisions, and video games) to see if they related to multiple risk behaviours in Canadian youngsters (10–16 years old), the results indicated that high computer use was associated with approximately a 50% increased engagement in multiple risk behaviours. High television use was also associated with modestly increased engagement in multiple risk behaviours. In this study, multiple risk behaviours referred to smoking, drunkenness, non-use of seatbelts, cannabis use, illicit drug use, and sex without condoms (Carson, Pickett, & Janssen, 2011).

CYBERBULLYING

Cyberbullying involves "sending or posting harmful or cruel text or images using the Internet (e.g., instant messaging, emails, chat rooms, and social networking sites) or other digital communication devices, such as cell phones. When it involves adults, it's called cyber-harassment, or cyberstalking. It can involve stalking, threats, harassment, impersonation, humiliation, trickery, and exclusion" (Feinberg & Robey, 2009). In British Columbia in 2012, 15-year-old Amanda Todd committed suicide one month after posting an eight-minute clip on YouTube about her life as a victim of cyberbullying. In the video (using cue cards), she explains that when in Grade 7, she showed her breasts to an unidentified man during an online chat, and describes the horror that her life had become since she fell into that trap. Canadians were in shock and saddened by the tragedy. Astoundingly, hecklers bullied her even in death, posting inappropriate comments on Internet memorial sites (Friscolanti, 2012). In 2013, a similar tragedy occurred in the case of Nova Scotia's Rehtaeh Parsons. She experienced repeated cyberbullying when a photo of her being sexually assaulted was made public through social media, leading to her suicide.

Technology is used for sexual purposes and for cyberbullying far more often than most people think. In a Massachusetts study of 835 respondents,

Cyberbullying: The practice of harassing someone online; includes sending threatening or aggressive messages, spreading malicious gossip through email or on websites, or using someone else's identity online.

Researchers found that approximately 23% of Grade 3 and 4 students had their own cellphones, as did 55% of Grade 5 students. Of those who responded to the survey, 11.4% indicated that they had received mean or hurtful email or text messages about them, and 45.6% were bullied in school (D'Antona, Kevorkian, & Russom, 2010). Results from the Pew Research Center show that nearly one-third (32%) of all teenagers who use the Internet say they have been targets of a range of annoying and potentially menacing online activities. Such activities include receiving threatening messages, having their private emails or text messages forwarded without consent, having an embarrassing picture posted without permission, and having rumours about them spread online (Lenhart, 2007). And, it's clear that girls (38%) are more likely than boys (26%) to report being bullied online. When teens were asked in a more recent study (2011) how often they saw other people being mean or cruel when social networking, 88% of the sample admitted to having seen someone being mean or cruel to someone else on a social media site (Lenhart, 2007).

Generation AO: Those individuals born around the turn of this century who are growing up in a highly technological world.

Transactive memory: Refers to one way of using our memory more efficiently, so that we rely on our family, friends, and co-workers as well as "things" to store information for us.

Computer-assisted instruction: Form of instruction that involves the use of computers to present various materials (such as practice drills or exercises) to engage the student interactively and to enhance learning.

Generation AO

The youngest of generations, known sometimes as **Generation AO** (for "always on"), are those individuals born around the turn of this century. They are growing up in a highly technological world. Recent research indicates that constantly having ready access to information deters people from memorizing information, and finds them instead relying on **transactive memory**—the idea that we rely on our family, friends, and co-workers as well as "things" to store information for us (Sparrow, Wenger, & Liu, 2011). How many telephone numbers can you recite, or remember? Probably not very many. This is just one of the consequences of increasingly relying on our transactive memories for information. When we know that we can readily get the information from another source, we're less likely to remember it.

A YouTube search of "babies using iPads" brings up numerous video clips that show children as young as eight months interacting with computer tablets in various ways. In one clip, a one-year-old can't figure out why her fingers won't make the images in a magazine move. She even presses her finger on her leg to make sure that her finger is working; then she goes back to trying to make the magazine as interactive as the tablet she was previously holding. The uploader's point in this video segment suggests: "Technology codes our minds, changes our OS (operating system). The video shows how magazines are now useless and impossible to understand, for digital natives" (UserExperiencesWork, 2011). The comments accompanying this video make for interesting reading, as users discuss the controversy surrounding young children and technological devices. Is a child ever too young to start learning technology?

In school curricula, children as young as two are using tablets in the classroom. The benefits of providing **computer-assisted instruction** (CAI) to children in junior kindergarten vary depending upon the kind of computer experiences offered, and how frequently children have access to computers. CAI involves computers presenting various materials (such as practice drills or exercises) to interactively engage

What are your strategies to stop cyberbullying? How do you use them?

At what age is it appropriate for children to have their own Facebook accounts?

the student and enhance learning. Children with access to computers showed greater developmental gains in intelligence, nonverbal skills, structural knowledge, long-term memory, manual dexterity, verbal skills, problem-solving, abstraction, and conceptual skills when compared to children who didn't have similar access to computers (Haughland, 1999). Newer research supports this earlier finding. By testing three- to six-year-old children, the authors of one study found that children at this age quickly developed the skills needed to use a stylus and tablet for drawing, although there were differences between ages, and skill level advanced with age. By the second learning session, all but one of the 41 children were able to draw a self-portrait using the tablet. What became paramount in this study was how the teachers chose to use the technology, since the children's Interest was continually peaked (Course & Chen, 2010).

The National Association for the Education of Young Children (NAEYC) and the Fred Rogers [Mr. Rogers] Center for Early Learning and Children's Media have recently affirmed that digital media and technology can be viewed as "learning tools that, when used in intentional and developmentally appropriate ways and in conjunction with other traditional tools and materials, can support the development and learning of young children" (Fitzgerald, 2011). The use of various forms of technology for children is inevitable, but the primary issue is, as always, how the technology is used.

ENDING THOUGHTS

Though Generations X and Y have more familiarity than Baby Boomers and Traditionalists with almost everything technology related, research indicates that all generations continue to adopt a digital lifestyle (Reisinger, 2010). As we become increasingly reliant on technology, however, are users (regardless of age) becoming increasingly capable and efficient?

Is using social media the same thing as being computer-literate? Even though we know that younger generations use more technology than older ones, for example, will they be just as capable of managing their health online? According to recent results from one European study, the answer is no. Researchers in the Netherlands studied the barriers that limit the Internet's adoption as a source of health information. They were trying to determine whether the general population was ready for an e-Health program, and they found that most people lack the skills to keep up with the constantly growing amount of online health-related information. Interestingly, these researchers found that younger generations, who are often skilled Internet users, also lacked the requisite skills (Van Deursen & Van Dijk, 2011).

Does technology, in fact, really connect people? Research from neuroscientist and author John Cacioppo shows that it depends on how you use it. If you use email or Facebook to arrange social engagements or interactions, the technology becomes a social connector. If, however, you have 3500 friends on Facebook but never see any of them face to face, there's really only a façade of being connected—it can actually make you lonelier (Cacioppo & Patrick, 2009). The heavy reliance on the use of all technologies has some corporations like Google and Nike installing space for employees to take naps or meditate—somewhere they can unplug and re-energize (Irvine, 2012).

In this fast-paced world of technological gadgets and gimmicks, then, have quiet thought and solitude lost their purpose? Are the times set aside for reflection and critical thought gone forever? When is the last time you just sat with yourself—no phone, no computer, no TV—just you and your imagination? As each generation faces the inevitability of aging, and the seeming onslaught of newer and faster ways to communicate, one can only hope that we haven't lost touch with ourselves.

READING

CLASH OF THE GENERATIONS

By Cindy Waxer

When Bill Horne sauntered into an evening meet-and-greet being held by a local packaging company in search of fresh IT talent, the retired computer engineer knew his chances of leaving the event with a job offer were slim. Now 56, Horne had spent 25 years working in the telecommunications industry before retiring from Verizon in 2002. Six years later, Horne says he knew that the IT field had changed dramatically, rendering him "out of step" with cutting-edge IT. But after watching his retirement savings dwindle and the demand for small side projects disappear, Horne says he was "economically motivated" to re-enter the workforce. A casual meet-and-greet seemed like a perfect opportunity for the baby boomer to get his feet wet. Horne was in for a shock, however. Expecting an informal recruiting event, he found himself in the thick of what "felt like a discotheque," surrounded by throngs of aggressive twentysomethings jostling for the attention of senior-level managers and barking into their cell phones.

"They were talking a lot, the noise was deafening, and the atmosphere was loud, confused and not very businesslike," Horne recalls. His experience is far from unique. Throughout busy job fairs, crowded boardrooms and hectic IT departments across the U.S., a battle royal is brewing between aging baby boomers and fresh-faced millennials—two distinct generations with differing work styles, conflicting cultures, and disparate skill sets.

On the one side stand the boomers: IT veterans valued for their unwavering work ethic, vast experience and institutional memory. On the opposing side, the millennials: Web 2.0 natives with technology in their DNA who would rather text and Twitter than talk and who have little patience with the way things have always been done.

IT managers are facing a tough predicament: a head-on collision between two vastly talented yet differing generations, both vying for full-time employment in a fast-shrinking economy. And it's happening everywhere. "Baby boomers coming back into the market is very common," says Brooke Kline, chief technology officer at iBank, a Costa Mesa, Calif.-based money management firm. "At the same time, we have just as many millennials coming out of college looking to explore new opportunities." Deciding whom to hire or lay off requires sorting through a minefield of competing technical expertise, business acumen, cultural preferences, and career expectations.

New Rules

Baby boomers and millennials might have eased by each other in the workplace with no clash at all, as boomers gradually retired and millennials moved in and up the ranks. But a faltering economy changed all that.

Over the past 15 months, the stock market has wiped out $2 trillion in Americans' retirement savings, according to the Congressional Budget Office. And even before the financial crisis hit full force, a February 2008 survey by job site *CareerBuilder.com* revealed that nearly three out of five U.S. workers age 50 or older were planning to look for work elsewhere after retiring from their current jobs.

And that can put them into competition with candidates their children's ages, says Home, because once an employee retires, he loses his seniority. "I have realistic expectations that I'm not going to be appointed vice president," he says.

As boomers struggle to resuscitate their careers and millennials flood the workforce, IT managers are having to rethink what it means to be an IT professional and to weigh the relative value of traditional and new-age skills.

That's not always easy. For example, millennials have a tendency to eat, sleep, and breathe Web 2.0 technologies, and the value of that may not be immediately clear to a hiring manager.

"When my boomer colleagues see me texting, blogging and using wikis, they see it as social" as opposed to work-related, says Brett Gardner Banner, a 26-year-old engineering specialist at FedEx Corp. "But they're just tools I use to achieve higher results by gaining consensus and connecting with others."

Yet it's precisely these tools—and users' proficiency levels—that are dividing the generations into warring factions. "A millennial is more likely to communicate electronically over more involved in social networking," says Sherry Aaholm, FedEx's vice president of IT. Take, for example, Banner, who practically showers with his BlackBerry Storm and claims his familiarity with Web 2.0 tools is "almost innate." He says he regularly relies on wikis, Twitter and microblogging services like Yammer to communicate with colleagues and swap information. "Boomers prefer conference calls and e-mails, whereas I prefer texting and wikis," says Bonner.

But it's not just the Web. "There's a lot of new technology—like agile software development and open source—that young kids have picked up, whereas some of the older folks are still working on migrating," says Jeff Schuster, a recruiter at IT consulting company Halo Group LLC in Novi, Mich.

Boomers are better known for their expertise in more traditional technologies such as IT infrastructure and operating systems. That's good news for FedEx, which is always on the lookout for IT professionals with the skills needed to support its largely mainframe-based package-tracking system. But that type of expertise can limit boomers' prospects elsewhere, Schuster says.

And it's not just about skills; attitude also plays a major role in who gets hired. For example, millennials' eagerness to adopt new technologies—and some boomers' tendency to resist doing so—may make recruiters think twice before bringing on an older candidate in need of extensive training.

"The boomer folks are a little more fixed in their ways and not as open to learning a new set of technology skills," says Aaholm. "That's the difference with the millennial generation—they're willing to expand their skill base."

This eagerness to learn is giving many millennials a leg up on the competition. But there's a managerial flip side to consider. Young IT workers who are bold enough to take on new technologies are also more likely to be impatient with the constraints of traditional workplaces. "There's an expectation on the part of millennials that the people who are managing them won't just see them as cogs in the machine but will be flexible with them and take their preferences into account," says Tom Clement, 54, an IT manager at application development firm Serena Software Inc. in Redwood City, Calif.

That kind of rugged individualism delivers enormous value to pioneering companies such as Serena, which is adopting innovative development trends, such as "business mashups" or composite applications, to stay ahead of the curve.

"It takes guts to build mashups, and that's what is great about the millennials," says Clement. "They've got the guts to go in and create a new application, whereas [boomers] aren't as emboldened."

Businesses that expect all employees to march to the beat of the same drummer, however, may have a tough time reining in millennials' more spirited work ethic and thirst for experimentation. And millennials' tendency to mix work with pleasure is another factor that could influence the hiring decisions of IT managers.

"Millennials really want a work-life balance that's seamless; they want to be able to communicate with their friends while they're working," says Kline. The older generation, in contrast, wants "to be productive from 8 a.m. to 5 p.m. and focus only on work." Those tendencies recently convinced Kline to hire a boomer—not a millennial—for a help desk maintenance job with the steady hours of 7:30 a.m. to 4:30 p.m.

"When we looked at the strengths and weaknesses of the candidates, we felt that a baby boomer was more equipped to handle that type of position," says Kline.

Cherry-picking aside, companies must still make some cultural adjustments to successfully mix millennials and boomers in the workplace. Your company's willingness to make those adjustments will affect its ability to recruit and retain talent.

"From a baby boomer's standpoint, it's a big change to see a really bright guy come in at 10:30 a.m. wearing shorts and sneakers and start work," says Kline. "Breaking down that barrier is a big challenge."

Just ask Home, who dedicated his entire career to a single employer. "Kids coming out of school have no work ethic," he says. "They think life is a video game and that you get paid because you show up."

John Martin, a 62-year-old iBank quality assurance specialist, is more artful. "My approach to working is much different than that of today's millennials," he says. "A great number of them think there are unlimited jobs out there, and so they approach work a little more casually than people of my generation."

Source: Cindy Waxer, "Clash of the Generations" (IT World Canada, 15 February 2009).

Defining "Professional"

It's this perception among boomers that deeply offends Nathan Williams, a 30-year-old Serena software engineer who identifies with the millennial generation. "There's the misconception that we're just not professional. But the truth is, we have different ideas of what it means to be professional, and a casual attitude is part of that."

In fact, Williams says millennials' easygoing disposition encourages creativity and "a willingness to break boundaries" that contributes to tasks such as product development. Millennials' casual approach to work can backfire in risky ways that managers also need to consider, however. According to a February 2008 study by security systems provider Symantec Corp., when asked whether they feel entitled to use whatever application, device or technology they like, regardless of source or corporate IT policies, 69% of millennials said yes while only 31% of other workers did.

Millennials and boomers may have to agree to disagree about what it means to be an IT professional today. But for IT managers, the trick is to weigh what each generation brings to the table and match the individual to the job. And that's a skill that they need to develop quickly. "The pressure on front-line managers nowadays with the millennials coming into the workforce is greater than it's ever been," says Lisa Orrell, a generational relations expert and author of *Millennials Incorporated* (Wyatt-MacKenzie, 2008). And, she warns, "the competition is only going to get more fierce as time goes on."

DISCUSSION QUESTIONS

1. What do you think about being categorized by a cohort—especially as it relates to technology? Do the characteristics that describe your generation seem like stereotypes to you? Explain.
2. How will your technology skills help or hinder your chances of finding employment in your chosen field? What about your social skills? In what ways do they affect how you relate to potential co-workers—especially those who are older or younger?
3. If you were in a position to hire an individual, what would matter more to you—their ability to work with the technology or their ability to interact with their co-workers?

KWIP

KNOW IT AND OWN IT: WHAT DO I BRING TO THIS?

Identifying yourself chronologically within the generations is the easy part here. What's a little more difficult is coming to terms with the characteristics that traditionally define each of the generations. If you've been labelled as a member of Generation Y, do you accept or deny the labels that come with it? Are the stereotypical traits that define the Generation Y cohort part of who you are, or do you stray from the pack?

WALKING THE TALK: HOW CAN I LEARN FROM THIS?

A better understanding of where people come from can help you to "get inside their heads" so you can know some of the outside influences that have helped shape their personalities. This inside information will assist you greatly when you try to relate to someone from a different generation. Knowing that someone might have lived through a war or has never used a computer might change the way that you begin a conversation with that person.

IT IS WHAT IT IS: IS THIS INSIDE OR OUTSIDE MY COMFORT ZONE?

Stepping outside our comfort zone is never easy, but when it comes to generations, it's like stepping in and out of a time machine. If your university program has a placement option, are you worried that you might not have anything in common with a co-worker or client—especially one who is much older or younger than you? Technology can be the common thread that weaves comfort into any social interaction.

PUT IT IN PLAY: HOW CAN I USE THIS?

Regardless of the generation to which you belong, the next time you decide to play an online game, consider visiting **http://freerice.com/#/english-vocabulary/1367** instead. On this site, you can challenge vocabulary skills while donating grains of rice to feed the hungry. Form a group if you like and set up challenges, or set your own personal goals. It's a win–win situation!

CourseMate Study Tools — Located at www.nelson.com/site/walkamile1e

- Consolidate your knowledge with the **Flashcards**.
- Gauge your understanding with **Picture This** and accompanying questions for reflection.
- Develop your critical thinking skills by working through **The Daily**.
- Apply your understanding with **KWIP** interactive!
- Develop your critical reading skills through compelling **Readings** and accompanying short answer questions.

REFERENCES

Adams, M. (2010). *Stayin' alive: How Canadian baby boomers will work, play and find meaning in the second half of their adult lives.* Canada: Viking Press.

Barratt, J., Chambers, L., Graham, T., Keefe, J., Meloche, A., O'Brien-Cousins, A. et al. (2006, September). Healthy aging in Canada: A new vision, a vital investment from evidence to action. Retrieved September 13, 2012, Newfoundland Labrador Department of Health and Community Services: http://www.health.gov.nl.ca/health/publications/vision_rpt_e.pdf

BBC. (2012). The BBC story. Retrieved from *BBC*: http://www.bbc.co.uk/historyofthebbc/

Beach, C. (2008, November). Canada's aging workforce: Participation, productivity, and living standards. Retrieved from *Bank of Canada*: http://www.bankofcanada.ca/wp-content/uploads/2010/09/beach.pdf

Behrstock-Sherratee, E., & Coggshall, J. (2010). Realizing the promise of Generation Y. *Educational Leadership*, 28–34.

Bowman, L. L., Levine, L. E., Waite, B. M., & Dendron, M. (2010). Can students really multitask? An experimental study of instant messaging while reading. *Computers & Education*, 927–931.

Buahene, A., & Kovary, G. (2007). *Loyalty unplugged.* Philadelphia: Xlibris.

Butler-Jones, D. (2010, October 28). The Chief Public Health Officer's report on the state of public health in Canada, 2010. Retrieved from *Public Health Agency of Canada*: http://www.phac-aspc.gc.ca/cphorsphc-respcacsp/2010/fr-rc/cphorsphc-respcacsp-06-eng.php

Cacioppo, J., & Patrick, W. (2009). *Loneliness: Human nature and the need for social connection.* New York City: W.W. Norton.

Canadian Communications Foundation. (2001). The history of Canadian broadcasting. Retrieved from *Canadian Communications Foundation*: http://www.broadcasting-history.ca/timeline/CCFTimeline.swf

Canadian Press. (2012). Baby boomers prepared to work longer to improve retirements. Retrieved from *Financial Post*: http://business.financialpost.com/2012/09/21/baby-boomers-prepared-to-work-longer-to-improve-retirements/

CARP. (2012, August 20). Most fiftysomethings plan to work in retirement to offset low savings. Retrieved from *CARP*: http://www.carp.ca/2012/08/22/most-fiftysomethings-plan-to-work-in-retirement-to-offset-low-savings/

Carrière, Y., & Galarneau, D. (2011, October 26). Delayed retirement: A new trend? Retrieved 2012, September 18 from *Statistics Canada*: http://www.statcan.gc.ca/pub/75-001-x/2011004/article/11578-eng.htm

Carson, V., Pickett, W., & Janssen, I. (2011). Screen time and risk behaviors in 10- to 16-year-old Canadian youth. *Preventative Medicine*, 99–103.

CIHI. (2012). The baby boom effect: Caring for Canada's aging population. Retrieved from *Canadian Institute for Health Information*: http://www.cihi.ca/CIHI-ext-portal/internet/en/Document/health+system+performance/quality+of+care+and+outcomes/RELEASE_01DEC11

Course, L., & Chen, D. (2010). A tablet computer for young children? Exploring its viability for early childhood education. *Journal of Research on Technology in Education*, 75–98.

D'Antona, R., Kevorkian, M., & Russom, A. (2010). Sexting, texting, cyberbullying and keeping youth safe online. *Journal of Social Sciences*, 521–526.

Dobbs, D. (2011, November). Beautiful brains. *National Geographic*, pp. 37–59.

Ellis, Y., Daniels, W., & Jauregui, A. (2010). The effect of multitasking on the grade performance of business students. *Research in Higher Education Journal*, 1–10.

Feinberg, T., & Robey, N. (2009). Cyberbullying. *Education Digest*, 26–31.

Fitzgerald, J. (2011, June 30). Child's play: Should preschoolers engage with technology or good-old fashioned fun? Retrieved from *Preschool Matters ... Today*: http://preschoolmatters.org/2011/06/30/child%E2%80%99s-play-should-preschoolers-engage-with-technology-or-good-old-fashioned-fun/

Foehr, U. (2006). Media multitasking among American youth: Prevalence, predictors and pairings. Retrieved from *Kaiser Family Foundation*: http://www.kff.org/entmedia/upload/7592.pdf

Friscolanti, M. (2012, October 29). Shunned in life, remembered in death. *Maclean's*, pp. 70–72.

Garrard, T. A. (2008). Remember, the force will be with you ... always: The electronic media and Star Wars and the socialization of Generation X. Dissertation Thesis. MI, USA.

Giedd, J. (2012). Inside the teenage brain. Retrieved from *Frontline*: http://www.pbs.org/wgbh/pages/frontline/shows/teenbrain/interviews/giedd.html

Goudreau, J. (2012, September 26). Top 5 interview mistakes millennials make. Retrieved October 16, 2012, from *Forbes*: http://www.forbes.com/sites/jennagoudreau/2012/09/26/top-5-interview-mistakes-millennials-make/

Gross, D. M., & Scott, S. (1990, July 16). Proceed with caution. *Time*, pp. 56–63.

Haughland, S. (1999). What role should technology play in young children's learning? *Young Children*, 26–31.

Hornblower, M. (1997, June 9). Slackers? Hardly. The so-called Generation X turns out to be full of Go-Getters who are just doing it—but their way. *Time*, pp. 58–65.

IMDb. (2012). IMDb charts: Top movies. Retrieved August 2, 2012, from *IMDb.com*: http://www.imdb.com/chart/

Infantry, A. (2012, June 19). Gen Y Canadians splurging on luxury items, despite high unemployment. Retrieved from *The Toronto Star*: http://www.thestar.com/business/article/1213344--gen-y-guess-who-s-driving-the-luxury-market

Irvine, M. (2012, October 29). Can true solitude be found in a wired world? Retrieved from *The Daily Herald*: http://www.heraldnet.com/article/20121029/NEWS02/710299975/0/sports01?page=single

Jones, S., & Fox, S. (2009, January 28). Generational differences in online activities. Retrieved from *Pew Internet and American Life Project*: http://www.pewinternet.org/Reports/2009/Generations-Online-in-2009/Generational-Differences-in-Online-Activities.aspx?view=all

Kane, S. (2012). Generation X. Retrieved from *About .com*: http://legalcareers.about.com/od/practicetips/a/GenerationX.htm

Keeter, S., & Taylor, P. (2009, December 11). The millennials. Retrieved from *Pew Research Center Publications*: http://pewresearch.org/pubs/1437/millennials-profile

Kraushaar, J. M., & Novak, D. C. (2010). Examining the effects of student multitasking with laptops during lecture. *Journal of Information Systems Education*, 241–251.

LaRose, L. (2011, October 26). More Canadians working longer into retirement years, StatsCan says. Retrieved from *Winnipeg Free Press*: http://www.winnipegfreepress.com/fpnewsfeatures/more-canadians-working-longer-into-retirement-years-statscan-says-132609108.html

Lawrence, D., & Zimmett, L. (2011, September 15). Generation X caught behind wall of boomers. Retrieved from *Financial Post*: http://business.financialpost.com/2011/09/15/generation-x-caught-behind-wall-of-boomers/

Lehtinen, V., Nasanen, J., & Sarvas, R. (2009). "A little silly and empty-headed"—Older adults' understandings of social networking sites. Retrieved from *Electronic Workshops in Computing*: http://www.bcs.org/upload/pdf/ewic_hci09_paper6.pdf

Lenhart, A. (2007, June 27). Cyberbullying. Retrieved from *Pew Internet*: http://pewresearch.org/pubs/527/cyber-bullying

Malcolm, M., Mann, W. C., Tomita, L. F., Fraas, L. F., Stanton, K. M., & Gitlin, L. (2001). Computer and Internet use in physically frail elders. *Physical and Occupational Therapy in Geriatrics*, 15–32.

McCrindle, M., & Wolfinger, E. (2010). Generations defined. *Ethos*, 8–13.

Meyer, T. (2011, July 5). Investigator: 'Granny cams' used to capture elder abuse. Retrieved from *WKYC*: http://www.wkyc.com/news/article/196420/45/Investigator-Granny-cams-used-to-capture-elder-abuse

Mitchell, M. A., McLean, P., & Turner, G. B. (2005). Understanding Generation X ... Boom or bust introduction. *Business Forum*, 26–31.

National Seniors Council. (2007, December 11). Report of the National Seniors Council on Elder Abuse. Retrieved from *National Seniors Council*: http://www.seniorscouncil

.gc.ca/eng/research_publications/elder_abuse/2007/
hs4_38/page00.shtml

NBC. (2012). NBC timeline: Key dates in its history.
Retrieved from *Media Biz on NBC News*: http://www
.msnbc.msn.com/id/33994343/ns/business-us_business/t/
nbc-timeline-key-dates-its-history/#.UBgpQqPCRe4

Netburn, D. (2012, February 29). Pew study: Is the Internet
ruining or improving today's youth? Retrieved from
Pew Internet: http://www.pewinternet.org/Media
-Mentions/2012/Is-the-Internet-ruining-or-improving
-todays-youth.aspx

O'Keefe, S. (2010, November 2). Technology trends for
seniors. Retrieved from *Minitrends*: http://minitrends
.com/technology-trends-for-seniors/

Pooley, E. (2006, January 6). Generation Y: How
twentysomethings are changing the workplace. Retrieved
from *Canadian Business*: http://www.canadianbusiness
.com/article/12625--generation-y-how-twentysomethings
-are-changing-the-workplace

Quitney Anderson, J. (2012, February 29). Millennials
will benefit and suffer due to their hyperconnected
lives. Retrieved from *Elon University School of
Communications*: http://www.elon.edu/docs/
e-web/predictions/expertsurveys/2012survey/
PIP_Future_of_Internet_2012_Gen_Always_ON.pdf

Reisinger, D. (2010, October 12). Forrester: Tech generation gap grows. Retrieved from *CIO Insight*:
http://www.cioinsight.com/c/a/Workplace/
Forrester-Tech-Generation-Gap-Grows-504206/

Rogers, M. (2009, October 28). Boomers and technology:
An extended conversation. Retrieved from *AARP*: http://
assets.aarp.org/www.aarp.org_/articles/computers/2009
_boomers_and_technology_final_report.pdf

Sheppard, G. (2006). *How to be the employee your company
can't live without*. New Jersey: J. Wiley and Sons.

Sorenson, C. (2012, September 24). Control-alt-reboot.
Maclean's, 38–40.

Sparrow, B., Wenger, D., & Liu, J. (2011). Google effects on
memory: Cognitive consequences of having information
at our fingertips. *Science*, 776–778.

Statistics Canada. (2001, April 17). Major social policy issues
for the 21st century. Retrieved September 18, 2012, from
Statistics Canada: http://www.statcan.gc.ca/pub/92-125-g/
html/4151217-eng.htm

Statistics Canada. (2010, May 26). Population projections: Canada, the provinces and territories. Retrieved

September 13, 2012, from *The Daily*: http://www.statcan.
gc.ca/daily-quotidien/100526/dq100526b-eng.htm

Statistics Canada. (2011, October 1). Canadian Internet use
survey, Internet use, by age group and Internet activity.
Retrieved July 16, 2012, from *Statistics Canada*:
http://www5.statcan.gc.ca/cansim/a26?lang=eng&
retrLang=eng&id=3580153&pattern=358-0152..358-0158&
tabMode=dataTable&srchLan=-1&p1=-1&p2=-1

Statistics Canada. (2012, May 30). Generations in Canada.
Retrieved July 18, 2012, from *Statistics Canada*: http://
www12.statcan.gc.ca/census-recensement/2011/as-sa/
98-311-x/98-311-x2011003_2-eng.cfm

Tal, B. (2012-25-09). Start-ups—Present and future. Retrieved
from *CIBC-Canadian Research Services*: http://research
.cibcwm.com/economic_public/download/if_2012-0925.pdf

Tapscott, D. (2009). *Grown up digital: How the net generation
is changing your world*. New York: McGraw-Hill.

Turcotte, M., & Schellenberg, G. (2007-07-02). A portrait of seniors. Retrieved July 6, 2012, from *Statistics
Canada*: http://www.statcan.gc.ca/pub/89-519-x/89-519
-x2006001-eng.htm

Ungar, L. (2012). Why swim with the sharks when you
can stay in the baby pool? Challenges facing Gen X.
Retrieved from *Affluent Magazine*: http://www
.affluentmagazine.com/articles/article/718

UserExperiencesWork. (2011, October 6). A magazine is an iPad
that does not work.m4v. Retrieved from *YouTube*: http://
www.youtube.com/watch?v=aXV-yaFmQNk&feature=plcp

Van Deursen, A., & Van Dijk, A. (2011, April 29). Internet
skills performance tests: Are people ready for eHealth?
Retrieved from *Journal of Medical Internet Research*:
http://www.jmir.org/2011/2/e35/

Waxer, C. (2009, February 16). Clash of the generations.
Computerworld, 17–20.

Williams, R. (2011, January 24). Baby boomers and technology. Retrieved from *Psychology Today*: http://www
.psychologytoday.com/blog/wired-success/201101/
baby-boomers-and-technology

World Health Organization. (2002). The Toronto declaration
on the global prevention of elder abuse. Retrieved from
World Health Organization: http://www.who.int/ageing/
projects/elder_abuse/alc_toronto_declaration_en.pdf

Zickuhr, K. (2011, February 3). Generations and their gad-
gets. Retrieved from *Pew Internet and American Life
Project*: http://www.pewinternet.org/Reports/2011/
Generations-and-gadgets/Report.aspx?view=all

Families

> "I love you, you love me, we're a happy family."
>
> (Lee Bernstein, a.k.a. Barney, 1983)

DIVERSITY COMPETENCIES

Diversity competencies are specifically learned behaviours that students can actively practise to promote equity and inclusion. By mastering this unit, students will gain the skills to become diversity-competent practitioners, including the ability to

- compare contrasting definitions of the family over time and between various organizations

- assess the amount of change each family form has experienced over time and explain plausible reasons for the changes

- identify barriers that each family form faces within the larger society

Do you recognize the opening song lyric and fondly remember that crazy purple dinosaur Barney? When you were growing up, did he in any way help you redefine or shape your concept of family? Did you grow up in a family that was firmly grounded in the traditional sense of what the word "family" meant—the traditional nuclear family—a mom and dad, a house, two kids, a picket fence, and a dog in the front yard? According to a 1994 Angus Reid poll, 68% of Canadians agreed that the "best type of family in which to raise children" has two heterosexual parents, with one at work and one at home (Nemeth, 1994).

Times have certainly changed in the past two decades. Maybe you've got a mom and a mom or a dad and a dad, with stepbrothers or sisters from a different cultural background, so that your family defies traditional definitions. There's little doubt that the "father as head of household" stereotype is a persistent one.

However you choose to define your family, there's no denying that it all begins and ends with your family. You belong to a family, and in doing so, you leave an indelible mark in the world that is traceable through your family roots—though not necessarily through bloodlines. When you die, whether or not you have children, you leave a legacy of relatives who mark your time here on earth. How far back can you trace your family roots? Can you trace your family back several generations? Or are you unsure about your heritage? What traditions does your family maintain, and what will you pass on to your own children? Do you speak or understand more than one language that you might teach to your children? Can you make a traditional food from your culture, which always reminds you of home?

Families exist in all forms, regardless of how they're defined, and we find them everywhere we look. Restaurants and businesses cater to families, television families like those from *The Simpsons* and *Modern Family* families fill our airwaves, and our neighbourhoods are inhabited with children from every kind of family. The face of the modern family has changed over the years, along with how we've come to define it. In this chapter, we'll look at some of the trends in Canada's families in the 21st century. Will your family be among them, or do you live in a family that defies convention? Regardless of how you choose to describe it, your family is uniquely yours; and in the quest for the perfect definition of a family, we quickly realize that maybe no such definition exists.

CENSUS DATA

Our family is usually our primary **agent of socialization**. We spend the most time with the people in our family, and consequently, they help to shape our values, ideals, and morals. Our **family of orientation** (the family you were born or raised in) gives us our heritage, social status, and history, while our **family of procreation** (the family you create when you're an adult) allows us to pass those traits—and possibly new ones—on to our children. How much difference will there be between the family you were born into and the one that you'll create when you're older and, possibly, married? If we look at how the composition of the family has changed over the past few decades in Canada, we see that there's a good chance that your birth family may not look like the family you'll end up with.

In 2006, the government made some significant changes to Canada's **census** and information-collection processes. Under the order of Prime Minister Stephen Harper, Statistics Canada switched to a short-form questionnaire for census-taking; and in 2010, information on the new **National Household Survey** became voluntary. Asked whether a voluntary survey could replace the long-form census, the chief statistician (who resigned in 2010, over this debacle) replied, "It cannot" (Daniel, 2012). The change from the long-form questionnaire to the short form hasn't affected the **validity** and **reliability** of the data from Statistics Canada, but it has affected the agency's ability to collect and analyze it, especially since the government made additional funding cuts to its operating budget. In February of 2012, Phil Cross, Statistics Canada chief economic analyst, also resigned over the controversy surrounding the abolition of the long form (Voices-Voix, 2012).

Agents of socialization: The people and institutions in society that create the social contexts where socialization takes place.

Family of orientation: The family someone was born or raised in; gives us our heritage, social status, and history.

Family of procreation: The family we create when we become adults.

Census: An official count of the population, with details as to age, sex, occupation, and so on.

National Household Survey: Information previously collected by the mandatory long-form census questionnaire; provides data to support federal, provincial, territorial, and local government planning and program delivery.

Validity: The ability of a measure to gauge or measure accurately what it sets out to measure.

Reliability: Whether or not the same results would be generated if an experiment were repeated.

The changes are crucial when you understand the importance of information and statistical analysis. The kind of information produced by Statistics Canada does three things:

- It tells us whether we are making progress or not.
- It shows us the kinds of changes that make things better for us as individuals and for society.
- It informs us about policy effectiveness when government policy is being considered or evaluated (Daniel, 2012).

Consider the issue of languages in Canada. Jean-Pierre Corbeil, a languages expert at Statistics Canada, finds it difficult to make sense of the recent numbers in the 2011 census data. The new data suggest that the number of Canadians who speak neither English nor French at home grew by just 100 000 between 2006 and 2011. During that time, however, more than 1.2 million immigrants entered Canada, the vast majority of whom spoke languages other than English or French. The unusual results may stem from the abolition of the long-form census, which contained a more detailed section on language (Friesen, 2012). This data can have an effect on policy and its implementation, since it will inevitably play a role when determining the number of required French- or English-speaking federal agencies that are needed in an area. Though the change from the long-form to the short-form questionnaire in gathering census data has created some controversy in Canada, the reality is that there is no other comparative data source, and Statistics Canada rates among the top statistical agencies in the world. What the change does is prompt us to question the policy decisions made based on the data.

Child care is another relevant issue here. Census data tell us that educated women with children have been increasingly entering the workforce, and the difficulties of finding affordable child care are painfully obvious in Canada. Even though the employment rate for women with children under three increased 233% between 1976 and 2009, and women moved from 32% of university graduates in 1971 to 60% by 2006, there have been no major advancements in child care policies to meet the growing needs of these women who require affordable child care (Decter, 2011).

DEFINING THE FAMILY

How do you define family? Does your definition include your pet or your best friend? Unfortunately, neither of those two made it to the definition that Statistics Canada uses when they gather information about families in Canada. For years, it was easy to define what a family was because marriage conferred legal status on the parents' children (Bird, 2010). Today however, the task of defining the family is much more difficult. Consider this definition from the 1971 census definition for family:

> A census family consists of a husband and wife (with or without children who have never been married, regardless of age) or a parent with one or more children never married, living in the same dwelling. A family may consist, also, of a man or woman living with a guardianship child or ward under 21 years for whom no pay was received. (Statistics Canada, 2012g)

How many families do you know of today that wouldn't be defined as families if you used the 1971 definition? Compare the 1971 definition to the one used in the 2011 census:

> A census family is composed of a married or common-law couple, with or without children, or of a lone parent living with at least one child in the same dwelling. Couples can be of the opposite sex or of the same sex. (Statistics Canada, 2012e)

Clearly, the definition has changed over four decades. What are some of the reasons that Statistics Canada has had to update how it defines the family? Do you agree with their definition? At its most basic level, Statistics Canada defines a family as a couple—married or common-law, with or without children—or a lone parent with at least one child in the same house. According to the 2011 census data, "it takes two people to make a family. Beyond that, anything goes" (Scoffield, 2012).

Statistics Canada uses that definition so that it can count the families in Canada—in all their various forms. If the definition seems a little stark to you, compare it to the definition that's used by the Vanier Institute of the Family Canada:

> Any combination of two or more persons who are bound together over time by ties of mutual consent, birth and/or adoption or placement and who, together, assume responsibilities for variant combinations of some of the following:
> - Physical maintenance and care of group members
> - Addition of new members through procreation or adoption
> - Socialization of children
> - Social control of members
> - Production, consumption, distribution of goods and services, and
> - Affective nurturance—love. (Vanier Institute of the Family, 2012a)

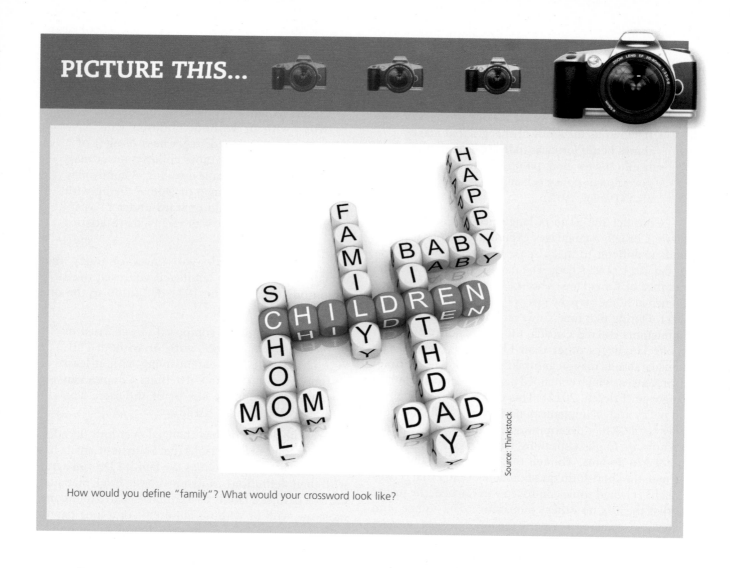

Source: Thinkstock

How would you define "family"? What would your crossword look like?

This definition clearly differs from the previous two. As you've probably noticed, Statistics Canada just counts the families and their composition, so as Canadians, we can see how the demographics or composition of the family has changed over time.

MARRIED FAMILIES

According to the 2011 census of population, there were 9 389 700 census families in Canada, up 5.5% from 8 896 840 families in 2006. Married couples remained the predominant family structure (67.0%) in 2011, but that share has decreased over time (Milan & Bohnert, 2012). This means that even though people are still getting married and having babies, couples are choosing other forms of cohabitation and child-rearing as well. Some claim that these changes don't bode well for the economy or the future, which seems to rest on the fate of the family. Sponsored by the Social Trends Institute,

the main message of the Sustainable Demographic Dividend is that "business, government, civil society, and ordinary citizens would do well to strengthen the family—in part because the wealth of nations, and the performance of large sectors of the modern economy, is tied to the fortunes of the family" (Wilcox & Cavalle, 2011). The partners in this global report see the traditional family unit as a vital component of the future survival of world economy, and base this proposition on these fundamental tenets:

- Children raised in intact, married families are more likely to acquire the human and social capital they need to become well-adjusted, productive workers.
- Men who get and stay married work harder, work smarter, and earn more money than their unmarried peers.
- Nations wishing to enjoy robust long-term economic growth and viable welfare states must

maintain sustainable fertility rates of at least two children per woman.

- Key sectors of the modern economy—from household products to insurance to groceries—are more likely to profit when men and women marry and have children. (Wilcox & Cavalle, 2011)

To what extent do you agree or disagree with their tenets? Do you think that alternative family forms are just as suited to meet these needs? Do you think that if traditional family forms—defined in the report as "children raised in intact married families"—continue to grow, that world economies will improve? Do you think that the traditional family form presupposes that traditional family roles are still intact?

Historically, men have been the head of the household, but as society changes, so do the roles assigned to men and women. Today's father can be single or divorced, gay, straight, adoptive, foster, a stepfather, or a co-parent. He may be a non-residential father, or he may be a stay-at-home dad. In short, he may not resemble the traditional notion of the head of the household at all, but he can still remain emotionally and financially invested in his children, while maintaining a stable, healthy, and loving relationship with them (American Psychological Association, 2012).

Women's roles have also been changing within the family. Mothers are still mothers, but a shift in societal attitudes has found women marrying later, having fewer children, obtaining an education, and entering the workforce—all of which have profound effects on their roles as the traditional primary caregiver (Kohen, 1981).

Do the changing roles of parents put the traditional family form in jeopardy? And if so, does our world economy hang in the balance, as suggested by some?

Changes within Married Families

Although married families continue to be the predominant family form in Canada, some changes are happening within those families. In 1961, married couples accounted for 91.6% of census families; by 2011, this proportion had declined to 67.0% (Statistics Canada, 2012c). The trend in divorce rates is partially to blame for the decline, especially since 2006 and the recession: fewer new divorce cases are entering the courts. The number of new divorce cases filed in civil courts has been declining in the reporting jurisdictions for several years. In 2010 to 2011, almost 54 000 new divorce cases were filed in the seven reporting provinces and territories, a decline of 2% from the year before (Kelly, 2012).

Divorce rates decline when times are tough for three specific reasons:

- two incomes during economic hardship are better than one;
- selling a house is difficult when no one has the money to buy it; and
- paying for a divorce can be very costly. (Adshade, 2012)

Perhaps for those reasons, some couples who separate never legally resolve their issues. Divorce cases may also involve issues that take significant time to resolve due to their complexity or the level of conflict between the parties. Other issues can return to court over time as family circumstances, such as income or living arrangements, change. Thus, divorce cases may span a number of years (Kelly, 2012).

The composition of the traditional married family is changing in other ways as well. According to the 2011 census, 42.3% of the 4 318 400 young adults aged 20 to 29 lived in their parental home, either because they never left it or because they returned home after living elsewhere (Statistics Canada, 2012d). Reasons for young adults staying at home or returning home include changes in relationship status (relationship breakdowns), cultural preferences, difficulties finding or securing long-term employment, and the high costs associated with education. This global phenomenon meets with different reactions, depending on the country in which it occurs. In North America, the **"boomerang generation"** is also known as the "accordion" family; in the United Kingdom, the adult children are known as "YUCKies" (young, unwitting, costly, kids); and Italians refer to the adult children as "bamboccioni," meaning "big babies" (Bartlett & LeRose, 2012).

In Italy, over one-third of 30-year-old men have never left home. Referring to this phenomenon as "delayed departure," the Italian government doesn't support this "cult of mammissimo," or "mamma's boys" (Newman, 2012). The longer the men stay with their parents, the less likely they are to marry and produce their own children. Fewer children translate into fewer workers to add to the retirement accounts in an aging society. Although the mothers seem to like it just fine, the politicians are not as happy (Newman, 2012). In Italy, there is a cultural belief that if the parents take care of the children, the children will, in turn, take care of the parents when they are old and frail.

In North America, parental views on boomerang kids are markedly

Boomerang generation: Term used to describe those young adults who return to their parental home after leaving for education, work, or a relationship.

An exaggeration, for sure—but in Italy, delayed departure is the norm for adult children.

different from those of Italian parents. With a Canadian unemployment rate of 14.7% for youths aged 15 to 24, leaving home for long-term employment is often not an option. The unemployment rate for that age group is twice that of the general working-age population, at 7.4% (Statistics Canada, 2012h). Western parents often find themselves funding their children's educational endeavours, simply because we live in a world that is much different from the one in which the parents themselves grew up in. Baby Boomers have a different relationship with their children than they had with their own parents; in many cases, it's more of a friendship than an authoritative relationship. Life for the adult children and their parents is very much a negotiation process, with a large degree of give and take. With the labour market turning a cold shoulder to young adults—even those with degrees—simply staying at home is sometimes the adult child's only option.

In the United States, there has been a 50% increase since the 1970s in the proportion of people aged 30 to 34 who live with their parents. Adult children who can't find jobs after getting a degree, divorced parents who can't afford rent, unemployed people, and adult children with their own children whom they just can't provide for—many are returning to their parents' homes (Newman, 2012). Whether or not this is a new stage in the life cycle is yet to be seen, but the existence of the boomerang generation is becoming more and more obvious. There still seems to be a stigma attached to adult children living with their parents, but there is a bit of a double standard as well, in that it's more acceptable for women to return home than for men.

NEWCOMER FAMILIES

Generally speaking, the immigrant population is similar to that of the non-immigrant population with respect to family type. Approximately 20% of both populations are single individuals, another 5% are lone parents, and the majority are married (Dempsey, 2006).

The Longitudinal Survey of Immigrants to Canada has tracked the progress of immigrants arriving in Canada for several years and has identified a number of barriers that they face. The four most difficult of these are finding employment, accessing training, finding housing, and accessing health care (Felligi, 2006). In many cases, it's difficult for newcomers to access training because of language barriers, costs, and accessibility. The high cost of housing, often coupled with the absence of a credit rating, makes it difficult to secure funding for housing, so accommodations are frequently problematic for immigrants; so many stay with family members or friends who are already in the country. Similar issues arise for health care—language barriers, costs, and wait lists prevent newcomers from using these services.

The settlement process for the newcomer family can involve many changes within the family unit, due to increasing rates of women's involvement in the workforce, increasing rates of unemployment for men, a rise in feminist attitudes among women, and the desire among men to be more involved in their children's lives (Stearns, 1991). Role reversal may occur between husband and wife, with both parents working, or the woman working while the man tends the home. For many fathers, the ability to provide food, shelter, and good prospects for the future are vital responsibilities (Bouchard, 2003). Any role other than head of household can often create conflicts that didn't exist in the country of origin. It can be difficult for a man when his wife has to go out to work to provide for the family, and in essence, take on the traditional role that was once his. It becomes more complicated when the domestic chores are factored in, since many men don't take part in these tasks when in their countries of origin. Learning how to adjust either to contributing to the household chores, or to living with a wife who goes to work and then must also complete her household chores, becomes a huge burden for many newcomer men. For many immigrant men especially, the role of father is one that is increasingly difficult to portray, because they're either underemployed or unemployed in their new environment (Shimoni, Este, & Clarke, 2003).

Some newcomer children and teens have to juggle between two different sets of beliefs and attitudes—the Canadian ones and those of their birth country. This often creates feelings of confusion, guilt, betrayal, and stress, as they virtually live two different lives. Whether it's the stress from the move, difficulties adjusting to a new educational system, or pressure from parents, at the heart of the issue is an identity crisis for the teen newcomer. Immigrant children and young adults face a risk of falling through the cracks in society, specifically because of a loss of identity (Roy, 2012).

Often, the role of the elderly in the family dynamics changes with migration to a new country; in some cases, families may also have to deal with the loss of a family member or support system (Este & Tachble, 2009). Grandparents have to adjust to grandchildren who are adopting the new values and traditions in their new country, and they sometimes view this as a loss of respect.

MULTIRACIAL FAMILIES

Once banned through legislative measures and seen as taboo through social norms, **mixed marriages** are a growing trend. In British Columbia, results from a new study indicate that mixed-union couples earn substantially better incomes than their non–mixed-union counterparts (Khan, 2010). In fact, unions of people from different ethnocultural backgrounds have been increasing in Canada as a whole. In 2006, there were 7 482 800 married and common-law couples, of which 289 400 were mixed unions, or about 4% of the population, indicating a 33% increase from 2001 (Milan, Maheux, & Chui, 2010). A major reason for the growth in mixed-union couples is the growth in visible minorities in Canada. The 2006 Census counted 5.1 million people who were members of visible minority groups, representing more than 16% of the population of Canada.

In Canada in 2006, individuals of Japanese descent had the highest proportion of coupling outside of their visible minority group. About 75% of the 29 700 couples that included at least one Japanese person involved pairings with a non-Japanese person. Latin Americans (47%) and Blacks (41%) followed Japanese with the next highest proportions of couples involving outgroup pairings. About one-third of couples involving a Filipino person (33%) were married or living common-law outside their visible minority group, and the proportions of mixed unions among Southeast Asians (31%), Arabs or West Asians (25%), or Koreans (19%) ranked somewhat in the middle of all visible minority groups (Milan, Maheux, & Chui, 2010).

The blending of cultures that comes from mixed unions can influence children and how they choose to see themselves. In 2006, a total of 293 600 children lived in two-parent mixed-union families. Among these children, two-thirds (66%) self-identified as a

The number of interracial families is increasing in Canada. How do you think this child will choose to self-identify?

visible minority, while one-third did not. Of the children who self-identified as a visible minority, the most common mixed-union family (137 700 children) was when the child and one parent belonged to the same visible minority group and the other parent wasn't a visible minority.

In terms of generational status, as the length of time spent in Canada increases, so does the proportion of mixed unions. Among first-generation visible-minority Canadians (those born outside of Canada), 12% were in mixed-union couples. For second-generation Canadians who were members of a visible minority group, the proportion in a mixed union was 51%. It reached 69% for third-generation visible-minority Canadians (Milan, Maheux, & Chui, 2010). What can explain the generational differences?

Many culturally diverse families have experienced and continue to experience prejudice, racial discrimination, and oppression, both in their countries of origin and in Canada. In a precedent-setting case in Nova Scotia in 2011, two teens received jail time after erecting a six- metre-high cross with a noose on it, and lighting it on fire, in the front yard of an interracial couple (Canadian Press, 2011). Acts like this one serve to remind us that even though the number of mixed unions continues to grow, these unions still risk defying social norms.

The investigation of mixed unions is important: they reflect another facet of the changing backdrop of Canada's familial landscape. In a situation like the one in Nova Scotia, for example, people will talk about it for years. Will this child's couple be bullied? Will he or she always be known as the "kid who had the cross burned in the front yard"? Or will feelings change, and if so, when?

Mixed marriages: Unions of people from different ethnocultural backgrounds.

This one isolated incident of social exclusion can be used to measure generational differences.

COMMON-LAW FAMILIES

Under Canadian law, couples aren't considered married if they live together; but if they separate, they may be entitled to the same rights as married people—only if certain conditions are met, however. The couple (either same-sex or heterosexual) must live together for a specified amount of time, which varies from province to province (usually two to three years). And, in some provinces, like Ontario, if the couple has a child together, regardless of the amount of time they've lived together, they're considered to be in a common-law marriage. (Canadian Divorce Laws, 2012).

Between 2006 and 2011, the number of **common-law couples** rose 13.9%, more than four times the 3.1% increase for married couples; as a result, common-law couples accounted for 16.7% of all census families (Milan & Bohnert, 2012). This growth was largely a result of the decline in divorce rates; but increasingly, couples are living together because they don't have enough money to live alone, and they aren't getting married until they have enough money. According to one large American study, marital status just isn't as important as achieving respect, happiness, career goals, financial security, or a fulfilling sex life. When it comes to having children, however, more than 75% of the sample of this study believed that they should be married first (Pew Research Center, 2010).

Attitudes about cohabitation are changing too. A 2009 survey of teens aged 15–19 indicated that over 75% approved of living together and at least 30% stated that they planned to live with someone at some point in their lives (Bibby, 2009). What do you think? Is living with someone the same thing as being married? Does it represent the same level of commitment?

Common-law couple:
Two individuals living together as a couple but who aren't considered married.

Simple stepfamilies:
Families with the children of one, and only one, of the married or common-law partners.

Complex stepfamilies:
Families with children of both parents and children of one parent only, families with children of each parent and no children of both parents, or families with children of both parents and children of each parent.

BLENDED FAMILIES

What famous family do you think of when you think of a blended family? Traditionally, the family that started it all was the *Brady Bunch* (1969). Mike and Carol each had three children when they married. The show was an instant success: watching the trials and tribulations of the Brady boys and girls kept television audiences all caught up in America's favourite stepfamily from 1969 until 1974—and then, of course, there were reunion shows. In the decades since then, television has offered numerous other blended families for our viewing pleasure. Shows like *Diff'rent Strokes* (1978–1986), *My Two Dads* (1987–1990), *Step by Step* (1991–1998), and more recently, *Modern Family* (2009–) have all offered a glimpse of what it's like to live in a non-traditional family setting.

In Canada, the 2011 Census counted stepfamilies for the first time. Statistics Canada separates this category into simple and complex stepfamilies. Of the 3 684 675 couples with children, 12.6% were stepfamilies (Milan & Bohnert, 2012). In 2011, 7.4% of couples with children were **simple stepfamilies**, in which all children were the biological or adopted children of one and only one married spouse or common-law partner. An additional 5.2% of couples with children were complex stepfamilies, most of which were comprised of at least one child of both parents as well as at least one child of one parent only (Milan & Bohnert, 2012). A simple stepfamily is a couple family with the children of one and only one, of the married or common-law partners. **Complex stepfamilies** can be any of the following:

- Families with child(ren) of both parents and child(ren) of one parent only—these families represent 32.2% of all stepfamilies in Canada.
- Families with child(ren) of each parent and no child(ren) of both parents—these families represent 7.7% of all stepfamilies in Canada.
- Families with child(ren) of both parents and child(ren) of each parent—these families represent 1.6% of all stepfamilies in Canada (Vanier Institute of the Family, 2012b).

In many ways, blended families are living in untested waters. Firmly entrenched societal norms that apply to these families simply don't exist, and in some areas, neither do laws. In some cases, policymakers and the courts are just now wrestling with decisions that surround the rights and responsibilities of stepparents (Preece, 2004). Living in a blended family often brings many changes and provides plenty of opportunities for new relationships to develop. Adjusting to a new family brings forth attachment, cultural, and conflict issues, which families must work together to overcome, as expectations and responsibilities are communicated.

IN THEIR SHOES

If a picture can say a thousand words, imagine the stories your shoes could tell! Try this student story on for size – have you walked in this student's shoes?

I come from a lower-middle-class family. My father is a pastor and does not receive a salary worthy of his educational calibre. My mother attended college for one year, but quit to get married and follow her husband to graduate school. Since then, my mother has worked hard in various part-time positions at minimum wage to help make ends meet. I know that my parents live paycheque to paycheque and often utilize their savings when they come up short at month's end. As a result, for my family going out for dinner, including fast-food, was a privilege. When my family did go out for dinner, we went to an average-priced restaurant (Swiss Chalet) and we were expected to order lower-priced meals. We all understood that steak was off-limits and that water was to be ordered. Appetizers were not even on our radar and dessert was a rarity. My siblings and I also knew never to ask our parents for money for anything "extra" such as movie tickets or money for shopping. In fact, we never begged our parents for anything. We understood at a young age that our parents were making daily sacrifices for us and we were always grateful.

Although I was grateful to my parents, somewhere mid-elementary school I began to take special note of other people's privileges and my wants. Other kids at school were more privileged than me. They had better and more cutting-edge toys and went on more luxurious vacations. There were the families who vacationed in Florida every year, and even worse were the families who went on cruises in Bermuda. My family's idea of a vacation was camping and we went every summer. I remember longing to visit Florida and being jealous of the kids with better clothes, better snacks in their lunches, and better Christmas presents. On some conscious level, I was aware that these kids were higher up on the social strata than me. However, it was not until I began to date my current husband that I realized the depth of differences between the lower middle class and upper middle class.

My husband comes from an upper-middle-class family. My father-in-law is a lawyer and owns his practice and my mother-in-law is a school teacher. Together they must make a pretty hefty sum of money. My in-laws do not worry about money. They travel to different parts of the world for spring break and eat at fancy restaurants. In fact, they eat out frequently. Not only that, they order *whatever* they want, including steak, appetizers, and alcoholic beverages. With my in-laws, ordering appetizers and alcoholic beverages is normal and encouraged. Eating out with my in-laws is still a culture shock for me.

My parents and in-laws make very different lifestyle choices, particularly in relation to eating, drinking, and spending habits. I believe these differences are directly correlated with socioeconomic status. My husband's family enjoys a range of foods of which my family has never heard, including calamari, quinoa, bulgur, couscous, rosé sauce, capers, and shallots. They also enjoy trying new recipes and types of foods. My parents eat a standard menu of meat and potatoes and do not make much use of recipes. My in-laws eat their spaghetti with a spoon and a fork and twirl it around their fork rather than cut it with a fork and knife. I was not even aware that this alternative way of eating spaghetti was a possibility. My in-laws also have a different attitude toward alcohol in comparison with my parents. My in-laws enjoy drinking and drink significantly more than my parents. I believe that this is partly because it is a value of the upper class to drink socially, but also because they can afford to drink wine at their meals and casually throughout the day. My family rarely drinks. For my family, alcohol is too expensive and is not high on their priority list of needs.

Lastly, my parents have a very different view on money in comparison to my in-laws. My family frowns upon frivolous and excessive spending. My parents taught me to be thrifty by weighing my needs and wants. As a result, I feel guilty for spending money in general. (How do you really define a *need* anyway?) In my family, one has to work to play and work very hard to deserve it, but in my husband's family, spending money is a pastime. My husband, as a result of his upbringing, enjoys "treating" me and having "nice things." I enjoy having nice things but I struggle with a guilty twinge. Since meeting my husband's parents, I have been exposed to a new world and have become aware of the differences between the lower-middle and upper-middle classes.

The lower-middle and upper-middle classes each have a different subculture and I have found these differences difficult to adjust to as a newlywed. I have often felt inadequate and out of place amongst my new family. I have felt jealous of the many privileges that my husband received as a child, such as his family vacations. My husband's family is the "Other" to me and I have struggled with "othering" them. It is easier for me to judge his family just because they are different, but that is not how I want to be.

After many years of struggle accepting the differences between my family of origin and my new family, I have learned to appreciate the best in both approaches. My husband and I have assimilated what we like from his family and mine and left behind what we do not. I have learned from both sets of parents. My lower-class upbringing taught me to be deeply grateful for all I have been given, but also to be wise in my spending. My husband's upbringing has taught me to *enjoy* what I have been given. I am thankful for both life lessons in my journey.

SAME-SEX COUPLE FAMILIES

Changes in social ideologies, laws, and medical technologies have allowed gay men and lesbians more opportunities than ever before to create families of their own. In 2005, Canada became the third country in the world to legalize same-sex marriage, following the Netherlands and Belgium. Same-sex marriage is now legal in Spain, South Africa, Norway, Sweden, Portugal, Iceland, Argentina, and Denmark. Additionally, parts of the United States and Mexico, have legalized same-sex marriage. The 2011 Census counted 64 575 same-sex coupled families, up 42.4% from 2006. Of these couples, 21 015 were same-sex married couples and 43 560 were same-sex common-law couples (Milan & Bohnert, 2012). The number of same-sex married couples nearly tripled between 2006 and 2011, reflecting the first five-year period for which same-sex marriage has been legal across the country. Same-sex common-law couples rose 15.0%, an increase slightly higher than the 13.8% increase for opposite-sex common-law couples (Milan & Bohnert, 2012).

For same-sex couples who can afford it and are willing to navigate the bureaucratic red tape, the choices for having children are better than they were before. Couples may choose to use a surrogate, adoption, or a fostering agency, or they may choose to co-parent with another gay or straight couple or single person (Ryan & Berkowitz, 2009). Although gay couples can legally adopt children in Canada, some international agencies will not allow adoption by same-sex couples (Adoption Council of Canada, 2012). Gay couples wanting to adopt children, however, face a number of barriers that heterosexual couples don't face. In one study, a social worker employed in the adoption unit of the British Columbia Ministry of Children and Family Development commented that "the reality is that sometimes some workers in our system are reluctant to choose same-sex couples or single applicants, and therefore, they tend to wait longer than do traditional couples in our system" (Sullivan & Harrington, 2009). Some of the perception that surrounds the prejudice against same-sex couples who want children focuses mainly on the children themselves and is manifested in three main arguments:

1. the risk for the children to be homosexual themselves;
2. the stigmatization of children with homosexual parents; and
3. the belief that children need both a mother and father (Pennings, 2011).

Heterosexism: Prejudicial attitudes and discriminatory practices against homosexuals.

American researchers (while admitting a small sample size) found that adopted teenagers' life satisfaction was positively related to attachment with adoptive parents but unrelated to their parents' sexual orientation. The results of this study found no significant differences between families based on sexual orientation, for variables including adolescent attachment to parents and peers, parent satisfaction with the relationship to their adopted children, and adolescent life satisfaction. Essentially, these findings challenge the misperception that children of homosexual parents have worse psychosocial outcomes than children of heterosexual parents (Erich, Kanenburg, Case, Allen, & Bogdanos, 2009). What do you think about these premises? Is it homosexuality that's the problem or society's reaction to it?

In the United States, just over half of the country is still opposed to legalized marriage for gay couples: in 2009, 37% were in favour while 54% were opposed (Pew Research Center, 2010). The lack of marital rights has a big influence on financial and legal status, once children are brought into a relationship. However, that doesn't stop over a million same-sex couples from raising over two million children in various states (Onderko, 2011). With so much opposition in the U.S., how do they manage to do it? If there's a biological parent, without a federally or state recognized union, the biological children of one partner have no legal connection to the non-biological parent. If the partner dies, in order for the non-biological parent to ensure medical benefits or custody, he or she must go through a process called second-adoption. Essentially, it involves a lawyer, several home visits from a social worker, testimony in front of a judge, and roughly $3000 (Onderko, 2011). (In Canada, this situation would not arise, as same-sex adoption is legal and open.)

Though same-sex marriage and/or families may still be illegal and/or not accepted in many countries, these families continue to thrive—but they do so as minority subcultures. Access to health care has become a guarded issue because of **heterosexism**, fear of discrimination, poor past health care experiences, and insensitivity. Many LGBT people are hesitant to disclose their sexual identity when looking for health care services because of the perceived risk of discrimination, and this can prevent them and their families from accessing quality health care (Chapman & Shields, 2012). Even in Canada, where attitudes toward homosexuality are more liberal, discrimination still affects those who live alternative sexual lifestyles. According to a major report compiled by Health Canada, LGBT people expressed many complaints about accessing health care, including the attitudes of health-care workers, ignorance of issues, and a lack of supportive providers. Hence, disclosure of sexual orientation was a major problem in consulting health-care professionals or gaining access to treatment (Ryan, Brotman, & Rowe, 2001).

LONE-PARENT FAMILIES

Lone-parent families exist because of a variety of circumstances including divorce, death of a spouse, adoption, and choice. Surprisingly, the proportion of lone-parent families has remained relatively consistent over the years. In 1931, 12% of families were headed by lone parents, compared to 15% in 1996 (Milan, 2000). Lone-parent families represented 16.3% of all census families in 2011, an increase of 8.0% between 2006 and 2011.

Although the rate of lone-parenthood doesn't seem to have increased by very much over the decades, the reasons for it have varied. In 1931, the main reason for the absence of a parent was widowhood. In 1996, the primary reason was divorce. Before the 1968 Divorce Act, marriage was, essentially, a permanent thing. Terminating the union was difficult, and it carried with it great social stigma; but that changed with the "no fault" laws, based on a separation for a least three years. In 1986, a further amendment reduced the separation period to one year, which made a divorce much easier to obtain (Douglas, 2008). The loosening of restrictions also eased societal reactions, diminishing the negative perceptions that once surrounded those whose marriages didn't quite live up to their expectations. Consequently, the divorce rates began to increase. In 1969, the percentage of marriages expected to end before their 30th anniversary was 13.6%, compared to 38% in 2004 (Lochhead & Tipper, 2008). The number of births outside of marriage also increased during this time, as the growing economic independence of women became evident. In 2006, about half (50%) of female lone parents were divorced or separated, 30% had never been legally married, and one-fifth (20%) were widowed (Milan, Keown, & Covadonga, 2012).

The make-up of lone-parent families has also changed. In earlier years, when a couple separated, custody of the children often went to the primary caregiver—usually the mother. Recently, we've seen an increase in the number of lone-parent families headed by males. In 2011, about 8 in 10 lone-parent families were female lone-parent families (12.8% of all census families), while male lone-parent families represented 3.5% of all census families (Milan & Bohnert, 2012). The increase in male lone-parent families was more than twice the increase in female lone-parent families

between 2006 and 2011, but it's hardly enough to even the distribution. In 2006, this was the household type/living style of 66% of recently divorced or separated mothers and 30% of fathers. After a divorce or separation, fathers are more likely (25%) to be living alone than mothers (6%). Within five years of their divorce or separation, a similar number of mothers and fathers find themselves living in stepfamilies (Lochhead & Tipper, 2008).

According to one American study, divorced and separated people relocate more than married people, which puts added stress and financial hardship on a lone-parent family (Pryor & Rodgers, 2001). That lone parents often struggle financially is evident. However, lone-parent mothers are more prone have a low income than are lone-parent fathers. More than half (52.1%) of female lone parents with children under six live in poverty (Statistics Canada, 2010). Many lone parents find themselves in a bind when it comes to finances, especially if they rely on social assistance programs. In addition to inadequate funding, lone parents face the stigma that's attached to relying on outside agencies to provide for their children, as well as a system that's often difficult to navigate (especially when there are language barriers), delays with cheques, and difficulties with careers (Pollack, 2009). While social assistance programs are designed to "lend a hand out, while you work your way up," any monies someone makes while collecting payments is subjected to "claw-backs," thus reducing the monthly cheque. This makes saving for the future very difficult. Policymakers have yet to come up with any programs that assist single parents who have unique economic and social needs, regardless of the time they spend as lone-parents (Press, 2012).

Researchers analyzed findings from a number of studies by comparing two-parent families with same- or different-sex co-parents and single-mother with single-father families. Although married families continue to be the dominant family form in Canada, these researchers found that compared to all other family forms, families headed by (at least) two committed, compatible parents are generally best for children (Biblarz & Stacey, 2010).

ADOPTION

Adopting a child is never an easy decision for parents who are unable to conceive a child naturally. The process can be lengthy, confusing, and—especially in the case of international adoption—very expensive.

It's estimated that 20% of couples in Canada experience infertility to some degree (Haaf, 2012). By the time couples have decided to adopt, many of them have already tried in vitro fertilization (IVF). With IVF, the woman's egg and the man's sperm are "mated" in a Petri dish where fertilization occurs. The fertilized egg is then placed back inside the woman's womb, where it will grow and naturally develop into a baby. While the process may not sound very complicated, it might take more than one or even several attempts or "cycles," and it is very expensive. Although the cost varies from clinic to clinic, IVF can cost as much as $30 000 for three cycles of treatment (Fidelman, 2010). Across Canada, the portion of costs covered by the provincial health care plan differs by jurisdiction.

Once the decision to adopt is made, however, the path to becoming a parent is fairly straightforward. Perhaps the greatest obstacle is time. From all accounts, the process seems to take much longer than anticipated. In Canada, couples (or in some cases, an individual) choosing to adopt can do so publicly or privately, domestically or internationally. A domestic adoption is arranged publicly or privately. If the applicants choose a public adoption, a government agency (for example, the Adoption Council of Canada) arranges and finances the adoption. The applicants contact the agency in their province that is responsible for adoptions (Children's Aid or another licensed facility) and register to begin the adoption process. Applicants who are willing to adopt a special-needs child or a child who has challenging circumstances (such as mental health issues or ADHD, for example) can register with Canada's Waiting Kids program. For applicants who wish to adopt privately, the rules differ from province to province, as does the meaning of "private adoption." Though these adoptions are facilitated by a private adoption counsellor or adoption agency, they must abide by all government regulations (Grove, 2001). Currently, there are over 80 000 children in Canada's child welfare system, roughly 30 000 of whom are available for free, legal adoption (Adoption Council of Canada, 2012).

International adoptions follow much the same process. They too can be private or public, but they are subject to a much more rigorous course of action, since there are government regulations of two countries involved. Each country that allows international adoption has its own laws and regulations, which determine eligibility requirements and the adoption process. Canadian laws state that the adoption laws of the sending country have to be followed before the child is allowed to enter Canada (Paul-Carlson, 2012). The Hague Convention of 1993 was pivotal in international adoption. Countries that sign this agreement must comply with strict international standards, such as ensuring that birth parents have truly given their

consent and haven't been paid, and that every effort has been made to find the child a permanent home in his or her country of origin. Canada made changes to the agreement in 1996, and countries like China continue to raise the standards of hopeful adoptive parents. No single parents, same-sex couples, obese parents, alcoholic parents, or those with cancer in the family can apply to be adoptive parents for a child from China (Pearce, 2012).

There's no doubt that international adoption is a complex and legally challenging process, but that doesn't stop couples from applying. Though international adoptions have declined over the years, a survey of the 23 countries receiving the most children through international adoption between 2003 and 2009, showed that Canada placed fifth, with 13 291 adoptees, or 4.8% of the total. The top five countries—the United States, Spain, France, Italy, and Canada—accounted for 229 433 international adoptions during that period, or 84% of the total international adoptions. The top five countries that send the highest number of adoptive children are China, Russia, Guatemala, Ethiopia, and South Korea (Hillborn, 2011).

On average, it now costs roughly $35 000 to $45 000 to complete an international adoption. About a third covers Canadian costs, a third goes to fees in the child's home country, and a third to travel (Pearce, 2012). While cost may seem paramount when considering whether or not to adopt internationally, it's also important to consider the child's cultural or racial differences. Though parents often feel that the child's culture or race isn't an issue, a child growing up in completely new surroundings may feel alienated, displaced, or uncomfortable in ways that the parents may not have imagined. After all, any adoption takes place with the best interests of the child in mind (Focus on the Family, 2011).

ENDING THOUGHTS

What kind of family is the best kind of family? Or, is there a best kind of family? It seems that the family form has diversified over the years, indicating a shift away from the traditional picture of the nuclear family, characteristically presented as a mom and a dad, two children, and a house with a white picket fence. And while this diversification of family type has led to some social policy reform (same-sex marriage, for example) and a re-examination and redistribution of gender roles within the family units themselves, there are those that see the "dilution" of the traditional family form as threatening to the good of society as whole. The Institute of Marriage and the Family argues that "a declining marriage culture is the wrong trend line for Canada ... all research points to the fact that married-parent families offer more stability for children and decreased poverty rates" (Mrozek, 2012). Commenting on the results of a newly released report, author Joel Kotkin sees a worrying global trend in the decline of the traditional family form:

> Today, in the high-income world and even in some developing countries, we are witnessing a shift to a new social model. Increasingly, family no longer serves as the central organizing feature of society. An unprecedented number of individuals—approaching upwards of 30% in some Asian countries—are choosing to eschew child bearing altogether and, often, marriage as well. (Kotkin, 2012, p. 1)

In Kotkin's view, this trend can lead to a diminished workforce and to fewer workers who will be able to contribute financially to those members of the population who will need funds in their retirement years. Additionally, he sees the traditional role of the family—something that we've built our society around for centuries—changing, as more and more people choose to stay single and childless.

In the end, does it really matter how you define a family? Whether it includes your best friend or your neighbour, your family consists of those people who have made a commitment to care and provide for each other, for an extended period of time. It's not about what a family looks like, but more about what a family does that makes a family. The bottom line is that your own family is the best kind of family—however you choose to define it.

READING

THE CHANGING FACE OF MATRIMONY: SAME-SEX CIVIL MARRIAGE IN THE TWENTY-FIRST CENTURY

By Adam Isaiah Green

As the second decade of the twenty-first century begins, civil marriage for same-sex couples is a legal option in parts of Western Europe, Africa, and North America, including the Netherlands, Belgium, Canada, Spain, South Africa, Norway, and in two states in the United States: Connecticut and Massachusetts. First legalized in the Netherlands in 2001, same-sex civil marriage is a hot-button issue throughout the Western world, vigorously contested in public discourse and policy. In the United States, for instance, a variety of legal measures designed to prevent same-sex marriage have been put into law, including federal Defense of Marriage Act (DOMA) legislation, which prohibits federal recognition of same-sex civil marriage by defining marriage as the explicit union of one man and one woman, and amendments to state constitutions with the same effect. Some countries sidestep the controversy associated with same-sex civil marriage with legal provisions that are roughly comparable with those of civil marriage. A handful of governments, for instance, grant same-sex couples the right to register as a domestic partnership, which confers many of the same rights and responsibilities as civil marriage. Parts of the United States and Western Europe offer civil unions for same-sex couples in place of civil marriage, although, like domestic partnership, the benefits of this legal arrangement vary widely from place to place.

Advocates of same-sex civil marriage typically reject these alternative, "marriage-like" measures because they regard them as a kind of second-class citizenship for lesbian and gay couples. They argue that state-sanctioned civil marriage is not just a legal status; it is also a symbolic arrangement that provides a vital source of societal legitimization to which same-sex couples are equally entitled (Hausknecht, 2003; Josephson, 2005; Sullivan, 1997). In contrast, opponents of same-sex marriage marshal a wide range of objections, often rooted in religious belief or historical precedent, to preserve the institution of marriage for opposite-sex couples. Legalizing same-sex marriage, they argue, threatens the sanctity of marriage, offends the moral beliefs of people opposed to homosexuality on religious grounds, and threatens the special social status afforded to the reproductive, heterosexual married couple (Baskerville, 2006; Gallagher, 2003). As well, not all lesbian and gay-identified activists support same-sex marriage. Some of them argue that the institution itself is inextricably tied to the historical subordination of women and the institutionalization of a heterosexual norm founded on reproduction, monogamy, and the nuclear family (otherwise known as heteronormativity) (Warner, 1999; Yep, Lovaas, and Elia, 2003). They see civil marriage as an institution that reproduces inequality and an outdated Judeo-Christian model of a moral intimate life.

These arguments aside, the arc of political history in the modern West bends toward the expansion of civil rights. Younger generations in liberal-democratic societies support same-sex marriage much more strongly than their older counterparts do. The lesbian and gay movements continue to mobilize support for same-sex marriage. Accordingly, same-sex civil marriage provisions are likely to become more widespread over time—albeit not without a fight. The twenty-first century has already witnessed dramatic battles over matrimony, and it is likely to continue to do so.

A BRIEF HISTORY OF CIVIL MARRIAGE AS A SOCIAL CONSTRUCTION

State-sanctioned or civil marriage has a thorny past, not least because, throughout history, it restricted who could marry, whom someone could marry, and the age at which a person could marry. In this sense, state sanctioned marriage has never been a simple entitlement but, rather, one bound to national ideologies concerning class, social status, and citizenship. For instance, Ancient Roman law held that the daughter, granddaughter, or great-granddaughter of a senator could not marry a freedman, an actor, or a man whose father or mother was an actor (Gamsey & Saller, 1987).

Modern civil marriages have been no less restrictive. Besides laws prohibiting same-sex partners to marry, the most common laws restricting marriage involve race, along with gender-specific restrictions on number of spouses and age of marriage. In the early nineteenth century in the United States, for instance, the government prohibited African Americans from civil marriage. Moreover, concern over racial inter-mixing, or miscegenation, fuelled a variety of anti-miscegenation laws that made it illegal to marry a person of a different race throughout most of the United States for the greater part of the twentieth century. In fact, a federal decree dissolved the anti-miscegenation only in 1967.

Nazi Germany also institutionalized anti-miscegenation policies to ward off the prospect of "mongrelism." The Nazis first outlawed marriages between Jews and non-Jewish Germans, and then between Germans and Roma ("Gypsies") or blacks. Similarly, under apartheid in South Africa (1948–92), the Prohibition of Mixed Marriages Act prohibited marriages between whites and blacks, and between whites and "coloureds" (Asians). Both Nazi Germany and apartheid South Africa even criminalized interracial sexual intercourse. In Nazi Germany, it was punishable by imprisonment or death. In both countries, antimiscegenation laws were repealed only after enormous political upheaval: the demise of the Nazi regime at the end of World War II and the collapse of apartheid in 1992.

Gender-specific restrictions on the number of spouses and age of marriage have also been common. For instance, in Utah before 1896, marriage was permissible between a man and a woman, or a man and multiple women, but never a woman and multiple men. Today, in many parts of the world, women are often encouraged—even coerced—to marry at a younger age than males. For instance, in Ethiopia, it is common for girls under 10 years of age to be married, whereas boys of this age are never married (Haberland, Chong, and Bracken, with Parker, 2005). In Afghanistan, a man must be 18 years old to marry, while a woman can marry at 16, and it is common for girls to be forced into marriage as young as 6 years of age (UNIFEM, 2008). Even in Ohio and Rhode Island, women can marry at 16 years of age, but men must be at least 18 years old.

The history of civil marriage, with its various and changing restrictions, provides sociological clues to the status of the institution of marriage more generally. First, sociologists view marriage as a social construction. The very fact that civil marriage has taken so many historical forms—including, according to some scholars, the inclusion of same-sex couples in early Ancient Rome (Boswell, 1980)— demonstrates the remarkable variety of ways a given society can organize the institution. Civil marriage is constructed out of the norms, values, and political commitments of a given society's policymakers and citizenry. It is not an institution with universal characteristics.

Second, sociologists note that civil marriage helps to institutionalize power relations. People who can marry enjoy advantages over those who cannot marry: certain tax breaks, healthcare benefits, and so on. Moreover, civil marriage serves an implicit legitimating function in that it regards certain two-person arrangements as superior to others and thereby worthy of legal support and protection. For instance, when the United States and Nazi Germany did not recognize interracial marriages, the state was making an explicit statement about which relationships were of value to the nation. Similarly, sociologists typically regard the exclusion of same-sex couples from civil marriage as a form of structural disenfranchisement reflecting national sentiments that devalue gay and lesbian relationships.

Historically, marriage has involved an exchange between spouses' families or clans, in which brides were traded for goods or as payment for debts (Levi-Strauss, 1969). Today, marriage typically institutionalizes gender inequality by relegating women to the roles of mother, domestic worker, and sex provider (Friedan, 1963; Hartmann, 1981; Rich, 1980). Thus, civil marriage often has gender-specific consequences that tend to disadvantage women. For instance, the fact that women can marry at a younger age than men is less a privileged status than a legal mechanism facilitating the institutionalization of women's roles as mothers and wives. When young women and girls are married off to much older men, often without the girls' consent, a husband typically regards his wife as his property, and she faces a relatively poor quality of life (UNIFEM, 2008). Until the twentieth century, women usually married for economic reasons, and even in postindustrial societies they are socialized to believe that marriage and motherhood are essential for a happy, fulfilling life (Rich, 1980). Thus, although, say, Canadian women are rarely forced to marry, neither are they entirely free to reject marriage. And once married, the institution typically cements a woman's subordination to a man, charging her with the responsibilities of bearing and raising children, keeping the household clean and orderly, and tending to her husband's emotional and sexual needs—all without remuneration. In this sense, civil marriage is a patriarchal institution of social control that establishes the conditions under which women are systematically disadvantaged and men systematically advantaged.

A third and related stream of scholarly analysis, sometimes called queer theory, suggests that widespread civil marriage for same-sex married couples may usher in an era of homonormativity, involving the consolidation of new lifestyle norms for lesbians and gays centred on domesticity, monogamy, reproduction, and the nuclear family (Duggan,

2002; Valverde, 2006). From this point of view, same-sex marriage may render lesbians and gays indistinguishable from their heterosexual counterparts, with marriages organized by the institutionalization of husband-wife gender roles, an unequal division of labour, and a conservative sexual politics indebted to Judeo-Christian interpretations of what constitutes a moral intimate life. The traditionalization of formerly queer lifestyles is regarded as problematic to the extent that it stigmatizes or renders less valuable lesbian and gay relationships that are not ongoing, monogamous, married, and reproductive (Johnson, 1996). In this sense, homonormativity threatens to dissolve the critical edge of queer culture, which drew attention to the repressive nature of dominant norms around gender roles and sexual sensibilities in the first place.

Some queer theory scholars are also critical of same-sex marriage insofar as the institution may align with broader transformations in political economy, most notably the transition from the era of centralized, governmental concern for the social welfare of its citizenry to neoliberal reforms that place the burden of social welfare on individuals and private entities (Foucault, 1991). From this perspective, same-sex marriage provisions are less an indication of a nation's social inclusiveness than a consequence of neoliberal reform, whereby the state increasingly cedes the care of citizens to the citizens themselves (Whitehead, 2006). Thus, same-sex civil marriage allows lesbian and gay spouses to look to each other, rather than to the welfare state, for care, support, and financial stability (Lessard, 2007).

I now offer a brief analysis of demographic and interview data to provide a statistical and qualitative portrait of same-sex marriage in Canada today.

A SNAPSHOT OF SAME-SEX MARRIAGE IN CANADA

Popular opinion among Canadians has only recently favoured same-sex marriage. In the first Gallup Canada survey of Canadian attitudes toward same-sex marriage in 1993, 76 percent of those surveyed opposed same-sex marriage. By 2000, that number had fallen to 48 percent.

In 2002, reflecting popular sentiment, the Ontario Supreme Court ruled that the opposite-sex stipulation for common-law marriage was unconstitutional. Similar decisions soon followed throughout Canada, and by 2004, courts in British Columbia, Quebec, Yukon, Manitoba, Nova Scotia, Saskatchewan, Quebec, and Newfoundland and Labrador fell in line with the Ontario ruling. That same year, the federal government of Canada put forward a request to the Supreme Court of Canada to deliberate on whether the exclusion of same-sex couples from civil marriage was permissible under the Charter guarantees of equality (Nelson, 2008). The Supreme Court ruled that the constitutional definition of marriage did not exclude same-sex couples and that the federal government was within its constitutional rights to redefine marriage to include same-sex couples. Subsequently, Parliament passed Bill C-38, which redefined marriage in line with the Charter. The chief justice of the Supreme Court of Canada signed the Civil Marriage Act into law on July 19, 2005. Same-sex marriage became the law of the land, making Canada only the third country in the world to do so, after the Netherlands and Belgium.

The 2006 census counted 45 345 same-sex couples in Canada, 84 percent of them common law (cohabiting for one year or more) and 16 percent legally married (between July 19, 2005, and the census date) (Statistics Canada, 2008). About 55 percent of same-sex couples were male and 45 percent were female. Eight percent of same-sex couples had children living with them; of these, 82 percent were female couples and 18 percent were male couples. Interestingly, 14 percent of same-sex married couples reported having one or more children, compared with just 7 percent of same-sex common-law couples. This difference suggests that parenthood may promote civil marriage among same-sex couples—that is, same-sex couples who choose marriage over common-law status may be motivated to do so because they have children or want to have them. Another possibility is that civil marriage promotes parenthood among same-sex couples—marriage may encourage samesex couples to want to have children. A third possibility is that both circumstances prevail.

The census is mute on such complex questions as whether and to what degree marriage promotes parenthood or vice-versa among same-sex couples. Until sociologists conduct more surveys and interviews of same-sex couples in Canada, we must rely partly on data from other countries to gain insight into many aspects of same-sex marriage. For example, one study found that nearly half of 812 married and registered gay and lesbian individuals in Denmark reported "legal rights" as the chief motivation for having their relationship formally recognized by the state (Eskridge and Spedale, 2006: 134). These legal rights include inheritance rights, tax breaks, and health and employment benefits. The Danish research also found that important intangible benefits derive from marriage, including increased commitment to the relationship, increased legitimacy, and increased social support from family and friends. Taken as a whole, these benefits seem to increase the durability of same-sex relationships.

My study of same-sex marriage in Ontario among 30 spouses, divided evenly by sex, yielded similar results (Green, 2008). Married spouses—men and women—were overwhelmingly surprised about the degree to which civil marriage conferred a sense of legitimacy and permanence to their relationship. In addition, some of these spouses found that the new sense of legitimacy extended beyond their immediate friends and families to the workplace. Co-workers and employers respected the individuals I interviewed—and their intimate relationships— more once they got married. In turn, marriage may produce conditions under which lesbian and gay employees can build better relationships with employers and clients. As one male respondent put it:

> There are honestly work benefits for us being married. When I interact with the partners (of the firm) in general ... it's probably more comfortable if they had us over for dinner. We could get invited as a couple. It's a different comfort aspect to it ... even how people interact and so on, even the signs of stability which is important to them when you get to the next level. ... And in contrast to the gay village boys that are at work who might even be at the same career level (but) can't talk about their

(partners) at all. ... For sure, there's a difference, the whole perception of stability is different between the two. Because even small-talk wise, even if you were gay and kind of semiin, semi-out at work, you just don't talk about your personal life. ... And part of the way you develop rapport with anyone is to talk about your personal life: "Are you married and do you have kids?" It's the standard small-talk question.

Although civil marriage may provide same-sex couples with benefits similar to those enjoyed by heterosexual couples, marriage forms are unlikely to be identical in the two cases. In particular, civil marriage may not produce the same level of monogamy as opposite-sex marriages, especially among male couples. In the United States, nearly all married couples expect sexual exclusivity from their spouses, and the situation is probably not very different in Canada (Laumann, Gagnon, Michael, and Michaels, 1994). In contrast, the Danish study cited earlier found that although some married same-sex male couples embraced monogamy, some did not. In my study, 40 percent of the women and 60 percent of the men reported that they do not believe that marriage must always be mono-gamous. Some 47 percent of male respondents reported an explicit policy of non-monogamous practice, as did a lone female same-sex spouse. However, half of the respondents with explicitly monogamous marriages believed that it is acceptable for marriages to be non-monogamous, while about one in five monogamous males and one in 10 mono-gamous females remained open to the possibility that their own marriages might one day become non-monogamous. Most interestingly, nearly half of the men with openly non-monogamous marriages decided to have an open marriage after getting married. Although my small sample size does not permit generalizing to the broader population of same-sex marriages in Ontario, much less Canada as a whole, the findings are consistent with research on the sexual norms of gay men and gay subcultures (Weeks, Heaphy, and Donovan, 2001; Woolwine and McCarthy, 2005). According to one study, gay men do not articulate a single moral code around sexual fidelity but rather a kind of "morally pragmatic stand" arising in the historical context of anti-homosexual sentiment and associated stigmatization (Woolwine and McCarthy, 2005: 399–400). Put another way, becoming gay is marked by a process of "unlearning" heterosexuality, including the expectation of a heteronormative lifestyle (Herdt and Boxer, 1992). In this light, it is perhaps not surprising that same-sex married couples, historically excluded from the institution of civil marriage, would draw from their prior experience in constructing married life.

If norms and practices around marital fidelity are, on average, different for same-sex couples and their heterosexual counterparts, norms and practices around the domestic divi-sion of labour might also represent a departure. In fact, the literature suggests that same-sex couples in general reject "husband-wife" roles in favour of a more egalitarian model of domestic work founded on choice and interest (Blumstein and Schwartz, 1983; Dunne, 1997; Green, 2008; Patterson, 1995). Thus, almost all the same-sex couples in my Ontario study reported sharing equally in housework and child care.

On occasion, housework was apportioned according to financial contributions; the partner who earned more money did less housework. However, in these circumstances, it was common for the partners to reverse roles when, for instance, the higher-earning partner lost his job or returned to school. In short, rather than accepting fixed husband-wife roles, the same-sex couples in my study negotiated domestic work on an ongoing basis determined by pragmatic concerns and per-sonal interests. The heavy hand of patriarchy was nowhere to be found. In sum, although more research is needed to explore whether the division of domestic labour among same-sex couples is consistent with their self-reports, preliminary findings suggest that same-sex marriage may differ signifi-cantly from heterosexual marriages in this way, too.

REFERENCES

Baskerville, Stephen. (2006). "The Real Danger of Same-Sex Marriage." The Family in America [Online Edition], 20 (5), 6. On the World Wide Web at http://www.profam .org/pub/fia/fia.2005.6.htm (retrieved 13 November 2008).

Blumstein, Philip and Pepper Schwartz. (1983). American Couples: Money, Work and Sex. New York: William Morrow.

Boswell, John. (1980). Christianity, Social Tolerance and Homosexuality: Gay People in Western Europe from the Beginning of the Christian Era. Chicago: University of Chicago Press.

Duggan, Lisa. (2002). "The New Homonormativity: The Sexual Politics of Neoliberalism." In Russ Castronovo and Dana Nelson, eds., Materializing Democracy: Toward a Revitalized Cultural Politics (pp. 175–94). Durham, NC: Duke University Press.

Dunne, Gillian A. (1997). Lesbian Lifestyles: Women's Work and the Politics of Sexuality. Toronto: University of Toronto Press.

Eskridge, William Jr. and Darren Spedale. (2006). Gay Marriage: For Better or for Worse? What We've Learned from the Evidence. New York: Oxford University Press.

Foucault, Michel. (1991). "Governmentality." In Graham Burchell, Colin Gordon, and Peter Miller, eds., The Foucault Effect: Studies in Governmentality with Two Lectures by and an Interview with Michel Foucault (pp. 87–104). Chicago: University of Chicago Press.

Friedan, Betty. (1963). The Feminine Mystique. New York: W.W. Norton and Company.

Gallagher, Maggie. (2003). "The Divorce Thing: A Diversion in the Marriage Debate." National Review Online (August 13). On the World Wide Web at http://www .dadi.org/divthing.htm (retrieved 13 November 2008).

Gamsey, Peter and Richard Saller. (1987). The Roman Empire: Economy, Society and Culture. Los Angeles: University of California Press.

Green, Adam Isaiah. (2008). "Same-Sex Marriage: Lesbian and Gay Spouses Marry Innovation and Change." Paper presented at the Annual Meeting of the American

Sociological Association, August 1–4, Boston, Massachusetts.

Haberland, Erica, L. Chong, and Hillary J. Bracken, with Chris Parker. (2005). "Early Marriage and Adolescent Girls." Youth Lens, 15 (August).

Hartmann, Heidi. (1981). "The Family as the Locus of Gender, Class and Political Struggle: The Example of Housework." Signs: Journal of Women in Culture and Society, 6, 366–94.

Hausknecht, Murray. (2003). "Gay Marriage and the Domestication of Sex." Dissent (Fall), 8–10.

Herdt, Gilbert and Andrew Boxer. (1992). "Introduction: Culture, History, and Life Course of Gay Men." Gay Culture in America: Essays from the Field. Boston: Beacon Press.

Johnson, Fenton. (1996). "Wedded to an Illusion: Do Gays and Lesbians Really Want the Right to Marry?" Harper's (November), 41–50.

Josephson, Jyl. (2005). "Citizenship, Same-Sex Marriage, and Feminist Critiques of Marriage." Perspectives on Politics, 3, 269–84.

Laumann, E.O., J.H. Gagnon, R.T. Michael, and S. Michaels. (1994). The Social Organization of Sexuality: Sexual Practices in the United States. Chicago: University of Chicago Press.

Lessard, Hester. (2007). "Family, Marriage, and Children: Neo-Liberal Choices and Conservative Values." Paper presented at the Annual Meeting of the Law and Society Association, July 25–28, Berlin, Germany.

Levi-Strauss, C. (1969). The Elementary Structures of Kinship. London: Eyre and Spottiswoode.

Nelson, Adie. (2008). "What Is a Family? New Challenges in Defining an Everyday Term." In Robert J. Brym, ed., Society in Question, 5th ed. (pp. 145–51). Toronto: Nelson.

Source: Adam Green.

Patterson, Charlotte, J. (1995). "Families of the Lesbian Baby-Boom: Parents' Division of Labour and Children's Adjustment." Developmental Psychology, 31, 115–23.

Rich, A . (1980). "Compulsory Heterosexuality and Lesbian Existence." Signs, 5 (Summer), 631–60.

Statistics Canada. (2008). "Status of Same-sex Couples (3), Sex (3) and Presence of Other Household Members (5) for the Same sex Couples in Private Households of Canada, Provinces and Territories, 2006 Census—20% Sample Data." On the World Wide Web at (retrieved 13 November 2008).

Sullivan, Andrew. (1997). Same-Sex Marriage. Pro and Con. New York: Vintage. UNIFEM. (2008). United Nations Development Fund for Women: Afghanistan Fact Sheet 2008. Kabul, Afghanistan: UNIFEM.

Valverde, Mariana. (2006). "A New Entity in the History of Sexuality: The Respectable Same-Sex Couple." Feminist Studies, 32, 155–63.

Warner, Michael. (1999). The Trouble with Normal: Sex, Politics and the Ethics of Queer Life. New York: Free Press.

Weeks, Jeffrey, Brian Heaphy, and Catherine Donovan. (2001) Same-Sex Intimacies. Families of Choice and Other Life Experiments. New York: Routledge.

Whitehead, Jaye. (2006). "Same-Sex Marriage as Risk Management." Paper presented at the Annual Meeting of the American Sociological Association, Montreal Convention Centre, August 11, Montreal, Quebec.

Woolwine, David, and E. Doyle McCarthy. (2005). "Gay Moral Discourse: Talking About Identity, Sex and Commitment." Studies in Symbolic Interaction, 28, 379–408.

Yep, Gust A., Karen E . Lovaas, and John P. Elia. (2003). "A Critical Appraisal of Assimilationist and Radical Ideologies Underlying Same-Sex Marriage in LGBT Communities in the United States." Jounal of Homosexuality, 45, 45–64.

DISCUSSION QUESTIONS

1. Why is same-sex marriage referred to as such? Why don't we refer to it as marriage? As a general rule, when a man and woman marry, we don't call it hetero-marriage, yet when homosexuals marry, it's usually called gay or same-sex marriage. What does that do to the institution of marriage, which in turn, affects how we define our families?

2. Legitimating civil same-sex marriages simply acknowledges one family form that has likely existed unofficially for a long time. Legitimacy is meaningful, but there are likely other family forms that exist that still don't have legal acknowledgement. Can you think of any?

3. From his small study, the author suggests that his respondents denied fixed husband–wife roles when it came to negotiating housework, rendering patriarchy all but invisible in this area. Elsewhere, it's argued, however, that women take on the greater role in domestic duties, which speaks directly to the presence of patriarchy. Where does patriarchy come from and does it need a "man's touch" to be enforced?

KNOW IT AND OWN IT: WHAT DO I BRING TO THIS?

Do you come from a traditional family, or one that's taken on a newer, more modern form? Are you aware of the changes that have taken place in how families have formed over the years, and have you examined your feelings surrounding issues like same-sex marriage and adoption, interracial or religious unions, and common-law partnerships? Knowing what your family situation is in relation to many other kinds of families that exist will go a long way in understanding the diversity that has changed the face of families today.

WALKING THE TALK: HOW CAN I LEARN FROM THIS?

Learning about different family forms and, consequently, various family traditions and values expands our world view and allows us to be more accepting of different cultures and diverse populations. How are non-traditional families treated in your community? When you were growing up, were many of your classmates' parents divorced? Were you raised by a single parent? All of these experiences are learning experiences that will help you connect with people you meet who are part of a diverse family.

IT IS WHAT IT IS: IS THIS INSIDE OR OUTSIDE MY COMFORT ZONE?

When we choose to change our world view and accept new ideas and values, it's bound to get uncomfortable, but that's all part of being different from each other. The first time you meet a new friend who has same-sex parents, it will likely be a little unsettling, but remember, your friend is likely to be a little unsettled too. How you socially construct the situation will determine the outcome, and the more you know and understand about changing family forms, the less uncomfortable you'll feel.

PUT IT IN PLAY: HOW CAN I USE THIS?

With the increasing diversity in family structures, many people don't know how children in different countries grow up, and what their family routines exist of. Visit **http://www.youtube.com/mastercommunications** and check out some of the short clips that show how children in over 50 countries spend their time. Although the segments are short, they give you a good idea of the food they eat, what they do in school, and the homes that they live in. The more that you learn about family life around the world, the easier it is to understand it—in all its various forms.

CourseMate Study Tools

Located at www.nelson.com/site/walkamile1e

- Consolidate your knowledge with the **Flashcards**.
- Gauge your understanding with **Picture This** and accompanying questions for reflection.
- Develop your critical thinking skills by working through **The Daily**.
- Apply your understanding with **KWIP** interactive!
- Develop your critical reading skills through compelling **Readings** and accompanying short answer questions.

REFERENCES

Adoption Council of Canada. (2012). FAQ's. Retrieved from *Adoption Council of Canada*: http://www.adoption.ca/faqs

Adshade, M. (2012, May 14). Good times means more divorces. *Canadian Business*, 17–18.

American Psychological Association. (2012). The changing role of the modern day father. Retrieved from *American Psychological Association*: http://www.apa.org/pi/families/resources/changing-father.aspx

Bartlett, S., & LeRose, M. (2012, November 17). Generation boomerang. Retrieved from *Doc Zone*: http://www.cbc.ca/doczone/episode/generation-boomerang.html

Bibby, R. (2009). *The emerging millennials: How Canada's newest generation is responding to change and choice.* Lethbridge: Project Canada Books.

Biblarz, T., & Stacey, J. (2010). How does the gender of parents matter? *Journal of Marriage and the Family*, 3–22.

Bird, A. (2010). Legal parenthood and the recognition of alternative family forms in Canada. *University of New Brunswick Law Journal*, 264–293.

Bouchard, C. (2003). Nurturing dads. In C. Bolte, A. Devault, M. St-Denis, & J. Gaudet, *On father's ground: A portrait of projects to support and promote fathering* (pp. 5–9). Montreal, Quebec: Canadian Institute of Child Health.

Canadian Divorce Laws. (2012). Common law marriage. Retrieved from *Canadian Divorce Laws*: http://www.canadiandivorcelaws.com/common-law-marriage/

Canadian Press. (2011, January 11). Cross-burning brother gets 2 months in jail. Retrieved from *CBC News*: http://www.cbc.ca/news/canada/nova-scotia/story/2011/01/11/ns-justin-rehberg-sentencing.html

Chapman, R., & Shields, L. (2012). An essay about health professionals' attitudes to lesbian, gay, bisexual and transgender parents seeking healthcare for their children. *Scandinavian Journal of Caring Services*, 333–339.

Daniel, S. (2012, October 27). Governing in the dark: Good policy-making requires reliable statistical data. Retrieved from *thestar.com*: http://www.thestar.com/opinion/editorialopinion/article/1278417--governing-in-the-dark-good-policy-making-requires-reliable-statistical-data

Decter, A. (2011, March 11). Educated, employed and equal: The economic prosperity case for national childcare. Retrieved from *YWCA Canada*: http://ywcacanada.ca/data/publications/00000047.pdf

Dempsey, C. (2006). Immigrant income and the family. Retrieved from *Citizenship and Immigration Canada*: http://www.cic.gc.ca/english/resources/research/income/section3.asp

Douglas, K. (2008, September 30). Divorce law in Canada. Retrieved from *Parliament of Canada*: http://www.parl.gc.ca/Content/LOP/ResearchPublications/963-e.htm

Erich, S., Kanenburg, H., Case, K., Allen, T., & Bogdanos, T. (2009). An empirical analysis of factors affecting adolescent attachment in adoptive families with homosexual and straight parents. *Child and Youth Services Review*, 398–404.

Este, D., & Tachble, A. (2009). Fatherhood in the Canadian context: Perceptions and experiences of Sudanese refugee men. *Sex Roles*, 456–466.

Felligi, I. (2006). A multicultural profile of Canada. *Transition*, 3–6.

Fidelman, C. (2010, March 5). IVF funding on way: Bolduc. Retrieved from *Canadian Fertility and Andrology Society*: http://www.cfas.ca/index.php?option=com_content&view=article&id=969:ivf-funding-on-way&catid=1:latest-news&Itemid=50

Focus on the Family. (2011, March 19). International adoption for Canadians. Retrieved from *Waiting to Belong*: http://waitingtobelong.ca/articles/international-adoption-canadians

Friesen, J. (2012, October 27). New language data may be skewed as a result of shift to voluntary census survey. Retrieved from *The Globe and Mail*: http://www.theglobeandmail.com/news/national/new-language-data-may-be-skewed-as-a-result-of-shift-to-voluntary-census-survey/article4709087/#

Green, A. I. (2014). The changing face of matrimony: Same-sex civil marriage in the twenty-first century. In R. J. Brym, *Society in question*, 7th ed. (203–213). Toronto: Nelson Education.

Grove, J. (2001, June). Waiting for parents: Canadian kids need homes. Retrieved from *Vanier Institute of the Family*: http://www.vanierinstitute.ca/modules/news/newsitem.php?ItemId=276#.UKvnKYatu-g

Haaf, W. (2012, March 12). IVF & infertility clinic costs across Canada - How much are we paying to get pregnant? Retrieved from *iVillage.ca*: http://www.ivillage.ca/pregnancy/fertility/ivf-costs

Hillborn, R. (2011, March 15). Global adoptions fall one-third in six years. Retrieved from *Family Helper*: http://www.familyhelper.net/news/110315global.html

Kelly, M. B. (2012, March 28). Divorce cases in civil court, 2010/2011. Retrieved November 5, 2012, from *Statistics Canada*: http://statcan.gc.ca/pub/85-002-x/2012001/article/11634-eng.htm#a10

Khan, F. K. (2010, March 5). Mixed race unions: The new power couples. Retrieved from *Colours of Love: Mixed Unions in Canada*: http://blogs.ubc.ca/mixedmarriages/

Kohen, J. (1981). Housewives, breadwinners, mothers, and family heads: The changing family roles of women. *Advances in Consumer Research*, 576–579.

Kotkin, J. (2012, October 10). The rise of post-familialism: Humanity's future? Retrieved from *newgeography.com*: http://www.newgeography.com/content/003133-the-rise-post-familialism-humanitys-future

Lochhead, C., & Tipper, J. (2008, September). A profile of recently divorced or separated mothers and fathers. Retrieved from *Vanier Institute of the Family*: http://www.vanierinstitute.ca/include/get.php?nodeid=737

Milan, A. (2000). One hundred years of families. Retrieved November 13, 2012, from *Statistics Canada—Canadian Social Trends*: http://www.statcan.gc.ca/pub/11-008-x/1999004/article/4909-eng.pdf

Milan, A., & Bohnert, N. (2012, September 18). Portrait of families and living arrangements in Canada. Retrieved October 2, 2012, from *Statistics Canada*: http://www12.statcan.gc.ca/census-recensement/2011/as-sa/98-312-x/98-312-x2011001-eng.cfm#a2

Milan, A., Keown, L., & Covadonga, R. (2012, February 24). Families, living arrangements and unpaid work. Retrieved November 19, 2012, from *Statistics Canada*: http://www.statcan.gc.ca/pub/89-503-x/2010001/article/11546-eng.htm#a5

Milan, A., Maheux, H., & Chui, T. (2010, April 20). A portrait of couples in mixed unions. Retrieved November 25, 2012, from *Statistics Canada*: http://www.statcan.gc.ca/pub/11-008-x/2010001/article/11143-eng.htm

Mrozek, A. (2012, September 12). Canada's declining marriage rate spells increasing poverty. Retrieved from *Institute of Marriage and the Family*: http://www.imfcanada.org/issues/canadas-declining-marriage-rate-spells-increasing-poverty

Nemeth, M. (1994, June 24). The family. *Maclean's*.

Newman, K. (2012, January 29). The accordion family. Retrieved from *The Chronicle of Higher Education - The Chronicle Review*: http://chronicle.com/article/The-Accordion-Family/130452/

Onderko, P. (2011, March 1). The (same-sex) family next door. *Parenting*, 62–65.

Paul-Carlson, P. (2012, May). Intercountry adoption in Canada: Does it protect the best interests of the child? Retrieved from *Adoption Council of Canada*: http://www.adoption.ca/publications

Pearce, T. (2012, September 6). The painful new realities of international adoption. Retrieved from *The Globe and Mail*: http://www.theglobeandmail.com/life/parenting/the-painful-new-realities-of-international-adoption/article547159/?page=all

Pennings, G. (2011). Evaluating the welfare of the child. *Human Reproduction*, 1609–1615.

Pew Research Center. (2010, November 18). The decline of marriage and rise of new families. Retrieved from *Pew Research Center*: http://www.pewsocialtrends.org/2010/11/18/the-decline-of-marriage-and-rise-of-new-families/6/

Pollack, S. (2009). Creating submissive subjects: Lone mothers and social assistance regimes in Canada. *The Policy Press*, 229–235.

Preece, M. (2004, December). When lone parents marry, the challenge of stepfamily relationships. Retrieved November 20, 2012, from *Vanier Institute of the Family*: http://www.vifamily.ca/library/transition/334/334.html

Press, J. (2012, September 12). Census: More single dads heading lone-parent families. Retrieved from *Canada.com*: http://www.canada.com/Census+More+single+dads+heading+lone+parent+families/7265375/story.html

Pryor, J., & Rodgers, B. (2001). *Children in changing families: Life after parental separation*. Massachusetts: Blackwell Publishers.

Roy, B. (2012, March 15). Six strategies to keep newcomer youth safe. Retrieved from *Canadianimmigrant.ca*: http://canadianimmigrant.ca/family/6-strategies-to-keep-newcomer-youth-safe

Ryan, B., Brotman, S., & Rowe, B. (2001). "Certain circumstances": Issues in equity and responsiveness in access to health care in Canada. Retrieved from *Health Canada*: http://www.hc-sc.gc.ca/hcs-sss/alt_formats/hpb-dgps/pdf/pubs/2001-certain-equit-acces/2001-certain-equit-acces-eng.pdf

Ryan, M., & Berkowitz, D. (2009). Constructing gay and lesbian parent families: Beyond the closet. *Qualitative Sociology*, 153–172.

Scoffield, H. (2012, September 18). Define the Canadian family? It'll require a flow chart. Retrieved from *Maclean's Online*: http://www2.macleans.ca/2012/09/18/define-the-canadian-family-itll-require-a-flow-chart/

Shimoni, R., Este, D., & Clarke, D. (2003). Paternal engagement in immigrant and refugee families. *Journal of Comparative Family Studies*, 555–568.

Statistics Canada. (2010, December 16). Women in Canada: Economic well-being. Retrieved November 19, 2012, from *The Daily*: http://www.statcan.gc.ca/daily-quotidien/101216/dq101216c-eng.htm

Statistics Canada. (2012a, May 22). Family violence in Canada: A statistical profile, 2010. Retrieved November 11, 2012, from *The Daily*: http://www.statcan.gc.ca/daily-quotidien/120522/dq120522a-eng.htm

Statistics Canada. (2012b, September 12). 2011 Census of population: Families, households, marital status, structural type of dwelling, collectives. Retrieved October 31, 2012, from *The Daily*: http://www.statcan.gc.ca/daily-quotidien/120919/dq120919a-eng.htm

Statistics Canada. (2012c, September 18). Fifty years of families in Canada: 1961 to 2011. Retrieved November 5, 2012, from *Statistics Canada*: http://www12.statcan.gc.ca/census-recensement/2011/as-sa/98-312-x/98-312-x2011003_1-eng.cfm

Statistics Canada. (2012d, September 18). Living arrangements of young adults aged 20 to 29. Retrieved November 5, 2012, from *Statistics Canada*: http://www12.statcan.gc.ca/census-recensement/2011/as-sa/98-312-x/98-312-x2011003_3-eng.cfm

Statistics Canada. (2012e, September 18). Portrait of families and living arrangements in Canada. Retrieved October 28, 2012, from *Statistics Canada*: http://www12.statcan.gc.ca/census-recensement/2011/as-sa/98-312-x/98-312-x2011001-eng.cfm

Statistics Canada. (2012f, September 19). 2011 Census of population: Families, households, marital status, structural type of dwelling, collectives. Retrieved November 9, 2012, from *The Daily*: http://www.statcan.gc.ca/daily-quotidien/120919/dq120919a-eng.htm

Statistics Canada. (2012g, October 28). Catalogue no. 93-716, Vol. II (1971 Census of Canada: Families). Retrieved October 28, 2012, from *Statistics Canada*: http://www5.statcan.gc.ca/bsolc/olc-cel/olc-cel?catno=95M0025XCB&lang=eng

Statistics Canada. (2012h, November 2). Labour force survey, October 2012. Retrieved November 5, 2012, from *The Daily*: http://www.statcan.gc.ca/daily-quotidien/121102/dq121102a-eng.htm

Stearns, P. (1991). Fatherhood in historical perspective: The role of social change. In F. Bozett, & S. Hanson, *Fatherhood and families in cultural context* (pp. 28-52). New York: Springer.

Sullivan, R., & Harrington, M. (2009). The politics and ethics of same-sex adoption. *Journal of GLBT Family Studies*, 235–246.

Vanier Institute of the Family. (2012a). Definition of family. Retrieved from *Vanier Institute of the Family*: http://www.vanierinstitute.ca/definition_of_family#.UIqWOVEwC-g

Vanier Institute of the Family. (2012b, November 5). Blended families: New challenges and opportunities. Retrieved from *Vanier Institute of the Family*: http://www.vanierinstitute.ca/modules/news/newsitem.php?ItemId=468#.UJlF5lGtu-g

Voices-Voix. (2012). Statistics Canada (mandatory long-form census). Retrieved from *Voices-Voix*: http://voices-voix.ca/en/facts/profile/statistics-canada-mandatory-long-form-census

Wilcox, B. W., & Cavalle, C. (2011). Sustainable demographic dividend: What do marriage and fertility have to do with the economy? Retrieved from *The Institute of Social Trends*: http://sustaindemographicdividend.org/wp-content/uploads/2012/07/SDD-2011-Final.pdf

"So why does it feel so wrong
To reach for something more
To wanna live a better life"

(Sick Puppies, 2010)

DIVERSITY COMPETENCIES

Diversity competencies are specifically learned behaviours that students can actively practise to promote equity and inclusion. By mastering this unit, students will gain the skills to become diversity-competent practitioners, including the ability to

- examine historic and contemporary patterns of immigration and resettlement in Canada

- analyze issues associated with Canada's immigration system that impact settlement and integration of ethnic groups

- assess barriers to acculturation faced by newcomers to Canada

- differentiate between the pre-migration and post-migration experiences of immigrants and refugees and the impact those experiences have on individuals and families

- reflect upon your own personal migration history and locate it within the context of Canadian immigration history

Source: Alex/Thinkstock

The best advice I ever got on how to begin to develop the skills I would need to work with refugees came one day while I was sitting across the kitchen table from an elderly woman. Her back was bent from what must have been arthritis. She looked up at me through her glasses with a mischievous glint in her eye and a sly grin on her face and told me that all I needed to work with refugees were my two ears and an open heart … oh, and also a thick skin and a silver tongue for the politicians. The wisdom of this woman remains with me to this day, and she defines for me what it means to be a global citizen and a world changer. She sprinkled love and compassion on the world's most vulnerable people, and I watched some of Canada's toughest politicians bend to the will of this "little old woman."

She was Nancy Pocock, known by refugees around the world simply as "Mama Nancy," and she opened her heart and her own home (Quaker House) to provide safe haven to them. A social activist who spent her life advocating for peace and justice, Nancy came to international fame when the United Nations awarded her the Pearson Peace Prize in 1987. She was also the recipient of the Order of Ontario in 1992. A medical clinic in Vietnam bears her name, as does a street in Toronto. But Nancy paid little attention to the awards and accolades she received. I wasn't with her in her final hours, but friends tell me that while she lay on a stretcher in the emergency room of Toronto's Women's College Hospital, she was writing a letter to a Member of Parliament on behalf of yet another refugee. Nancy always took the time to listen with her heart to a refugee's personal story; I suspect she listened to thousands throughout her lifetime.

THE POWER OF "THE STORY"

Twenty years of working in the field of **refugee** protection and resettlement confirm that the greatest moments of revelation, realization, and change are precipitated by the narrative—in this instance, the story of the lived experiences of those who choose and those who are forced to **migrate**. Allen Say, in a wonderful children's story titled *Grandfather's Journey*, documents a compelling family history of life between Japan and the United States and the desire to be in both locations that is often at the heart of migration stress for many families: "So I return now and then, when I cannot still the longing in my heart. The funny thing is, the moment I am in one country, I am homesick for the other" (Say, 1993, p. 31). The push–pull resettlement issues ranging from **culture shock** to homesickness are the theme of many stories about immigrants, refugees, **refugee claimants**, **Cross Culture Kids** (CCKs), and **Third Culture Kids** (TCKs).

The stories of **asylum seekers** and others forced to migrate also expose the limits of human endurance, the courage to survive, and the indomitable human spirit. It is this same courage and spirit you will discover in Mariatu Kamara's story in her book *The Bite of the Mango*—a story representative of the children victimized during the ten-year civil war in Sierra Leone. It is a different story of struggle Ishmael Beah recounts in *A Long Way Gone: Memoirs of a Boy Soldier*, but it shares the same courage in his journey to heal. Stories of the indomitable human spirit bind the narratives of exile and quests for asylum detailed in the book *Refugee Sandwich* (2006), written by Peter Showler, former chair of the **Immigration and Refugee Board** (IRB) and professor of refugee law at the University of Ottawa. It is a story of courage you will read about as you walk a mile in this chapter's narrative *In Their Shoes*. These narratives give testament to the importance of the Canadian **Immigration and Refugee Protection Act**'s objective in fulfilling our humanitarian obligations under international law (Immigration and Refugee Protection Act, 2001). They are representative of thousands of

Refugee: Person who is forced to flee from persecution and is outside of his or her country of origin.

Migrate: To move from one country, place, or region to another.

Culture shock: Negative consequences of intercultural contact; more specifically refers to the stress and confusion that individuals feel from being immersed in a new environment where cultural and communication patterns are foreign to them.

Refugee claimants: Term used in Canadian law for asylum seekers; they receive a decision on whether they are refugees after they arrive in Canada.

Cross Culture Kid (CCK): A child who has lived in or meaningfully interacted with two or more different cultures during his or her childhood.

Third Culture Kid (TCK): Children who move with parents from one culture to another due to a parent's career choice.

Asylum seeker: An individual who is seeking refuge (i.e., political asylum) in a foreign country and whose case is not yet decided.

Immigration and Refugee Board (IRB): Independent tribunal established by the Parliament of Canada the mission of which is to resolve immigration and refugee cases efficiently, fairly, and in accordance with the law.

Immigration and Refugee Protection Act (IRPA): Legislation whose mission is "respecting immigration to Canada and the granting of refugee protection to persons who are displaced, persecuted or in danger."

Convention refugees who have found protection in Canada and have subsequently gone on to make significant contributions as global citizens.

As you learn about the history of our immigration policy, some of the different ways in which people come here to live, a few of the commonly held myths and facts about immigrants and refugees, and the contemporary issues they face in their **resettlement** here, it is important to remember that behind all of these issues are human stories that are worth exploring. They are stories that can be learned through your grandparents, parents, aunts, uncles, cousins, friends, and colleagues. This is an opportunity to use your imagination to explore the relationship between **immigration**, your personal biography, and your cultural identity. It is a chance to explore two important questions: "Who am I?" and "Where do I come from?" As Nancy Pocock once said, all you need for this journey are your ears and an open heart.

HISTORY OF CANADIAN IMMIGRATION POLICY

Look at the contributions made to Canada's social, cultural, political, and economic landscape by immigrants such as Thomas Bata, Alexander Graham Bell, Olivia Chow, Adrienne Clarkson, Tommy Douglas, Michaëlle Jean, Peter Mansbridge, and Joe Schlesinger, to name only a few. Successive waves of immigrants throughout Canada's history have made extraordinary contributions to our nation. The Canadian immigration process has significantly contributed to our evolving character as a multicultural nation and will likely continue to contribute to significant demographic changes in the future.

An analysis of Canada's immigration policies helps us to understand some of our nation's greatest controversies around inclusion and exclusion—essentially, who gets in and who doesn't. The history of Canadian immigration policy can best be summarized in eight periods—a model formulated by Geneviève Bouchard in a presentation by the Canadian Institute for Research on Public Policy on Canada's immigration system (Bouchard, 2007).

PERIOD ONE

Period One (1867–1913) was a time when the main goal of immigration was to secure farmers and labourers to populate and settle western Canada. During this time, immigration was encouraged from source areas such as Great Britain, the United States, and northwestern Europe. The Canadian Pacific Railway was completed, and Chinese labourers were no longer required—this is important because, at this time, the government imposed a **head tax** on new Chinese immigrants. The first head tax imposed by the federal government in 1885 was $50 (Canadians for Redress, 2002). In 1900, the Canadian government doubled the head tax to $100, and then increased it once again to $500 in 1903. In 1913, over 400 000 immigrants arrived in Canada, marking the largest influx of immigrants in Canadian history (Citizenship and Immigration Canada, 2006a).

PERIOD TWO

Period Two (1919–1929) was a time when revisions to the Immigration Act resulted in more restrictive and selective procedures based on the country's "absorptive capacity," which is essentially a country's perceived saturation level—the level at which it cannot take on any more immigrants without risking peril to its own inhabitants. Immigrants had to pass a literacy test, and the government could limit the number of immigrants allowed into Canada. Source countries were officially divided into preferred and non-preferred groups. Preferred source countries included Great Britain, the United States, the Irish Free State, Newfoundland, Australia, and New Zealand. The Chinese were formally excluded from immigrating to Canada from 1923 until 1947.

PERIOD THREE

Period Three (1930–1945) was during the time of the Great Depression and World War II. When the Canadian unemployment rate reached 27% in 1933, the door was closed to most newcomers (except those from Britain and the United States) and active immigration recruitment ended.

Convention refugee: Individual who has been granted asylum by the 1951 Geneva Convention Relating to the Status of Refugees; someone who has reason to fear persecution in his or her country of origin due to race, religion, nationality, membership in a social group, or political opinion.

Resettlement: The process of settling in another place or country to live; resettlement generally refers to newcomers' acclimatization and the early stages of adaptation.

Immigration: Entering into and becoming established in a new place of residence; usually means entering a country that one was not born in.

Head tax: Tax imposed by the Canadian government on anyone immigrating to Canada from China between 1885 and 1923.

PERIOD FOUR

Period Four (1946–1962) was significant, as Canada saw a large influx of displaced persons from Europe. Approximately 70 000 war brides (foreign wives of Canadian soldiers) and their children arrived in Canada. Canada's immigration policy now had very clear ethnic/racial and economic goals. In 1947, Prime Minister William Lyon Mackenzie King stated that the purpose of immigration was to improve Canada's standard of living, but that immigration should not change the basic character of the Canadian population.

PERIOD FIVE

Period Five (1962–1973) was a time when the government abolished what it acknowledged as racist immigration policy: "Henceforth any unsponsored immigrants who had the requisite education, skill, or other qualifications were to be considered suitable for admission, irrespective of colour, race, or national origin" (Citizenship and Immigration Canada, 2006b). One of the most significant changes in immigration policy occurred in 1967 with the creation of a point system that facilitated the immigration of skilled workers based on an assessment of factors such as education, employment opportunities in Canada, adaptability, and language proficiency. The point system is still the method of selection used today for skilled workers.

PERIOD SIX

Period Six (1974–1984) was the time of a new Immigration Act (1976), which defined the three objectives of Canada's immigration policy: family reunification; humanitarian concerns; and the promotion of Canada's economic, demographic, social, and cultural goals. These same objectives have endured as part of today's immigration policy.

PERIOD SEVEN

Period Seven (1985–1993) was a time when a landmark decision made by the Supreme Court of Canada changed the refugee determination system, resulting in the eventual creation of the Immigration and Refugee Board. This decision, known as the Singh decision, required that all people seeking asylum in Canada be provided with a full oral hearing on the merits of their claim. This decision, rendered on April 4, 1985, is now commemorated annually on this date as Refugee Rights Day. During this period, immigration policy increased the inflow of economic immigration to 250 000 people, but not at the expense of humanitarian obligations.

PERIOD EIGHT

Period Eight (1993–2010) was a time that saw the 1976 Immigration Act replaced with the Immigration and Refugee Protection Act of 2002. The desire to increase the number of skilled workers continued during this period, with only a few changes in the point system, which was designed to draw a younger and bilingual demographic. The definition of refugee was expanded to include a class of protected persons, honouring international obligations under the **Convention against Torture** (Danelius, 2002). There was an increased use of temporary foreign workers and a decrease in the number of family class sponsorships approved.

PERIOD NINE

We are adding Period Nine (2010–) to the model, as Parliament has recently passed two new immigration acts, namely the **Balanced Refugee Reform Act** and the **Protecting Canada's Immigration System Act**. At the same time, Canada announced it will settle an additional 500 government-sponsored refugees from overseas refugee camps and urban slums and will increase the number of private sponsorships by an additional 2000. Projections estimate that the Canadian government and private sponsors would annually resettle up to 14 500 UN-selected refugees.

CANADA APOLOGIZES

Despite the outstanding contributions made to Canada by successive waves of immigrants throughout our history, Canada's immigration policy has not always been an open door. Broad claims about the Canadian government's long-standing humanitarian tradition suffer from historical amnesia. The Canadian government overtly discriminated through an exclusionary

Convention against Torture: United Nations international human rights agreement signed on December 10, 1984, as a commitment against the use of torture in their country for any reason; signatory nations also agree not to use any evidence obtained under torture and not to deport or return people to countries where they are at risk of being tortured.

Balanced Refugee Reform Act: Immigration legislation that, together with the Protecting Canada's Immigration System Act, makes changes to the Immigration and Refugee Protection Act and the refugee claimant process in Canada.

Protecting Canada's Immigration System Act: Immigration legislation designed to make the review and determination of refugee claims faster and to expedite removals of those who do not qualify.

immigration policy designed to keep out certain ethnicities who were deemed "unfit" to enter—some call it a history of "whites only" immigration.

The "Undesirables"

The Canadian Immigration Act of 1910 stated that the government could exclude immigrants of any race; in 1919, language was added to the act to provide a rationale for deeming some immigrant groups undesirable "owing to their peculiar customs, habits, modes of life and methods of holding property and because of their probable inability to become readily assimilated" (Matas, 1985). This legislation was used at points throughout the period of 1910–1962 to prohibit, restrict, or expel immigrants from Germany, Austria, Hungary, Bulgaria, Turkey, India, Pakistan, Ceylon, China, Japan, and other nations (Matas, 1985). It was also used to exclude religious groups like Doukhobors, Hutterites, Mennonites, and Jews (Matas, 1985).

An Apology for *Komagata Maru*

The incident involving a ship named the *Komagata Maru* is one example of the way the Canadian government applied exclusionary immigration policy to bar entry to those deemed "undesirable." As Ali Kazimi (2012) suggests, the *Komagata Maru* is not just an incident, it is part of a continuum in creating Canada as a white settler state.

When the *Komagata Maru* dropped anchor in the Vancouver harbour in 1914, aboard were 376 passengers from British India, many bearing the Sikh ceremonial name of Singh (Bissoondath, 1994). Many of the men on board were veterans of the British Indian Army, who believed their military service would support their right to settle anywhere in the empire that they had fought to defend. They were wrong (Kazimi, 2012).

Using the "continuous journey" regulation, immigration officials held passengers on board for over two months, and eventually only 24 passengers were allowed to remain in Canada. The other 352 passengers were forced to sail back to India, where upon arrival 29 passengers were shot and 20 were killed. Others were jailed. On August 3, 2008, Prime Minister Stephen Harper issued an apology on behalf of the government of Canada for the *Komagata Maru* incident. There was some disappointment among some members of the Sikh community, who expected a formal apology to be made in Parliament.

Source: Project Photo: Komagata Maru Memorial Company: LEES+Associates Photographer: Scott Massey

"The immigration restrictions experienced by some people of Indian descent mark an unfortunate period in our nation's history. This monument commemorating the *Komagata Maru* incident recognizes this past."—Citizenship, Immigration and Multiculturalism Minister Jason Kenney, July 24, 2012

An Apology for the Chinese Head Tax and Exclusion

Another example of Canada's racially motivated exclusionary immigration policies was the Chinese head tax levied by the Canadian government in 1885 through the Chinese Immigration Act as a means of discouraging new Chinese immigrants from entering Canada after the completion of the Canadian Pacific Railway. By today's standard, the tax would be the equivalent of $100 000 per person (Canadians for Redress, 2002). This act was replaced by the Chinese Exclusion Act, which specifically prohibited Chinese immigration to Canada from 1923–1947. In 2006, Prime Minister Stephen Harper issued a formal apology and financial redress to the Chinese Canadian community.

An Apology for Japanese Internment

Following the bombing of Pearl Harbor during World War II, the Government of Canada confined Japanese immigrants and Canadian citizens of Japanese descent in internment camps, confiscated their personal property, and forced their repatriation (deportation) from Canada. Once again, Canadian immigration policy was used to exclude a particular group of people—this time those of Japanese descent.

Anyone listening to Raymond Moriyama, one of Canada's most famous architects, tell the story of his internment as a boy in Slocan Valley, British Columbia, is left with a feeling of horror and disbelief that this could have happened in Canada. It is an experience

Source: THE CANADIAN PRESS/Fred Chartrand

"For over six decades, these malicious measures, aimed solely at the Chinese, were implemented with deliberation by the Canadian state ... we have the collective responsibility to build a country based firmly on the notion of equality of opportunity, regardless of one's race or ethnic origin."—Prime Minister Stephen Harper, 2006

Source: THE CANADIAN PRESS/Dave Noble

Japanese Canadians demand redress. Between 1942 and 1949, some 23 000 Japanese Canadians, labelled "enemy aliens," were forcibly removed from their homes, dispossessed of their properties, and placed in internment camps across the country.

Moriyama shares with another well-known Japanese Canadian, David Suzuki. Moriyama and Suzuki were among the 23 000 Japanese taken to internment camps in British Columbia, branded as "enemy aliens." Their personal property was confiscated; Price Waterhouse estimated the value of this property in 1986 dollars at $443 million (Roberts-Moore, 2002). Regulations passed under the authority of the War Measures Act restricted immigration from Japan and also provided for the deportation of Japanese Canadians.

In 1988, Prime Minister Brian Mulroney issued a formal government apology to the Japanese-Canadian community:

> Mr. Speaker, I know I speak for members of all sides of the House in offering to Japanese Canadians the formal and sincere apology of this Parliament for those past injustices against them, their families, and their heritage, and our solemn commitment to

Canadians of every origin that they will never again be countenanced or repeated. (National Association of Japanese Canadians, 2008)

Under the terms of the Japanese Canadian Redress Agreement signed in 1988 between the Government of Canada and the National Association of Japanese Canadians, the federal government agreed to create a Canadian Race Relations Foundation to help eliminate racism. The federal government proclaimed the Canadian Race Relations Foundation Act into law on October 28, 1996, and the Foundation officially opened in 1997.

No Apology for the Voyage of the Damned

Another example of **xenophobia** manifest in Canadian immigration policy was the systematic exclusion of Jews as immigrants or refugees during the period of 1933–1948. During this period, Canada's immigration policy is best summarized in the words of an immigration agent, who, when asked how many Jews would be allowed into Canada, replied, "None is too many." This phrase has become the title of a book by Irving Abella, a Toronto history professor, who argues that from 1933–1948, Canada had the worst record of any immigration country in the world in providing asylum to Jews, despite mounting reports of Adolf Hitler's genocide (Abella, 2008). The closed-door policy on Jewish immigration was led by Frederick Blair, the head of immigration in the King administration. In one letter, Blair compared Jews clamouring to get into the country to hogs on a farm at feeding time (CBC, 2011).

Xenophobia: Hostility toward anything foreign.

In 1939, 907 Jewish refugees aboard the *St. Louis* were refused asylum by Canada, and many returned to Europe where they faced death (Thomas & Witts, 1974). This incident is remembered in history as the "voyage of the damned." A memorial for these Jewish refugees was unveiled in Halifax at Pier 21 in 2011, but no official government apology was ever issued. In 2000, a group of Canadian clergy gathered with 25 survivors to issue an apology. One of those clergymen was Douglas Blair, a Baptist minister whose great uncle was none other than Frederick Blair (CBC News, 2000).

IMMIGRATING TO CANADA

According to the most recent Canadian Census data available, **immigrants** made up nearly one-fifth (19.8%) of Canada's population, a percentage that is expected to reach at least 25% by 2031 (Malenfant, Lebel, & Martel, 2010). More than half (54%) of the adult immigrant population in Canada lives in the cities of Toronto, Montreal, or Vancouver (Ng, 2011). Canada is now home to people from more than 200 countries, who speak over 200 languages (Statistics Canada, 2012).

People come to live in Canada in a variety of different ways on either a temporary or a permanent basis. They come to work, study, visit, set up a business, reunite with family, be adopted, or find protection. The legislation currently used to regulate immigration in Canada is called the Immigration and Refugee Protection Act (IRPA). Passed in 2001, some of the objectives of this act are to support the development of a strong and prosperous Canadian economy, family reunification, and fulfillment of international humanitarian obligations. Recently, Canada passed new legislation to deal with refugee migration to Canada, namely the Balanced Refugee Reform Act and Protecting Canada's Immigration System Act. Receiving Royal Assent on June 29, 2010, the Balanced Refugee Act is intended to improve the expediency and fairness of the refugee determination process. Some of the changes include the launch of a Refugee Appeal Division, the designation of countries considered safe to live in, and an expedited removal process for failed refugee claimants. The Protecting Canada's Immigration System Act, implemented on December 15, 2012, brings further reform to the refugee determination process, but it is also intended to address issues of human smuggling and adds a requirement of biometric data for temporary resident visas, work permits, and study permit applications.

Immigrants: People residing in Canada who were born outside of Canada; this category excludes Canadian citizens born outside of Canada and people residing in Canada on temporary status, such as those with a student visa or temporary foreign workers.

Family class: Immigration category used to described immigrants who have been sponsored to come to Canada as a spouse, partner, dependent child, parent, or grandparent.

Ways of Immigrating to Canada

For people looking to come to Canada permanently, there are three basic ways to do this. First, they can reunite with family members in Canada if someone sponsors them. This is called a **family class** sponsorship. A Canadian citizen or permanent resident of Canada can sponsor a spouse, common-law partner, conjugal partner, dependent child, or other eligible relative (e.g., a parent or grandparent; Citizenship and Immigration Canada, 2009). Sponsors sign a legal undertaking promising that they will support the family member financially in Canada and that they will not seek financial assistance from the government for this purpose.

The second way to apply to come to live in Canada permanently is through a category referred to as the economic class. An immigrant can apply independently to come as a skilled worker, an entrepreneur, an investor, or a self-employed person (Citizenship and Immigration Canada, 2010). As a skilled worker, an applicant is assessed under a point system based on education, work experience, knowledge of official languages, and other criteria that prove the person can make an economic contribution to Canada (Citizenship and Immigration Canada, 2010). An entrepreneur must be able to demonstrate the business knowledge, experience, and assets to be able to own and manage a business in Canada, a business that will create employment and contribute to the economy (Citizenship and Immigration Canada, 2010). Someone who applies to come to live in Canada as a permanent resident through the Immigrant Investor Program must have a net worth of $1.6 million and make an $800 000 investment in the Canadian economy (Citizenship and Immigration Canada, 2010).

The third way someone can apply to come to Canada permanently is as a Convention refugee or person in need of protection (Citizenship and Immigration Canada, 2013). Canada will offer protection to those who fear persecution or who could be tortured or suffer cruel and unusual punishment and are therefore unable to return to their home country (Citizenship and Immigration Canada,

2013). There are three ways that people come to Canada as refugees. The first way is as a **Government Assisted Refugee** (GAR)—a government-sponsored refugee selected overseas for resettlement in Canada. The second method is to be privately sponsored as a refugee by a group within Canada that has been approved by the government. The third way to seek asylum is to make a refugee claim upon arrival in Canada. In this situation, the person will have an oral hearing to decide, based on testimony and evidence presented, whether he or she meets the criteria as a **protected person,** according to Canada's Immigration and Refugee Protection Act (Citizenship and Immigration Canada, 2013).

An Overview of the Number of Immigrants Coming to Canada

The majority of immigrants come to Canada as members of the economic class or the family class (see Table 11.1). The Protected Persons class, which includes all refugees, protected persons, and their dependants abroad, is a comparatively smaller group.

Government Assisted Refugee (GAR): A government-sponsored refugee selected overseas for resettlement in Canada.

Protected person: Someone who, according to the Immigration and Refugee Protection Act, meets the definition of a Convention refugee and can also mean a person in Canada who, if they were sent home, would be tortured or at risk of cruel and unusual treatment or punishment.

TABLE 11.1
Immigration Overview

ECONOMIC CLASS	
skilled workers	100 828
business immigrants	10 080
provincial and territorial nominees	40 899
live-in caregivers	9 012
Total economic class (including dependants)	**160 819**
FAMILY CLASS	
spouses, partners, children, and others	43 193
parents and grandparents	21 815
Total family class	**65 008**
PROTECTED PERSONS	
government-assisted refugees	5 430
privately sponsored refugees	4 220
protected persons in Canada	8 586
dependants abroad	4 858
Total protected persons	**23 094**
OTHER	**8 966**
TOTAL	**257 887**

Source: Statistics Canada, Facts and Figures, 2009. Reproduced and distributed on an "as is" basis with the permission of Statistics Canada.

DECIDING WHO GETS IN

Myths and Facts about Refugees and Immigrants Coming to Canada

Unfortunately, there are many enduring myths about refugees and immigrants coming to and living in Canada. Here are some of the statements and questions people make around refugee and immigrant issues, and some of the facts to consider in response.

When Someone Asks ... Why don't refugees have to line up and wait like other immigrants?

This question refers to the practice known as queue jumping—like when someone cuts in front of you in the coffee line. Refugees need to come to Canada more quickly than ordinary immigrants because their lives are usually in danger. Many refugees come to Canada's borders to apply because they can't safely apply overseas. In many countries where there is conflict, Canadian embassy or consulate offices are not accessible. Time needed for processing applications can endanger lives and safety. There are also situations where Canadian embassies and consulates are watched by those perpetrating violence in that country; obviously, they do not want their citizens talking to the international community about human rights violations. Sometimes, waiting in line can mean the difference between life and death for the asylum seeker.

When Someone Asks ... Doesn't Canada already do enough to help refugees?

This is really a question about what Canada's role is in terms of its international obligations. The **United Nations High Commissioner for Refugees** in the 2012 Global Trends Report (2013) notes some of the following facts:

- At the end of 2012, some 45.2 million people worldwide were forcibly displaced due to conflict and persecution.
- This number included 10.5 million refugees, 27.1 million **internally displaced persons**.

United Nations High Commissioner for Refugees (UNHCR): Agency mandated to lead and coordinate international action to protect refugees and resolve refugee problems worldwide.

Internally displaced person: Person who has fled his or her home because of war, violence, or human rights violations, but who remains in his or her country in another location.

Developing countries: Designation used only for statistical convenience in measuring countries against the United Nation's Human Development Index; the term is used to replace the terms "Third World" or "underdeveloped countries."

- Almost half (46%) of the world's refugee population in 2012 were children under 18.
- **Developing countries** hosted 80% of the global refugee population.

According to estimates of the United Nations High Commissioner for Refugees (UNHCR), the majority of the world's refugees at the end of 2012 were being hosted in countries like Pakistan, the Islamic Republic of Iran, Germany and Kenya (see Figure 11.1). In 2012, Canada sponsored approximately 5430 refugees, private individuals and organizations sponsored 4220 refugees, and Canada accepted 13 444 asylum seekers.

Given the UNHCR's global statistics on world refugees, to suggest Canada needs stricter limits so we don't end up hosting millions of refugees is not valid. In fact, the evidence would suggest that Canada could be doing more in terms of its international obligation to world refugees. However, no one, including the UNHCR, is suggesting that all the world's refugees should be resettled in a third country, when **voluntary repatriation** and settlement of countries of first asylum are preferred.

When Someone Asks ... It's nice that we help, but shouldn't we look after people in our own country first?

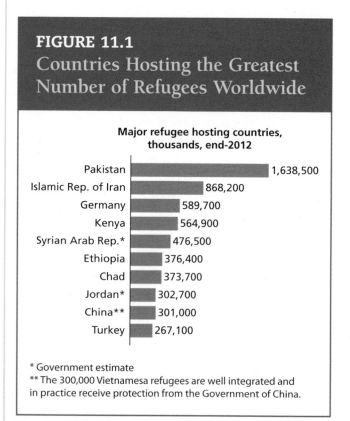

FIGURE 11.1
Countries Hosting the Greatest Number of Refugees Worldwide

Major refugee hosting countries, thousands, end-2012

Pakistan	1,638,500
Islamic Rep. of Iran	868,200
Germany	589,700
Kenya	564,900
Syrian Arab Rep.*	476,500
Ethiopia	376,400
Chad	373,700
Jordan*	302,700
China**	301,000
Turkey	267,100

* Government estimate
** The 300,000 Vietnamesa refugees are well integrated and in practice receive protection from the Government of China.

Source: UNHCR Global Trends Report 2012.

Canada has a legal obligation under international law as a signatory to the UN Convention on Refugee Protection (1951) and the 1967 Protocol. The spirit of the Convention and the Protocol suggests that all human beings have a right to seek asylum from persecution in other countries. As such, refugee protection is a universal responsibility for all of us as global citizens.

When Someone Asks … If a refugee can afford to wear nice clothes and drive a car, is that person a genuine refugee?

Refugees are not **economic migrants**. Economic status has no bearing on refugee status. A refugee is someone who has a well-founded fear of being persecuted because of his or her race, religion, nationality, membership in a particular social group, or political opinion. It makes no difference to the granting of status whether a refugee is rich or poor—the point is that the person is at risk of, or has experienced, persecution. Many refugees are well-educated professionals in their own countries, such as doctors, nurses, judges, lawyers, professors, journalists, and so on.

When Someone Asks … Why can't these people just go to refugee camps?

This is not a question anyone might ask who has visited or worked in a refugee camp overseas or even participated in a simulation exercise of life for a refugee in a camp. The average length of time spent in a refugee camp is 17 years. Security of food and water in camps is unpredictable. Refugees living in camps are often not allowed to leave or work outside the camp. (UNHCR, 2010).

When Someone Asks … Aren't there a lot of bogus refugees coming to Canada abusing our system? Shouldn't they apply to be a refugee before they come to Canada?

Persons who seek protection onshore and are granted status are no less "genuine" than refugees who are resettled from offshore. Refugees who are resettled in Canada, regardless of whether they apply onshore or offshore, must meet the criteria for refugee status outlined in the UN Refugee Convention (UNHCR, 2010). A decision by the Supreme Court of Canada, referred to as the **Singh decision**, requires all people seeking asylum in Canada to be provided with a full oral hearing of the merits of their claim (Immigration and Refugee Board of Canada, 2013). Unfortunately, the terms "bogus refugee," "phoney claim," and "abuser" are often used when governments are looking to make restrictive changes to the refugee determination process. Some of the reforms to this process throughout history have

A bundle of belongings isn't the only thing a refugee brings to his new country.

Einstein was a refugee.

UNHCR

Source: USA for United Nations High Commissioner for Refugees

Can you imagine a world without the contributions of Albert Einstein, a Jewish refugee to America from Germany?

been positive and necessary. Unfortunately, the use of this language and rationale brands all asylum seekers indiscriminately.

When Someone Asks … Don't refugees bring crime and pose a terrorist threat to Canada?

The UN Refugee Convention excludes people who have committed war crimes, crimes against peace, crimes against humanity, or other serious non-political crimes from obtaining refugee status. All asylum seekers must undergo rigorous security checks before being granted protection. Applicants with a serious criminal record or considered to be a security risk because of suspected involvement in terrorism, organized crime, espionage, or human rights violations are not eligible for a refugee hearing in Canada. The Canadian Security Intelligence Service (CSIS) Security Screening program manages the *Refugee Claimant Screening Program*, providing security

Voluntary repatriation: The process of returning voluntarily to one's place of origin or citizenship.

Economic migrant: Person who moves to another country for employment or a better economic future.

Singh decision: Landmark decision in refugee determination made by the Supreme Court of Canada in 1985; the decision protects the right of every refugee claimant to an oral hearing.

assessments on refugee applicants to **Citizenship and Immigration Canada** (Canadian Security Intelligence Service, 2013). This program is designed to ensure that those who are inadmissible to Canada for security reasons under the Immigration and Refugee Protection Act are identified early and prevented from taking up residence in this country (Canadian Security Intelligence Service, 2013).

When Someone Asks ... We don't have enough jobs for Canadians, so why are we inviting immigrants to come in?

Citizenship and Immigration Canada: Government department that is responsible for immigration, settlement, resettlement, citizenship, and multiculturalism programs and services.

Lump of labour fallacy: The false belief that the amount of work available to labourers is a fixed amount and, therefore, there is no capacity to absorb more labourers into an economy.

Newcomer: Blanket term used to refer inclusively to all immigrants and refugees who have recently arrived in the country to settle on a permanent basis.

Host country: A country where representatives or organizations of another country co-exist either because they've been invited by the government or because an international agreement exists.

Acclimatization: The process of beginning to adapt to a new environment.

Integration: The long-term, multidimensional process through which newcomers become full and equal participants in all aspects of society. As part of this process, newcomers interact with the larger society and also maintain their own identity. Integration is not a linear process.

Whenever we experience hard times economically in Canada, the first target we generally look to is immigrants. The fear is that immigrants will come into the country and take jobs away from Canadians who have lived here all their lives. Economists refer to this as the **lump of labour fallacy**. The lump of labour theory suggests that there is only a fixed amount of labour within a country for a fixed number of workers, but economists know this is a fallacy. Immigrants make a positive contribution to the economy through the goods and services they buy and the taxes they pay. They also have an important contribution to make towards filling skilled labour shortages in Canada. The Canadian Council of Human Resources Associations explains:

> [R]esearch has shown that without immigration there

would be only two ways to fuel the workforce: natural increase (more births than deaths) or movement from rural to urban areas. Both have levelled off in Canada in recent years, making the role of immigrants more important for the Canadian economy. (Canadian Council of HR Associations, 2008)

CONTEMPORARY MIGRATION ISSUES IN CANADA

Settlement Process

The need for a comprehensive, collaborative approach to the successful settlement and integration of newcomers in Canada is something that private, public, and voluntary sectors agree on. The Ontario Council of Agencies Serving Immigrants (1991, p. 8) defines the term "settlement" as a long-term process of change, adaptation, and integration for both the **newcomer** and Canada as a **host country**. Through this two-way process, newcomers achieve equity and the freedom to actively participate in Canada, and in return, Canada, as a host country, gains access to the full human resource potential in its newcomer communities.

The Canadian Council for Refugees describes settlement as a continuum whereby newcomers move from **acclimatization**, to adaptation, to **integration** (see Figure 11.2).

Newcomers to Canada have a wide variety of issues they must deal with upon arrival as part of their acclimatization stage. Learning or improving proficiency in English and/or French is one of the first steps in this process. The ability to communicate is integral to successful settlement and integration in Canada. Other critical issues include finding housing and employment, enrolling children in schools, finding a doctor, and making new friends (see Figure 11.3).

At the other end of this continuum is integration—a long-term process whereby newcomers become full, equal, and active participants in the institutions of their new host country (see Table 11.2). It is important to remember that while this continuum provides a model for newcomer settlement, each newcomer's experience is multifaceted and unique (Canadian Council for Refugees, 1998, p. 3).

While these are things we all must do in moving to a new community, it is a more complex process when coming from a different culture where the customs, norms, values, beliefs, and language may all be different. Newcomers' ability to adjust to a new culture can also be affected by how different their culture is from the culture of the host country. If, for example, their language, religion, and value system is radically

FIGURE 11.2
The Settlement/Integration Continuum

Acclimatization   Adaptation   Integration

Settlement is a multidimensional process and does not occur at a similar rate across all aspects of a newcomer's life. The model developed here illustrates a continuum of phases in the process, but it is important to remember that settlement is not a linear process. Settlement issues can arise long after newcomers arrive in Canada; issues evolve with changing needs. Newcomers may also be acclimatized in one dimension of their life, but not well integrated in other aspects.

Source: "Best Settlement Practices," Settlement Services for Refugees and Immigrants in Canada, Canadian Council for Refugees (February 1998).

FIGURE 11.3
Newcomer Needs and Challenges

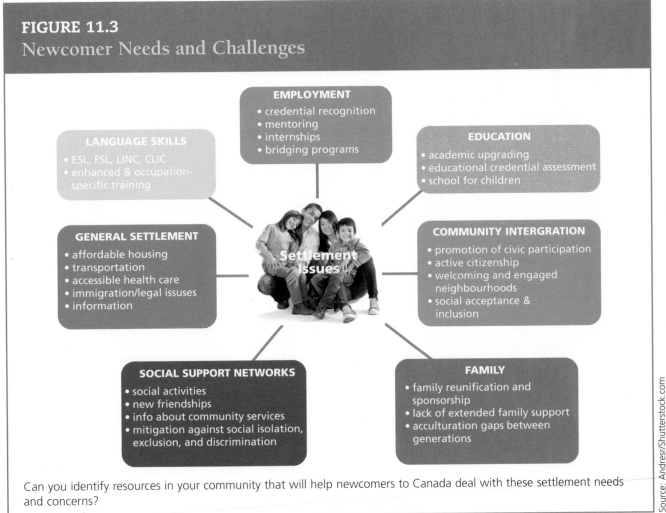

Can you identify resources in your community that will help newcomers to Canada deal with these settlement needs and concerns?

Source: Andresr/Shutterstock.com

different from the culture they are moving to, one could expect that their adjustment will take more time and may present other difficulties.

Other factors affecting settlement in a new country can include a person's pre-migration experiences (whether that person voluntarily chose to move or was forced to move), the individual attitude and personality of the newcomers, how receptive and welcoming a new culture is, and the support services available to help newcomers adjust. Many believe that the stress of the settlement process in Canada can affect the health of immigrants. There

TABLE 11.2
Possible Indicators of Settlement and Integration

DIMENSION	SHORT TERM (SETTLEMENT)	LONGER TERM (INTEGRATION)
Economic	entering job market financial independence	career advancement income parity entry into field of prior employment
Social	established social network diversity within social network	accessing institutions engaging in efforts to change institutions
Cultural	adaptation of various aspects of lifestyle (e.g., diet, family relationships)	engaging in efforts to redefine cultural identity adapting or reassessing values
Political	citizenship voting	participation in political parties participation in socio-political movements

Source: "Best Settlement Practices," Settlement Services for Refugees and Immigrants in Canada, Canadian Council for Refugees (February 1998).

IN THEIR SHOES

If a picture can say a thousand words, imagine the stories your shoes could tell! Try this student story on for size – have you walked in this student's shoes?

I will never forget my first day at work. No one talked to me. I was shown where the dishwasher was and shortly explained what to do. I worked ten hours that day; no one offered help or kind words. As I realized later, everyone assumed I was stupid. Because my language skills were basic, I was judged as without knowledge about anything. I was asked (in the period of the two months that I worked there) if we had a refrigerator back home and it was just collectively assumed that I had no exposure to technology and the modern world. I was at the bottom of the lowest class.

Today, I am not angry. I am aware of who I am and very proud of my ethnic background. However, I do feel a need to ask you to change and open up your views toward other people from different cultures. They have values and beauty specific to them as a group that can add variety, beauty, knowledge, etc., if you are willing to accept and respect them for who they are: great individuals and citizens of the world.

Healthy immigrant effect: Immigrants' health is generally better than the health of those born in Canada, but this declines as their years spent living in Canada increase.

is a complex relationship between migration and health, but research generally supports the conclusion that while recent immigrants' health is generally better than that of people who are born in Canadian (known as the **healthy immigrant effect**), this declines as their years in Canada increase. It is believed that the difficulties of settling and integration into Canada contribute to this phenomenon (Ng, 2011).

Canada's Receptivity to Newcomers

It would appear that with some exceptions, Canada has generally become a more welcoming nation for newcomers. Perhaps we have learned from moments in our history as a nation when our policies were clearly exclusionary. At first, Canada moved ideologically from xenophobia to **assimilation**, telling new immigrants that they would now be welcomed but they would have to melt into what was thought of as "Canadian" at that time. In 1947, for example, Prime Minister King stated in the House of Commons that "the people of Canada do not wish as a result of mass immigration to make a fundamental alteration in the character of our population" (Canadian Council for Refugees, 2000). Canada's receptivity to newcomers at that time is described by the former governor general of Canada, Adrienne Clarkson (2011, p. 32), in her recent book titled *Room for Us All*. She characterized Canada's receptivity as one of benevolent neglect—"so that people find themselves, sometime stumbling but without obstacles put in their way." As a result, many immigrants who arrived in Canada during the 1950s and 1960s relied upon their families and their ethnic communities to assist them with initial settlement, with the expectation that they would become self-sufficient as quickly as possible (Anzovino, 2009). In 1971, Canada implemented a new national policy called multiculturalism, and the celebration of our cultural diversity as a nation became one of the policy's underlying principles. Four decades later, Clarkson's book, a collection of immigrants' stories, continues to embrace the theme that Canadian culture has been enriched by the diversity of its immigrants. But today, the Canadian government provides significant funding for the language training and settlement services necessary to support the settlement and integration process of newcomers to Canada. While years from now, we may have to apologize for some exclusionary aspects of recent refugee law and policy changes, the process of settlement has certainly evolved from one of benevolent neglect.

Forced vs. Voluntary Pre-Migration

The motivation of an individual to come to live in Canada as a **permanent resident** has different implications for settlement here. For refugees or protected persons who are displaced, their settlement in Canada is often challenging. Forced to migrate, they do not have time to prepare for departure. They must learn to live in a new country while also dealing with issues that may include uncertainty about their future, **acculturative stress**, effects of war, effects of torture, loss of loved ones, and **post-traumatic stress disorder (PTSD)**. Immigrants who *choose* to come to this country, on the other hand, have time to prepare before their arrival. They usually have the opportunity to sell their homes, say goodbye to family members, and bring all of their documents and belongings.

Internationally Trained Immigrants

One of the biggest frustrations for immigrants remains credential recognition and employment in Canada. We invite highly trained immigrant professionals into Canada each year, only to deny them employment because their credentials are not recognized or equivalent here. This frustration is very palpable within immigrant communities.

CREDENTIAL RECOGNITION

The Canadian Council of Human Resources Associations notes that Canada's population and its workforce are undergoing demographic changes that will impact employers. We have a significant portion of our workforce made up of aging baby boomers who are getting close to retiring. There are fewer young people in the workforce, because of a declining birthrate (CCHRA, 2008). The demand for more highly skilled and educated workers is increasing at the same time as we have skilled immigrants arriving in Canada who have higher

Assimilation: Total re-socialization of individuals from one culture to another, such that traces of the former culture eventually deteriorate.

Permanent resident: According to the Canadian Immigration and Refugee Protection Act (2002), a person who has come to Canada and successfully applied and received immigration status to live here permanently.

Acculturation: The process of adaptation to a new culture, whereby prolonged contact between two cultures begins to modify both cultures.

Acculturative stress: Immigrants experience this stress when there are difficulties resulting from the *acculturation* process. The stress of this process increases when immigrants experience discrimination, language difficulties, and incongruencies in non-material aspects of culture.

Post-traumatic stress disorder (PTSD): A psychological disorder caused by a traumatic event involving actual or threatened death or serious injury to oneself or others; symptoms may include anxiety, depression, survivor guilt, sleep disturbances, and nightmares, impaired use or loss of memory, concentration difficulties, hyperarousal, hypersensitivity, suspiciousness, fear of authority, and paranoia.

levels of education and international expertise (CCHRA, 2008). Despite labour market demands, one of the most significant challenges faced by internationally trained immigrants is finding employment (OCASI, 2012).

This disconnect is highlighted in a series of television advertisements titled *Recognize Immigrant Credentials*, which dramatize this question: If Canada is a land of opportunity, then why is a doctor driving a cab, an MBA cleaning offices, and an engineer serving fast food? People applying to immigrate to Canada through the federal skilled worker program are assessed using a point system that is based on six selection factors: official language ability, education, employment experience, age, adaptability, and arranged employment in Canada. The individuals featured in these television advertisements have presumably received the maximum points allotted to potential applicants for their educational qualifications and

employment experience. Yet the likelihood that a new immigrant will work in his or her chosen profession in Canada is a dream that generally takes many years and much effort to realize (see Picture This). The cliché of overqualified immigrants driving taxis is supported to some extent in a study entitled *Who Drives a Taxi in Canada?*—taxi drivers do include internationally trained physicians, architects, engineers, and other highly trained professionals (Xu, 2012).

In recent years, for example, Canada's chronic shortage of physicians and increasing patient wait times could logically be mitigated by removing the institutional barriers and challenges that prevent internationally trained physicians from practising in Canada. Yet, we fail to make these connections. Internationally trained immigrants in the Canadian labour market boost innovation and reflect the markets in which Canadian organizations operate, thereby

PICTURE THIS...

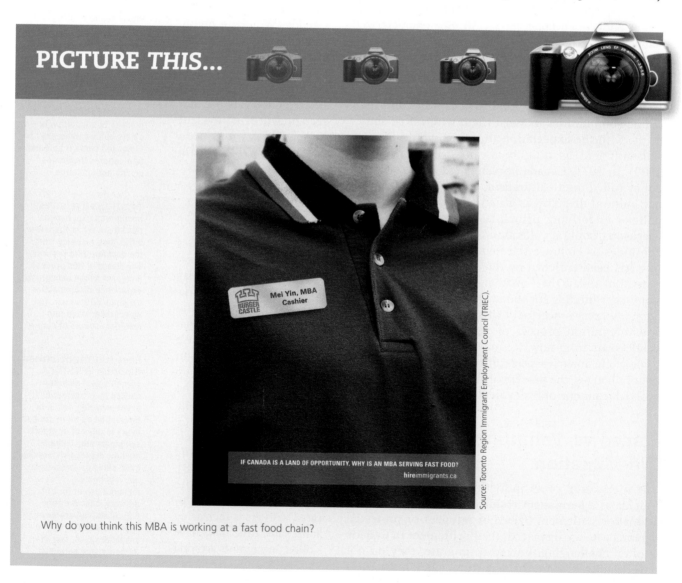

Source: Toronto Region Immigrant Employment Council (TRIEC).

IF CANADA IS A LAND OF OPPORTUNITY, WHY IS AN MBA SERVING FAST FOOD?
hireimmigrants.ca

Why do you think this MBA is working at a fast food chain?

ensuring that Canada remains competitive in the global marketplace and in a knowledge-based economy. According to the Conference Board of Canada (2001, p. 2), between "$4.1 and $5.9 billion is lost to the Canadian economy each year because of unrecognized qualifications." More than 340 000 Canadians possess unrecognized credentials, most likely to have come from China, India, and the Philippines (Conference Board of Canada, 2001). Canada is a nation with an aging population and declining birthrate, so we must resolve these labour force issues if Canadian businesses are going to be able to compete in the global marketplace.

Canada is a nation with emerging and growing labour shortages at the same time that it is a nation with a highly educated pool of skilled immigrants who are underemployed and unemployed. Why the disconnect? How do we fix it? Some suggest that the disconnect is a result of discrimination in hiring practices. Others suggest that the disconnect happens as a result of the way Canada selects skilled workers from overseas, further suggesting that the skilled workers program needs to meet existing labour shortages in the same way that temporary workers programs do. Simply put, this means that if, for example, there is a shortage of masons in Canada, then the applications of skilled workers who are masons would be prioritized.

WORK EXPERIENCE

There is a great deal of discussion and training happening among human resource professionals in Canada regarding the recruitment and selection of internationally trained professionals. Some of this activity is precipitated by labour market demands and the realization that the failure to recognize foreign credentials and experience is costing the Canadian economy billions of dollars. Human resources training is looking at strategies such as overcoming bias in resumé screening, inclusive interviewing strategies, and skills for managing a diverse workforce. The implementation of formalized bridging and internship programs have begun to address employers' concerns about lack of "Canadian experience."

There is a great deal of hope within the business sector, particularly the banking industry, which provides leadership in leveraging diversity and the skills of immigrants in a global economy. Take, for example, the Smart City Business Show in Halifax, which recently featured strategies used by the Royal Bank of Canada for recruitment of internationally trained immigrants. "Diversity for growth and innovation" is one of the Royal Bank's core values.

RBC Regional Vice President Glenn Doherty has highlighted the business case for hiring immigrants and the belief that having a workforce that reflects the population and the communities they serve and a workplace that offers all employees the opportunity to reach their potential, is simply the right thing to do. Greeted by employees who speak many different languages, the Royal Bank is using linguistic and cultural diversity as a business advantage (Smart City News, 2012).

Scotiabank is another example of an employer utilizing skilled immigrant talent as smart business. As a spokesperson for Hire Immigrants Ottawa, Denis Jackson, a senior executive with Scotiabank, discussed the importance of Ottawa's culturally diverse immigrant talent pool, and the ways in which Hire Immigrants Ottawa supports employers in hiring internationally trained immigrants. Similarly, IBM Canada's values include a workforce that is enriched by internationally trained immigrants who bring an indigenous understanding of consumers from a variety of cultures around the world and the linguistic competencies required for effective intercultural business communication.

The public sector provides numerous examples of mentorship and bridging programs for internationally trained immigrants. St. Michael's Hospital in Toronto is an exemplary public sector pioneer for programs that it has developed for internationally trained healthcare professionals. In 2003, the hospital created a formal mentorship program for internationally educated professionals (IEPs). In 2004, the hospital began a program to create paid internships for skilled immigrants, and this program is now embedded in St. Michael's recruitment practices. Later, the hospital created a new position of Specialist of Internationally Educated Professionals, which focuses on internal education programs for IEPs, increasing cultural sensitivity throughout the hospital, and advancing immigrant employment in the broader community. Also embedded in the organization's human resource practices is an IEP bridging program that offers support to skilled immigrants in integrating into the workplace, as well as training for managers and staff mentors on the challenges and opportunities IEPs experience. Its Newcomer Volunteer Program allows IEPs to gain Canadian experience with the benefit of feedback and insight from mentors. St. Michael's also participates in the CARE Centre for Internationally Educated Nurses, a program that helps internationally educated nurses prepare for an Ontario licence, among other career and education services. St. Michael's Hospital also provides mentoring, job shadowing, and bursaries (Toronto Region Immigrant Employment Council, 2011).

CANADA THIRTY YEARS FROM NOW

The federal election Leaders' Debate in 2011 highlighted the importance of immigration issues for Canadians. Jade Calver, a student at McGill University in Montreal, asked the candidates:

As a leader, how do you envision the social make-up of our country over the next thirty years? Where do you stand on reasonable accommodation? Do you think that immigrants should adopt the social practices of Canadians already living here or not? (Immigration Watch Canada, 2011)

The discussion and debate that ensued touched on everything from multiculturalism as a unifying social framework to the failure to adequately support newcomer settlement in Canada. Included in the debate were questions about whether family reunification remains an immigration priority when it is taking five to ten years to reunite family members separated through migration, and given the number of family class sponsorships that have been dropped.

Is Canada doing enough to fulfill our international obligations to the world's internally displaced persons and asylum seekers?

Is the increased use of temporary foreign workers the human resource strategy needed to fill skilled labour demands of the Canadian workplace? While temporary foreign workers may fill immediate skill shortages, is this a short-sighted strategy in terms of the business investment in human capital and retention of skilled employees in Canada? (Canadian Council of Human Resources Associations, 2008). Some suggest that the use of temporary workers is simply a method of importing cheap labour to Canada and that it disadvantages Canadian workers and undermines the long-term contributions made to the Canada economy by economic class immigrants.

Given Canada's demographic pressures resulting from a declining **birth rate**, an aging population, and resulting labour shortages, we will need to continue to look to immigration as a solution. Canada will need to find a real solution to the underemployment and unemployment of immigrants, beginning with foreign credential and work experience recognition. At the top of the humanitarian response agenda are concerns that Canada will need to engage in "the situation of unaccompanied and separated children, sexual and gender-based violence, the recruitment of children into armed forces, girls' schooling, equal access to services for women and men, and the participation of refugee women in decision-making bodies" (UNHCR Global Trends, 2010 p. 13). If we want to move forward as socially responsible global citizens, we will have to critically examine the "brain drain effect" of our immigration policies. A comprehensive and collaborative approach to settlement and international development will be key.

Birth rate: The number of live births per year per 1000 population.

ENDING THOUGHTS

Sam Richards is a sociology professor at Penn State University who teaches the largest race relations class in the United States. As he stands before his class of 700 students, he tells them that the one thing he will not stand for is hypocrisy. No one in the room self-identifies as Aboriginal, so Richards tells his students that everyone in the room is an immigrant, that all are there living on someone else's land. Someone let them or their ancestors enter the country, or forced them there, so the hypocrisy arises in saying to a would-be immigrant, "No, you can't come in" (Richards, 2009).

"No, you can't come in" is something that potential newcomers to Canada have heard since the first immigration act was implemented in 1867. Unless you are Aboriginal, you or your ancestors have immigrated here—some by choice and some by force. When settlers arrived in the "new world," Canada's Aboriginal communities did not say, "No, you can't come in." Rather, they often established treaties (usually oral agreements) with them. One such an agreement between the Haudenosaunee nation and Dutch settlers was solidified symbolically in a wampum belt made of two rows of purple wampum beads against a background of white beads.

Perhaps we can learn from the symbolism of the wampum beads as we welcome newcomers to Canada. The purple wampum beads symbolize the course of two vessels—a Haudenosaunee canoe and a European ship—which are travelling together in a parallel direction down the river of life, but which never touch. The parallel course of these vessels is an agreement that neither nation will try to steer the vessel of the other, stressing the importance of non-interference between the two nations. The three white rows of beads between the purple rows keep the nations bound together but separate; they symbolize respect, peace, and friendship (Iroquois Indian Museum, n.d.).

THE BITE OF THE MANGO

By Mariatu Kamara

The following is an excerpt taken from the book The Bite of the Mango, *which details Mariatu Kamara's unforgettable story as a child affected by war. Kamara was 12 years old when armed rebels attacked her village.*

Forward

By Ishmael Beah, New York, June 2008

In my culture, every story is told with the purpose of either imparting knowledge, repairing a broken bond, or transforming the listener and the teller. Mariatu's story embodies all of those elements. I have been waiting for such a story, one that reminds us all of the strength and resilience of the human spirit ... The light and joy in Mariatu's face don't show you that she is someone whose heart once said goodbye to everything she knew. Meeting this remarkable young woman changes one's idea of what it means to be a victim of war. The media often focus on the trauma people suffer, forgetting to tell us about their ability to recover and the humanity that remains intact. Mariatu's story gives that necessary human context to what it means to be both victim and a survivor, to transform your life and continue to live with vigor. I am deeply thankful that the world will be able to meet Mariatu through this book.

My name is Mariatu, and this is my story. It begins the year I was 11, living with my aunt and uncle and cousins in a small village in Sierra Leone.

I'd lived with my father's sister Marie and her husband, Allie, since I was a baby. I called them Ya for mother and Pa for father, as terms of endearment. It was common in my country for children in the rural areas to be raised by people other than their birth parents.

Our village of Magborou was small, like most villages in Sierra Leone, with about 200 people living there. There were eight houses in the village, made out of clay, with wood and tin roofs. Several families lived in each house. The adults slept in the smaller rooms, and we kids usually slept together in the living room, which we called the parlor. Everyone chipped in and helped each other out. The women would all cook together. The men would fix the roofs of the houses together. And we kids played together.

None of the kids in my village went to school. My family, like everyone else in Magborou, was very poor. "We need you to help us with chores on the farm," Marie explained ... Even though not everyone who lived in Marie and Allie's house was related by blood, we thought of each other as family, calling one another uncle, aunt and cousin. Mohamed and Ibrahim, two of my cousins, were already living in the village when I arrived as a baby. Magborou was a lively place, with goats and chickens running about and underfoot. In afternoons I played hide-and-seek with my cousins and friends, including another girl named Mariatu ... But then the rebels invaded our lives and everything changed ...

It all started during the dry season when I was 11. War had come to Sierra Leone, and our chairman heard that the violent rebels who were destroying villages and killing people in eastern Sierra Leone were headed toward Magborou. The rebels wanted to overthrow the government, which they accused of being corrupt and not helping people. The rebels were from different tribes across Sierra Leone, including Temne, like us, and I couldn't understand why they wanted to kill poor people or take over our villages, eat all our food and sleep our houses. But apparently they did.

Whenever we heard a rumor that the rebels were close, the chairman would order all of the villagers in Magborou to flee into the bush. The first time it happened, we abandoned our homes and took nothing with us, hiding in the bush for several days as we listened to our stomachs moan in hunger ... After a while, the hiding began to seem normal. We would spread out our straw mats in a forest clearing and stay there, sometimes for as long as a month ... As the rumors about the rebels grew more frequent, we had to keep quiet during our time in the bush. We stopped cooking our food so the rebels wouldn't see the smoke from our fires and sometimes all we ate for an entire day was raw cassava, which is very hard and dry and bland. Everybody talked in whispers. Chills ran through me whenever I'd hear a noise, such as a twig breaking in the bush behind the clearing. A few times I overheard the adults talking. They were saying that the rebels didn't just kill people, they tortured them. I didn't talk a lot in the forest after that ...

Then we saw them, coming out of one of the houses— soldiers of some sort, bare-chested, wearing khaki pants, with bullets wrapped around their muscled bodies. Adamsay began to run away. But a man came out of nowhere and caught her by the waist. He carried her back and threw her down in the dust beside me. He wore a red bandana around his head and had several guns slung over his shoulders.

I froze. "This is it," I thought. "Today is the day the rumors of the rebels prove to be true."

The soldier ordered me to take the palm oil down from my head. Behind him, I could see why everything was still: the soldiers had taken over the village, and they were going in and out of all the houses, looting them of people's possessions. They tossed most of the items onto a pile in the middle of the road.

Another soldier joined the first one, and the two pushed us into the village, to a spot by the side of the house. They ordered Adamsay and me to sit side by side on the ground. One of the men tied our hands behind our backs with a piece of scratchy rope. "Do you know who we are?" he asked with a toothy grin ...

Then everything began to happen fast. Too fast.

I heard voices coming from the house beside me. The rebels had blockaded the doors and windows with big wooden planks. Inside, one of the rebels told me, were about 20 people. A single voice stood out, that of my friend Mariatu. She was wailing, calling for help, trapped with the others.

My eyes darted away from the house to a terrifying sight. Two rebels were shoving Ibrahim and Mohamed up the road toward us. They were punching the boys in the back to get them to move faster. When my cousins were directly in front of us, the rebels grabbed them by the neck and pushed them down hard into the dirt. Using their gun barrels, the rebels nudged the boys until they were back to back. Then they tied Mohamed and Ibrahim together.

Next, the rebels forced the boys to stare up into the blinding noonday sun.

"Are you the soldiers watching the village?" one rebel yelled at them. "Are you the soldiers? Are you the soldiers?" he shouted over and over again. Mohamed and Ibrahim shook their heads, but the rebel would not relent.

The boys started crying. Ibrahim had wet his pants, and I watched the stain grow. I had to look away when the rebel began waving a knife around their bare backs and scalps.

I tried to find somewhere my eyes could rest, but the first place they landed was back on the house. Three young rebels, no older than me, were walking alongside it, brandishing torches that set the thatched roof on fire. Everyone inside started to scream as the fire became an inferno. A woman with a baby tied on her back managed to punch through the wooden planks blocking one of the windows. The baby had curly black hair and big eyes that were looking all around. One of the young rebels threw down his torch and grabbed the machete slung on his back. In one violent swoop, he chopped off the woman's head. The baby wailed as the woman's body fell back into the house on top of him. Her head rolled onto the road toward me. I started to cry again, and my body convulsed. "Do you want to join them?" the rebel watching over me threatened. Part of me did …

The rebel guarding us grabbed Adamsay by her braids and yanked her into a standing position. He shoved her into the arms of another rebel, who spun her around and dragged her by the hair down the road. I saw her, like a shadow, being pushed into the doorway of a house on the other side of the bonfire.

"Goodbye," my heart said to her. "Goodbye."

… After Adamsay disappeared into the house with the rebels, I closed my eyes and began to pray and pray and pray. This time, it wasn't for new clothes. "Please let me die quickly. Let it be over quickly. Let my family, if they have been captured by the rebels all die quickly, too. Don't let the rebels cut my body piece by piece."

I prayed hard, so hard my head began to throb. When I opened my eyes, there was a group of rebel boys staring right at me. If it hadn't been for their red eyes, their guns, and the knives in their hands, it would have been like opening my eyes after counting to a hundred during a game of hide-and-seek and finding the village kids smiling in front of me.

I felt dizzy. My eyes wouldn't focus. I stopped hearing things, and then my vision went too. I passed out.

When I came to, the first thing that struck me was the music. It pounded in my head. The men and boys were singing along to it, some even screaming lyrics that I couldn't understand. Above the singing, the rebels were yelling some words to each other that I recognized only later, when I moved to North America. *Rambo. Red Eye. Killer …*

I knelt down in front of my captors, lowered my head and waited. I wanted to show the older rebel that I would be obedient.

"Okay, little one," said the rebel as the second man walked away. "Get lost. We don't want you after all."

I wasn't sure I had heard the words correctly, so I remained still.

"You can go," the man repeated, waving his hand this time. "Go, go, go!"

I stood up slowly and turned my body toward the soccer field.

"Wait!" the rebel hollered. I stood motionless as a couple of the boys grabbed guns from their backs and pointed them at me. "You must choose a punishment before you leave," he said.

"Like what?" I mumbled. Tears I could no longer hold back streamed down my face.

"Which hand do you want to lose first?"

The knot in my throat gave way to a cream. "No," I yelled. I set off at a run for the soccer field, but it was not use. The older rebel caught me, his big arm wrapping around my belly. He dragged me back to the boy rebels and threw me to the ground in front of them.

Three boys hauled me up by the arms. I was kicking now, screaming and trying to hit. But though they were little boys, I was tired and weak. They overpowered me. They led me behind the outhouse and stopped in front of a big rock …

"Please, please, please don't do this to me, "I begged one of the boys. "I am the same age as you. You speak Temne. So you might be from around here. We could have been cousins had we lived in the same village. Maybe we can be friends."

"We're not friends," the boy scowled pulling out his machete. "And we are certainly not cousins."

"I like you," I implored, trying to get on his good side. "Why do you want to hurt someone who likes you?"

"Because I don't want you to vote," he said. One of the boys grabbed my right arm, and another stretched my hand over the flat part of the boulder.

"If you are going to chop off my hands, please just kill me," I begged them.

"We're not going to kill you," one boy replied. "We want you to go to the president and show him what we did to you. You won't be able to vote for him now. Ask the president to give you new hands."

Two boys steadied me as my body began to sway. As the machete came down, things went silent. I closed my eyes tightly, but they popped open and I saw everything. It took the boy two attempts to cut off my right hand. The first swipe didn't get through the bones, which I saw sticking out in all different shapes and sizes. He brought the machete down again in a different spot, higher up on my arm. This time, my hand flew from the rock onto the ground. The nerves kept it alive for a few seconds and it leapt from side to side, as trout did when we caught them from the river, before we knocked then on the head and killed them to cook for our evening meal.

I had not energy left as a boy took my other arm and held it down on the boulder. It took three attempts to cut off my left hand. Even at that, some of the flesh remained and hung precariously loose.

I didn't feel any pain. Maybe that was because my hands were still numb from having been tied together for so long. But my legs gave way. I sank to the ground as the boy wiped the blood off the machete and walked away.

As my eyelids closed, I saw the rebel boys giving each other high-fives. I could hear them laughing. As my mind went dark, I remember asking myself: "What is a president?"

The rebels during Sierra Leone's 10-year civil war cut off the arms and legs of civilians as a means of terrorizing the population.

Kamara survived having her own arms cut off and began an unimaginable journey that took her from the African bush to begging in the streets of Freetown to college in Canada. Today, Kamara is the UNICEF Special Representative for Children and Armed Conflict.

Source: *The Bite of the Mango* © 2008 by Mariatu Kamara and Susan McClelland, published by Annick Press. Reproduced by permission.

DISCUSSION QUESTIONS

1. What other countries use children as soldiers? Once a war is over, what do you think happens to these children? Do you think their emotional scars can ever heal? What can we do as global citizens to reduce the number of children fighting in armed conflict around the world?
2. Mariatu eventually immigrated to Canada as a refugee. What do you think are some of the major challenges she will face during her resettlement?
3. Pick a country anywhere in the world where you neither speak the language nor know much about its culture, history, people, and so forth. Imagine you are going to immigrate there voluntarily. What would you do to prepare before you moved there? What questions would you need answered? What would be some of your fears about immigrating there? What would you miss most about home? How would your migration experience be different from Mariatu's?

KWIP

KNOW IT AND OWN IT: WHAT DO I BRING TO THIS?

Unless you are an Aboriginal student, you may want to begin by knowing and owning that you have a personal history as an immigrant to Canada. Understanding this aspect of who you are may help you to understand and respect the migration experience of others. If you are an Aboriginal student, you may want to begin by examining your ancestors' history since inviting others to live on your land.

WALKING THE TALK: HOW CAN I LEARN FROM THIS?

As a non-Aboriginal student, you share a common history as an immigrant to Canada. As you reflect on what it was like for you or your ancestors coming to Canada, can you begin to identify with the experiences of others as immigrants? In moving from an *us-and-them* mentality, can you envision how *we* will build an inclusive society for Canada 30 years from now? As an Aboriginal student, how can you continue to teach the non-Aboriginal ancestors who came to live on your land respect for nations bound together but separate?

IT IS WHAT IT IS: IS THIS INSIDE OR OUTSIDE YOUR COMFORT ZONE?

Don't be surprised if you find that you have been challenged to move outside your comfort zone in this chapter.

Immigration is about the power to decide who gets to live where. Take the "Come to Canada" test on the Citizenship and Immigration Canada website at **http://www.cic.gc.ca/ ctc-vac/cometocanada.asp** to see if you have enough points to immigrate to Canada as a skilled worker. If you don't think immigration is about power, then try imagining a world without borders where you could move anywhere and live any place you wanted at any time—no visas, no applications, no hearings. The words "undocumented immigration" and "illegal migrants" would cease to exist.

PUT IT IN PLAY: HOW CAN I USE THIS?

Talk to your relatives and see where your family members came from. In many cases, an individual has to go back generations to find that a relative came to Canada from another country. If you can't find any starting information, then you should start from scratch. Go to one of the family tree websites (e.g., **http://www.ancestry.ca** has a free trial) to find out if any of your relations migrated here from another country. If that's the case, try to pinpoint the period in immigration history when they came to Canada. What was going on during that time? Has it in any way affected your family's name or occupation?

Use your sociological imagination to examine your own personal migration history. As we examine the history of Canada's policies, situate your own personal history within that framework.

CourseMate

Study Tools

Located at www.nelson.com/site/walkamile1e

- Consolidate your knowledge with the **Flashcards**.
- Gauge your understanding with **Picture This** and accompanying questions for reflection.
- Develop your critical thinking skills by working through **The Daily**.
- Apply your understanding with **KWIP** interactive!
- Develop your critical reading skills through compelling **Readings** and accompanying short answer questions.

REFERENCES

Abella, I. (2008). *None is too many: Canada and the Jews of Europe 1933–1948.* Toronto: Key Porter Books.

Anzovino, T. (2009). A national movement begins with one man named Isaac. World Cafe Presentation. Fort Erie, Ontario.

Beah, I. (2007). *A long way gone.* Vancouver: Douglas and McIntyre.

Bissoondath, N. (1994). *Selling illusions: The cult of multiculturalism in Canada.* Toronto: Penguin Books Canada.

Bouchard, G. (2007). The Canadian immigration system: An overview. Retrieved from *Institute for Research on Public Policy*: http://archive.irpp.org/miscpubs/archive/bouchard_immig.pdf

Canadian Council for Refugees. (1998). Best settlement practices. Retrieved from http://ccrweb.ca/bpfina1.htm

Canadian Council for Refugees. (2000). A hundred years of immigration to Canada 1900–1999. Retrieved from *Canadian Council for Refugees*: http://ccrweb.ca/en/hundred-years-immigration-canada-1900-1999

Canadian Council of Human Resources Associations. (2008). Integrating new Canadians into Canada and the workplace: Maximizing potential–white paper. Retrieved from *National Forums*: http://www.ccarh.ca/uploadedFiles/Content_-_Primary/National_Forum/CCHRA_White_Paper_FINAL.pdf

Canadian Security Intelligence Service. (2013, June 11). Security screening. Retrieved from *CSIS*: http://www.csis-scrs.gc.ca/prrts/scrt-scrnng-eng.asp#bm05

Canadians for Redress. (2002). History of Chinese head tax. Retrieved from *Canadians for Redress*: http://www.ccnc.ca/redress/history.html

CBC. (2011). Life after Auschwitz. Retrieved from CBC Digital Archives: http://archives.cbc.ca/war_conflict/second_world_war/topics/1579-10644/

CBC News. (2000, November 6). Canadian clergy apologize to 'Voyage of the Damned' survivors. Retrieved from *CBC News Canada*: http://www.cbc.ca/news/canada/story/2000/11/06/holocaust001106.html

Citizenship and Immigration Canada. (2006a, July 1). Forging our legacy: Canadian Citizenship and Immigration, 1900–1977. Chapter 1. Retrieved from *Citizenship and Immigration Canada*: http://www.cic.gc.ca/english/resources/publications/legacy/chap-1.asp

Citizenship and Immigration Canada. (2006b, July 1). Forging our legacy: Canadian Citizenship and Immigration, 1900–1977. Chapter 6. Retrieved from *Citizenship and Immigration Canada*: http://www.cic.gc.ca/english/resources/publications/legacy/chap-6.asp#chap6-3

Citizenship and Immigration Canada. (2009, May 6). Sponsoring your family. Retrieved from *Citizenship and Immigration Canada*: http://www.cic.gc.ca/english/immigrate/sponsor/index.asp

Citizenship and Immigration Canada (2010, September 9). Immigration overview: Permanent and temporary residents. Retrieved from *Citizenship and Immigration Canada*: http://www.cic.gc.ca/english/resource/statistics/facts2009/permanent/01.asp#category

Citizenship and Immigration Canada. (2013a, August 1). Facts and figures 2012 – Immigration overview: Permanent and temporary residents. Retrieved from *Citizenship and Immigration Canada*: http://www.cic.gc.ca/english/resources/statistics/facts2012/permanent/02.asp

Citizenship and Immigration Canada. (2013, August 23). Refugees. Retrieved from *Citizenship and Immigration Canada*: http://www.cic.gc.ca/english/refugees/

Clarkson, A. (2011) *Room for us all.* Toronto: Penguin Books Canada.

Conference Board of Canada. (2011). How Canada performs: A report card on Canada. Retrieved June 23, 2011, from *Conference Board of Canada*: http://www.conferenceboard.ca/e-library/abstract.aspx?did=4423

Danelius, H. (2002, December 18). Convention against torture and other cruel, inhuman or degrading treatment or punishment. Retrieved June 14, 2011, from *Audiovisual Library of International Law*: http://untreaty.un.org/cod/avl/ha/catcidtp/catcidtp.html

Harper, S. (2006, June 22). Prime Minister Harper offers full apology for the Chinese Head Tax. Retrieved May 21, 2011, from *Prime Minister of Canada Stephen Harper*: http://pm.gc.ca/eng/media.asp?id=1219

Immigration and Refugee Board of Canada. (2013, July 31). Immigration and Refugee Board of Canada's twentieth anniversary: The landmark Singh decision. Retrieved from http://www.irb-cisr.gc.ca/Eng/NewsNouv/NewNou/2009/Pages/singh.aspx

Immigration and Refugee Protection Act. (S.C. 2001, c 27). Retrieved from *Justice Laws Website*: http://laws-lois.justice.gc.ca/eng/acts/1-2.5/index/html

Immigration Watch Canada. (2011, April 15). The leaders' immigration debate. Retrieved June 2, 2011, from *Immigration Watch Canada*: http://www.immigration watchcanada.org/2011/04/19/april-15-2011-the-leaders-immigration-debate-how-things-went-downhill-fast/

Iroquois Indian Museum. (n.d.). What is wampum? Retrieved from *Iroquois Indian Museum*: http://www.iroquoismuseum.org/ve11.html

Kamara, M. (2008). *The bite of the mango*. Canada: Firefly Books.

Kazimi, A. (2012). *Undesirables: White Canada and the Komagata Maru*. Toronto: Douglas & McIntyre.

Komagata Maru incident [Gurdit Singh with passengers]. (1914). Retrieved from http://komagatamarujourney.ca/node/14661

Matas, D. (1985). Racism in Canadian immigration policy. *Refuge*, v5, n2.

Malenfant E.C., Lebel A., & Martel L. (2010). *Projections of the diversity of the Canadian population, 2006-2031* (Statistics Canada, Catalogue 91-551-X). Ottawa: Statistics Canada.

National Association of Japanese Canadians. (2008). The 20th Anniversary of the Japanese Canadian Redress Settlement Celebration and Conference. Retrieved May 2011 from *Japanese Canadian Redress Anniversary*: http://redressanniversary.najc.ca/redress/

Ng, E. (2011). Longitudinal health and administrative data research team. Insights into the healthy immigrant effect: Mortality by period of immigration and place of birth (Statistics Canada, Catalogue 82-622- X, Number 8) Ottawa: Statistics Canada.

Ontario Council of Agencies Serving Immigrants. (1991). Immigrant settlement counselling: A training guide. Toronto: OCASI.

Ontario Council of Agencies Serviing Immigrants. (2012). Making Ontario home 2012: A study of settlement and integration services. Toronto, Ontario, Canada. Retrieved from http://www.ocasi.org/downloads/OCASI_MOH _ENGLISH.pdf

Richards, S. (2009, September 9). Close that door. Retrieved from *YouTube*: http://www.youtube.com/watch?v=iyxWGqFQalY&feature=related

Roberts-Moore, J. (2002). Establishing recognition of past injustices: Uses of archival records in documenting the experience of Japanese Canadians during the Second World War. Archivaria: *The Journal of the Association of Canadian Archivists, 53* (2002), 64–75.

Say, A. (1993). *Grandfather's journey*. Boston: Houghton Mifflin Company.

Showler, P. (2006). *Refugee sandwich: Stories of exile and asylum*. Kingston: McGill-Queen's University Press.

Smart City News. (2012, September 12). Smart City Business: "Diversity for Growth and Innovation" feat. RBC, Season 2: Episode 1. (C. Layton, Ed.) Halifax, Nova Scotia.

Statistics Canada. (2007, September 10). The Immigrant Labour Force Analysis Series. Retrieved June 12, 2011, from *Statistics Canada*: http://www.statcan.gc.ca/pub/71-606-x/2007001/4129573-eng.htm

Statistics Canada. (2007, September 10). Study: Canada's immigrant labour market. Retrieved April 2, 2011, from *Statistics Canada*: http://www.statcan.gc.ca/daily-quotidien/070910/dq070910a-eng.htm

Statistics Canada. (2012, October 24). 2011 census of population: Linguistic characteristics of Canadians. Retrieved from *The Daily*: http://www.statcan.gc.ca/daily-quotidien/121024/dq121024a-eng.htm

Thomas, G., & Witts, M. M. (1974). *Voyage of the damned*. Konecky & Konecky.

Toronto Region Immigrant Employment Council. (2011). The mentoring partnership. Retrieved from *Toronto Region Immigrant Employment Council*: http://triec.ca/?nr=1

United Nations High Commissioner for Refugees. (2013). 2012 global trends: Refugees, asylum-seekers, returnees, internally displaced and stateless persons. Retrieved from http://www.unhcr.org/4c11f0be9.html

United Nations High Commissioner for Refugees. (2010a). The 1951 Refugee Convention: The legislation that underpins our work. Retrieved from *UNHCR*: http://www.unhcr.org/pages/49da0e466.html

Xu, L. (2012, March). Who drives a taxi in Canada? Retrieved from *Citizenship and Immigration Canada*: http://www.cic.gc.ca/english/pdf/research-stats/taxi.pdf

Multiculturalism

> *"It takes every kinda people to make the world go round"*
>
> *(Robert Palmer, 1978)*

DIVERSITY COMPETENCIES

Diversity competencies are specifically learned behaviours that students can actively practise to promote equity and inclusion. By mastering this unit, students will gain the skills to become diversity-competent practitioners, including the ability to

- trace the history and various definitions of multiculturalism

- distinguish between multiculturalism and diversity

- assess whether or not multiculturalism is working in Canada

- reflect upon multiculturalism as a unifying and inclusive national identity and as a divisive and marginalizing reality

Upon the death of one of this century's greatest moral leaders, Nelson Mandela, we recall the inspiration he found in Canada's respect for diversity. In Mandela's first address to Canadian parliament (McQuigge, 2013) he remarked, "your respect for diversity within your own society and your tolerant and civilized manner of dealing with the challenges of difference and diversity had always been our inspiration." As a nation, we take pride in the fact that we were the first country in the world to adopt multiculturalism as an official policy that affirmed the value and dignity of all citizens of this racially, ethnically, linguistically and religiously diverse society. And while we know that Canadian multiculturalism creates a sense of belonging and is interwoven with our belief that all citizens are equal, the framework and definition of multiculturalism continues to change.

What does it mean to live in a country where hundreds of thousands of immigrants are welcomed each year? Is multiculturalism a fundamental right or freedom? Is it a policy or a law? Is it a political ideology that is mandated differently through varying government factions?

For some, multiculturalism simply boils down to traditions, customs, and costumes that are worn at folk festivals and annual celebrations—like Canadian Multiculturalism Day, celebrated on June 27 of each year. Others see it as a movement toward the inclusion of all people who are marginalized or disenfranchised—yet welcomed—into Canada every year. Still others see it as an imposition on what they view is "their" Canada. Whatever your viewpoint is, two things are certain. First, as a society, we will likely never agree on a universal definition of multiculturalism. Second, we must never stop trying to create one.

IN THEIR SHOES

If a picture can say a thousand words, imagine the stories your shoes could tell! Try this student story on for size – have you walked in this student's shoes?

"Where are you from?" I can't begin to count the number of times I have been asked this question. I am Canadian. I was born in Canada and have lived here all of my life. I have a Canadian passport and am proud to call myself Canadian. I know that I am privileged to be born in this great nation. I am bilingual in English and French. My parents are originally from Africa, but came to Canada before I was born. I attended elementary and secondary school in Canada. I am now attending college, studying in a Police Foundations program. I hope to one day be employed as a police officer where I will uphold the laws of Canada. So why do people frequently ask me the question, "Where are you from?" Why do they assume that my sense of belonging and my national identity are acquired elsewhere?

Since about grade three, I remember teachers talking about Canada as a multicultural country. They used metaphors like mosaics and mixed green salads to illustrate how as a nation, Canada too was made up of distinct pieces and ingredients. We were taught that with the exception of Aboriginal peoples, all Canadians are immigrants to Canada or descended from immigrants. People have labelled me as a second-generation Canadian. One person even labelled my oldest brother as 1.5-generation Canadian because he was born in Africa but came to Canada with my parents when he was 10 years old. You can only imagine how many jokes were made about "one and a half."

So why are people so eager to identify others by their migration history? Is it relevant? I have friends who are "second-generation Canadian" and the only things we have in common are that our parents immigrated to Canada and we love soccer. I don't come from the same country as them. We don't share the same religion, culture, customs or traditions. I spoke English at home with my parents growing up; they didn't. They attended ESL classes in elementary school. I didn't. In fact I have more in common with friends who are "fourth- and fifth-generation Canadian," so why not just identify us as Canadian—period. Isn't that what multiculturalism is all about—we can be different but we still "belong" as part of the whole?

If ethnic and racial diversity and integration are really part of Canadian multiculturalism, then why do people still ask me on a regular basis where I come from? When I tell them I am Canadian, I can usually predict their next question: "But where were you born?" When I tell them Fort Erie, I can usually predict their next question: "Is that in Canada"? And you might think it would end there. But I have had people ask me where I learned to speak such good English, how long have I been in Canada, if they had McDonald's restaurants back where I came from and where did I learn to skate?

Now I just wear a t-shirt that says, "My name is John and I am CANADIAN."

Debating what multiculturalism is and what it is not means questioning the value and rights of immigrants as they attempt to rebuild their lives in new surroundings. As the face of Canadian society continues to change, we must continue to ask ourselves if multiculturalism in Canada is working. Conversations surrounding multiculturalism in Canada must continue to be open and ongoing until inclusion and equality for all become the norm.

CANADIANS ARE NOT AMERICANS

It's not always easy living next door to the world's largest economic, military, and cultural giant. Canada can often feel like a satellite in America's planetary orbit. But in many ways, Canada defines itself and its culture specifically by distinguishing itself from its neighbour. In 1990, sociologist Seymour Martin Lipset proposed that one of the most important defining elements of Canadian identity was that Canadians have historically defined themselves as "not Americans" (Lipset, 1990).

Though many have contested this, it's hard not to use the United States as a point of reference against which to determine our own national culture. Nowhere is this matter better illustrated than with Canada's stance on multiculturalism. Recent polls show that Canadians consider multiculturalism a fundamental Canadian value (Mosaic Institute, 2012). Further, they are quick to point out the distinction between "our multiculturalism" and "their multiculturalism." The United States has the famous **melting pot model**, where newcomers are expected to dissolve that which makes them different into a "pot" mixed with everyone else. This model was formally rejected in the Canadian Charter of Rights and Freedoms in favour of the **mosaic model**, where newcomers maintain their unique and distinct cultures and live alongside other Canadians with other distinct cultures. The important difference centres around how much newcomers to Canada are expected to shed their traditional cultures in order to **assimilate** into the broader majority culture. The mosaic model, in theory, asserts that all Canadians have the right to maintain their own distinct cultures, as long as the values expressed do not clash with Canadian laws and values. And that's where multiculturalism gets messy.

Is Multikulti a Failure?

In 2010, German Chancellor Angela Merkel announced to the world that the so-called "*multikulti*" concept—where people would "live side-by-side" happily—did not work, and immigrants needed to do more to **integrate** (Evans, 2010). Her comments came alongside a rising wave of anti-immigration sentiments that were sweeping across Europe at the time, and which are continuing to do so. Here, decades after Pierre Trudeau's government enshrined multiculturalism as a national value and a law in Canada, social and political commentators claim we have gone too far with the experiment. Multiculturalism has been called a cult and a governmental money-drain, and it has been blamed for ethnic ghettos, violence against women, a lack of a cohesive national identity, and **home-grown terrorism**. Nor is it just extreme right-wing politicians blowing the whistle on immigration. According to Transatlantic Trends (an annual survey of American and European public opinion), the strongest opposition to multiculturalism in Germany and France comes from the left (Todd, 2011a).

Great Britain's commitment to multiculturalism naturally took a sharp blow after the subway bombings in July of 2005. Overnight, low-grade grumblings became full-fledged and feverish protests against the nation's perceived over-acceptance of "foreigners." There was an immediate demand for newcomers (and long-established ethnic ghettos) to start assimilating and dropping any allegiances to other countries. Months later, ethnic riots erupted in North African and Arab neighbourhoods in France after a French police chase of a group of North African teenagers ended in two fatal electrocutions. Nine thousand cars and hundreds of buildings were destroyed in the ensuing race riots. But in France's case, multicultural policy could hardly be blamed: France has always insisted on a strict **assimilationist policy** (Gregg, 2006) for immigrants.

In the Netherlands, a country which prides itself on its broad tolerance towards immigrants and which took on an aggressive multicultural policy in the 1980s, the

Melting pot model: Immigration model, made famous by the United States, wherein newcomers are expected to dissolve that which makes them different into a "pot" mixed with everyone else.

Mosaic model: The Canadian immigration model in which newcomers are encouraged to maintain their unique and distinct cultures and live alongside other Canadians with other distinct cultures.

Assimilation: The process by which minority group members adopt the culture of the dominant group until they become indistinguishable from the dominant group; often referred to as the "melting pot."

Integrate: Become an accepted part of mainstream culture.

Home-grown terrorism: Acts or plans of mass violence for political purposes that are initiated and/or carried out by residents or citizens as opposed to foreign nationals.

Assimilationist policy: Policy that encourages immigrants to integrate into the mainstream culture.

retreat has been swift and startling. The nation has now instituted a restrictive visa system; unless immigrants come from one of the exempt (wealthy) nations, anyone wishing to live in the Netherlands now must submit to a rigorous civic-integration examination, including components that test their compatibility with liberal Dutch values in the form of films depicting homosexuality and nude beaches. Under the new policy, Dutch men and women of foreign descent would not be able to sponsor a spouse if that spouse did not also pass the exam. The government claims that it is simply responding to public opinion, where polls show 90% of Dutch citizens wanting a more assimilationist integration policy (Bransten, 2006).

Even intergovernmental groups have joined in the condemnation of multiculturalism, with the Council of Europe calling it "the flip side of assimilation, equally based on the assumption of an irreconcilable opposition between majority and minority" (Kymlicka, 2010) and blaming the naïve acceptance of a live-and-let-live attitude for increasing ethnic **segregation** and marginalization throughout the continent.

The high unemployment rates, low education levels, and general view that immigrants are not successfully integrating in many European countries have put Canada in the spotlight. Some countries, such as Sweden, recognizing that what they've done historically has not worked, are looking westward. In their book *Kanadamodellen* ("The Canada Model"), editors Peter Hojem and Martin Adahl examine the various factors that have allowed Canada to be seen as the promised land where people of hundreds of different backgrounds are able to live and work together in relative peace and prosperity (Saunders, 2011).

Ironically, just as Canada is being presented as a possible solution to Europe's ethnic conflicts, Canadian policymakers are considering adopting a more European model of immigration, favouring temporary guest workers as future residents (Saunders, 2013). **Guest workers** are immigrants who come in essentially as guests of their employers, with few rights and even fewer opportunities for permanent residency. Their numbers are now starting to eclipse the numbers of traditional economic immigrants whose goal is eventual Canadian citizenship (Saunders, 2013; Yalnizyan, 2011).

Canadians themselves have become somewhat ambivalent about their own multicultural reality. Almost half of Canadians polled in 2010 believed immigrants should give up their customs and traditions and more closely assimilate to the majority culture (Angus Reid, 2010). But this view is the exact opposite of what the nation has been known for. Is *multikulti* failing in Canada too?

Because one of the perceived goals of the Canadian model of multiculturalism is to allow diverse communities to retain their various backgrounds without

Bhola Chauhan and Harnarayan Singh broadcast *Hockey Night in Canada* in Punjabi. They may not be as flashy as Don Cherry, but they manage to draw a lot of fans.

having to assimilate to succeed in Canada, there was always the possibility that historic ethnic tensions would find their way to Canadian soil. When a Canadian politician of Croatian descent appeared on television in 1991 and proclaimed, "I don't think I'd be able to live next door to a Serb," it was immediately taken as proof that this fear was already a reality: that Canada was **balkanizing**, or dividing into hostile groups (Bissoondath, 1988).

Backlash against multiculturalism is not simply a matter of anti-immigrant sentiment. Opponents of multiculturalism claim that the Canadian model doesn't so much respect the diversity of its population as it treats its various ethnic groups as archetypes, not individuals—viewing the superficial differences as exotic, and turning various ethnic traditions into an amusement park ride (Bissoondath, 1994). There is also the danger that ethnic minorities themselves do not want recognition as such. A study of recent Colombian immigrants found that 13% of the sampled group responded that they rarely, if ever, listened to Colombian music, read Colombian periodicals, or ate Colombian food. That same group indicated that they spend little or no time with other Colombians. More importantly, over 90% of the study respondents felt that interacting with other ethnic groups was particularly important (Urzúa, 2010). Is multiculturalism putting Canadians in boxes they don't want to be in?

While immigrants often do better in Canada than they do elsewhere, it could be a result not

Segregation: Imposed separation of different groups, usually unequally.

Guest worker: Foreign worker who is only allowed to live in the country as a "guest" of his or her employer on a temporary basis.

Balkanize: Divide into hostile groups; refers to what happened when Yugoslavia was dissolved.

of our multicultural policy, but of the fact that our immigration policy cherry-picks the best and brightest of those seeking to come. After all, refugees make up only a small fraction of Canada's immigrant numbers, especially compared to other Western countries who either share a land border with poorer nations (such as the United States) or are an obvious sea voyage port (such as Australia; Kymlicka, 2012). Canada does not have to worry about illegal immigration. Essentially, immigrants who come to Canada are those whom the government has allowed to come.

In 2005, Bernard Ostry, one of the original architects of Trudeau's multiculturalism policy, sounded a tepid retreat from the direction Canada had been going for the past 40 years (Kymlicka, 2012). Was multiculturalism just forcing everyone into different corners?

DIVERSITY VS. MULTICULTURALISM

One often hears these words used interchangeably. "Come join our diverse workforce!" "Toronto is so multicultural!" "Look at all those ethnic markets; so much culture!" Most people have come to believe "diversity" and "multiculturalism" mean the same thing. They don't.

Diversity is a fact; multiculturalism is a policy—or in some cases, a theory. It is entirely possible to have a diverse population that maintains one distinct **monoculture**—essentially, a culture that contains no diversity. Similarly, there may very well be areas within Canada that have enthusiastically signed on to multicultural policies, but have no ethnic, religious, or other diversity to show for it.

Monoculture: Culture containing little or no diversity.

Cultural relativism: Assumption that all cultures are essentially equally valuable and should be judged according to their own standards.

Anglo- or Franco-conformity: Policy that informed early Canadian immigration; immigrants were expected to conform to dominant British-based or French-based culture as opposed to retaining their own.

That Canada is a culturally diverse nation is undeniable. Whether in major metropolises like Vancouver, Montreal, or Toronto, or in far-flung rural Northern communities, the near-homogeneity found at the turn of the 20th century is now almost impossible to find. Where the population once consisted of almost 90% British or French origin, the 2011 National Household Survey reports respondents from over 200 ethnic origins (Statistics Canada, 2013).

In addition to the two official languages sanctioned and protected by name in the Constitution, there are now over 200 languages spoken in homes across Canada (Canadian Press, 2012b); and some of these languages have now escaped the confines of the home and made their way onto street signs and shop windows. One has only to walk along almost any street in Canada to find ample evidence of the diversity of this nation.

But diversity is a fact, not a moral choice. To return to a comparison with the United States, for every Caribana festival in Toronto, there is an equally colourful and "ethnic" festival in the United States—Carifest in Baltimore, Bayou Bacchanal in New Orleans, and dozens of other Caribbean festivals throughout the country. So what makes Canada different? When multiculturalism became an officially recognized policy in our Constitution, did we automatically become more diverse? More tolerant?

One way to understand multiculturalism and its relationship to diversity is that multiculturalism can refer to governmental policies that aim to manage a diverse population. Multiculturalism can be descriptive or prescriptive: demographics or policy. For this textbook, we will examine the issues from the prescriptive angle.

Multiculturalism is often characterized as an "anything-goes" celebration of superficial differences where **cultural relativism** allows independent subcultures to live outside the bounds of the law. But neither the architects nor the proponents of multicultural policy ever intended or allowed for a flouting of the law. Anything that violates federal law—regardless of whether it is a cultural norm elsewhere—remains illegal for anyone living in Canada.

The Architecture of Multiculturalism

Now that multiculturalism is a buzzword, it's hard to remember a time when it wasn't even mentioned. No matter the future direction Canada takes with regard to its diverse population, it will forever retain the distinction of being the first nation to implement an official policy of multiculturalism. How did this happen? Where did this come from?

Perhaps a historical rather than a geographic comparison would clarify matters. Though not enshrined in official federal documents, the general policy that informed early Canadian immigration and that preceded multiculturalism was known as **Anglo- or Franco-conformity**.

Immigrants were expected to conform to dominant British-based or French-based culture as opposed to retaining their own. In the years leading up to World War II, English-speaking Canada had no identity crisis. Canada was a British outpost and proud of it. The only acceptable "ethnic" affiliation was to England and to a lesser degree, France; all other ethnic identities were to be purged, and new immigrants were encouraged to assimilate—and the sooner the better. This was relatively easily done, as the immigration policies discouraged large numbers of visible minorities ("non-Caucasian") unless they were needed as cheap labour (e.g., the building of the Canadian Pacific Railway). The Empire Settlement Scheme of the 1920s explicitly stated the preference of British immigrants to the prairies. Although not preferred, central and Eastern Europeans were considered acceptable, but only in limited number and capacity—namely, as agricultural and domestic workers (Belanger, 2006). But in addition to the hostility and **xenophobia** that many of these new immigrants faced (including the internment of 5000 Ukrainian men in enemy camps during World War I), official laws were enacted to enforce English-only instruction in schools (Stoddard, 2012).

The final "caste" of undesirables consisted of all **visible minorities**. Section 38 of the Canadian Immigration Act of 1910 gave the federal government the right to forbid entry "of immigrants belonging to any race deemed unsuited to the climate or requirements of Canada." Among those deemed unsuited to immigrate to Canada were those from "warm climates"—in other words, those who could fully assimilate but would never really be "Canadian" (Belanger, 2006).

By the 1960s, the federal government introduced the idea of the non-racist points system allowing for immigration from non-European countries to increase (Belanger, 2006). While this changed the demographics of Canada, it would still be a decade before the ideology caught up. At this point in the story, the assumption is that multicultural policy was enacted as a direct result of this demographic shift. History, however, tells a different story.

Early Multiculturalism

THE QUIET REVOLUTION

Ironically, **Quebec nationalism** is at least partly responsible for Canada as we know it today. In the 1960s, rumblings of the **separatist movement** that sought separation from Canada to form a smaller independent nation could be heard throughout the province. Campaigning under slogans of "Maîtres chez nous" ("Masters of our house") and "Il faut que ça change" ("Things must change"), the **Quiet Revolution**, a period in the 1960s, was poised to split the

nation in two. This spurred Prime Minister Lester B. Pearson's government to engineer policies that would enshrine the place of both England and France as "founding nations" and woo Quebec back from the brink of secession. This included making the country officially bilingual at all levels of government with the Official Languages Act of 1969 (Stoddard, 2012). But in trying to appease one group, the Canadian government awoke another group who watched these developments with concern.

Did making Canada officially **bilingual** and **bicultural** mean that there was no room for other ethnicities? This was the message that "white ethnics"—Ukrainians, Poles, Germans, Jews—across Canada received. Many of these groups were the ones forced to give up their own languages shortly upon arrival in Canada. Why should they now be forced to recognize French? These groups mobilized and began to put pressure on the government to ensure that they would be included as full Canadians in the "new Canada," and that French-speaking Quebec wouldn't be given higher accord at their expense. After all, they had proven themselves as model citizens, building the country in its early years, and fighting in two world wars. In response, the federal government commissioned a report clumsily entitled "The Cultural Contributions of Other Ethnic Groups in Canada," which laid out 16 recommendations to recognizing the "other ethnic groups" (Kymlicka, 2010).

THE FORMATIVE STAGE OF MULTICULTURALISM: PLURALISM

This is how the current formulation of Canada's

Xenophobia: An irrational fear attached to anyone or anything perceived as foreign.

Visible minority: People, other than Aboriginal people, who are non-Caucasian in race or non-white in colour.

Quebec nationalism: The belief that Quebec should be recognized as a sovereign and separate nation.

Separatist movement: A movement that seeks separation from a nation to form a smaller independent nation, as with Quebec nationalism.

Quiet Revolution: Period during the 1960s when Quebec saw rapid secularization and an increased sense of nationalism.

Bilingual: Able to speak two languages; in Canadian history, the official recognition of English and French as equal official languages.

Bicultural: Retaining two distinct cultural identities; in Canadian history, it often refers to the recognition of England and France as primary cultures within Canada.

multicultural policy started to emerge. The government's attempts at a bilingual country expanded to include a somewhat broader multiculturalism within that framework. As Will Kymlicka put it, "The formula which gradually emerged—namely multiculturalism within a bilingual framework—was essentially a bargain to ensure white ethnic support for the more urgent task of accommodating Quebec" (Kymlicka, 2004, p. 7). What this means is that Canada's multiculturalism was not initially an attempt to be inclusive of a diverse nation of visible minorities. Perhaps it could be argued that we didn't quite know what we were in for with this bargain.

The period between 1971 and 1985 is considered the formative stage of multiculturalism (Urzu'a, 2012). Prior to this period, the default policy in most cases was Anglo-conformity. But before it became a nationally recognized value, in its earliest form, official Canadian multiculturalism only existed in the context of Prime Minister Pierre Trudeau's speech to the House of Commons:

> Cultural **pluralism** is the very essence of Canadian identity. Every ethnic group has the right to preserve and develop its own culture and values within the Canadian context. To say that we have two official languages is not to say we have two official cultures, and no particular culture is more official than another. (Trudeau, 1971)

The resulting policy pledged to do the following:

1. Recognize and respect the multicultural nature of Canada's population.
2. Eliminate any barriers to full participation for all Canadians, regardless of ethnic origin.
3. Enhance the development of communities with shared origins and recognize their contributions to Canada.
4. Ensure equality of all Canadians.
5. Preserve the use of languages other than Canada's two official languages.
6. Foster multiculturalism through social, cultural, economic, and political institutions (Hyman, Meinhard, & Shields, 2011).

Much of the early support went into funding folk festivals and artistic programs. It's important to recognize that the early policy was intent on new Canadians retaining their heritage; no funding was provided for the Métis, First Nations, or long-established black Canadian communities. That was to come in the next iteration of multicultural policy in the 1980s (Hyman, Meinhard, & Shields, 2011).

THE EXPANSIONIST (INSTITUTIONALIZATION) STAGE

After the formative stage, Canada entered the **expansionist** or **institutionalization** stage of official multiculturalism, where multiculturalism was formally recognized and institutionalized as law (Urzu'a, 2012). The 1988 revamp of the policy saw Parliament's passing of the **Canadian Multiculturalism Act**, which aimed to preserve and enhance multiculturalism in Canada. In addition to the continued emphasis on the celebration of diversity, the act recognized the changing nature of Canadian demographics and placed special emphasis on eliminating the growing racial tensions and subsequent social exclusion of new visible minorities. This era saw the birth of the **Employment Equity Act** of 1986, which specifically addressed the barriers faced by women, Aboriginal peoples, persons with disabilities, and members of visible minorities. The legislation insists that it is not enough to merely treat everyone the same, but that an effort must be made to accommodate differences (Abella, 1984).

In 1996, the Heritage Department began a review of multicultural policy, and the resulting findings concluded that the "non-diverse" segments of the population had a duty to allow immigrants and minorities to more fully integrate, including a more aggressive push towards hiring quotas (Gingrich, 2004). The backlash to this was seen almost immediately in cries of reverse-discrimination, and this period witnessed the lowest satisfaction with multiculturalism since its inception.

Ensuing budget cuts began chipping away at the funding for multiculturalism, and today it is a subprogram within the Department of Canadian Heritage, encompassing a far wider category of diverse groups (Nilsen, 2001).

Pluralism: Existence of recognized diverse groups within a single (peaceful) society.

Expansionism: A country's practice or policy of getting bigger, usually in terms of territory or currency.

Institutionalization: The process of making something part of an already established, formalized system.

Canadian Multiculturalism Act: Law passed in 1988 that aims to preserve and enhance multiculturalism in Canada.

Employment Equity Act: Law that requires employers in Canada to eliminate barriers to and increase the hiring of women, people with disabilities, Aboriginal people, and visible minorities.

PICTURE THIS...

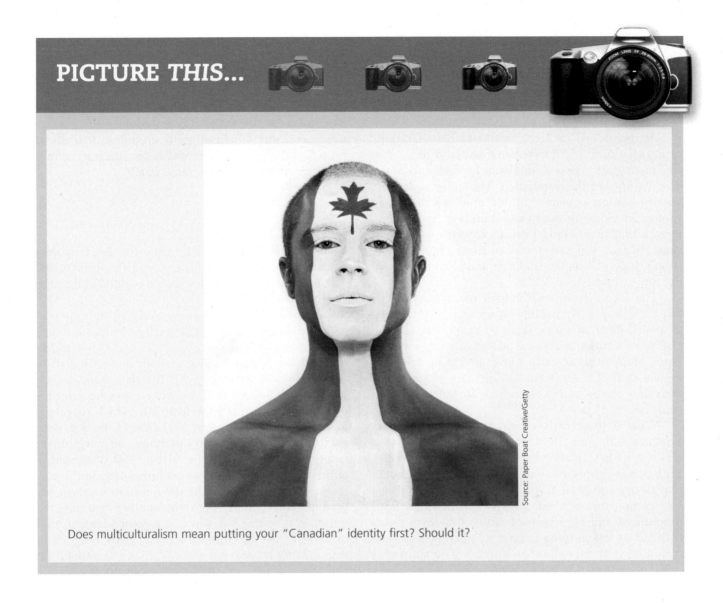

Does multiculturalism mean putting your "Canadian" identity first? Should it?

Source: Paper Boat Creative/Getty

DOES CANADIAN MULTICULTURALISM WORK?

Canada has been hailed all over the world as a successful, functioning model of multiculturalism done right. They are perhaps too polite to admit it, but Canadians—in government, in the press, in the streets—take pride in this and wonder why other Western countries seem to keep getting it wrong. A statistical outlier, Canada has managed to maintain all the markers of modern success—economic prosperity, a thriving democracy, and individual freedom—with high levels of immigration, without resorting to assimilationist policies. It is no wonder that Canadians have taken such pride in their reputation.

International leaders and organizations ranging from former U.S. president Bill Clinton to the United Nations have looked to Canada as the leader in the field of multiculturalism and have set up think tanks to examine why and how it works. All the indices of success are there: high intermarriage rate, high citizenship rate, high levels of acquisition of one or both official languages, and a significantly high level of political participation at the voter level as well as in terms of elected officials.

But one of Canada's leading scholars of political philosophy argues that far from Canada's success resulting from unique policy, it is a set of fortunate circumstances that have allowed Canada's multiculturalism to work while other Western countries have faced emphatic anti-immigrant backlash. Some governments—of Australia, England, and the Netherlands, for example—are sounding the retreat from their attempts. In fact, Australia, the only country that accepts more immigrants per capita than Canada, jettisoned the term "multiculturalism" altogether from its federal vocabulary. In 2007, it replaced the Department of Multicultural Affairs with the Department of Immigration and Citizenship (Kymlicka, 2012).

As mentioned earlier, Canada's earliest iterations of multiculturalism referred to "white ethnics." For the most part, these Canadians looked and acted like majority of the population. The differences were mostly benign—cuisine, ethnic clothing, language spoken by elders in the home—and they had already proven that they would provide no clash of civilizations. In fact, most, if not all of these groups, came from a Judeo-Christian tradition and shared many of the same values.

The face of multiculturalism today is very different. These early ethnic groups have now been absorbed as "real Canadians" to make way for the visible minorities who now take centre stage in the issue. Many of these early ethnic groups, in fact, feel a great deal of resentment towards later immigrants who they see as taking advantage of their hard-won gains in acceptance.

What if these early ethnic groups were seen as bringing with them illiberal ideas and practices that clashed with Canada's Western democratic ideals? This is not simply the early prejudicial xenophobia that all newcomers to Canada faced when the country was young; this is a real question with which both proponents and opponents of multiculturalism today contend. It is one thing to have a Polish perogy festival; it is another to allow cock-fighting—a sport that is widely engaged in all over the world, particularly in Latin American countries. It is one thing to build a museum to recognize the suffering of Jews during World War II; it is another to allow female genital mutilation (FGM), a practice that is common in many parts of Africa and Asia Minor. These are the kinds of issues that are simmering and have flared up repeatedly since the 1970s.

But a simple comparison between immigrants of similar backgrounds coming to Canada and the United States illustrates that—all other things being equal—immigrants to Canada are more quickly able to feel "Canadian," despite being allowed and encouraged to retain their ethnic heritage, than immigrants to the United States are able to feel "American." Irene Bloemraad, a sociology professor at the University of California at Berkeley, conducted studies comparing Vietnamese and Portuguese immigrants of similar socioeconomic and language backgrounds coming to Boston and Toronto. In both cases, the Toronto group was found to have a far higher sense of citizenship in their new country and was more actively participating in civic life. After examining all the alternative reasons for this disparity, Bloemraad concludes that it is indeed the mechanism of Canada's institutionalized multiculturalism that allows for a healthier, smoother, and faster integration into mainstream society (Bloemraad, 2010).

What Do the Numbers Tell Us?

There are two ways to determine the diversity of a country. One is by simple, unscientific observation. The other seemingly more reliable method is through census reports.

Canada is one of the few Western nations that collect data on the ethnic and religious backgrounds of its residents. But even with the previously more-detailed long-form census, statisticians struggled to make cohesive pictures with the data. One reason for this problem is that a checked box for country of origin does not tell the degree to which that individual identifies with that background. In fact, with the official inclusion of "Canadian" as a legitimate response for ethnic origin in the 1996 census, it is entirely possible to have two siblings respond in different ways—one assuming the question is asking for grandparents' country of origin, another assuming the question is asking for where the respondent himself or herself grew up. Interestingly, in 1996, only 4% of respondents considered their ethnicity Canadian, up to 23% in 2001, and close to 33% in 2006—despite the increase in immigrant population (Satzewich & Liodakis, 2010).

Many visible minorities claim that what others consider them to be is equally—if not more—important in determining ethnic labels. Most visible minorities who have been in Canada for at least a generation have stories where they were asked where they are "really" from. Does **phenotype**—the visible traits a person displays—trump citizenship?

As diverse as Canada may sometimes feel, the vast majority of the population is still of European heritage, with only 13% of the total population reporting non-European descent. But official ethnicity does not determine a person's ethnic identity. The Ethnic Diversity Survey found that—not surprisingly—ethnic identification varied among diverse groups and tended to decline with subsequent generations. Seventy-eight percent of Filipinos reported a strong sense of ethnic affiliation compared to 58% of Chinese (Statistics Canada, 2003). Presumably, this means that

Phenotype: The visible traits a person (or organism) displays.

the remaining 42% of Chinese Canadians consider themselves primarily Canadian. Consider the dissonance created when someone feels Canadian, but their "Canadian-ness" is repeatedly questioned.

Statistics Canada projects that by 2031, at least one out of every four people in Canada will be foreign-born and over half this number will likely be from Asia. Compared to the rest of the population, the foreign-born segment will be increasing at four times the rate.

As for visible minorities, the 2006 report (Statistics Canada, 2010b) documented just over 5 million, and the projections by 2031 nearly double, meaning that almost one-third of the population will belong to a visible minority group. The question remains as to whether the minority continues to have any meaning in this context, especially in cities like Toronto and Vancouver where visible minorities are expected to represent 63% and 59% respectively of the cities' populations (Statistics Canada, 2010b).

South Asian minorities will continue to be the most numerous visible minority, with the Chinese population likely doubling as well. However, the Chinese population will lose some of its percentage of representation of the visible minority segment due to low fertility rates among Chinese women. The second and third largest visible minority groups in 2006, black and Filipino Canadians, will also possibly double in size. The fastest growing groups of all will be Arabs and West Indians, who are predicted to triple their current numbers by 2031 (Statistics Canada, 2010b).

Is "Ethnic Enclave" Just a Fancy Name for "Ghetto"?

Almost every ethnic group that has immigrated to Canada has some claim to a particular geographic concentration. According to Statistics Canada projections, by 2031, more than 71% of all visible minority Canadians will live in Canada's three largest census metropolitan areas: Toronto, Vancouver, and Montreal (Statistics Canada, 2010b). In the Greater Toronto Area alone, there are numerous well-established ethnic neighbourhoods: Italians in Woodbridge and Vaughan, Chinese in Richmond Hill, and South Asians in northern Brampton. Sociologists call these focussed areas of homogenous ethnic groups, which are usually coupled with some business and institutional activity, **ethnic enclaves** (Keung, 2013). People don't need charts or maps to tell them they have entered into an ethnic enclave; a quick look at the storefronts, billboards, and religious buildings is usually enough.

Source: © Purestock/Thinkstock

Some Canadians believe that ethnic enclaves, such as Chinatown in Toronto, divide cities in a way that prevents cohesion; others believe that ethnic enclaves invite co-mingling among all Canadians, while providing newcomers with some familiar features of their home countries.

To some, these enclaves proclaim the beauty of diversity and the triumph of capitalism, where demand meets previously non-existent supply. To others, these enclaves are the harbingers of the impending cultural wars Canada faces if it does not resume its policy of assimilation. With each ethnic group crouched behinds its walls, how can we hope to have a cohesive national identity?

Ethnic enclaves serve a number of positive functions. Far from balkanizing their respective residents, these neighbourhoods help new immigrants acculturate slowly into their new home country. Minimizing culture shock, they allow various

Ethnic enclave: Focused areas of homogenous ethnic groups, usually coupled with some business and institutional activity.

ethnic groups to establish stores and places of worship; they make it easier to deliver civic services in a culturally appropriate way; and, in many cases, they transform the landscape, adding numerous vibrant tourist attractions—Little Italy, Little India, Chinatown; all distinct, yet all Canadian.

In 1981, Canada had only six ethnic enclaves; today there are more than 260 throughout the country, half of which are found in metropolitan Vancouver (Hopper, 2011). But what differentiates them from the ethnic ghettos seen in the United States and Western Europe is that, by and large, these enclaves are enclaves of choice—not the result of discriminatory housing practices or poverty (Kymlicka, 2010). Another radical difference is the mobility both in and out of these enclaves. While many of the previously homogeneous neighbourhoods are now being **gentrified**, causing housing prices to rise as wealthy young urbanites populate them, many ethnic minorities are moving out of urban areas and into the suburbs.

That's the good news. The bad news is far louder—and it's the bad news that makes the actual news. Segregation, social exclusion, lack of language acquisition—all these issues are blamed on ethnic enclaves, which are viewed as the enemies of integration. Although not necessarily determined by socio-economics, some ethnic enclaves were historically indistinguishable from slums, and many still are. When ethnic neighbourhoods get large and dense enough, they are able to support their own schools, thereby eliminating one of the fastest means of civic integration and allowing minority groups to socialize almost entirely with "their own." Despite reports that Canada's immigrant population has gotten high marks on all the standard benchmarks of assimilation—home-ownership, language acquisition, and attainment of citizenship (Kymlicka, 2004)—Canada's former Minister of Immigration and Citizenship, Jason Kenney, worried that the government's commitment to preserving and enhancing Canada's multicultural heritage and allowing the continuation of nearly autonomous ethnic enclaves threatened national cohesion and did a disservice to new immigrants (MacDonald, 2013). And though some of these neighbourhoods remain prosperous, newcomers to Canada today—earning on average 61 cents to the dollar of their Canadian-born counterparts—have nowhere near the economic mobility that they had in the early 1990s (Hopper, 2011).

University of Victoria scholar Zheng Wu found that although ethnic enclaves can help recent immigrants feel more comfortable and protected, they also decrease a resident's sense of belonging to Canada (Todd, 2011b). Ethnic segregation and economic inequality are ripe conditions for exacting the kind of cultural warfare that some right-wing politicians often warn about as a result of multicultural "political correctness."

There are also serious issues of violence in ethnic communities. For example, a number of Aboriginal communities are being exploited by criminal elements, according to the RCMP's Aboriginal division (Canadian Press, 2010). Groups involved in drug distribution, prostitution, and theft manipulate and coerce younger members of these economically depressed and culturally isolated neighbourhoods. As a result, there has been a proliferation of violent Native gangs. The Indian Posse, the Manitoba Warriors, the Native Syndicate and other Aboriginal gangs have now spread to almost every major metropolis in Canada (Canadian Press, 2010).

Violence has been reported in other ethnic communities as well. When a Punjabi teenager was stabbed to death in Brampton in 2007, residents voiced their concerns that "Vancouver-style" violence was spreading into their communities. What they were referring to was the hundreds of Punjabi-on-Punjabi murders in British Columbia's ethnic gang warfare (Grewal, 2007).

Canadians were horrified when they learned of Pakistani-Canadian teenager Aqsa Parvez being murdered by her father for supposedly violating the family's honour. Soon after, other stories of so-called "honour killings" started appearing in the headlines. Many feared that the perpetrators would get a lighter sentence, hiding behind a cultural defence.

A Canadian blogger recently told Canadians that they should "consider ourselves fortunate that Canada's Somali settlers seem more or less content with killing each other" (Shaidle, 2011). In 2011, Edmonton led the nation in homicide rates, and a significant number of those murdered were young Somali men. With Alberta pledging close to $2 million to address the issues surrounding the Somali communities' integration, many, like then-Minister Jason Kenney, wondered if it was time to restructure Canada's multicultural stance (Sun News, 2011).

CANADA'S MULTICULTURAL FUTURE: DOES IT EXIST?

One of the reasons the debate around multiculturalism is so heated stems from lack of a cohesive definition for what multiculturalism actually is.

Gentrified: Improved so as to appear more middle class.

Opponents equate multiculturalism with political correctness and a war on "real Canadian" culture. Further, they say multiculturalism divides Canada into ethnic silos and doesn't promote national unity. Speaking to the Trudeau Foundation conference in Nova Scotia, a European critic of the Canadian model contends that

> multiculturalism undermines much of what is valuable about the lived experience of diversity. Diversity is important because it allows us to expand our horizons, to think about different values and beliefs, and to engage in political dialogue and debate that can help create a more universal language of citizenship. But it is precisely such dialogue and debate that multicultural policy makes so difficult by boxing people into particular ethnic or cultural categories. (Malik, 2011)

At the federal level, in the 1990s, the Reform Party of Canada (an early branch of today's Conservative party) explicitly stated its aim to cut any and all funding to multicultural programs and to abolish the entire department. Some have even made the link between "homegrown terrorism" and multicultural policy (Wong, 2011).

Proponents, on the other hand, define multiculturalism as part of the Canadian identity and a necessary component of a modern liberal society. Tom Axworthy, one of the main architects of Trudeau's original policy calls it "our Alamo, without the original war," referring to the unifying rallying cry of the war between Texas and Mexico (Fleras & Elliot, 2007). Without it, Canada's immigration drive would not be successful, and the nation would find itself with a rapidly declining population. With 84% of recent immigrants reporting a strong sense of belonging to Canada, it is clear that Canada must be doing something right. On the other hand, 20% of visible minorities report experiencing some degree of discrimination, and **racialized** Canadians are at least twice as likely to be poor as non-racialized Canadians (Galabuzi, 2006).

To further illustrate Canada's struggle with its cultural identity, consider the range of opinions that come in through polls. For a decade, research has continued to affirm that Canadians overwhelmingly support multiculturalism and proudly consider it one of the nation's defining features. Compare that to recent findings that as many as 30% of Canadians think that multiculturalism has been bad or very bad for Canada. Perhaps even more surprisingly, a strong majority (54%) support a "melting pot" model as opposed to the traditional "mosaic" model that Canada made famous (Angus Reid, 2010).

Social scientists are attempting to reinvigorate Canada's multicultural policies to address not only the reality of new groups coming in greater numbers to Canada, but also the accusations or fears of cultural isolation as a result of emphasizing the differences between various ethnic groups. Sociologist Lloyd Wong proposes including programs that foster inter-ethnic cohesion, manufacturing forums where different groups would regularly interact, and—it is hoped—develop bonds based on their allegiance to Canada. Instead of funding groups that simply promote entrenchment in their own heritage identity, he proposes that the federal and provincial governments begin funding groups and programs that get different groups meeting on common ground—whether that be politically, artistically, or simply socially (Wong, 2011).

Others propose a most cosmopolitan approach that essentially erases the categories of ethnicity altogether. Neil Bissoondath, author of the highly controversial and best-selling book *Selling Illusions: The Cult of Multiculturalism in Canada*, illustrates with his own example:

> I feel greater affinity for the work of Timothy Mo—a British novelist born of an English mother and a Chinese father—than I do for that of Salman Rushdie, with whom I share an ethnicity. ... Ethnically, Mo and I share nothing, but imaginatively we share much. (Bissoondath, 1994)

Still others, like Phil Ryan, author of *Multicultiphobia*, propose a blending of both the mosaic and melting pot model with a few guiding principles. Among these principles, he counsels that we should avoid comparing the best of one ethnic group with the worst of another; that respecting multiculturalism does not necessitate signing a "non-interference clause," where everyone is forced to remain silent in the face of illegal or immoral activities committed under the guise of cultural relativism; and that we stop considering white Canadians the default and stop measuring everyone else by that mark (Todd, 2010). This last point has recently been brought to light in a number of headlines. For example, when the Bank of Canada commissioned an artist to portray a female Canadian scientist on the new polymer $100 bills, focus groups responded to the first draft with concerns that the scientist looked "too Asian." The Bank withdrew this version and replaced it with

Racialized: Characteristic of people, other than Aboriginal people, who are non-Caucasian in race or non-white in colour, as defined by the Employment Equity Act.

one depicting a more "neutral"-looking scientist (Canadian Press, 2012a).

In a study conducted on behalf of Metropolis British Columbia—entitled "Why Do Some Employers Prefer to Interview Matthew, But Not Samir?"—researchers collected evidence from Toronto, Vancouver, and Montreal, and confirmed what was perhaps already anecdotally obvious: that resumés with English-sounding names had a far better chance getting a call back—in some cases, a 40% greater chance (Oreopoulous & Dechief, 2011). Whether this is evidence of **latent discrimination**, or of recruiters' attempt to avoid a "bad hire" with language-skill deficiencies, the study echoes the Bank of Canada focus group findings. An Anglo background is still the default in Canada. The report ends with numerous suggestions for avoiding this sort of discrimination without resorting to a quota system or resulting in unqualified hiring (Oreopoulos & Dechief, 2011).

ENDING THOUGHTS

Latent discrimination: Discrimination that is hidden and may not even be obvious or known to the discriminator.

Ethnic identity: The extent to which someone identifies with a particular ethnic group.

As Canadians become more self-conscious about their country's multicultural policy, it is natural to wonder if the bloom is off the rose. Evidence is coming to light that challenges former assumptions about the early days and motivations for multiculturalism, and there is a growing cynicism that we are perhaps not as tolerant as we once believed. Recent research is promising, however. Studies have shown that multiculturalism in Canada prevents national identity turning into xenophobia as it often does and has in other countries. With the Canadian policy, national identity is inextricably linked to the stance towards immigrants and visible minorities. The mythology, well founded or not, means that to be Canadian is to take pride in the country's multiculturalism:

> Multiculturalism provides a locus for the high level of mutual identification among native-born citizens and immigrants in Canada … the fact that Canada has officially defined itself as a multicultural nation means that immigrants are a constituent part of the nation that citizens feel pride in. (Kymlicka, 2010)

Reciprocally, according to the "multicultural hypothesis," immigrants integrate into mainstream society more successfully when they feel their **ethnic identity** or their ancestral roots are publicly acknowledged and respected (Kymlicka, 2010).

If Canadians' interactions with the federal government become increasingly limited, coupled with a lack of any other defining narrative, there are those who believe multiculturalism may be the unifying rallying point for the nation. Still others fear that years of encouraging segregated cultural identities have fundamentally weakened the fabric of national cohesion. Whether Canada will go the way of European multiculturalism, melt into the more American model, or chart its own course, will be determined in the upcoming generation.

READING

AN IMMIGRANT'S SPLIT PERSONALITY

By Sun-Kyung Yi

I am Korean-Canadian. But the hyphen often snaps in two, obliging me to choose to act as either a Korean or a Canadian, depending on where I am and who I'm with. After sixteen years of living in Canada, I discovered that it's very different to be both at any given time or place. When I was younger, toying with the idea of entertaining two separate identities was a real treat, like a secret game for which no one knew the rules but me.

I was known as Angela to the outside world, and as Sun-Kyung at home. I ate bologna sandwiches in the school lunch room and rice and kimchee for dinner. I chatted about teen idols and giggled with my girlfriends during my classes, and ambitiously practised piano and studied in the evenings, planning to become a doctor when I grew up. I waved hellos and goodbyes to my teachers, but bowed to my parents' friends visiting our home.

I could also look straight in the eyes of my teachers and friends and talk frankly with them instead of staring at my feet with my mouth shut when Koreans talked to me.

Going outside the home meant I was able to relax from the constraints of my cultural conditioning, until I walked back in the door and had to return to being obedient and submissive daughter.

The game soon ended when I realized that it had become a way of life, that I couldn't change the rules without disappointing my parents and questioning all the cultural implications and consequences that came with being a hyphenated Canadian.

Many have convinced me that I am a Canadian, like all other immigrants in the country, but those same people also ask me which country I came from with great curiosity, following with questions about the type of food I ate and the language I spoke. It's difficult to feel a sense of belonging and acceptance when you are regarded as "one of them." "Those Koreans, they work hard … You must be fantastic at math and science." (No.) "Do your parents own a corner store?" (No.) Koreans and Canadians just can't seem to merge into "us" and "we."

Some people advised me that I should just take the best of both worlds and disregard the rest. That's ideal, but unrealistic when my old culture demands a complete conformity with very little room to manoeuvre for new and different ideas.

After a lifetime of practice, I thought I could change faces and become Korean on demand with grace and perfection. But working with a small Korean company in Toronto proved me wrong. I quickly became estranged from my own people.

My parents were ecstatic at the thought of their daughter finally finding her roots and having a working opportunity to speak my native tongue and absorb the culture. For me, it was the most painful and frustrating 2-1/2 months of my life.

When the president of the company boasted the he "operated little Korea," he meant it literally. A Canadian-bred Korean was not tolerated. I looked like a Korean; therefore, I had to talk, act, and think like one too. Being accepted meant to totally surrender to ancient codes of behaviour rooted in Confucian thought, while leaving the "Canadian" part of me out in the parking lot with my '86 Buick. In the first few days at work, I was bombarded with inquiries about my marital status. When I told them I was single, they spent the following days trying to match me up with available bachelors in the company and the community.

I was expected to accept my inferior position as a woman and had to behave accordingly. It was not a place to practise my feminist views, or be an individual without being condemned. Little Korea is a place for men (who filled all the senior positions) and women don't dare speak up or disagree with their male counterparts.

The president (all employees bow to him and call him Mr. President) asked me to act more like a lady and smile. I was openly scorned by a senior employee because I spoke more fluent English than Korean. The cook in the kitchen shook her head in disbelief upon discovering that my cooking skills were limited to boiling a package of instant noodles. "You want a good husband, learn to cook," she advised me.

In less than a week I became an outsider because I refused to conform and blindly nod my head in agreement to what my elders (which happened to be everybody else in the company) said. A month later, I was demoted because "members of the workplace and the Korean community" had complained that I just wasn't "Korean enough" and I had "too much power for a single woman." My father suggested that "when in Rome do as the Romans." But that's exactly what I was doing. I am in Canada, so I was freely acting like a Canadian, and it cost me my job.

My father also said, "It doesn't matter how Canadian you think you are, just look in the mirror and it'll tell you who you really are." But what he didn't realize is that an immigrant has to embrace the new culture to enjoy and benefit from what it has to offer. Of course, I will always be Korean by virtue of my appearance and early conditioning, but I am also happily Canadian and want to take full advantage of all that such citizenship confers.

But for now I remain slightly distant from both cultures, accepted fully by neither. The hyphenated Canadian personifies the ideal of multiculturalism, but unless the host culture and the immigrant cultures can find ways to merge their distinct identities, sharing the best of both, this cultural schizophrenia will continue.

Source: "An Immigrant's Split Personality" by Sun Kyung Yi. Reprinted from *The Globe and Mail* (April 12, 1992). Reprinted by permission of the author.

DISCUSSION QUESTIONS

1. Sociologist Erving Goffman's (1956) theory of impression management suggests that we divide ourselves into our "front stage" selves, which we use to wind through the realities of everyday life, and our "back stage" selves, which allow us to take off our masks and exist as who we really are, when we are not "acting." In some ways, this division becomes a coping mechanism. For those who live their lives as "hyphenated Canadians," how and when can they experience their "back stage" self?

2. As an ideal, multiculturalism was supposed to alleviate the author's notion of "cultural schizophrenia," but what can be done to merge the opposing views of her elders, employers, and the author herself?

3. The author identifies herself in dimensions that include other factors besides her ethnicity; for example, she indicates that she's a feminist, single, and not a very good cook. Her parents, however, seem to identify themselves strictly in terms of their heritage. Do you think that this is a generational phenomenon, or do you think this is because the author is "hyphenated"?

One of the fundamental truths about diversity is that it involves as much learning about oneself as it does learning about others. Let's use the KWIP process to look at how our identities are shaped through social interaction.

KNOW IT AND OWN IT: WHAT DO I BRING TO THIS?

As a member of Canadian society, you likely have your own views when it comes to multiculturalism, based on your own personal experiences. Those experiences will make excellent points of entry when discussing this topic in conversation, provided you couch your stories of those experiences in some new-found knowledge. For example, you may be new to Canada, and your experiences of assimilation or of retaining your unique identity may be completely different from someone who is a Canadian visible minority, but who has lived here since birth and yet has often been mistaken for an immigrant. Regardless of your story, it's an important one to share, especially since Canada is internationally known as a multicultural society.

WALKING THE TALK: HOW CAN I LEARN FROM THIS?

Familiarizing yourself with Canada's policies as they relate to multiculturalism and diversity will help give you a better understanding of the complexities that surround this issue and how the policies impact Canadians today and in the future. Whether or not they relate specifically to your personal experiences, an awareness of the "multicultural experience" is a must for anyone discussing diversity and inclusion and hoping to become culturally competent.

IT IS WHAT IT IS: IS THIS INSIDE OR OUTSIDE MY COMFORT ZONE?

It's not easy to discuss concepts like multiculturalism when they are surrounded by such controversy in the news and the literature. How do you decide what's right when you read so many different views and definitions? Admitting that the debate exists is half the battle won, and it shouldn't discourage you from discussing the issues pertaining to multiculturalism and diversity. The contentious nature of a topic doesn't diminish the topic's importance—if anything, it often increases it. Set aside your uneasiness in the knowledge that perhaps in this area, there are several right answers—and several wrong ones too. Add yours to the mix in a respectful manner and see where things lead! Do you have a wide circle of friends, which might include newcomers, to help develop your thoughts in this area?

PUT IT IN PLAY: HOW CAN I USE THIS?

Put your new-found knowledge to use and have some fun while you're at it—if you can, that is. Go to **http://www.cic.gc.ca/english/games/index.asp**. On this site, you'll find a host of games that relate to multiculturalism, citizenship, and immigration. How easy are these games to understand and play, and what are the chances that a newcomer with language barriers might complete them? Do they need to be more inclusive and user-friendly?

**CourseMate
Study Tools**

Located at www.nelson.com/site/walkamile1e

- Consolidate your knowledge with the **Flashcards**.
- Gauge your understanding with **Picture This** and accompanying questions for reflection.
- Develop your critical thinking skills by working through **The Daily**.
- Apply your understanding with **KWIP** interactive!
- Develop your critical reading skills through compelling **Readings** and accompanying short answer questions.

REFERENCES

Abella, R. (1984). Equality in employment: A Royal Commission report. Retrieved from http://epe.lac-bac .gc.ca/100/200/301/pco-bcp/commissions-ef/abella1984 -eng/abella1984-eng.htm

Angus Reid Public Opinion. (2010, November 8). Canadians endorse multiculturalism, but pick melting pot over mosaic. Retrieved from *Angus Reid Global*: http://www.angus-reid.com/wp-content/ uploads/2010/11/2010.11.08_Melting_CAN.pdf

Belanger, C. (2006, May). Canadian immigration history: Lecture plan. Retrieved from *Marianopolis College*: http:// faculty.marianopolis.edu/c.belanger/quebechistory/

readings/CanadianImmigrationPolicyLectureoutline.
html

Bissoondath, N. (1988, September 5). Multiculturalism.
Retrieved from *New Internationalist*: http://newint.org/
features/1998/09/05/multiculturalism/

Bissoondath, N. (1994). *Selling illusions: The cult of multiculturalism in Canada*. Toronto: Penguin Books.

Bloemraad, I. (2010, October 28). Multiculturalism has been
Canada's solution, not its problem. Retrieved from *The Globe
and Mail*: http://www.theglobeandmail.com/commentary/
multiculturalism-has-been-canadas-solution-not-its-problem/
article4330460/

Bransten, J. (2006, April 5). Netherlands leading trend to more
stringent immigration rules. Retrieved from *Radio Free
Europe*: http://www.rferl.org/content/article/1067418.html

Canadian Press (2010, March 16). Native gangs spreading
across Canada. Retrieved May 2013, from *CBC
News*: http://www.cbc.ca/news/canada/manitoba/
story/2010/03/16/mb-native-gangs-manitoba.html

Canadian Press (2012a, August 17). Asian-looking woman
scientist image rejected for $100 bills. Retrieved
from *CBC News*: http://www.cbc.ca/news/canada/
story/2012/08/17/pol-cp-100-dollar-bills-asian-scientist
-image.html

Canadian Press (2012b, October 24). Census trends: Canada's
many mother tongues. Retrieved from *CBC News*: http://
www.cbc.ca/news/interactives/cp-census/index-oct
-mother-tongues.html

Evans, S. (2010, October 17). Merkel says German multicultural society has failed. Retrieved from *BBC News*: http://
www.bbc.co.uk/news/world-europe-11559451

Fleras, A., & Elliott, J. L. (2007). *Unequal relations: An introduction to race, ethnic, and Aboriginal dynamics in Canada*.
5th ed. Toronto: Pearson.

Galabuzi, G.-E. (2006). *Canada's economic apartheid: The
social exclusion of racialized groups in the new century*.
Toronto: Canadian Scholars' Press.

Gingrich, P. (2004, September). Sociology 211: History
of multiculturalism in Canada. Retrieved from
http://uregina.ca/~gingrich/211s2904.htm

Goffman, E. (1956). *The presentation of self in everyday life*.
Anchor Books.

Government of Canada (1988, July 21). Canadian
Multiculturalism Act. Retrieved from *Justice Laws
Website*: http://laws-lois.justice.gc.ca/eng/acts/C-18.7/
page-1.html

Gregg, A. (2006). Multiculturalism: A twentieth-century dream
becomes a twenty-first-century conundrum. Retrieved
from *The Walrus*: http://walrusmagazine.com/article
.php?ref=2006.03-society-canada-multiculturism&page=

Grewal, S. (2007, March 9). Punjabis in Peel warn of teen
violence. *Toronto Star*. Retrieved from http://www.thestar
.com/news/2007/03/09/punjabis_in_peel_warn_of_teen
_violence.html

Hopper, T. (2011, December 2). Canada: As immigration
booms, ethnic enclaves swell and segregate. Retrieved
from *National Post*: http://news.nationalpost.com/
2012/02/11/canada-as-immigration-booms-ethnic
-enclaves-swell-and-segregate/

Hyman, I., Meinhard, A., & Shields, J. (2011). The role of
multiculturalism policy in addressing social inclusion
processes in Canada. Retrieved from *Centre for Voluntary
Sector Studies*: http://www.ryerson.ca/content/dam/
cvss/files/new-WORKING-PAPERS/2011-3%20The%20
Role%20of%20Multiculturalism%20Policy%20in%20
Addressing%20Social%20Inclusion.pdf

Keung, N. (2013, May 7). Toronto's immigrant enclaves
spread to suburbs. Retrieved from *Toronto Star*: http://
www.thestar.com/news/immigration/2013/05/07/
torontos_immigrant_enclaves_spread_to_suburbs.html

Kymlicka, W. (2004). The Canadian model of diversity in a
comparative perspective. University of Edinburgh; Eighth
Standard Life Visiting Lecture.

Kymlicka, W. (2010, January 12). The current state of multiculturalism in Canada and research themes on Canadian
multiculturalism 2008-2010. Retrieved from *Citizenship
and Immigration Canada*: http://www.cic.gc.ca/english/
resources/publications/multi-state/section1.asp#evidence

Kymlicka, W. (2012, February). Multiculturalism: Success,
failure, and the future. Retrieved from *Migration Policy
Institute Europe*: http://www.migrationpolicy.org/pubs/
multiculturalism.pdf

Lipset, S. M. (1990). *Continental divide: The values and institutions of the United States and Canada*. New York: Routledge.

MacDonald, A. (2013, March 20). Canada worries over 'deep-
ening ethnic enclaves.' Retrieved from *The Wall Street
Journal*: http://online.wsj.com/article/SB10001424127887
324557804578372483418341140.html

Malik, K. (2011, December 6). Canada's multiculturalism
is no model for Europe. Retrieved from *The Guardian*:
http://www.guardian.co.uk/commentisfree/2011/dec/06/
canada-multiculturalism-europe

McQuigge, M. (2013, December 5). *Mandela said he found
inspiration in Canadian respect for diversity*. Retrieved
from The Gazette: http://www.montrealgazette.com/news/
Mandela+said+found+inspiration+Canadian+respect/9252452/
story.html

Mosaic Institute. (2012, April 24). Younger Canadians believe
multiculturalism works; older Canadians, not so sure.
Retrieved from *Mosaic Institute*: http://mosaicinstitute
.wordpress.com/2012/04/24/younger-canadians-believe
-multiculturalism-works-older-canadians-not-so-sure

Nilsen, K. (2001). Deconstructing multiculturalism: How
government policy is reflected in current education
and practice. Retrieved from *Canadian Association of
Information Science*: http://www.cais-acsi.ca/proceedings/
2001/Nilsen_2001.pdf

Oreopoulos, P., & Dechief, D. (2011, September). Why do
some employers prefer to interview Matthew, but not

Samir? Retrieved from *Metropolis British Columbia*: http://mbc.metropolis.net/assets/uploads/files/wp/2011/WP11-13.pdf

Ryan, P. (2010). *Multicultiphobia*. Toronto: University of Toronto Press.

Satzewich, V., & Liodakis, N. (2010). *'Race' & ethnicity in Canada: A critical introduction* (2nd ed.). Canada: Oxford University Press.

Saunders, D. (2011, October 13). Sweden's big immigration idea: The 'Canada model.' Retrieved from *The Globe and Mail*: http://www.theglobeandmail.com/news/world/worldview/swedens-big-immigration-idea-the-canada-model/article618559/

Saunders, D. (2013, April 13). Time to make temporary foreign workers permanent. Retrieved from *The Globe and Mail*: http://www.theglobeandmail.com/commentary/time-to-make-temporary-foreign-workers-permanent/article11142634/

Shaidle, K. (2011, August 8). Canada's Somali problem. Retrieved from *Taki's Magazine:* http://takimag.com/article/canadas_somali_problem/print#axzz2UWI01PWE

Statistics Canada. (2003, September). *Ethnic diversity survey: Portrait of a multicultural society. Catalogue no. 89-593-XIE.* Retrieved from http://publications.gc.ca/Collection/Statcan/89-593-X/89-593-XIE2003001.pdf

Statistics Canada. (2010b, March). Projections of the diversity of the Canadian population 2006–2031. Retrieved from *Statistics Canada*: http://www.statcan.gc.ca/pub/91-551-x/91-551-x2010001-eng.pdf

Statistics Canada. (2013). Ethnic origin reference guide, National Household Survey, 2011. Retrieved from *Statistics Canada*: http://www12.statcan.gc.ca/nhs-enm/2011/ref/guides/99-010-x/99-010-x2011006-eng.cfm

Stoddard, A. (2012). The birth of Canada's multicultural policy: Plotting the official acceptance of diversity. Retrieved from *Dalhousie Faculty of Arts and Social Sciences*: http://arts.dal.ca/Files/Froese_Stoddard_Birth_of_Canada's_Multiculturalism_Policy_FA.pdf

Sun News Video Gallery. (2011, July 19). Edmonton worries. Retrieved from http://www.sunnewsnetwork.ca/video/search/somali/edmonton-worries/1066103814001

Todd, D. (2010, June 26). Multicultiphobia in Canada and beyond. Retrieved from *Vancouver Sun*: http://blogs.vancouversun.com/2010/06/26/multicultiphobia-in-canada-and-beyond/

Todd, D. (2011a, August 8). Trans-Atlantic poll shows Canadians have much to learn about immigration. Retrieved from *Vancouver Sun*: http://blogs.vancouversun.com/2011/08/08/trans-atlantic-poll-shows-canadians-have-much-to-learn-about-immigration/

Todd, D. (2011b, December 20). Ethnic mapping conclusion: As enclaves grow, will Metro residents' trust fade? Retrieved from *Vancouver Sun*: http://blogs.vancouversun.com/2011/10/20/ethnic-mapping-conclusion-as-enclaves-grow-will-metro-residents-trust-fade/

Trudeau, P. E. (1971, October 8). On multiculturalism: To the House of Commons. Retrieved from *Canada History*: http://www.canadahistory.com/sections/documents/Primeministers/trudeau/docs-onmulticulturalism.htm

Urzu'a, F. (2012, March). The Canadian multiculturalism policy within the Colombian community. Retrieved from *Concordia Working Papers in Applied Linguistics*: http://doe.concordia.ca/copal/documents/4_Soler-Urzua.pdf

Wong, L. (2011). Questioning Canadian multiculturalism: Debunking the fragmentation critique of multiculturalism. Retrieved from *Diverse*: http://www.diversemagazine.ca/Culture-Questioning%201.htm

Yalnizyan, A. (2011, February 18). Canada's immigration policy: Who is on the guest list? Retrieved from *The Globe and Mail*: http://www.theglobeandmail.com/report-on-business/economy/economy-lab/the-economists/canadas-immigration-policy-who-is-on-the-guest-list/article1913178/

Yi, Sun-Kyung. (2004). An immigrant's split personality. In *The maple collection*. Toronto: Nelson Education Ltd.

Practising Diversity

"There is a crack in everything. That's how the light gets in."

(Leonard Cohen, 1992)

DIVERSITY COMPETENCIES

Diversity competencies are specifically learned behaviours that students can actively practise to promote equity and inclusion. By mastering this unit, students will gain the skills to become diversity-competent practitioners, including the ability to

- scaffold increased self-awareness and knowledge to develop diversity-competent practice and achieve equity and justice at a personal, professional, and global level

- analyze tools for social change that challenge injustice and embrace social inclusion and equity in local, national, and global systems

- construct strategies to combat prejudice and discrimination against diverse populations

- reflect upon moving from social analysis to social action to make a difference in the world

While Canada remains committed to multicultural-ism, as evidenced by the increasing numbers of newcomers each year and changing legislation sur-rounding diverse populations, there is still a long way to go. The ability to engage in social interaction on an inclusive level goes far beyond a person's cultural make-up and includes a wide variety of factors not determined by heritage. Do you see how crucial it is to develop skills that will allow you to feel comfortable socializing, communicating, and doing business with all individuals, regardless, for example, of their race, gender, size, or ability? What about the organization that you'll be working for? How savvy should they be when it comes to diversity awareness? And, what role does power play in how well you and larger institu-tions institute social change?

The interplay that exists between individuals and the larger society is best explained by what sociolo-gist C. Wright Mills calls the **sociological imagination**. Mills coined the term sociological imagination to refer the "quality of mind" that allows a person to grasp "history and biography and the relations between the two within society" (Mills, 1959, p. 3). Essentially, what Mills means by the sociological imagination is that it's impossible to look at the world—or your place in it—without looking at the past, and beyond the borders of your "being." When we engage our minds to think beyond the scope of our "private" selves, we must also consider the implications of "public" goings-on in the world. By doing so, we can better situate ourselves to investigate and, ultimately, influence what's going on around us. For example, suppose you were going to meet a friend for coffee. When you use your sociological imagination to think about an event that wouldn't normally be thought pro-voking, you might see it in a different light. What are the implications of the language in the café's menu? Can everyone read and understand it? Is it exclu-sionary to some people? Do you realize that when you meet the barista—by extension—there's a whole history of other people you also meet, including the person who delivered the beans? What about the exploited Ethiopian coffee farmers who picked the beans for your coffee—how do they affect your life? Is the "fair-trade" coffee you're drinking really fair-trade

coffee? Caffeine is an addictive substance, yet no one gives you a dirty look for being addicted to it—why is this? What if your friend decided to have a cup of tea instead of coffee, would that be okay with you? (Spencer, 1993).

For Mills (1959), using our sociological imagin-ation is all about being able to take ourselves away from the reality of a situation and look at it in a new—or old—light. It's about being able to see ourselves as **agents of change** on a private, or individual, level, but also being aware of the potential to make change and see the changes as they occur within societal institu-tions and organizations on a public level—nationally, internationally, and globally. Sociological imagination is an awareness that change happens on an individual level and on a societal, systemic level—and that you can be an agent of change at every level. By practising diversity competency skills, you will become an agent of change—inevitably, unavoidably, and unquestion-ably. Whether it begins with a smile, an attitude, or a gift, you will become someone who has the power to include or exclude an individual—from a line-up, a conversation, or a group. Use your power wisely, and you can change the world.

SOCIAL CHANGE THROUGH EQUITY AND JUSTICE

What Is Social Change?

Can you make a lasting difference in the world? That's a tricky question and the answer is even trickier. The reality is that every single person makes a differ-ence—but it takes a lot of time, a lot of effort, and a lot of people to effect real social change in society. Use your sociological imagination here, and think of change happening on two levels. When you pass by street people and feed them, or work at a local shelter, you're changing their worlds on a personal level, but you're changing your world too—because it makes you feel good, or it provides volunteer hours on a resumé. But what are the chances that your work is going to solve the homeless problem in Canada? Prob-ably not very good. In order for **social change** to occur in any lasting way, it has to be embedded in the values, beliefs, policies, and procedures of the institutions of a society. In essence, there must be a change to the social order of things in society. If you apply your soci-ological imagination, donating money or time to street people is an action that occurs in the private realm of things, but social change occurs in the public realm of your sociological imagination—way beyond indi-vidual acts of charity.

Sociological imagination: A term coined by C. Wright Mills meaning the use of your imagination when both asking and answering sociological questions.

Agents of change: Individuals, groups, or organizations that use their various skills to bring about change.

Social change: Any major alterations in the behaviour, cultural values, and norms of a society over time.

Sociologists try to explain social change using a number of varying theories. Evolutionary theories of social change by thinkers like Auguste Comte (1798–1857) and Émile Durkheim (1858–1917) saw society progressively moving forward in a set of predictable stages. Consequently, change was viewed in a linear model, moving from simpler to more complex forms of organization, based on human knowledge (Maryanski, 2007; Schaefer, Smith, & Grekul, 2009).

Functionalist theorists believe that everything in society has a function—and that each institution works together to maintain balance and harmony in society. When explaining social change, Talcott Parsons (1902–1979), a leading functionalist of his time, stated that society tries to preserve equilibrium by using four different approaches. For Parsons, when there's a change in one area of society, others will adjust to accommodate those changes. His equilibrium model includes four processes:

1. Differentiation—social organization become more and more complex (e.g., the transition from barter system to capitalism)
2. Adaptive upgrading—social institutions become more specialized (e.g., areas of specialty in medicine)
3. Inclusion—groups that were previously excluded are included (e.g., women gaining the right to vote)
4. Value generation—new values develop that tolerate and legitimate a wider range of activities (e.g., increased acceptance of same-sex marriage)

For functionalists, social change is all about maintaining order in society. We can see this operate in today's economy. When there's a shortage of a product, the price of the product increases, causing the producers to make more of the product, which eliminates the shortage. With the shortage eliminated, prices return to normal (Schaefer, Smith, & Grekul, 2009).

Conflict theories, stemming mainly from the work of Karl Marx (1818–1883) are more proactive, focusing on the ability of human beings to determine their own fate, through political activity. These theorists explain social change as the result of a struggle between classes, races, or other groups, rather than society's quest for balance. Historically, society has relied on exploitation—ancient societies exploited slaves, the estate system of feudalism exploited serfs, and modern capitalism exploits the working class. For Marx, it would be a socialist revolution, led by the "underclass," or proletariat, that would cause society to move toward utopia—a classless society. He insisted that men transform history, and in the process, transform themselves—an experiential process that requires conflict in order to bring about change. For as much as he despised the oppressive workings of the rich against the poor, he saw them as a necessary means to bring about social change—for without this conflict, there would be nothing to oppose (Scott & Marshall, 2005; Schaefer, Smith, & Grekul, 2009).

Feminist theories are rooted in the feminist understanding of society and aim to make lasting changes in the world. Deeply vested in **social justice** and a desire to promote change for the marginalized and disenfranchised who are disadvantaged by their various statuses, feminist research uses gender as a "basic organizing principle which profoundly shapes/mediates the concrete conditions of our lives. ... Through the questions that feminism poses and absences it locates, feminism argues for the centrality of gender in shaping our consciousness, skills, and institutions as well as in the distribution of power and privilege" (Lather, 1988, p. 571). The theory of the "matrix of domination" suggests that because of people's social location or status (e.g., race, gender, sexual orientation), they can be oppressed in some ways or privileged in others. Further, for every act of subjugation, there is an interconnected, opposing act of domination (Hill Collins, 1990). For feminist theorists like Patricia Hill Collins and others, social change is sought for individuals, who, because of their social locations, find themselves facing political, social, cultural, economic, or any other kind of injustice.

Social change has often come about because of collective actions or **social movements**, which have included the civil rights movement, unionism, and feminism (Scott & Marshall, 2005). Change has taken place because of migration, war, colonialism, and technology. Inventions—such as the printing press, antibiotics, the automobile, and the computer—have also led to lasting social change. Today, social change can be measured in short-term and long-term effects—on a small scale and on a large scale. Sociologists measure change on a global level (public) and in families (private).

Any way you look at social change, it's important to remember that it affects everyone. Consider unemployment. You might have a job, so you think you don't have to worry. But when you live in a city where unemployment rates are skyrocketing, you'll soon find that the shops on Main Street are closing, your friends are moving away to find work, and people you thought would never use the food bank are suddenly lining up there. Your personal

Social justice: An interactive process where members seek equitable treatment for all members of society, regardless of their social locations.

Social movement: An organized attempt by a number of individuals either to change or to resist change in society.

issue soon becomes a much bigger issue—and it's one that you find yourself caring about, especially since you've developed a social conscience, much like the relationship between public and private, called to mind from the sociological imagination. But how do we get to a place where we move from actions on the individual level to actions on a grander scale—actions that will lead to lasting, meaningful change?

Charity or Social Justice?

Consider the old adage: "Give a man a fish and you feed him for a day; teach a man to fish, and you feed him for a lifetime." Now consider the following scenario: once, during a summer gathering in a small village, someone noticed a small baby, struggling and crying in the river. As the village people rushed to save the baby, additional babies appeared in the waters. As frenzied village people tried saving all the babies in the water, two people walked upstream and put a stop to the person throwing babies in the river (Difference-Between.net, 2013).

Is the lesson in these two examples the same, or do they say different things? The characteristics of these two examples also outline the features that mark the differences between charity and social justice. **Charity** happens when someone provides immediate help or relief to those in need. It might consist of an individual or an organization voluntarily donating its time or resources to a person or group of people who have fewer resources, like money, food, or shelter. When it's done in an organized, efficient, loving, honorable manner—and delivered to those who are in need—it can literally save lives, prevent misery, and preserve the dignity of the recipients. Conversely, social justice refers to a state of institutional or structural arrangements where any inequities that exist can be explained or justified in terms of the greater social good. When your goal is social justice, you try to change the structural policies or practices that created the inequities in the first place (Marullo & Edwards, 2000).

In the first example about the man and fish, if hunger is the problem, charity is the immediate solution by feeding the man a fish, but social justice is the long-term solution by teaching him how to fish. Hence, he becomes self-sufficient, and is no longer reliant on repeated one-time fish donations. In the second story, the village people provided an immediate solution to the problem by rescuing babies (charity), but the two individuals who stopped the baby-thrower employed a social justice approach when they

Charity: Actions or donations to provide immediate help to those in need.

ceased the problematic behaviour altogether. This is not to say that there is no place in society for charity—but it is a stop-gap measure, a band-aid on the plight of oppressed. Charity focuses more on the immediacy of a problem or issue; social justice addresses a long-term resolution in a move toward social change.

TOOLS FOR ACHIEVING EQUITY AT A PERSONAL LEVEL

Thinking

SOCIAL CONSCIOUSNESS

Are you wondering if you have the tools for achieving equity? Are you a socially conscious individual? Social consciousness seems to be one of the "in" terms these days, and telemarketers will often use it when soliciting funds over the phone—"Are you a socially conscious individual, who cares about the future of your children?" The reality is that you can insert virtually any word in place of "children" and the speech works fine. The solicitor already had your attention by using the words "socially conscious." But do you really know what these words mean, and who lives by them? According to eminent sociologist Charles Horton Cooley (1864–1929):

> Social consciousness, or awareness of society, is inseparable from self-consciousness, because we can hardly think of ourselves excepting with reference to a social group of some sort, nor of the group except with reference to ourselves. The two things go together, and what we are really aware of is a more or less complex personal or social whole, of which now the particular, now the general aspect is emphasized. In general, then, most of our reflective consciousness—of our wide-awake state of mind—is social consciousness, because a sense of our relation to other persons, or of other persons to one another, can hardly fail to be a part of it. Self and society are twin-born, and we know one as immediately as we know the other. (Cooley, 1907)

For Cooley, to be socially conscious is to be one with society in your waking life. As you are aware of your own surroundings on a personal level, you are also aware of—in tune with—the surroundings of the larger society as a whole simultaneously, both unconsciously and consciously. It is both the manifestation and culmination of Mills's concepts of the private and public spheres playing out in real time as we act on the choices we make to effect social change. If we believe in Cooley's definition, then everyone is a socially conscious individual—since the premise is that individuals cannot be separate from society.

So, just as individuals are conscious of the state of society, are they also responsible for it? Is social consciousness akin to **social responsibility**? And, if so, how many people take this responsibility seriously? This was the focus of a recent study (Trudel & Cotte, 2012), which had researchers wondering if consumers would pay higher prices for "ethically" produced goods. (Corporate social responsibility has become media fodder in recent years, especially with examples like the BP oil spill in 2010 and the 2013 clothing factory that collapsed in Bangladesh, killing over 1100 workers.) The researchers took to the streets to determine just how much more "socially conscious" individuals would pay for products that were produced by ethical companies. A company was determined to be "ethical" if it met three criteria:

1. It had to have progressive stakeholder relations, such as a commitment to diversity in hiring and consumer safety.
2. It had to follow progressive environmental practices, such as using eco-friendly technology.
3. It had to have demonstrated respect for human rights (e.g., no child labour or forced labour in overseas factories).

The researchers asked respondents two questions:

1. How much more would you pay for an **ethically produced product?**
2. How much less would you spend for a product you think is unethical?

In this case, the product was coffee, and consumers were given information to read, which offered either positive, negative, or no commentary about the producers' ethical practices. After reading about the company and its coffee, the people said they were willing to pay from $5 to $15 on an 11-point scale. The results showed that the mean price for the ethical group ($9.71 per pound) was significantly higher than that of the control group ($8.31) or the unethical group ($5.89), illustrating that the unethical group punished the coffee company's bad behaviour more than the ethical group rewarded its good behaviour. The unethical group's mean price was $2.42 below the control group's, while the ethical group's mean price was $1.40 above. So, negative information had almost twice the impact of positive information on the participants' willingness to pay (Trudel & Cotte, 2012). Would you pay more for "fair trade" coffee? Would you buy a shirt at a higher price if you knew that it wasn't made by child labourers? Your answers to these questions tell you something about your social consciousness.

Consciousness, awareness, responsibility—really, they are all the same thing. To be socially conscious is to be aware of your responsibility in taking care of the world that you live in—just as you would take care of yourself. But, how do you even begin? Can you imagine working alongside your favourite professor to create a project that will benefit you, other students, and the whole university community? That's exactly what's happening at Birmingham City University in the United Kingdom, where teams of staff and students have partnered equally to create projects meant to strengthen the learning and teaching activities for the university community as a whole, ultimately allowing the students to influence their own education (Birmingham City University, 2012). One such project found two disabled students working with faculty members to create a "first day" video for incoming students with disabilities. This is an excellent example of how people can create change at an individual level, which then becomes embedded at the institutional level and affects the lives of countless others. Although we don't often recognize it, this is social change! Craig Keilburger's equation of Issue + Gift = Better World (Me to We, 2013) applies perfectly to this situation, as we see a group of students (and, in this case, faculty) who saw something they decided was wrong. Social consciousness is embodied in the lives and work of the Kielburger brothers and the countless numbers of people they have inspired. Theirs is a community of caring and sharing founded on a very simple principle. Imagine that you were going to apply the Me to We equation to your life. Once you've filled in the Issue + Gift = Better World equation, you're well on your way to being a new and improved socially conscious individual.

The "Aha! Moment"

Nearly everyone can remember an "Aha! moment" in their lives. It happens when something clicks and you know that something has just happened that will transform your life forever. In the In Their Shoes story, it happened when a young student went to Africa and found her life's purpose.

Social responsibility: The idea that corporations and individuals have an ethical duty to protect the earth and protect society as a whole.

Ethically produced products: Goods that were produced in such a way that their production function or activities were not harmful to the consumer or to society.

IN THEIR SHOES

If a picture can say a thousand words, imagine the stories your shoes could tell! Try this student story on for size – have you walked in this student's shoes?

I just wanted to be like everyone else growing up. If I had known what diversity really meant back then, I would have said it sucks and I want no part of it. I hated being different with every fiber of my being. I was the fat kid who had a "unique" name, black curly hair and always looked tanned. I stuck out like a sore thumb.

It has always amazed me that when I confided in someone about the horrific things I went through as a child, a teen and an adult, they always say, "Wow, I had no idea." Over the years I have perfected an art of being okay on the outside, even though inside I am barely hanging on. I hid my hurt and despair behind humour. This was a skill I learned early on and I have become the David Copperfield of that skill. At the age of two, I remember being sexually abused by my step-brother and stepfather. This type of abuse continued throughout my childhood by different people in my life. As an adult, I was raped. I did go to counselling, and I did love it. I was 10 and my counsellor was amazing. She worked from home, as did her husband. She also had twin babies and when we were finished with our session, my grandma would go in and talk to her about me. I would wait in the living room where her husband would read to me or sometimes let me play with the babies. It wasn't long before he started molesting me. After a while I threw fits so I wouldn't have to go anymore. I never told my grandma why. I was a really easy-going kid but my poor grandma was so shocked at my unusual behaviour she wouldn't make me go. This had happened for as long as I could remember and I just thought that's how little girls were treated. That was my role in life. I did tell a few times, and each time I was told I was lying. So I decided no one could be trusted—I now hated police, social workers, and counsellors of any kind. You couldn't pay me to go near them.

I didn't finish high school. I couldn't—I needed to get out of my town. I was so lost, angry and hurt. I began travelling the world. Really I was just distracting myself because it was too overwhelming to deal with my feelings. I was at a point when I didn't care if I died. I had been through so much that death would not be the worst thing to happen. I dared it to come and get me. About five years ago I came home, I was tired of running, I was ready to put the past behind me, but how? New beginnings are not easy and I felt more lost, trying to figure out a direction for my life.

Three years ago I found myself in Africa on a mission trip; it changed my life. We were bringing food, water and clothes into various villages across Kenya. I spent a lot of time with children in those villages and finally I knew my place in the world. I wasn't going to let anything stop me. When we came back, I decided it was time to achieve my high school diploma, and I did. Then after several conversations and a ton of tears, I applied for college. I was accepted into the Social Service Worker Program. How ironic to become something I hated. I promised myself to be that beacon of hope to those who thought life was no longer worth living. I want to help people who are vulnerable, the way I was. I want to be the person that I wished had been there for me when I was little. I graduated the program with President's Honours, and I was accepted to university to achieve my BA of Social Work. Plus I have a job that I love. I work with adults who have acquired a brain injury. They have to relearn how to live their lives. I am so privileged to be a part of this agency.

As an adult I am so thankful for diversity. I am who I am today because of what I went through. They didn't break me; in fact, because of them I am stronger. I'm proud to be me.

It was Africa, too, for Sir Bob Geldof, singer, author, and social activist. During a concert, he told the audience of the impoverished conditions he saw for the first time. For the lead singer of the Boomtown Rats, this was his "Aha! moment," one that sparked him to partner with others to create the charity concerts, Live-Aid in 1985 and Live 8 in 2005.

Australia's Young Social Pioneers club is a year-long leadership program dedicated to young, budding Australian social change-makers. The 18–20 social entrepreneurs who participate in this program often do so knowing that they want to make a difference, but not having any specific goal or future plans intact. They're very civic-minded and community-based, and they have a strong sense of social justice, often working in areas as diverse as education, the environment, health, human rights, the arts, and technology (Foundations for Young Australians, 2013). They break the myth of the "lone entrepreneur," highlighting instead the reality that teams, not individuals, are the leading force behind entrepreneurial start-ups (Reuf, 2010). Although the ideas of individuals are of fundamental importance to a group, their work doesn't rely on the group, but rather is embedded in the social intergroup processes and relationships (Reuf, 2010). A recent ethnographic study on the Young Social Pioneer's program recounts experiences from the participants' retreats, and highlights some of their "Aha! moments":

> It's just that sort of moment where everyone has that understanding that there is something, that there are people out there who want to support us and who want to help us and we do have friends in wider networks. Just to be able to share that feeling with a bunch of 20 disengaged young people; it's just incredible and they love it and they feed off it and that's fantastic (Daniel, final retreat, 2010) (Berman & Mellon, 2012).

The authors of this study found that participation in the Young Social Pioneer's program provided the youth with a variety of tools for social change, including the value of participating in a community of like-minded change-makers, the refinement of their initiative focus, and gaining insight and expertise in the area of sustainable business practices (Berman & Mellon, 2012). What about you? Have you got a vision? Has your "Aha! moment" happened, but you're not sure what to do with it? Perhaps the answer lies in finding someone who shares your idea!

Doing

How do you go about putting an idea into practice? How do you know your risk will pay off? The bottom line is that you don't; but by making informed decisions, you can choose to take informed action, which will increase the chances of success, regardless of the size of the endeavour that you choose. An example here will detail the concrete steps that one particular organization uses in their informed actions. It is the steps that are important, as they can be applied to any such query or problem.

INFORMED ACTION

Engineers Without Borders is a registered Canadian charity dedicated to human development in Africa and Canada. They work with various partners to build maximum efficiency in rural areas in Africa as they relate to water and sanitation, food production and processing, and energy. They operate under the rubric of four major outcome goals: supporting rural African capacity, advocating for improved Canadian policies toward Africa, helping the engineering profession serve global society, and engaging Canadians to contribute and connect to Africa (Engineers Without Borders, 2010).

Use your sociological imagination and social conscience to see how an idea on an individual level (in your mind, for example) becomes transformed into an action that plays out in the real world on a bigger scale—out in the public realm. In this example, there's an individual who may not be concerned about issues in Africa, so the first step in informed action is simply to become aware of the problem. The second step involves empathy—feelings of what it might be like to be hungry or thirsty, and to live in a country that's not industrialized. In the third step, turn your imagination into reality as you read about what goes on in that country, or watch a video/documentary to learn about a situation that you know very little about. Remember the "Aha! moment"? That's the fourth step in this practice, and it finds you realizing that you're drawn into the process, and that you've committed yourself to making an informed decision about your participation. The fifth step finds you sharing your information with others—mostly because you're excited, but also because you want feedback. Lastly, you're ready to move—take action—and do what you've set your mind to do.

Whether it's a trip to Africa to volunteer with Engineers Without Borders or starting with something on a smaller scale, the actions that you take will be more fruitful—for you and those you choose to help—if they are based in sound judgment and information. Spend some time inside your head and keep going through the steps, using a variety of scenarios to practise. Get wild and crazy with your ideas and travel the world in your mind. Remember that as a diversity-competent practitioner, you have the skills to situate yourself comfortably with people from all walks of life.

DOING PERSONAL ADVOCACY

Deborah Boutilier writes, "A couple of years ago, my sister Larry and I were driving down the street. We were at a stop sign when Larry, who was driving, noticed that some children were picking on another child. I rolled down my window and hollered for the bullies to leave the other child alone, but one of the bullies just hollered some curse words back at us. Do you think my sister drove away? Not a chance. She pulled over and got out of the car. The bully got on his bike and started riding away, and my sister (who was 45 years old at the time) started chasing this kid down the street, asking him if he wanted a "piece" of her. On countless other occasions, my sister has advocated for international students, often providing them with transportation, food, or clothing. I love my sister Larry because of the kindnesses she does without a second thought. In many ways, my sister is my hero."

Boutilier's sister is what Anne Bishop (2011) calls an ally, and what others would call an **advocate**. Are you an advocate? Are you someone who will you speak up for others, or for yourself? For Bishop, allies include "men who work to end sexism, white people who work to end racism, heterosexual people who work to end heterosexism, able-bodied people who work to end ableism ... [it] is also recognizing one's own experience of oppression" (Bishop, 2011).

Bishop's model for being an ally consists of the following steps:

- understanding oppression, how it came about, how it is held in place, and how it stamps its pattern on the individuals and institutions that continually recreate it;
- understanding different oppressions, how they are similar, how they differ, how they reinforce one another;
- consciousness and healing;
- becoming a worker for your own liberation;
- becoming an ally; and
- maintaining hope (Bishop, 1994).

When a diversity-competent practitioner leaves the realm of simply thinking about an issue and enters the world of doing, personal advocacy becomes of paramount importance. The private and public spheres of the sociological imagination become separated. The practitioner can see the differences that privileges make. The lines of power become clearly demarcated, differentiating the dominant from the subordinate groups, and indicating the consequences that accompany the divisions. At this point, the practitioner leaves the solely private sphere and moves into the public sphere, moving from idea to action, from Me to We.

Every year, men in all shapes, sizes, and colours are "scrunching" their feet into a pair of lady's shoes to "Walk a Mile in Her Shoes," in an organized event to raise money and raise awareness about the serious causes and effects of sexualized violence, and the potential for **remediation** (Baird,

Advocate: Person who writes or speaks in representation for something, or someone, else.

Remediation: Working to fix or correct something that's been broken or damaged.

2013). The walks, which began in 2001, were organized to bring assistance and healing to all people that have experienced sexual violence in some form—directly or indirectly. What originally started as a small grass roots movement, involving mostly men, has grown into public theatre, involving women and children and families who participate in the walks, and audience members who interact with the participants. And, it's not just about women anymore. The collective that participates in this event is an example of what Bishop (1994) means when she uses the word "ally." These are individuals understand the oppression of being victimized by sexual violence and they have chosen to speak out against it, with both words and actions. After the walk, individuals hold an education session, where they can choose to speak about their experiences and bring hope to the lives of others. Every year, police officers, fire fighters, local radio personalities and other men find themselves walking in the trademark red shoes and asking other men if they're "man enough to walk a mile in her shoes"?

What about you? As a diversity-competent practitioner, do you have the skills to become an ally? Are you grounded in the knowledge of what it means to be oppressed—even if in your own life, you have not experienced oppressive conditions? Can you recognize social injustice and make a socially conscious decision to work toward alleviating it? Can you speak for those who cannot find their voices? Will you bring them hope?

Doing Kindness

Canadians are well known for their manners—and their love of Tim Hortons. A recent trend sees both of these traits playing out in real time, as an excellent example of doing kindness, Canadian style. In a practice dubbed "pouring it forward," one patron at the Tim's drive-thru pays for their order and at the same time, leaves some money to pay for a coffee for someone in the car behind them. When the next person drives up, the cashier tells them that their coffee's already been paid for by the car in front of them, and they can choose to accept the gift or continue to "pour it forward." "At a restaurant in Winnipeg, there were 228 orders. That means it happened 228 times through our drive-thru. That went on for three hours. It was amazing," said spokeswoman Nadia McDonald (CTV News, 2013).

Kindness has distinctly beneficial side effects. Spiritually, we feel better when we are kind—our heart swells and we take a sense of pride in ourselves. On a biochemical level, our body produces higher levels of dopamine, often resulting in what some call "helper's high."

Through the release of **oxytocin**, blood vessels expand, actually causing us to feel more emotional warmth. On a social level, kindness connects people, causing new relationships to develop or strengthening the bonds of existing ones. And as seen in the Tim Hortons example, kindness is contagious, often inspiring others to perform acts of kindness when at first they had no such intent on their agendas (Hamilton, 2011).

Now consider the case of Hanna Brencher. She's the 2013 Kindness Challenge winner selected by Random Acts of Kindness Foundation (Random Acts of Kindness Foundation, 2013). Feeling a little despondent herself, she saw on older woman on the subway one day and recognized that the woman was feeling the same way she did. Pulling a notebook out of her bag, she wrote the woman a letter—a love letter—and gave it to her. That simple gesture changed the woman's life and in the process has transformed the lives of thousands. Hanna started a website (**http://www.moreloveletters.com/**) informing people that if they need a "love letter"—a letter of support—that she would write one to them. People from all over the world wrote to Hanna in hopes of receiving a love letter in return. She now has many writers writing love letters, and volunteer kits are available on her site so that you can participate in this act of kindness too. That one simple act of kindness has rejuvenated "snail mail," and brought love to so many people around the world. Here is the very private act of writing a love letter—one of the most private things that you can imagine—yet it's affecting hundreds of thousands of people across the globe. How far can we travel without crossing any borders at all? Evidently, socially conscious individuals who want to make a positive change in the lives of other people can become world travellers by simply walking to their mailbox.

Random acts of kindness—and even not-so-random acts of kindness—are crucial for the diversity-competent practitioner. Not just for the recipient, but for the practitioner as well. In addition to the good feeling that comes from doing kindness, acts of kindness have the power to turn socially conscious practitioners of today into role models for others, and champions for the cause of their choosing. Are you a budding champion?

DOING LEADERSHIP

In 1999, when she was 15 years old, Amanda Belzowski created "Amanda's Lemonade Stand," a fundraising initiative that started out on her front lawn and grew into an annual event that would raise over $181 000 for several charities. After seeing the discrimination that job candidates face, 19-year-old Jared Valdron worked with recruiters in the IT field; he ultimately created his own company—Careers in Code—that works toward minimizing the discrimination that often accompanies the hiring process (Youth in Motion, 2013). These are only two of recipients of the 2013 "Top 20 Under 20" Award, a national award given out annually by Youth In Motion—an organization devoted to developing the leadership skills of diverse young Canadians. Offering programs like Career Days, Leading the Way, and Opportunities Unlimited, and partnered with a host of impressive organizations (e.g., Yonge St. Mission and Partnership for a Drug-Free Canada), Youth In Motion offers a variety of cognitive and experiential learning opportunities for young people who aspire to make a difference (Youth In Motion, 2010).

Working toward social justice is more than just an idea or a dream. The "Aha! moment" is crucial, but putting your ideas in place doesn't happen overnight. ACTIVATE (Motivate Canada, 2013) is a national leadership camp that inspires, trains, and supports Canadian youth from every province, so they can return to their communities with the skills to implement their ideas. Participants spend time together learning about grant writing, for example, while bonding with each other and sharing stories of each others' communities. Youth from every province share the characteristics, stories, and traditions of their communities, and talk about how they plan to implement change. This time that they spend together creates a lasting bond and social network of support for them, as they return to their homes—the public spaces—to implement their dreams and visions, toolkits in hand.

Doing leadership involves leading, but just as there is no "I" in "team," there is no "I" in "leader." Increasingly, young people are joining together to make a difference in their own lives and in the lives of others. Ginwright and James (2002) offer a set of principles and strategies that can act as guidelines for youth who have the drive and desire to work toward social justice:

- Analyzing power within social relationships—encourages young people to get at the root of social problems and understand that the misuse of institutional power is what creates inequality.
- Making identity central—often, identity is linked to inequality and this becomes the starting point for collective action.
- Promoting systemic change—changes the focus away from blaming the individual and on

Oxytocin: A hormone that promotes a feeling of connectedness and bonding.

to making change at the institutional level by focusing on the root cause of the problem.

- Encouraging collective action—without action, there is no change, and the capacity to change oppressive conditions lies in collective efforts, not individual ones.
- Embracing youth culture—youth culture shares a world view different from the dominant ideology (Ginwright & James, 2002, pp. 36–37).

Doing leadership is not a solitary role, although it is often portrayed as such. In leadership camps across the country, like-minded youths learn the skills to become leaders—people who want to make change. As a socially conscious individual, you have the dreams to make changes in your private and public communities. And as a diversity-competent practitioner, you have the skills to make those dreams a reality. How will you champion your cause and become a leader today?

TOOLS FOR ACHIEVING EQUITY AT A PUBLIC LEVEL

Thinking

How can social justice be achieved at the public level? What are some community partners and organizations doing in order to address the quality of life in their communities? Most organizations (like municipal, provincial, and federal governments; large corporations; and even small businesses) have **civic engagement** as a priority on their agendas for change. But involving participants or stakeholders in the community is no easy task. Don't individuals get their say when they vote? Shouldn't that be enough? Not really. The reality is that people—all people—have the right to be involved in their communities' decision-making processes. And, when done properly, civic engagement leads to better decisions (Ruf, 2013).

Civic engagement: Political or non-political participation and promotion of the well-being of a community.

Aggregation: Gathering individual pieces of information and bundling them into a whole.

Stakeholders: Often refers to organizations, community, or more formal associations within the community.

STRATEGIES FOR CIVIC ENGAGEMENT AND SOCIAL INCLUSION

James Surowiecki outlines four guidelines for maximizing the wisdom of group interaction:

1. Diversity—The best decisions come from difference and discussion, not from like-minded individuals sharing the same experiences.
2. Independent thought and opinion—People need unbiased information and the time to process it and form their own judgments about it.
3. Inclusion—Everyone should be represented; people have their own specialization and skills they bring to the table and without those, key puzzle pieces are missing.
4. **Aggregation**—There has to be a system in place to organize individual input so that it's representative of a community decision (Surowiecki, 2004).

Although many governments realize the benefits of good governance and civic engagement, few have taken the steps to formalize their approach to it. The City of Victoria is one of those municipal governments that realizes the benefits of civic engagement and takes the practice of it seriously. The City of Victoria set a task to improve civic engagement and realized it had six distinct challenges:

1. confusion about roles and responsibilities in engagement;
2. how to set priorities when resources are scarce;
3. how to ensure that engagement efforts are consistent and coordinated across city departments and initiatives;
4. how to allocate resources for engagement;
5. how to ensure effective communication about city issues; and
6. how to engage a diversity of **stakeholders** and citizens in civic engagement (City of Victoria, 2012).

What kinds of problems get solved with civic engagement? In Victoria, the city was having challenges with a large student population: with little night-time transit and most evening activities centred on drinking, an increase in the number of barroom fights in the downtown core resulted. Stakeholders (the bar owners, for example), citizens (patrons, residents), and city employees (police officers) all wanted a voice. Something needed to change, and it had to happen at the city level. That's where civic engagement comes in. How, as a city official, do you develop bonds and lines of communication that will unite all of these people, including the patrons? Try applying Surowiecki's (2004) model to Victoria's problem and see if you can come up with some solutions.

Listening

Would you sit and listen to the story of an Aboriginal residential school survivor? Would you listen to someone who has experienced sexual assault and needed to tell others, as part of the healing process? Would you laugh (and cry) with someone who recounted tales of adventure travelling from another country to Canada, with just the clothes on his or her back? A fairly recent study suggests that there is untapped power in storytelling—something that Aboriginal peoples have known since time began. By scanning the brain of a professional storyteller, recording her story, and then scanning the brains of respondents while they listened, researchers found that by simply telling a story, the woman could plant ideas, thoughts, and emotions into the listeners' brains (Stephens, Silbert, & Hasson, 2010). Telling stories brings people together, allowing them to empathize with each other.

Stories are very powerful tools for social action and social change. Nadja Halilbegovich may not define herself as such, but she is a storyteller of magnificent proportions. Deborah Boutelier writes, "I was privileged (in every sense) to be part of a small group who listened as she told of her childhood during the war in former Yugoslavia." Halilbegovich was 12 when the siege began, and for three and half years, along with her family, the whole of Bosnia suffered the atrocities of war. In 1992, she endured a serious shrapnel injury; and in 1995, she entered the United States. Ultimately, she started speaking with **Free The Children** and penned a novel that details her experiences (Halilbegovich, 2008). She also supports YES!, a non-profit organization that connects, inspires, and collaborates with change-makers to join forces for thriving, just, and sustainable ways of life for all (YES!, 2012). Her story touched the minds and hearts of everyone who listened that day. We laughed when she laughed, and cried when she cried. She was speaking at the general meeting for a non-profit organization, and the value of stories was not lost on the crowd, as clients, volunteers, workers, guests, and MPs listened. Yes, facts and numbers are vital to provide evidence, make estimates and evaluations. However, when told from the heart, nothing is more effective than a good story.

In this instance, a storyteller brought together like-minded community members who had the desire to make changes within the mandate of that particular non-profit organization. Other work in storytelling shows that storytelling is a powerful tool in neighbourhoods as well. Researchers studied individuals' civic engagement (neighbourhood belonging, collective effectiveness, and civic participation) and their interconnectedness to what they call "critical neighbourhood storytellers" (CNS). These CNS include local media, community organizations, and talking with other neighbours. Results of the study indicated that levels of civic engagement were indeed related to interconnectedness with critical neighbourhood storytellers; in fact, this interconnectedness was the most important individual-level determinant (Yong-Chan & Ball-Rokeach, 2006).

Stories are important—and need to be heard—from the grassroots level to the institutional top. One popular saying today is "everything happens for a reason." Of course, it does—or else it wouldn't happen. To make social change happen, we have to know the stories behind the reasons why everything happens. And, to do that, we must listen.

PUBLIC EDUCATION

Listening also involves looking at what's going on in the world and making socially responsible choices about the relationships between communities and their stakeholders—regardless of how you define the memberships. You are likely familiar with the Dove campaigns, which were initially aimed at improving the self-esteem of young girls and women. Started in 2004, the first campaign was based on a study (funded by Unilever, of which Dove is a subsidiary) that presented a disturbing major finding: only 2% of women around the world choose the word "beautiful" to describe their looks. Some women chose "attractive" (9%), "feminine" (8%), "good-looking" (7%), or "cute" (7%) (Etcoff, Orbach, Scott, & D'Agostino, 2004). Another important finding was that answers from the 3200 female respondents indicated that real beauty was a concept that came from inside a woman's heart and mind—that in reality, it had nothing to do with what was portrayed as "physical beauty," as depicted by mass media and popular culture. Essentially, authentic beauty was a concept that was left untouched by the paparazzi. Fully two-thirds of women strongly agreed that "the media and advertising set an unrealistic standard of beauty that most women can't ever achieve" (Etcoff, Orbach, Scott, & D'Agostino, 2004).

The first campaign began announcing Dove's "unprecedented movement to make beauty a source of confidence, not anxiety" (PRNewswire, 2004). The Dove Movement for Self-Esteem included celebrities like Maria Shriver and Katie Couric. It partnered with the Boys and Girls Clubs of America and provided free downloadable tools on their websites for individuals. Billboards, workshops, seminars, videos, and chat lines were fully functional in an all-out blitz to make the message heard. The "Evolution" video, which shows the "before and

Free The Children: A global charity and youth movement founded by Craig Kielburger.

after" of cosmetic and digital enhancement processes that a young female model undergoes, won the prestigious Cyber Lion award at Cannes. The concept for the video's writer came, oddly enough, from his girlfriend, who was always primping with her make-up (Mudhar, 2007). A different campaign focused on aging women; and the latest campaign, which featured a criminal sketch artist drawing women as they described themselves and as other people described them, won yet another prestigious award. Committed to educating the public about distorted images of beauty, Dove continues to hold seminars, workshops, and public awareness campaigns.

While the Dove campaigns continue to create a more inclusive culture of beauty and simultaneously educate the public about issues of self-esteem and eating disorders, Malala Yousafzai will be supporting the Raise Your Hand campaign for the Because I am a Girl organization. Malala is a young schoolgirl when she was shot by the Taliban while on her way to school in Pakistan in 2012. Since then, she has become an international symbol of girls' right to an education (Because I am a Girl, 2013). Focusing on educating young girls, the goals of this international organization include education and health care, clean water and food security, and livelihood initiatives to support the young girls' future.

Whether it's standing up for the education of young girls, or creating an awareness of the need for it, communities, organizations, and institutions have a duty to work toward informing all members of society about the goals of diversity and inclusion.

Doing

Are **institutions** and **organizations** the same thing? Surprisingly, even though the terms are often used interchangeably, they do not have the same meaning. The distinctions between the two are important, especially when it comes to effecting any kind of change. Institutions have both a formal side (laws, rules, regulations) and an informal side (norms, values, and mores); North (1991) characterizes institutions by the following traits:

Institution: A governing body through which social order and basic societal needs are met.

Organization: A formal or informal group of like-minded people working together to meet an agreed-upon goal.

- They are socially determined and govern social, political, cultural, and economic exchanges and interactions.
- They define a range of choices, regulate risk and uncertainty, and determine transaction

and production costs and, hence, the feasibility and profitability of engaging in economic activity.
- They evolve, incrementally, linking the past with the future.
- They provide the incentive structure of an economy, and set the tone of societal development.

Organizations, on the other hand, refer to either a formal or informal group or association, in which there are defined and accepted roles, positions, and responsibilities, structured in some relationship to each other, in order to achieve a specific objective (Uphoff, 1992).

By these definitions, you can see that the institutions are rather like the "rules" and the organizations are rather like the "players" (North, 1993). Organizations and their members work within an institutional framework while simultaneously attempting to influence that framework to achieve greater advantages and benefits. Organizations can be private (families, commercial enterprises, and corporations), civil (associations, non-governmental organizations, and membership-based groups), and public (government and government-owned enterprises) (Lobo, 2008). They exist on the private and public level, the local and international level.

In terms of addressing social change, institutions and organizations tackle the same problems but they approach them differently. By way of example, consider the recent directives toward addressing racism in the workplace. In a 2012 edition of *Canadian Diversity Magazine* devoted strictly to racism, the guest editor used the introduction to comment on the all the articles written. Determining what actions were being taken to alleviate racism, she summarized the suggestions from the articles. At the government, or institutional, level, the following mechanisms were addressed:

- Employment equity legislation
- Federal racism-free workplace program
- Fair assessment of foreign credentials
- The role of unions

On the same issue of racism in the workplace, redress to discrimination at the organizational level included the following:

- Diversity training
- Councils and networks
- Mentoring
- Rewarding managers for having a greater range of behaviours to work with a diverse workforce
- Best practices
- Intercultural leadership (Weiner, 2012).

Change at the organizational level is often change that is transformative, and it requires time and a recognition of power relations and, to some extent, healing. It often means challenging the existing norms and reshaping or rebuilding current policies and procedures. In some cases, it could mean the physical reconstruction of existing spaces to accommodate the individual needs of people—for example, transgender washrooms or the addition of ramps. At the institutional level, laws may have to be changed or enacted, which can be a lengthy, time-consuming process. There is no right or wrong answer to whether social change is better implemented at the organizational or institutional level. What is of greater importance is that the process of change begins. If no seeds are planted, then nothing will grow; but if just one seed lands, even in the most barren soil, there's always a chance that the rains will fall.

DOING THE BEST: BEST PRACTICES MODELS

The Bank of Montreal annually compiles a list of Canada's Best Diversity Employers. This list recognizes employers across the country that have exceptional workplace diversity and inclusiveness programs. The competition examines a range of diversity initiatives, including programs for five major employee groups:

1. Women
2. Members of visible minorities
3. Persons with disabilities
4. Aboriginal peoples
5. Lesbian, gay, bisexual, and transgendered/transsexual (LGBT) people (Canada's Top 100 Employers, 2013).

One of the winners in 2013 was the University of Toronto. In 2013, the University of Toronto was also recognized as one of Greater Toronto's Top Employers, as a Top 100 Employer for Canadians Over 40, and as one of Canada's Top 100 Family Friendly Employers.

The University of Toronto 2012 Employment Equity Report provides several concrete examples of why this institution has won these awards. A few of the university's initiatives are as follows:

- An increase in Indigenous programming—organized monthly learning circles, led by Elders, were open to staff, students, and faculty.
- The Anti-Racism and Cultural Diversity Office (ARDCO) in partnership with the Organizational Development and Learning Centre (ODLC) presented Culture, Conflict and Inclusion, which provided employees with information on creating a respectful, equitable, and inclusive environment.

- The Family Care Office (FCO) offered a Queer and Trans Family Planning 101 workshop where the university's community members were able to interact with facilitators of Toronto-based queer and trans family-planning courses. Participants enjoyed a productive dialogue regarding the practical, emotional, social, and legal issues involved with becoming LGBTQ parents (University of Toronto, 2012).

In addition, the Human Resources and Equity Offices at the university include assistance in the following areas:

- Accessibility for Ontarians with Disabilities Act (AODA) Office
- Anti-Racism & Cultural Diversity Office
- Community Safety Office
- Director, Faculty & Academic Life
- Employment Equity Office
- Equity Resources
- Family Care Office
- Health & Well-Being Programs & Services
- Quality of Work-Life Advisor
- Sexual & Gender Diversity Office
- Sexual Harassment Office
- Status of Women Issues Advisor

Doing diversity at the public level requires having a strategy and the people that will put it into practice. Human resource policies and practices should be equitable, just, and diversity- competent. The University of Toronto strives to "cultivate a teaching, learning and working environment that is equitable, accepting, inclusive and free from discrimination and harassment" (University of Toronto, 2013). By adopting a set of best practices and principles, and by building them into their daily operations, it seems that the university has succeeded.

The Conference Board of Canada rates Canada very high in terms of overall diversity acceptance—based on a 2011 Gallup survey of World Values, Canada rates an A, in fact. Canada's future prosperity depends on its people, including an increasing number of visible minorities. Canada's visible minority population (mainly Chinese) is projected to increase much faster than the rest of the population. Japan and Italy, on the other hand, rated a D in terms of acceptance, and only 52% of Japanese and 59% of Italians said their community was accepting of people from different racial, ethnic, and cultural groups (Conference Board of Canada, 2013). Accepting diversity is crucial if our labour force will depend on the new influx of immigrant workers, but how far up the ladder will those workers rise? How far is Canada ahead when it really comes to social inclusion?

Regardless of your chosen profession, what diversity skills will you use to interact effectively with the wide array of clients that make up Canada's diverse population?

Source: © Wavebreakmedia Ltd/Thinkstock

The Canadian Board Diversity Council (CBDC) is the leading Canadian organization promoting diversity on Canada's boards of directors (Canadian Board Diversity Council, 2012). In 2010, the CBDC reported results from surveying the directors of 450 FP500 companies (Canada's biggest companies as reported by the *Financial Post*). Those findings revealed that the majority of respondents did not have a written diversity policy nor did they feel the need to adopt one. In 2011, the results were much the same, with the exception that respondents felt as though diversity was important. The 2012 findings showed some advancement in the area of women on board—but not much (Jeffery, 2012).

When you consider the implications, the numbers are not promising. We are referring to individuals who sit on the boards of directors for the top 500 companies in Canada—very powerful people, who have the ability to promote social change and social equity on both the organizational and institutional levels. In 2012, the CBDC reported that women continue to lag far behind men in terms of representation on boards of directors. Overall, only 14.4% of FP500 corporate directors are women. Worse yet are the numbers of the three other protected groups in society. The percentage of directors who were visible minorities was less than 5%. Only 2.7% of board members self-reported as having disabilities, and board members of Aboriginal descent barely registered at 1.1% (CBDC, 2012). Speaking at a Conference Board of Canada

conference on diversity challenges in the workplace, then-president of Pitney Bowles and current CEO of Canada Post Deepak Chopra remarked:

> There are too many companies that are busy admiring the problem of diversity. We don't take that approach. When you walk onto our premises, you will never see a diversity poster. We think the ultimate recognition is our own people who are a living example of our practices. (Chopra, 2010)

Traditionally, organizations flaunt their efforts toward an inclusive workforce with signage, annual reports, and open HR policies. But for Chopra, in essence, the proof is in having a diverse workforce. As a diversity-competent practitioner, do you think that Chopra's approach to diversity is a wise one? Do you support this approach, or is it wiser to emphasize the marketing approach, and let consumers and users know that your company is aware and working toward inclusion. If you were the head of a large-scale organization or institution, what would you do to make your workforce more inclusive?

ENDING THOUGHTS

Ultimately, diversity-competent practitioners can have all the necessary tools, all the required experience, and all the learning that money can buy; but if they don't have the right attitude, they aren't going to be effective. A guiding principle that might be included in any practitioner's toolkit is this:

> I believe the single most significant decision I can make on a day-to-day basis is my choice of attitude. It is more important than my past, my education, my bankroll, my successes or failures, fame or pain, what other people think of me or say about me, my circumstances, or my position. Attitude keeps me going or cripples my progress. It alone fuels my fire or assaults my hope. When my attitudes are right, there's no barrier too high, no valley too deep, no dream too extreme, no challenge too great for me. Words can never adequately convey the incredible impact of our attitude toward life. The longer I live the more convinced I become that life is 10 percent what happens to us and 90 percent how we respond to it. (Swindoll, 2009)

As diversity-competent practitioners, you will face extraordinary circumstances in your futures. In many of these situations, you will find yourself to be privileged—the individual who holds the power—but in others, you might be the one who is powerless. For example, when preparing a grant proposal, you may have tried your best, but the ultimate decision rests in the hands of someone else. If your funding is denied, your reaction plays a big role in the strategy of your plan. The key to maintaining dignity and energy for yourself and those for whom you advocate, even in the face of adversity, lies in your ability to maintain a positive attitude.

You will make a lot of choices in your academic, personal, and professional careers. Choose wisely and you WILL change the world.

READING

Me to We: Turning Self-Help on Its Head

Excerpted from Chapter Ten—Help Yourself to a Better World: Join the Movement

By Marc and Craig Kielburger

"Never doubt that a small group of thoughtful, committed citizens can change the world. Indeed, it is the only thing that ever has." Margaret Mead (1901–1978), Anthropologist

If reaching out and helping others is so beneficial for us socially, emotionally, mentally and physically, then why aren't all people doing it? Why don't we have a world full of interactive and cooperative communities, in which everyone gets along, helps one another, and feels good?
Well, first, our society's tragic underconsumption of broccoli appears to indicate that we haven't yet arrived at the stage of evolution where we all do what's good for our health.

Second, we're stuck. In Grade 10 science class, we called it "inertia": the tendency of a body to remain in a uniform, perpetual state of rest or motion until acted upon by an external force. Millions of us are bystanders on a massive, worldwide scale. We know there are problems. We know people need help. We know we *can* help. But most of us continue to stand by.

Moving beyond our societal inertia won't be easy. The problems we see every day in the media are often intimidating because of their sheer size and complexity, and our self-help culture makes it difficult for us to even care. We feel paralyzed by the conflicting choices that we think we have to make between what is popular and what is right. Often without real grounds, we fear that others will see us as "abnormal" or "radical" if we begin to question the injustices around us. What will happen if we stand out from the crowd and no one follows? What will happen if we don't succeed?

Those same risks stood before women seeking equality with me, African Americans seeking civil rights, South Africans seeking an end to apartheid, countless countries around the world (including Americans) seeking self-determination and independence from colonialism, and peace activists seeking a ban on the use of landmines. The realities they face were different from their vision of a better world. Colossal barriers lined their path to a just society. Inertia appeared overwhelming. But it was *not* insurmountable.

The precise reasons for the success of the world's most celebrated social movements are hotly debated in academic literature and activist circles. But their beginnings are uncontestable: somebody *did* something. A bystander acted. Inertia was pushed into action.

THE MOVEMENT FROM *ME* TO *WE*

This movement is characterized by a spirit of compassion and justice, where we look out for not only our own individual interests, but also those of others—people in our local and global communities, our environments, our families and ourselves.

When people think of movements they immediately envision marches and demonstrations, public protests, petitions, and the changing of laws. While these activities are elements of a social movement, they are not its end goal. ... Renowned activist Bill Moyer, defines social movements as "Collective actions in which the populace is alerted, educated, and mobilized, sometimes over years and decades, to challenge the powerholders and the whole society to redress social problems or grievances and restore critical social values." A movement is thus built upon values, and its goal is to bring about a fundamental shift in the psyche of a people.

In writing this book, we, too, are seeking a shift in the social psyche, in how individuals think about themselves and others. The movement from Me to We means living our daily lives as socially conscious and responsible citizens, engaging in daily acts of compassion and kindness, building meaningful relationships and community, and considering the impact on We when making decisions in our own lives. It challenges us to see ourselves as part of a greater entity and to lie with the realization that all our actions or inactions affect not only us, but also others in our evolving world. This may not seem as dramatic as the social movements of the past. These acts will probably not capture front page of the paper. But the end result will be just as powerful and important—a shift in the thinking of people, their values, beliefs, attitudes, and, yes, daily decisions. As we go from being detached spectators to active participants in our community, we move from Me to We with the understanding that we are all interconnected and that helping others is better for us all.

We may not reach the end of this thousand-mile journey in our lifetime, but as Lao Tzu said, one has to take the first step. We know that each and every positive step makes the world a better place. ... Yes, we are idealists. Yes, the world we envision seems difficult to achieve. Yes, we realize that we have a lot of people to convince. But sometimes it takes a little bit of idealism to change the world.

Women voting? Yeah right, Harriet Taylor. An end to slavery? Surely you jest, Frederick Douglass. An international ban on landmines? Get out of town, Jody Williams. A black president of South Africa? Nelson Mandela, you are too much!

When studying the history of social movements, we remember major events like the Storming of the Bastille during the French Revolution, the "March on Washington" when Martin Luther King gave his impassioned "I Have a Dream" speech, or the Rivonia Trial when Nelson Mandela was sentenced to life imprisonment. But we usually overlook the smaller, daily actions and sacrifices of thousands of ordinary people that provided the foundation for these social movements to become a reality.

The civil rights movement was fueled by the actions of individuals like Rosa Parks, who in 1955 refused to move to the back of the bus in her hometown of Montgomery, Alabama. This small action sent forth a ripple and grew into a wave that spread to the hearts of millions of people prompting them to speak about the issue in fields and factories, on their front porches and around kitchen tables, in town halls and churches. Small groups of people came together, discussed and debated, struggled and strived, organized and spoke out. They lived through pain, setbacks, abuse, and distress before a single civil rights marcher ever placed a foot on the Washington Monument. Every action taken by an individual and group to stand up against segregation and systemic discrimination contributed to the success of the movement, the work of which is still not finished, but has profoundly altered the course of American history ...

Social movements like the civil rights and women's movements are not just for the history books. Struggles continue today over these issues and others, including aboriginal issues, disability rights, poverty and hunger, the environment, and numerous other global problems. They have built on the actions and energy of thousands of individuals and groups striving to create a better world, step by step.

We have seen the power of social movements to bring about change. Free The Children is an example of what a small group of ordinary people—even children—can do when they are willing to take that first important step to help another.

Ten years ago, we would have laughed if someone had told us that Free The Children would grow to be so large today, having already affected the lives of over one million children worldwide. We started with small actions—giving speeches to local schools, a neighbourhood garage sale to raise money to improve the lives of poor children, and a petition to call for more government intervention to protect children's rights.

SETTING THE STAGE FOR A SOCIAL MOVEMENT

The key to success was three-fold. First we were willing to take a risk. By taking a stand, we put ourselves "on the line" and faced the possibility of failure. When Craig stood up in front of his Grade 7 class and spoke about the article that had inspired him regarding the young boy sold into child labour, he took a risk. There was a risk he would be laughed at by his peers. There was a risk that no one would join him. There was a risk that no one would care. But he decided to speak up anyway. It wasn't that he was without anxiety—in fact, he was incredibly nervous! But he was able to overcome his fear because this story had touched him so deeply, and because he was so firm in his belief that he had to act.

We were nervous the first time we challenged an adult on a social justice issue. We were uneasy the first time we asked someone for a donation. We were scared when we first boarded a plane to travel to Asia and leave behind the friends and family whom we had come to rely upon throughout our childhood. It was difficult for us to take these first steps. And it may be equally difficult for you to take your first step— whether it be reaching out to a neighbor in need, walking into a hospital to volunteer, or stepping outside your comfort zone and taking action on an issue that is important to your community. But that first step is critical. Once the inertia is broken, each act builds upon the foundation of the previous one, and each step becomes a little easier. In the same way, every social movement has its setbacks and triumphs. Although standing up for what you value is not an easy task, it can be a very rewarding one.

The second reason for the success of Free The Children is that we were not alone in this journey. The organization grew beyond our initial vision and became a movement shared by many people—especially children who realized that they, too, had the power to change the world.

In taking the first step you may feel alone—we certainly felt that way when we started. However, people quickly began to take note of our activities and offered to help. Support first came from the individuals who were closest to us: our parents and our family members. Then our energy and passion became contagious and our friends and classmates began to help. Then our friends' friends did as well. The organization grew by word of mouth and we soon began to receive e-mails from complete strangers who had heard about the movement and wanted to be of assistance.

The third and perhaps most important reason for the success of Free The Children is also arguably the most simple: it was a movement whose time had come. Previously organizations espousing children's issues had worked *for* children, but rarely *with* children, denying young people a voice in decisions that affected their future. Can you imagine a conference on women's rights that excluded women? The idea of a network of children helping children was part of the growth of a larger movement that recognized the valuable contributions that young people could make in helping themselves and their peers.

Social movements—a pivotal change in thinking—wait for the right set of circumstances to be present before they emerge. People involved in mediation in conflict areas have told us that only when both sides accept the fact that their current situation is causing them pain and recognize that neither side can change the situation alone—something they call a hurting stalemate—are they willing to move ahead. The question is whether we as a society have reached the stage where people feel unfulfilled, frustrated, and unhappy enough to willingly make change in their own lives. This is the point of impasse from which all movements begin. For generations, people knew that slavery was wrong, that African Americans and women should have the right to vote, and that apartheid was evil. However, there finally came a time when social, political, and economic factors made the women's rights, civil rights and anti-apartheid movements possible. This hurting stalemate, an inner readiness for change,

is the first stage in the emergence of a social movement. The second stage is the trigger that sets it in motion.

In his well-known book, *Tipping Point,* Malcolm Gladwell argues that large-scale changes in societal attitudes and behaviours are like epidemics. The slightest action or change in environment has the power to tip society's attitude and behaviour with respect to an issue. Either through the extraordinary actions of a few people, the overwhelming pervasiveness of a message or idea, or an unrelated change in the overall environment, a widespread social trend can sweep into existence; the result is that inertia is blown off the map. The message behind the *Tipping Point* is that any small action can be the one to tip a situation into what becomes a far-reaching phenomenon. And more importantly, every small action that is taken contributes to creating the perfect environment for the tipping point to occur.

The *Me to We* philosophy is an idea whose time has come. It is the alternative for which we have been searching, and the foundation of a happier, more compassionate, and more fulfilling community for all of us. To participate in the movement from *Me to We*, you have to be willing to take action, however small, to improve the life of another. You do not have to start with a major world problem. As hard as it might seem to believe, your one letter, one dollar, one smile, or one act could be the tipping point in the life of one person. You may never know how many others are engaging in similar actions, but you will not be alone. You can only begin to imagine the ripples you send forward as others are inspired to join you in this movement.

What we often forget about Grade 10 science is that inertia also refers to the capacity of an entity to move relentlessly forward forever. All it takes is one small force—one tipping point—to give it a push, and it will carry itself forth into eternity.

Source: Craig and Marc Kielburger, *Me to We: Turning Self-Help on Its Head.* © Craig and Marc Kielburger, 2004.

DISCUSSION QUESTIONS

1. In this reading, philanthropists Marc and Craig Kielburger explain why they think people aren't reaching out and helping each other more often. What are your reasons? How do you explain the fact that so many people are not willing to "help a brother or sister out"?
2. What do you think it takes to make the transition from contributing on a personal level to making contributions on a larger scale? Have you ever organized a fundraiser or taken part in social change beyond your individual practices? If so, describe the differences between the two.
3. Does everyone have the capacity to start a revolution for change? Does it go back to nature vs. nurture? Does it take a certain personality type, and if so, what's a crucial character trait?

KWIP

KNOW IT AND OWN IT: WHAT DO I BRING TO THIS?

All of us at some point in our lives experience oppression because of certain aspects of our identity; and at other times we experience privilege because of certain aspects of our identity. Hopefully, you now bring to the table greater

self-awareness of this issue. You may through your own lived experience understand the personal and social consequences of being marginalized or socially included. You have listened to the voices of other students and empathized with their diverse lived experiences as you walked a mile in their shoes. You have learned that diversity competency is a life-long journey of self-discovery, learning, and experiencing. So what are you doing in your everyday life to practise diversity?

WALKING THE TALK: HOW CAN I LEARN FROM THIS?

For most people, in order to walk the talk, they need to understand why diversity matters. There needs to be some relevance to individuals' lives in order for them to embrace its practice. There also needs to be an opportunity to continue to learn and grow. The opportunity to marry knowledge with action helps to ground diversity competencies in meaningful ways that impact on the lived experiences of other people and create social change. On a personal level, meaningful action may be as an ally to someone who needs support or it may be a random act of kindness. On a structural level, it could mean that you become an agent of organizational change in your workplace.

IT IS WHAT IT IS: IS THIS INSIDE OR OUTSIDE YOUR COMFORT ZONE?

Few people are comfortable with all forms of visible and invisible difference. Developing awareness, understanding, and competency can at times be a scary journey. For some, the fear originates in lack of exposure or limiting social experiences. Perhaps your map of the world has been limited to a rather small geographical area. Or maybe you have a very large map with numerous interconnections and relationships. Some of these connections could be negative and thereby influence your perceptions and assumptions. All of us are challenged by the process of diversity competence to move outside our comfort zone, to question assumptions, to critically analyze what we know, and to have the courage to act.

PUT IT IN PLAY: HOW CAN I USE THIS?

Why are we interested in becoming diversity-competent practitioners? The Conference Board of Canada (2008) has found that diversity and inclusion are competencies that many corporations consider in hiring new employees, and diversity management is considered an essential component of their organizational structure. As we move into an ever more pluralistic and multicultural society, diversity competency is also considered valuable in the helping professions, as service outcomes are dependent upon effective service delivery to diverse populations. The diversity-competent practitioner is able to act equitably and justly with diverse populations, and becoming diversity-competent can help to make you, on a personal level, a skilled candidate for potential employers, and, on a public level, an informed global citizen making a difference in the world.

CourseMate Study Tools

Located at www.nelson.com/site/walkamile1e

- Consolidate your knowledge with the **Flashcards**.
- Gauge your understanding with **Picture This** and accompanying questions for reflection.
- Develop your critical thinking skills by working through **The Daily**.
- Apply your understanding with **KWIP** interactive!
- Develop your critical reading skills through compelling **Readings** and accompanying short answer questions.

REFERENCES

Baird, F. (2013). The international men's march to stop rape, sexual assault and gender violence. Retrieved from *Walk a Mile in Her Shoes*: http://www.walkamileinhershoes.org/index.html#

Because I am a Girl. (2013). Malala raises her hand for girls! Retrieved from *Because I am a Girl*: https://becauseiamagirl.ca/malala-raises-her-hand-for-girls-education

Berman, N., & Mellon, E. (2012). Contextualising the self and social change making: An evaluation of the Young Social Pioneers Program. *Cosmopolitan Civil Societies Journal*, 52–70.

Birmingham City University. (2012). Student academic partners. Retrieved from http://www.bcusu.com/learning/academicpartnerships/saps/; http://www.bcusu.com/pageassets/learning/academicpartnerships/saps/downloads/BCU-Student-Engagement-brochure.pdf

Bishop, A. (1994). *Becoming an ally: Breaking the cycle of oppression*. Halifax: Fernwood Publishing.

Bishop, A. (2011). Tools for achieving equity in people and institutions. Retrieved from *Becoming an Ally*: http://www.becominganally.ca/Becoming_an_Ally/Home.html

Canada's Top 100 Employers. (2013, February 19). Canada's best diversity employers. Retrieved from *Recognizing the employers that offer Canada's most inclusive workplaces*: http://www.canadastop100.com/diversity/

Canadian Board Diversity Council. (2010). Vision and mandate. Retrieved from *The Canadian Board Diversity Council*: http://www.boarddiversity.ca/vision-mandate

Canadian Board Diversity Council. (2012). 2012 annual report card. Retrieved from *Canadian Board Diversity Council*: http://www.boarddiversity.ca/sites/default/files/CBDC-Annual-Report-Card-2012-ENG.pdf

Chopra, D. (2010, March 10). Workplace diversity and inclusion. Retrieved from *Conference Board of Canada*: http://www.conferenceboard.ca/onboard/onboard-november-2010.aspx

City of Victoria. (2012). Civic engagement at the city of Victoria. Retrieved from *City of Victoria*: http://www.victoria.ca/assets/Departments/Communications/Documents/engaging-foundations-for-success.pdf

Conference Board of Canada. (2008). Creating a competency model for diversity and inclusion practitioners. Retrieved from *Conference Board of Canada*: http://www.conference-board.org/pdf_free/councils/TCBCP005.pdf

Conference Board of Canada. (2013). Acceptance of diversity. Retrieved from *How Canada Performs*: http://www.conferenceboard.ca/hcp/details/society/acceptance-of-diversity.aspx

Cooley, C. H. (1907). Social consciousness. *Proceedings of the American Sociological Society*, (pp. 97–109). Michigan.

CTV News. (2013, March 29). Canadians 'pouring it forward' at Tim Hortons drive-thrus. Retrieved from *CTV News*: http://www.ctvnews.ca/canada/canadians-pouring-it-forward-at-tim-hortons-drive-thrus-1.1216358

DifferenceBetween.net. (2013). Difference between justice and charity. Retrieved from *DifferenceBetween.Net*: http://www.differencebetween.net/language/difference-between-justice-and-charity/

Engineers Without Borders. (2010, September 6). Steps to informed action. Retrieved from *Orangeapedia*: http://wiki.ewb.ca/en/Steps_to_Informed_Action

Etcoff, N., Orbach, S., Scott, J., & D'Agostino, J. (2004, September 1). The real truth about beauty: A global report. Retrieved from *Club of Amsterdam*: http://www.clubofamsterdam.com/contentarticles/52%20Beauty/dove_white_paper_final.pdf

Foundations for Young Australians. (2013). Young social pioneers. Retrieved from *Foundations for Young Australians*: http://www.fya.org.au/initiatives/young-social-pioneers/

Ginwright, S., & James, T. (2002). From assets to agents of change: Social justice, organizing, and youth development. *New directions for youth development*, 27–46.

Halilbegovich, N. (2008). *My childhood under fire: A Sarajevo diary*. Toronto: KidsCan Press.

Hamilton, D. R. (2011, June 2). 5 beneficial side effects of kindness. Retrieved from The *Huffington Post*: http://www.huffingtonpost.com/david-r-hamilton-phd/kindness-benefits_b_869537.html

Hill Collins, P. (1990). *Black feminist thought: Knowledge, consciousness and the politics of empowerment*. London: HarperCollins.

Jeffery, P. (2012). Founder's message. Retrieved from *Canadian Board Diversity Council*: http://www.boarddiversity.ca/founders_message

Kielburger, C., & Kielburger, M. (2004). *Me to We: Turning self-help on its head*. Mississauga: John Wiley & Sons.

Lather, P. (1988). Feminist perspectives on empowering research methodologies. *Women's Studies International Forum*, 569–581.

Lobo, C. (2008). *Institutional and organizational analysis for pro-poor change: Meeting IFAD's millennium challenge*. Rome: International Fund for Agricultural Development.

Marullo, S., & Edwards, B. (2000). From charity to justice: The potential of university-community collaboration for social change. *American Behavioral Scientist*, 895–912.

Maryanski, A. (2007, September 15). Evolutionary theory. Retrieved from *Encyclopedia of Social Theory*: http://knowledge.sagepub.com/view/socialtheory/n97.xml

Me to We. (2013). Our story. Retrieved from *Me to We: We Live the Change*: http://www.metowe.com/about-us/our-story/

Mills, C. W. (1959). *The sociological imagination*. Oxford: Oxford University Press.

Motivate Canada. (2013). ACTIVATE. Retrieved from *Motivate Canada*: http://www.motivatecanada.ca/en/activate

Mudhar, R. (2007, June 22). Dove's "evolution" ad wins at Cannes. Retrieved from *The Toronto Star*: http://www.thestar.com/entertainment/2007/06/22/doves_evolution_ad_wins_at_cannes.html

North, D. (1991). Institutions. *Journal of Economic Perspectives*, 97-112.

North, D. (1993). Institutions and credible commitment. *Journal of Institutional and Theoretical Economics*, 24-28.

PRNewswire. (2004, September 16). Dove® launches unprecedented movement to make beauty a source of confidence, not anxiety. Retrieved from *PRNewswire*: http://www.prnewswire.com/news-releases/dove-launches-unprecedented-movement

Random Acts of Kindness Foundation. (2013). 2013 kindness challenge winner. Retrieved from the *Random Acts of Kindness Foundation*: http://www.randomactsofkindness.org/kindness-videos/6810-2013-kindness-challenge-winner

Reuf, M. (2010). *The entrepreneurial group: Social identities, relations, and collective action*. New Jersey: Princeton University Press.

Ruf, E. (2013, March 13). Why is civic engagement important? Retrieved from *TMI: Inclusion for Innovation*: http://tmiconsultinginc.com/civic-engagement/765/

Schaefer, R., Smith, E., & Grekul, J. (2009). *Sociology*. Canada: McGraw-Hill.

Scott, J., & Marshall, G. (2005). *Oxford dictionary of sociology*. New York: Oxford University Press.

Spencer, M. (1993). *Foundations of modern sociology*. Toronto: Prentice Hall.

Stephens, G., Silbert, L., & Hasson, U. (2010). Speaker-listener neural coupling underlies successful communication. *National Academy of Science*, 14425–30.

Surowiecki, J. (2004). *The wisdom of crowds*. Toronto: Random House.

Swindoll, C. (2009, January 9). The value of a positive attitude. Retrieved from *Insight for Living*: http://daily.insight.org/site/News2?page=NewsArticle&id=13123

Trudel, R., & Cotte, J. (2012, 06 19). Does being ethical pay? Retrieved from *Wall Street Journal*: http://online.wsj.com/article/SB121018735490274425.html

University of Toronto. (2013). Human resources and equity. Retrieved from *University of Toronto*: http://www.hrandequity.utoronto.ca/about-hr-equity/diversity.htm

University of Toronto. (2012). University of Toronto 2012 employment equity report. Retrieved from *University of Toronto—Human Resources and Equity*: http://www.hrandequity.utoronto.ca/Assets/HR+Digital+Assets/Employment+Equity+Annual+Reports/2012eer.pdf

Uphoff, N. (1992). *Local institutions and participation for sustainable development*. London: International Institute for Environment and Development.

Weiner, N. (2012, Winter). Introduction. *Canadian Diversity (9)*1. Retrieved from *Metropolis*: http://canada.metropolis.net/pdfs/Diversite_Racism_2012_ACS.pdf

YES! (2012). Connecting, inspiring and collaborating with young changemakers. Retrieved from *YES!*: http://www.yesworld.org/

Yong-Chan, K., & Ball-Rokeach, S. (2006). Community storytelling network, neighborhood context, and civic engagement: A multilevel approach. *Human Communication Research*, 411– 439.

Youth In Motion. (2010). Our programs. Retrieved from *Youth in Motion*: http://youth-in-motion.ca/

Youth In Motion. (2013). Top 20 Under 20. Retrieved from Youth in Motion: http://www.youth-in-motion.ca/uploads/files/2013_top_20_bios.pdf

Glossary

A

ableism The set of attitudes and behaviours that allocate inferior status and or value to individuals who have developmental, emotional, physical, or psychiatric disabilities. Discrimination based on ability; occurs when a society has a set of ideas about the "normal" abilities of people. p. 32, 143

Aboriginal peoples The original peoples of North America and their descendants, consisting of three groups of people—First Nations, Inuit, and Métis. p. 81

absolute homelessness Situation of individuals who live either in emergency shelters or on the street. p. 52

absolute poverty Situation where an individual lacks even the basic resources that are necessary for survival; people who live in absolute poverty live without food, clothing, or a roof over their heads. p. 46

accessibility The degree to which a product, device, service, or environment is available to as many people as possible. p. 153

acclimatization The process of beginning to adapt to a new environment. p. 212

accommodation The specialized design of products, environments, and individualized strategies that are uniquely adapted to an identified limitation for the purpose of ensuring access. p. 146

acculturation The process of adaptation to a new culture, whereby prolonged contact between two cultures begins to modify both cultures. p. 215

acculturative stress Immigrants experience this stress when there are difficulties resulting from the acculturation process. The stress of this process increases when immigrants experience discrimination, language difficulties, and incongruencies in non-material aspects of culture. p. 215

achieved status A status that is not given at birth; for example, occupation, education, or marital status. p. 43

advocate Person who writes or speaks in representation for something, or someone, else. p. 248

ageism Stereotyping, prejudice, and discrimination against individuals or groups because of their age; it also refers to the tendency to view seniors as unable to work, confused, and fragile. p. 32

agents of change Individuals, groups, or organizations that use their various skills to bring about change. p. 242

agents of socialization The people and institutions in society that create the social contexts where socialization takes place. p. 182

aggregation Gathering individual pieces of information and bundling them into a whole. p. 250

ambiguous genitalia A birth defect where the outer genitalia don't have the appearance of either a male or a female. p. 126

androgynous Having the appearance of not being clearly masculine or feminine; applies to someone who could be either or both. p. 125

anglo-conformity Policy that informed early Canadian immigration; immigrants were expected to conform to dominant British-based culture as opposed to retaining their own. p. 228

antiracist Against or opposed to racism. p. 62

apartheid Any system or policy that divides people based on their race. p. 44

arbitration Occurs when two disputing parties call in a third, neutral party to help them settle their dispute. p. 110

ascribed identity Identity based on traits and characteristics that others use to define an individual. p. 15

ascribed status Status given at birth, such as gender, age, or race. p. 43

Asian Heritage Month Observed annually in Canada (and the United States where it is called Asian-Pacific American Heritage Month) in May. The purpose of the month is to learn about and acknowledge the historical and contemporary contributions made by Canadians of Asian heritage. p. 74

assimilation The process by which minority group members adopt the culture of the dominant group until they become indistinguishable from the dominant group; often referred to as the "melting pot "; total re-socialization of individuals from one culture to another, such that traces of the former culture eventually deteriorate. p. 215, 226

assimilationist policy Policy that encourages immigrants to integrate into the mainstream culture. p. 226

asylum seeker An individual who is seeking refuge (i.e., political asylum) in a foreign country and whose case is not yet decided. p. 203

avowed identity Identity based on traits and characteristics that individuals use to define themselves. p. 15

B

Baby Boomers Those individuals born between 1946 and 1964 and raised by Traditionalists. p. 169

Balanced Refugee Reform Act Immigration legislation that, together with the Protecting Canada's Immigration System Act, makes changes to the Immigration and Refugee Protection Act and the refugee claimant process in Canada. p. 205

balkanize Divide into hostile groups; refers to what happened when Yugoslavia was dissolved. p. 227

barriers Policies or practices that prevent full and equal participation in society; barriers can be physical, social, attitudinal, organizational, technological, or informational. p. 153

best practice A benchmark, process, strategy, system, approach, policy, procedure, program, or design that has been proven to work well and produce positive outcomes and then is used as a model or optimal standard. p. 11

bicultural Retaining two distinct cultural identities; in Canadian history, it often means the recognition of England and France as primary cultures within Canada. p. 229

bilingual Able to speak two languages; in Canadian history, the official recognition of English and French as equal official languages. p. 229

birth rate The number of live births per year per 1000 population. p. 218

bisexual Sexual orientation in which one is sexually attracted to members of both sexes. p. 124

Black History Month Observed during the month of February in Canada, the United States, and the United Kingdom to commemorate the important people and events and history of the African diaspora. p. 73

boomerang generation Term used to describe those young adults who return to their parental home after leaving for education, work, or a relationship. p. 185

C

Canadian Charter of Rights and Freedoms Referred to as the Charter, it is a bill of rights and the first part of the 1982 Constitution Act; it is considered the highest law of Canada and, as such, supersedes any other federal or provincial law that conflicts with it. p. 145

Canadian Human Rights Act Statute passed in 1977 to ensure equal opportunity; protects Canada's citizens against discrimination based on race, national or ethnic origin, colour, religion, age, sex, sexual orientation, marital status, family status, disability, and conviction for a pardoned offence. p. 145

Canadian Multicultural Act Law passed in 1988 that aims to preserve and enhance multiculturalism in Canada. p. 230

caste system A closed stratified system in India that is premised on ascription or birth. p. 43

castes Fixed groups that individuals are born into based on their societal roles; a caste is an unalterable social status, passed on through heredity. p. 44

cede Surrender or forfeit possession of something, usually by treaty. p. 85

census An official count of the population, with details as to age, sex, occupation, and so on. p. 182

charity Actions or donations to help those in need. p. 244

chronic disease A disease that lasts a long time and progresses slowly; examples are arthritis and heart disease. p. 165

Citizenship and Immigration Canada Government department that is responsible for immigration, settlement, resettlement, citizenship, and multiculturalism programs and services. p. 212

civic engagement Political or non-political participation and promotion of the well-being of a community. p. 250

classism The systematic oppression of dominant class groups on subordinate classes in order to gain advantage and strengthen their own positions. p. 33

closed system society Society where status is based largely on ascription and individuals are restricted in their movements between and within strata. p. 43

cognitive disorders Category of mental disorders that affect memory, perception, learning, and problem-solving; examples include dementia and Alzheimer's disease. p. 166

cohort Any group of people who share a time-specific period, such as graduating in the same year. p. 164

common-law couple Two individuals living together but who aren't considered married. p. 188

complex stepfamilies Families with children of both parents and children of one parent only, families with children of each parent and no children of both parents, or families with children of both parents and children of each parent. p. 188

comprehensive claims A modern-day "treaty-making process," where Aboriginal land rights have not been dealt with by past treaties or through other legal means. p. 87

computer-assisted instruction Form of instruction that involves the use of computers to present various materials (such as practice drills or exercises) to engage the student interactively and to enhance learning. p. 174

Convention against Torture United Nations international human rights agreement signed on December 10, 1984, as a commitment against the use of torture in their country for any reason; signatory nations also agree not to use any evidence obtained under torture and not to deport or return people to countries where they are at risk of being tortured. p. 205

Convention refugee Individual who has been granted asylum by the 1951 Geneva Convention Relating to the Status of Refugees; someone who has reason to fear persecution in his or her country of origin due to race, religion, nationality, membership in a social group, or political opinion. p. 204

creed A doctrine or system of beliefs—very much like dogma. p. 107

Cross Culture Kid (CCK) A child who has lived in or meaningfully interacted with two or more different cultures during his or her childhood. p. 203

cultural competency The ability of an organization or individual to practise in a manner that is respectful of and consistent with a client's or a patient's culture. p. 3

cultural genocide The deliberate destruction of the cultural heritage and traditions of a group of people or a nation. p. 94

cultural imperialism A form of oppression where the dominant group has made their beliefs and values the norms of a society (for example, heterosexuality or Christianity). p. 31

cultural racism Includes both individual and systemic forms of racism. p. 67

cultural relativism The idea that no cultural standpoint is privileged over another; assumption that all cultures are essentially equally valuable and should be judged according to their own standards. p. 7

culture The total of everything in our social environment that we learn through socialization, that is passed down from one generation to the next, and that continues to change throughout our lives. p. 6

culture shock Negative consequences of intercultural contact; more specifically refers to the stress and confusion that individuals feel from being immersed in a new environment where cultural and communication patterns are foreign to them. p. 203

cyberbullying The practice of harassing someone online; includes sending threatening or aggressive messages, spreading malicious gossip through email or on websites, or using someone else's identity online. p. 173

D

developing countries Designation used only for statistical convenience in measuring countries against the United Nation's Human Development Index; the term is used to replace the terms "Third World" or "underdeveloped countries." p. 210

difference In a social context, it is a term used to refer to difference in social characteristics. p. 3

disability A universal human experience that anyone can experience at any time; disabilities can limit a person's ability to engage in daily activities; disabilities can be visible or invisible, temporary or permanent. p. 140

disablism A term that is used to refer to discrimination based on disability; while Canadians are more apt to use the term *ableism*, the term *disablism* is used more frequently internationally. p. 160

discrimination The unequal treatment of individuals or groups based on their characteristics or behaviours. It involves actions or practices of dominant group members that have a harmful impact on members of a subordinate group. p. 29

diversity A framework used to acknowledge difference-based guiding principles of social equity, social justice, and anti-oppression. p. 2

diversity competency The ability to work effectively with diverse populations in a manner that protects and preserves their dignity and recognizes, affirms, and values differences, similarities, and worth. p. 9

diversity wheel A tool developed by Marilyn Loden to analyze different social aspects and dimensions of a person's identity. p. 17

dogma A system of beliefs or bodies of knowledge believed to be true by a particular group—often a church. p. 104

dominant group A group in a society with social power. p. 4

duty to accommodate A legal principle that requires employers to identify and change any rules, practices, expectations, or procedures that have or may have a discriminatory impact based on the Canadian Human Rights Act's prohibited grounds—namely, race, national or ethnic origin, colour, religion, age, sex (including pregnancy), sexual orientation, marital status, family status, and disability. p. 146

E

eagle feather A great honour among Aboriginal peoples; represents a mark of distinction. p. 98

economic migrant Person who moves to another country for employment or a better economic future. p. 211

elder abuse A single or repeated act against an older person in which harm or distress is caused. p. 166

employment equity Requirement under the Employment Equity Act of Canada that employers use proactive employment practices to increase representation of four designated groups: women, people with disabilities, Aboriginal peoples, and racialized communities in the workplace. Employment equity mandates the accommodation of difference with special measures when needed. p. 67

Employment Equity Act Law that requires employers in Canada to eliminate barriers to and increase the hiring of women, people with disabilities, Aboriginal people, and visible minorities. p. 230

enfranchisement The process whereby an individual gets the right to vote or become a citizen. p. 91

equality Fairness and justice achieved through same treatment. p. 4

equity Principle based on fairness, justice, access, opportunity, and advancement for everyone, while recognizing historically underserved and unrepresented populations, identifying conditions needed to provide effective opportunities for all groups, and eliminating barriers to their full participation. p. 4

equivalency State of being equal to another. p. 5

ethically produced products Goods that were produced in such a way that their production function or activities were not harmful to the consumer or to society. p. 245

ethnic cleansing The process or policy of eliminating unwanted ethnic, racial, or religious groups by deportation, forcible displacement, mass murder, or threats of such acts, with the intention of creating a homogenous population. p. 64

ethnic enclave Focused areas of homogenous ethnic groups, usually coupled with some business and institutional activity. p. 233

ethnic identity The extent to which someone identifies with a particular ethnic group. p. 236

ethnicity A person's or his or her ancestors' country of origin; includes material and non-material aspects associated with a culture and social identity. p. 72

ethnocentrism A tendency to regard one's own culture and group as the standard, and thus superior, whereas all other groups are seen as inferior. p. 28

expansionism A country's practice or policy of getting bigger, usually in terms of territory or currency. p. 230

experiential affinity A feeling of closeness and understanding that someone has for someone else because of their similar experience. p. 155

exploitation The unfair use of people's time or labour without compensating them fairly. p. 31

F

false consciousness Friedrich Engels originally coined this term to attach thought to social action, but it becomes problematic when used in the context of victim/saviour. In a modern context, false consciousness refers to a view of social problems as the fault of the individual rather than society. p. 7

family class Immigration category used to described immigrants who have been sponsored to come to Canada as a spouse, partner, dependent child, parent, or grandparent. p. 208

family of orientation The family someone was born or raised in; gives us our heritage, social status, and history. p. 182

family of procreation The family we create when we become adults. p. 182

fiduciary A person who holds power or property in trust for another person—usually for the benefit of the other person. p. 91

First Nations A term used to refer to those Aboriginal people who are of neither Inuit nor Métis descent; First Nations refers to the ethnicity, while a band may be a grouping of individuals within that ethnicity (e.g., Seneca or Oneida). p. 81

fluidity Characteristic of identity that describes it as something that can change and be shaped. p. 11

Free The Children A global charity and youth movement founded by Craig Kielburger. p. 251

G

gay Someone who is emotionally and physically attracted to a member of the same sex. p. 121

gender The social and/or cultural aspect of masculinity and femininity. p. 123

gender dysphoria A condition where a person feels as though their physical self contradicts their sense of gender identity. p. 126

gender identity A person's perception or conception of him- or herself, in terms of masculine or feminine. p. 123

gender inequality The disparities (either obvious or hidden) that people experience based on their gender, as opposed to their biological sex. p. 132

gender roles Preconceived sets of behaviours, norms, and values that are associated with males and females in any given culture. p. 123

gender stereotypes Exaggerated, one-sided images by which the media repeatedly portray men and women in the same typical roles. p. 121

gender variants Individuals whose expressions of gender don't conform to the traditional norms of masculine and feminine. p. 126

generation A cohort or group of people who share similar chronological ages (usually in 15-year time spans) and who were shaped by the events, trends, and developments of a particular span of time p. 164

Generation AO Those individuals born around the turn of this century who are growing up in a highly technological world. p. 174

Generation X Those individuals born between 1965 and 1980. p. 170

Generation Y Those individuals born between 1981 and 2006; also known as Millennials. p. 172

genocide The intentional extermination or killing of an identifiable group. p. 64

gentrified Improved so as to appear more middle class. p. 234

Gini index A commonly used measure of income inequality, which measures inequality on a scale of 0 to 1; a Gini index of 0 represents exact equality (i.e., every person in a certain society or nation has the same amount of income), while a Gini index of 1 represents total inequality (i.e., one person has all the income and the rest of the society has none). p. 48

glass ceiling An invisible barrier that prevents women and minorities from advancement in organizations. p. 133

global citizenship Developing the competencies to actively engage with the world, and help to make it a more just, equitable, and sustainable place to live in. p. 9

Government Assisted Refugee (GAR) A government-sponsored refugee selected overseas for resettlement in Canada. p.209

granny cams Security cameras intended to monitor for elder abuse by caregivers. p. 166

guest worker Foreign worker who is only allowed to live in the country as a "guest" of his or her employer on a temporary basis. p. 227

H

hate crimes Crimes that are committed against people or property that are motivated solely by hate or prejudice against a victim's racial, ethnic, religious, or sexual identity; they can involve intimidation, harassment, destruction of property, vandalism, physical force or threat of physical force, or inciting hatred in other people. p. 66, 111

head tax Tax imposed by the Canadian government on anyone immigrating to Canada from China between 1885 and 1923. p. 204

healthy immigrant effect Immigrants' health is generally better than the health of those born in Canada, but this declines as their years spent living in Canada increase. p. 214

heterosexism Prejudicial attitudes and discriminatory practices against homosexuals; the belief in the natural superiority of heterosexuality as a way of life and therefore its logical right to dominance. Comprised of a system of ideas and institutionalized beliefs, it leads to the oppression of any non-heterosexual form of behaviour, identity, relationship, or community. p. 33, 190

heterosexuality The state of being sexually attracted to members of the opposite sex. p. 124

hidden or concealed homelessness State of those without a place of their own who live in a car, with family or friends, or in a long-term institution such as a prison. p. 52

home-grown terrorism Acts or plans of mass violence for political purposes that are initiated and/or carried out by residents or citizens as opposed to foreign nationals. p. 226

homelessness Social category that includes anyone who cannot obtain and sustain long-term, adequate, and risk-free shelter, for any reason. p. 51

homosexuality The state of being sexually attracted to members of the same sex. p. 125

host country A country where representatives or organizations of another country co-exist either because they've been invited by the government or because an international agreement exists. p. 212

human rights commission A national or international organized body that investigates, protects, and advocates for the rights of human beings. p. 107

I

identity Social construction of a person's sense of self that is based upon social categories that influence self-perception and the perception of others. p. 14

immigrants People residing in Canada who were born outside of Canada; this category excludes Canadian citizens born outside of Canada and people residing in Canada on temporary status, such as those with a student visa or temporary foreign workers. p. 208

immigration Entering into and becoming established in a new place of residence; usually means entering a country that one was not born in. p. 204

Immigration and Refugee Protection Act (IRPA) Legislation whose mission is "respecting immigration to Canada and the granting of refugee protection to persons who are displaced, persecuted or in danger." p. 203

Immigration and Refugee Board (IRB) Independent tribunal established by the Parliament of Canada the mission of which is to resolve immigration and refugee cases efficiently, fairly, and in accordance with the law. p. 203

impairment According to the biomedical perspective, a medical condition that leads to disability; according to functional perspective, it is any loss or abnormality of physiological, psychological, or anatomical structure or function, whether permanent or temporary. p. 141

inclusion Creating an environment that embraces diversity and where everyone is made to feel welcome, invited to participate, and valued and respected for their contributions. p. 6

inclusive language A policy or practice that includes and reflects the diversity of communities in an accurate and respectful way. p. 68

individual or direct discrimination The denial of a right or freedom, by an individual, against another individual, institution, or group. p. 30

Indian Act of 1876 Assimilatory Canadian federal legislation, first passed in 1876, and subsequently amended, which details certain federal government obligations and regulates the management of reserve lands, money, and other resources previously negotiated with Canada's first peoples. p. 81

Indian Register Document that kept track of all of the existing records of people recognized by the federal government as members of an "Indian" band; started in the 1850s. p. 91

indigenous Term used to describe a variety of Aboriginal groups and, in very broad terms, refers to any group of people that are known to have initially settled in an area. p. 81

individual racism Individual discriminatory attitudes or behaviour motivated by negative evaluation a person or group of people using a socially constructed concept of race. p. 66

information communications technology (ICT) The various uses of digital technology in assisting individuals to access, store, transmit, and manipulate information. p. 164

institution A governing body through which social order and basic societal needs are met. p. 252

institutionalization The process of making something part of an already established, formalized system. p. 230

institutionalized racism Direct and intentional system of inequality based on race, which is built into societal institutions. p. 75

integrate Become an accepted part of mainstream culture. p. 226

integration The long-term, multidimensional process through which newcomers become full and equal participants in all aspects of society. As part of this process, newcomers interact with the larger society and also maintain their own identity. Integration is not a linear process. p. 212

intercultural Relating to different cultural groups. p. 2

internalized oppression Occurs when targeted people internalize (or begin to believe) the negative stereotypes and misinformation that the larger society communicates to them, either as individuals or part of a larger group. p. 32

internally displaced person Person who has fled his or her home because of war, violence, or human rights violations, but who remains in his or her country in another location. p. 210

interreligious marriages Occur when two individuals who believe in different faith marry. p. 112

intersectionality Refers to the way various aspects of identity interact on multiple and often simultaneous levels; can include how identity interacts with multiple systems of oppression. p. 11

intersex Having the sexual characteristics of both a male and a female. p. 126

intra-generational mobility Mobility measured over an individual's career, such as someone's first job compared to his or her last job. p. 45

Inuit The Aboriginal peoples who live in the far north or Arctic regions of Canada. p. 81

J

Jim Crow racism Anti-black racism that existed in the United States during the period of 1877–1960s; Jim Crow laws enforced racial segregation and a racialized social order that resulted in the subjugation, oppression, and death (through lynching and other violence) of African Americans. p. 62

L

language-related discrimination Discrimination that is based on a person's accent or some manner of speech (such as a person's fluency). p. 68

latent discrimination Discrimination that is hidden and may not even be obvious or known to the discriminator. p. 236

lesbian A woman who is sexually attracted to women. p. 121

low-income cut-off (LICO) Measure established by Statistics Canada annually that refers generally to what people call a poverty line; it represents the income level at which a family may face hardship because it has to spend a greater proportion of its after-tax income on food, shelter, and clothing than the average family of similar size. p. 46

low-income measure (LIM) A measure of poverty that is commonly used for making international comparisons. p. 46

lump of labour fallacy The false belief that the amount of work available to labourers is a fixed amount and, therefore, there is no capacity to absorb more labourers into an economy. p. 212

M

marginalization The process of pushing groups with less social power to the margins of society; an act of exclusion that forces minority groups to the fringes of society, most commonly based on race. p. 4, 31

market basket measure (MBM) A measure of low income based on the cost of a specified basket of goods and services representing a modest, basic standard of living in comparison to the standards of its community. p. 46

material culture The physical aspects of a culture or society; for example, food, clothes, buildings, religious objects, homes, places of worship, music, art and so on. p. 2

medicine wheel Ceremonial tool of the Indigenous people of North America; symbolizes the interconnected, circular journey of all living things. p. 82

melting pot model Immigration model, made famous by the United States, wherein newcomers are expected to dissolve that which makes them different into a "pot" mixed with everyone else. p. 226

Métis People with mixed Aboriginal and European ancestry. p. 81

migrate To move from one country, place, or region to another. p. 203

Millennium Development Goals (MDG) A set of eight goals established by a global partnership committed to reduce extreme poverty by 2015; the goals are to eradicate extreme poverty and hunger, to achieve universal primary education, to promote gender equality and empower women, to reduce child mortality, to improve maternal health, to combat HIV/AIDS, malaria, and other diseases, to ensure environmental sustainability, and to develop a global partnership for development. p. 49

mixed marriages Unions of people from different ethnocultural backgrounds. p. 187

monopoly Situation where someone has exclusive control over goods or services, allowing them to set any price. p. 85

mosaic model The Canadian immigration model in which newcomers are encouraged to maintain their unique and distinct cultures and live alongside other Canadians with other distinct cultures. p. 226

multiculturalism The practice of creating harmonious relations between different cultural groups. p. 3

N

National Aboriginal History Month Observed annually in Canada during the month of June to recognize the past and present contributions of First Nations, Inuit, and Métis peoples to the birth and development of Canada. p. 74

National Day of Action Day devoted to raising the awareness of serious issues facing Aboriginal people in Canada; first organized on June 29, 2007. p. 96

National Household Survey Information previously collected by the mandatory long-form census questionnaire; provides data to support federal, provincial, territorial, and local government planning and program delivery. p. 182

neo-Nazism A post–World War II movement related to the white nationalist and white power skinhead movements, which seeks to revive elements of Nazi ideology such as racism, xenophobia, homophobia, holocaust denial, and anti-Semitism. p. 70

newcomer Blanket term used to refer inclusively to all immigrants and refugees who have recently arrived in the country to settle on a permanent basis. p. 212

non-material culture The non-physical aspects of culture or society, including customs, traditions, symbols, language, values, beliefs, norms, and sanctions. p. 2

O

omnibus bills Proposed laws or legislature that can cover a number of different subjects, but are packaged together in one bill. p. 95

open system society Society where status is based largely on achievement and individuals have the ability to move between and within different strata. p. 43

oppression Describes policies, practices, norms, and traditions that systematically exploit one group at the expense of another. p. 30

oral-based knowledge systems Ways of knowing that provide an account of a group's origins, history, and spirituality, passed on through the tradition of oral storytelling. p. 82

organization A formal or informal group of like-minded people working together to meet an agreed-upon goal. p. 252

overt racism Racism that is direct, open, and often public; examples of this are found in hate crimes, the ideology of white superiority as voiced in white power music, and blatant racist statements. p. 70

oxytocin A hormone that promotes a feeling of connectedness and bonding. p. 249

P

paradigm A model, typical pattern, or framework. p. 9

Participation and Activity Limitation Survey A national survey the purpose of which is to gather information on all people whose daily activities are limited by a physical, mental, or other health-related condition or problem. p. 148

pathologization Characterization as medically or psychologically abnormal. p. 143

patriarchy Historically, any social system that was based on the authority of the heads of the household, which were traditionally male; recently, the term has come to mean male domination in general. p. 130

people of colour Term intended to be more positive and inclusive of people than the terms "non-white" or "visible minorities"; refers to people who may share common experiences of racism. p. 63

permanent resident According to the Canadian Immigration and Refugee Protection Act (2002), a person who has come to Canada and successfully applied and received immigration status to live here permanently. p. 215

personal identity The part of person's identity determined by his or her individual attributes and characteristics. p. 14

phenotype The visible traits a person (or organism) displays. p. 232

pigmentocracy A social hierarchy based on skin pigmentation that places light skin on the top. p. 68

pluralism Existence of recognized diverse groups within a single (peaceful) society. p. 230

"post-Christian" society A society in which the traditional values, beliefs, and symbols of Christianity are declining in meaning, leading toward secularization. p. 106

post-traumatic stress disorder (PTSD) A psychological disorder caused by a traumatic event involving actual or threatened death or serious injury to oneself or others; symptoms may include anxiety, depression, survivor guilt, sleep disturbances and nightmares, impaired use or loss of memory, concentration difficulties, hype arousal, hypersensitivity, suspiciousness, fear of authority, and paranoia. p. 215

potlatch Organized meeting for special ceremonies, such as name-giving, birth, rites of passage, treaties, and weddings; practised mainly by First Nations of the west coast. p. 91

power The ability to do want you want even in the face of opposition. p. 4

powerlessness Lack of authority or capacity to act; occurs when the dominant group has left the subordinate group with virtually no access to the rights and privileges that the dominant group enjoys. p. 31

precarious employment Employment that differs from the traditional ideal of a stable, full-time job. p. 133

prejudice A negative attitude based on learned notions about members of selected groups, based on their physical, social, or cultural characteristics. p. 27

privilege Benefits or advantages that are often unearned and can occur unconsciously because of social power; a special right or benefit that only certain people have access to by birth or ascription. p. 4

protected person Someone who, according to the Immigration and Refugee Protection Act, meets the definition of a Convention refugee. p. 209

Protecting Canada's Immigration System Act Immigration legislation designed to make the review and determination of refugee claims faster and to expedite removals of those who do not qualify. p. 205

Q

Quebec nationalism The belief that Quebec should be recognized as a sovereign and separate nation. p. 229

questioning Refers to individuals who are uncertain about their gender, sexual identity, or sexual orientation; individuals who may be unsure of their sexuality or are still exploring their feelings. p. 121

Quiet Revolution Period during the 1960s when Quebec saw rapid secularization and an increased sense of nationalism. p. 229

R

race Concept no longer recognized as valid except in terms of its social consequences; for many years, the concept of race referred to biological divisions between human beings based primarily on their skin colour. p. 64

race card Term that refers to the use of race to gain an advantage. p. 62

racial discrimination Behaviour that has a discriminatory effect based on race; there does not have to be an intention to discriminate. p. 63

racial harassment Pattern of behavioural conduct that isolates, humiliates, or intimidates racialized individuals; can include name calling, slurs based on racial or ethnic stereotypes, racial or ethnic jokes, cartoons, drawings or graffiti based on demeaning stereotypes, unwanted letters or phone calls of a racist nature, vandalism or damage to your property, spreading rumours, or staring at someone in an intimidating manner because of their race or colour. p. 68

racial prejudice Prejudgment or negative attitude based on a set of characteristics associated with the colour of a person's skin. p. 63

racial profiling Any action undertaken for reasons of safety, security, or public protection that relies on stereotypes to treat a person differently; while it is most often relevant in policing practices, it is not limited to the context of criminal justice. p. 68

racial stereotyping Using the concept of race or ethnicity to attach a generalized concept that all members of a group have a particular characteristic or ability. p. 66

racialization The way in which society makes the concept of race seem real; used to differentiate groups of people as unequal. p. 75

racialized Referring to people, other than Aboriginal peoples, who are non-Caucasian in race or nonwhite in colour, as defined by the Employment Equity Act. p. 96, 235

racialized persons or communities Persons or communities of persons, other than Aboriginal peoples, who are non-Caucasian in race or non-white in colour. p. 73

racism A set of ideas that entails the supremacy of one social group over another based on biological or cultural characteristics, combined with the power to put these beliefs into practice to the exclusion of minority men and women; negative attitudes of a person or group of people using a socially constructed concept of race; racism can manifest itself as feelings or behaviours that can give advantages, privilege, and power to certain groups of people, and conversely, can disadvantage or limit the opportunities of racialized individuals or racialized groups. p. 33, 62

refugee Person who is forced to flee from persecution and is outside of his or her country of origin. p. 203

refugee claimants Term used in Canadian law for asylum seekers; they receive a decision on whether they are refugees after they arrive in Canada. p. 203

relative homelessness State of those who have housing, but who live in substandard or undesirable shelter and/or who may be at risk of losing their homes. p. 52

relative poverty Situation where an individual or group lacks basic resources for survival when compared with other people in the society as a whole; relative standard of living when measured to others. p. 46

reliability Whether or not the same results would be generated if an experiment were repeated. p. 182

religious accommodation Arrangements made by an employer so that employees can do their jobs and practise their faith at the same time. p. 104

remediation Working to fix or correct something that's been broken or damaged. p. 248

resettlement The process of settling in another place or country to live; resettlement generally refers to newcomers' acclimatization and the early stages of adaptation. p. 204

reverse discrimination Discrimination against whites, usually in the form of affirmative action, employment equity, and diversity policies; the concept of reverse discrimination, specifically reverse racism, is considered by many to be impossible because of existing power structures in society. p. 62

Royal Proclamation of 1763 One of the most important documents pertaining to Aboriginal land claims. p. 85

S

segregation Imposed separation of different groups, usually unequally. p. 227

self-fulfilling prophecy Situation where a belief in something that's false actually sparks a behaviour that makes the original false assumption come true. p. 92

separatist movement A movement that seeks separation from a nation to form a smaller independent nation, as with Quebec nationalism. p. 229

settlement See resettlement. p. 204

sex The biological components that make up who we are. p. 123

sex reassignment surgery The surgical procedure where a person's physical appearance and functioning of their sex organs are modified to resemble that of the other sex. p. 123

sexism The attitudes or behaviours based on the belief that one sex is superior to the other, often resulting in the discrimination or devaluation of that sex and the roles related to it. p. 34

sexual orientation Orientation based on whom a person is attracted to affectionately and sexually. p. 124

sexuality All the ways in which individuals experience and express themselves in relation to sex and gender. p. 124

shadeism Intra-racial discrimination based on skin tone that currently privileges lighter skin tones. p. 68

shaman Aboriginal healer or spiritual counsellor. p. 82

simple stepfamilies A couple-family with the children of one, and only one, of the married or common-law partners. p. 188

Singh decision Landmark decision in refugee determination made by the Supreme Court of Canada in 1985; the decision protects the right of every refugee claimant to an oral hearing. p. 211

sizeism Discrimination against individuals based on their body size, including height and weight p. 34

social change Any major alterations in the behaviour, cultural values, and norms of a society over time. p. 242

social class Any group of people who share the same situations in a common social structure. p. 44

social construction of reality The sociological theory that proposes that how we present ourselves in any given situation is shaped by the interactions of our all our past relations and the social interactions that we have with others p. 25

social enterprise A business organization whose primary mission is social benefit to people or the environment as opposed to making profit. p. 8

social identity The part of a person's identity that is determined by attributes and characteristics of groups the person aligns him- or herself with. p. 14

social inequality The unequal distribution of tangible or intangible goods or services to individuals or groups in society. p. 42

social justice An interactive process where members seek equitable treatment for all members of society, regardless of their social locations. p. 243

social mobility The degree of opportunity that individuals have to move from one position in a stratified system to another; these moves can be vertical (upward or downward mobility) or horizontal (movement within a class). p. 45

social movement An organized attempt by a number of individuals either to change or to resist change in society. p. 243

social responsibility The idea that corporations and individuals have an ethical duty to protect the earth and protect society as a whole. p. 245

social stratification Division of people into categories or strata that are rewarded unequally in terms of power, property, and prestige. p. 43

socially stratified Refers to the hierarchical social layers of a society where those at the top have the greatest amount of social power and privilege and those underneath have descending levels of power and privilege. p. 7

sociological imagination A term coined by C. Wright Mills meaning the use of your imagination when both asking and answering sociological questions. p. 242

specific claim Process to deal with past grievances, mainly of First Nations; related to unfairly distributed treaty lands or mismanagement of First Nations funds by the Crown. p. 87

stakeholders Often refers to organizations, community, or more formal associations within the community. p. 250

standpoint Using the experiences of social groups as the basis of a theory or explanation. p. 7

starlight tours Alleged police practice of picking up Aboriginal people and taking them to some location far way and leaving them there to get home on their own. p. 71

stereotype A stereotype is a label that may have some basis in fact, but that has been grossly over-generalized and applied to a particular segment of the population, or situation. p. 26

stratification See social stratification.

structural discrimination The policies in the institutions of the dominant groups and the behaviour of the individuals who control the policies are neutral in intent, but end up having a differential or harmful effect on the minority groups. p. 30

systemic or institutionalized discrimination Refers more to the policies of the dominant group's institutions and the behaviours of the individuals who control these policies, which tend to have a harmful or undesirable effect on the members of a minority group. p. 30

systemic racism Behaviour, policies, or practices that disadvantage racialized persons; can be intentional or unintentional. p. 66

T

theo-cons Conservative thinkers who believe that religion (specifically Christianity) should inform public policy. p. 113

Third Culture Kid (TCKs) Children who move with parents from one culture to another due to a parent's career choice. p. 203

tokenism The practice of including one or a small number of members of a minority group to create the appearance of representation, inclusion, and non-discrimination, without ever giving these members access to power. p. 6, 74

totem pole A pole or post usually carved from red cedar and painted with symbolic figures, erected by Indigenous people of the northwest coast of North America. p. 82

Traditionalists Refers to those born specifically between the years 1925 to 1945. p. 164

transactive memory Refers to one way of using our memory more efficiently, so that we rely on our family, friends, and co-workers as well as "things" to store information for us. p. 174

transcultural Transcending cultural differences. p. 3

transgender Category that includes cross-dressing males, cross-dressing females, and inter-or bi-gendered individuals, as well as trans-sexed individuals. p. 121

transsexual Person who permanently identifies with the role of the opposite gender or someone who has had sex reassignment surgery to alter his or her external sex organs to those of the opposite sex. p. 121

transman An individual born biologically female who has transitioned into a man. p. 121

transvestites Men and women who express their sexuality by wearing the clothes of the opposite sex; often, the behaviour has nothing to do with whom they are attracted to physically. p. 125

transwoman A transgendered woman or a transsexual woman; an individual who is born biological male who has transitioned into a woman. p. 123

treaty A formal agreement between two parties that has been negotiated, concluded, and ratified. p. 84

two-row wampum belt A treaty of respect for the dignity and integrity of both parties involved; stresses the importance of independence and non-interference. p. 90

two-spirited Having a male and female spirit living in the same body; recently, the term was adopted by contemporary gay, lesbian, bisexual, and transgender Native Americans and Canadian First Nations people to describe themselves and the traditional roles they are reclaiming. p. 126

U

underserved Disadvantaged because of structural barriers and disparities. p. 2

United Nations Convention on the Rights of Persons with Disabilities A human rights instrument adopted by the United Nations in 2006 for the purpose of protecting the human rights and dignity of persons with disabilities; signatories are required to ensure that people with disabilities are equal under the law. p. 141

United Nations High Commission for Refugees (UNHCR) Agency mandated to lead and coordinate international action to protect refugees and resolve refugee problems worldwide. p. 210

universal design "The design of products, environments, programs and services to be usable by all people, to the greatest extent possible, without the need for adaptation or specialized design (but does not exclude assistive devices for particular groups of persons with disabilities where this is needed)" (United Nations, 2006) p. 153

V

validity The ability of a measure to gauge or measure accurately what it sets out to measure. p. 182

visible minorities Term used primarily in Canada by Statistics Canada to refer to a category of persons who are non-Caucasian in race or non-white in colour and who do not report being Aboriginal. p. 63

voluntary repatriation The process of returning voluntarily one's place of origin or citizenship. p. 211

W

wampum White or purple shells that come from whelk (white ones) or quahog clams (purple ones); has a multitude of meanings and uses in Aboriginal cultures, including jewellery, healing, and decoration. p. 90

war crimes Serious violations of international law applicable during armed conflict, such as ill treatment of prisoners of war, killing of prisoners of war, and so on; as of 2002, those arrested for war crimes have been tried in the International Criminal Court. p. 64

War Measures Act 1914 statute that gives emergency powers to the federal government, which allows it to govern by orders when there's a real or perceived threat of war or invasion. p. 88

white nationalism A political ideology that advocates for a racialized identity for "white people." p. 70

white supremacy An ideology that supports the superiority of whites over all others and is embraced by members of white supremacist organizations. p. 70

World Health Organization (WHO) United Nations authority on health issues. p. 140

world view The ways in which a group of people perceive and understand their place in the universe, often in relation to their interconnectedness with others. p. 84

X

xenophobia Hostility or an irrational fear attached to anyone or anything perceived as foreign. p. 63, 207

Index

Note: Page numbers with f's and t's refer to figures and tables